How to...

Exchange 2000 Server

24seven™

Exchange 2000 Server
24seven™

24seven™

Jim McBee

San Francisco   London

SYBEX

Associate Publishers: Richard Staron, Neil Edde

Acquisitions and Developmental Editor: Maureen Adams

Editor: Emily K. Wolman

Production Editor: Liz Burke

Technical Editor: Andy Webb

Book Designer: Bill Gibson

Graphic Illustrator: Tony Jonick

Electronic Publishing Specialist: Judy Fung

Proofreaders: Nancy Riddiough, Nanette Duffy, Yariv Rabinovitch, Emily Hsuan, Laurie O'Connell

Indexer: Ted Laux

Cover Designer: Ingalls + Associates

Cover Illustrator/Photographer: Hank Osuna

Library of Congress Card Number: 200193083

ISBN: 0-7821-2797-5

Manufactured in the United States of America

10 9 8 7 6 5 4

This book is dedicated to Computer Training Academy's Jeff Bloom, the consummate businessperson, community leader, educator, and friend.

Acknowledgments

Wow! How can I even begin to write acknowledgments for this book? I began researching this book almost two years ago, and along the way dozens of talented people have had an effect on it. My name goes on the cover, but the others involved in the production of the book remain silently anonymous. These people deserve my profound gratitude. Even starting a list is difficult to do.

First, I would like to say that I am in awe of Andy Webb, the technical editor. Andy skillfully and patiently read the entire book (twice!). He is not only technically proficient in programming and Exchange 2000 deployment, but he understands business needs. I'm sure Andy would have thought twice about accepting the technical editor's position if he knew up front about the time it would consume. Thanks for being there at 3:00am when I needed to e-mail you questions and ideas.

Emily Wolman, the editor, is the most skilled "non-technical" person I know. Secretly, I think she knows more about Exchange than I do. Emily, my friend, my editor, thank you for agreeing to do this project with me; I know it's been challenging. Acquisitions and Development Editor Maureen Adams and Production Editor Liz Burke have been extremely patient and are critical to the success of this book. I missed almost every deadline that Maureen and Liz outlined, and they are still nice to me.

A number of people helped me with content for different parts of the book, and I could not have done this without them. Many kudos and thanks to Chris Fox and Joe Kvidera of Rainer Technology's Messaging Team for assisting with clustering and performance monitoring. Brian Eiler helped with client troubleshooting, and ISA Server guru Dr. Thomas Shinder provided the material on ISA Server. Also thanks to Siegfried Weber for helping with scripting, and to Goga Kukrika for reviewing the book and helping with workflow. Maureen McFerrin provided valuable insight on the outline as well as feedback on the manuscript. Also thanks to Deb Danielsen, Greg Lynd, and Fred Unsworth, from Compaq, for providing information about cluster hardware sizing.

Still others reviewed different pieces of the book, answered questions, and provided feedback and insight into different topics. Thanks to Paul Bowden, Lyle Bullock, Cynthia Randall, Chris Scharff, Kim Cameron, Andrew Riehemann, KimKim Ditto-Ehlert, Tibor Soos, Russ Kaufmann, Regi Hill, Ilan Joosten, Missy Koslosky, Pam McKickin, Pete Koehler, John Bradley, Gary Renzi, Ryan Tung, Clayton Kamiya, Tom Meunier, and Amy Styers.

On the Sybex side, many people lent their skills to the production of this book. These folks include Judy Fung, Nancy Riddiough, Nanette Duffy, Yariv Rabinovitch, Laurie O'Connell, Ted Laux, Tony Jonick, and Emily Hsuan.

To Jeff Bloom and all the folks at Computer Training Academy who put up with my surfer-like eccentricities, you guys "no ka oi!" And finally, thanks to Suriya Supatanasakul, who put up with me while I was trying to write this. Aloha!

Jim McBee
Honolulu, Hawaii

Contents at a Glance

Contents

Introduction

Exchange Server is my favorite Microsoft product. (Active Directory comes in a close second.) It is a phenomenal product, and I never stop learning new things about it.

I began researching this book in August 1999, when I received an early beta copy of what was then called Platinum. Now I have file boxes and binders full of notes, white papers, presentations, and magazine articles on Platinum (now known as Exchange 2000). I have a mailbox folder with several hundred e-mail messages that have been sent back and forth between myself and Exchange administrators, former students, Microsoft consultants, and others regarding Exchange 2000 features, deployment, and questions. Add to that a CD-ROM full of documents and presentations on Exchange 2000. All in all, I'm guessing that I have about 6000 pages of research. Out of that I have had to disseminate about 900 pages for this book. Sometimes the decision of what to leave in and what to leave out was very difficult. Exchange is a wonderful product and I want to cover every possible aspect of it if I can.

Exchange has been not only a revolution, but also an evolution. The product has continued to improve since the day it was released in 1996. Even Exchange 2000 has continued to evolve with the release of Service Packs 1 and 2. As I am putting the finishing touches on this book, SP2 is being released. This service pack will once again improve scalability, fix bugs, and add a few new features to Exchange 2000.

This Book and the Development Process

During the initial development of this book (and the entire 24seven series), an emphasis was placed on conveying what you, as an administrator, need to know to keep your Exchange server healthy, happy, and operational 24 hours a day, 7 days a week. This book is the sequel to *Exchange 5.5 24seven*, which I wrote in 1999. In researching this book, I listened to many of the readers of the first one, and asked experienced Exchange administrators a few questions:

- What do you do to keep your Exchange servers up and running?
- What lessons did you learn the hard way?
- What have you done wrong (and right)?
- What would you like to share with other Exchange administrators?

It is with this information that I assembled this book. I focused primarily on Exchange Server operations issues—due to space and time constraints associated with this book, there were issues I had to avoid or only partially cover. For example, I skipped client-related issues except when necessary; the Outlook family is the subject of its own book.

Nor did I go into depth on NNTP, due to the fact that I rarely see it deployed in the field. Microsoft Exchange 2000 Conference Server is now becoming an interesting topic, but I felt that I could not cover it adequately in the few pages I would have been able to devote to it in this book. I also avoided the topic of application design and development (except where relevant) to show some of the capabilities of Exchange 2000 event sinks and workflow.

Throughout this book are Exchange@Work sidebars. These contain specific situations and problems that I have encountered in the field while deploying Exchange. I felt it important to emphasize how other companies are approaching problems. (The actual names of the companies have been changed.)

In several chapters, I included a Frequently Asked Questions section, which address a lot of the typical questions I am asked about those topics. The Exchange administrator's mailing list also has a FAQ maintained by Andy Webb, at www.swinc.com/resource/e2kfaq.htm.

And throughout each chapter you will find references to other books, white papers, RFCs, and Microsoft Knowledge Base articles. I hope you will find the time to review this supplementary reference material.

Most of the scenarios and the instructions for this book were tried out on my test network, though some were taken from how I had implemented something for a customer. My test network consists of six Pentium III computers with 266–700MHz processors and between 128MB and 256MB of RAM. Yes, the machines with only 128MB of RAM were pretty slow. Almost all of the screen captures were taken on these systems except for a few provided by Dr. Thomas Shinder (who provided the ISA Server content) and by Brian Eiler, Chris Fox, and Joe Kvidera.

Should I Buy This Book?

If you are standing in your neighborhood bookstore asking yourself this question, then ask no further. Maybe you are just starting a pilot deployment of Exchange. Perhaps you have just come back from a Microsoft Certified Technical Education Center class and you want to know more. Maybe you are currently running Exchange and you want to know what you can do better, or you are curious about some of the pitfalls and sticky situations that can happen with Exchange. If you match any of these descriptions, this book is for you.

Maybe the mysteries of how Exchange 2000 and Active Directory interact are keeping you awake at night. Are you wondering about the best management practices for Exchange Server? What events indicate that the Exchange server is having problems? How often should you run backups? Have you given any consideration to what would happen if disaster strikes? What you can do to proactively prevent problems? Are you wondering what Microsoft recommends versus what works in the real world? If you answered yes to any of these questions, this book is for you.

Are you looking for ways to further customize your Exchange organization? Are you trying to figure out the best Exchange connectors to use? Or maybe you are trying to track down a problem with a connector? Do you know what to do if the Exchange server fails to restart or if you lose a disk drive? Maybe you are concerned about messaging security? If you are seeking answers to any of these questions, this book is for you.

I have endeavored to keep the topics in this book useful for you whether you are supporting 10 mailboxes or 100,000. For those of you with larger sites, you are already aware that any guidance I can provide in a 900-page book will have to be generic enough for you to customize to your own environment.

This book is not for beginners. Its readers should have networking experience in Exchange or some other messaging system, including knowledge of network operating systems, communications media, and related technologies. If you want to understand how to install Exchange, create mailboxes, or perform other basic Exchange Server administration tasks, then this book is *not* right for you. For a good generic Exchange 2000 reference, pick up a copy of *Mastering Exchange 2000 Server* by Barry Gerber (Sybex, 2000). It is an excellent introduction to the world of installing, configuring, and administering Exchange Server. After you learn the basics, I hope you will consider purchasing this book to take you up to the next level.

If you are studying for the MCSE exams, this book will be helpful, but should not be considered an exam study guide. If that is what you are seeking, purchase a copy of *MCSE: Exchange 2000 Server Administration Study Guide*, by Walter Glen and James Chellis (Sybex, 2001).

Assumptions

This book is centered around Exchange 2000 SP1 at a minimum, but I have noted some of the specific features of SP2 when relevant. Most places I avoided talking about the bug with the RTM (release to manufacturing) version and how SP1 fixes those issues; instead I'm assuming that you are using SP1 or later. In many places, I have drawn contrasts to how something was handled in Exchange 5.5 versus how it now works in Exchange 2000. If you did not run Exchange 5.5, I apologize ahead of time for boring you with some details of an older version of the product.

In the text, I assume that the Windows NT directory is located on the C drive in the \WinNT directory. Also, I assume that the \exchsrvr\bin directory is on the C: drive. The Exchange 2000 Setup program now puts the \Exchsrvr directory into \Program Files, but I still refer to it simply as \Exchsrvr.

Anytime you see HKLM in a Registry path, it is a shortened version of \HKEY_Local_ Machine. The same is true for HKCU (HKEY_CURRENT_USER).

How This Book Is Organized

This book is divided into six parts that consist of 17 chapters. The topics and complexity of the book vary from chapter to chapter. Each chapter was intended to stand on its own, but you should read Chapters 1 and 2 first. If you are interested in Exchange Server and security, you should read Chapters 11, 12, and 13. Though overall, you can read the chapters in just about any order you wish.

Part I: Building a Foundation

The first part of this book covers important facts that you need to know when preparing your Windows 2000 environment, planning Exchange 2000, understanding Active Directory, and migrating/upgrading from a previous version of Exchange. These chapters emphasize things that have gone wrong with installations I've been exposed to, including common design mistakes with Windows 2000, Active Directory forests, and Exchange organizations, and suggestions for how to plan, deploy, and migrate to Exchange Server.

Part II: Operations

Part II covers Exchange server operations. This is my favorite topic, because I love to figure out how to make things run better (ever since I was a little kid taking apart my mom's vacuum cleaner). Particularly popular with the reviewers is Chapter 4, which covers typical Exchange 2000 operations. Chapter 5 covers different approaches to monitoring your Exchange organization's health and well being, while Chapter 6 covers performance monitoring and optimization. This topic may be particularly useful if you believe your Exchange servers are overburdened. Chapter 7 covers disaster prevention, backup and disaster recovery; in my opinion, this is one of the most important chapters in the book. Chapter 8 is an overview of the Exchange 2000 clustering. Public folders, building a public folder hierarchy, and developing a replication strategy are covered in Chapter 9, and Chapter 10 covers automating tasks and using scripts to perform tasks.

Part III: Security

Any server that has a user community presents a certain amount of challenge to keep it secure. And any server connected to a public network presents an even bigger challenge with respect to security. That is why I enjoyed writing this section. Chapter 11 discusses basic messaging security and implementing proper administrative permissions. Securing message content using the Key Management Service is discussed in Chapter 12. Chapter 13 covers topics such as securing Windows 2000, virus protection, and putting Exchange behind a firewall.

Part IV: Connectivity

Part IV discusses connectivity and Exchange 2000. This section has two focuses: server SMTP connectivity and Internet client connectivity. Chapter 14 discusses Exchange 2000's use of SMTP, connecting routing groups, the Routing Group Connector, and the SMTP Connector. Chapter 15 covers Internet clients such as POP3 and IMAP4 clients, Outlook Web Access, and Instant Messaging.

Part V: Troubleshooting

My goal with Part V was to provide you with some basic tools for troubleshooting problems with Exchange 2000 and clients. Let's face it, a lot can go wrong in a complex environment such as with Exchange 2000/Active Directory. But usually there are a few root causes to those problems. Chapter 16 looks at client connectivity issues for Outlook and Internet clients, while Chapter 17 covers topics related to Exchange 2000 server problems.

More to Come

I could not fit everything I wanted to in this book. There is just too much information to share. However, I do have a website onto which I will periodically post additional information such as sample documentation sheets, a sample Service Level Agreement, and anything else that may be relevant to the topics covered in this book. Right now, my poor, content-impaired website can be found at www.somorita.com. Also visit the Sybex website (www.sybex.com) as they maintain a special section for this and other 24seven books. Here you'll find this book's two appendices, covering registry settings and offering additional reading and resources.

I hope that the material in this book answers some of those nagging questions you have had and that it helps you to prevent problems in the future. And I hope that this book helps get you out of the office by 5:00 P.M.!

Part 1

Building a Foundation

Topics Covered:

- Exchange 2000 Architecture
- Picking the Right Edition
- Storage Considerations
- Synchronization and Standardization
- Server Hardware Considerations
- User Education
- Active Directory and DNS
- Basics of Active Directory Operation
- Preparing the Active Directory Forest and Each Domain
- Exchange 2000 and Active Directory Groups
- Customizing Active Directory
- Importing and Modifying Active Directory Data
- Preparing for a Migration/Upgrade to Exchange 2000
- Understanding the Active Directory Connector
- The Site Replication Service and the Recipient Update Service

Getting Started with Exchange 2000

A successful Exchange 2000 deployment hinges on many elements; these include a strong dependency on Windows 2000 Active Directory (AD), Windows 2000 Internet Information Server (IIS), a properly configured DNS (Domain Name Service) infrastructure, sufficient and reliable hardware, and good operational practices. Your Exchange 2000 installation will have serious problems unless you have a good understanding of not only Exchange 2000, but also Windows 2000, AD, and DNS. Exchange 2000's destiny is much more intertwined with Windows 2000 than earlier versions of Exchange. A basic understanding of the Exchange 2000 architecture and deploying Exchange 2000 on the proper hardware platform will also be crucial to your success.

One of the most important parts of deploying any Exchange system is making design decisions that relate to supporting your organization. This includes choosing the right edition of Exchange 2000 Server, deciding how to best store your data, maintaining time synchronization, setting reasonable standards (Active Directory, Exchange performance, user space allocation, etc.), and picking the right hardware. Placing your Exchange 2000 system on appropriately sized and configured hardware will also help to keep you happy and safe from end-user lynch mobs.

Finally, providing your user community with good documentation, notification, and training will help to minimize your administration woes. Most experienced Exchange administrators will tell you that educating their users, keeping them informed, and managing their expectations are some of the most powerful tools in their operations arsenal.

Yet perhaps first and foremost, essential tools to have in your bag of tricks are solid operations practices that will help reduce the likelihood of downtime and improve the recoverability from disasters—and help keep you sane. One particularly wise Exchange guru once said his secret to Exchange success was the following:

- Perform daily backups of Exchange.
- Check the event logs.
- Make sure the server does not run out of disk space.
- Check the queues.
- Then leave Exchange alone.

So, is that all there is to say about Exchange administration? If so, why have volumes of information been written about it, and why am I writing more? The answer is simple: We all benefit from shared experiences. Combine that with the fact that software documentation and training do not always make matters crystal clear, and you have good reasons for a book about skillfully maintaining Exchange.

The Makings of a Good Exchange Administrator

I have tended to a number Exchange "disasters" where the clients were running either Exchange 5.5 or Exchange 2000. These were situations in which I was called in to fix a pretty serious problem. I classify these as disasters because in each case the user community was without e-mail services for more than half of a business day. In one case, the user community was without e-mail for more than a week before I was called. One of the strengths I look for in system administrators is the ability to know when they are in over their heads and when to call for help. This includes not being afraid to call Microsoft Product Support Services.

With a few exceptions, the aforementioned disasters were either caused or compounded by administrators who were not prepared for the disaster, did not know what they were doing, or did not call for help when they should have. The administrators did not have a clear understanding of Exchange, Active Directory, and the steps to successfully manage an Exchange system, nor had they documented or practiced disaster recovery beforehand.

Disaster prevention involves two major steps. The first is recognizing that you cannot solve every problem in the world (and not being afraid to admit it). The second step—and the one you are taking now, by reading this book—is to do everything you can to improve your knowledge of Exchange 2000 (and Windows 2000).

Exchange 2000 Architecture Basics

If you lived the life of an Exchange 5.5 administrator, you should have a strong understanding of the primary differences between Exchange 5.5 and Exchange 2000. Any time a systems administrator or network engineer is troubleshooting a problem, knowledge of the system's architecture as well as of the system dependencies is essential.

Exchange 2000 for Exchange 5.5 Administrators

The differences between Exchange 5.5 and Exchange 2000 are staggering considering that the two products are merely one generation apart. For one, Exchange 5.5 is a complete messaging system. It includes not only a message store, but also a directory service and components to deliver messages to other systems. Also, Exchange 5.5 relies on Windows NT as an operating system platform and for authentication.

Exchange 2000 still relies on Windows 2000 as an operating system and for authentication, but essentially Exchange 2000 is a message storage engine with interfaces to AD and IIS. Directory services and message transport is no longer the concern of Exchange 2000; they have been offloaded to Windows 2000. There are many other differences between Exchange 5.5 and Exchange 2000, such as more storage scalability, message routing, and an improved Outlook Web Access (OWA) interface.

Hey, Who Took My Directory?

The most striking change between Exchange 5.5 and 2000 Server is that Exchange 2000 does not have its own directory service. Rather, Exchange 2000 relies entirely on Windows 2000 Active Directory. Some of the information that is now stored in AD includes:

- User-specific information, such as telephone number, title, department, e-mail addresses, Instant Messaging home server, and mailbox home server
- Access Control Lists (ACLs) for accessing mailboxes, public folders, and administrative rights
- Server configuration, including what mailbox and public folder stores are on each server, SMTP configuration, connectors, routing group configuration, and administrative group configuration
- Exchange 2000–specific classes of objects and attributes of those objects that are unique to Exchange

Also, Active Directory, not Exchange 2000, now controls all replication of user and configuration data. In my opinion, AD is the most important component of Exchange 2000, even though it is actually part of Windows 2000.

> **NOTE**   Active Directory is covered in more detail in Chapter 2, "Active Directory for Exchange 2000 Administrations."

Message Transport

The Exchange 5.5 message transfer agent (MTA) is responsible for delivery of all messages that are "leaving" the server, whether the message is going to a connector (such as the Internet Mail Service), another Exchange server, another Exchange site, or a foreign connector such as X.400. Further, the Exchange 5.5 MTA expands recipients of distribution lists.

In Exchange 2000, SMTP is now the message transport used for most inter-server message transport. The Exchange 2000 MTA is responsible for delivery of messages to Exchange 5.5 servers, Exchange 2000 routing groups connected via X.400, and foreign X.400 Connectors.

Unlike Exchange 5.5, all messages delivered by Exchange 2000 are routed through the Advanced Queuing Engine, a component of Internet Information Server. This includes local deliveries as well as messages destined for other Exchange servers (both 5.5 and 2000), distribution lists, foreign connectors, third-party gateways, and the Internet. The Advanced Queuing Engine is covered in more detail later in this chapter.

Is It a Site, a Routing Group, or an Administrative Group?

An Exchange 5.5 site serves two primary purposes. First, the site is a boundary of high-speed, full-time connectivity. Second, the site is a boundary of administrative control.

Exchange 2000 introduces the concept of *administrative groups* and *routing groups*, which effectively separate administrative permission requirements and message routing requirements. The administrative group is a boundary of administrative control; the routing group is a boundary of reliable, full-time connectivity. In a native Exchange 2000 organization, administrative and routing groups can have different boundaries; a server can be in one administrative group but in a routing group that is contained in another administrative group. Grouping servers (for administrative purposes) based on bandwidth is no longer necessary.

Waiter, There's an STM File in My Data Directory!

All Exchange 5.5 message data is stored in either the PUB.EDB file or the PRIV.EDB file, depending whether the message was to be stored in the public or private information store, respectively. With the release of Exchange 2000, message data is now split between two types of files: the EDB file and the STM file. Each public and private information store has an STM file and an EDB file.

- The EDB file is also known as the *rich-text store* or *MAPI store*; I have even seen it referred to as the *property store*. This file contains all messages sent by MAPI clients as well as folder content listings, indexes, and a subset of properties of each message stored in the STM file.

- The STM (streaming) file is also known as the *native content store*. Messages that are sent to Exchange by clients other than Outlook, such as from MIME (Multipurpose Internet Mail Extensions) or non-MIME clients, are stored in this file, as are messages inbound from the SMTP service. For performance reasons, only a subset of properties is converted to and stored in the MAPI store.

Storage of data between these two files is transparent to the client. When a client retrieves a message located in either file, the message content is converted to the appropriate format as necessary and passed on to the client.

Where Are Link Monitor and Server Monitor?

One of my favorite (and often one of the most unreliable) Exchange 5.5 tools is the Exchange Administrator's Link Monitor. Running a close second is Server Monitor. These two tools let me ensure that messages are flowing to different parts of my organization and that services I have designated are running on my Exchange servers. However, historically these tools have been inaccurate due to slow WAN links, message delays, and incorrect administrative permissions.

Exchange 2000 has replaced Server Monitor and Link Monitor with the other tools found in the Exchange System Manager console in the Tools ➢ Monitoring And Status folder. The Notifications and Status tools allow you to monitor the availability of connectors, the availability of servers, queue growth, free disk space, and other Windows 2000 services. Though I originally liked the old tools better, I have now found the new tools to be both reliable and flexible.

Other Enhancements and Changes

Other enhancements and changes found in Exchange 2000 include:

- The Gateway Address Routing Table (GWART) has been replaced by the much more robust Link State Table, which includes information about whether a specific route is currently available.

- All administration is now performed through Microsoft Management Console (MMC) snap-ins. These can be run from any Windows 2000–based computer.

- OWA has been completely rewritten to use more efficient, modern Internet technologies such as HTTP/DAV (Distributed Authoring and Versioning), DHTML (Dynamic HyperText Markup Language, and XML (Extensible Markup Language).

Exchange 2000 Dependencies

There are a number of Windows 2000 services that must be started before you can start the first Exchange service. There are still other services that Exchange 2000 requires to be installed prior to Exchange installation (IIS services including the web service, SMTP, and NNTP.) Table 1.1 lists the Windows 2000 services that must be started in order to start the principal services.

Table 1.1   Exchange 2000 Dependencies

Exchange 2000 Service	Windows 2000 Services (Dependencies)
Microsoft Exchange System Attendant (mad.exe)	Event log NT LM Security Support Provider Remote Procedure Call (RPC) Remote Procedure Call (RPC) Locator Server Workstation
Microsoft Exchange Information Store (store.exe)	IIS Admin Service Microsoft Exchange System Attendant
Microsoft Exchange MTA Stacks (emsmta.exe)	IIS Admin Service Microsoft Exchange System Attendant
Microsoft Exchange IMAP4 (part of inetinfo.exe)	IIS Admin Service Microsoft Exchange Information Store
Microsoft Exchange POP3 (part of inetinfo.exe)	IIS Admin Service Microsoft Exchange Information Store
Simple Mail Transport Protocol (SMTP) (part of inetinfo.exe)	IIS Admin Service (The SMTP service is actually part of Windows 2000, but is enhanced during the installation of Exchange 2000.)
Network News Transport Protocol (NNTP) (part of inetinfo.exe)	IIS Admin Service (The NNTP service is actually part of Windows 2000, but is enhanced during the installation of Exchange 2000.)
Microsoft Exchange Event (events.exe)	Microsoft Exchange Information Store

Table 1.1   Exchange 2000 Dependencies *(continued)*

Exchange 2000 Service	Windows 2000 Services (Dependencies)
Microsoft Exchange Routing Engine (part of `inetinfo.exe`)	IIS Admin Service
Microsoft Search (`mssearch.exe`)	NT LM Security Support Provider Remote Procedure Call (RPC)
Microsoft Exchange Key Management Service (`kmserver.exe`)	Microsoft Exchange Information Store
Microsoft Exchange Site Replication Service (`srsmain.exe`)	Event log NT LM Security Support Provider Remote Procedure Call (RPC) Remote Procedure Call (RPC) Locator Server Workstation
Microsoft Exchange Connectivity Controller (`lscntrl.exe`)	Event log Microsoft Exchange System Attendant
Microsoft Exchange Connector for Lotus cc:Mail (`ccmc.exe`)	Event log Microsoft Exchange Information Store
Microsoft Exchange Connector for Lotus Notes (`dispatch.exe`)	Event log Microsoft Exchange Connectivity Controller Microsoft Exchange Information Store
Microsoft Exchange Directory Synchronization (`dxa.exe`)	Microsoft Exchange MTA Stacks
Microsoft Exchange Router for Novell GroupWise (`gwrouter.exe`)	Event log
MS Mail Connector Interchange (`mt.exe`)	Event log Microsoft Exchange MTA Stacks
MS SchedulePlus Free-Busy Connector (`msfbconn.exe`)	Event log Microsoft Exchange Information Store

Table 1.1   Exchange 2000 Dependencies *(continued)*

Exchange 2000 Service	Windows 2000 Services (Dependencies)
Microsoft Exchange Connector for Novell GroupWise (dispatch.exe)	Event log Microsoft Exchange Connectivity Controller Microsoft Exchange Information Store Microsoft Exchange Router for Novell GroupWise
Microsoft Active Directory Connector (adc.exe)	Event log NT LM Security Support Provider Remote Procedure Call (RPC) Remote Procedure Call (RPC) Locator Server Workstation

Other network services that must be available in order for Exchange 2000 to function properly include:

- Windows 2000 domain controller
- Windows 2000 Global Catalog server
- DNS server that will resolve service records for the Windows 2000 forest, MX (mail exchanger) records, and A (address or host) records

An In-Depth Look at Exchange 2000 Architecture

Now that we have covered the basics, let's take a closer look at the Exchange 2000 architecture. This includes a more in-depth examination of Exchange 2000 message storage, message access with Exchange Installable File System (ExIFS) and IIS, and Advanced Queuing Engine, as well as connectors and the System Attendant service.

Message Storage

A number of improvements were made in the database engine that ships with Exchange 2000; the current database engine is called ESE98 (Extensible Storage Engine). More information on the database engine and storage technology is in Chapter 4, "Maintenance and Management."

Exchange breaks down storage into either public or private information stores. All mailbox data is stored in a mailbox store (private information store) while all public folder data is stored in a public folder store, and these stores each have two separate components, an EDB file and an STM file.

> **NOTE** A MAPI (Messaging Application Programming Interface) client is any
> client that sends and reads messages where the message properties are defined
> as MAPI properties. MAPI clients include the original Exchange client, Outlook 97/
> 98/2000/ and Outlook 2002.

As mentioned earlier in this chapter, the EDB file is called the MAPI store. This is a rich, hierarchical property store; messages sent by MAPI clients are stored here. Thus all messages stored here have MAPI properties associated with them.

The STM file is not nearly as structured as the EDB file. Messages are not converted to MAPI messages when they arrive, but instead are stored in their native format (typically MIME). This includes messages sent by SMTP clients. However, the EDB file does contain a list of *all* messages stored in each folder, so certain MAPI properties for messages in the STM file are promoted to the EDB file. To improve performance, the STM file data is accessed through a kernel-mode device driver called ExIFS; a Windows Explorer extension that uses this device driver also allows the entire store to be accessible through the file system.

> **NOTE** By now, you have probably seen the term "Web store" or "Web storage
> system" used (or overused) in technology media. The Web store is not actually a
> single database but a technology for providing access to data through HTTP/DAV
> or the ExIFS.

Figure 1.1 illustrates two examples of message storage, a MAPI message and a MIME message.

Figure 1.1   Messages arriving in a mailbox store

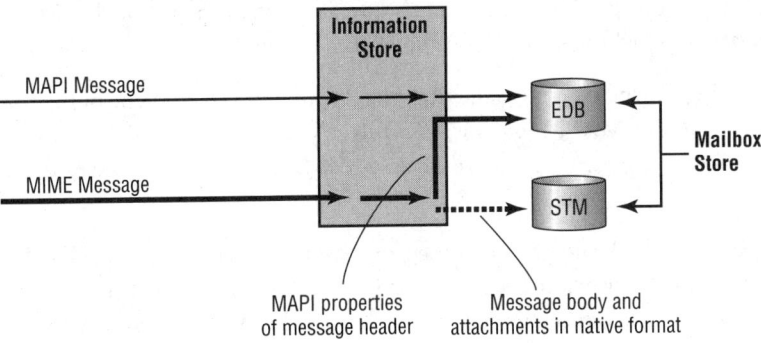

The first message shown in Figure 1.1 is sent by a MAPI client such as Outlook 2000. The client designates most of the message's MAPI properties, and the client sends the message to the Exchange server; the message transport and the store may also set some of the message properties. The information store saves the entire message in the EDB file.

The second message is formatted by a client such as Outlook Express as a MIME message. The Internet Mail Service in Exchange 5.5 would have converted this message, but the Advanced Queuing Engine in Exchange 2000 simply passes it along to the information store in its native format. The information store determines that the message is in native format, then "promotes" certain properties of the message header (such as the To, From, Subject, and Date information) to MAPI properties, and finally stores this information in the EDB file along with a "pointer" that points to the message body and attachments in the STM file. Technically, there are actually three separate phases of property promotion: The initial properties are promoted when the message is sent to the server by the client, the second set when the messages is accessed, and finally if the content is changed by a MAPI client.

NOTE   In a pure MAPI environment with no SMTP connectivity to the outside world, your STM files will hardly grow in size at all. In an environment with all POP3 and IMAP4 clients, the STM file will grow significantly while the EDB file will hardly increase in size.

Content Conversion on Demand

The obvious question now is "What happens if a MAPI client reads a message that was sent to the Exchange server via SMTP and is formatted as a MIME message?" Simple. The information store retrieves the message into memory on the Exchange server and performs an "on-the-fly" conversion. The message is *not* converted in the STM file, merely in the copy in memory. The message is saved as a MAPI message only if a MAPI client modifies the message. If the message contains an attachment but the attachment is not modified, then it is not moved into the EDB data file.

The same holds true of a message that was sent by a MAPI client but is now being retrieved by a non-MAPI client such as Outlook Express. The information store converts the message on-the-fly to a MIME or non-MIME message and passes it on to the client.

So why all the conversion? Why not just store all messages in a common format? In Exchange 5.5, all inbound SMTP message content was converted to MDBEF message format by the information store's IMAIL process. If the message was retrieved by a POP3 or IMAP4 client, it was once again converted by the IMAIL process. If your environment is a pure environment of one type or another (all MAPI or all MIME clients), converting to another format would be too much overhead compared to keeping the content in its native format.

Microsoft's developers recognize the changing nature of the messaging world and that in the future we will have more mixed-client environments, which achieved better performance than if they simply stored the message in its native format and converted the message only when necessary. OWA and IMAP4 clients are becoming increasing popular, and future versions of Outlook will more than likely provide the ability to access data using HTTP/DAV rather than MAPI. With a steady turn toward an emphasis on XML, HTTP/DAV, and other "Internet" clients, it makes sense to figure out how to keep data stored in its native format without content conversion. Further, the streaming store provides much higher performance access for message attachments. Messages stored in the EDB file are written in 4K page reads, whereas the STM file is accessed using kernel-level I/O in 64K streamed chunks. This is much more efficient.

Storage Groups and Multiple Stores

In Exchange 5.5, you are limited to a single private information store and a single public information store. If you are running Exchange 2000 Enterprise Server, you can create up to 20 separate mailbox or public folder stores. Storage groups are used to organize these mailbox and public folder stores. Exchange 2000 Server allows for only a single mailbox store (maximum EDB size of 16GB), but up to four public folder stores.

Storage Groups   Storage groups are the building blocks for multiple stores. Exchange 2000 Enterprise Server allows you to create up to four separate storage groups, each of which can contain up to five mailbox stores or public folder stores and has its own set of transaction logs. Circular logging can be turned on for some storage groups depending on the requirements of the data stored in the storage group.

> **TIP**   For optimal performance, each storage group's transaction log files should be placed on a separate physical hard disk. The transaction logs should not share this hard disk with any other application or data.

When the first database in a storage group is mounted, a new instance of the ESE database engine is started. All instances of ESE run as part of the `store.exe` process.

Multiple Stores   What possible uses can there be for additional mailbox stores? Here is a list of possible advantages to using more than one mailbox store:

- Company executives or VIPs can be placed in a separate mailbox store to allow for quicker backup and restoration times.
- The overall size of any specific mailbox store can be reduced by splitting up the storage load between two stores.

- You can specify separately which stores need to be full-text indexed and which do not.
- Additional public folder stores can be used to store data that is accessed exclusively via OWA or the ExIFS driver.

However, be cautioned that if you choose to have more than one private mailbox store on a single server, there are a few things you should consider:

- Each additional store that you mount consumes at least another 10MB of RAM.
- Single-instance storage is preserved only within a single store. Recipients across multiple stores will cause multiple copies of a message to be created.
- Backup and recovery scenarios require more diligence and testing in this more complicated environment.

Message Access

Exchange 2000 introduces an entirely new approach to accessing message storage. In addition to being able to access message and public folder data through MAPI, POP3, IMAP4, NNTP, and HTTP clients, you can now access Exchange data directly through the file system. (The POP3, IMAP4, NNTP, and HTTP processes are all part of IIS.)

Exchange 2000 Installable File System (ExIFS)

One of the new features of Exchange 2000 is the Exchange Installable File System (ExIFS), which allows mailboxes or any public folder tree to be accessed as if it were another network resource. When the Exchange information store starts, it also starts a kernel mode device driver called EXIFS.SYS, which interacts with the information store and allows access to the public folders and mailboxes.

From the server console, you can see a new drive letter (the M: drive by default). Figure 1.2 shows the M:\ drive and its root folder, SOMORITA.NET. Exchange takes SOMORITA.NET from the default recipient policy's default SMTP address. Under SOMORITA.NET, you can see the MBX folder and the Public Folders that allow access to the mailboxes and public folders.

The M: drive is available only from the Exchange server console unless it is shared. Once shared, any user can access any mailbox or public folder to which they have permissions.

WARNING Do not back up your mailboxes and public folder stores using the M: drive. Make sure that any file-based virus-scanning software that might be on the Exchange server excludes the M: drive entirely.

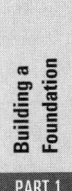

Figure 1.2   The M: drive with a mailbox open

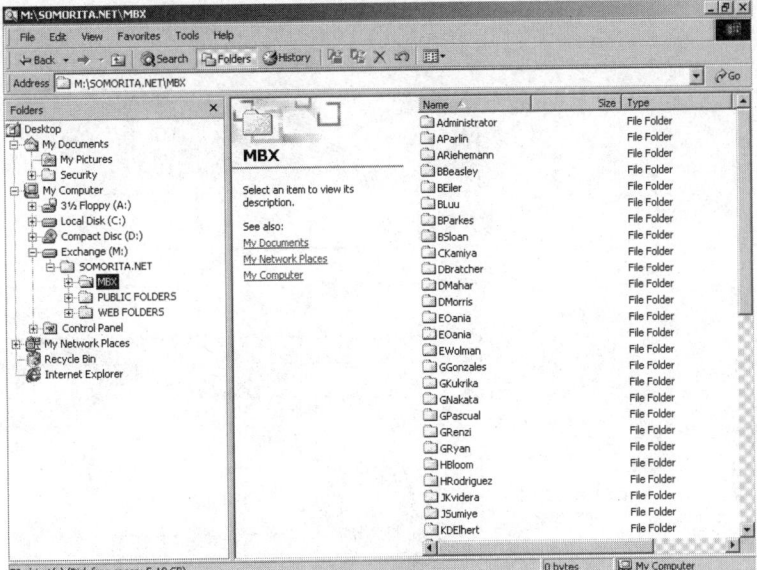

The ExIFS feature may be useful if you want users to be able to access their mailboxes or public folders through the file system. OWA and the Web storage system use ExIFS to access data stored in the Exchange mailbox and public folder stores.

Internet Information Server and Exchange 2000

Internet Information Server (IIS) 5 plays an important role in the accessing and storing data in Exchange 2000. All Internet protocol support is now handled by IIS rather than by Exchange 2000 components. Figure 1.3 shows a basic architectural diagram of IIS and the Exchange 2000 information store.

All communication for POP3, IMAP4, SMTP, HTTP, and NNTP is now handled by IIS rather than being integrated into other Exchange components. IIS receives Internet protocol requests and messages, and passes these on to the information store. In order to achieve optimal performance, the Exchange developers implemented a shared memory layer between IIS and the information store called the Exchange Inter-Process Communication (ExIPC) layer. This layer is also referred to as EPOXY because it's the glue that holds the information store and IIS together, and thus the ExIPC DLL name is EXPOXY.DLL.

Figure 1.3   IIS and Exchange 2000 information store interaction

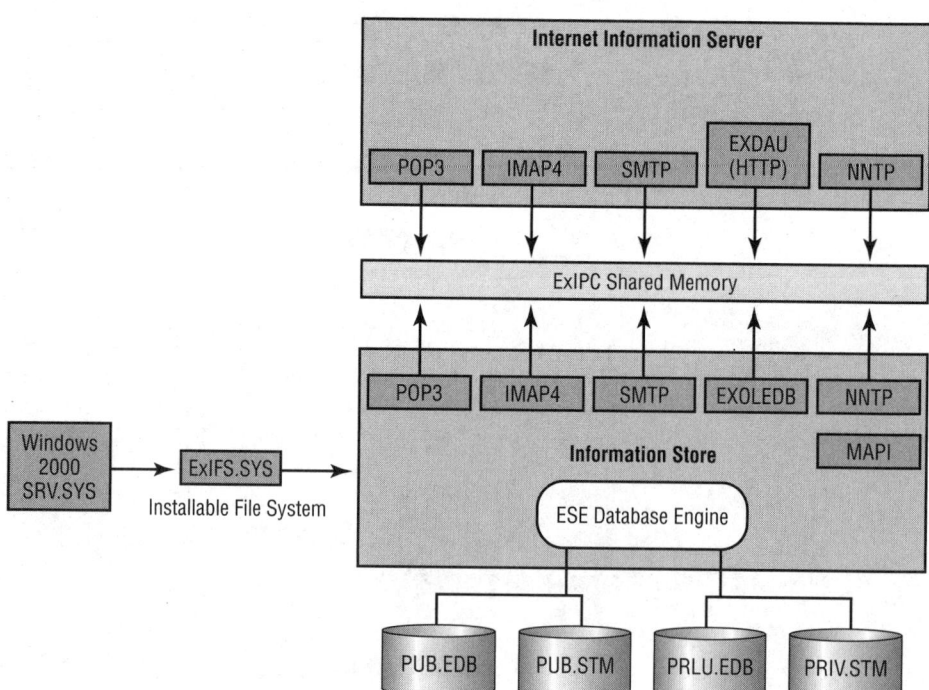

Essentially, ExIPC is nothing more than an area of memory that the two processes share for queuing data and requests between them. Since it is shared memory, data and requests are transferred quickly and efficiently.

The Advanced Queuing Engine

Perhaps one of the most dramatic changes between Exchange 5.5 and Exchange 2000 is the change to the message transport architecture. With Exchange 2000, all message transfer is the responsibility of the Message Transport System of which the Advanced Queuing Engine is a part. One of the design goals for the Exchange 2000 message transport system was to ensure that all messages were processed exactly the same. To that end, all messages are delivered through the Advanced Queuing Engine—even those that are destined for local delivery.

To do this without affecting performance and scalability is something of a monumental task. Further, all message transport in a native Exchange 2000 organization is via SMTP rather than RPC, so all Exchange 2000 servers must have the capability to transfer SMTP messages between servers in the same routing group. The Exchange 5.5 MTA used RPCs to transfer messages between servers in the same site.

In 1996, when Exchange 5.5 was released, Microsoft had three separate teams of developers working with SMTP: the Exchange team, the IIS team, and the Microsoft Commercial Internet System team. When Windows 2000 was being developed, Microsoft decided to combine these three teams into one group that would develop a single SMTP transport system to be used by all Microsoft components requiring SMTP transport.

> **NOTE** All messages including those destined for local delivery are handled by the Advanced Queuing Engine.

Message Transport Components

The IIS SMTP component is required prior to the installation of Exchange 2000. When Exchange 2000 is installed, it enhances (not replaces) several of the existing SMTP components so that they can work with Exchange 2000 more effectively. The SMTP transport components include:

ExIPC Provides the queuing layer that transfers message header information quickly and efficiently between IIS and the information store.

Advanced Queuing Engine Creates and manages the queues through which a message passes when it is being delivered. These queues include per-domain queues, the pre-categorization queue, the post-categorization queue, and the local delivery queue.

Message Categorizer Provides features specific to Exchange, such as checking recipient home servers, checking recipient limits, checking sender limits, and expanding distribution lists. This is an enhancement to the Advanced Queuing Engine. The IIS SMTP component has a basic message categorizer (`cat.dll`) that is disabled by default. When Exchange 2000 is installed, the Exchange categorizer (`phatcat.dll`) replaces the IIS categorizer.

Routing Engine Maintains the Link State Table, which is used by the Advanced Queuing Engine to determine the "next hop" through which a message needs to be routed. The Routing Engine also maintains information about whether or not a link is currently available.

SMTP Service Handles transmission of messages between hosts using the SMTP protocol.

When a message is transferred to the Advanced Queuing Engine, each component has specific functions that it performs to move the message to its next hop. Figure 1.4 shows a basic diagram of the Advanced Queuing Engine.

Figure 1.4   SMTP Advanced Queuing Engine

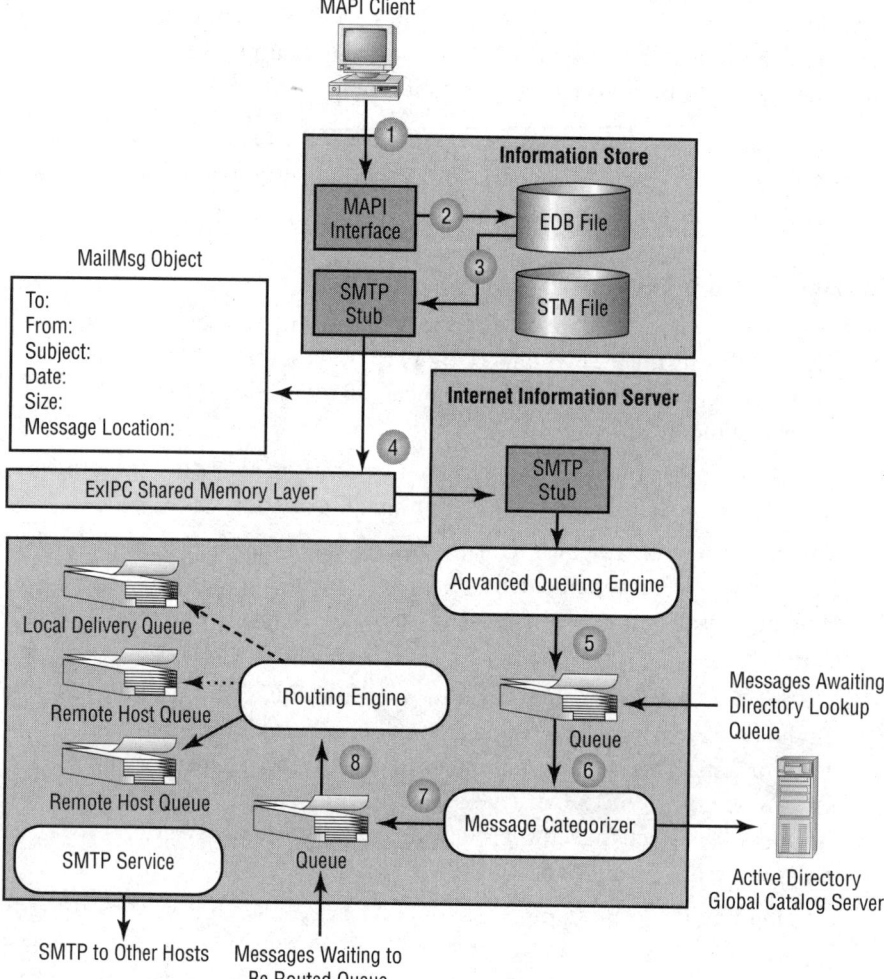

If we follow the message through its path as it travels through the information store and Advanced Queuing Engine, it looks something like this:

1. A MAPI client submits a message through the information store's MAPI interface.

2. The information store determines that the message is a MAPI message and stores the entire message in the EDB portion of the mailbox store.

3. The information store creates an object that represents the message called the *MailMsg* object (also called the IMsg or IMailMsg object). This object is merely a small chunk of memory that identifies information such as the To, From, Subject, Date, Size, and other message properties, as well as where the actual message content is stored. In this case, the message content is stored in the EDB portion of the mailbox store. Only the MailMsg object, not the entire message content, is passed to the SMTP memory stub in the information store. The SMTP memory stub is a queuing location provided by the ExIPC queuing layer between IIS and the information store.

4. The information store's SMTP stub passes the MailMsg object through the ExIPC shared memory layer to the SMTP stub in IIS.

5. The MailMsg object is passed to the Advanced Queuing Engine, which stores the message in the Messages Awaiting Directory Lookup queue (Microsoft also refers to this queue as the Pre-Categorizer queue). You can see messages in this queue by using the Exchange System Manager and viewing the queues in the SMTP virtual server.

6. The MailMsg object proceeds to the Message Categorizer component, which takes message information—such as the sender, recipient, and size—and performs AD queries (to a Global Catalog server) to determine if the message exceeds the sender's or recipient's limits. Also at this point, gateway and routing restrictions are determined. If the message is sent to a distribution list, the Message Categorizer also expands the distribution list. If the message is being sent to both external and internal recipients, the Message Categorizer performs a bifurcation of the message (two or more copies are created) so that an RTF copy is sent to internal recipients and a MIME copy is sent to external recipients.

TIP When the Message Categorizer component is performing directory lookups, connectivity to the Global Catalog server is critical. Any location that contains an Exchange 2000 server should also have a local Global Catalog server.

7. The MailMsg object is placed in the Messages Waiting To Be Routed queue (I also refer to this queue as the Pre-Routing queue).

8. The MailMsg object is handed off to the Routing Engine, which examines the destination domain or server and compares the destination with routes that are available in the Link State Table. If the message is for a local recipient, the MailMsg object is placed in the local delivery queue and the object is passed back to ExIPC. If the message is for remote delivery, the message is placed in the appropriate outgoing queue, and the SMTP service delivers the message off of the server. If the message is to be delivered by the message transfer agent (MTA) to Exchange 5.5 server

or to an X.400 connection, the message is routed back to the local store and placed in the MTA mailbox's MTS-OUT folder. Only when the message delivery to a remote host begins are the actual contents of the message moved out of the information store.

NOTE   Only the MailMsg object—not the entire message—is passed through the Advanced Queuing Engine. The message content is moved only when the message is ready to be delivered to another server or store.

There are slight variations on this message routing process for inbound messages, but the process is essentially the same.

Event Sinks

If all messages, regardless of whether or not they are destined for local delivery, are routed through the exact same message routing components, you might think this would be a good place to handle other types of message processing needs. If you thought this, you are not alone. The Exchange developers have introduced the concept of event sinks to Exchange 2000. An *event sink* is a small program that runs when a specific type of event occurs, such as a message arrival or the completion of categorization. In fact, the Exchange 2000 extensions to the IIS SMTP service are implemented as event sinks.

Types of Event Sinks

There are three major categories of event sinks: information store events, transport events, and protocol events. When dealing with the Message Transport system, we are concerned mostly with the protocol and transport events.

Protocol events are used to extend SMTP functionality by enhancing or providing additional SMTP command verbs. Possible uses include rejecting all messages from domains that do not have a reverse lookup record, changing the behavior of an existing SMTP command verb, or adding a custom SMTP command verb.

Transport events can be used when the message is passing through the Message Transport system. Uses include content inspection, adding message disclaimers, anti-spam features, or message compression. Another use might be a virus-scanning service, but the Exchange 2000 antivirus API provides much better virus-scanning performance. Transport events can be fired at the following points:

- When a message is submitted to the Message Transport system (inbound from the information store or from the SMTP service)
- When a message is placed in the Pre-Categorizer queue

- When a message is in the categorizer
- When a message is in the Pre-Routing (Post-Categorizer) queue
- When a message is being processed by the Routing Engine

Writing an Event Sink

The keys to writing a successful event sink are speed and accuracy. The accuracy part comes with comprehensive testing. However, the speed part comes with your choice of a programming language (and of course, writing efficient code). Development platforms include any programming language that is compatible with the Component Object Model (COM), including VBScript, JavaScript, Visual Basic, C, and C++.

If the event sink you want to develop will fire only for a select few messages an hour, then you can use Visual Basic, VBScript, or JavaScript. However, if your event sink will fire for all messages being processed, then you should use C or C++ to ensure maximum performance.

Exchange 2000 Connectors

By default, SMTP is used between Exchange servers in the same routing group. There is no need to set up any special configuration since an SMTP virtual server is configured by default on all Exchange 2000 servers. However, like connectivity to other Exchange 5.5 sites, connectivity to other Exchange 2000 routing groups requires a messaging connector. Exchange 2000 offers these options:

Routing Group Connector   The preferred method of communication between routing groups. It uses SMTP to connect between routing groups unless it is being used to communicate between an Exchange 2000 routing group and an Exchange 5.5 site, in which case it uses RPC. The Routing Group Connector is sort of like the old Exchange 5.5 site connector on steroids and using SMTP. It uses multiple bridgehead servers, can be scheduled, and can defer large messages to a time when WAN connectivity is not at a premium.

SMTP Connector   Typically used when you want to focus outbound SMTP connectivity to the Internet. If the SMTP Connector is not installed, then *any* Exchange 2000 server can deliver an SMTP message to the Internet. Once an SMTP Connector is installed, an SMTP address space is added to the Link State Table, indicating that all SMTP messages not destined for another Exchange 2000 server in the organization should be routed to this connector, but only if the address space is set to "*". The SMTP Connector can also be used to connect to Exchange 2000 routing groups.

Message transfer agent (MTA)   Used to communicate with other Exchange 2000 routing groups using X.400 and with foreign X.400 systems such as the U.S. Department of Defense's Defense Messaging System (DMS).

Other connectivity options that are part of Exchange 2000 include:

- Connector to Microsoft Mail
- Connector to Lotus Notes
- Connector to Lotus cc:Mail
- Connector to Novell GroupWise

Though Exchange 5.5 shipped with the connectors for PROFS- and SNADS-based systems, these are not included with Exchange 2000. If you require these connectors, you must keep your organization in Mixed mode and continue to operate an Exchange 5.5 server. If you are starting from scratch, you must install the Exchange 5.5 server first and then install your Exchange 2000 servers into the Exchange 5.5 organization.

Exchange 2000 System Attendant

The Exchange System Attendant (MAD.EXE) is essentially the general manager of the Exchange server. It is the first Exchange service that starts and the last one that shuts down. While a novice might actually think that this service performs few, if any, useful functions, it actually is responsible for a lot of odd yet important jobs. Some of the tasks that the System Attendant runs include:

- Performing offline address book generation.
- Running the DS2MB (Directory Service to Metabase) update process to keep the IIS Metabase in sync with the information in Active Directory.
- Generating proxy addresses for X.400, SMTP, and other address types based on the defined Exchange 2000 recipient policies.
- Emulating the Exchange 5.5 directory service through a process called DSProxy for MAPI clients prior to Outlook 2000 that cannot receive referrals.
- Passing referrals for Outlook 2000 and later clients that need to be referred to a Global Catalog server for querying address information.
- Running the Recipient Update Service to make sure that AD objects are included in the appropriate address lists.
- Running the DSAccess cache, which caches information about AD objects. This cache is available for Exchange 2000 to query rather than querying the AD directly for each lookup request.
- Inserting data into and managing the message tracking logs.

Exchange 2000 Modes

Like Windows 2000 Active Directory, Exchange 2000 has two modes in which the organization can operate: Mixed mode and Native mode. AD Native mode and Exchange 2000 Native mode have no effect on each other; they are completely independent.

By default, the organization is in Mixed mode, which allows Exchange 2000 to interoperate with Exchange 5.5 servers. Several limitations are imposed on an Exchange 2000 organization that is operating in Mixed mode, including:

- Windows 2000 Administrative groups are mapped directly to the Exchange 5.5 site architecture.
- Routing group membership can consist only of the servers that are in the administrative group containing that routing group.
- Exchange 2000 servers cannot be moved between routing groups.
- RPCs are used between Exchange 2000 servers and Exchange 5.5 servers.

To switch the organization to Native mode, check that all Exchange 5.5 servers have been upgraded or removed from service, and remove all ADCs and site replication services (SRSs). (Make sure to remove the SRS from the Tools container in Exchange System Manager.) Then display the Exchange organization's properties using Exchange System Manager and click the Change Mode button.

WARNING Changing to Exchange 2000 Native mode cannot be reversed.

Once you are in Native mode, you will have a little more flexibility than you do in Mixed mode. Some of its features include:

- Each administrative group can have multiple routing groups or no routing groups.
- A routing group can contain servers from any administrative group.
- Servers can be moved between routing groups.
- SMTP is used as the default message transport protocol between all Exchange 2000 servers.

Picking the Right Edition of Exchange

Now that you understand some of the basics of Exchange 2000 and how it differs from Exchange 5.5, it's important that you understand the differences between the two editions of Exchange 2000: Exchange 2000 Server and Exchange 2000 Enterprise Server.

You must pick the right version to meet the needs of your organization. Table 1.2 lists available features and which edition of Exchange 2000 provides them.

Table 1.2   Features with Exchange 2000 Server and Exchange 2000 Enterprise Server

Feature	Exchange 2000 Server?	Exchange 2000 Enterprise Server?
Active/Active clustering (Clustering can be either Active/Active or Active/Passive depending on the number of nodes.)		✓
Active Directory integration	✓	✓
Chat services		✓
Content indexing and searching	✓	✓
Database size larger than 16GB		✓
Exchange Installable File System (ExIFS)	✓	✓
Exchange policies	✓	✓
Front-end/back-end configuration	Can only function as a back-end server, but can be "front-ended" by an Exchange 2000 Enterprise server.	Can function as a front-end server or a back-end server.
Instant Messaging	✓	✓
Multiple mailbox stores		✓
Multiple storage groups		✓
Routing Group Connectors	✓	✓
SMTP Connector	✓	✓

Table 1.2   Features with Exchange 2000 Server and Exchange 2000 Enterprise
Server *(continued)*

Feature	Exchange 2000 Server?	Exchange 2000 Enterprise Server?
Web storage system	✓	✓
Windows 2000 security	✓	✓
Workflow Designer for Exchange 2000	✓	✓
X.400 Connector		✓

Building a Foundation

PART 1

> **NOTE**   Exchange 2000 Conference Server is not included with either edition of Exchange 2000; it is a separately licensed product. Exchange 2000 Conference Server requires at least one Exchange 2000 server and one Windows 2000 domain controller.

Upgrading between Editions

You can easily upgrade from Exchange 2000 Server to Enterprise by simply running the Exchange 2000 Enterprise Server Setup program and choosing the Reinstall option.

However, you cannot "downgrade" from the Exchange 2000 Enterprise Server version to Exchange 2000 Server. If you must do this, consider installing an additional server using Exchange 2000 Server and moving the mailboxes over to that new server.

> **TIP**   How can you tell which edition you have? Check under the server's Protocols container and see if you have an X.400 container. If so, that server is an Enterprise Server. You can also review your event logs and look for event 1217 from the MSExchangeIS Mailbox Store. This indicates that the mailbox store has unlimited capacity.

Storage Considerations

Exchange 2000 is far more scalable than its predecessors. Some Exchange 2000 administrators are reporting that they are now supporting nearly a terabyte of mailbox data on single servers. As the number of mailboxes on servers increases, you need to plan carefully to make sure that you're keeping a manageable amount of storage and that the mailbox data is backed up—and backed up in a reasonable amount of time.

Storage Limits

During the first Exchange 4 beta, I discovered storage limits, a feature sadly missing from other messaging platforms I had supported in the past. I asked a Microsoft consultant what the recommended limit was for mailboxes. His reply? 50MB per mailbox. As a cc:Mail administrator, I would have panicked if my entire database approached 50MB!

The changing nature of messaging systems has launched the need for more and more storage. E-mail messages are more and more complex with the advent of RTF and HTML formatting. And users love to send attachments. A typical Microsoft Word document with a few pages of text can easily be 40KB without any graphics. Several Exchange administrators report to me that they see 100MB Microsoft PowerPoint attachments all the time. The increasing popularity of digital signatures also increases the average message size. I know numerous people who include their company logos in their personal message signatures—and even one person who includes his picture (every message he sends is automatically 72KB!).

Many Exchange installations have embraced third-party add-on products, which include fax gateways, work-flow solutions, and voicemail integration—all potential space hogs. A standard two-page fax received into my mailbox is about 80KB, and a typical one-minute voicemail message is about 125KB.

Even simple, innocuous looking forms can put a burden on storage requirements. The "While You Were Out" form that is included with Outlook creates a message that is nearly 80KB. Messages that contain a form that is not in the organizational forms library can be 100KB or greater simply because the form is stored with the message.

Additional features of Outlook such as calendaring, contacts, journaling, notes, and tasks continue to drive the need for larger mailbox storage limits. A quick glance at my own Exchange mailbox shows that I have over 5MB of data in my Contacts folder, nearly 2MB of data in my Calendar folder, and 10MB in my Journal folder.

WARNING   Outlook's Journal folder can easily accumulate many megabytes of data if the journaling feature is turned on. Advise your users not to turn on this feature unless they require it. Alternatively, configure a Windows NT policy that disables this feature.

Exchange@Work: Setting Storage Limits

What does the typical organization do with respect to storage limits? Well, the only consensus is that there is no consensus. I still know a few organizations that require their users to use personal folders (PST files); all received e-mail is downloaded to the user's PST file storage in their personal profile or home directory.

I also know of a few companies that do not set any limits other than the Prohibit Send And Receive limit, but they use the Mailbox Manager (available with Exchange 2000 SP1) to automatically clean out all Sent items and Inbox items that are older than 60 or 90 days.

Still other folks set mailbox limits fairly low (20MB Issue Warning limit, 25MB Prohibit Send limit), but require that the users keep their own mailboxes clean. Some of these will configure Outlook's auto-archive feature to automatically move messages older than 30 days to a PST file.

I do know one administrator who purges older messages in users' mailboxes with the exmerge.exe utility from the Exchange 2000 CD-ROM (found in the Support\ Utils\I386\exmerge directory). She archives messages older than 120 days from the mailboxes and then backs up on tape the PST files that are created.

Obviously there are numerous approaches to handling storage issues (even more options are discussed in Chapter 4!), but the majority of administrators I know set their Issue Warning and Prohibit Send limits between 40MB and 75MB, and then override these limits for individual mailboxes. Keep in mind that when setting limits on mailbox storage, you have to have balanced the need to have a manageable amount of mailbox data with making sure the system remains usable to end users. Applying a policy that gives users only 5MB or 10MB of server-based storage will certainly help reduce your server-based storage requirements, but it may not allow the user anything more than a few days' worth of e-mail on the server.

TIP Even if you set no warning or send limits on mailboxes, configure Prohibit Send And Receive limits to prevent a mailbox from being spammed and possibly causing the server to run out of disk space. On several occasions, I have seen a single mailbox cause an entire server to shut down.

Server-Based Storage Versus Local Storage

One of the age-old questions that Exchange administrators have been facing since Exchange 4 was released in 1996 is "Where should users store their mail?" Both the original Exchange client as well as all versions of Outlook provide a storage option called a personal store (PST file). These clients give the user the option of automatically downloading all mail that was sent to the user's mailbox on the server to the local PST file.

The PST file is a simple B-tree database that can be located on either the user's local hard disk or server-based home directory. Yet based on the experiences of many Exchange administrators as well as my own, I strongly recommend that the primary message storage medium be the Exchange information store, not the local PST file. Table 1.3 compares PST-file storage and Exchange server-based storage.

Table 1.3   PST-Based Mail Storage vs. Server-Based Mail Storage

PST-Based Mail	Server-Based Mail
Reduced storage capacity is required on server.	Single instance storage is maintained.
PST files can be password protected, but the password can be cracked easily.	Mailbox security is centrally controlled and audited by the Exchange administrator.
Locally stored PST files may not be backed up if the local machine's hard disk is not being backed up.	Backups are centralized and administrator controlled.
A PST file may consume twice as much or more disk space as server-based storage because messages are stored twice in the PST file—once in RTF and once in plaintext—to maintain compatibility with older clients, and all forms are stored with each message.	Message storage is limited by the administrator.
Maximum PST file size is 2GB or 64,000 entries per folder. When the file size nears 2GB, it becomes corrupt, and you may not be able to recover any information from it.	
PST files are subject to database corruption.	

Table 1.3   PST-Based Mail Storage vs. Server-Based Mail Storage *(continued)*

PST-Based Mail	Server-Based Mail
PST cannot be shared or accessed by multiple systems.	
PST files can't be accessed from OWA.	

Time Synchronization

When using Windows NT 4 and Exchange Server 5.5, time synchronization was not required. Even with Windows 2000, AD replicates and synchronizes directory entries, not based on time, but by using *update sequence numbers (USNs)*. Exchange 2000 public folder replication is still based on a list of changes to each item called the *predecessor change list*. Time values for changes are used only in the event of public folder design change conflicts.

Based on this information, you might believe that time synchronization is not necessary. However, Windows 2000–based networks use Kerberos authentication, which requires that computers have their time synchronized to within five minutes. This means that all Windows 2000–based computers that are part of an AD forest must have their time synchronized to a common time source.

Synchronizing Windows 2000 Computers

Unlike previous version of Windows, Windows 2000 includes a service (the *W32Time service*) that ensures all Windows 2000 computers in an organization use a common time. Understanding how the time is synchronized is helpful, especially if you want to synchronize your network's time to an outside source.

In order to maintain proper time synchronization between Windows 2000 computers, the following hierarchy is used:

- Windows 2000 Professional computers use the domain controller that authenticated their login as their time source.
- Windows 2000 member servers use the domain controller that authenticated their login as their time source.
- Windows 2000 domain controllers use the PDC (primary domain controller) Flexible Single Master of Operations (FSMO) as their time source.

- Windows 2000 PDC FSMOs in child domains use the Windows 2000 PDC FSMO in their parent domain as their time source.

- The Windows 2000 PDC FSMO in the root domain of the forest is considered the authoritative time source for the entire forest.

Since the root domain's PDC FSMO is the master time source for all Windows 2000 computers in the forest, it should be configured to use an external time source. The easiest way to do this is simply to keep this server set to the correct time. Though not terribly accurate, you can call your local time and temperature telephone number periodically and set this server's time accordingly. You can get more accurate time information from the United States Naval Observatory (USNO) at tycho.usno.navy.mil/what.html.

If you have Internet connectivity, you can automate this process by setting the preferred time source for the root domain's PDC FSMO. If you want to set the server to use the USNO SNTP *(Simple Network Time Protocol)* time server, type the following at the command prompt:

```
NET TIME /SETSNTP:TOCK.USNO.NAVY.MIL
```

> **WARNING**   Setting the SNTP server name on Windows 2000 member servers and Windows 2000 Professional computers will appear to work, but it won't actually set the time. Only Windows 2000 PDC FSMO computers can use an external time source using the NET TIME command.

In order for this command to work, the PDC FSMO must have Internet connectivity. If you have a firewall, SNTP must be allowed through it. SNTP uses UDP port 123.

> **NOTE**   For a list of NTP and SNTP servers around the United States, visit tycho.usno.navy.mil/ntp.html.

Synchronizing Non–Windows 2000 Computers

If you have Windows NT 4, Me, 98, 95, or (shudder) 3.*x* computers on your network, you may also want to synchronize their system clocks. While this is not required for authentication, it is a good practice to make sure all the clients on the network have the same time. The simplest way to this is from the command prompt. Pick a server on your network as the master time server for these computers (in my example it is called HNLDC01) and type the following at the command prompt:

```
NET TIME \\HNLDC01 /SET /Y
```

This works fine for Windows 9*x* and 3.*x* based computers, but you must be a member of either the local Administrators, Power Users, or Server Operators group in order to make this change on Windows NT 4 computers. If you don't want to assign a user membership in one of these groups, you can simply assign them the local right "Change the system time."

Since some computer's time settings drift as much as 10 minutes per week (as one of my notebook computers does), in order to keep the time synchronized automatically, consider placing the NET TIME command in the logon script.

Automatically Synchronizing Windows NT 4 Computers

The Windows NT Server 4 Resource Kit has a tool called the Time Synchronization Service. At certain intervals, this tool gets the current time from a time source that you have defined. The time service tool can use a TCP/IP network or a modem to contact a time source.

There are two types of time sources. A *primary time source* is usually an external and highly accurate time source located somewhere like the Naval Observatory or the National Institute of Standards and Technology (NIST). A *secondary time source* is set from a primary time source.

When I use the Time Synchronization Service, I pick a server on my network that has a connection to the Internet to designate as my primary server. Then I install the time server software and edit the timeserv.ini file to set the time source type to INTERNET and to set the default period to 12. This points my server to the US Naval Observatory to get time updates every 12 hours. When I start the time service, an optional parameter in the timeserv.ini file tells the time service to log events to the Application event log.

On all other servers on the network, I install the time-server software and edit the timeserv.ini file to designate those servers as SECONDARY. I designate the primary server that I have just installed as the PrimarySource and set the period to 12 hours in the timeserv.ini. Every 12 hours, these servers will contact the primary server and get the updated time.

Standardization

One of the most important and useful things you can do for your organizations is establish standards. Perhaps one of the biggest mistakes I saw for organizations implementing Exchange 5.5 was a lack of common standards for hardware, the Exchange organization, site names, alias names, display names, SMTP addresses, group names, and server names.

To say that a lack of planning and standardization will be a stumbling block for the implementation of Exchange 2000 would be the biggest understatement I have ever made. Without planning and standardization, Exchange 2000 (and Active Directory) implementations don't hit stumbling blocks—they hit brick walls.

Active Directory

Windows 2000 Active Directory is the single biggest factor affecting the successful implementation of Exchange 2000. Exchange 2000 uses AD to store all Exchange 2000 configuration information, mailbox attributes, connector information, administrative permissions, and routing information, just to name a few. Some important facts and factors to keep in mind when planning your organization's Active Directory include:

- A single Exchange 2000 organization cannot span multiple AD forests.
- Only one Exchange 2000 organization can exist in any AD forest.
- The AD schema is replicated to *all* domain controllers in the entire forest.
- Create a single AD forest that will contain all Exchange 2000 servers and mailboxes.
- Use a common DNS namespace for all servers and workstations.

Exchange@Work: Three Forests, One Company

XYZ Corporation was an early adopter of Windows 2000. They installed three separate Windows 2000 forests; each forest contained a single domain. Each of these domains was in a different physical location, and the local administrators performed most day-to-day administrative work.

When it came time to upgrade their Exchange 5.5 servers, they were disappointed to learn that they were going to have to migrate two of the Windows 2000 domains into a common forest. While there are tools available to help migrate accounts to a new domain, this is not the same as moving the domain into a new forest. Many hours were spent preparing for and carrying out this migration. The ultimate forest design consisted of a single Windows 2000 domain with users from the different locations split into multiple organizational units.

If XYZ Corp. had initially created a single AD forest, they would have saved themselves many hours of additional work reconfiguring their AD domain structure.

> **NOTE** More information on Active Directory is found in Chapter 2. For in-depth information on Active Directory, consult *Mastering Active Directory* by Robert R. King (Sybex, 2000) or *Mastering Windows 2000 Server* by Mark Minasi (Sybex, 2000).

Usernames

Active Directory becomes the global directory service for your entire organization. Every user account you create in AD is visible to the entire organization, including the information that you input for that user. The standard you develop for creating user accounts should include:

- Alias name
- Display name appearance
- Additional information that's entered into Active Directory, such as SMTP addresses, mailing address, title, department, manager, etc.

Alias Names In most organizations, the alias name is exactly the same as the Windows user account name. There are a number of possible standards you could choose to implement:

NKarasuda	First name initial followed by last name
KeithS	First name followed by first initial of the last name
JWM	Initials
US2632	Employee number or job code

In any organization with more than a few dozen employees, you are most definitely going to run into problems with duplicates. Make sure that your standard allows for duplicate names and provides a standard formula for conflict resolution that creates unique names.

> **TIP** Some organizations are now choosing a separate e-mail address from their Windows user account. The reason is simple security. If you choose the same Exchange alias (and thus the SMTP address) as your Windows user account, you are giving a potential hacker half of the equation (hopefully, given strong passwords, the easier half) for accessing your network.

Display Names The display name is one of the most important directory attributes to keep consistent. Why? Because this attribute is the one that users see when they display the global address list and that users of foreign systems see when they receive a message from your users. Many organizations that have multiple domains and administrators have unfortunately seen each administrator creating their own standards for how a display name should look. And something as simple as commas being placed in different places or displaying the first name before the last name can make finding a mailbox difficult.

When choosing a standard for the display name, keep in mind that the display name is the user's relative distinguished name (RDN) and is designated by the "CN" value in the distinguished name (DN). Creating complex DNs may make it difficult to build custom Active Directory applications. Here are a number of standards that I have seen implemented:

Keith Sanchez	First name, last name (the default display name)
Sanchez, Keith	Last name, comma, first name
Sanchez Keith SFC 30 SigBn Ft Shafter	Last name, first name, title/rank, department, user location (a popular structure in the military)
Sanchez, Keith (DFW – Systems Engineer)	Last name, comma, first name, user location, job title (a popular structure among larger organizations)
Sanchez, Keith M.D.	Last name, comma, first name, title

Figure 1.5 shows the global address list as it appears in an organization that has not established any standards for display names. Note that there is no consistency in how the names are displayed.

Figure 1.5   Global address list for an organization with no display naming standards

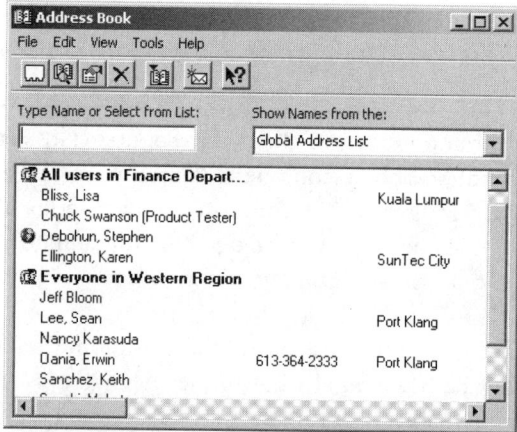

SMTP Addresses Depending on your organization, standards in SMTP addresses may also be important. I have worked in a number of organizations that were all over the board with respect to what the SMTP address actually is. Again here, a predetermined sequence of naming rules is useful for resolving conflicts that arise. Here are some examples of possible SMTP address standards:

GKukrika@somorita.com	First initial, last name (the most common SMTP naming standard)
GogaK@somorita.com	First name, last initial
Goga.Kukrika@somorita.com	First name, period, last name

> **NOTE** SMTP addresses cannot contain spaces or commas. They are not case sensitive.

Group Names

Active Directory enables you to create two types of groups. Either of these groups can be "mail-enabled" for use with Exchange 2000. These group types are:

- A *security group* allows permissions and user rights to be assigned to the membership of the group by assigning the permission or right to the group. Security groups are also used for assigning public folder permissions.

- A *distribution group* is used only for sending e-mail messages. Permissions and rights cannot be assigned to a distribution group.

> **NOTE** Don't confuse group types (security or distribution) with group scopes (Domain Local, Global, or Universal). These are discussed in more detail in Chapter 2.

Any group that is "mail-enabled" will appear in the Exchange global address list and can be used as a distribution list. The Exchange global address list does not differentiate distribution groups from security groups. When creating display names for these groups, a good practice to consider is using some type of special character to control where these groups display in the address list.

Figure 1.6 shows the Outlook address book view of an organization's global address list. Note that the mail-enabled security groups all have an underscore character (_) in front of them. The conference room resources contain a pound symbol (#), and system accounts have a dollar sign ($) in front of them. These special characters cause the different types of objects to be sorted together.

Figure 1.6 Outlook address book showing security groups sorted together

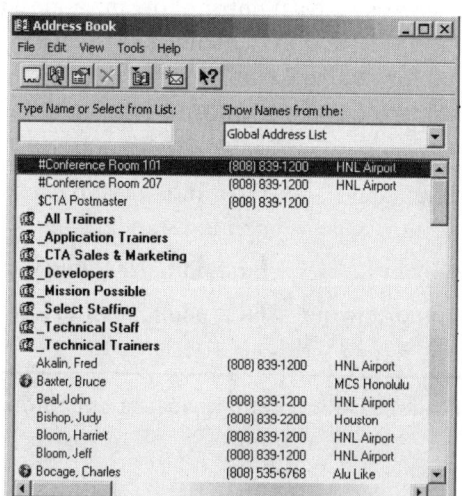

Server Names

Windows computer names should be standardized to avoid conflicts. You should develop a standard that will be meaningful to your organization and prevent conflicts. I have found administrators who are fond of using server names such as SERVER1 or using the user's name who works at a particular workstation. However, SERVER1 may be duplicated at another location. Users often move to new computers, or the computer is replaced with an upgrade model.

You should develop a standard that is independent of the user's name and does not allow for duplicates between offices or locations. Additionally, the standard should include a location code to identify the location of the computer (I am fond of the city's airport code), as well as an identifier showing what type of server it is. Below are some examples of naming that I have found to be useful and versatile:

Server Name	Explanation
SFODC01	San Francisco domain controller 01
HNLEXCH02	Honolulu Exchange server 02
KULSQL01	Kuala Lumpur SQL server 01
SINPROX03	Singapore proxy server 03
LJUISA02	Ljubljana ISA server 02
NRTWS0644	Tokyo workstation 0644

> **WARNING** Do not use spaces or the underscore (_) character in server names.

Server Hardware Considerations

Do you want 99.9% uptime on your Exchange 2000 servers? We all do, but most people don't realize that 99.9% uptime allows you only about nine hours of downtime per year. 99% uptime gives you about $3\frac{1}{2}$ days per year that you can actually be down. Three things will help move you toward that 99.9% uptime category:

- Good operational procedures.
- A reliable, well designed hardware platform.
- A good operational definition of "downtime" and "uptime." Make sure that you note the difference between scheduled/planned outages and system failure. There is no shame in having 10–15 hours of planned downtime if it means you have zero unplanned downtime.

Though most of this book is dedicated to helping you establish good operational procedures, this section will help you make the right decisions when choosing server hardware for Exchange 2000.

Choosing Hardware Components

Choosing the right brand of server hardware and the components for that hardware will help you achieve significantly better uptime. I believe the most important decision with respect to hardware choice is the choice of the hardware manufacturer. Further, I highly recommend that once you have chosen a manufacturer for your major components, you use that manufacturer for your minor components (disks, RAM, network adapters, SCSI adapters, tape drives, etc.) as well.

Sure, this may prove to be a little more costly in the short term. But any systems engineer who has tried to integrate components from different manufacturers will tell you that integration time for components from a single manufacturer is significantly less than the time it takes to build a server containing components from many different manufacturers. Further, if there are problems with any of the components, you have only a single vendor that you have to work with. So when making hardware decisions, pick a reputable hardware manufacturer and stick with them for all of your components.

Preventing Disasters with Hardware

As I stated earlier, most of the disasters that I have helped recover recently have been due to the inexperience of the system administrator, or the problem has been compounded by incorrect user actions. However, the other system failures that I have had to help recover in the past year have been a result of poor choices with respect to server, disk, and network hardware. These disasters have included a failed server that had run out of disk space, a disk failure on an unmirrored transaction log disk, debugging performance problems, and a bizarre case of Windows 2000 blue-screening a few times a week. This was one of the easiest problem-solving gigs of my career: The customer was running a Windows 2000 domain controller, DHCP, DNS, and Exchange 2000 on a single Pentium 700MHz system with 128MB of RAM. Their vendor swore that they had 1GB of RAM, but never bothered to physically check.

Disk Redundancy

The system component that fails the most often is the hard disk. Sometimes you are lucky and a server can operate for many years without a single disk failure. Other times you can be remarkably unlucky (like one of my clients), and two of the three disks in a RAID 5 array will fail inside of one week.

When configuring a new server, one hard and fast rule you should live by is this: All hard disks should be configured with *redundancy*. This includes the operating system disk, log file disks, mailbox and public store disks, and swap file disk.

Recently, I reviewed a proposal from a large, international consulting firm that recommended disk redundancy for only the database disks and the operating system disk. The consultancy's logic was that if the log file disk failed, the data would still be intact on the other disks. This is true to a certain degree, but the server will still shut down. And how long will that server be offline before the disk is replaced? Data redundancy is certainly important, but keeping the server online and available to the users is just as vital.

Disk Space Requirements

How much disk space should you plan for? And should you purchase the disk space immediately, or add the disk space as you need it? Typically, I recommend the following formulas for calculating how much disk space is required:

- Provide at least a 4GB system disk.
- The transaction log file should be able to store at least five days' worth of transactions without being purged.
- Each database disk should have free space that is at least the size of the largest database on the disk available. For example, if the largest database on the disk is 100GB, then there should be 100GB of free disk space in addition to the 100GB database.
- The disk that contains the SMTP \Mailroot\Queue directory should contain enough disk space to store at least 12 hours' worth of incoming mail. If you don't know how much this is, then plan for at least 2GB.

As for adding disk space as it is required, this is one recommendation I would *not* make. Purchase all the disk space you think you will need for a few years. For most servers, adding additional disk space means downtime and administrative overhead.

Exchange@Work: Disk Space Usage

ABC Corporation supports a site with four Exchange 2000 servers. Two of these servers have mailboxes, the third is dedicated to public folders, and the fourth is their bridgehead server (containing the fax connector and the SMTP Connector).

Each of the two mailbox servers has approximately 2300 mailboxes, most of which are accessed on a daily basis. The average user has a 65MB Send And Receive limit on their mailbox and a 50MB Warning limit. The largest mailbox store is nearly 95GB.

It's interesting to note that each of the mailbox servers generates 650 transaction log files per day, on average. When the nightly backup runs, the transaction log disk has about 3.5GB of transaction logs. The transaction log disk has approximately 16GB of usable disk space, so the server can run for about 4½ days without performing a normal or differential backup. Each volume that is used by a mailbox store is partitioned (on a storage area network) with 200GB of usable store. I think this is a great setup; it gives ABC a good safety net in a number of areas, including the transaction log disk and the mailbox stores.

> **WARNING**   Running out of disk space on the transaction log disk is one of the most common reasons for Exchange servers going offline.

Tape Backup Hardware

Today's tape backup hardware is very impressive. The choices of available backup technology include DLT tape arrays, auto-loader systems, and more. Many companies choose to perform centralized backups rather than installing backup devices on their Exchange servers. The advantage of centralized backups is that they require less administration, and you can purchase more sophisticated loader and tape library management systems if you are supporting one centralized system.

The disadvantage of centralized backup and restore systems is that they must back up the data across the network, which typically means that it takes longer. One of my clients implemented a centralized DLT backup. This centralized system could back up remote

Exchange data at a rate of about 3GB per hour. They found this rate to be unacceptable, so they moved this backup hardware into a storage area network that was attached to each of the Exchange servers locally. The backup rate improved to almost 2.5GB per hour. They later found out that the backup server was actually on a 10MB network, not a 100MB network. Once the backup server was moved to a 100MB switched network, the backup rate improved to almost 15GB per hour.

The points I try to follow when I recommend or purchase tape backup hardware include:

- The hardware must be able to perform a full (normal) backup of the all Exchange information stores each night and allow each store to complete at least one pass of nightly maintenance.
- The restoration time of the largest mailbox or store must fall well within the maximum continuous downtime limit specified by the service level agreement.

Uninterruptible Power and Power Supply Redundancy

Though providing an uninterruptible power supply (UPS) for all server hardware seems like an obvious recommendation, it is one that is often overlooked. Uninterruptible power is essential for not only Exchange servers, but for all components in your computer room. This includes hubs, switches, and routers. Exchange should continue to operate normally and have access to the necessary domain controllers and Global Catalog servers after a power failure.

Even if you have a building power supply and generator, the UPS is still a good investment. One of my customers recently had a commercial power failure and found that the generator system took a full five seconds to cut over. Naturally, all of the servers were offline about five seconds before the generator kicked in.

Further, UPS monitoring should be configured so that all servers will shut themselves down if the commercial power is not restored in a timely fashion. Note that active Exchange servers can take significantly longer to shut down cleanly than other servers, like file or print servers. If you must commence an automated shutdown, make sure that your servers have enough time to completely shut down prior to the battery power being exhausted.

How much battery life should the UPS provide? Here in Hawaii, our typical power outage, however infrequent, usually lasts no more than 10 minutes. So I feel that 15 minutes of battery power should be sufficient. However, living in the U.S., I am lucky to have consistently reliable power. Many people around the world are not as fortunate. Overseas, I have experienced power outages between five minutes and two or three days. If your primary electrical power source is frequently unavailable for more than 15 minutes, consider generator backup solutions.

If you are running complex disk storage systems such as storage area networks or network appliances, an emergency generator or a UPS that will keep you up longer than 30 minutes is essential. Some of the new SAN (storage area network) solutions I have worked with are about as complex to shut down as a mainframe and can take upwards of 20 minutes for a controlled shutdown!

> **TIP**   Vendors that ship server class hardware today provide the ability to configure the server with multiple power supplies. Make sure that the server can run with a failed power supply. And learn how to monitor the power supplies so that you can determine if one has failed.

Cold Standby Servers

One of my favorite things to do in an environment that is installing several Exchange servers is to make sure that they are all configured identically and to specify an additional server that has no specific function. This server has two purposes. The first and official job is to act as the cold standby server. If any hardware failure occurs to any of the other servers, I can simply move the disks over to the standby server and bring it back online.

The second purpose of the cold standby is to be used for disaster recovery practice and training. Disaster recovery practice and test data restores are essential for a healthy organization. Ideally, we hope that we will never have to restore data from tape or use our disaster recovery skills, but I promise you that your first disaster will go much more smoothly if you have some practice.

> **TIP**   Make sure that you have written (and hard-copy) instructions of the procedures for switching a server over to a cold standby in the event the production server fails. In one site, I developed meticulous documentation for this, but left it stored on one of the servers. When we got ready to test the switchover, we had to bring the original server back up in order to print the documentation.

Hardware and Performance Tuning

Purchasing the right hardware and setting it up for disaster prevention is not enough; the hardware must be configured properly, and Exchange 2000 must be configured to use the hardware effectively. This includes which disks Exchange Server uses for mailbox and public folder stores and transaction logs as well as making sure the RAM on the server is configured properly.

One Server, One Task

Want to avoid problems? Do not overlap tasks on the same machine. Exchange Server should be on a member server; it should not be installed on the same server as a Windows 2000 domain controller or Global Catalog server, nor should other application servers such as SQL Server, SMS components, or ISA Server be installed on the same machine.

RAM Requirements

How much memory is enough for Exchange? How much memory does your server hold? Max it out, and you'll probably have enough. Seriously though, I recommend a starting point of 512MB of RAM. For servers that are going to support more than 300 mailboxes, plan to go to a minimum of 1GB of memory. For more than 500 to 1000 mailboxes, go ahead and max out the server at 4GB of RAM.

> **NOTE** Exchange 2000 will attempt to allocate all of the free memory with the information store processes (store.exe) using the most memory. It is not unusual to see the store.exe consuming almost all of the memory on a server. If the server has 1GB of RAM, the store process may well have allocated over 800MB of RAM. This is normal and should not be a source of concern.

If memory is at a premium on your Exchange server, create fewer mailbox and public folder stores. Create all of your mailbox stores and public folder stores in a single storage group. Each mounted mailbox store allocates a minimum of 10MB of RAM. The first store in a storage group allocates even more memory. So with some innovative creation of mailbox stores in a single storage group, you can reduce your overall memory consumption.

If your server hardware has more than 1GB of memory, you should add the /3GB switch to the BOOT.INI file of your server. Windows NT and Windows 2000 allocate 2GB of virtual address space for the Windows NT kernel and 2GB of virtual address space to user mode processes. Windows 2000 Advanced Server and Windows 2000 Datacenter allow you to change this allocation with the /3GB switch in the BOOT.INI. This feature is not available with Windows NT 4 or Windows 2000 Server.

The Exchange information store is typically the memory hog on an Exchange server. If the server has 2GB of RAM, the store will attempt to use as much of that memory as it can. However, as it allocates RAM, the amount of virtual memory it has allocated will be greater than the actual amount of RAM. It will run out of virtual memory even though there is still RAM available. Memory allocations will begin to fail, and the information store service will have to be shut down in order to resolve the problem. However, the problem will recur when the information store has restarted. The solution is to make sure that Windows 2000

Advanced Server or Windows 2000 Datacenter has the /3GB switch in the BOOT.INI file. If you are not using Windows 2000 Advanced Server or Datacenter, you should upgrade the operating system.

NOTE For more information about the /3GB switch, see Microsoft Knowledge Base article Q266096.

Locating Exchange Data and Transaction Log Files

One of the keys to improving Exchange performance is to ensure that Exchange database and transaction logs are located on separate physical hard drives, as shown in the simple server configuration in Figure 1.7. The operating system and Exchange binaries are located on one physical disk (hopefully mirrored), the Exchange transaction logs are located on a separate physical disk (also mirrored), and the Exchange public folder and mailboxes stores are located on a separate physical disk (in this case, a RAID 5 array).

Figure 1.7   Disk drive configuration for Exchange

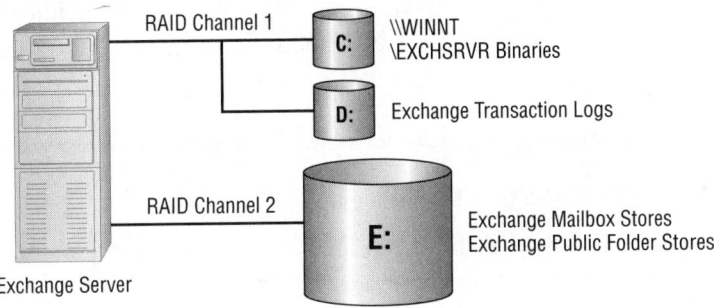

Significant performance improvements will always be realized by placing the transaction log files on a separate physical disk. The disk should not be shared by any other application. If you create more than one storage group, each storage group's transaction log files should be placed on a separate physical disk drive. The volume on which you place the transaction log files will best perform on a mirrored volume or a RAID 0+1 volume (mirrored, striped sets). During normal server operations, log file usage is exclusively write-intensive, so RAID 5 drive arrays will hurt transaction log file performance.

If the Exchange server functions as a bridgehead server, then the \EXCHSRVR\MTAData and \EXCHSRVR\Mailroot directories should be located on a separate physical hard disk. A single physical disk dedicated to the Mailroot and MTAData directories should be sufficient for all but the most extreme circumstances (thousands of message per hour to both the MTA and the SMTP message system).

User Education

An area that is often overlooked during deployment of a new messaging system is end-user training. When you are a technical person managing the Exchange deployment, it is easy to rationalize that your end-user community can "figure things out." This is a bad assumption. My advice is to plan for two phases of training.

The first run of training should address equivalent functionality issues. Show the users how to use Outlook and Exchange to get the identical functionality that they had previously. Your user community is going to have enough worries adapting to a new software product; teach them just what they need to know to do exactly what they were doing with the old system. Many companies also provide "floor support" for their users immediately after training. This is a trainer or person who is already comfortable with the new system. Throughout the workday, the floor support person checks with the users who have just started using the new system to see if they have questions or need assistance.

Once your user community has become accustomed to the new system and to the basic features of Outlook, the second phase of training introduces them to features they may not have had previously, including group scheduling, rules, journaling, and task assignment. Additional phases of training can introduce new features such as using forms and public folders.

Exchange@Work: A Training Plan

What is one great way to reduce your help desk costs? Turn your end users into power users! Company GHI migrated a 2400-node network from Lotus cc:Mail to Exchange. Prior to migration, the cc:Mail users had no features such as calendaring or group scheduling available to them.

The first phase of user training introduced the basic abilities of Outlook. The three-hour mandatory training session covered:

- The acceptable use policy for using the system, keeping mailboxes cleaned up, password and confidentiality issues, and help desk procedures. Also discussed were the introductory training materials, which included a short "How to..." guide and frequently asked questions section.

- Message formatting, attachments, and other features of an Outlook message such as delivery and notification receipts.

Exchange@Work: A Training Plan *(continued)*

- How to send, receive, reply to, and forward e-mail messages using Outlook; how to manage the Inbox and Sent Items folders; and how to create subfolders to better organize messages. Searching features and views were also introduced.

- Contact and Calendar folders (with the promise to users of future calendar training).

- Exchange's public folders feature vs. cc:Mail bulletin boards. Three public folders were discussed: a system announcements public folder, a Microsoft Office tips and questions public folder, and a classified ads public folder. (This last folder was specifically designed to stimulate people's interest in public folders.)

Once all users had been migrated and trained on basic functionality, another two-hour mandatory training session was held for all users that included:

- Group scheduling and calendaring (as promised)

- Scheduling shared resources such as conference rooms, laptops, and so on

- Creating a personal folder (PST file) and archiving messages to it

- A vacation/time-off request form

- A new public folder application, departmental In/Out boards

After the system had been in production for nearly nine months and users had been given time to get very comfortable with the basic features of Outlook, weekly training sessions were offered. Each "no nonsense" session covered one particular topic in detail. The sessions were offered five times during a week (at lunchtime), and the users were encouraged to bring their own lunch (they were called Brown Bag sessions). Though this got off to a slow start, the Brown Bag sessions became immensely popular and were often standing-room only. These one-hour meetings included topics such as:

- The Rules Wizard and the Inbox Assistant

- The Outlook Journal feature

- Accessing other users' mailboxes (calendars, contacts, and so on) or giving other users access to a user's mailbox

Exchange@Work: A Training Plan *(continued)*

- Outlook usage for remote or home users

- Outlook refresher courses

Well, you get the idea. GHI had implemented this particular strategy when converting from WordPerfect to Word with excellent results, and they continue to offer Brown Bag sessions for Word, Excel, and Outlook. This is a great example of a company doing whatever it takes to turn their user community into power users. GHI realizes that in the long term, better-educated users will reduce the total amount of IS support they'll require.

Messaging Champions

In any department or workgroup, a few users inevitably arise from the ashes of a new mail system as champions of the new technology. These folks see early on the benefits of Exchange and Outlook and become evangelists for your cause. You should identify these people early on and encourage them. Often, these users will end up being your "on-the-spot help desk."

Getting the Training Done

A lot of companies today have an in-house training staff. If this is the case with your organization, make sure that your in-house trainers are brought into the Exchange design process early. The trainers should have been using the server and client features long before they start training the user community.

If you decide to contract an outside organization, carefully select both the company and the individual(s) who will be providing your client training. The trainers should understand the client (such as Outlook) as well as Exchange Server. If possible, look for a training company that has experience with your legacy system and is amenable to customizing the training to suit your users' level of expertise and needs.

Once you have selected your training company, ask if you can work with the same trainers throughout your training process so you'll have an opportunity to familiarize them with your existing system and procedures. The more comfortable the third-party trainers are with your organization, the better training your users will receive.

Other Training Topics

What should be covered in training other than using the messaging system? What can you do in end-user training that will help keep your Exchange system healthy? I am betting that there is a long list of things you wish your users knew, and many of those things are not technical. In addition to the obvious, some things that I would make sure to cover during training are

- Showing users how to use distribution lists (or to use the appropriate public folder rather than a distribution list).
- Instructing users to double-check their To, Cc, and Bcc fields to make sure that the message is addressed to the proper recipient(s).
- Teaching users the difference between the Reply button and the Reply To All button. Discourage the use of Reply To All. Users should ask themselves "Does everyone who originally received this message need to see my reply?" Inevitably, a few times a year, a user will hit the Reply To All function by accident and reply with a message like: "I'd like to make it to the company picnic, but I'm getting a wart removed." For the accidental recipients of this message, this is too much information.
- Discouraging large message signatures and signatures with graphics in them.
- Showing users how to send shortcuts or links to large files rather than attaching the files directly to the message.
- Storing files in personal folders, archiving messages and other Outlook data to these files, and retrieving data from personal folders.
- Reviewing the acceptable use policy.
- Educating users about chain letters and urban legends so that they will not be so quick to forward "Good Times" virus warnings, pictures of naked celebrities, free money ads, and warnings of kidney theft rings.
- Teaching users to delete messages once they have acted on them and to keep their Sent Items folder clean.

Documentation for End Users

Another integral part of the training process is providing your user community with detailed documentation. This guarantees that you don't leave your users out in the cold during and after the migration. Their first line of defense will be your help desk, but you want to give your users something they can use *prior* to calling the help desk. This may be a simple handout or a complete manual. This documentation should include:

- "How to..." guides for common tasks
- Frequently asked questions (and answers)

- Common problems and how to resolve them
- Special notes on what you learned during the pilot project

For example, one small company that I worked with assembled this material in a very professional, bound booklet. The user was given this booklet a few days prior to attending training. I personally like hard copies of my reference material, but a web site or an Exchange public folder is also an excellent location for posting this material.

Exchange@Work: Can You Give Me Just a Hint?

A particularly resourceful network administrator created one-page handouts describing how to perform certain tasks in Outlook, Word, Excel, and so on. These handouts focused on a single hint or task, included a graphic or picture, and were never more than a single page.

She posted these in the employee kitchens, photocopy rooms, above the fax machines—any place people would stop for a few minutes and might have idle time. I suspect she even tried posting these in the elevators and bathrooms.

At first, the user community did not know quite what to think. However, her writing style, humor, the concise nature of each "page," and the usefulness of the information proved quite effective. She recently created an internal web site of her "greatest hits"; unfortunately it is not accessible outside of her company.

And a Little Bit of Therapy on the Side...

Migration to a new message system is a stressful experience. As system administrators and network engineers, we all recognize this type of stress. We have deadlines to meet, executives and managers demanding successful implementations in one or two days, and impatient users.

As technical people, we often overlook the fact that a migration is also stressful for the end users. We technophiles view upgrades as a way to get to work with new things. Every few months I have to listen to one of my friends complain about changes in their computer system at work. "Nothing works the way it used to." "The IT department never tells us anything; they just show up and change things." "Why do I have to learn something new?"

End users do not view system upgrades with the same optimism that we do. They view technology as the means to do their job, not the job itself. Once they learn to manipulate a tool to do something, even if it is a poor tool, they are often reluctant to upgrade to a better tool.

Some larger organizations have someone on staff who analyzes the changes in people's work environments. If this modification will introduce too much stress, this staff member works with the facilitators of the change to make sure that the negative impact is minimal.

You can help minimize stress on your user community by providing them with good documentation as well as by getting their input—and letting them know what is going to happen and when. Once you create a schedule, stick to it! Let the users know that you care and that you will do everything you can to make sure they are happy with the things that are about to change. If all else fails, the users are burning you in effigy, and things are going terribly wrong, I suggest a little Rocky Road ice cream, a chili dog, and some time with a surfboard.

2

Active Directory for Exchange 2000 Administrators

Active Directory (AD) is one of the most complex and powerful products that Microsoft has ever released. Writing about even a small part of it can fill an entire book. This chapter serves merely as an introduction to Active Directory that is targeted toward Exchange 2000 administrators. A successful installation of Exchange 2000 depends on the successful deployment of Windows 2000 Active Directory. Since Exchange 2000 has no directory service of its own, it is entirely reliant on Windows 2000.

Exchange 5.5 administrators seem to grasp the concepts of Active Directory fairly quickly due to the fact that AD is similar in some respects to the Exchange 5.5 directory. And it should be; many of the Exchange 5.5 developers also worked on Windows 2000 Active Directory.

Since the first betas of Exchange 2000, I have noticed two different schools of thought arising with respect to Active Directory. The first group is made up of the Windows 2000/ Active Directory gurus. These folks believe in multiple domains and looking for ways to reduce replication in any way possible (such as the choice of the scope of Active Directory groups). The second group, into which I reckon I now fall, believes in fewer domains in the forest and using Universal groups (both distribution and security).

Regardless of the group into which you fall, a solid understanding of Active Directory is important, as is locating the tools that will help you to solve AD- and DNS-related problems. Understanding things such as your choice of group scope (Universal, Global, or Domain Local) and how that will affect AD is helpful when performance turning. When troubleshooting, you should understand the structure of your forest when explaining things like why a user's name is not yet appearing in the entire directory. And finally, understanding what type of load Exchange 2000 is going to place on the domain controllers and Global Catalog servers will help you design a better, more reliable Active Directory infrastructure, whether AD is your responsibility or someone else's.

> **TIP** Even if Exchange 2000 administrators are not responsible for maintaining Windows 2000 Active Directory, they should be consulted on questions regarding the design and AD infrastructure.

> **NOTE** This chapter and this entire book assume that you are running Windows 2000 Service Pack 2 on all of your domain controllers and member servers. Further, it assumes that you have installed Exchange 2000 Service Pack 1. There are two excellent white papers, "Microsoft Exchange 2000 Internals Service Pack 1 Deployment Guide" and "Microsoft Exchange 2000 Internals Service Pack 1 Component Guide," that you should download and read from www.exinternals.com.

Active Directory and the Domain Name Service

Though not explicitly part of Exchange, successful Exchange administrators must understand the use of DNS (Domain Name Service) as well as how Active Directory and Exchange depend on it. Many of the problems I have experienced in early deployments of Windows 2000 and Exchange 2000 have been related to name resolution and locating the appropriate Active Directory resources.

> **NOTE** Though Windows 2000 and Active Directory can work with the latest versions of BIND, I still recommend using the Windows 2000 DNS server. This chapter assumes that you are using the Windows 2000 DNS server.

> **TIP** I recommend that you enable dynamic updates. You can increase the security of dynamic updates by creating Active Directory integrated zones (the zone data is stored in AD, not in a zone file).

> **WARNING**   I will repeat myself on a couple of points several times in this book, but they deserve to be repeated. The first point is that a Windows 2000 Active Directory forest can host only *one* Exchange organization. The second is that an Exchange 2000 organization *cannot* span multiple Active Directory forests. These facts must be fully assimilated into your organization's mindset before you begin designing your Active Directory and Exchange 2000 infrastructure.

Active Directory Partitions

Exchange 2000 is completely reliant on Active Directory, not only for looking up information about mail Active Directory objects (mailbox-enabled users, mail-enabled users, mail-enabled contacts, distribution lists, and public folders), but also for storage of Exchange 2000 configuration information. To better understand this, let's first look at the different partitions of the Active Directory database. A *partition* is a unit of replication with respect to Active Directory. There are three partitions in Active Directory:

- Domain partition
- Configuration partition
- Schema partition

Though each partition is a boundary of replication, they all exist within the same database file (NTDS.DIT). Exchange 2000 uses each of these partitions for different purposes.

Domain Partition

The *domain partition* of Active Directory contains information about users, contacts, public folders, resources, groups, workstations, servers, and domain controllers. When a new Active Directory user account is created, it is created in the domain partition of Active Directory.

All data in the domain partition is replicated to all domain controllers in the domain. For organizations with a single Active Directory site, replication can take between five and 15 minutes depending on the number of domain controllers. For organizations with multiple AD sites in their organization, replication will be based on the schedule set up on the site replication links.

A subset of the user, contact, and group attributes in the domain partition is replicated to all domain controllers in the forest that have been assigned the role of a Global Catalog server. These attributes include first name, last name, logon name, user principal name, city, state, and others.

Configuration Partition

The *configuration partition* is a forest-wide resource. Data in the configuration partition is replicated to all domain controllers in the entire forest. AD-aware software (such as Exchange) can use this partition to store configuration data that may be necessary anywhere in the forest. Regardless of how many domains or trees you have in your AD forest, this container is always the same in all domains.

When using the Exchange System Manager console, this utility is actually making changes to a nearby domain controller's copy of the configuration partition. Thus the administrator does not have to be in direct contact with the Exchange 2000 server in order to modify most configuration options. This brings up an important point. Since the changes are made to the one domain controller's configuration container and the Exchange 2000 server is using a different domain controller to retrieve its configuration information, changes may not take effect immediately. Patience, my friends. If you need to see which domain controller an Exchange server is using, you can use the DSADiag utility, discussed later in this chapter.

The configuration partition contains information such as data about AD sites, Windows 2000 public key services, routing and remote access, and, of course, Exchange 2000. When the first Exchange 2000 server is installed into Active Directory, a new container called Microsoft Exchange is created in the CN=Services,CN=Configuration,*<domain context>*. For example, in an organization whose forest root domain is called somorita.net, this path will look like this: CN=Microsoft Exchange,CN=Services, CN=Configuration, DC=somorita, DC=net. Get used to these container name paths—they are used frequently with Active Directory and Exchange 2000. This container will hold information about the Active Directory Connector (ADC) and the Exchange organization. (The ADC is discussed in detail in Chapter 3, "Exchange 2000 Migration and Upgrades.") Figure 2.1 shows the Microsoft Exchange container being viewed by ADSI Edit.

The organization captured in Figure 2.1 is Somorita Surfboards, and in CN=Administrative Groups,CN=Somorita Surfboards,CN=Microsoft Exchange, there can be only one Exchange organization object in the Microsoft Exchange container. Since the configuration container is replicated to the entire forest, there can be only one Exchange organization in the entire forest.

Almost all Exchange 2000 configuration information is stored in the configuration container; this includes routing and administrative group information, address list definitions, recipient policies, virtual server configuration (SMTP, POP3, HTTP, IMAP4, NNTP, IM), Exchange 2000 system policies, and server configuration.

Figure 2.1 ADSI Edit showing the Microsoft Exchange configuration container

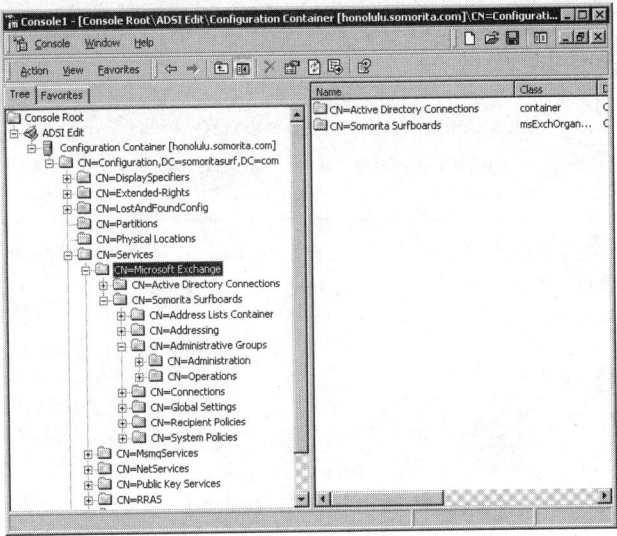

The Exchange System Manager console may create and store information about virtual servers in the AD configuration partition, but the information is updated to the appropriate server's Internet Information Server (IIS) Metabase by the DS2MB process that runs as part of the Exchange System Attendant.

Here is an example of how IIS would be updated. An administrator makes a change to one of Exchange 2000 Server's STMP virtual servers. The change is stored in the configuration container and then replicated to all domain controllers. The DS2MB process monitors the AD configuration container for changes that affect the local server. When the change is replicated to the domain controller that the affected Exchange server uses for configuration information, the DS2MB service updates the local IIS Metabase. This update is one-way, meaning changes are made only from AD to IIS, not the other way around.

Each Exchange 2000 server selects a Windows 2000 domain controller in its own domain to use for configuration data lookup. The Exchange server picks a configuration domain controller by doing a DNS query for service location (SRV) records; Exchange will pick a domain controller in the same AD site as it is in. If this server becomes unavailable, the Exchange server does a DNS query and picks another domain controller. Exchange 2000 seems to prefer selecting a domain controller that is not a Global Catalog server.

In some production environments, administrators are noting that failover to another domain controller is not happening quickly. Check your Exchange 2000 servers to make sure they are still functioning after an AD domain controller fails. You can use the DSAdiag utility to force an Exchange server to re-select a domain controller. If no domain controllers are available in the Exchange server's domain, it cannot start. If a domain controller fails and there is not another domain controller available, Exchange 2000 will cease to function properly.

You can determine which domain controller an Exchange server is using for its configuration partition by using DSADiag or viewing the server's properties in Exchange System Manager.

NOTE Viewing the configuration domain controller as well as the Global Catalog servers that a server is using is easily accomplished with the DSADiag utility, which is described later in this chapter.

Schema Partition

The third partition of Active Directory is the *schema partition*. The schema is a set of rules about the AD database that defines what classes (objects) are available and what attributes of each object can be or must be used. Examples of AD classes include a user, contact, public folder, or Exchange server. Each of these classes has attributes associated with it; for example, the user object's associated attributes may include given name, home mail server, and e-mail addresses. A class can have mandatory and optional attributes associated with it. Data for mandatory attributes must be entered in order to save the new object that is being created.

Figure 2.2 shows the Schema Management MMC with the user class highlighted in the left pane and some of the user class's attributes in the right pane.

Figure 2.2   Schema Management console showing the user class and some of its attributes

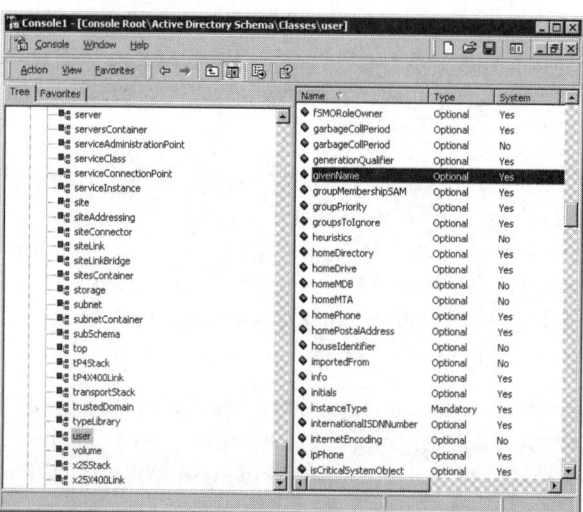

NOTE For a complete list of the classes and attributes that the Exchange 2000 Setup creates and modifies, view the schema0.ldf through schema9.ldf files on the Exchange 2000 CD-ROM or the Exchange 2000 schema class and attribute extensions document on the Web at www.somorita.com.

The schema partition is also replicated to all domain controllers in the forest. Only certain administrators can modify the schema (members of the root domain's Schema Admins group). Exchange must update the schema in order for the required classes and attributes to be in AD. This is done during the installation of the first Exchange 2000 server, during the ADC installation, or when the ForestPrep setup option is run.

Exchange@Work: Surfing and Troubleshooting Active Directory

Are you planning on taking a tour through Active Directory? I encourage you to do so, but with these words of caution: Just as with the Registry or Exchange Server 5.5 raw mode, you can prematurely end the life of Active Directory by changing the wrong thing. However, with caution and following instructions exactly, you can learn a great deal about AD, customize it, and possibly even fix some problems that cannot be fixed through the standard administrative utilities. Following is a list of utilities that may prove useful when browsing AD in raw mode. Some of these tools are found with the Windows 2000 Support Tools located on the Windows 2000 CD-ROM in the \Support\Tools directory. I highly recommend installing these tools on all of your Windows 2000 servers.

ADSIEDIT is a Microsoft Management Console (MMC)–based utility that allows you to view or edit any object in Active Directory. ADSIEDIT uses the Active Directory Services Interface (ADSI) to access Active Directory. This tool is part of the Windows 2000 Support Tools. Once installed, you must register the adsiedit.dll so that it can be loaded into an MMC console. To register the DLL, type **regsvr32 "c:\program files\system tools\adsiedit.dll"**. Once this is done, you can add the ADSIEDIT snap-in to any MMC console.

LDP is a low-level AD tool that uses LDAP commands to access Active Directory. You can search, modify, and create new entries in Active Directory using LDP, but it is not a user-friendly utility and should be used only if you know exactly what you're doing. This utility is found in the same directory as the adsiedit.dll utility, once the Windows 2000 support tools are installed. It is not an MMC snap-in. For more information on using the LDP utility, read Microsoft Knowledge Base articles Q260745 and Q255602.

Exchange@Work: Surfing and Troubleshooting Active Directory *(continued)*

Active Directory Schema Management is an MMC-based utility that allows you to view the properties of object classes and attributes. It is part of the standard Windows 2000 installation. From this utility, you can configure an attribute to be indexed or to include it in the Global Catalog. It uses the `schmmgmt.dll`, but it must be registered first before the console snap-in will work. To do so, at the command prompt, type **regsvr32 c:\winnt\system32\schmmgmt.dll**. Once this is done, you can add the Active Directory Schema tool to any MMC console. Only members of the Schema Admins group in the forest root domain can actually update the schema.

Replication Monitor, or ReplMon, is included with the Windows 2000 Support Tools. This utility lets you connect to any domain controller and check its replication status, view its replication partners, force replication, view FSMO (flexible single master of operations) roles, locate Global Catalog servers, and much more. FSMOs are discussed later in this chapter.

Active Directory Sites

Active Directory organizational units, domains, trees, and forests represent the administrative structure of your network. This structure does not consider the physical network, bandwidth between locations, or the need to control directory replication. This is where Active Directory sites come into the picture.

An AD site is much like an Exchange 5.5 site: It is a collection of Windows 2000 domain controllers (from one or more domains) that are separated by reliable, full-time, high-speed connectivity. Active Directory sites do not follow the logical structure of the AD trees; an AD site can contain more than one domain, and a domain can span multiple sites. Sites are defined by one or more IP subnets using the Active Directory Sites And Services console.

Active Directory sites allow you to control two types of traffic that are generated on a Windows 2000 network: logon traffic and directory replication traffic. When a Windows 2000–based user logs on to a Windows 2000 network, the client will attempt to find a domain controller in the same site. Further, the administrator can control directory replication traffic by scheduling replication between sites and by using SMTP rather than RPCs to replicate directory updates. Most of the AD sites I have seen to date have used RPCs to replicate directory updates because SMTP is less versatile and more difficult to configure.

Each Active Directory site should have at least one (but preferably two for redundancy) Global Catalog servers. This is because Exchange 2000 will try to use a Global Catalog server in its own site before attempting to use one from another site. This will help control directory lookup traffic on your wide area network.

> **NOTE**   Exchange 2000 administration and message routing are not based on Active Directory sites.

> **WARNING**   If you choose to control Active Directory replication using sites, you must assign the correct IP subnets to each site you are building, move the domain controllers into the appropriate sites using the Active Directory Sites And Services console, and create site links between the AD sites.

Global Catalog Servers

A *Global Catalog server* is a Windows 2000 domain controller that contains the entire domain partition from its own domain as well as specific attributes of all objects from all other domains. While the Exchange 2000 server will use any domain controller in the domain for configuration information, it must use a Global Catalog server for information about mailboxes, mail-enabled users, mail-enabled contacts, and public folders. This is because these types of objects are stored in the domain partition of the database, not in the configuration partition of the AD database. Information about mail-enabled objects in other domains will only be found in the Global Catalog.

> **WARNING**   If an Exchange 2000 server cannot contact or loses contact with a Global Catalog server, it will not deliver e-mail.

If an organization had only a single domain, the Exchange server could query any domain controller and find all the information about the objects it wants. However, Exchange 2000 had to be designed to work effectively in organizations that have multiple domains. When the first Exchange server is installed, certain attributes of some classes are marked for replication to the Global Catalog servers.

For example, an attribute that all Exchange servers in the organization would need to know is a mailbox's home server. During Exchange installation, an attribute is created called msExchHomeServerName that will contain the name of the user's home server. This attribute is associated with the user class. Further, this attribute is flagged for replication to all Global Catalog servers.

You can view which attributes are flagged for replication to the Global Catalog servers using the Schema Management MMC. Figure 2.3 shows the properties of the msExchHomeServerName as viewed from the Schema Management MMC.

Figure 2.3   Properties of an AD attribute viewed through Schema Management

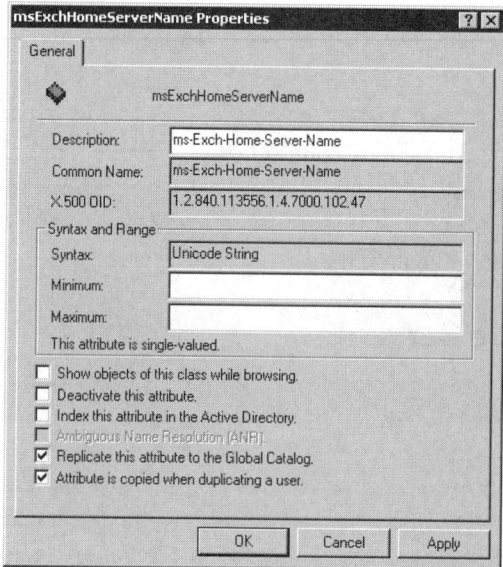

Note in Figure 2.3 that the Replicate This Attribute To The Global Catalog check box is checked, which means that this data will be available to all Global Catalog servers.

WARNING   Do not randomly change attributes in the Schema Management MMC to be replicated to the Global Catalog. Doing so forces a complete replication of all data to all Global Catalog servers.

Attributes in the Global Catalog

Understanding the attributes that are flagged to be included on Global Catalog servers is important because you need to know what types of expectations to set for your users. If you have multiple domains, the only attributes that your Outlook users will be able to view for mailboxes in another domain are those included in the Global Catalog.

For example, when viewing the properties of a mailbox, the user will not be able to view the department of a user in another domain. This is because the department attribute is not included in the Global Catalog. Table 2.1 includes some of the common attributes that a user can see through an Outlook client.

Table 2.1   Common User Account Attributes

Display Name	LDAP Name	In Global Catalog?
First Name	GivenName	✓
Initials	Initials	
Last Name	sn	✓
Display Name	DisplayName	✓
Address	Streetaddress	
Title	title	✓
Company	Company	✓
City	L	✓
Department	department	
State	st	✓
Office	PhysicalDeliveryOfficeName	✓
Zip code	PostalCode	
Country/Region	C	✓
Phone	TelephoneNumber	✓
Manager	Manager	✓
Fax	FacsimileTelephoneNumber	

NOTE   For a larger list of common user account attributes and their LDAP names, see the document called "Object Attributes and Samples" on the Web at www.somorita.com.

You can use the Active Directory Schema console to flag additional attributes to be included in the Global Catalog, but be aware that each time a new attribute is included in the Global Catalog, all Global Catalog servers re-replicate everything from scratch.

This can take hours or even days in an organization with many user objects, domains, and Global Catalog servers.

NOTE Custom messaging applications may use certain user attributes. If your organization spans more than one domain, make sure that you include these attributes in the Global Catalog.

Where Are My Global Catalog Servers?

Do you know where your Global Catalog servers are? Though you can designate others, the only default Global Catalog server is the first domain controller installed into the forest root domain. You can assign the Global Catalog role to additional domain controllers using the Active Directory Sites And Services console. Browse through the AD sites and find the domain controller; in the right pane, select the NTDS Settings object and display the properties. You can promote this computer to be a Global Catalog server by clicking the Global Catalog check box.

If you need to determine which domain controllers are Global Catalog servers, the Windows 2000 Support Tools includes a fantastic utility called ReplMon (Replication Monitor). Connect to any domain controller using ReplMon and right-click the server name. Choose Show Global Catalog Servers In Enterprise to display a list of all Global Catalog servers in the entire forest.

How Many Global Catalog Servers Should Be Designated?

One of the more common questions that is asked during the design of both a Windows 2000 Active Directory infrastructure and an Exchange organization is "How many Global Catalog servers should I create?"

Placement of Global Catalog servers is critical for not only Exchange 2000, but also Active Directory. The Global Catalog server is critical for a number of operations in Active Directory, including verification of Universal security group membership and verifying User Principal Names (UPNs). Even in a simple Windows 2000 Active Directory forest, the Global Catalog server is contacted by the domain controllers when a user logs in to verify this information.

If other applications are installed that require the additional data stored in the Global Catalog, then they will also perform queries to the Global Catalog servers. Exchange 2000 makes heavy use of the Global Catalog server for looking up information about user accounts, mailbox home server location, and e-mail addresses.

Each Active Directory site should have two Global Catalog servers. In Active Directory sites with more than four back-end Exchange 2000 servers, consider adding an additional Global Catalog server. However, this is purely a "textbook" recommendation, for I have not considered other factors that may affect the usage of a Global Catalog server and the consequences of installing additional ones. Each additional Global Catalog server in a forest with more than one domain will increase the amount of data that must be replicated between the two domains.

Exchange@Work: All Domain Controllers Are Global Catalog Servers

Company XYZ went to great pains to design their Active Directory forest. Their Windows NT 4 domain structure supported 26,000 user accounts and consisted of 11 separately managed Windows NT 4 domains. Many of these domains existed because the company was concerned about bandwidth between the company's offices, but a number of the domains existed merely for political reasons. Everyone agreed that the number of domains was excessive, but no one was willing to give up their own domain.

The Active Directory design process revealed that the excessive domains would create a unnecessarily large tree. After a lot of debate, administrator education, an increase in several remote office's WAN bandwidth, and an executive order from the company president, the company chose a single domain model.

Each smaller office location (fewer than 500 users) had a domain controller. Locations with more than 500 users had at least two domain controllers. Each of these domain controllers was designated as a Global Catalog server. Since the organization had a single domain, there was no additional AD replication overhead between the domain controllers, so making them Global Catalog servers was an easy decision. This design works well since as long as a domain controller is near the Exchange servers or users, there will always be a Global Catalog server.

Troubleshooting with DSADiag

Would you like to know which domain controllers and Global Catalog servers your Exchange Server is currently using? The DSAccess process maintains this information and can be queried using a utility called DSADiag. To run it, copy the dsadiag.exe utility in the Exchange server binaries directory (\exchsrvr\bin) and type **dsadiag 1**. The output includes a list of up to 10 known domain controllers and 10 known Global Catalog servers, and will be similar to this:

```
C:\exchsrvr\bin\dsadiag 1

.......
Working DC's:
UP FAST DOWN InSync     Name
```

```
X  X        X        honolulu.somorita.com
X  X        X        hilo.somorita.com
X  X        X        sanfrancisco.somorita.com
X  X        X        singapore.somorita.com
Working GC's:
UP FAST DOWN InSync   Name
X  X        X        honolulu.somorita.com
X  X        X        hilo.somorita.com
X  X        X        sanfrancisco.somorita.com
X  X        X        singapore.somorita.com
Config DC:
X  X        X        honolulu.somorita.com
Done
```

This listing includes information about whether the domain controller is currently available (UP or DOWN), if it responds to LDAP queries within five seconds (FAST), and if it is fully replicated (InSync). You can also use DSADiag to force an Exchange 2000 server to rediscover domain controllers and Global Catalog servers. To do this, type **dsadiag 2**.

Locating Domain Controllers, Global Catalog Servers, and Servers Using DNS

Take a quick tour through the Microsoft Knowledge Base and search for "DNS" and "error"; you will find a number of articles relating to problems with DNS. Ask anyone who has implemented Active Directory and Exchange 2000, and they will tell you that your servers must be able to query DNS properly. Additionally, the information that the DNS server returns must be accurate.

When Windows 2000 servers boot, they dynamically register their hostname and IP address with their DNS server. This will automatically create a host record (A record) for this server.

When Windows 2000 domain controllers boot, not only do they register their hostname and IP address with the DNS server, but they also register service location (SRV) records that indicate which services that domain controller is supporting (domain controller, Global Catalog, and Kerberos). Windows 2000 member servers and clients use these SRV records to locate domain controllers and Global Catalog servers. Further, the client will determine which Active Directory site it is in and attempt to contact a domain controller or Global Catalog server in that site first.

So how can we verify that connectivity is working properly to both DNS and Active Directory? Well, try installing Exchange 2000. If there are any issues, then the Exchange installation will find them. Actually, that is probably not the best recommendation in the world, since you don't want to find out you have problems with DNS and Active Directory on the day of the installation.

Alternatively, you could use some complex NSLOOKUP queries to verify that you can indeed find the names and IP addresses of domain controllers, Global Catalog servers, and Kerberos servers. This *will* verify that DNS is working, but not necessarily that your client is interpreting the results properly.

However, there is a utility included with the Windows 2000 Support Tools called NLTEST; this utility has saved me a lot of pain several times by showing me ahead of time what I could and could not query. There are many command-line options for this utility, but I have found the following three to be most useful. In these examples, let's assume that my Windows 2000 domain name is Somorita.

This first example confirms that the computer from which I ran NLTEST is in the Southeast-Asia-Network:

```
C:\tools\W2K Support Tools\nltest /dsgetsite
Southeast-Asia-Network
The command completed successfully
```

If the /dsgetsite option does not return your site name or returns an incorrect site name, make sure that the site definition in Active Directory Sites And Services includes the correct IP subnet information.

This second example uses the /dsgetdc option to confirm that the computer can locate a nearby domain controller for the SOMORITA domain:

```
C:\tools\W2K Support Tools\nltest /dsgetdc:Somorita
            DC: \\KLANG-DC01
       Address: \\172.16.201.7
      Dom Guid: 35ce13bf8c-a87d-4e10-e9cd-763ae83c34001d
      Dom Name: SOMORITA
   Forest Name: somorita.net
  Dc Site Name: Southeast-Asia-Network
 Our Site Name: Southeast-Asia-Network
         Flags: PDC GC DS LDAP KDC TIMESERV WRITEABLE DNS_FOREST
CLOSE_SITE
The command completed successfully
```

If you cannot locate a domain controller, verify that you have the correct domain name and that the AD site and subnet information is correct.

This final example uses the /dclist option to allow you to list all of the domain controllers in a specific domain:

```
C:\tools\W2K Support Tools\nltest /dclist:Somorita
```

```
Get list of DCs in domain 'somorita' from '\\KLANG-DC01'
    klang-dc01.somorita.net [DS] Site: Southeast-Asia-Network
    sing-dc01.somorita.net [DS] Site: Southeast-Asia-Network
    jaka-dc01.somorita.net [DS] Site: Southeast-Asia-Network
    hono-dc01.somorita.net [PDC] [DS] Site: Central-Pacific-Network
```

Note that the server hono-dc01 is the PDC emulator for this domain.

NOTE   These examples covered three of the most useful NLTEST options. You can see others by typing **nltest /?**.

Operations Master Roles

In order for Exchange 2000 to operate well with Active Directory, there are a few things you should do beforehand. These preparations include making sure you have domain controllers and Global Catalog servers located near the Exchange servers, and that you have sufficient Global Catalog servers. This means that you must have a basic understanding of the roles that certain Windows 2000 domain controllers play in a Windows 2000 forest, including certain roles that a domain controller assumes either for its own domain or for the entire forest.

The first server installed into the first domain in the forest (called the forest root domain) assumes the role of master of operations for certain tasks, much like the PDC does for the entire domain in Windows NT 4. I know you are probably saying to yourself "Self, I thought all domain controllers contained 'writeable' copies of the domain database, so why are there operations masters?" You are correct, each domain controller has a write-able copy of the domain database, but there are still certain tasks that should be handled only by specific domain controllers.

Such a domain controller is known as an operations master, or a *flexible single master of operations (FSMO)*. Operations masters' roles are summarized in Table 2.2 and are discussed in more detail below.

Table 2.2   Operations Masters Roles in an Active Directory Forest

Role	All Domains	Forest Root Domain
Schema master	No	Yes
Domain naming master	No	Yes

Table 2.2 Operations Masters Roles in an Active Directory Forest *(continued)*

Role	All Domains	Forest Root Domain
PDC emulator	Yes	Yes
RID master	Yes	Yes
Infrastructure master	Yes	Yes

There are five different types of operations masters; some encompass the entire forest, while others are specific to a single domain. There are two operations master roles for the entire forest, and each domain has three operations master roles. The FSMO roles include:

The *schema master* is the only domain controller that can modify the AD schema for the entire forest. There is only one schema master for the entire forest and it is, by default, the first domain controller installed into the first domain in the forest. Updates to the schema master domain controller will replicate to all other domain controllers in the forest. Understanding where the schema master resides and how it behaves is important. When it comes time to install Exchange 2000 for the first time in the forest, the schema must be upgraded.

The *domain naming master* is the only domain controller in the forest that can add or remove domains in the forest. There is only one domain naming master for the entire forest and it is, by default, the first domain controller installed into the forest.

The *primary domain controller (PDC) emulator* is the only domain controller in a domain that acts as a Windows NT 4 primary domain controller. There is one PDC emulator in each Windows 2000 domain and it is, by default, the first domain controller installed into the domain. In Mixed mode, this domain controller is responsible for replication to Windows NT 4 domains. In Native and Mixed modes, this domain controller is responsible for accepting password changes from older clients. The PDC emulator in the root domain of the forest is also the master time source for the forest.

The *relative identifier (RID) master* is the domain controller that is responsible for giving pools of available security identifiers to the other domain controllers in the domain; these identifiers can be used by those domain controllers when creating objects in Active Directory. The RID master is also the only domain controller that can move objects out of the domain. There is one RID master for each domain.

The *infrastructure master* is the domain controller that is responsible for updating the security identifiers (SIDs) and domains of objects that are moved out of the domain. There is one infrastructure master per domain.

NOTE The PDC emulator in the forest's root domain maintains the "master time" used for time synchronization to all Windows 2000 computers in the forest.

Whose Line Is It, Anyway?

So which domain controller is currently in each operations master role? If you have a single domain and you have not moved anything, then all operations master roles are still being held by the original domain controller. If you do not know which roles specific domain controllers hold, then you can determine this using your new best friend, ReplMon.

Launch ReplMon and connect to one of the domain controllers in your domain. Right-click the domain controller name, choose Properties, and click the FSMO Roles property tab. The FSMO roles for the domain that the selected domain controller is in are shown (see Figure 2.4).

Figure 2.4 ReplMon showing FSMO roles

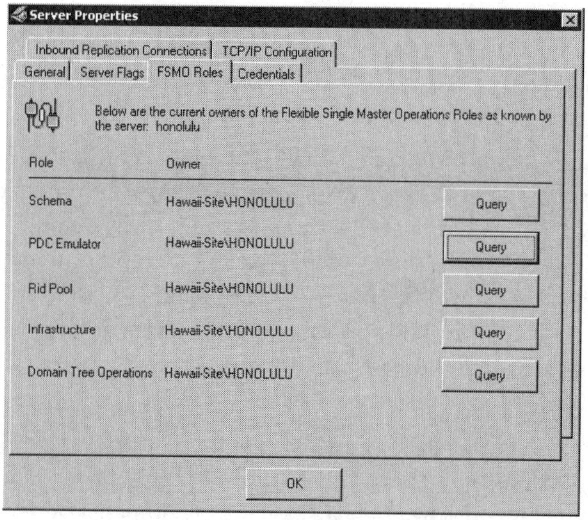

Operations masters can also be viewed from the built-in MMCs. To view a specific domain's FSMOs (infrastructure master, RID master, and PDC emulator), launch the Active Directory Users And Computers console, highlight the domain you are interested in viewing, right-click, and choose Operations Masters from the context menu.

To view the forest-wide FSMO role schema master, launch the Active Directory Schema console, right-click the Active Directory Schema console root, and choose Operations Masters.

To view the forest-wide FSMO role domain naming master, launch the Active Directory Domains And Trusts console, right-click the Active Directory Domains And Trusts root, and choose Operations Masters.

Assignment of Operations Masters Roles

Which domain controllers should be assigned which roles? By default, the first domain controller into the forest has all of the FSMO roles for both the forest and the first domain. The first domain controller into each additional domain in the forest has the infrastructure master, PDC emulator, and RID master roles for that specific domain. In an organization with more than one domain controller, you should make changes to the role assignments to better distribute the load that these roles place on each domain controller.

Domain-Specific FSMO Roles

In each domain, the domain-specific FSMO roles are the RID master, PDC emulator, and infrastructure master. In the root domain, the RID master, PDC emulator, and infrastructure master should be moved to another domain controller. The RID master and PDC emulator should be on the same domain controller.

The infrastructure master should be on a domain controller that is not a Global Catalog server, but that has good connectivity to a Global Catalog server.

Forest-Wide FSMO Roles

The two forest-wide FSMO roles are the schema master and the domain naming master. These two roles should be on the same domain controller. Further, the domain controller that supports these two FSMO roles should be close (from the perspective of the network) to the person responsible for the schema. The server that holds the schema master and domain naming master must be a Global Catalog server.

Changing FSMO Roles

There are a couple of circumstances under which you may be changing FSMO roles. You may be retiring a domain controller and need to move the role to another server. You may be taking steps to better tune your domain controllers by distributing the load. Or you may be simply reconfiguring your domain after initially installing your domain controllers.

The other reason you may have to transfer a domain role is when an FSMO master has failed. This is called "seizing" an FSMO role. You should do this only if the original FSMO master will not be coming back online and only under the guidance of Microsoft Product Support Services (PSS).

You can transfer FSMO roles of the domain roles using either the NTDSUTIL command-line utility or through the built-in MMC consoles. To transfer the domain naming FSMO role, use the Active Directory Domains And Trusts console, right-click the Active Directory Domains And Trusts root, and choose Operations Masters; the Change Operations Master dialog box appears. Click Change and select a new domain controller to be the operations master.

To change the schema master, use the Active Directory Schema console (which must be registered, as described earlier in this chapter). Right-click the Active Directory Schema console root, choose Operations Masters, and click Change.

To transfer FSMO roles of the domain-specific roles, launch the Active Directory Users And Computers console, right-click the domain to which you want to transfer the FSMO role, select either the RID, PDC, or Infrastructure tab, and click Change to select the new operations master for the role you desire to change.

Exchange 2000's Effect on Active Directory

It's difficult to ascertain the exact effect that Exchange 2000 will have on Active Directory. There are many factors involved in determining the load that Exchange will place on AD, including the number of simultaneous users, the number of MAPI clients versus Internet clients, and the number of messages sent over busier periods of time.

To understand the types of loads that Exchange is placing on Active Directory, let's look at some of the operations that take place.

Configuration Queries and Address Lookups

Periodically, Exchange needs to be able to query information about its configuration. Further, components such as the System Attendant and SMTP message transport must look up mailbox information such as e-mail address, home server, etc. Rather than have all components executing queries to Active Directory whenever they need, the Exchange 2000 designers designed a process called DSAccess that runs as part of the System Attendant. DSAccess is used by Exchange components such as the information store, System Attendant, and other internal components; clients do not use DSAccess. The Advanced Queuing Engine's message categorizer (phatcat.dll) performs its own queries; it uses DSAccess only to get a list of available Global Catalog servers.

DSAccess keeps a list of the domain controllers in its domain; if there is more than one domain controller, DSAccess will perform a "round-robin" query. When querying information about mailbox-enabled users, mail-enabled users, mail-enabled contacts, public folders, or other mail recipients, DSAccess first sends a query to a domain controller; if this query fails, DSAccess then queries a Global Catalog server.

This information is held in the DSAccess cache in order to improve performance and reduce the number of queries to Active Directory. The DSAccess cache holds up to 50MB of data and holds entries for five minutes. The DSAccess cache, when set at the default 50MB, will hold approximately 6500 entries; each entry consumes approximately 7.5KB. The DSAccess cache process requires approximately 2.5MB, which leaves about 47.5MB for data caching. Never set the DSAccess cache size below 2.5MB.

> **NOTE** Both the DSAccess cache timeout and size as well as the default domain controllers that it uses can be manually entered in the Registry. These values are covered in Appendix A.

The DSAccess cache can be preloaded with specific base-distinguished names; preloading the DSAccess cache can improve performance and reduce the load on the domain controllers and Global Catalog servers. This is not a process that most administrators will have to do. Instructions for configuring DSAccess to preload certain containers can be found in Microsoft Knowledge Base article Q250572.

> **TIP** If you suspect that there is stale data in the DSAccess cache, you can flush the cache using an Exchange 2000 Resource Kit utility called DSCFlush. This utility must be run from the Exchange 2000 server, and you should only flush one server at a time to prevent the domain controllers and Global Catalog servers from being overwhelmed. This is often the problem when you have just changed an SMTP address or home server, or enabled Instant Messaging.

MAPI Client Lookups

With the release of Exchange 2000, MAPI client directory lookups have been broken down into two categories: pre–Outlook 98-SR1, and those released after Outlook 98 (Outlook 2000 and Outlook XP). Both clients initially contact the Exchange server, but the Outlook 2000 and XP clients are capable of being referred directly to an Active Directory Global Catalog server. Outlook 98-SR1 and earlier (hereafter referred to as Outlook 98 clients) do not have the capability to be referred to another directory source.

The component of Exchange 2000 that handles these referrals and performs directory lookups for Outlook 98 clients is called DSProxy, which operates as part of the System Attendant service.

Outlook 98 and Earlier MAPI Clients

When an Outlook 98, Outlook 97, Exchange, or Macintosh client performs a directory lookup request to an Exchange 2000 server, the server appears to these clients as if it were an Exchange 5.5 directory service. These clients cannot accept referrals, so DSProxy takes these MAPI requests and redirects them to a Global Catalog server. The Active Directory Global Catalog server accepts the MAPI request, performs the directory lookup, and sends the query back to the Exchange 2000 server's DSProxy process, which returns the requested data to the client. Figure 2.5 illustrates this process.

Figure 2.5 DSProxy process in action

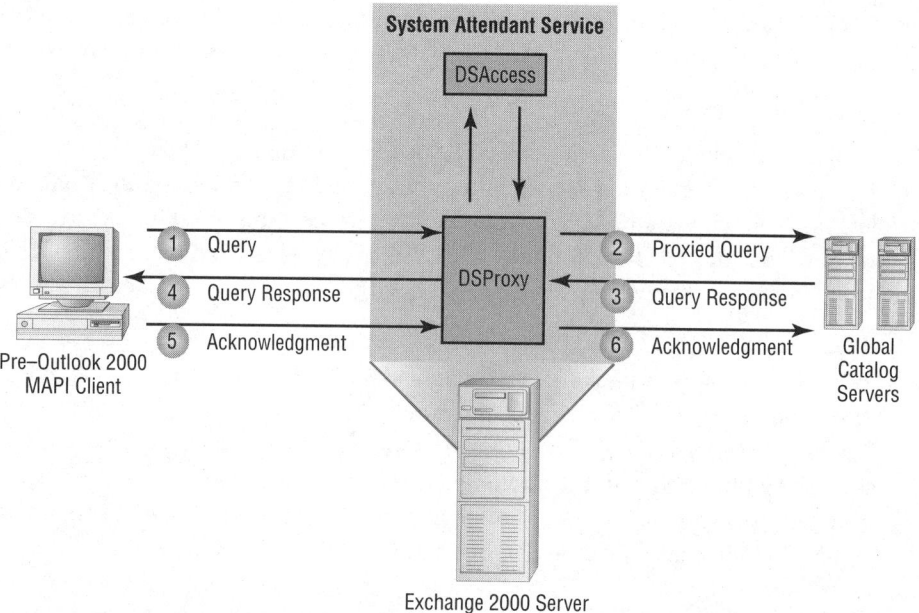

Exchange 2000 Server

The entire process takes six frames of network traffic and is transparent to the user. DSProxy does *not* cache data. DSProxy gets a list of Global Catalog servers from the DSAccess process described earlier in this chapter. You can view this list of Global Catalog servers using the DSADiag utility discussed earlier in this chapter.

NOTE For the sake of better performance, DSProxy passes MAPI requests from the client to the Global Catalog server; MAPI requests are not converted to LDAP requests.

NOTE DSProxy will also be used by Outlook 2000 and Outlook XP clients that cannot contact a Global Catalog server directly, such as in the case of the Global Catalog server being behind a firewall.

Outlook 2000 and Outlook XP Clients

When an Outlook 2000 or Outlook XP (a.k.a. Outlook 2002) client queries an Exchange 2000 server when it first connects to the server, it connects to the DSProxy process. The DSProxy process answers the client's request, but then it gives the client a referral to a Global Catalog server. Future queries by this client will be directed to the Global Catalog server, not the Exchange server.

Once the Outlook client has received a referral, it adds a new (and cryptic) entry to the user's messaging profile that indicates which Global Catalog should be used. On a Windows NT or Windows 2000 client, this entry is found in: HKCU\Software\Microsoft\WindowsNT\CurrentVersion\Windows Messaging Subsystem\Profiles\profilename\dca740c8c042101ab4b908002b2fe182. Look for a value called 001e6602, which contains the name of the Global Catalog server. This Registry key is shown in Figure 2.6.

Figure 2.6   Registry entry for Outlook 2000 referrals

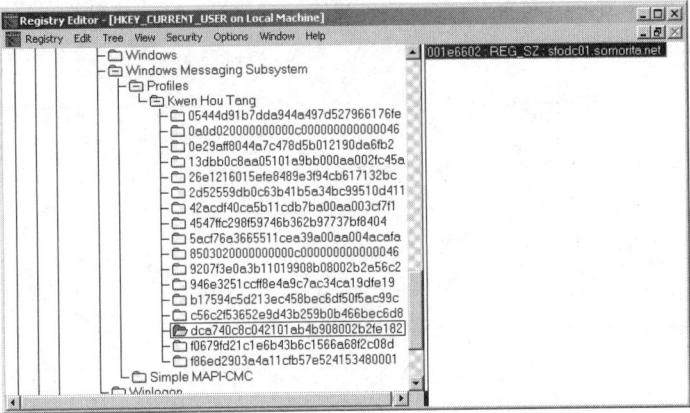

> **NOTE**   If the Global Catalog server that the client has been referred to fails or becomes inaccessible, the Outlook client will have to be restarted.

The referral process can be disabled at the server with a Registry key, but it must be disabled at each Exchange 2000 server in order to disable it for all clients. You can disable it for a single server if you wish for only that server to not participate in the referral process. The Registry key, No RFR Service, is found in HKLM\System\CurrentControlSet\Services\MicrosoftSA\Parameters. To disable referrals, set this key to 0x1.

Outlook XP introduced a new feature that automatically causes the client to negotiate a new Global Catalog server on every restart. There is a hot fix for Outlook 2000 that incorporates this change. (See Microsoft KB article Q272290 for more information.) One implication of this is for laptop users; they will automatically get a closer Global Catalog server. This will also cause your clients to get a new Global Catalog server that may be closer if you have recently designated a new domain controller as a Global Catalog server.

Preparing the Active Directory Forest and Each Domain

Before an Exchange 2000 server is installed in an Active Directory forest, there are a few steps you need to take. First, you should perform a number of pre-installation checks to ensure that Exchange 2000 will install and operate properly.

Second, there are two processes that must be run. During the first installation of Exchange 2000, the Active Directory schema must be updated to support the additional classes and attributes necessary for Exchange 2000. The second process involves making changes to each domain; in each domain that will support Exchange 2000, certain changes must be made before an Exchange 2000 server is installed.

NOTE   If you are already running Exchange 5.5, the ADC must have been installed prior to extending the schema. See Chapter 3 for more information.

Pre-Installation Checks

Prior to installing Exchange 2000, there are a number of things that you should do to ensure that the installation will go smoothly:

- Confirm that the IIS SMTP and NNTP services have been installed. The Exchange 2000 installation will fail without them.

- Make sure the server is running Windows 2000 Service Pack 2 or later.

- Confirm DNS and Active Directory connectivity (discussed earlier in this chapter).

- Set the server's initial and maximum page file size to RAM+500MB; setting the initial and maximum page file size to the same value will prevent the page file from growing and help prevent exacerbating disk fragmentation problems. Monitor the Memory object's Committed Bytes to make sure you do not approach the maximum page file size. If you do, increase the initial/maximum size.

- Gain knowledge of the Active Directory site infrastructure (number of sites and the replication schedule between the sites).

- If an Exchange 5.5 system exists and must be upgraded, learn the Exchange 5.5 site services account and password. Also learn the Exchange 5.5 site infrastructure and server names. If upgrading, the ADC must be in place.

- Make sure that you have the necessary permissions for the type of installation you are performing.

Additionally, make sure that you have the necessary permissions to install the components you are installing. To extend the schema, you must be a member of the forest root domain's Schema Admins and Enterprise Admins groups. Installing an Exchange server that is a Windows 2000 member server requires only that you be a member of that server's local Administrators group and that you have the Exchange Full Admin permission. Table 2.3 shows a summary of these permissions.

Table 2.3   Exchange 2000 Installation Actions and the Necessary Permissions

Action	Root Domain Schema Admin	Domain Admin (in the Affected Domain)	Local Server Administrator	Organization Level Full Exchange Admin
Extend the Schema.	Yes	Yes (in the root domain)	No	No
Prepare the domain.	No	Yes	No	No
Install an Exchange 2000 Server.	No	No	Yes	Yes

WARNING   Exchange 5.5 cannot be installed into an Exchange 2000 organization that has only Exchange 2000 servers, even if it is in Mixed mode. If you will require an Exchange 5.5 server, you must install it first. You might require an Exchange 5.5 server in a pure Exchange 2000 environment if one of your third-party gateways or applications does not yet support Exchange 2000.

Forest Prep

A newly created Active Directory forest contains 142 classes and 863 attributes. During the first Exchange 2000 Setup installation, a process called *forest prep* creates 160 additional classes and 887 new attributes. This process also promotes 124 additional attributes to the Global Catalog. All in all, over 2000 changes are made to AD.

The forest prep process automatically runs the first time you install Exchange 2000 server in a new Windows 2000 forest. However, it may be desirable to prepare the forest at a separate time from the actual Exchange installation. Reasons to do this include:

- The schema changes may need to be run prior to installation to allow them to propagate to the entire forest.

- The person installing Exchange may not have the permissions necessary to extend the Active Directory schema.

- The root domain in the forest may need to be prepared separately because there will be no Exchange 2000 servers in the forest root domain.

The Exchange 2000 Setup program has an option that allows the schema to be extended separately from the regular installation process. To extend only the schema, run the Exchange Setup program with the /forestprep command option. During the forest prep process, Exchange Setup will do the following:

- Prompt to join an existing Exchange 5.5 organization or create a new one. If the organization is new, then the organization name must be provided.

- Create the Exchange organization object in the Active Directory configuration container.

- Request the user or group name of the first Exchange administrator and set the permissions for that user or group.

- Request the Exchange 5.5 service account password, which is to be used for interoperability with Exchange 5.5 servers.

- Extend the forest schema.

The first question you are prompted for during the forest prep process is whether this is a new installation or part of an existing 5.5 organization. If it is the latter, you will have to provide the name of an existing Exchange 5.5 server.

WARNING Your Exchange 5.5 organization name and site names must contain only characters that are legal characters in Active Directory. Essentially, all the special characters on the keyboard except for the space and the hyphen are not supported when upgrading to Exchange 2000. If your Exchange 5.5 organization name or any site names have any special characters, you can change the display name to a legal name; that name will be used when the Active Directory Connector is installed. For more information, see the Exchange 2000 release notes or Knowledge Base article Q277844. This also provides you an excellent opportunity to change your organization and site names by adjusting the display names in the Exchange 5.5 Administrator program prior to installing the Active Directory Connector.

Further, you will have to provide the site services account password (the site services account will be retrieved from the 5.5 organization you have specified). This information will be used by the Site Replication Service (SRS) and the message transfer agent (MTA) when communicating with Exchange 5.5 sites and servers. If this is a new Exchange organization, you will be prompted for the name of the Exchange organization.

> **WARNING**   The Exchange 2000 organization name cannot be changed without completely uninstalling Exchange 2000 from all Exchange servers in the forest.

You will also be asked for the username or group name that should be given full Exchange administrative permissions. By default, this user or group will be given all permissions to the entire organization.

> **TIP**   I recommend creating a group in the forest's root domain called something like Exchange Full Administrators and assigning this group Exchange Administrator permissions to the organization. This way all the initial permissions are assigned to a group rather than to an individual user who might be deleted later.

The Exchange 2000 Setup program will go through the schemax.ldf files found on the Exchange 2000 Setup directory and import each of them using the Windows 2000 LDIFDE utility. There are 10 of these files, numbered schema0.ldf through schema9.ldf; they contain all of the changes needed to extend the schema. A summary of these changes can be found on the Web at www.somorita.com in a document called "Exchange 2000 Active Directory Schema Changes."

> **WARNING**   Exchange 2000 can be uninstalled, but the schema changes are irreversible.

Are We There Yet?

Whether you have a single domain or many trees in your Active Directory forest, you will have to wait until the schema changes have replicated to all domain controllers in the forest (or at the very least to all domain controllers to which your new Exchange server may connect). If you have only two or three domain controllers, this may take fewer than 10 minutes. However, in a large Windows 2000 forest, these schema changes can take between 15 minutes and many hours. The amount of time will depend on the number of domain controllers and AD sites that you have configured as well as the number of replication intervals defined between the AD sites.

When Exchange 2000 Setup is run, it will locate a nearby domain controller. If the schema changes are not incorporated into that domain controller's copy of the AD database, either the installation will fail or the Setup program will try to contact the AD schema master and make the changes again. Thus it is imperative that the schema changes be replicated to the domain controllers in the domain into which Exchange 2000 is being installed.

How can you be sure that the changes have replicated? Well, when the schema changes are made, the last change in the `schema9.ldf` file is setting the ms-Exch-Schema-Version-Pt (the Pt stands for Platinum, the code name of Exchange 2000) attribute to an upper range value of 4397. Locate a domain controller in the far reaches (from a replication perspective) of your forest and use either ADSIEDIT or LDP to view ms-Exch-Schema-Version-Pt. Locate the rangeUpper attribute; if this attribute is not found or is a value other than 4397, then the schema changes have not fully replicated to this domain controller. If you are a scripting whiz, you can easily write a WSH script that would query the domain controllers and confirm this value.

> **NOTE** There is a utility called `getschemaver.exe`, written by Andy Webb, that you can download from www.swinc.com. This utility allows you to quickly check the version of the ms-Exch-Schema-Version-Pt attribute on any domain controller in your forest.

> **NOTE** Exchange 2000 Service Pack 1 does not modify the schema, though future service packs might.

Domain Prep

Each domain that will have Exchange 2000 objects (servers, mail-enabled users, mail-enabled contacts, or mail-enabled groups) must have certain changes made to it so that the proper administrative permissions are granted. These changes are made automatically the first time an Exchange server is installed into a domain. The person installing the first Exchange server must be a member of that domain's Domain Admins group in order to make these changes.

The changes can be made separately from the actual Exchange setup process by running Exchange 2000 Setup with the `/domainprep` option. If the `/domainprep` option is used to prepare the domain for Exchange installation, then the only permissions required to install Exchange server are to be a member of the local machine's Administrators group and to be a Full Exchange Administrator in the administrative group into which you want to install the Exchange server.

The domain prep process makes certain domain-wide changes including:

- Creating a Domain Local security group called Exchange Enterprise Servers and a Domain Global security group called Exchange Domain Servers

- Making the Exchange Domain Servers Global group a member of the Exchange Enterprise Servers group
- Assigning the Manage Auditing And Security Log right (`SeSecurityPrivilege`) to the Exchange Enterprise Servers group
- Granting the Exchange Enterprise Servers group full read and write permissions to the AdminSDHolder Active Directory system object
- Creating a Microsoft Exchange System Objects container in the root of the domain's domain naming context

Why are all of these security-related changes made? Essentially, there are two reasons. The first is that Exchange 2000 does not have its own service account; rather, each Exchange service uses the Windows 2000 local system account. This account has no permissions on any other Windows 2000 computer other than its own. Exchange 2000 servers must be able to connect to one other and be authenticated properly. The Exchange Domain Servers and Exchange Enterprise Servers groups are used to this end.

In each domain that will contain an Exchange 2000 server or Exchange 2000 recipients, the local Exchange Enterprise Servers security group will contain all the Exchange Domain Servers security groups from the other domains in the forest.

WARNING The Exchange Enterprise Servers and Exchange Domain Servers groups are created in the domain's Users container. These groups should *not* be moved to another container under any circumstances.

The second reason is that the System Attendant service runs a process called the Recipient Update Service (RUS), which is discussed later in this chapter. The RUS must be able to modify objects found in the domain in order to include those objects (such as user accounts, contact objects, groups, and public folders) in address lists or to assign them proxy addresses. Thus, each Exchange server must have the permissions to modify objects in its domain.

A new container in the root of the domain's domain naming context is also created; this container is the Microsoft Exchange System Objects container. This container is used for mail-enabled public folders, Active Directory Connector public folder connection agreements, and Microsoft Exchange 2000 Conference Server conferencing objects.

NOTE If a domain will contain mail-enabled objects, even if it will not have any Exchange servers installed there, the /domainprep option must be run. Otherwise, the RUS will not have permission to update the account objects in that domain.

Is the Domain Ready?

The domain prep changes are made to a single Windows 2000 domain controller. You must wait until all of these changes have replicated to the other domain controllers in the domain before you can install the first Exchange 2000 server. Like forest prep, this can take as few as five minutes to 10 minutes or significantly longer depending on the number of domain controllers or Active Directory sites you have.

You can confirm that the changes have replicated by using the ADSIEDIT utility. Connect to a domain controller somewhere in the farthest reaches of your AD site structure. Open the domain naming context within ADSIEDIT and locate the newly created container Microsoft Exchange System Objects. If the container does not appear, then you are certain that the replication changes have not completed. If it does appear, examine the objectVersion attribute; it should be set to a value of 4406. If it is not yet at 4406, then wait a while longer.

Another change that you should confirm is that the security policy change has been made. This is because Microsoft includes a utility on the Exchange 2000 CD-ROM called `policytest.exe`, which is found in the `\support\utils\i386` directory. Simply run the utility while logged in as a member of that domain's Domain Admins group (no command-line options necessary). It will contact each domain controller in the domain and verify that the Exchange Enterprise Servers security group has been given the Manage Auditing And Security Log right.

> **NOTE** When installing Exchange 2000, you will notice a new user account that is created in either the local member server's account database (if Exchange 2000 is installed on a member server) or in Active Directory (if Exchange 2000 is installed on a domain controller). This user is EUSER_EXSTOREEVENT and was used to provide OLE DB functionality during beta testing, but it is not used with the RTM version. Exchange 2000 SP 1 removes this user; this is normal and should not be cause for concern. See Knowledge Base article Q278523 for more information.

Active Directory Groups

One of the challenges that an Active Directory designer or administrator faces is the choice of which types of Active Directory groups to use. The introduction of Exchange 2000 compounds this challenge by introducing additional issues. This is because Exchange 2000 does not have its own distribution lists, but rather relies on mail-enabled groups within Active Directory.

> ***NOTE*** See the "Exchange 2000 and Active Directory Groups" document at
> www.somorita.com for more information on Active Directory Groups. This
> document covers group types and things to consider when picking a group
> scope.

Creating a Mail-Enabled Group

Groups that are used by Exchange clients are known as *mail-enabled groups*. Both security groups and distribution groups can be mail enabled; in fact, a security group cannot be used to set permissions on a public folder until it is mail enabled. To mail-enable a group, follow these steps:

1. Locate the group in Active Directory Users And Computers, right-click the group, and choose Exchange Tasks.

2. From the Exchange Task Wizard, choose Establish An E-mail Address, and click Next.

3. On the next screen, confirm that the Alias and the Associated Administrative Group are correct, and click Next.

4. Click Finish.

Figure 2.7 shows a mail-enabled security group's properties; notice that the box has some additional property tabs including Exchange General, E-mail Addresses, and Exchange Advanced, which are not found on a group that is not mail-enabled.

Figure 2.7   Exchange general property tab of a mail-enabled group

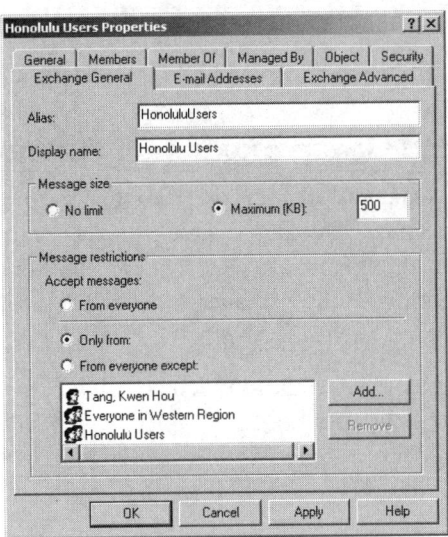

The Exchange-specific property tabs and their properties are outlined in Table 2.4.

Table 2.4   Exchange-Specific Property Tabs for Mail-Enabled Groups

Property Tab	Function
Exchange General	Alias name.
Exchange General	Display name.
Exchange General	Message size (sets maximum message size that can be sent to this group).
Exchange General	Message restrictions (determines which recipients can send messages to this group).
E-mail Addresses	Proxy addresses for SMTP, X.400, etc.
Exchange Advanced	Simple display name.
Exchange Advanced	Expansion server designates the Exchange 2000 server that is responsible for expanding this mail-enabled group.
Exchange Advanced	Hides group from Exchange address lists.
Exchange Advanced	Sends out-of-office messages to originator.
Exchange Advanced	Designates to whom to send delivery reports.
Exchange Advanced	Sets custom attributes.

The Mail-Enabled Group Expansion Quandary

The major issue that Exchange 2000 introduces concerns group expansion in multidomain environments. The Advanced Queuing Engine's message categorizer is responsible for expanding the group membership and performs its own queries rather than using the DSAccess process to perform an LDAP query. Unlike DSAccess, the Advanced Queuing Engine does not maintain a cache of recently queried directory objects.

In a single domain, when the Advanced Queuing Engine's message categorizer needs to expand a distribution list, it sends an LDAP query to a local domain controller to enumerate the group membership. Since this is a single domain environment, the local domain controller will have membership information for all groups.

In multi-domain environments, the message categorizer attempts to enumerate the group membership from the Global Catalog. If the group is Universal, then the membership will be retrieved. If the group is Domain Local or Global, the membership is not in the Global Catalog, and thus the delivery of the message will fail. Other than the fact that the message will not be delivered to its intended recipients, no one will ever know. To resolve this, an expansion server in the Domain Local or Global group's home domain must be designated. Otherwise, the message will not be delivered to the intended recipient.

Possible Solutions

How can you provide mail-enabled groups to your organization while reducing the overhead associated with replication and cross-domain LDAP queries? There are a couple of possible solutions, but they all have their caveats.

Use Universal Groups   The first solution is to use Universal groups when creating groups that must be mail-enabled. Administration is simple: The mail-enabled group can be enumerated by any Global Catalog server. And a Universal group's membership can include user accounts from any domain in the forest.

The downside to this approach is that changes to the Universal group membership cause replication traffic between Global Catalogs. If a list changes infrequently (fewer than five times per day), this additional replication traffic may not be an issue.

Use Global Groups and Specify Expansion Servers   The second solution is to use Global groups within each domain, but specify an Exchange 2000 server as an expansion server. The Exchange 2000 server must be located in the domain in which the Global group is created in order to be able to enumerate group membership without crossing domain boundaries. Figure 2.8 shows the Exchange Advanced property tab of a mail-enabled group. Here you can specify a specific server that is responsible for expanding the mail-enabled group.

In Figure 2.8, for the mail-enabled group Singapore Users, all messages sent to this group in the entire organization will be forwarded to server SFOEX001 designated in the Expansion Server drop-down list box.

The drawback to this approach is that the Global group can contain only members from the domain it was created in, and thus it is not very useful in environments where group lists must span domains.

Figure 2.8 Specifying an Exchange 2000 server that will be used as an expansion server

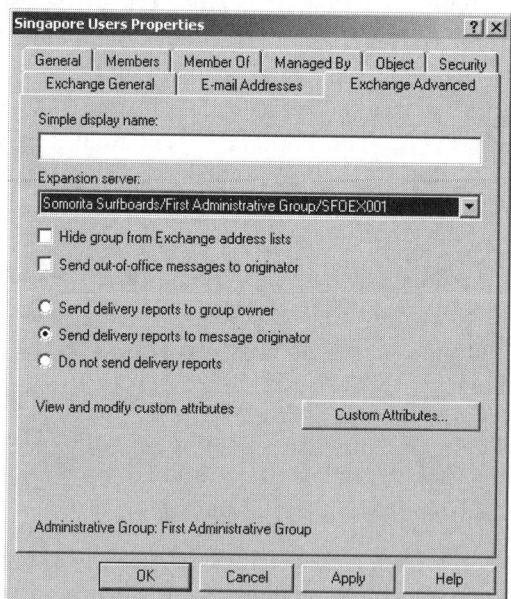

Try a Combination Approach For large organizations, a combination of Universal and Global groups may be the best solution. However, in order to prevent group enumeration across domains, the mail-enabled Global groups should have an expansion server designated.

To illustrate this point, let's look at an example. Somorita Surfboards has a single Active Directory tree with a parent domain (somorita.net) and two child domains (asia.somorita.net and usa.somorita.net). They require a mail-enabled group that they can use to assign permissions to the design department's worldwide resources as well as to send messages to the entire design department. For Somorita Surfboards to create a mail-enabled group for everyone in the Design Department, they would follow these steps:

1. Create and mail-enable a Global group in the somorita (the root) domain called Design Department HQ. Designate a server in the somorita domain as the expansion server for this group.

2. Create and mail-enable a Global group in the asia domain called Design Department Asia. Designate a server in the asia domain as the expansion server for this group.

3. Create and mail-enable a Global group in the usa domain called Design Department USA. Designate a server in the usa domain as the expansion server for this group.

4. Create a Universal group in the somorita (the root) domain called Design Department Worldwide. Mail-enable this group and assign the three Global groups from each of the domains as members of this domain.

While a little harder for an administrator to keep track of, this approach will eliminate LDAP queries between domains to enumerate group membership—and it will keep the Universal group from growing too large.

Other Group-Related Issues

Creating mail-enabled groups is both a blessing and a curse. They enable your user community to quickly and easily communicate with other mail-enabled users and contacts that share a common purpose or task. But they introduce some potential problems that you should avoid, including restricting who can use a mail-enabled group, setting the maximum message size, and giving users permissions to manage group membership.

Controlling Membership

Any administrator who has the Account Operator permissions or has been delegated the Modify The Membership Of A Group role to the Active Directory organizational unit that contains the group is capable of adding members to or removing members from a group. In Exchange 5.5, the administrator could assign a distribution list an "owner" who was capable of modifying the membership of a distribution list from the Outlook address book. Though the Active Directory group object allows administrators to assign a Managed By attribute, this attribute is merely the contact person for this group.

NOTE The Managed By attribute of a group grants no administrative rights.

If you wish to duplicate this functionality, you will have to assign some Active Directory rights to the group. Display the properties of the group and select the Security property tab. Click the Add button and add the user or group that you wish to have control of the membership. Assign this user or group the following permissions: Read, Write, Add/Remove Self As Member, Read Phone And Mail Options, and Write Phone And Mail Options. In the example in Figure 2.9, user Kwen Hou Tang has been given the permissions to manage the Singapore Users group membership.

Figure 2.9 Permissions to manage group membership

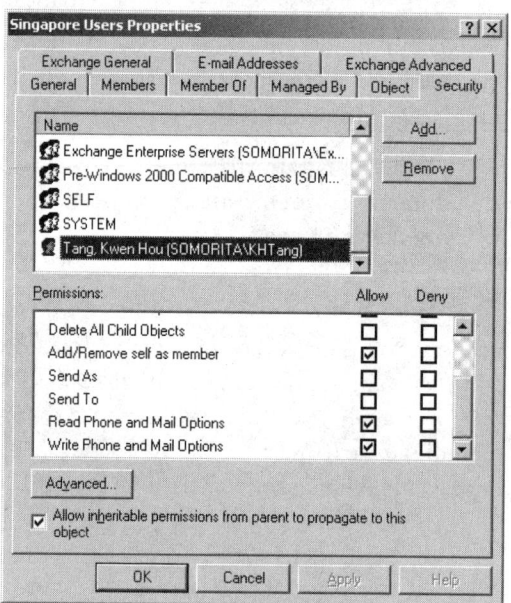

Once you have assigned these permissions, the user should be able to change the group membership from within Outlook by selecting the address book icon, locating the mail-enabled group in the address list, and displaying its properties (shown in Figure 2.10). Click the Modify Members button to add or remove members from the group.

Figure 2.10 Outlook 2000 interface for modifying group membership

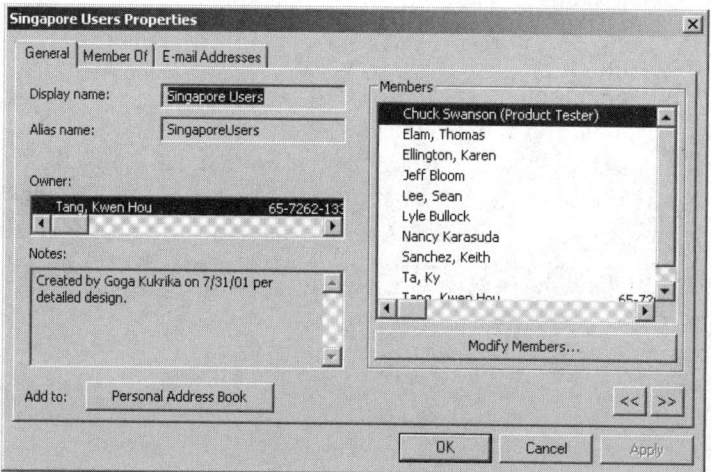

Exchange@Work: Allowing End Users to Control Membership

BCD Corporation has nearly 8500 mailboxes and 153 distribution lists. While running Exchange 5.5, the MIS staff decided that controlling membership in many of these distribution lists was becoming difficult. Many of the distribution lists were for departments, and the department managers wanted the membership changed often.

The MIS assigned many of the department managers to be the owners of their respective distribution lists and then trained them to assign and remove members using Outlook as they found necessary.

This worked fine when using Exchange 5.5, but when BCD Corporation migrated to Windows 2000 and Exchange 2000, one of the goals of the migration was to consolidate the Exchange 5.5 distribution lists and the Windows NT Global groups. Since BCD had only a single domain, there was no need to consider the use of Universal groups, so Global groups were chosen.

BCD's administrators duplicated the Exchange 5.5 distribution list owner functionality that allowed department managers to manage their own distribution lists.

During a security audit a few months after the migration was completed, administrators noticed some unauthorized users had permissions to Windows 2000 resources such as file shares and printers. For example, several users outside of sales had permission to access the sales department's lead-tracking database.

The cause of the problem? The sales department manager decided to include several non-department users into the sales department group. Since BCD was using security groups, the users received the permissions that this group was assigned, even though that was not the manager's intention.

The departmental managers had to undergo some additional training so that they fully understood the ramifications of adding someone to a mail-enabled group. Since they were using security groups, membership included not only receiving mail from this group, but also receiving any permissions to files, directories, shared folders, printers, databases, and public folders to which the group had been assigned permissions.

Conflicts in Group Management

If the management of group membership is widely distributed in your organization, you may have a problem. Under certain circumstances, group membership could be modified by two different administrators at approximately the same time, but on different domain controllers. Active Directory uses a last-update-wins decision if there is a conflict in modifying a single attribute of an object.

Restricting who can manage group membership can help to alleviate this problem. Configuring the Active Directory Users And Computers console to connect to a single domain controller will also help. If you have many administrators who may need to manage group membership, this may be a good argument for designing and implementing some type of Web-based management tool for group administration so that all groups are managed from a single point.

The Exchange 2000 Resource Kit includes a tool called AutoDL that provides a Web interface for group management. This interface allows administrators to manage group membership and allows users to request that they be added or removed from a group. You should install version 2.0 of this product from the Exchange 2000 Resource Kit first, then download the version 2.1 update from `www.microsoft.com/exchange/downloads/2000/AutoDL.asp`.

> **NOTE** For more information about using AutoDL, see the document "Using AutoDL," located at `www.somorita.com`.

Maximum Group Size

Though not enforced, the recommended maximum number of members in any group is 5000. Larger distribution lists can place a significant burden on Active Directory replication, the Advanced Queuing Engine (which expands mail-enabled groups), and the Global Catalog server to which the LDAP query is directed.

Five thousand is not really a hard limit, but rather a restriction on Active Directory replication. A single property (such as the member property) must be able to replicate in a single AD replication transaction. The limit really has to do with the minimum free resources in the Active Directory's ESE (Extensible Storage Engine) version store. Once the member property reaches about 5000 entries, there will no longer be enough free resources to handle the transaction atomically, and the local security authority subsystem (LSASS) will no longer have a valid copy of the member attribute. I suspect that this issue will be addressed in the final release of Windows.NET or a subsequent service pack. Though this will not fix the overall issue of expanding a huge distribution list, it will fix the problems associated with replicating it. Until then, large distribution lists will need to be built by nesting smaller distribution lists.

> **WARNING** Per-message recipient limits restrict the maximum number of recipients (To, Cc, and Bcc) that a MAPI or HTTP client can include in a single message. The default global option is 5000. Individual users can have separate restrictions configured. Each member of a group is part of this limit. If a user is restricted to a maximum of 100 recipients per message, but a mail-enabled group has 101 members, the user will not be able to address a message to that group.

Other Group Restrictions

Other restrictions that you may be wise to place on a group include the following:

- Restrict the maximum message size (I recommend 100K) that can be sent to a group, especially to groups with more than 10 or 15 members. Large messages generally do not need to be sent to large groups of people.
- Restrict who can send messages to groups. The larger the group, the fewer people should be able to send a message to the group.
- Hide the membership of sensitive groups.

Active Directory Customization

As you become more comfortable with Active Directory, there are a number of things that you will want to do to make your job easier and to customize the behavior of Active Directory for your environment. These include customizing display names, creating additional global address lists (GALs), making custom address lists, and restricting access to some address lists.

Further, for better administration of Exchange 2000, you may want to create administrative groups to customize administration. Other modifications include the extended attributes, adding additional recipient policies, enabling additional attributes to be used with automatic name resolution (ANR), and allowing users to manage certain Active Directory attributes.

Creating Administrative Groups before Exchange Installation

During the first Exchange server installation, the Exchange Setup program automatically creates an administrative group called First Administrative Group and a routing group called First Routing Group. Subsequent installations automatically put new servers into this administrative group and routing group unless there are other administrative groups created, in which case you are given a choice of into which administrative group and routing group you want to install the server. Much to my chagrin, this administrative group cannot be changed after it is chosen. And to my profound disappointment, Exchange 2000 servers cannot be moved between administrative groups.

NOTE   If you are joining an Exchange 5.5 organization, the administrative groups are the same as your site names.

What is a poor administrator to do if you want to have a more meaningful administrative group name than First Administrative Group? After running the forest prep process outlined earlier in this chapter, run the Exchange Setup program again and choose a custom installation type. Make sure that the *only* component being installed is the Microsoft

Exchange System Management Tools. Once Exchange System Manager is installed, you can display the administrative groups and routing groups by viewing the Organization object properties.

There will not be any administrative groups or routing groups created since there are no servers installed. Create the administrative groups and routing groups that you require (or at least the first one). During the first server installation, you will now be prompted for which administrative and routing groups you want the server to join.

> ***TIP***   New administrative groups and routing groups are added to the Active Directory's configuration partition. Like all changes to AD, make sure you give them ample time to replicate to the appropriate domain controllers.

Customizing Automatic Display Name Generation

When you create a new user or contact in Active Directory Users And Computers, the display name that is automatically created is in the form of *first_name last_name*. You can simply overwrite the automatically created name when you create the user, or you can modify it later; I find this tedious after about the second one I have to change. One recommendation that I sometimes make is to change this so that the automatically created display name (shown in the interface as Full name) is *last_name, first_name*.

However, if you change the display name generation, the CN portion of the distinguished name is also changed to be *last_name, first_name*. This may cause problems if you must create custom ADSI tools to manipulate your AD later on. Possibly a better solution, though it involves a little bit more work, is to develop an ADSI tool that creates the user, enables the mailbox, and sets all the properties explicitly the way you want them to be set.

> ***TIP***   Chapter 10, "Automated Tasks," includes a simple ADSI script that will change the display name from *first_name last_name* to *last_name, first_name* provided you have both the first_name and last_name fields populated in Active Directory.

To change the automatically created display name, you will have to use the ADSIEDIT utility discussed earlier in this chapter. You will also need to know the language locale code for the language you are using; U.S. English is 409. Follow these steps to change the display name creation rules for U.S. English:

1. Load ADSIEDIT and connect to the configuration container.
2. Locate and display the properties of cn=DisplaySpecifiers,cn=409,cn=User-Display.

3. In the Select A Property To View drop-down dialog box, choose CreateDialog (see Figure 2.11).

4. In the Edit Attribute box, type *%<sn>, %<givenName>*.

5. Click the Set button and then click OK.

NOTE   The syntax *is* case-sensitive when adding entries to the CreateDialog box.

Figure 2.11   Changing the display name generation for the user object.

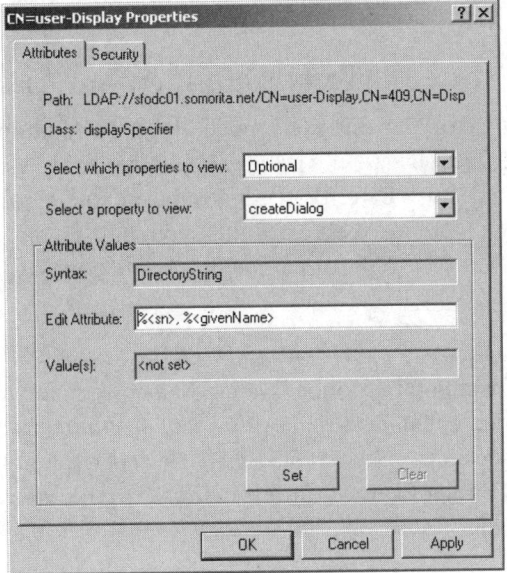

To change the display name generation for a contact object, change cn=User-Display to cn=Contact-Display. To change the display name generation for a locale other than U.S. English, change cn=409 to the appropriate locale code.

NOTE   See Microsoft Knowledge Base article Q250455 for more information.

You can further customize the display name generation by instructing the Active Directory Users And Computers console to only put in part of the name. Here are a couple of examples that you could use to create a display name (see in Step 4) where the username is Anna Madrigal.

Specified Attributes	Resulting Display Name
%<*sn*>, %<*givenName*>	Madrigal, Anna
%1<*givenName*>%<*sn*>	AMadrigal
%<*givenName*>%2<*sn*>	AnnaMa
%1<*givenName*>%7<*sn*>	AMadriga

NOTE   Remember that if you are going to do any ADSI scripting to manipulate Active Directory, commas in the distinguished name will make your coding more complex.

Adding Exchange Mailbox Management Extensions

Once the Active Directory schema is extended, there are additional attributes associated with mailboxes, contact objects, and groups; you'll find another menu choice added to the context menu within Active Directory Users And Computers (just right-click to open the menu). In order to see and use these attributes, you must do one of two things: Install the Exchange System Manager tools, or manually copy the required files and register them yourself.

TIP   Prior to installing Exchange System Manager or copying the files manually, you must have installed the Windows 2000 administration tools. This is done by right-clicking the ADMINPAK.MSI file found in the \I386 directory of the Windows 2000 Server CD-ROM or the \Winnt\System32 directory of any Windows 2000 server.

To install the Exchange 2000 administration extensions, run the Exchange 2000 Setup program, choose a custom installation type, and install only the Microsoft Exchange System Management tools. This will copy all the DLL files required to use the extensions necessary to create mailboxes for users, to mail-enable groups, to mail-enable contact objects, to enable instant messaging for users, and more. This process will also install the files necessary to use the Exchange System Manager tool.

For many administrators, the Exchange System Manager tool will be unnecessary, because their primary task will be only managing user's mailboxes. For these administrators, you can copy and register only the appropriate DLL files. To do this, from a Windows 2000 machine that already has the Exchange System Manager tools installed, locate and copy maildsmx.dll, escprint.dll, address.dll, and exchmem.dll to the \winnt\ system32 directory. Then run regsrv32.exe and register each of these DLL files. For example, to register maildsmx.dll, type **regsvr32 maildsmx.dll** from the command prompt.

TIP Exchange System Manager and Active Directory Users And Computers only run on Windows 2000–based computers. You can use Windows 2000 Terminal Services to remotely administer Windows 2000 servers. I highly recommend enabling Windows 2000 Terminal Services in remote administration mode for all Windows 2000 servers. This will allow you to remotely administer your server just as if you were sitting at its keyboard.

Global Address Lists and Address Lists

Exchange 5.5 supported a single GAL and address book views. The address book view gives the Exchange administrator a way to categorize or sort the GAL based on attributes such as city, department, site, etc. Exchange 2000 introduces the capability to support multiple GALs and address lists.

These address lists are built using LDAP queries. Users are then added to appropriate address lists by the Recipient Update Service based on the query results. When an address list or GAL is created, the RUS performs a query in each domain and modifies the mail-enabled object's showInAddressBook attribute. This attribute is a multi-valued property; the RUS adds the distinguished name (DN) of the address list to this attribute.

Global Address Lists

Outlook clients are presented with the *global address list (GAL)* when they address a message. By default, the only GAL available is the aptly named default global address list, which includes all mail-enabled, unhidden recipients in Active Directory. It may be useful to build more than one GAL; this would be good for organizations that don't want the entire organization to be visible in the global address list. Multiple GALs are also useful for application service providers (ASPs) that host more than one company in the same Exchange organization.

To create a custom GAL, create the GAL in the Global Address Lists container under Recipients in Exchange System Manager. Before the users will see the new global address list, you will have to change some permissions on both the default global address list as well as the one you have created.

The first step is to make sure that the users do not have permission to open the default global address list. To do this, follow these steps:

1. Display the properties of the default global address list and select the Security property tab.

2. Click the Advanced button and locate the permission that allows the Authenticated Users group to Open Address List (see Figure 2.12).

3. Click the View/Edit button and scroll down to the Open Address List permission. The Allow button should be checked; uncheck this button.

WARNING   Do not click the Deny button. Doing so will deny *all* authenticated users the right to view this address list.

Figure 2.12   Customizing permissions on an address list

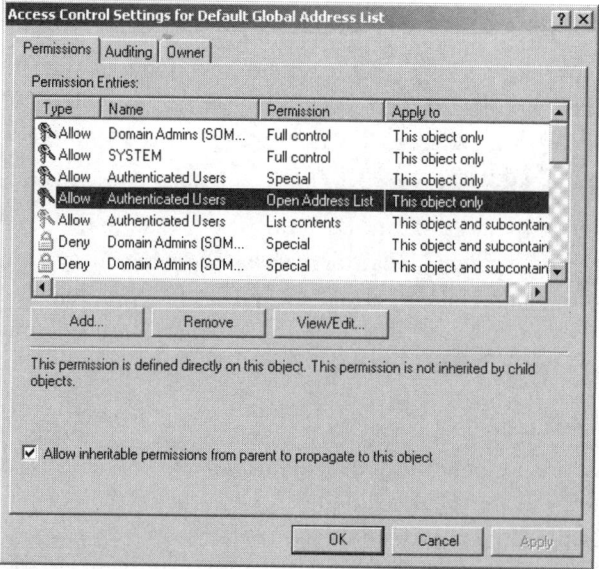

Once you have removed the Open Address List permissions to the default global address list that the authenticated users are granted, you need to grant permission for the users or groups to open your newly created GAL. You may want to grant these permissions to a few users (such as test users) or a security group just in case the administrator or test user needs to log on and see the contents later.

On the security page, add the group that needs to see the GAL and assign that group the Open Address List permission. Note that if you want to permit only certain users to access this newly created GAL, make sure that you remove the Open Address List permission to the new GAL that Authenticated Users is automatically granted.

NOTE   Outlook clients must exit Outlook and reload in order to see new address lists or for permissions changes to an address list to take effect.

Picking the Right Global Address List   Outlook clients can view only one global address list. If a user has rights to more than one GAL, which GAL will the client actually view? Following is a list of criteria that is used to determine which GAL is presented to the client:

- Which GAL does the user have permissions to access?
- If user has permissions to more than one GAL, of which GAL is the user a member?
- If the user has permissions to more than one GAL and is a member of more than one of those GALs, then the one that is the highest alphabetically is displayed.

NOTE   In Exchange 2000 RTM, Outlook Web Access (OWA) users do not have per-user rights for Active Directory applied to them, and thus they can see the entire directory regardless of what rights have been granted or restricted in the Active Directory DACLs (Discretionary Access Control Lists). While this has been fixed in Exchange 2000 SP1, there is a directory attribute for each user object that allows you to control the scope of a search that is done by OWA users. This attribute is msExchQueryBaseDN, and it must point to the organizational unit for the user's virtual organization or address list. Note that this attribute must be set for each OWA user and can only be set through ADSI scripts, ADSIEDIT, or an LDAP tool; it cannot be set through the Active Directory Users And Computers console.

Address Lists

Replacing Exchange 5.5 address book views, *address lists* allow you to create custom views of the directory based on any of the LDAP query filters described earlier in this chapter. Address lists are found in the Recipients ➢ Address Lists container. To create an address list, you must have Exchange Administrator permissions at the organization level.

Address lists are more versatile in that you can create only the specific address lists that you require. If you require only an address list of everyone in the Human Resources department, you can create that list. However, you may find that the address list is less flexible since it only generates a list for a particular query; whereas with address book views you could create a view on a specific property. Address lists make you create an address list based on a condition where a specific property equals a certain value (such as City = "Austin"). With an address book view, the first user whose city field was equal to Austin would cause an Address Book View container to be created for that city. With address lists, you will have to create a new address list that contains users whose city attribute equals Austin.

Additionally, you can restrict a user's or group's permissions to view an address list. However, even if you restrict their ability to view the recipients in the address list, they will still be able to see the address list container. If you need to create several address lists that will be restricted, create a parent address list container and restrict permissions to access that container.

Offline Address Lists   Offline address lists are the equivalent of Exchange 5.5 offline address books (OABs). Outlook clients use these lists when working in offline mode. The Outlook client synchronizes the offline address list into a series of OAB files located in the \WINDOWS or \WINNT directory (Outlook 97 and 98) or the user's application data directory (Outlook 2000 or 2002).

The offline address lists are found in the Recipients ➢ Offline Address Book container. Creating an OAB involves associating one more address lists or global address lists with the offline address book and designating an Exchange 2000 server to be responsible for generating it. The properties of an offline address book are shown in Figure 2.13, which shows that you can customize it by adding specific address lists to it.

Figure 2.13   Offline address book properties

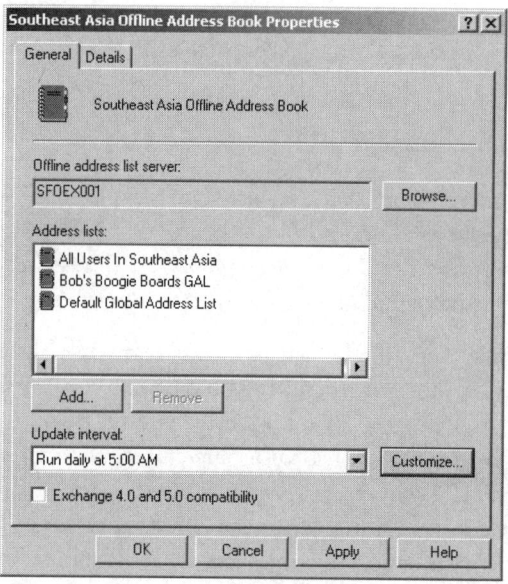

Users are assigned an offline address book based on which mailbox store their mailbox is located in. The default offline address book contains the default global address list.

TIP You can create an offline address book that contains a filtered view of an address list. See Knowledge Base article Q280435 for more information.

Address Lists and LDAP Queries

Address lists (including GALs and offline address books) as well as recipient policies are built using LDAP queries. The Exchange System Manager gives you the ability to build these LDAP queries from the graphical user interface (GUI). Figure 2.14 shows the Find Exchange Recipients interface (you get this by clicking the Filter button), which will help you build the necessary LDAP query to build an address list.

Figure 2.14   Building an LDAP query

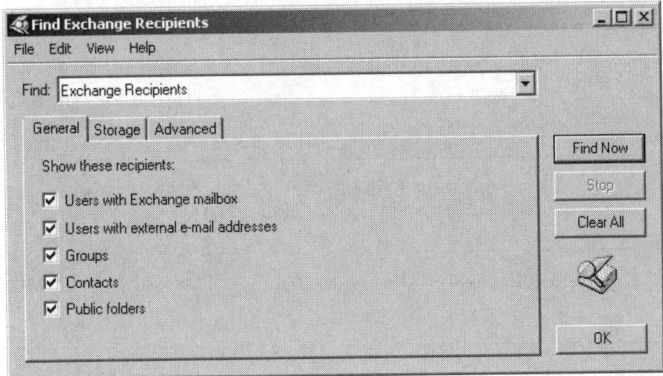

From the interface in Figure 2.14, you can build a query that includes the characteristics found in Table 2.5.

Table 2.5   Property Pages, Options, and Search Criteria Found on the Find Exchange Recipients Interface

Property Page	Option	Search Criteria
General	Users with Exchange mailbox	If checked, includes users with Exchange mailbox (mailbox-enabled users).
General	Users with external e-mail addresses	If checked, includes users with external mail address (mail-enabled users).

Table 2.5   Property Pages, Options, and Search Criteria Found on the Find Exchange Recipients Interface *(continued)*

Property Page	Option	Search Criteria
General	Groups	If checked, includes mail-enabled groups.
General	Contacts	If checked, includes mail-enabled contacts.
General	Public Folders	If checked, includes any mail-enabled public folders that are not hidden from the address lists.
Storage	Mailboxes on any server	If checked, searches mailboxes on any server (default).
Storage	Mailboxes on this server	Mailboxes on a specific server.
Storage	Mailboxes in this mailbox store	Mailboxes on a specific mailbox store.
Advanced	Field	Allows you to specify custom search.

Creating Customized Search   The complaint that I have with creating a filter through the GUI is that when I want to specify a custom filter, the interface only allows me to specify an AND. For example, I want to create an address list called All Users In Southeast Asia; I would use the custom search feature on the Advanced property tab to include the search City begins with Singapore *and* begins with Kuala Lumpur. This custom filter is shown in Figure 2.15.

NOTE   The LDAP name for city is I, which is short for locality.

Figure 2.15   A custom filter for all users whose City attribute is Singapore and Kuala Lumpur

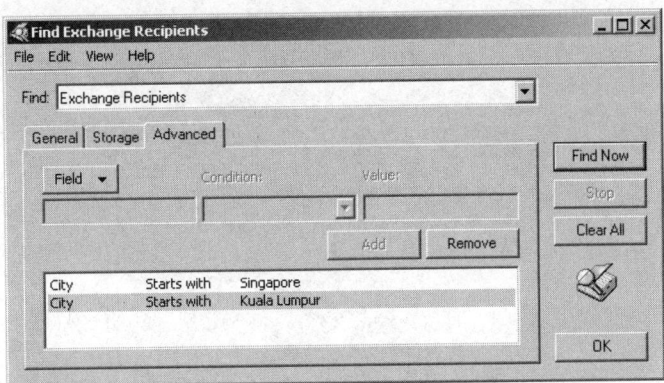

However, the custom search generates the following LDAP query:

```
(&(&(&(& (mailnickname=*) (| (&(objectCategory=person)(objectClass=user)
(|(homeMDB=*)(msExchHomeServerName=*))) ))) (objectCategory=user)(l=Singapore*)
(l=Kuala Lumpur*)))
```

This LDAP query will include all mailboxes whose City attribute is Singapore *and* Kuala Lumpur. If the City attribute contains *only* Singapore or Kuala Lumpur, the mailbox will not be included in the list. The interface provides only an AND query, not an OR.

To make this query include users whose City attribute begins with either Singapore or Kuala Lumpur, I have to edit the LDAP query and include an operator that will indicate that the query is an OR, not an AND. The only modification I have to make is to tell the equation that I want to search for l=Singapore OR l=Kuala Lumpur. The change is subtle, instead of (l=Singapore*)(l=Kuala Lumpur*), I add an additional set of parentheses and the OR operator |. The last part of the query looks like |(l=Singapore*)(l=Kuala Lumpur*). The entire modified LDAP query looks like this:

```
(&(&(&(& (mailnickname=*) (| (&(objectCategory=person)(objectClass=user)
(|(homeMDB=*)(msExchHomeServerName=*))) ))) (objectCategory=user)(|(l=Singapore*)
(l=Kuala Lumpur*))))
```

Prior to editing the query, use the GUI to get the query as close as possible to the query you need to perform. Then block and copy the query from the Filter Rules box on the General property tab of the address list (see Figure 2.16). Paste the query into Notepad and make the changes, then copy the modified query into the paste buffer.

Figure 2.16 Filter rules widow

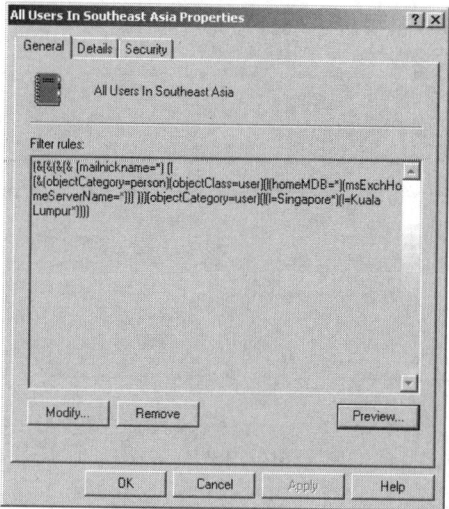

Next, using ADSIEDIT, locate the address list in the configuration partition. This will be located in the Configuration partition (CN=All Address Lists,CN=Address List Container,CN=*Organization Name*>,CN=Microsoft Exchange,CN=Services). Display the properties of the address list, locate the purportedSearch attribute, paste the edited query into the Edit Attribute box, and click the Set button (shown in Figure 2.17).

Figure 2.17 ADSIEDIT purportedSearch value for address list

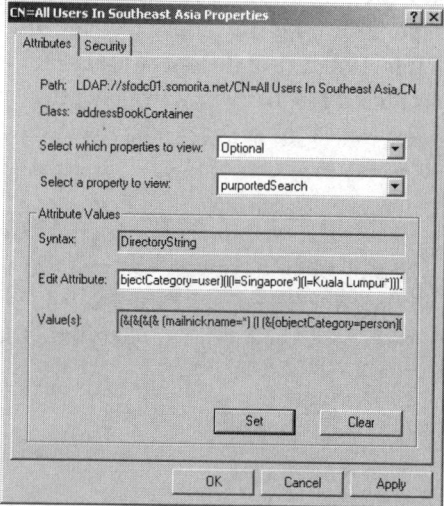

NOTE Custom searches can be performed from the Find dialog box that you can access when modifying the search criteria, but custom searches are limited to 270 characters.

NOTE Request for Comments (RFC) 2254 covers the syntax and operators used for custom LDAP searches. This RFC can be viewed at www.rfc-editor.org.

Sample Queries

To better understand LDAP queries, I have found it useful to review sample queries from which I can better create my own custom queries. Table 2.6 has some sample queries including those that generate the default address lists. In one of the queries, I am taking advantage of the fact that each mail-enabled object has an attribute called legacyExchangeDN. This attribute consists of the Exchange 2000 organization and the administrative group name.

Table 2.6 Sample LDAP Queries

What Is Being Queried	LDAP Query
Default global address list	(& (mailnickname=*) (| (&(objectCategory=person) (objectClass=user)(!(homeMDB=*))(!(msExchHome-ServerName=*)))(&(objectCategory=person)(object-Class=user)(|(homeMDB=*)(msExchHomeServerName=*)))(&(objectCategory=person)(objectClass=contact))(objectCategory=group)(objectCategory=publicFolder)))
All mail-enabled objects	(& (mailnickname=*) (| (&(objectCategory=person)(objectClass=user)(!(homeMDB=*))(!(msExchHomeServerName=*)))(&(objectCategory=person)(objectClass=user)(|(homeMDB=*)(msExchHomeServerName=*)))))
All contacts	(& (mailnickname=*) (| (&(objectCategory=person)(objectClass=contact))))
All groups	(& (mailnickname=*) (| (objectCategory=group)))
All public folders	(& (mailnickname=*) (| (objectCategory=publicFolder)))

Table 2.6   Sample LDAP Queries *(continued)*

What Is Being Queried	LDAP Query
All mailbox-enabled users in Honolulu	(&(&(&(& (mailnickname=*) (| (&(objectCategory= person)(objectClass=user)(|(homeMDB=*) (msExchHomeServerName=*)))))) (objectCategory=user)(l=Honolulu*)))
All users in the Southeast Asia admin group	(&(mail=*) (legacyExchangeDN=/o=Somorita Surfboards/ou=Southeast Asia/*))
All users whose mailbox is on SFOEX001 or SFOEX002	(&(mail=*)(|(homeMDB=cn=SFOEX001)(homeMDB= cn=SFOEX002)))
All mail-enabled objects whose extended attribute 10 equals March	(&(&(mailnickname=*)((extensionAttribute10=*March*))))
All mail-enabled users whose User Principal Name suffix is bobsboogieboards.com	(&(&(mailnickname=*)((userPrincipalName= *@bobsboogieboards.com))))

You cannot query based on the OU in Windows 2000, though this is supposed to change in Windows.NET. The operators that are found in LDAP queries include:

Operator	Function
&	AND
|	OR
!	NOT

Extended Attribute Names

Once the Active Directory schema is extended, there are 15 additional extension attributes that you can use to assign other fields to users. These are the same types of attributes that you could use with Exchange 5.5. The values for each of these extension attributes can be set on the Exchange Advanced property tab of mail-enabled objects (click the Custom Attributes button).

The custom attributes are named extensionAttribute1 through extensionAttribute15, but you can change these to be something more meaningful. To change the attribute names, you will need to use ADSIEDIT. The following example steps through changing the display name of the custom attribute extensionAttribute1 to JobCode.

1. Log in as a user who is a member of the Schema Admins group.

2. Launch ADSIEDIT and connect to the Schema partition.

3. Locate and display the properties of the attribute called CN=ms-Exch-Extension-Attribute-1 (properties are shown in Figure 2.18).

4. Select Both in the Select Which Properties To View drop-down list box.

5. Select lDAPDisplayName in the Select A Property To View drop-down list box.

6. In the Edit Attribute box, enter **JobCode**, and then click the Set button.

NOTE   Spaces are not allowed in attribute names.

Figure 2.18   LDAP display name properties for extension attribute 1

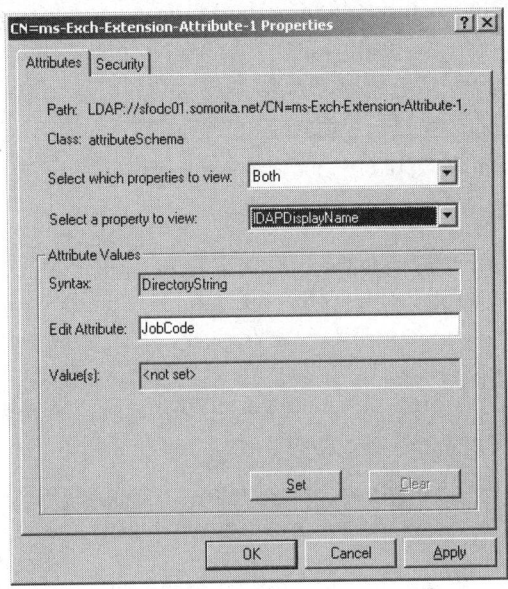

Recipient Policies

Recipient policies allow you to assign more than one proxy address to mail-enabled recipients. These are roughly comparable to the Exchange 5.5 site addressing object. However, you could only create a single proxy address for each type of address you supported, and that address applied to the entire site.

Exchange 2000 recipient policies provide three basic functions to Exchange 2000:

- Creating proxy addresses (SMTP, X.400, etc.) for mail-enabled objects in Active Directory
- Enabling SMTP virtual servers to accept mail for a specific domain
- Setting the default SMTP domain name that is used by the Exchange Installable File System (ExIFS)

Creating Additional Recipient Policies

When Exchange 2000 is installed, there is a single recipient policy called the *default policy*, which sets a single X.400 and SMTP address. The default policy affects all SMTP recipients in the organization and cannot be changed. Further, the default SMTP address is the folder name that will be found in the M: drive. For example, if the default SMTP domain name is SOMORITA.NET, then the first folder found in the ExIFS drive will be M:\SOMORITA.NET.

NOTE The default recipient policy is always the lowest priority policy. It cannot be deleted.

You can add additional proxy addresses for users using the default policy, but that policy affects all mail-enabled objects. If you want to create an additional recipient policy that affects only a specific group of users, you can create a policy and set a filter that determines which recipients this policy affects. Also, recipient policies can be assigned a priority. If a mail-enabled object is affected by more than one policy, then the policy with the highest priority takes precedence.

Recipient policies are an organization-wide resource, and you must have at least the Exchange Administrator role at the organization level to create recipient policies. Recipient policies are found in the Recipients ➤ Recipient Policies container. The following example creates a recipient policy named Asia Users that will apply an STMP address of @asia.somorita.com to all users located in Singapore, Kuala Lumpur, and Tokyo:

1. Locate the Recipients Policies container, right-click, and choose New ➤ Recipient Policy.

2. Name this policy Asia Users and then click Modify button.

3. In the Find Exchange Recipients dialog box, you can generate the criteria for this policy. For this example, choose all the defaults on the General tab, and click the Advanced tab.

4. Click the Field button and select the City user attribute. Specify that the condition starts with a value of Singapore. Repeat this step for Kuala Lumpur and Tokyo. Once you have entered all three city values, click OK to get out of this screen.

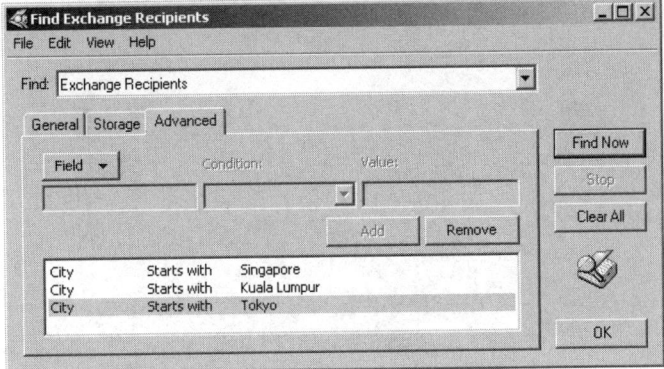

5. The LDAP query necessary to find the mail-enabled recipients you are specifying will now show up in the Filter Rules screen. However, you will need to modify the query slightly since the city portion of the query is querying for mail-enabled objects whose city attribute is Singapore AND Kuala Lumpur AND Tokyo. Block and copy this query.

6. Run ADSIEDIT, locate the new recipient policy, and locate the purportedSearch attribute. You will have to modify the portion of the search that says (1=Singapore*)(1=Kuala Lumpur*)(1=Tokyo*) so that it says (|(1=Singapore*)(1=Kuala Lumpur*)(1=Tokyo*)). This procedure was discussed earlier in this chapter.

7. Click the E-mail Addresses property tab and insert a new e-mail address for @asia.somorita.com. Remember to click the check box next to the e-mail address so that it will be included in the policy.

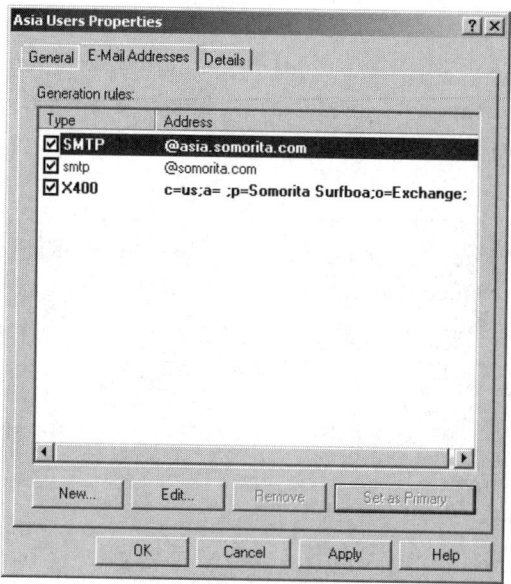

Once this policy is in place, the organization's SMTP virtual servers will now accept mail destined for the asia.somorita.com domain. In Exchange 5.5, this was handled on each Internet Mail Service by adding additional inbound domains to the Routing property tab.

The recipient policy will affect only newly created users. If you want it to affect existing users, right-click the policy and choose Apply This Policy Now. These additional proxy addresses are applied to each mail-enabled recipient by the RUS.

Proxy addresses are added to each mail-enabled object's proxyAddresses directory attribute. This attribute is used by the Advanced Queuing Engine message categorizer to determine where to route inbound messages from external connectors (SMTP, Lotus Notes, GroupWise, etc.).

NOTE   If a recipient policy is deleted, the proxy addresses that it created will remain with the mail-enabled objects.

Ambiguous Name Resolution (ANR)

The Exchange and Outlook clients are capable of performing something called *Ambiguous Name Resolution (ANR)*; this is turned on by default. (Though I define ANR as Ambiguous Name Resolution, I have seen the "A" referred to as Ambiguous, Automatic, and Address.) You can type an ambiguous name into the message To, Cc, or Bcc fields, and Outlook will search the Exchange directory for mailboxes and custom recipients whose alias, office, e-mail addresses (such as SMTP addresses), last name, or the first word of the display name matches the ambiguous name. If there is more than one result, the Exchange and Outlook clients will display the results, allowing you to choose the correct display name.

Just entering a name will return all matches, including partial matches. You can also enter an equal sign (=) in front of the name you are looking for, and the client will return only exact matches.

If you want to include other fields in the search criteria for ANR, you can do this through Active Directory's Schema Management MMC. Locate the attribute you wish to use for ANR, such as Title, and display its properties as shown in Figure 2.19. Select the Ambiguous Name Resolution (ANR) check box.

Figure 2.19   Changing the ANR property for the Title attribute

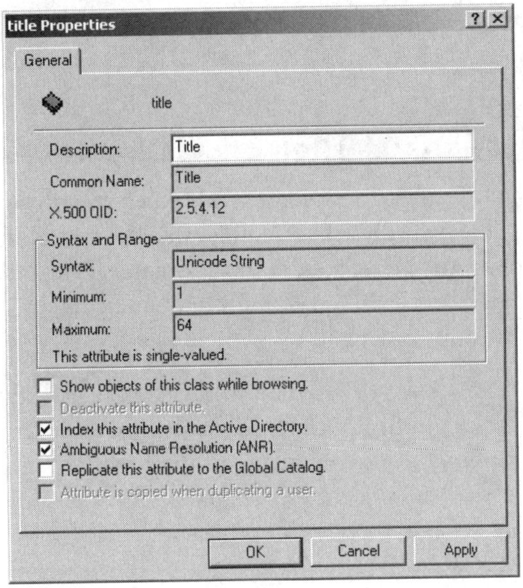

If the attribute is not flagged to be indexed in Active Directory, you must also check the Index This Attribute In The Active Directory check box. Like all changes to AD, only a member of the Schema Admins group can change these attributes. Further, the change should be made from the schema master. If you get an error message stating that you cannot make these changes, the most common cause is incorrect permissions.

Also, make sure that changes to the schema can currently be made. To do this, right-click the AD Schema object in the MMC, choose Operations Master, and confirm that the Schema May Be Modified On This Domain Controller check box is checked.

Exchange@Work: Using Automatic Name Resolution on Other Attributes

One of my customers is a large military installation in which users often use their job code rather than their name when exchanging correspondence. This is because people change positions frequently, but the job requirements for a specific job code are always the same. My client wanted to be able to type the person's job code into the To field and have Outlook automatically resolve to the correct display name.

To achieve this, we created a custom attribute field, renaming it to Job Code. Then, using the Active Directory Schema Management console, we enabled the Ambiguous Name Resolution and Index This Attribute In Active Directory check boxes. This allowed ANR to automatically search using a person's job code.

Letting Users Manage Their Own Directory Attributes

I am a big proponent of using the mailbox fields when creating a mailbox. I will enter the address, city, state, phone number, fax number, title, and more. For a number of organizations I have worked for, AD is also serving as the organization-wide phone book. However, the biggest problem is that this information is quite dynamic in a larger organization, and someone has to keep it up-to-date.

The Exchange 2000 Resource Kit's GAL Modify tool (shown in Figure 2.20) lets users change their own personal information that is displayed in the global address list. With this tool, users can modify a selected group of their mailbox attributes, including the street address, city, state, zip code, business phone, home phone, mobile phone, pager number, fax number, title, company, office, assistant, and notes.

The GAL Modify tool uses MAPI, not LDAP, to modify the user's properties, so the user must have some version of Outlook installed on their computer and a MAPI profile for their mailbox.

Figure 2.20   The GAL Modify tool

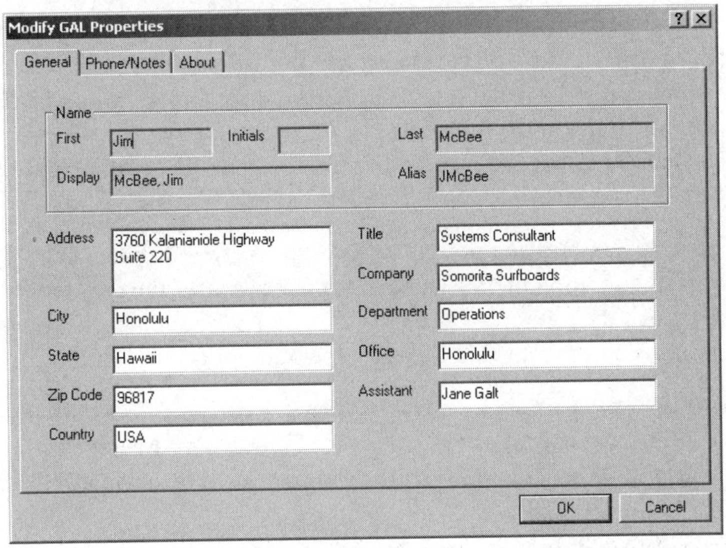

The program is simple to install. When the Resource Kit is installed, it is copied into `\Program Files\Exchange 2000 Server Resource Kit\Tools\Client\Galmod32` directory. From there, copy the `GALMOD32.EXE` program to a directory where the client can access it.

> **NOTE**   The GAL Modify tool is used only with MAPI clients. A more robust and generic alternative would be to create an internal Web page that used ASP (Active Server Pages) and ADSI (Active Directory services interface) to look up user attributes and make changes to those attributes.

Importing and Modifying Active Directory Data

There may come a time when you need to make bulk changes to the Active Directory data, such as adding many new users or changing a group of users' addresses. In Exchange 5.5, the Exchange Administrator program allowed us to import and export data from using a comma-separated value (CSV) file.

Windows 2000 provides two tools that can be used to make bulk changes or additions to AD. The first tool is the Comma-Separated Value Directory Exchange (CSVDE) tool. I was immediately fond of CSVDE since it uses CSV files—the same format that I used with Exchange 5.5. However, I was devastated when I discovered that it could only be used to add new objects to the directory, not to make changes.

I switched over to using the LDAP Data Interchange Format Directory Exchange (LDIFDE) tool, which can not only add new objects, but also delete and modify existing objects. My main beef with LDIFDE is that it is just a little more complicated to use. LDIFDE is also very picky about the format of the data, but as long as you know the LDAP attribute names of the values you need to populate or modify, you can change anything in Active Directory using LDIFDE.

Another approach to creating objects in AD is to use the Exchange 2000 Migration Wizard in two-step migration mode. This mode creates a CSV file that can be used to create accounts in much the same way as the Exchange 5.5 Administrator program's import/export feature. You can edit this CSV file and add your own columns to it.

> **NOTE**   RFC 2849 describes the format for LDIFDE files. Microsoft Knowledge Base article Q263991 outlines how to set a password using an LDIF file.

Common LDAP Attribute Names

The first challenge to using LDIFDE is learning all of those LDAP attribute names. While the LDAP attributes are not case sensitive, you must have the attribute names correct in the import file. Table 2.7 describes the common LDAP attributes. A more complete list of LDAP attribute names can be found at www.somorita.com.

Table 2.7   Some LDAP Attributes Used in AD

Attribute	Description
DN	The distinguished name of the object. The DN is unique throughout the entire forest.
SAMAccountName	User account for compatibility with pre–Windows 2000 systems.
userPrincipalName	The logon name for the account that will be unique throughout the forest.
displayName	The full name of the object. This is the name that appears in the GAL.

Table 2.7   Some LDAP Attributes Used in AD *(continued)*

Attribute	Description
MailNickName	Exchange alias; required if creating a mailbox for a user.
HomeMDB	Distinguished name of the home mailbox store; required if creating a mailbox for a user.
givenName	First name.
Initials	Initials.

Other entries you can place in an LDIFDE file control the changes that are being made. Some of these are described in Table 2.8.

Table 2.8   LDIFDE Entries Used to Control LDIFDE

Entry	Description
changeType	Controls what action is being taken on the object specified in the DN line. Valid options are add, modify, or delete.
objectClass	Specifies the type of object being configured. Valid options include user and contact.
userAccountControl	Specifies whether the user object being created is enabled or disabled. Valid options include 512 if the user account should be enabled or 514 if the user account is to be disabled. If this is not specified, the account is disabled.

Sample LDIFDE Files

The simplest way to learn how to use LDIFDE and learn the format of the LDIFDE files is to look at sample files. The following example is the minimum number of fields required to create two user account objects in Active Directory. Note that the user accounts must be separated by a blank line for them to import properly.

```
DN: cn="Tang, Kwen Hou",ou=Operations,dc=Somorita,dc=net
changeType: add
objectClass: user
sAMAccountName: KHTang
```

```
DN: cn="Suzuki, Makoto",ou=Operations,dc=Somorita,dc=net
changeType: add
objectClass: user
sAMAccountName: Msuzuki
```

WARNING   Do not create your LDF files using a word processor such as Microsoft word. Word will create special characters that LDIFDE cannot process.

NOTE   If you are adding objects to the Users container, use CN=Users instead of OU=.

The above example will create two disabled user accounts. If you want to create a user account that is enabled, simply add userAccountControl: 512 to each user's section of the file.

Let's look at a somewhat more complex example. Here we're incorporating some additional attributes and including the mailNickname and homeMDB attributes. *Both* of these are required to mailbox-enable this user account.

```
DN: cn=Karen Ellington,ou=Operations,dc=Somorita,dc=net
changeType: add
objectClass: user
sAMAccountName: Kellington
displayName: "Ellington, Karen"
givenName: Karen
sn: Ellington
street: 1401 Raffles Avenue
l: Singapore
postalCode: 8763
co: Singapore
title: Regional Director
Department: Operations
physicalDeliveryOfficeName: SunTec City
mailNickname: KEllington
homeMDB: cn=mailbox store (SINGEX01),cn=First Storage Group,
  cn=InformationStore,cn=SINGEX01,cn=Servers,cn=South East Asia
 Admin Group,cn=Administrative Groups,cn=Somorita Surfboards,cn=Microsoft
Exchange,cn=Services,cn=Configuration,DC=Somorita,
   DC=net
UserAccountControl: 512
```

How about modifications to existing objects? Changes are a little more complicated. The LDIFDE file must specify not only the DN of the object that will be affected, but also the attribute that will be modified. Multiple changes can be made in a single file, but changes must be separated by a hyphen (-) *and* a blank line. Here is an example that changes two user's city attributes:

```
DN: CN="Ta, Ky",ou=Operations,dc=Somorita,dc=net
changeType: modify
replace: 1
1: Kuala Lumpur
-

DN: CN="Lee, Sean",ou=Operations,dc=Somorita,dc=net
changeType: modify
replace: 1
1: Kuala Lumpur
```

At the end of each entry, remember to include the hyphen, even if you are modifying only one object.

This final example creates an LDF file to delete an object. This file is quite simple since it need contain only the distinguished name (DN) and the changetype filed.

```
DN: CN="Supatanasakul, Suriya",ou=Sales,dc=Somorita,dc=net
changeType: delete
```

> **NOTE** For more information on using LDIFDE files, see Microsoft Knowledge Base article Q237677.

Using the LDIFDE Utility

Now that you have created your LDIFDE file, you are ready to use the LDIFDE utility. Table 2.9 lists the utility's command-line options.

Table 2.9 LDIFDE Command-Line Parameters

Parameter	Description
-i	Specifies that LDIFDE run in import mode. If -i is not specified, the utility runs in export mode.
-k	Instructs LDIFDE to continue to process entries even if an error occurred on one of the entries in the file. Used on import only.

Table 2.9 LDIFDE Command-Line Parameters *(continued)*

Parameter	Description
-f *filename*	Specifies the filename to read from or export to.
-s *servername*	Specifies a domain controller to bind to.
-v	Runs in verbose mode to generate more detailed messages.
-j *path*	Specifies the path for log files.
-t *portnumber*	Specifies an LDAP port other than 389.
-d *RootDN*	Specifies the DN from which to begin exporting. Used on export only.
-r *filter*	Allows the specification of an LDAP search filter so you can export only specific objects. Used on export only.
-l *list*	Specifies a comma-separated list of attributes to export. Used on export only.
-o *list*	Specifies a comma-separated list of attributes not to export. Used on export only.
-g	Disables paged search.
-n	Specifies that binary values are not exported.

> **NOTE** Active Directory does not support the following characters: *, (,), \, and =.

LDIFDE creates an LDIF.LOG file that is all the lines that LDIFDE will process for each entry in the LDF file. If there are problems during the import, an LDIF.ERR file is created for entries that caused errors. Review this log carefully if you have errors.

Sample LDIFDE Commands

Just like learning how to use the LDF files, learning LDIFDE works best if you have examples to go by. This example is used to import the NEWUSERS.LDF file:

```
ldifde -i -v -f newusers.ldf
```

This command exports only the objects found in the Accounting organizational unit to a file called accountingusers.ldf:

```
Ldifde -v -f accountingusers.ldf -d ou=accounting,dc=Somorita,dc=net
```

This command exports all objects in the directory, but only the givenname, surname, and title attributes to a file called usernames.ldf:

```
Ldifde -v -f usernames.ldf -l dn, givenname,surname
```

The Recipient Update Service

When managing Exchange 2000, the administrator can make changes that will affect user, contact, public folder, message store, or other Active Directory objects. When such a change occurs, there must be an Exchange 2000 component responsible for updating the affected objects in Active Directory. The Exchange 2000 System Attendant runs a process called the recipient update service, which handles these updates. The Exchange 2000 RUS is responsible for:

- Ensuring that mail-enabled objects belong to the correct address lists.
- Creating proxy addresses for mail-enabled objects based on recipient policies.
- Applying Exchange 2000 system policies to mailbox stores, public folder stores, and Exchange 2000 servers.
- Changing the relevant group's security descriptor if the Hide DL Membership option is set.
- Populating the legacyExchangeDN and displayName attributes for mail-enabled recipients. For mailbox-enabled recipients, it populates legacyExchangeDN, displayName, msExchHomeServerName, homeMDB, homeMTA, displayName, msExchUserAccountControl, and msExchMailboxGuid if any of these attributes are missing.

> **NOTE** The RUS was known as the Address List Service during the beta cycle of Exchange 2000. You may still see references to the Address List Service (WLDAP32.DLL), or it may be shortened to just MSExchangeAL.

Recipient Update Service and Address Lists

The RUS runs once a minute checking for changes that affect address list membership. These changes would include adding new address lists, adding new users, changing address list filter criteria, or changing an existing attribute on a user that would require that the user be a member of an address list.

The RUS does an LDAP query based on each address list's filter and checks to see if any mail-enabled object has not been made a member of the list. If it finds one that needs to be part of an address list, it inserts the distinguished name of the address list into the object's showInAddressBook directory attribute (see Figure 2.21).

Figure 2.21   A user's showInAddressBook attribute

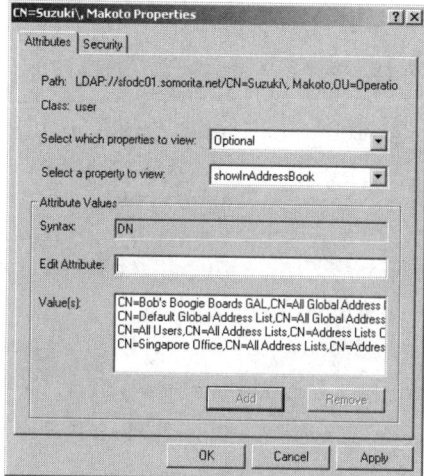

Figure 2.21 shows that the user is a member of the Bob's Boogie Board GAL, the Default Global Address List, the All Users address list, and the Singapore Office address list.

If the user's msExchHideFromAddressList attribute is set to TRUE, the RUS will remove all address lists from the showInAddressBook attribute. The user's showInAddressBook attribute *must* contain at least one address list; otherwise the user will not be able to find the mailbox from a MAPI client. This means that the user must also wait until the RUS has run at least once before they can access their mailbox. Depending on the Active Directory replication interval, this can be 15 minutes or more before updates that the RUS has made are replicated to all domain controllers.

Configuring the Recipient Update Service

When you install the first Exchange 2000 server, you will find two recipient update services in the RUS container; one is for the domain in which the Exchange server is located, and the second is for the enterprise configuration. The RUS for the domain that the server is located in is responsible for updating all of the objects in the domain naming partition of Active Directory (mailbox-enabled users, mail-enabled users, mail-enabled contacts, mail-enabled public folders, etc.). There is only one enterprise configuration; it is responsible for updating objects found in the configuration container.

As you install additional Exchange servers into other domains, there will be one RUS automatically created for each additional domain. You can create additional RUSs that work with each domain; however, each must point to a different domain controller. You might want to create multiple RUSs if you have a large, geographically dispersed domain whose replication interval between AD sites would cause significant delays for users to appear in the address lists or receive new proxy addresses.

Figure 2.22 shows the RUS for the Asia domain; SFOEX001 is the Exchange server from which the RUS will be run, and the Windows 2000 domain controller that this RUS will connect to is `singex01.asia.somorita.net`. Both of these options can be changed.

Figure 2.22   RUS for the Asia domain

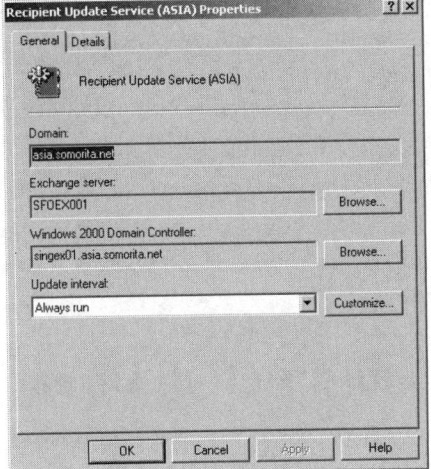

In this figure, the Update Interval is set to Always Run. This can be configured to run on a custom schedule, every few hours, or to never run. If the interval is set to Always Run, the RUS will run once per minute; however it only checks for changes. The RUS will not process the entire directory again unless the administrator explicitly selects the Rebuild option from Exchange System Manager.

Figure 2.22 also shows a bad design. In the network from which Figure 2.22 was captured, there is not an Exchange server in the Asia domain. The Exchange 2000 server that runs the RUS is located in San Francisco, and the domain controller is located in Singapore. This is a poor design because all of the LDAP queries and updates that the SFOEX001 server would generate would occur across the WAN link. If bandwidth was an issue, a better solution might be to place an Exchange Server in the Singapore office or place an Asia domain controller in the San Francisco office.

If you have a Windows 2000 domain that does not have an Exchange 2000 server but will have recipients whose mailbox server is in another domain, you must do the following:

- Run the Exchange 2000 Setup program on a domain controller in that domain with the /domainprep option. This will give the Exchange servers in the other domains the necessary permissions to change the attributes of mail-enabled objects in that domain.
- Manually create a RUS that services the recipients in the domain.

Managing the Recipient Update Service

Typically, there is nothing that the administrator needs to do to manage the Recipient Update Service. By default, it will process changes once per minute. You can force the RUS to run manually by right-clicking the desired RUS and on the context menu, choosing Update Now or Rebuild.

If you choose Update Now, the RUS will process any changes. However, if you choose Rebuild, the RUS will recalculate all address list memberships and policies during the next scheduled update interval. A large domain could take several hours to process.

I have seen problems with pre–Exchange 2000 SP1 servers where I had to occasionally force the RUS to run in order for recipients to appear in the address lists or have their proxy addresses generated. Typically, though, if I am waiting for a user to appear in the address lists or get their proxy addresses, I am waiting for my domain controllers to replicate, not for the RUS to run.

Exchange 2000 and Active Directory FAQ

Following are some commonly asked questions relating to Exchange 2000 and its interaction with Active Directory. This list is by no means a substitute for reading this chapter or for having a better understanding of Active Directory, but it does provide a good starting place and a quick reference.

How many domain controllers and Global Catalog servers should I have in my forest? The number of domain controllers will depend partially on the number of domains you have and the number of domain controllers required for authentication. I recommend a minimum of one domain controller and one Global Catalog server in each Active Directory site. Two domain controllers and Global Catalog servers provides redundancy and fault tolerance. Additionally, you should have, on average, one Global Catalog server for every four Exchange servers in a particular site to handle the mail routing load.

Is there a maximum number of mail-enabled recipients that can be put in a group? You should never put more than 5000 mail-enabled recipients in any type of group.

Does each domain in the forest need an Exchange 2000 Recipient Update Service? If a domain will have either an Exchange server located in it or objects that will be mail-enabled, then you must create a Recipient Update Service for it.

3

Exchange 2000 Migration and Upgrades

Are you running Exchange 5.5 and want to upgrade? If you haven't started installing Exchange 2000, then you're in the right place. There are several approaches to installing or upgrading to Exchange 2000. The method you choose will depend on your upgrade goals, the environment you're working in, and whether your migration process is a single phase (in which you move your entire organization) or a multiphase process (in which Exchange 5.5 and Exchange 2000 coexist).

Upgrading to Exchange 2000 is a complex topic that certainly deserves more coverage than this single book can offer, but I will at least attempt to cover the high points. The decisions you make during setup or upgrade will determine what features and options are available. This chapter provides a broad overview of the process, workload, and other key factors involved in upgrading a Windows NT 4 and Exchange 5.5 environment to a Windows 2000 and Exchange 2000 environment.

> **NOTE** Microsoft Consulting Services and the Exchange team have assembled volumes of information on upgrading and migrating to Exchange 2000. These papers are available on the Web at www.microsoft.com/exchange; look in the Technical Resources ➤ Deployment and Migration section.

Both managers and IT teams tasked with upgrading or migrating to Exchange 2000 will be relieved to know that Exchange 2000 has been designed to simplify integration and migration to the Active Directory (AD) service while providing backward compatibility and interoperability with Exchange 5.5. Further, Exchange 2000 can upgrade Exchange 5.5 mailboxes without losing data. In fact, the primary difference between Exchange 5.5 and Exchange 2000 is that Exchange 2000 relies entirely on Windows 2000 Active Directory for all directory and security information. Integration of the Exchange 5.5 and Windows 2000 directory services offers deployment teams many benefits, including:

- Shared network security and messaging, which can dramatically improve administration flexibility.

- Strong coordination between Exchange and Windows administrators. These teams must now cooperate and coordinate their formerly separate administrative responsibilities for successful Active Directory Connector (ADC) and Exchange 2000 deployment.

- Expanded attributes for mail delivery and storage, in addition to a new Windows 2000 group model, which merges Exchange 5.5 distribution list and Microsoft Windows NT 4 group functionality.

- New components, such as the ADC, Site Replication Service (SRS), and Recipient Update Service (RUS), which are all integrated with Active Directory.

In order to successfully move to Exchange 2000 either in a new environment or as an upgrade from an earlier messaging system, the deployment team must understand the integration of the Exchange 2000 services with Windows 2000. Exchange 2000 now relies heavily on Windows 2000 and AD services for the following areas:

- Directory services (Active Directory)
- Message transport (SMTP via IIS)
- Message access (POP3, IMAP4, and NNTP via IIS)
- Security

Here are the basic steps, in a nutshell, to upgrading an existing Exchange 5.5 server to an Exchange 2000 server. Before diving in, take the time to review the first several pages of this chapter to make sure you fully understand the upgrade process.

1. Upgrade at least one of the domain controllers on your network to Windows 2000 Service Pack 2 and upgrade the domain to an Active Directory domain.

2. Upgrade the operating system of the Exchange server to Windows 2000 Service Pack 1.

3. Install the ADC.

4. Create a connection agreement between Active Directory and the Exchange 5.5 directory, and allow time for replication to occur.

5. Install Exchange 2000 and confirm that you want the upgrade to occur.

Does this list leave out some critical steps? You bet it does! If you don't feel comfortable without a lot more detail, then this chapter and the references to other material will give you the information you need to upgrade your organization properly.

> **NOTE** Installing the RTM (release to manufacturing) version of Exchange 2000, I encountered a number of errors and glitches, most of which have been addressed with Exchange 2000 SP1 or Windows 2000 SP2. Therefore, this chapter assumes you are running one of those versions and doesn't address many of the RTM problems.

As you prepare to upgrade or migrate from Exchange 5.5, there are many factors to consider. There may even be some changes needed, depending on your environment and what you want to get out of Exchange 2000. Prior to upgrading to Exchange 2000, you should do the following:

- Take note of the factors that may affect your upgrade or migration strategy.
- Successfully deploy Windows 2000.
- Create a deployment plan.
- Design your Active Directory and Exchange 5.5 organization.
- Check permission consistency.
- Clean up the Exchange 5.5 directory.
- Check for Outlook Web Access compatibility.
- Make sure you have the right permissions.
- Change your site architecture.

Considering Factors before Migrating/Upgrading

Before delving into a migration or upgrade, it's important to look at some of the options and steps involved so you can be as prepared as possible. In the days or weeks prior to migration or upgrade, check out the following items:

- Confirm that your organization's site model matches the administrative model you want to use for administrative groups in Exchange 2000.

- You must have a Windows 2000 AD forest, and the servers that will host Exchange 2000 must be on Windows 2000 member servers (or domain controllers) in that forest. The domains can be Mixed mode or Native mode (preferably). All Windows 2000 servers and domain controllers should be running Windows 2000 SP2 or later.

- Inventory and confirm that you have Exchange 2000 versions of any third-party Exchange add-in products you have, such as antivirus solutions, fax gateways, pager gateways, messaging gateways, and voicemail integration.

- Inventory any Microsoft connectors that you may currently be using, such as the Internet Mail Service, Microsoft Mail Connector, GroupWise Connector, cc:Mail Connector, Lotus Notes Connector or mainframe mail system connectors. Exchange 2000 does not provide PROFS/Office Vision and SNADS connectors, so you must continue using the Exchange 5.5 version of these connectors, which means you must continue running an Exchange 5.5 server.

- There must be at least one Exchange 5.5 SP3 or later server in each Exchange 5.5 site, though my personal preference is that all servers be running at least Exchange 5.5 SP3.

- Exchange servers that will be upgraded in place must be running Exchange 5.5 SP3 or later.

- If you will be performing a migration by moving mailboxes or upgrading a server in place, then you must install the ADC.

- Exchange servers that will be the source/target server for an ADC configuration agreement (CA) must be running Exchange 5.5 SP3 or later.

- Ensure that Windows 2000 servers with more than 1GB of physical memory are using the /3GB startup switch. For example:

  ```
  [Boot Loader]
  Timeout=30
  Default=multi(0)disk(0)rdisk(0)partition(2)\WINNT
  [Operating Systems]
  multi(0)disk(0)rdisk(0)partition(2)\WINNT="Microsoft Windows 2000
  Server" /fastdetect /3GB
  ```

- Windows 2000 servers that will host Exchange 2000 Server must have proper DNS connectivity and be able to resolve domain controller and global catalog server SRV records (see Chapter 2, "Active Directory for Exchange 2000 Administrations," for more information).

- Windows 2000 servers that will host Exchange 2000 Server must have Internet Information Server installed including Web services, NNTP, and SMTP.

- Confirm that you know each Exchange 5.5 site's site services account username and password.

- Make sure that each Exchange 5.5 mailbox has a unique Windows user account associated with it. No Windows user account should be the primary Windows NT user account for more than one mailbox. (This can be checked using the NTDSATRB tool, discussed later in the chapter.)

- The last Exchange 5.5 server that should be upgraded is the one that provides Outlook Web Access (OWA) services, since Exchange 2000 OWA will not access Exchange 5.5 servers.

- The Exchange 5.5 organization and site names must adhere to the Exchange 2000 naming standards. If they do not, you can change the display names using Exchange Administrator prior to installing the first ADC.

NOTE   All future references to Exchange 5.5 assume that you are using Exchange 5.5 SP3 or later, unless otherwise noted.

Exchange@Work: Renaming an Exchange Organization

Company XYZ had been using Exchange Server since Exchange 4.0. In the past few years, they merged with a smaller company, changed their site architecture, and changed their name. The smaller company's users had merely been imported into the existing Exchange 5.5 servers, but the managers often complained that they wanted to see the new company name everywhere. However, the Exchange organization name is essentially etched in stone.

When time for migration to Exchange 2000 came, XYZ were elated to find that they could change the name of the organization and the sites. To do this, they changed the display name of the organization and the sites prior to installing the Active Directory Connector. When the ADC first begins to create Exchange-specific information in Active Directory, it will use the display names to create the corresponding Exchange 2000 organization and administrative group names, not the Exchange 5.5 directory names.

As you approach the big day, the following steps are helpful when preparing to upgrade or migrate from an Exchange 5.5 server:

- Run the DS/IS Consistency Adjuster.

- Remove the antivirus software from the Exchange 5.5 server. Disabling the software will probably work, but I prefer to remove it completely so that it can be reinstalled once Exchange 2000 is running.

- If Exchange 5.5 is running on a server that is a Windows 2000 domain controller, change the LDAP (Lightweight Directory Access Protocol) port number to 3389 (Microsoft recommends port 390). Though port 390 is assigned to a fairly obscure service (UIS), I believe it is never a good idea to pick a port below 1024 for any application.

Exchange@Work: Don't Proceed with Connectivity Solutions

One early adopter of Exchange 2000 upgraded both of their Exchange 5.5 servers to Exchange 2000 in a single night. They did this on the assumption that all of their connector software would continue to work. I think you can see where this is going; naturally, the fax connector software was not compatible with Exchange 2000. Inbound and outbound network faxing was out of commission for a week while the customer waited for their upgrade. Since they had upgraded both of their Exchange 5.5 servers to Exchange 2000, they could not add a new Exchange 5.5 server to continue hosting this service.

This all could have been avoided if adequate planning and preparation had been done. Each connector that an organization uses, whether to another messaging system or a service such as fax service, should be thoroughly researched to determine the exact version that is necessary to work with Exchange 2000. If a version is not available, plans must be made for how to handle this.

Successfully Deploying Windows 2000

You won't be able to successfully deploy Exchange 2000 in your organization if you haven't worked out the kinks with your Windows 2000 installation. Whether in Mixed or Native mode, your Windows 2000 installation should be stable and working as expected *before* you begin to upgrade or migrate to Exchange 2000.

NOTE   An Exchange 2000 organization cannot span more than one Active Directory forest, and a single AD forest cannot support more than one Exchange 2000 organization. You cannot have some Exchange servers in one forest, and some in another. All Exchange resources—mailboxes, servers, public folders, and so forth—must be in the same forest. For more information, see Chapter 2.

As part of your Windows 2000 AD deployment, make sure that the AD domain controllers are replicating properly, that the AD site architecture is in place, and that all of your IP subnets have been defined and associated with the appropriate AD site. DNS name resolution should also be working properly; confirm this using the tools such as NLTest and NSLookup discussed in Chapter 2.

The most significant thing you can do to determine the ultimate success of your Exchange 2000 migration or upgrade is to create a deployment plan that identifies your goals. If you think a quick sketch will work, you better think again. Introducing Exchange 2000 Server to your organization is a serious undertaking; after all, we're talking about an application that has enterprise-wide implications! When developing your deployment plan, you should do the following:

- Understand your existing organization and where data is located.
- Map out the existing network infrastructure.
- Identify the existing messaging and directory structures.
- Determine the functional requirements to be met after the upgrade.
- Determine the order in which domains and servers will be upgraded.
- Identify available resources and obtain any necessary new hardware.

In short, your deployment plan needs to reflect your understanding of how Exchange and Windows interoperate and the Exchange 2000 dependencies on Active Directory and Windows 2000 (see Chapters 1 and 2). In addition, you'll want to consider the relationships between Windows 2000 sites and domains, domain controllers, global catalog servers, and Exchange 2000 administrative and routing groups. Finally, make sure that you're up to speed on the ADC, Site Replication Service, and Recipient Update Service (all of which are discussed later in this chapter as well as in Chapter 2).

Understanding Your Current Organization

As with any upgrade, there is information you need to gather from your current organization. The following sections outline the information you need to gather regarding how your Active Directory and current Exchange 5.5 organization are designed.

Windows 2000 Domain Architecture

Before you install your first Exchange 2000 server, you must prepare the Windows 2000 domains and schema. This is a two-step process: Prepare the Microsoft Windows 2000 forest, and then prepare the Windows 2000 domains. Preparing the Windows 2000 forest is a multi-step process as well. First you must prepare the forest schema, then install and configure the ADC, and then you prepare each of the domains.

> **_NOTE_** For more information about how to make these preparations, see the "Preparing the Active Directory Forest and Each Domain" section in Chapter 2. For more information about ADC, see "Understanding Active Directory and the AD Connector," later in this chapter.

This section will help you identify your current Windows 2000 environment and determine additional steps that may be necessary to perform an upgrade. Review each section to determine which situation applies to your environment.

- If you do not have Windows 2000 domains in your organization, you must build a Windows 2000 AD plan before you can consider how to upgrade your Exchange 5.5 messaging system to Exchange 2000. This should be a comprehensive plan. You will have to work with your network, DNS, AD, messaging, and security administrators to be sure you capture all the necessary information.

- Each AD site should have at least one (but preferably two) Active Directory Global Catalog server.

- If you have only one Windows 2000 domain installed, prepare the Microsoft Windows 2000 forest and then prepare the Windows 2000 domains. Then review the "Exchange 2000 Architecture Basics" section in Chapter 1, "Getting Started with Exchange 2000."

- If you have more than one Windows 2000 domain installed, perform the steps below in each of your Windows 2000 domains, as applicable. These include installing the ADC and running Exchange 2000 Setup with the /ForestPrep switch. (For more information about the /ForestPrep switch, see the "Preparing the Active Directory Forest and Each Domain" section in Chapter 2. The steps in that section must be completed before you install your first Exchange 2000 server.)

  - If all your Windows 2000 domains are in Native mode, you will be able to take advantage of all Windows 2000 features in all domains, including Universal groups and nested groups. Windows 2000 Universal security groups replace Exchange 5.5 distribution lists (DLs) during the upgrade of your messaging system. This is the preferred mode to be in before upgrading or migrating to Exchange 2000.

  - If you have at least one Native-mode Windows 2000 domain, you will be able to use much of the native Windows 2000 functionality, but it must be used in this domain or from this domain.

  - If you have no Native-mode Windows 2000 domains, you will not be able to take advantage of some new features in Windows 2000, such as Universal security groups, nested groups, and directly updating Exchange 5.5 distribution lists with Windows 2000 distribution groups.

- If users will manage mail-enabled groups using in Outlook, you must ensure that the domain controllers and global catalogs to be used by Exchange 2000 are in the same domain on which universal groups are managed.
- If you will use Exchange Key Management Service (KMS), ensure that the domain controllers and Global Catalogs to be used by Exchange 2000 are in the same domain as users who will update keys on the domain controllers and Global Catalogs.

Existing Exchange 5.5 Architecture

This section will help you determine how to upgrade your environment. For those of you in a hurry, you'll be happy to know that the upgrade process is very fast—about 30GB per hour, though this may vary dramatically depending on the hardware you have.

If you have an Exchange 5.5 server or if you can upgrade at least one Exchange server in your organization to Exchange 5.5, you will be able to upgrade using one of the following:

- If you have fewer than 500 mailboxes and public folders combined and a single Internet mail connector (no other messaging connectors), you can upgrade your Exchange 5.5 server in place.
- If you have more than 500 mailboxes or a large amount of public folder data, you can upgrade your Exchange 5.5 server in place. Before you jump on this bandwagon, make sure the amount of downtime required for your upgrade is acceptable for your organization. Plan for at least a half an hour for system preparation and 30GB per hour for the upgrade.
- If you have a dedicated server for use with Outlook Web Access, this server should be upgraded last; Exchange 2000 OWA cannot be used with Exchange 5.5 mailboxes, but Exchange 5.5 OWA can be used with Exchange 2000 mailboxes.
- If you determine that the length of time your system will be unavailable for user access is unacceptable, you can join your server with a new server that is running Exchange 2000 and move the mailboxes and resources between the two systems. This type of upgrade isn't for the faint of heart; it's difficult due to the larger number of steps involved.
- If you have several messaging connectors and use this server mostly as a bridgehead between other messaging systems, you can upgrade your old Exchange 5.5 server or, with a second system, you can install a new Exchange 2000 server and migrate the connectors from the old server. To do this, you must determine if the messaging systems to which this server connects have native Exchange 2000 connectors. Currently, native connectors are available for Lotus Notes, Lotus cc:Mail, Microsoft Mail, and Novell GroupWise. Native Exchange 2000 connectors are *not* available for mainframe-based messaging systems.

What Order in Which to Upgrade? If you have specialized Exchange servers (such as mailbox servers, public folder servers, connector servers, etc.) in a single-site environment, the following may apply with regard to the order in which you need to upgrade those servers:

Mailbox servers You can upgrade your Exchange 5.5 server in place or move users to a new Exchange 2000 server to upgrade the mailbox servers.

Public folder servers You can upgrade these servers in place or by moving the public folders to a new Exchange 2000 server.

> **WARNING** During either of the above two processes, do not remove the first Exchange 5.5 server, which hosts folders and responsibilities that are vital to the Exchange organization. For more information on the first Exchange server, read the following Microsoft Knowledge Base articles: Q152959 ("XADM: How to Remove the First Exchange Server in a Site") and Q152960 ("XADM: Rebuilding the Site Folders in a Site").

Connector servers Because Exchange 2000 and Exchange 5.5 can connect concurrently to external systems, you can build and test new Exchange 2000 servers with your existing hardware. This allows you to use old connectors during testing to ensure that inbound and outbound messages can travel through the new connectors.

Upgrading Multi-Site Servers Servers in multi-site Exchange 5.5 environments are similar to those in a single-site scenario, and the upgrade order is no different. However, in a multi-site organization, you will have an additional type of server that handles site-to-site connectivity. On an Exchange 5.5 server, the connector is often the site connector; the Exchange 2000 version of the site connector is known as the Routing Group Connector (RGC); it requires capabilities separate from the external messaging connectors in Exchange 2000. These messaging connectors require that the Site Replication Service (SRS) function properly in a mixed environment. For this reason, you should perform an upgrade of the current servers. The upgrade process configures the site connectors and installs an SRS on these servers.

If you plan to join your current Exchange 5.5 site with a new one that is running Exchange 2000, at least one server must be running Exchange 5.5 SP3 or higher in order for Exchange 2000 to join the systems. If this is not the case with your architecture, you must install at least one new server running Exchange 5.5 SP3, and then move resources (mailboxes, connectors, and public folders) to this new server.

Checking Permission Consistency before Upgrading

Before upgrading an Exchange Server 5.5 to Exchange 2000, you should run DS/IS Consistency Adjuster on the server you are upgrading. Select only the options necessary to verify that all users deleted in Exchange Server 5.5 do not retain permissions on mailboxes and public folders. If you forget to do this, then when you upgrade to Exchange 2000, folders that give permissions to unknown user accounts (mailboxes that may have been deleted) will be accessible only to the owner of the folder. Don't fret if you forget to do this, because event logs will be generated to alert you to the inconsistency.

> **TIP**   If you have public folders that are no longer allowing users to access them after an upgrade, edit the user permissions list using Exchange System Manager and reapply the permissions.

To check permission consistency, follow these steps:

1. In the Exchange Server 5.5 Administrator program, click the server you are upgrading, and then select File ➢ Properties.

2. On the Advanced tab, select the Consistency Adjuster check box (shown in Figure 3.1).

3. Verify that only the Remove Unknown User Accounts From Mailbox Permissions and Remove Unknown User Accounts From Public Folder Permissions check boxes are selected.

4. Choose the All Inconsistencies radio button and click OK.

5. On the dialog box that warns you of public folder rehoming, click OK. If you did not select the Synchronize With The Directory And Reset The Home Server Value For Public Folders Homed In Unknown Sites option, public folders will not be rehomed.

6. You can view the Windows Event Viewer's application log for information about what inconsistencies were fixed.

> **NOTE**   When running the DS/IS Consistency Check, only the permission options need to be checked. If public folders need rehoming, Consistency Adjuster will warn you; however, you do not need to rehome public folders to correct permission settings for deleted users. You will not need to rehome public folders if you fix permissions for unknown user accounts.

Figure 3.1   DS/IS Consistency Adjustment options to fix permissions inconsistencies

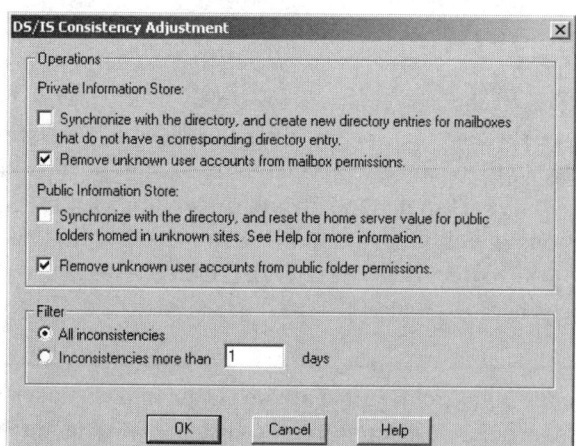

Cleaning Up the Exchange 5.5 Directory

In Exchange 5.5, a Windows NT 4 user can have permissions on multiple mailboxes. In AD, however, a mailbox-enabled user can have only a single mailbox attribute. When you prepare the Exchange 5.5 directory by running ADC, a one-to-one relationship must exist between Windows NT 4 user accounts and Exchange 5.5 mailboxes. When two mailboxes are associated with the same Windows account, usually one of them is a "resource mailbox," a mailbox for a resource such as a conference room. It may also represent a mailbox with revolving ownership such as the company "information" mailbox or a "help desk" mailbox. In Exchange 2000, every mailbox in the information store must have a matching user object in AD.

When resource mailboxes are manually marked with a certain attribute, new accounts will be created for them in Active Directory, after the ADC replicates the information. If you have many mailboxes to locate, you can automate this process and populate this attribute using a utility called NTDSNoMatch (or NTDSATRB.EXE).

> **NOTE**   NTDSATRB.EXE can be found on the Web at www.exinterals.com in the Tools section.

To mark resource mailboxes manually, locate each Exchange 5.5 mailbox that has no Primary Windows NT Account associated with it or that has duplicate accounts associated with it. Then, on the Custom Attributes tab, add the string *NTDSNoMatch to Custom*

Attribute 10. If the ADC finds an Exchange 5.5 mailbox that has a Custom Attribute 10 with a value of NTDSNoMatch, then it will create a new user object instead of trying to match it to an existing user. Companies that are using Custom Attribute 10 for something else can change this, but it should be identified at the beginning of the cleanup process.

> **NOTE** If you don't clean up the Exchange 5.5 directory before you run ADC, you may have to clean up Active Directory afterward, because Windows 2000 accounts may be associated with the wrong mailboxes.

To mark the resource mailboxes with *NTDSNoMatch to Custom Attribute 10* automatically, download and decompress the NTDSATRB.ZIP file, and run the Setup program. This will install the program to your C:\Program Files\Ntdsnomatch directory. Locate the NTDSATRB.EXE program file. To run this program, you will need to specify the name of the Exchange 5.5 server you are working with; if you have changed the LDAP port number, you must also specify it (this got me the first time I ran NTDSATRB.EXE on an Exchange 5.5 server that was also a Windows 2000 domain controller). For example, to run NTDSATRB.EXE for a server called HNLEX001 whose LDAP port is 3389, type **ntdsatrb.exe hnlex001:3389**.

If you get an error running this utility, confirm that you are using the correct LDAP port number, that the Exchange server's directory service is started, and that you are indeed contacting the Exchange server.

Running NTDSATRB.EXE creates two files in the current directory:

- The first file, NTDSNOMATCH.CSV, is essentially a log file of each ntdsatrb session.
- The second file created is the business end of this process; it will be named whatever the local site name is with a CSV on the end of it. In the example above, the file that was created was PACIFIC.CSV (shown in Figure 3.2).

Figure 3.2 A CSV file produced by NTDSATRB.EXE

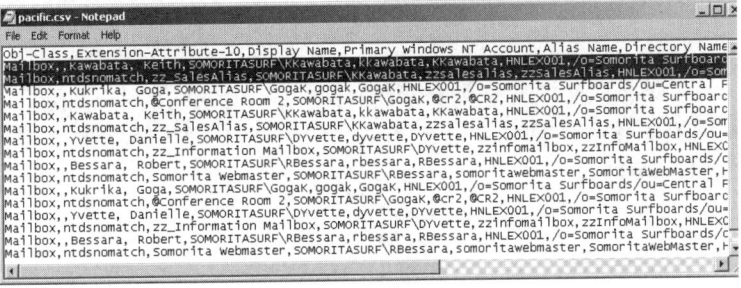

The file shown in Figure 3.2 is kind of hard to read using Notepad, but you get the general idea. Notice the two lines that I have highlighted: The first is for Keith Kawabata's mailbox, but the second is for the sales department's alias. Keith's user account is the Primary Windows NT Account for both of these mailboxes. Note that the second mailbox contains NTDSNoMatch for Extension-Attribute-10 (Custom Attribute 10). NTDSNoMatch chooses the first mailbox that it finds (alphabetically) to be the one to match up with an AD user account.

The next (and final) step is for the administrator to import this file using the Exchange 5.5 Administrator utility. Once this is done, each duplicate mailbox will have NTDSNoMatch for Custom Attribute 10.

NOTE For more information on the NTDSNoMatch process, consult Microsoft Knowledge Base article Q274173. If you have already created an ADC connection agreement (CA) and have run it for the first time, then consult Q256862.

Outlook Web Access 2000 and Exchange 5.5

Outlook Web Access for Exchange 2000 is not compatible with Exchange 5.5 mailboxes. (Exchange 5.5 OWA can read Exchange 2000 mailboxes, but Exchange 2000 OWA cannot read Exchange 5.5 mailboxes.) If you choose to upgrade some of your Exchange 5.5 servers to Exchange 2000, and if your OWA server is separate from your Exchange mailbox servers, then you must keep your OWA server running Exchange 5.5 until the last Exchange mailbox server is upgraded.

Making Sure You Have the Right Permissions

While much of this permissions-related information is covered elsewhere in this book, it is worth repeating here, in the migration/upgrade chapter. The following sections describe the permissions needed to prepare Active Directory and Exchange 2000.

First Exchange 2000 Server Installation Permission Requirements

To install your first Exchange 2000 server, you will need to be logged on to AD with the following permissions:

- Exchange Full Administrator role
- Member of the local Administrators group on the destination computer

> **NOTE** This assumes that the Active Directory schema has already been extended. If not, you will also need to be a member of the forest root domain's Schema Admins and Enterprise Admins groups.

Additionally, if you are joining an existing Exchange 5.5 site, the logged-on account must have the following permissions to access the Exchange 5.5 directory, and the person installing Exchange must know the Site Services account name and password:

- Admin role in the site naming context
- Admin role in the configuration naming context

Subsequent Exchange 2000 Servers Installation Permission Requirements

To install subsequent servers, you will need to be logged on to AD with the following permissions:

- Either as Exchange Full Administrator or as a delegated Exchange Full Administrator at the organization level
- Member of the local Administrators group on the destination computer

Exchange 5.5 Server to Exchange 2000 Upgrade Permission Requirements

The Exchange 5.5 server must be installed on a computer running Windows 2000 in an Active Directory domain. You will need to be logged on to AD as a user who has the following permissions:

- Exchange 5.5
- Admin role to the Exchange organization naming context
- Admin role to the Exchange site naming context
- Admin role to the Exchange configuration naming context
- Active Directory
- Either as Exchange Full Administrator (as defined during ForestPrep) or as a delegated Exchange Full Administrator at the organization level
- Member of the local Administrators group on the destination computer

Distribution Lists and Permissions

In Exchange 5.5, you can assign permissions to any type of recipient in the global address list. Some administrators use distribution lists widely to build systems for access permissions to public folders.

With Exchange 2000, you can assign permissions only to a Windows 2000 user or security group. When Exchange 2000 upgrades the public folder store and mailbox store, it must be able to replace Exchange 5.5 distribution lists that appear in ACLs with Windows 2000 security groups.

Permission issues don't end there. When upgrading to Exchange 2000, you must also consider the following:

- ADC replicates Exchange 5.5 distribution lists to AD as Universal distribution groups (UDGs), which are not security groups.

- Exchange 2000 needs to evaluate group membership when applying permissions, but only one type of Windows 2000 group—the Universal group—has its membership replicated to all global catalog servers.

- Universal security groups can be created only in Native-mode Windows 2000 domains.

There must be at least one Native-mode Windows 2000 domain in the forest in which the security groups can be created, because Windows 2000 Universal security groups must replace Exchange 5.5 distribution lists. You can create a special Native-mode child domain specifically for the purpose of holding Universal security groups, rather than having the entire forest in Native mode. For ease of upgrade, you should convert your Windows 2000 domains to Native mode as early as possible.

Changing Your Site Architecture

Are you happy with your Exchange 5.5 site infrastructure with respect to server administrative concerns? Would you like to move servers to other sites? Do you want your administrative group structure to mimic your Exchange 5.5 sites, or do you want to change it?

If you want to move servers between sites, now is the time to do it. After you install your first Exchange 2000 server, and thus create a Mixed-mode Exchange organization, you cannot move servers between sites in the same organization. Further, Exchange 2000 servers cannot be moved between administrative groups, even once you have switched to Exchange 2000 Native mode.

NOTE You should change your site architecture before moving to Exchange 2000 since Exchange 2000 does not permit you to move servers between administrative groups. One way to change your existing Exchange 5.5 site architecture is to use the Exchange 5.5 Move Server Wizard. For more information on the Move Server Wizard see the Move Server Wizard document located at www.somorita.com.

Understanding Active Directory and the AD Connector

Up until now, to use some type of directory services within your organization, you have had to do way more work than you should. With the introduction of Active Directory, directory services are now tightly integrated not only with the operating system, but also with network resources and, of course, with Exchange 2000. Exchange 2000 relies upon AD in Windows 2000, rather than having its own directory service, to provide functionality such as the global address list, Address Book Views, and Offline Address Books. AD offers many benefits for those in the thralls of deploying Exchange 2000. For instance, rather than having to manage multiple directory services, now all you'll have to manage is Active Directory.

In the past, organizations had to maintain multiple directory services such as the Exchange 5.5 directory service, which many organizations leveraged as their corporate directory service, and the Windows NT SAM (Security Accounts Manager). Exchange 5.5 directory information can be viewed by Outlook MAPI clients, Outlook Web Access, and LDAP clients.

Any Exchange 5.5 administrator will tell you that the information they populated into the Exchange 5.5 directory is tough to keep updated. Windows 2000 attributes for much of the information that is tracked in Exchange 5.5, but it is not automatically placed into AD. Figure 3.3 shows the attributes of a user's Exchange 5.5 mailbox.

Figure 3.3   An Exchange 5.5 user's mailbox attributes

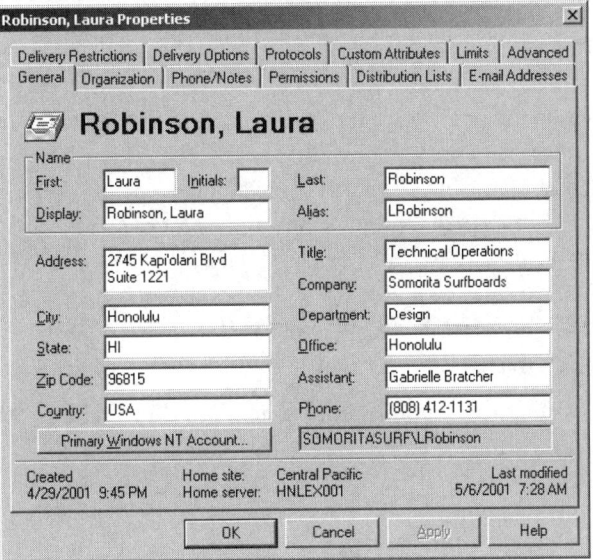

Notice in Figure 3.3 that someone has filled in all of the user attributes for this mailbox. This is quite an investment of time and energy. Figure 3.4 shows the Exchange 5.5 user's AD user account attributes (the General property tab). This Active Directory domain was upgraded from a Windows NT 4 domain, so there is no information associated with this user except for the display name.

Figure 3.4 Active Directory properties of a user who was upgraded from Windows NT 4

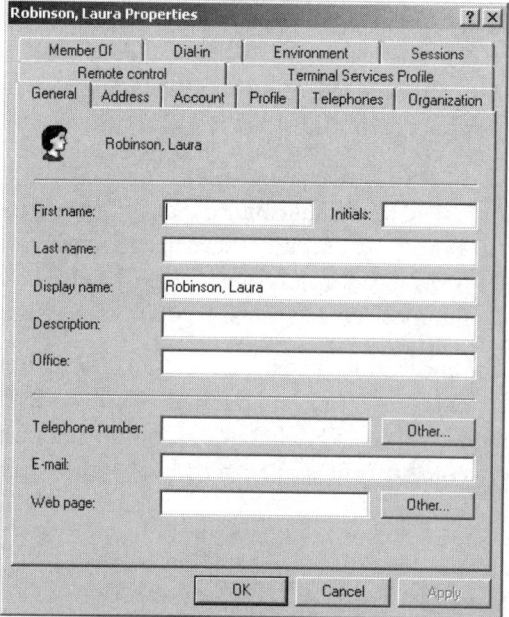

How does an organization leverage the "rich" information that has been populated into the Exchange 5.5 directory? That responsibility befalls the Active Directory Connector. Understanding the ADC and how it interacts with Exchange 5.5 and Windows 2000 is important. The ADC is not an Exchange 2000 tool, but rather an Exchange 5.5/Windows 2000 directory connectivity tool.

Permissions Needed by Active Directory and the Active Directory Connector

The following outlines permission requirements as they relate to AD, the ADC and Exchange 2000.

First ADC Installation Permission Requirements

To install the first ADC, you will need to update the schema of the Active Directory service as well as copy the binaries across to the local computer. Therefore, you will need to be logged on as a user with the following AD permissions:

- Schema Admins
- Enterprise Admins
- Member of the local Administrators group on the destination computer

As an alternative, an administrator in the Schema Admins group can use the /SchemaOnly switch with the ADC Setup program to make the additions to AD. In this scenario, the person who actually installs the ADC service does not need to be a member of the Schema Admins group. An advantage to this method is that if a company has very strict control over the schema, these people can make the adjustments required, and the ADC/Exchange administrator can perform his or her job independently.

If you want to apply the schema extensions required by the ADC, follow these steps.

1. Log on as user account that has the appropriate permissions; this will run fastest if you run it from the domain controller that currently holds the Schema Master operations master role.

2. Insert the Exchange 2000 CD-ROM, and run the ADC Setup program with the \ADC\i386\setup /schemaonly switch.

3. Click the Next button to start the schema extensions. The process should take 20 to 40 minutes, depending on the speed of the machine.

4. Click Finish.

The ADC can operate on any Windows 2000 computer, but it should be placed close to the Exchange 5.5 server that it will use as its Exchange 5.5 source server and close to the Windows 2000 Active Directory domain controller that it will use as its AD source server.

Subsequent ADC Installation Permission Requirements

Because the schema has already been updated, you will need the following AD permissions to install additional ADCs:

- Enterprise Admins
- Member of the local Administrators group on the target machine

---

NOTE   Most organizations will need only a single ADC.

Service Account Permission Requirements

The ADC requires a service account because a subset of the ADC technology is shipped with the Windows 2000 operating system. Exchange 2000 has features to prepare the Active Directory forest and domains for installation of the server (with the use of ForestPrep and DomainPrep). Part of this preparation involves granting permissions for the LocalSystem account to AD. As the ADC can be used without Exchange 2000 installed, a separate service account is used to give the ADC the required permissions.

The ADC service account requires the following permissions:

- Member of the built-in Administrators group
- Member of Enterprise Admins if the ADC is used in a Windows 2000–based environment without Exchange 2000
- Either a member of the Enterprise Admins group or have the role of Exchange Full Administrator if the ADC is used with Exchange 2000 and not just Windows 2000

NOTE Do not call the service account SERVICE, but rather use something like ADCService. Of course, the service account should also have a strong password.

Active Directory and Exchange 5.5 Directory Service Access Permission Requirements

The permissions that you need to create ADC configuration agreements and mange the ADC are as follows:

- Exchange 5.5
- Admin role to the Exchange 5.5 site naming context
- Admin role to the Exchange 5.5 organization naming context
- Active Directory
- Domain Admins (of the local domain)
- Exchange View Only Administrator role to the Exchange 2000 organization (if it exists)

The Active Directory Connector

It's likely that a key requirement during the migration period is preserving the data currently housed in the Exchange 5.5 directory. In any large environment, the migration will take some time, and during the transition the Exchange Server 5.5 directory and Windows 2000 Active Directory must be kept synchronized. A temporary but critically important step in that migration is deployment of the Exchange 2000 Active Directory Connector.

The ADC is the Exchange 2000 component responsible for synchronizing Active Directory with the Exchange Server 5.5 directory during the migration period. You may not be familiar with a directory service, but I'm sure you're familiar with the white pages of a telephone book. A directory service is very similar to a telephone book. For example, if you want to find a person's address and telephone number (output), you would use the person's name (input) and look it up in the white pages. Similarly, using a directory service, you can find out an employee's phone number, office location, distribution list membership, and more. Directory services also provide the functionality of yellow pages. Using general input such as "where are the printers?" would result in a listing of printer resources nearest to you. With the deployment of Windows 2000, AD provides all this information and more.

The Exchange 2000 ADC is fundamentally a replication and attribute-mapping engine, taking information from one LDAP directory (Exchange 5.5) and replicating it to another LDAP directory (Active Directory); this is illustrated in Figure 3.5.

Figure 3.5   Operation of the Active Directory Connector

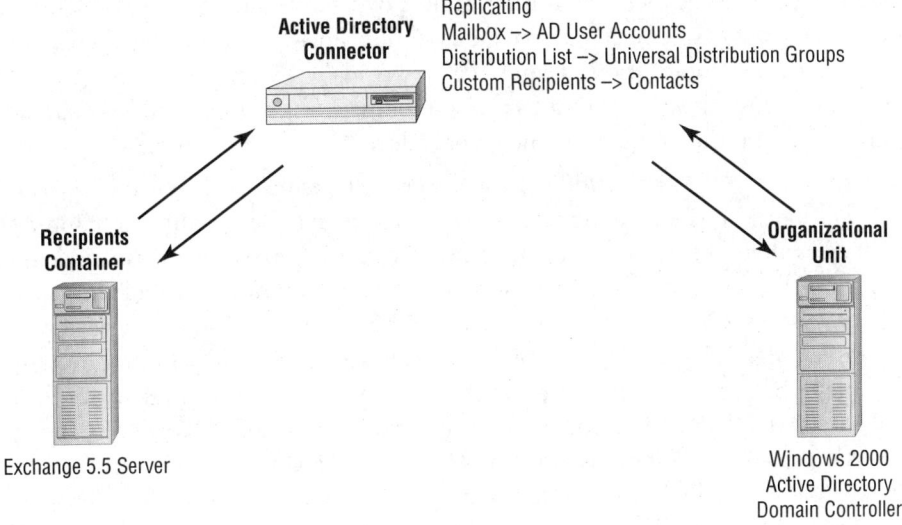

The ADC can operate on a domain controller or an Exchange 2000 server, but in any environment where more than a few dozen changes are going to be replicated per hour, I recommend installing the ADC on its own computer. In the example in Figure 3.5, the ADC is responsible for taking directory objects and their attributes from an Exchange 5.5 recipient container and replicating those objects and their attributes to an organizational unit (OU) in AD. The connector can also do bi-directional replication.

Functions of the ADC include:

- Leveraging the standard replication mechanism of querying for changes based on the last known update sequence number (USN)
- Running on a scheduled or continual basis
- Merging objects with similar semantics
- Linking Exchange 5.5 mailboxes to AD mailbox-enabled users
- Creating AD mail-enabled contacts based on Exchange 5.5 custom recipients
- Creating Active Directory UDGs based on Exchange 5.5 distribution lists
- Replicating Exchange 5.5 site configuration information to Exchange 2000 administrative and routing groups

Deploying the ADC is the first step in the process of unifying information in the two directories and consolidating two separate entities (Exchange 5.5 mailbox and Windows 2000 user) into one—a Windows 2000 mailbox-enabled user.

With an ADC, you can replicate directory objects between Exchange 5.5 and Active Directory. However, the ADC is not installed by default during Windows 2000 installation. The Windows 2000 AD schema must be extended to support the diverse attributes found in the Exchange 5.5. Exchange 2000 extends AD with new Exchange classes and attributes. Existing AD attributes are also modified, and some of these modifications affect what Outlook users see in the global address list. To extend the schema, you must:

- Install the Exchange 2000 version of the ADC, which adds the ability to exchange configuration information between the Exchange 5.5 organization and AD. This will extend the Active Directory schema with the classes and attributes required by the ADC and *some* of the classes and attributes required by Exchange 2000. The Windows 2000 version of the ADC will perform replication of data between Exchange 5.5 and AD, but it will not replicate public folder information or instantiate the necessary configuration connection agreement (CA). If all you really need to accomplish is directory synchronization between Exchange 5.5 and Active Directory, the Windows 2000 version of the ADC is sufficient. However, since it must be installed prior to the installation of Exchange 2000 in order to replicate a configuration CA and public folder information, I recommend installing it initially anyway.

- Run the ForestPrep mode of Exchange 2000 Setup. For more information about ForestPrep, see "Preparing the Forest" in Chapter 2. This extends the Active Directory schema with *all* of the classes and attributes required by Exchange 2000. This is not really necessary when you install the ADC, but it is a good thing to go ahead and get out of the way.

> **WARNING**   In order to have coexistence with Exchange 5.5 in your organization, you must install ADC before running ForestPrep.

The schema is partially extended with Exchange attributes if you install the Windows 2000 version of ADC; you must install the Exchange version of ADC to obtain all required Exchange attributes. If you have already installed the Windows 2000 version of ADC, you must still install the Exchange ADC in order to appropriately extend your schema.

> **NOTE**   There are two versions of the ADC; one ships with Windows 2000, and one is found on the Exchange 2000 CD-ROM. You must use the version that ships with Exchange 2000 for Exchange 2000 upgrades/migrations.

Microsoft Exchange Server and the ADC must be installed and running before you can use the Exchange extensions to Active Directory Users And Computers. To run the ADC, you must connect to a computer running Exchange Server 5.5. If you are running multiple versions of Exchange Server 5 or earlier within a site, you must first upgrade at least one server to Exchange Server 5.5. All Windows 2000 servers and domain controllers should be Windows 2000 SP2 or later.

Installing the Active Directory Connector

Installing the ADC is a simple process, but it requires several Windows 2000 permissions (as discussed earlier in the "Permissions Needed by Active Directory and the Active Directory Connector" section). Before you begin installing the ADC, be sure you are logged on to an account with Schema Administration, Enterprise Administration, and Domain Administration permissions.

Before you upgrade or migrate to Exchange 2000, you should create CAs between Exchange and each of the child domains that contains user accounts (if any child domains exist). To do this, you must first extend the Active Directory schema by running the ADC Setup from a command line in the domain where the schema master is located and using the /schemaonly flag. The root domain is used by default. In addition, keep the following things in mind:

- It helps if you are logged on to a domain controller/global catalog (DC/GC) when you perform these steps.
- You need to install an ADC configuration agreement to each domain in your organization that contains user accounts.

- If you plan to use a separate Windows 2000 account as the service account for the ADC, you must create it with the Active Directory Users And Computers tool.

- If Exchange 2000 is installed before replication of all information on users is complete, those users whose mailbox information has not been synchronized will not be viewable by those whose mailboxes have been upgraded. Mail will not be able to reach those unsynchronized Exchange 5.5 mailboxes.

Once you're set up with necessary permissions and other considerations, follow these steps to install the ADC:

1. Log on to the server to which you want to install the ADC, and insert the Exchange 2000 Server CD.

2. On the CD, change to the ADC directory. Run the `setup.exe` file.

3. On the Welcome To The Active Directory Connector Installation Wizard page, click Next.

4. On the Component Selection page, select the Microsoft Active Directory Connector Service Component and the Microsoft Active Directory Connector Management Components options, and click Next.

> **NOTE** Most administrators select both check boxes to install the ADC *and* its management components. Additionally, you can install just the ADC administrative tools on any Windows 2000 computer by running the ADC Setup on that system and selecting only the Microsoft Active Directory Connector Management Components item.

5. On the Install Location page, click Next to choose the default location, or click Browse to choose another location. If you enter a directory that does not exist, a message box appears. Click Yes to close the message, and then click Next.

6. On the Service Account page, enter the account name that you want the ADC to use for its operation. The default is your logon account, but this might not be the preferred account. If the default account is acceptable, click Next, and go to step 8. If you already have created an account for this service, click Browse and continue to step 7.

7. Select the account you want to designate as the new ADC service account, and then click OK.

8. On the Service Account page, type the password for the account you have designated as the ADC service account.

9. After you have selected your service account, the setup process starts copying files from the Exchange 2000 Server CD onto your system.

10. Click Finish to complete the ADC installation.

> **NOTE** ADC installation can take 20 minutes or more. During installation, you will see the installer process 10 files of AD schema updates. These may take some time to complete, especially if you are not running the installation on the DC/GC that is the schema master. These schema updates are only performed the first time you install the ADC in your organization. After the AD schema has been modified, Registry modifications are made that allow the system to run the AD management tool, and additional files are copied. If you are curious about the changes to AD, the LDIF files that are used to update the AD can be found in the files adcschema0.ldf through adcschema9.ldf on the Exchange 2000 CD-ROM in the \ADC\I386 directory.

Now it's time to configure ADC. If your organization is small, read on; if it contains more than a few servers, skip down to the "Configuring the ADC in a Large Environment" section.

Configuring the ADC in a Small Environment

When you configure the ADC for a small environment, you create a single recipient CA, which populates Active Directory with the Exchange 5.5 directory information. The CA can be configured for two-way synchronization, but if there is only one server, this is not necessary. However, if you are configuring only a one-way connector, then all information has to be managed at whichever source the connection agreement is replicating from.

Follow these steps to create a simple connection agreement:

1. Open the Active Directory Connector MMC snap-in (found in the Programs ➤ Administrative Tools or the Programs ➤ Microsoft Exchange menu.)

2. Right-click the icon representing the ADC on your server and choose New ➤ Recipient Connection Agreement. This creates a CA that allows the ADC to transfer recipient information between Active Directory and Exchange 5.5.

3. On the General tab, type a meaningful name for this CA. Then, in the Replication Direction area, select the type of CA you want to use. If you select Two-Way or From Windows To Exchange, you will see a warning message. Click OK. If you are going

to replicate from Windows to Exchange or implement a two-way CA, make sure that you don't accidentally configure the CA to create duplicate entries in the AD or Exchange 5.5.

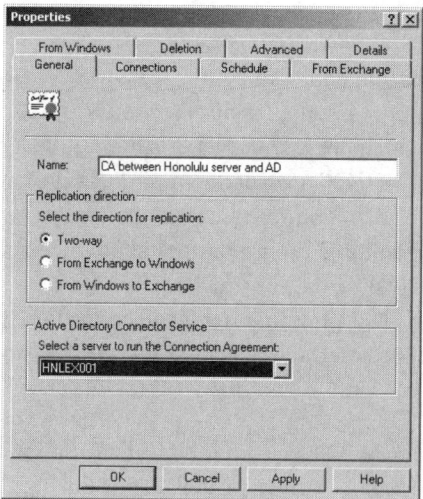

4. On the Connections tab, you will be required to enter different information depending on whether the CA is one-way or two-way. Specify an account that has read-write access to the items in the Exchange directory that will be modified and an account that has permissions to modify the AD accounts. The Exchange 5.5 account might be the Exchange 5.5 service account or another account that has been granted the necessary permissions.

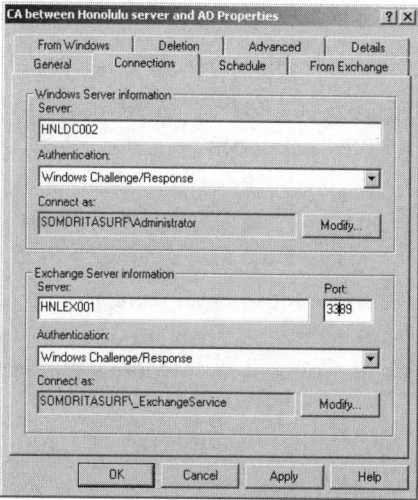

5. Click Modify and enter the accounts to be used by this CA to connect to the respective directories.

6. Enter the names of the Exchange server and the domain controllers, and specify the LDAP port number if the port number has been changed from the default of 389.

> **NOTE** You can use the Port setting for the Exchange 5.5 server to modify the port this server uses for its LDAP queries, because it might be running on a DC. If you have Exchange 5.5 running on a DC, the most common port to use is 390, but check your system to see how it is configured. I personally believe it is a bad practice to pick ports below 1024 for general use, so I recommend port 3389.

7. On the Schedule tab, you can choose the timing for replication. The default is early mornings, but you can select Always.

> **NOTE** On the Schedule tab, you can force a full replication by selecting the Replicate The Entire Directory The Next Time The Agreement Is Run check box.

8. On the From Exchange tab, configure the Exchange recipient containers that are replicated into AD. You can also specify what types of objects should be replicated (mailboxes, custom recipients, and/or distributions lists). Click Add.

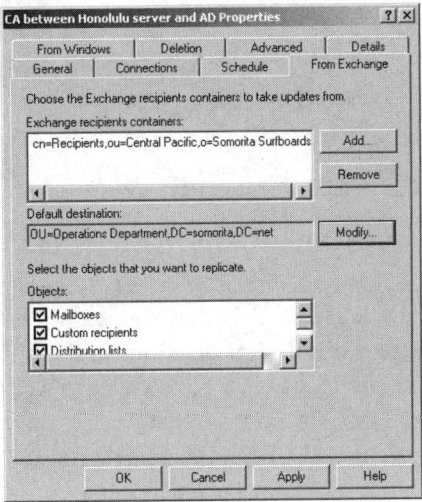

9. In the Choose A Container dialog box, select the containers you want replicated to AD. You can have subcontainers replicate, even though the root container does not. If you haven't given proper access to the accounts on the Connections tab, you will receive an error message. Ensure that the permissions for the accounts you entered on the Connections tab are sufficient and that you have entered the proper passwords.

10. On the From Windows tab, you specify the organizational units that you want to replicate to AD, the default container for these objects in Exchange 5.5, and the types of objects to replicate to Exchange 5.5 (mail-enabled users, contacts, and/or groups). Click Add to specify the OUs that should be replicated to Exchange 5.5.

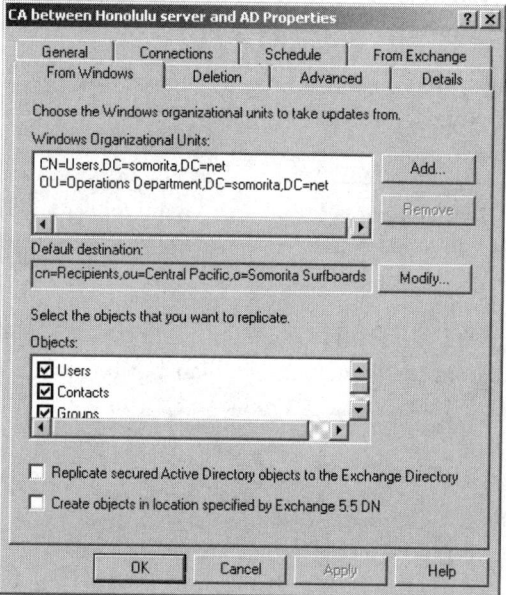

11. Click the Modify button to select the default destination for objects replicated to Exchange 5.5.

12. On the Deletion tab, determine whether you want the ADC to automatically delete entries in one directory if it detects deletions in the other directory. For instance, if you delete mailboxes in Exchange 5.5, do you also want the Windows 2000 account to be deleted? If you don't want this automatic connection between the directory objects, you can have the ADC write these deletions to a file that can be used to perform the deletions after they have been checked for accuracy.

13. On the Advanced tab, you can designate whether a CA is primary or not. A *primary* CA replicates information about existing objects and creates necessary new objects. A *nonprimary* CA replicates information about existing objects only. This means that if you have two primary CAs, each will create a new AD account if you have added an Exchange account, causing duplicate accounts in AD.

CA between Honolulu server and AD Properties

| General | Connections | Schedule | From Exchange |
| From Windows | Deletion | Advanced | Details |

Paged results

Windows Server entries per page: 20

Exchange Server entries per page: 20

☑ This is a primary Connection Agreement for the connected Exchange Organization.

☑ This is a primary Connection Agreement for the connected Windows Domain.

☐ This is an Inter-Organizational Connection Agreement

When replicating a mailbox whose primary Windows account does not exist in the Domain:

Create a disabled Windows user account ▼

Initial replication direction for two-way Connection Agreements:

From Exchange ▼

OK   Cancel   Apply   Help

14. On the lower portion of the Advanced tab, the When Replicating A Mailbox Whose Primary Windows Account Does Not Exist In The Domain drop-down list tells the ADC what sort of object to create in AD if an Exchange mailbox is created. If you are in a mixed Microsoft Windows NT 4/Windows 2000 environment, you might want to create disabled accounts, which would be used to access the Exchange 2000 mailbox with a Windows 4 account.

> **NOTE** You should never have the ADC create contacts in AD unless you are using the ADC to connect two Exchange 5.5 organizations or unless you want to migrate your Exchange 5.5 custom recipients to AD mail-enabled contacts.

15. Create the Windows 2000 groups that are used for Exchange administration. Click OK in the message box that appears.

WARNING   If you are installing ADC in a Mixed-mode Windows 2000 domain, a message box appears if your CA will be replicating DLs. When the ADC replicates DLs between the two directories, it tries to create Universal groups, which are accessible to all users in the organization. Because the CA cannot create these groups in a Mixed-mode domain, this warning says you cannot replicate your DLs to Windows 2000 groups. After you have installed your first Exchange 2000 server, Exchange 2000 users will use these groups in place of DLs. So, if the DLs are necessary for your Exchange 2000 users, you must create a native Windows 2000 domain to host them.

In the example in Figure 3.6, once the CA has been processed, you'll see the operations department OU in AD. Notice that a number of disabled user accounts have been created. These are accounts that represent mailboxes that did not have a Primary Windows NT user account(s) that I used the NTDSNoMatch process to identify as having duplicate accounts associated with them.

Figure 3.6   Active Directory Users And Computers OU after the ADC CA has run for the first time

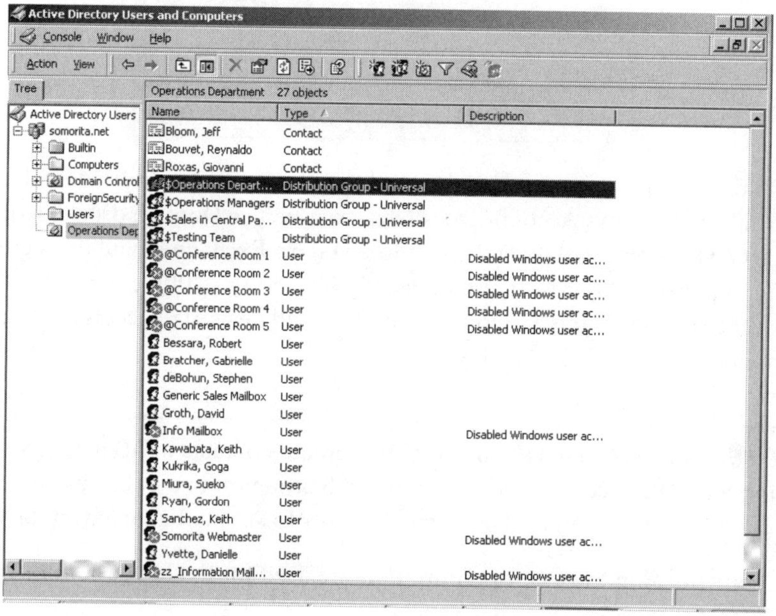

Earlier in this section, Figure 3.4 showed user Laura Robinson's Active Directory account that displayed only the display name in AD. However, all of her attributes were fully populated in the Exchange 5.5 directory. Once the ADC connection agreement runs for the first time, Laura's AD account will be populated with the information. Figure 3.7 shows Laura's now populated AD user account.

Figure 3.7   Active Directory user account after the ADC CA is processed

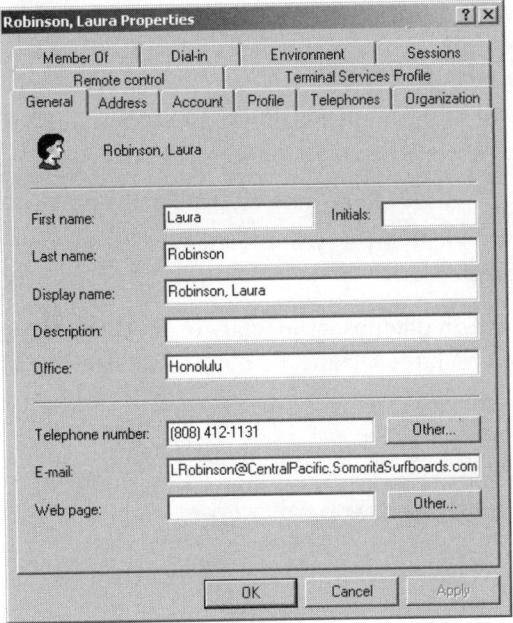

Configuring the ADC in a Large Environment

The main difference between configuring CAs for a single-site Exchange 5.5 implementation and a multi-site one is that you may need additional ADC CAs for the additional Exchange sites. In addition, you should run the ADC on Exchange 5.5 servers (which is not possible if they are running on Windows NT 4) or on DC/GC servers. This will improve the performance of the ADC.

You need multiple connection agreements between AD and the Exchange 5.5 organizations if there are multiple Exchange 5.5 sites and Active Directory domains and you want to perform two-way synchronization between AD and multiple Exchange sites. This is because each Exchange 5.5 site is responsible for only the directory information in that site and cannot change data in the directories of other sites.

You may also want to create multiple ADC CAs to replicate different types of objects on different schedules. Once the ADC is configured with multiple CAs, it can replicate information between containers in multiple Exchange 5.5 sites.

Another consideration is the Exchange 5.5 distribution lists, which replicate to the AD as Universal distribution groups. However, if these distribution lists have been assigned permissions to public folders, Exchange 2000 will try to automatically convert these universal distribution lists to Universal security groups. You may want to create a separate CA that replicates distribution lists to an Active Directory domain that is in Native mode.

Troubleshooting with the ADC

There are a couple of tools on the Exchange 2000 Resource Kit that can help with problems related to the Active Directory Connector. These include:

- AWP is a command-line tool that will remove the passwords that the ADC is using.
- LPADC helps to identify password-related problems when troubleshooting ADC connection agreements.

Further, you can turn on diagnostics logging for the ADC by right-clicking it and choosing Properties. Then click the Diagnostic Logging tab to see the categories that are available (Figure 3.8).

Figure 3.8   ADC diagnostics logging categories

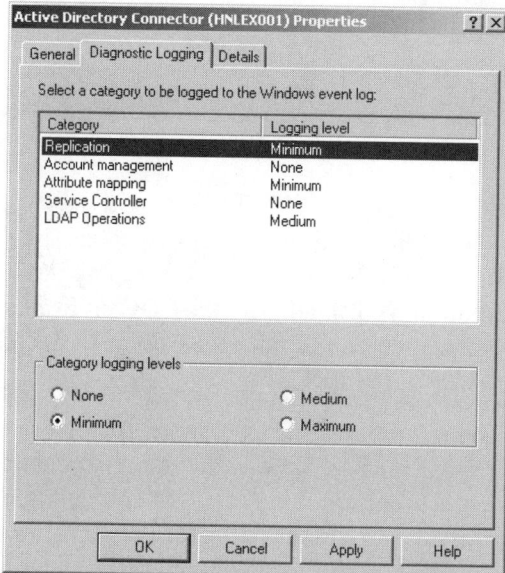

Active Directory Connector Customization

You can further customize the attributes that are replicated between Exchange 5.5 and AD. To do this, launch the Active Directory Connector MMC, right-click the console root (Active Directory Connector Management), and choose Properties. Then click either the From Windows or From Exchange property page; the From Exchange property page is shown in Figure 3.9:

Figure 3.9   Active Directory Connector Management's From Exchange tab

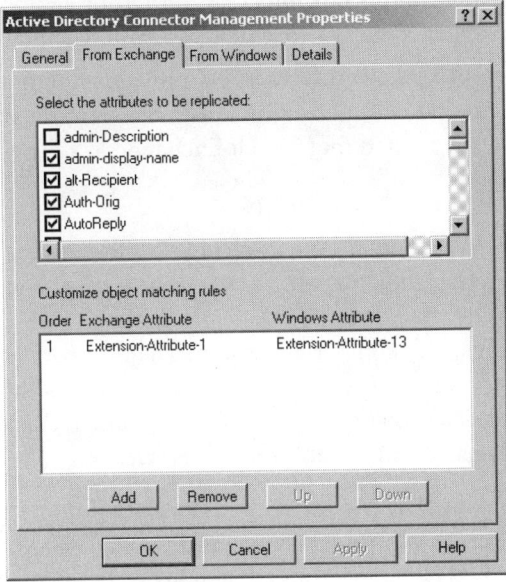

From the From Windows and From Exchange property pages, you can select which object attributes are replicated and specify additional matching rules for matching objects in the Exchange directory with objects in AD.

> **NOTE**   For more information about the ADC, there are several excellent articles on the Exchange Administrators Newsletter website (www.exchangeadmin.com). These include "Planning for and Configuring the Active Directory Connector," by Bill English, "5 Things They Never Told You about the ADC," by Kieran McCorry, and "The Active Directory Connector," by Tony Redmond.

Synchronizing Objects with Connection Agreements

Connection agreements (CAs) synchronize objects and specify what is replicated between AD and the Exchange 5.5 directory. In addition a CA specifies the containers to which the information is replicated.

NOTE Don't confuse ADC connection agreements with a Certificate Authority. They use the same acronym, but the two CAs are completely different.

The following three types of information get synchronized by the ADC:

Recipient Connection Agreement   Mailboxes, distribution lists, and custom recipients

Public Folder Connection Agreement   Information required for mailing purposes, such as public folder name, hierarchies, permissions, and e-mail address

Configuration Connection Agreement   Connectors, monitors, protocols, topology information, and other configuration information (for example, administrative and routing groups are created that match Exchange 5.5 site names)

Public Folder Connection Agreements

There are a number of changes within Exchange 2000 that deal with how public folders are represented in Active Directory. In Exchange 5.5, *all* public folders are found in the information store and in the directory. The information store is where the public folder hierarchy, permissions, and content are stored. The directory is used primarily so that public folders can appear in the global address list, and thus the public folders can have an e-mail address. Replication of hierarchy, permissions, and content is the responsibility of the Microsoft Exchange Information Store service.

A Native-mode Exchange 2000 organization does not automatically have mail-enabled public folders (these are public folders that appear in AD). While interoperability between Exchange 5.5 and AD is being maintained, I highly recommended that you keep a public folder CA between Exchange 5.5 and AD. The public folder CA is much simpler to create since it has far fewer options to configure.

Configuring the ADC public folder CA is quite simple—most of it is already configured for you. The defaults for the public folder CA includes the fact that they are two-way connection agreements, the From Windows and From Exchange tabs are pre-populated, and deletions are turned on. You should create a public folder CA between AD and each of the Exchange 5.5 sites to ensure that all Exchange 5.5 public folders are accurately represented in AD. The destination Active Directory domain does not matter, so I recommend using the forest root domain. The following situations would dictate Exchange sites that need a public folder CA:

- Any Exchange 5.5 site that currently has or will have Exchange 2000 servers
- Any Exchange 5.5 site that has public folder that are visible in the address lists

- Any site that where a server or servers will soon be upgraded
- Sites that have public folders that are created in Exchange 2000, but will need to be mail-enabled and visible to users in the Exchange 5.5 global address list
- Sites that will be administering public folders created in Exchange 2000 using the Exchange 5.5 Administrator program

If you fail to configure public folder CAs for any of the above circumstances, the following may occur:

- Public folder content may not be available to all users.
- An Exchange 5.5 administrator may accidentally rehome public folders to an incorrect site.
- E-mail addresses for mail-enabled public folders may not work properly.
- Users may not have proper permissions to public folders once the public folders are replicated to Exchange 2000 servers.
- In-place upgrades of Exchange 5.5 servers may fail.

TIP If you have changed the public folder container (the container in which the site's public folders appear) to something other than the Exchange 5.5 Recipients container, you will need to manually override the From Windows and From Exchange property tabs on the public folder's CA.

The public folder CAs must work in concert with the recipient CA. If you have put public folder CAs in place, but have not yet put in place the proper recipient CAs, the information store will not be able to properly match up the Exchange 5.5 attribute (legacyExchangeDN) with an AD user object. This may prevent users from accessing public folders.

To Migrate Or to Upgrade?

There are several migration and upgrade options—so which is right for you? For instance, you can migrate using the "move mailbox" method, in which you install new servers to an existing site and mailboxes. Alternatively, you can migrate using the "swing-server" method, which allows you the flexibility of the "move mailbox" method but does not require that you purchase new hardware for each existing server. Finally, you can simply upgrade your existing servers. Each of these methods is described in detail later in this chapter; this section of the chapter outlines the different options.

Upgrading to Exchange 2000

I'm sure that there are folks out there who would disagree with my choice of terminology when I use the word *upgrade*, so I want to clarify what this approach means to me. An upgrade (or in-place upgrade) is the process of overwriting an existing copy of Exchange 5.5 with a new copy of Exchange 2000 using the same hardware. There are several advantages and disadvantages to this method:

Advantages	Disadvantages
You can use existing hardware without many changes.	Some Exchange 5.5 configuration items do not upgrade, such as X.400 connected sites and some IMS configuration information.
It's a straightforward approach.	Upgrades can be time consuming and interrupt users for long periods.
You convert the entire server at one time.	Difficult to back out of an in-place upgrade.
Entire migration time is shorter.	If you have a badly designed organization, you are keeping it.
	Granularity of migration is at the server level.

There are a few requirements for using this upgrade method:

- Existing hardware must be powerful enough for Windows 2000 and Exchange 2000.
- Exchange 5.5 servers are running on Windows 2000.
- The Active Directory Connector is configured.

Migrating to Exchange 2000

An Exchange migration entails installing a new Exchange 2000 server and moving the existing Exchange 5.5 data over to this new server. Migrations from Exchange 5.5 to Exchange 2000 where a new server is involved are often called *swing migrations*. There are two possible approaches to migration:

- Install a new Exchange 2000 server in the existing Exchange 5.5 site and use the Move Mailbox feature. This process encompasses using move mailbox tools to move a mailbox over to a newly installed server.
- Install a completely new Exchange 2000 organization and Active Directory, and migrate mailboxes to PST files and then into a new Exchange 2000 organization.

Migration is a usually a lot more work than an in-place upgrade, but it offers some distinct advantages (and disadvantages):

Building a
Foundation

PART 1

Advantages

Permits some restructuring of existing configuration.

Creates minimal user disruption.

Granularity of migration is at the mailbox level.

Back out of a migration if a problem occurs is easier than when upgrading.

Provides the opportunity to test and verify the design a little at a time.

Disadvantages

Requires new hardware (though I think this is an advantage!).

Can be more time-consuming.

There are a number of requirements for using this method:

- At least one server is running Exchange 5.5.
- The Active Directory Connector is configured.

Moving Train Migrations

Moving train migrations, or leapfrog migrations, are used when you have limited hardware for migration. In some cases, you may only have a single extra server, in which case you can use the extra server as your currently installed server. Simply install that server as a new Exchange 2000 server, and move mailboxes from one of your existing servers to that server. Once a respectable amount of time has passed after you have moved the mailboxes, you can shut down the old server.

> **TIP** Once you have migrated all of the mailboxes off of an Exchange 5.5 server, wait until you are sure that all Outlook clients have accessed their mailboxes on the new Exchange 2000 server. When the Outlook client contacts the original server, it will be informed that the mailbox has been moved and thus will update its local profile.

When you remove the Exchange 5.5 server from service, you can now reformat that server and use it to install your next Exchange 2000 server into the organization.

Hybrid Migrations

Most people who have more than a few servers will probably be faced with some combination of upgrades and migrations. In an environment with more than a few servers and sites, some of your hardware simply won't support Exchange 2000, while some of it will. Some of these servers will easily be upgraded, while others will have to be replaced.

Hybrid types of migrations are most useful when Exchange 2000 deployments will begin before the Windows 2000 deployments are finished.

The total number of permutations that a hybrid migration introduces is too numerous to mention here. When planning for a hybrid migration, you need to make sure that you are planning a migration path that will be the least complex for both administrators and the end users. I would focus on trying to minimize user impact at the cost of additional administrative overhead.

Installing New Servers into an Existing Site and Moving Mailboxes

One way of upgrading to Microsoft Exchange 2000 is to move mailboxes from an existing Microsoft Exchange Server 4 or 5.x computer to an Exchange 2000 server. This is called the Move Mailbox method and involves installing Exchange 2000 in the existing Exchange 5.5 site and then moving all mailboxes and public folders to the new Exchange 2000 server.

Some advantages to this method include:

- The only downtime is the time required to move the user, which is minimal.
- You can easily move mailboxes on Exchange Server 4 and 5 computers to Exchange 2000.
- Not all users have to be upgraded to Exchange 2000 at the same time.

If there is a problem during installation, none of your users will be affected, because initially none of your user accounts are enabled on the new server. For instance, if you could install a new server you would run the installation wizard and choose an Exchange server in the Exchange 5.5 site that you want to join. Exchange would collect the information it needs to create CAs. The server would then join that site, and the Setup program would automatically configure CAs, create a Recipient Update Service (RUS), and create a Site Replication Service (SRS).

Some disadvantages to this method include:

- Key Management Server (KMS) cannot be moved.
- Connectors cannot be moved.

If you have KMS or old connectors on the Exchange server, you may want to run an in-place upgrade. Otherwise, KMS and the connectors must be reconfigured on the Exchange 2000 server.

NOTE   When upgrading the Exchange 5.5 KMS, you must have an Enterprise Certificate Authority installed in Windows 2000.

Before starting any upgrade or mailbox move operation, here are a couple of things you should consider or have completed:

- All Exchange 5.5 servers should be running Exchange Server 5.5 SP3 or later.
- Verify that the source server or the server to be upgraded has been backed up.
- Verify that there is enough disk space to accommodate the moved mailboxes and that the transaction logs that will be generated when messages are moved to the destination server.
- Verify that you have accurate documentation on your server's current configuration and current software versions.

Installing a New Exchange 2000 Server

If you do not want to upgrade your Exchange 5.5 servers or if your current Exchange servers are not capable of running Windows 2000, this section covers how to install a new server with Exchange 2000 in an existing Exchange 5.5 site. After this server is installed, you can move services, resources, and mailboxes to it with minimal impact, if any, to the current systems.

If you have performed the forest prep and domain prep processes already, your Exchange 5.5– and Windows 2000–based organizations will be ready for you to install Exchange 2000. If you haven't run these processes yet, see Chapter 2.

Installing Exchange 2000 in an Exchange 5.5 Site

The installation process consists of three phases: the pre-installation phase, the installation phase, and the post-installation phase. These processes can take a long time, depending on the speed of your system and network, the amount of RAM on your system, and the number and type of components you are installing. Follow these steps to install Exchange 2000 in an Exchange 5.5 site:

1. Insert the Exchange 2000 Server CD in the server on which you want to install Exchange 2000. Close the Autorun window, and open a command prompt.

2. From the command prompt, type *F:\SETUP\I386\SETUP* (where *F:* is your CD-ROM drive).

3. Follow the instructions on the setup wizard, but note the following:

   • On the Component Selection page, you can change the options that are installed without having to rerun the Setup program. You can select from three different installations: Typical (Microsoft Exchange Messaging and Collaboration Services and Microsoft Exchange System Management Tools), Minimum (Messaging and Collaboration only), or Custom.

   • If you try to install to a directory that doesn't exist, a message box appears. Click Yes to create the new directory and return to the Component Selection page of the wizard.

NOTE   A message box appears to warn you that the test for prerequisite conditions may take a few minutes. During this check, Setup determines whether your Exchange 5.5–and Windows 2000–based organizations have been prepared. Then it verifies whether the installer has the information required to join the Exchange 5.5 organization. Click OK to start the check.

NOTE   If you receive any system messages warning of an unsuccessful installation, you must ensure that your organizations have been configured properly (see the sections on ForestPrep and DomainPrep in Chapter 2).

If this is the first Exchange 2000 server you have installed in the Exchange 5.5 site, you will see a new ADC Configuration CA after the installation completes. This is the connection agreement that replicates the Exchange 5.5 configuration information into AD, and the Exchange 2000 configuration information from AD into the Exchange 5.5 directory. The Exchange endpoint for the Configuration CA is the SRS on the Exchange server you just installed (see Figure 3.10). Note in Figure 3.10 that the LDAP port used is TCP port 379, which is the LDAP port used by the SRS.

The Exchange 2000 has an alternative LDAP port because the first server you upgrade in an Exchange 5.5 site, or the first Exchange 2000 server you join into an Exchange 5.5 site, or any directory replication server that you upgrade in an Exchange 5.5 site, has a "replica" of the Exchange 5.5 directory.

The SRS is created only on the first Exchange 2000 server installed or upgraded in Exchange 5.5 sites in your Exchange 5.5 organization. For more information on the SRS, see "Site Replication Service and Recipient Update Service," later in this chapter.

Figure 3.10 Configuration CA to the newly installed Exchange 2000 server

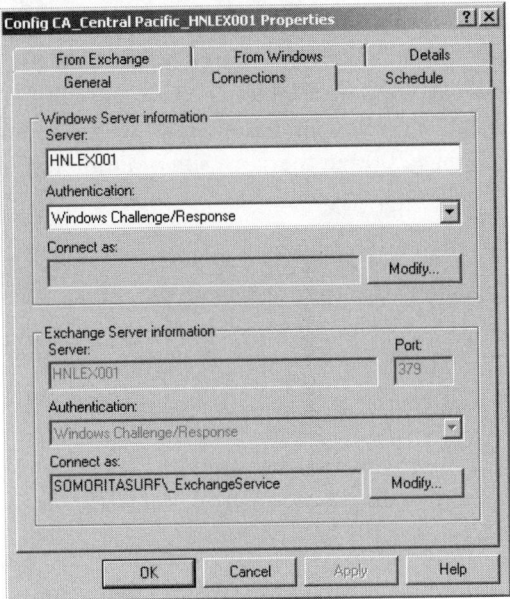

TIP After you install the first server in to the organization, you can run the Exchange 2000 Administration Delegation Wizard, which simplifies the process of delegating the appropriate permissions to Exchange administrators. You may want to initially set up permissions for other administrative activities. The Administration Delegation Wizard is installed with Exchange and cannot be run until the first instance of Exchange 2000 is installed in the organization. This wizard is the preferred means for designating administrators in your Exchange 2000 organization and is discussed in more detail in Chapter 11, "Security within the Network."

After you introduce the first Exchange 2000 server to an Exchange 5.5 organization through an upgrade or a fresh installation, the Exchange organization is in Mixed mode. The organization stays in Mixed mode until all the Exchange 5.5 servers have been upgraded or decommissioned. Once all Exchange 5.5 servers are gone, you can switch the organization to Native mode.

Moving Mailboxes

To move mailboxes, you must use a system on which the Exchange 2000 management tools have been installed. You use the Windows 2000 Active Directory Users And Computers snap-in to move the mailboxes between Exchange 5.5 and Exchange 2000 servers.

If you plan to move a mailbox from Exchange 5.5 to Exchange 2000 in the same site or administrative group, you will need certain permissions. When you use Active Directory Users And Computers, the mailbox is transferred between the two servers, and then the current credentials are used to update the Home-MTA and Home-MDB attributes on the user or mailbox object. The following permissions are needed to move a mailbox from Exchange 5.5 to Exchange 2000 in the same site or administrative group:

- Permissions for Exchange 5.5:
  - Admin to the site naming context
- Permissions for Active Directory:
  - Either a member of the Domain Admins or the Account Operators group to the local domain
  - Exchange Administrator role to the administrative group

To move mailboxes between Exchange 5.5 servers and Exchange 2000 servers, follow these steps. You should run this procedure from the Exchange 2000 server to which you are moving the mailboxes for the best performance.

1. Before starting any procedure to move mailboxes or make changes, confirm that you have a recent backup.

2. Using Active Directory Users And Computers, select the account or accounts that have the mailboxes you wish to move. Right-click and choose Exchange Tasks.

TIP You can select several mailboxes at once and move them together. I recommend moving between 10 and 50 mailboxes at a time. You can move more than this, but I find smaller numbers of mailboxes easier to track.

---

3. On the Welcome To The Exchange Task Wizard page, click Next.

4. On the Available Tasks page, select Move Mailbox and click Next.

5. On the Move Mailbox dialog box, select the Exchange 2000 server to which you want to move the mailbox, verify the correct storage group and mailbox store into which the mailbox should be moved, and click Next.

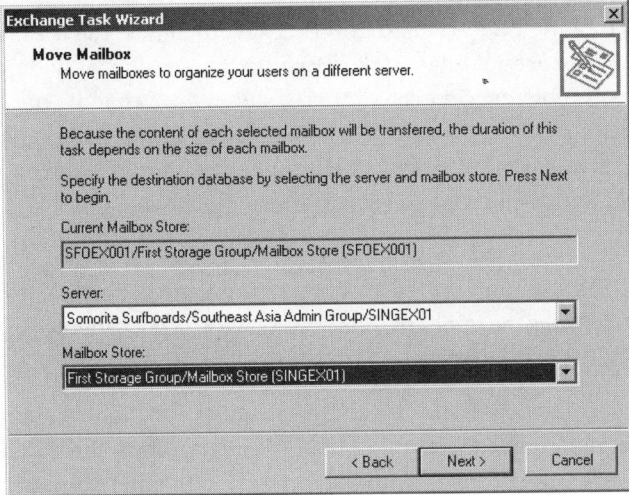

> **NOTE** All Exchange servers, not just the new Exchange 2000 servers, are listed in the Move Mailbox page.

6. On the Task In Progress page, click Next once the mailboxes have been moved.

7. On the Completing The Exchange Task Wizard page, you can review which mailbox was moved and whether the task was successful.

Repeat this process for all the mailboxes you want to move.

> **NOTE** You can also move mailboxes using scripts. To do so, use Collaborative Data Objects for Exchange Management. For more information on CDOEXM and other Exchange development topics, visit msdn.microsoft.com/exchange.

Exchange@Work: Failures when Moving Mailboxes

Company XYZ decided to install new Exchange 2000 servers into their existing site and to move the mailboxes from their existing Exchange 5.5 servers. Most of the mailboxes moved just fine, but a handful of them generated MAPI error messages part of the way through the move process and could not be moved.

Exchange@Work: Failures when Moving Mailboxes *(continued)*

The site administrator suspected corruption in the Exchange 5.5 private information store. After running ESEUTIL and ISINTEG several times, the messages would still not move. So she used Veritas Backup Exec to back up the individual mailboxes that were causing problems. On each of these, she noticed that the backup took an inordinate amount of time to back up a relatively small amount of data (for example, 45 minutes to back up a 20MB mailbox). However, the Backup Exec report indicated that there was a corrupt message in each of these mailboxes.

The administrator opened each of these mailboxes and found an attachment that was corrupted. Once she removed the attachment from one of the mailboxes, she was able to successfully move the mailbox. This method works, but it involves quite a bit of work on the part of the administrator.

A better way to do this is to use the ExMerge utility and archive the mailbox data out to a PST file, then move the empty mailbox and re-import the data back to the new server. However, the problem with this method is that the corrupted attachment would have remained. If the message or attachment is truly corrupted, ExMerge will not be able copy it out of the mailbox, so the corrupted attachment will remain in the mailbox. If this is the case, you will still have to open the mailbox using the Outlook client or the MDBVUE32.EXE utility and remove the message.

Make sure that you are using the version of ExMerge that ships with Exchange 2000 SP1 or later.

Moving Public Folder Resources to Exchange 2000 Servers

When you move public folder resources to Exchange 2000 servers, you perform a replication to the new server and then rehome the item to the Exchange 2000 server. This replication can be performed with either the Exchange 5.5 or Exchange 2000 tools.

To move public folder data to newly installed Exchange 2000 servers, follow these steps:

1. Use the Exchange Server 5.5 Administrator program to replicate existing public folders on the Exchange Server 5.5 computer to the new Exchange 2000 server, though I recommend using the Exchange System Manager when managing public folders on Exchange 2000 servers.

2. Browse the sites (administrative groups) to locate the new destination server, and add that server to the Replicate Folders To list:

> **TIP**   You can replicate a parent folder and all of its child folders by adding the new server to which you want to replicate and, on the parent folder's General property page, click the Propagate These Properties To All Subfolders check box. When you click OK, confirm that the Replicas button is checked.

3. Allow enough time for replication to finish. The amount of time necessary for replication depends on how many folders you are replicating, how much data is going across, scheduled time for replication, and bandwidth.

4. Verify that replication has completed successfully. The most accurate way to do this is to use the Outlook client or the OWA client to verify that the content is stored on that instance of the server. You can also use Exchange System Manager and view the number of items stored for that folder on that particular public folder store.

5. Remove the replicated instances from the Exchange Server 5.5 computer.

A directory replication between the Exchange 5.5 directory and AD is not an immediate process. After the replication is complete, the public folder is homed on the Exchange 2000 server.

The Performing Directory Replication Update page updates Exchange 2000 AD with public folder information. This is necessary because Exchange public folders typically do not exist in Windows 2000 AD. The reason for this is that unless a public folder is given an address, it does not exist in AD. This is not the case with Exchange 5.5.

> **NOTE**   Unlike Exchange 5.5, there is no obvious way to set a home server for a public folder. Any replica acts as a primary server for the data it holds, and any public folder server can be removed from the replica list. There is no concept of an Exchange 2000 site outside the legacy Exchange 5.5 system. Thus you cannot orphan a public folder, because the server where it was homed in the site was removed, and the replica in the other site still exists.

Migrating to Exchange 2000 Using the Swing Method

Another way to upgrade to Microsoft Exchange 2000 would be to purchase one or two new servers while upgrading the whole organization to Exchange 2000. This method is called the moving train method or *swing method*. The swing method is closely related to the Move Mailbox process, which is used to move data onto the new servers, and then the old Exchange Server 5.5 computers are upgraded to or reinstalled with Exchange 2000, verified as stable, and redeployed into production. However, with the swing method, you can upgrade existing hardware to make it more powerful and then reintroduce it into the production environment with minimal disturbance to your users.

Some advantages of the swing method include:

- The only downtime is the time it takes to move data between servers, which is minimal. Note that if you are using Exchange 2000, the Exchange 2000 information store may cache information about which mailboxes are on each store for up to two hours. This cache timeout has been reduced to 15 minutes in Exchange 2000 SP1.
- You can upgrade users on Exchange Server 4 and Exchange Server 5.x computers by moving them to an Exchange 2000 server.
- No operating system, Exchange, or hardware upgrades take place on the existing server until users are fully moved to another server.

Some disadvantages to the swing method include:

- The server name changes as users are moved onto new equipment.
- Key Management Server (KMS) cannot be moved.
- Connectors cannot be moved.

If you have KMS or old connectors on the Exchange Server 5.5 computer, you may want to choose to run an in-place upgrade. Otherwise, you must reconfigure KMS and connectors on the Exchange 2000 server.

The following steps guide you through the process of installing Exchange 2000 using the swing method:

1. Back up the server.

2. Verify that the users being moved have Microsoft Windows 2000 accounts in AD. If they do not, you may need to set up an ADC connection agreement to populate the accounts from Exchange Server 5.5 into Active Directory. You may also need to force the RUS to run.

3. Install Exchange 2000 Server on the swing server, and join the existing Exchange Server 5.5 site.

NOTE For Exchange 2000 to join a site, there must be a server running Exchange Server 5.5 SP3 or later in that site.

4. Use Active Directory Users And Computers to move the mailboxes from the server that currently exists to the swing server. To do this, follow these steps:

   a. Start the Active Directory Users And Computers Microsoft Management Console (MMC) snap-in.

   b. Right-click the user being moved, and then click Exchange Tasks.

   c. In Select A Task To Perform, click Move Mailbox.

   d. In the Move Mailbox pane, verify that Current Mailbox Store is the Exchange Server 5.5 computer and that the server in the Server drop-down list is the new Exchange 2000 server name. Choose the storage group and mailbox store where you want to move the user.

5. Verify that the mailboxes have been moved successfully; the easiest way to do this is to look at the mailbox store's Mailboxes container and verify that the mailbox you moved now has messages on the mailbox store.

6. Have the users log on to Exchange using a client. As long as the original server is still up, their profiles can be automatically updated.

Moving Public Folders to the Swing Server

To move public folders to the swing server, follow these instructions:

1. Use the Exchange Server 5.5 Administrator program to replicate existing public folders on the Exchange Server 5.5 computer to the new Exchange 2000 server.

2. Allow enough time for replication to finish. The amount of time necessary for replication depends on how many folders you have to replicate, how much data is going across, scheduled time for replication, and bandwidth.

3. Verify that replication has completed successfully. The most accurate way to verify replication content is to use the Outlook client or the OWA client to verify that the content is stored on that instance of the server. You can also use Exchange System Manager and view the number of items stored for that folder on that particular public folder store.

4. Remove the replicated instances from the Exchange Server 5.5 computer.

After all users have moved successfully over to the swing server and have logged on, you can then proceed with upgrading the original server. Throughout this process, you do not have to change the server name.

   a. Upgrade or add new hardware.

   b. Upgrade or reinstall the operating system.

   c. Upgrade Exchange or install a fresh copy of Exchange 2000.

   d. Verify that the server is stable and functional.

Swinging Back to the Original Server

When you finish the upgrade of the original server, you must move all users and public folders back to that server. Simply follow the same steps that are listed above, but this time go from the swing server back to the original server. This swing server can then be reused to upgrade another Exchange server If you don't want to move all the mailboxes back to the original server, you could keep them on the new destination server and turn the server you have just migrated from into the new swing server.

A slight modification of this process would be to move only a portion of the mailboxes from the source server to the swing server. Then run on offline defragmentation on the original source Exchange 5.5 server to decrease the size of the database. You could then upgrade the original Exchange 5.5 server. This may help to make the swing/migration process more manageable and allow you to rebalance some of the server load in the process.

Upgrading an Existing Exchange 5.5 Server

The following steps explain how to perform an in-place upgrade of an Exchange 5.5 server. Remember, you must be running Exchange 5.5 to perform this upgrade. There is no direct upgrade path from any other version of Exchange.

To upgrade on Exchange 5.5 server, follow these steps:

1. Insert the Exchange 2000 Server CD in the server you wish to upgrade.

2. If the Autorun menu does not appear, you can run Setup from the command prompt by typing *F:*\SETUP\I386\SETUP (where *F:* is your CD-ROM drive).

3. As with forest prep and domain prep, all the upgrade and installation processes have the same first three wizard pages. On the first page, click Next; on the second page, click I Agree and click Next; and on the third page, type the product ID found on your Exchange 2000 Server CD and click Next.

4. On the Component Selection page, there are several components that are pre-selected. If a feature was installed on the Exchange 5.5 server, it will be included as an Upgrade option. You cannot change the status of these items, nor can you add items to the list. To accept the default installation path, click Next and skip to step 6. To choose another path, click Change Folder and go to step 5.

5. To change the installation path, select or type the folder name into which you want to install the Exchange system files, and then click OK. If the folder does not exist, click Yes in the message box that appears to create the folder. Then, on the Component Selection page, click Next.

6. On the Service Account page, type the Exchange 5.5 Service Account password and click Next.

7. On the Component Summary page, ensure that the items you want to upgrade are included in the component summary. Click Next to accept the default installation path, or click Change Folder to choose another path.

8. As with the previous processes, you now see the Component Progress page, which indicates the current phase of the installation.

TIP During each of these phases, the upgrade process performs several functions on the items being upgraded. If you want detailed information about what happens in each step, you can open the Exchange Server Setup Progress.log log file in the root of drive C of the system you have upgraded. However, like most log files, it is fairly cryptic.

NOTE The databases are not actually upgraded during the installation of Exchange 2000. After the upgrade is complete and Exchange 2000 starts, the tables and indexes in the database are converted on demand. This means that the server may be a little slower during the first 24 hours after it is upgraded.

If this is the first server you have upgraded on a server that hosted Exchange 5.5 site directory replication connectors, open the ADC MMC snap-in and look at the new CA that has been created in the ADC. This ConfigCA is the connection agreement that replicates the Exchange 5.5 configuration information to Active Directory, and the Exchange 2000 configuration information from AD to the Exchange 5.5 directory. The Exchange 5.5 endpoint for the ConfigCA is the server on which you just completed the upgrade. The first server in the site that is upgraded is the endpoint for the ConfigCA, because this server hosts a replica of the Exchange 5.5 directory database. The replica is hosted by the Site Replication Service (SRS).

NOTE The SRS is created only on the first Exchange 2000 server installed or upgraded into your Exchange 5.5 organization, or on the Exchange 5.5 directory replication bridgeheads that you upgrade. If your ADC public folder CAs and recipient CAs are pointing to a different server than this Exchange 2000 server, you might consider changing the end points to the SRS service merely to reduce your dependency on your old Exchange 5.5 server. Just remember that the SRS LDAP port number is 379.

Decommissioning Your Last Exchange 5.5 Server

When you have upgraded your servers, you might want to decommission the last Exchange 5.5 server in your organization. If you migrated the data on this server or have removed or replicated any First Server information it might have contained, you can simply turn it off.

However, before you remove this server from service, you should ensure that nothing of importance still requires this server. For example, there is the ADC, which is no longer needed, and possibly some SRSs that can be deleted.

Switching to Exchange 2000 Native Mode

Once you have removed all of the Exchange 5.5 servers, ADCs, and SRSs from all servers in your Exchange 2000 organization, you can now switch from Mixed mode to Native mode.

The switch to Native mode is made in the Properties of the organization itself. To do this, select your organization root and click Action ➤ Properties. On the General tab of the organization's Properties dialog box, you will see the Change Mode button. If there are still Exchange 5.5 servers in the organization, it will be disabled. However, as soon as you have removed the last Exchange 5.5 server, you can use the Exchange 5.5 Administrator tool to delete it from the information stored in the SRS. This activates the Change Mode button, which you can use to take full advantage of a Native-mode Exchange 2000 organization.

Site Replication Service and Recipient Update Service

Two new services, which are crucial to the Active Directory Connector functions, are installed by Exchange 2000 Server Setup: the Site Replication Service (SRS) and the Recipient Update Service (RUS).

Site Replication Service (SRS)

When you upgrade a server that hosts any directory replication connections, the SRS is installed on the upgraded server. The SRS is an Exchange 2000 tool that is used to replicate data between Exchange 5.5 servers and Exchange 2000. The Exchange 2000 SRS allows the Exchange 2000 system to emulate an Exchange 5.5 system (as viewed by the rest of the Exchange 5.5 organization).

The SRS translates directory information between the Exchange 5.5 directory service (including Exchange 5.5 intrasite and intersite information) and the Exchange 2000 SRS database; the SRS also incorporates data from AD. It has complete knowledge of the organization topology and adapts itself to any changes, preventing any interruption of service or loss of data.

The SRS is a modified Exchange 5.5 directory on the Exchange 2000 server, allowing replication between SRS (Exchange 2000) and remaining Exchange 5.5 servers as before. It is used as the Exchange 2000 side of the ADC Configuration CA. The SRS allows upgrade/migration teams to avoid reconfiguring the endpoint of a CA every time an Exchange 5.5 server in a site is upgraded to Exchange 2000 during the migration. The SRS was specifically built to replicate the Exchange 2000 directory to Exchange 5.5, which is why it is required for directory-upgraded replication servers. These servers replicate the directory between their sites.

Granting SRS Rights to New Administrator Accounts

When the SRS is enabled during or after installation in Exchange System Manager, SRS Administrator rights are granted to the user enabling the SRS. Exchange administrators created after initially enabling the SRS do not have any administrative rights to the SRS, such as disabling or reinstalling the Exchange server. Thus after enabling the SRS, whenever you use Delegation Wizard to create a new Exchange Administrator account, you must manually grant SRS rights to that new account.

An SRS is installed automatically on the first new Exchange 2000 server that you install into an Exchange 5.5 site, or on the first server in an Exchange 5.5 site that is upgrade to Exchange 2000. (An SRS is also installed automatically when you upgrade an Exchange 5.5 server that is a directory replication bridgehead server.) To existing Exchange 5.5 servers, the SRS functions like an Exchange 5.5 directory service; it participates in directory replication just as any Exchange 5.5 server does, and it displays in the Exchange 5.5 Administrator program as an Exchange 5.5 directory service. (No directory service is listed for those Exchange 2000 servers that do not host an SRS.)

The SRS uses a directory database that is compatible with the Exchange 5.5 `Dir.edb` file. Because it mimics an Exchange 5.5 directory, the SRS can be configured to provide AD information to all Exchange 5.5 servers in its site.

> **NOTE** There's an excellent article on the Exchange Administrator's Newsletter's website (www.`exchangeadmin`.com) called "The Site Replication Service" by Kieran McCorry.

Recipient Update Service (RUS)

The RUS component of the System Attendant operates on a continuous polling basis, determines which objects appear in the various Exchange address lists. The RUS component of the System Attendant, which operates on a continuous polling basis, determines which objects appear in the various Exchange address lists. During the polling period, the service searches for all objects matching a set of specified rules and associates them with address lists or makes sure they have the correct Active Directory attributes. The RUS is responsible for creating mail addresses and other Exchange attributes on the recipient objects in Active Directory. The RUS can also be used to set additional proxy address for users, as well as other Active Directory attributes required by Exchange 2000 such as the msExchUserAccountControl attribute.

> **NOTE** The RUS is discussed in more detail in Chapter 2.

> **NOTE** For information removing Exchange 2000 or rolling back a failed upgrade, see the document "Removing Exchange 2000" at www.somorita.com.

After the Upgrade

This section outlines what steps you'll need to take after upgrading your environment to Exchange 2000. This includes determining the source of problems that occurred during the migration or upgrade or switching the organization to Native mode.

Debugging an Installation

If you have problems during the installation, there is a file created called the Exchange Server Setup Progress.log. This file, found in the root of the C: drive on the Exchange server, contains a very detailed record of the entire Exchange 2000 installation or addition of any components. Each time Exchange 2000 Setup is run, this file is appended.

> **TIP** Don't confuse this file with the Exchange Server Setup.log that is generated when Exchange 5.5 is installed.

This is not the easiest file in the world to browse through. A simple Exchange 5.5 server upgrade generated a log file that was just over 1.2MB in size and had 9500 lines.

If you have to read through this log, I highly recommend that you download the Log Parser utility from www.exinternals.com. The Log Parser lets you view the Setup log and easily sort for fatal errors, general information, prerequisites, configuration problems, warnings, errors, and more. Figure 3.11 shows the Log Parser in action. I have only selected the General Information, Fatal Errors, and Prerequisites to be displayed. The utility is simple—just run it and open the log file you wish to view.

Figure 3.11 Log Parser utility

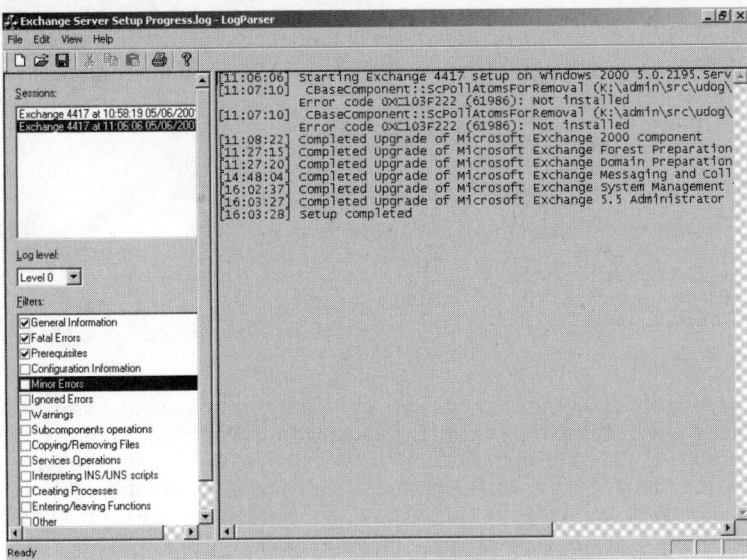

Note in Figure 3.11 that there are actually two sessions in the log file. The first one (started at 10:58) failed because I had forgotten to install NNTP. The second one started at 11:06, but did not complete the entire upgrade until 16:03. (I started the upgrade and went surfing. Naturally, the Setup program prompted me to overwrite some files while I was not watching it.)

Problems If a Domain Is Not in Native Mode

When the ADC creates Exchange 5.5 distribution lists in the Active Directory, it creates them as Universal distribution groups. The Exchange 2000 information store service will periodically try to upgrade these groups to Universal security groups. If it is not successful in upgrading these groups, the permissions that the groups are assigning will not be effective.

Further, you will notice the following event IDs in the application event log, which indicate problems converting groups or assigning permissions.

```
Event type: Error
Event Source: MSExchangeIS Public Store
Event Category: General
Event ID: 9556
```

Description:

Unable to set permissions for DL /O=SomoritaSurf/OU=Southeast Asia/ cn=Recipients/cn=Sales Department because it could not be converted to a security group. This is mostly likely because your system is Mixed mode.

Or

Event type: Error

Event Source: MSExchangeIS Public Store

Event Category: General

Event ID: 9552

Description:

While processing public folder replication, moving user, or copying folders on database "First Storage Group\Public Folder Store (SFOEX001), DL /O=SomoritaSurf/OU=Southeast Asia/cn=Recipients/ cn=Sales Department could not be converted to a security group. Please grant or deny permissions to this DL on Folder (Public Folders)/Sales Department/Forecasts again. This is most likely because your system is a Mixed mode domain.

The ramification of the above messages is that if an Exchange 2000 organization is in Native mode, distribution groups will be converted to security groups. See Microsoft Knowledge Base article Q274046 for more information.

NOTE   There is a setting you can configure in Active Directory that prevents Exchange 2000 from attempting to upgrade Universal distribution groups to Universal security groups. See Appendix A, "Registry Settings," on www.sybex.com for more information.

Problems with Public Folder Access and Domain Admins

If your public folders have permissions assigned using members of the Domain Admins, Enterprise Admins, or Schema Admins global groups, the folder will not be accessible. This is because these groups are not converted to Universal security groups.

Switching to Exchange 2000 Native Mode

You have finally arrived at the junction where all of your Exchange 5.5 servers have been upgraded or migrated off of the network. Now you can switch to Exchange 2000 Native mode. This will allow you to create routing groups that more closely match your message routing requirements.

WARNING   The switch to Exchange 2000 Native mode is irreversible.

Before you can switch to Exchange Native mode, you must:

- Delete any ADC connection agreements.
- Remove the SRS from Exchange System Manager.

Once you have done this, highlight the Exchange organization in Exchange System Manager, display its properties, and click Change Mode. Notice in Figure 3.12 that the Change Mode button is not available. This indicates that the SRS is still configured.

Figure 3.12   Changing to Exchange 2000 Native mode.

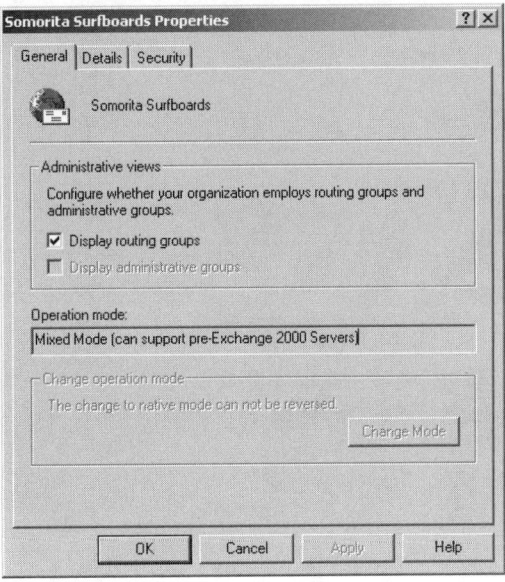

> **NOTE**   For more information about Exchange 2000 Native and Mixed modes, see Microsoft Knowledge Base article Q270143.

Manually Configuring Message Journaling

Per-server message journaling, as described in the Exchange Server 5.5 SP1 Release Notes, is no longer configured per message transfer agent (MTA). Instead, it is configured per mailbox store. When upgrading an Exchange Server 5.5 server, the message journaling settings are not upgraded. You must manually configure message journaling (called "message archival" in Exchange 2000) on the mailbox store object.

To do this, using Exchange System Manager, locate a mailbox store on the Exchange 2000 servers and display its properties (shown in Figure 3.13). Click the Archive All Messages Sent Or Received By Mailboxes On This Store button, and then click Browse to locate the mailbox that should have an archive of these messages.

Figure 3.13   Mailbox store properties with an archive mailbox specified

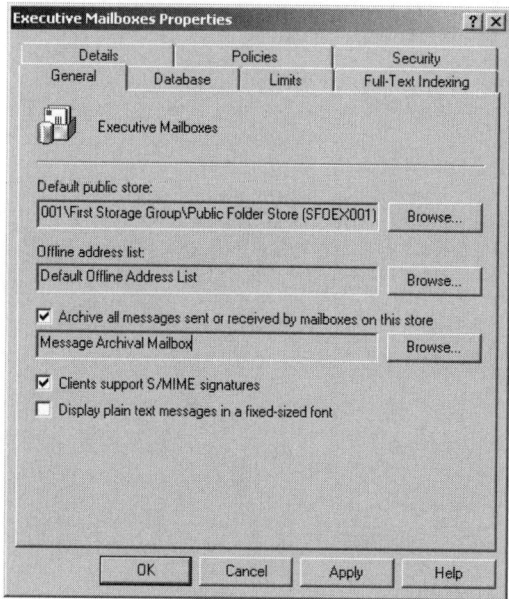

Deleting Uninstalling Servers from Active Directory

After you uninstall the last Exchange Server 5.5 server from a mixed site topology, the server you uninstalled will still appear in the Exchange 2000 server's Active Directory, and in any other Exchange Server 5.5 server's directory. You must use Exchange Server 5.5 Administrator to delete the uninstalled server from all other Exchange servers.

To install Exchange Server 5.5 Administrator, use Exchange 2000 Setup, select Custom, and then select Install For Exchange Server 5.5 Administrator. Use Exchange Server 5.5 Administrator to connect to the SRS on an Exchange 2000 server that is in the same site as the server you uninstalled. Delete the entry for the uninstalled server from the list of site servers. Once removed from the SRS, ADC will replicate the change to AD. Verify if that this change has replicated to AD before making the topology changes.

Enabling Secure Sockets Layer

After you upgrade from Exchange Server 5.5, Secure Sockets Layer (SSL) will not function because the certificate information is not upgraded. To enable SSL, you can either request a new certificate, or use the existing Exchange Server 5.5 certificate. To use your existing certificate, you can use Key Manager (`Keyring.exe`) to create a backup file.

To install a backup file, on the Access tab, select Certificate, and then import a certificate from a Key Manager backup file.

Frequently Asked Questions

Following are some questions that I am frequently asked with respect to migrations and upgrades.

Is the Active Directory Connector required?

The ADC is required if you are upgrading an existing Exchange 5.5 server or if you are installing an Exchange 2000 server into an existing Exchange 5.5 site.

What does the Active Directory Connector do?

The ADC replicates directory information between the Exchange 5.5 directory service and AD, including user information, contact objects, distribution lists, public folder properties (e-mail addresses), and Exchange 5.5 configuration information.

Should I upgrade an existing server or install a new Exchange 2000 server?

Thus far, I have had better results when I install a new Exchange 2000 server into an existing Exchange 5.5 site and move the mailboxes to the new server.

What are the most common mistakes people make when moving to Exchange 2000 from Exchange 5.5?

I am not seeing any single common mistake, but I do have a Top Four list. This includes (in no particular order):

- Improperly configuring the ADC
- Failing to confirm that their current third-party software and connector will work with Exchange 2000
- Failing to have a good migration/upgrade plan in place with reasonable milestones
- Failing to consider organization-wide AD impacts when installing Exchange 2000

Which ADC should I install?

While the ADC that ships with Windows 2000 is sufficient for synchronizing user data between Exchange 5.5 and AD, it is not sufficient for performing an upgrade to an Exchange 5.5 server, nor for adding an Exchange 2000 server to an Exchange 5.5 site. If you have previously installed the Windows 2000 ADC, you must upgrade it to the Exchange 2000 ADC before upgrading or installing any Exchange 2000 servers. The ADC that ships with Windows 2000 cannot create a public folder CA, while the version that ships with Exchange 2000 can.

Part 2

Operations

Topics Covered:

- Daily and Weekly Maintenance
- Managing Storage Groups, Mailbox Stores, and Public Folder Stores
- Managing Mailboxes
- Using Full-Text Indexing
- Monitoring Exchange
- Tracking Messages
- Performance Monitoring Windows 2000 and Exchange 2000
- Optimizing Exchange 2000
- Implementing Backup
- Disaster Recovery
- Clustering Basics
- Building Exchange 2000 Clusters
- Public Folder Replication
- Public Folder Security
- Implementing NNTP
- Automating Server Tasks
- Using ADSI Scripts

4

Maintenance and Management

The most important operational responsibility of an Exchange administrator is make sure that the e-mail system is up and available to the user community during the expected availability window. To that end, part of the administrator's job entails keeping a watchful eye on Exchange Server. This includes confirming that the backups have run, watching event logs, and monitoring disk space; this may also include applying policies that will control how the messaging system is used. Controlling mailbox storage and message recipients is also an important role of an Exchange administrator, as is understanding what the Windows 2000 event logs are telling you. Some of the tasks that are part of Exchange 2000 administration includes:

- Performing daily and weekly maintenance tasks
- Restricting access to the Exchange server
- Applying Exchange system policies
- Managing the Exchange 2000 databases
- Managing stores and storage groups
- Managing mailboxes
- Dealing with users who have recently left
- Customizing templates
- Implementing full-text indexing
- Understanding the steps to preventing disasters

Daily and Weekly Maintenance

The Exchange administrator has one of the IT industry's simplest and most complicated jobs all rolled into one package. A few years ago, I was polling Exchange administrators about their daily, weekly, and monthly maintenance procedures. One administrator's advice stands out: "I leave Exchange alone and let it do its job."

Up until Exchange 5.5 had been released for about a year, I still clung desperately to my beliefs that an e-mail system had to have intensive maintenance, including offline backups and database maintenance. This is partly because I was a cc:Mail administrator and consultant for several years. Lotus cc:Mail, like many other shared-file e-mail systems, required regular database integrity checks and compression to keep the database healthy and happy. Large Exchange 4 installations reiterated this in my mind because to keep Exchange 4, you still had to take it offline for maintenance every few weeks.

However, the days of regular downtime and offline maintenance are past, and the advice "Leave Exchange alone!" now rings true. Mind you, this does not mean you can grab your surfboard and head to the beach every day; Exchange still requires a certain amount of daily and weekly attention. This maintenance includes reviewing event logs, performing backups, checking virus signatures, and monitoring queues, but fortunately it does not include having to shut down the system once every few weeks. There may also be a few long-term maintenance tasks that you will want to perform every few months.

Daily Maintenance

Does Exchange truly require a hands-free administrative approach? Let's just say almost. There are things that an administrator should do on a daily basis to ensure that the Exchange server remains healthy, happy, and processing e-mail messages. These include:

- Ensure that the nightly backup has been run and has completed without errors.
- Review the event logs.
- Check the available disk space.
- Make sure that your virus signatures are up-to-date.
- Check the SMTP and MTA queues to make sure that no queue is growing excessively.

NOTE   Backup, an essential part of daily operations, is discussed in Chapter 7, "Backup and Recovery."

Monitoring the Event Logs

On your daily scan through the application and system event logs, there are events you should watch out for. In general, any error events (red) should catch your eye, and the cause should be investigated *immediately*. Warning events (yellow) should also be looked into as soon as possible. Though yellow events are generally not as critical as red events, they may indicate a problem that will later on become critical.

What events should you watch for that will indicate normal daily operation? Table 4.1 lists some of these events, many of which occur during a mailbox store or public folder store's maintenance interval. The default maintenance interval is 1 A.M. to 5 A.M. Maintenance-related events should complete at least once nightly.

Table 4.1   Events That Indicate Normal Operation

Event ID	Source	Description
1206	MSExchangeIS Public MSExchangeIS Mailbox Store	Beginning cleanup of deleted items on a public folder store or mailbox store. See event description to determine which store.
1207	MSExchangeIS Public MSExchangeIS Mailbox Store	Completing cleanup of deleted items. Event description contains summary of how many deleted items were cleaned up and on which public folder store or mailbox store the cleanup occurred.
9531	MSExchangeIS Mailbox	Beginning cleanup of mailboxes (deleted mailboxes) that are past retention date for the mailbox store listed in the event description.
9535	MSExchangeIS Mailbox	Completing cleanup of mailboxes that are past their retention date. Description includes mailboxes that have been removed and the mailbox store affected.
700	ESE98	Beginning online defragmentation of database listed in the event description.

Table 4.1 Events That Indicate Normal Operation *(continued)*

Event ID	Source	Description
701	ESE98	Online defragmentation of database listed in the event description has completed.
1221	MSExchangeIS Public MSExchangeIS Mailbox Store	Report of how much free space is available in the database listed in the event description.
210	ESE98	Starting a backup of one or more stores in a single storage group. The description does not reveal which storage group, but rather the instance of ESE (Extensible Storage Engine).
213	ESE98	Completing a backup pass of one or more stores in a single storage group.
8000	NTBackup	Indicates that the Windows NT Backup program is beginning the backup of one or more stores in a storage group.
8001	NTBackup	Completing backup of one or more stores in a storage group.
9551	MSExchangeIS Public	A warning event that indicates that a mail-enabled distribution group has been assigned permissions to a public folder and the store is trying to convert it to a mail-enabled security group. It is probably failing because the Active Directory domain is in Mixed mode. There is an ADSIEDIT setting discussed in Appendix A that can be used to disable the auto-conversion feature.

Table 4.1 Events That Indicate Normal Operation *(continued)*

Event ID	Source	Description
101	W3SVC	This error indicates that IIS could not find the /Exadmin, /Exchange, or /Public virtual directories. This is normal and is due to the fact that these directories are found on the ExIFS, and the Exchange information store service is not yet started.
5008	MSExchangeSA	This is not an error, but merely reports that an old message tracking log file is being deleted.

Note that the events in the table relating to backup and restore (events 210, 213, 8000, and 8001) are not terribly descriptive. For an accurate representation of what was backed up and whether or not the backup was successful, consult the backup software's logs.

Reporting Mailbox Access by Other Users   When someone other than the primary owner of a mailbox (such as a delegate or an administrator with Receive As permissions) accesses it, the application log displays event ID 1016 (the source for this event is the MSExchangeIS Mailbox). This event message can be annoying, especially if you have anti-virus software or other third-party add-on products that access the mailboxes. However, the message is also useful for determining if anyone other than the authorized user account is accessing a mailbox.

Exchange 2000 SP1 changed the behavior of this feature, and now you must enable diagnostics logging on the information store in order to see these messages. You must choose a logging level of at least Minimum to the Logons category found under the MSExchangeIS ➢ Mailbox service. This is found on the Diagnostics Logging property page of the server's properties. Once enabled, you will see 1016 events as well as 1009 events, which indicate that a specified user is accessing a specified mailbox.

Events That Indicate Potential Problems

No list of Windows 2000 events is complete without looking at events that warn you of a problem. Table 4.2 lists some of the events that indicate you may have an Exchange-related issue.

Operations

PART 2

Table 4.2 Events That Indicate a Potential Problem

Event ID	Source	Description
102, 103	ESE98	ESE has started/stopped an instance of the ESE database engine. This suggests that the first database in a storage group has been mounted or the last database has been dismounted.
9539	MSExchangeIS Mailbox MSExchangeIS Public	A mailbox or public folder store has been dismounted. The affected store is listed in the event description. If you see this event, ask yourself if this was something that was authorized or scheduled.
9523	MSExchangeIS Mailbox MSExchangeIS Public	A mailbox or public folder store has been mounted. The affected store is listed in the event description. Confirm that this event was something that was authorized or scheduled.
200, 201	ESE98	Indicates that ESE (Extensible Storage Engine) is generating JET read/verify errors. You should see –1018 mentioned in the event description. This is not a good message to see and almost always indicates either a hardware problem with the disk subsystem or a disk system device driver.
2028	MSExchangeIS Public	Indicates that an inbound message to a public folder should have been responded to automatically, but the folder did not have permissions to respond. This is seen often when an administrator has directed an SMTP virtual server's NDR reports to a mail-enabled public folder.

Table 4.2   Events That Indicate a Potential Problem *(continued)*

Event ID	Source	Description
2075	MSExchangeDSAccess	Indicates that applications are requesting data from the DSAccess cache, but DSAccess is unable to bind to a domain controller. Confirm that this server has reliable connectivity to a domain controller and a Global Catalog server.
8026, 8026	MSExchangeAL	The domain controller that the Recipient Update Service (RUS) is trying to use is not available or has been demoted to a member server. Reconfigure the RUS to use a valid domain controller.
8024	MSExchangeAL	E-mail queues are backing up and are not being delivered. Indicates that the server is not in contact with a Global Catalog server.
9562	MSExchangeIS	Indicates that the information store cannot read some mailbox attributes. Most likely, this is seen immediately after an upgrade. Force the RUS for the domain that contains the user accounts referenced to do a rebuild.
6004, 9003	MSExchangeTransport	Generated when an SMTP Connector is installed on a front-end server, but the information store service is not running, or the mailbox store is dismounted. Mount the mailbox store or move the SMTP Connector to another server.
16387	MSExchangeIM	A user is attempting to access Instant Messaging but is using the wrong credentials.

Operations

PART 2

Table 4.2   Events That Indicate a Potential Problem *(continued)*

Event ID	Source	Description
9519	MSExchangeIS	If an error 0xfffffb3a is reported, this means you are trying to mount a database that is already mounted. This can happen if you make a copy of database files and try to mount them in another storage group.
8022	MSExchangeAL	The RUS has tried to access a distribution list but does not have the Modify Permissions right. See Microsoft Knowledge Base article Q287137 for more information.
9188	MSExchangeSA	System Attendant may be trying to read information about the Exchange Domain Servers group. It expects to find this group in the Users container, but it has been moved. Move the group back into this container.
904, 8003, 8012	NTBackup	Windows NT Backup has attempted to restore a database that does not match the name in Active Directory. See Microsoft Knowledge Base article Q296841 for more information.
2060	MSExchangeSA	The DSProxy component of the System Attendant failed to start because it could not contact a Global Catalog server. Confirm that the Exchange server has connectivity to a Global Catalog server. If any Global Catalog servers have recently been designated as such, reboot them.
115	POP3Svc IMAP4Svc SMTPSvc	The specified service could not start a virtual server. This is mostly likely due to a conflict with the IP address and/or port number of another virtual server.

Table 4.2 Events That Indicate a Potential Problem *(continued)*

Event ID	Source	Description
619	ESE98	ESE attempted to mount a database that had been restored from backup, but the Last Backup Set check box had not been selected during restoration. See Chapter 7 for recovery steps.
9405	MSExchangeMTA	The Microsoft Exchange MTA Stacks service is attempting to start on a server that has no local mailbox stores. This can happen on front-end servers. Disable this service on servers with no mailbox stores.
8024	MSExchangeAL	An LDAP query was attempted to a domain controller and failed. Confirm connectivity to domain controllers and that the DNS is resolving the IP addresses of domain controllers properly.
1022	MSExchangeIS Mailbox	A user is denied access to their mailbox. This is probably because the user is trying to access their mailbox while it is currently being moved to another mailbox store.

One of the reasons that many critical events are missed in the event logs is that administrators don't (or can't) make the time to scan through the event logs on each of their Exchange servers each day. Another problem is that often the event log sizes are set so small than only a few hours worth of events can be recorded. I recommend setting each event log to a maximum size of 15,360KB (15MB).

Further, if you have more than two or three Windows 2000 servers, you should invest in an event log management tool. Some of these tools even allow you to set specific errors that you want to be notified about when they occur. Software vendor Sunbelt Software has information and evaluation software on their website (www.sunbeltsoftware.com) for Event Log Monitor, a product I really like.

Exchange@Work: Is the Problem Hardware or Software?

Everyone has heard this joke: How many software engineers does it takes to change a light bulb? None, that's a hardware problem! I often agree with this punch line, yet when a database becomes corrupt, I tend to blame the software.

One of my clients starting having error messages popping up in the application event log: "Event Id 23. Description: MSExchangeIS ((455)) Direct read found corrupted page error -1018 ((1:251563) (0-2295758), 251563 379225672 381322824). Please restore the database from a previous backup."

Not very pretty, eh?

Twice within a three-month period, we had to restore the database from a previous backup. After the first time, we made sure we had the latest service pack and hot fixes. Only after the second backup did we notice there had been SCSI errors in the system event log that closely corresponded to the database failures. We replaced the SCSI controller, and the problem did not recur.

What is the moral of the story, kids? Don't be so quick to blame the software, and check your system event logs daily!

NOTE −1018 and −1811 errors in the application event log (in the event description, not the Event ID) indicate some type of database corruption, yet the cause is almost always linked back to failing hardware or buggy device drivers. An exception to this would be where NTFS compression is enabled on the Exchange databases.

Weekly Maintenance

On top of daily maintenance, an additional series of checks should be run on each of your Exchange servers about once a week:

- Check the Windows NT Performance Monitor to ensure that the server is not running out of memory or exceeding other resources such as the capacity of the disk system or processor. See Chapter 6, "Performance Monitoring and Optimization," for more information.

- If message tracking is enabled, check the message tracking log directory (\exchsrvr\ tracking.log) to make sure that the System Attendant is indeed purging older log files. Though these log files are typically never larger than 10–20MB, on heavily used Exchange servers, I have seen them grow to more than 100MB. By default, these log files are deleted after they are seven days old, but I prefer to keep them for 10 to 15 days. If you are using a tool that imports these log files in to a database, confirm that you are importing them before they are purged. Many administrators also like to keep these files for capacity planning purposes. If that is the case, then this is one directory on which you could consider implementing NTFS file compression.

- Confirm that directory replication is occurring to the Exchange 5.5 servers and sites through either the Site Replication Service (SRS) or the Active Directory Connector (ADC) and to external mail systems such as Microsoft Mail and Lotus cc:Mail.

- Check the public folder replication properties to make sure that the public folders are being replicated and are up-to-date.

- View each public folder store's Public Folders container and the mailbox store's Mailboxes container to make sure that user mailbox and public folder storage usage is meeting expectations. Take note of mailboxes and public folders that are over their storage limits. You can automatically provide mailbox cleanup services using the Mailbox Manager, described later in this chapter.

- If necessary, archive the application event log. Though I don't keep copies of the old event logs, many administrators archive event logs (especially the security logs) for later review.

- If applicable, run mailbox cleanup routines manually or on a schedule with Mailbox Manager.

- Clean your tape drives according to the manufacturer's recommendations. The time required can vary from once a week to once every six months depending on the tape drive manufacturer and the tape technology (8mm, DAT, DLT, etc.).

Long-Term Maintenance

Some little part of the cc:Mail administrator in me still wants to take Exchange services offline once a week and do a database integrity check and offline compaction of the databases. Under most circumstances, this is not necessary. The online maintenance routines that Exchange 2000 runs are good and will generally keep the database tidy. For most organizations, any sort of offline database maintenance is not ever necessary, and certainly not in the weekly or monthly intervals in which it had to be performed with earlier mail systems.

Some people are not comfortable until they are sure that everything is compressed and checked. If you feel it is necessary, then compacting your database and checking your database's integrity might be useful. However, I strongly recommend that you avoid this process, because the possibility of causing problems is increased every time you take a server offline to perform unnecessary maintenance. I will sanction offline maintenance only when a large number of mailboxes have been moved or deleted, or when the server is about to undergo an upgrade.

Database Compaction

Though the database is defragmented during the nightly online maintenance routines, the database file size will never shrink. If you have a 50GB mailbox store and move all of the mailboxes to another mailbox store, the mailbox store will still consume 50GB of disk space. Online maintenance will rearrange the "white space" in the database files in order to make reads more efficient, but the file will still contain empty space.

To reduce the size of the file, you will need to perform this operation offline. Further, you need to plan to have *at least* as much available disk space as the file itself takes up. This is not always the case, especially if there is a lot of white space in the database file, but it is a good estimate. You can direct the temporary database files to another disk if necessary, but this will increase the amount of time it takes to compact the database.

> **NOTE**   If you have recently deleted a large number of mailboxes, the disk space that those mailboxes consumed may not be reclaimable immediately. This is because, by default, the mailbox store keeps deleted mailboxes for 30 days.

The utility you use to compact the database is the eseutil.exe program, which lives in the \exchsrvr\bin directory. To compact a database, run eseutil.exe in defragment mode using the /d switch. There are a number of options that can be used with this switch:

- *edbfilename* is the name of and path to the rich-text (EDB) file. The path to the native content (STM) file is not necessary.
- /ss*stmfilename* specifies the name of and path to the native content (STM) file. This option is necessary only if the STM file is not in the same location as the EDB file.
- /b*filename* specifies that a backup of the database should be made before starting the compacting process.
- /t*tempdatabase* specifies the name and location of the temporary database file. You can redirect the temporary files to another drive on the same server or even a network drive. I don't recommend redirecting to a network drive, as this can cause the offline maintenance to take a very long time.

- /ftempstmfile specifies the name and location of the temporary streaming file.

- /i specifies that ESEUTIL should skip the streaming file and only defragment the EDB file.

- /o suppresses the ESEUTIL logo.

- /p instructs ESEUTIL not to replace the newly compacted files with the original. This means you will have to do this yourself.

You may find it useful to include >c:\eseutil-report.txt on the end of the ESEUTIL command line. This will direct all output from the ESEUTIL command to the eseutil-report.txt file. Having this file may be helpful if ESEUTIL reported errors.

> **NOTE** The database must be dismounted prior to running ESEUTIL, and the information store must remain started. This process is slightly different than with Exchange 5.5, which required that the information store service be stopped.

Figure 4.1 shows an example that compacts both the rich-text store (priv1.edb) and the native content store (priv1.stm). Since I did not specify temporary names for the STM or EDB files, random temporary names were generated.

Figure 4.1   Compacting the default mailbox store.

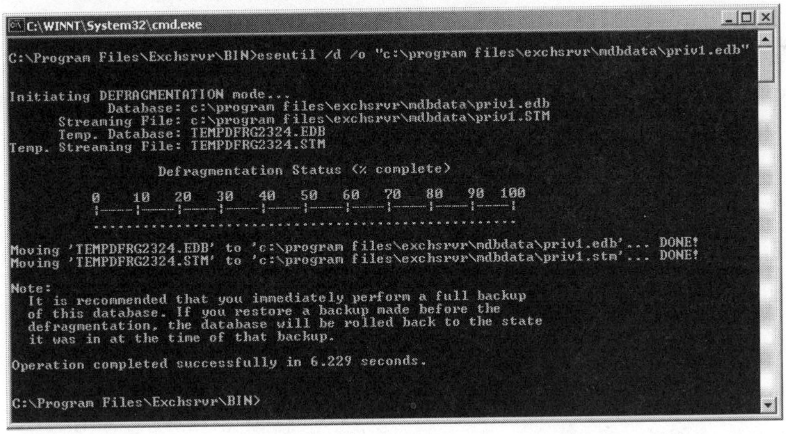

The only times I recommend performing an offline defragmentation is after a large number of mailboxes or messages have been deleted. However, you will need to wait until after those deleted mailboxes and messages have *really* been deleted, since they may not be purged immediately. The other metric I use to determine if this should be run is if event ID 1221 (generated nightly during online maintenance) indicates that there is more than about 25 percent free space in the store.

TIP Perform a backup prior to starting any offline compaction, and then perform an immediate backup of the entire storage group once you have performed
an offline compaction. The old transaction log files cannot be used to recover the
database once it has been compacted.

Database Integrity Check

Performing a database integrity check is another operation that is not typically necessary, but
it makes some administrators feel better. When an online backup is run, each page in the database is checked to make sure that it is not corrupted. However, if you are running only offline
backups, or if you are using some other backup solution such as a "snapshot" type backup,
you may not be assured that the database is always completely corruption free. One of the reasons I object to snapshot backups is that they do not perform integrity checks.

NOTE I advise against running offline data integrity checks. The information
they give you (corrupted data in the ESE databases) will generally be reported
during online backups. Besides, there are many other things that administrators
are better suited to do with their time, such as running disaster recovery drills.

There is a utility on the Exchange 2000 CD-ROM in the \Support\Utils\i386 directory
called esefile.exe. This utility will scan an EDB file and perform a checksum on each
database page. This is the same process that backup programs take advantage of in the
Exchange ESE backup API. Following is a sample of running this utility on the default
priv1.edb data file:

```
C:\Program Files\Exchsrvr\BIN>esefile /s ..\mdbdata\priv1.edb

Microsoft(R) Exchange Server(TM) Database Utilities
Copyright (C) Microsoft Corporation 1999-2000.  All Rights Reserved.
Checksumming

          0    10   20   30   40   50   60   70   80   90  100
          |----|----|----|----|----|----|----|----|----|----|
          ..................................................

1538 pages seen
0 bad checksums
383 uninitialized pages
0 wrong page numbers

esefile completes successfully after 1 seconds
```

The ESEFILE utility does not make any changes to the database. The useful /d option will allow you to dump a particular page of the database.

> **NOTE** For more information about the ESEFILE utility, refer to Microsoft Knowledge Base article Q253325.

Two options of ESEUTIL that are useful are the options to perform an integrity check and to dump the header of the database file. The /g option performs an integrity check by checking tables, rebuilding all of the indexes in a temporary file, and comparing the production indexes with the temporary indexes. This is a read-only option; it makes no changes to the database. There are several options that can be used with the `eseutil /g` command:

- *edbfilename* is the name of and path to the rich-text (EDB) file. The path to the native content (STM) file is not necessary.
- */sstmfilename* sets the name and the location of the native content (STM) file. This option is only necessary if the STM file is in a separate location from the EDB file.
- */ttempdbfile* sets the temporary database filename and location that is created while ESEUTIL checks the indexes.
- */flogprefix* specifies the prefix name to use to create the report that will be generated. The default is the *databasename*.`integ.raw`.
- /o suppresses the ESEUTIL logo.

The following is an example that performs an integrity check on the default mailbox store:

```
eseutil /g \exchsrvr\mdbdata\priv1.edb
```

Another useful feature for checking the integrity of the database is the /m option, which allows you to dump the database header information. I use this often to see if a database file is actually consistent (all transactions have been properly flushed). Several /m options are listed below (at least one must be specified):

- /mh dumps the header of the specified database file.
- /mk dumps the header of the specified checkpoint file.
- /ml dumps the header of the specified log file or a set of logs.
- /mm dumps the metadata of the specified data file.
- /ms dumps the space usage information.

Other options for `eseutil /m` include:

- *filename* is the name of and path to file in question. This can be a checkpoint file, log file, STM file, or EDB file.

- /sstrmfile sets the name and path for the STM file.
- /ttablename specifies to dump nodes only from specific table.
- /v lists detailed information about the file being dumped.
- /o suppresses the ESEUTIL log.

Here is an example of dumping the header of the default mailbox store (priv1.edb):

```
eseutil /mh \exchsrvr\mdbdata\priv1.edb
```

NOTE Other options used for disaster recovery and database repair are discussed in Chapter 7.

Restricting Access to the Exchange Server

Exchange 2000 allows you to restrict access to the information store in one of two ways: either based on the legacy distinguished name (DN) of the mailbox-enabled user, or based on the MAPI-client version. Restricting access to the information store is a pretty obscure feature, but I had a couple of opportunities to use it, and it is pretty cool.

Restricting Access to Specific Users Only

You may want to restrict access to the information store only to a specified list of mailboxes. By default, the information store will allow all mailboxes to access the store; however there is a Registry setting that allows you to restrict store access to only a few users. I have used this feature when I have had to perform a rebuild on a server or when I have had to reformat a disk, but first want to make absolutely sure that I have a current backup.

WARNING Make absolutely sure you have a complete, up-to-the-minute backup prior to reformatting the server hard disks.

Before you can use this feature, you will need the legacyExchangeDN of the mailboxes that will be allowed to access the information store. You can find this on each user's Active Directory account by using ADSIEDIT and looking for the legacyExchangeDN attribute. To restrict access to the Exchange server, follow these steps:

1. Run the Windows NT Registry Editor (REGEDT32, *not* REGEDIT).
2. Locate the HKLM\System\CurrentControlSet\Services\MExchangeIS\ ParametersSystem Registry key.

3. Select Edit ➢ Add Value, type **Logon Only As**, and select REG_MULTI_SZ in the Data Type box.

4. In the Data box that appears, enter a list of legacy Exchange DNs of mailboxes that are allowed to access the server. If you leave this box empty, *no one* will be able to access the server. The DNs should be in the following format:

   ```
   /O=Somorita/OU=Honolulu/CN=Recipients/CN=NancyM
   ```

5. Stop and restart the information store service for the change to take effect.

WARNING When you are finished backing up the server or performing whatever maintenance required you to restrict access, make sure that you delete the entire Logon Only As value.

Restricting Access to Specific MAPI Clients

A new feature introduced with Exchange Server 2000 SP1 allows you to restrict which versions of MAPI clients can access the information store. This is an incredibly useful feature if an administrator wants to restrict access to only a certain list of approved clients. Perhaps you want to make sure that everyone who uses your servers is using at least Outlook 2000. Or perhaps you want to make sure that no one installs a later version of Outlook until you have tested it. This feature allows you to do this.

This feature must be enabled in the Registry of each Exchange 2000 server, and you must know the MAPI version of the client (which will not necessarily correspond to the actual Outlook version). To restrict logon based on the client's MAPI version, run the Registry Editor and locate the following key:

```
HKLM\System\CurrentControlSet\Services\MSExchangeIS\ParametersSystem
```

In this key, create a new value of type REG_SZ called Disable MAPI Clients. You then populate this key with a list of MAPI clients that are *not* allowed to access the server. Table 4.3 lists some of the MAPI client versions that are currently available. This list is by no means inclusive of all MAPI clients, since each service release and security fix may update this version. The best way to determine the MAPI client version is to look at the Client Version field in the Logons container of the information store. This will not necessarily correspond to the Help ➢ About screen of Outlook.

Table 4.3 MAPI Client and Outlook Versions

Client	Help ➤ About Version	MAPI Version	Value Required to Restrict Logon
Exchange 4	4.0.993.3	4.0.993.3	4.993.3
Exchange 5	5.0.1457.3	5.0.1457.3	5.1457.3
Outlook 97 (from Office 97 CD)	8.02.4212	5.0.1457.3	5.1457.3
Outlook 97 8.03 (with Exchange 5.5)	8.03.4629	5.0.1960.0	5.1960.0
Outlook 98	8.5.5104.6	5.0.2178.0	5.2178.0
Outlook 2000 (with Office 2000)	9.0.0.2711	5.0.2819.0	5.2819.0
Outlook 2000 SR-1	9.0.0.3821	5.0.3121.0	5.3121.0
Outlook 2000 SR-1 (after Office 2000 SP2 applied)	9.0.0.4527	5.0.3144.0	5.3144.0
Outlook 2002/XP	10.2627.2625	10.0.0.2627	10.0.2627
Exchange 2000 SP1 components	N/A	6.0.4712.0	6.4712.0

TIP Always make sure that MAPI version 6 components are allowed to log on. These are Exchange 2000 components such as the System Attendant.

The MAPI version number looks much like an IP address, except that each decimal place is a 16-bit number, so the range can be between 0 and 65,535. The number is in the form of $W.X.Y.Z$. When determining which version number to put in to the Disable MAPI Clients Registry value, use only the $W.Y.Z$ format (leave out the X).

You can mix and match values in the Registry key to allow certain ranges of clients to access the information store. Additionally, you can put in multiple values by separating them with commas. Here are some examples:

Registry Value	Function
-6.0.0, 7.0.0-	Allows only the Exchange 2000 components to access the information store by blocking all clients before version 6 and all clients after version 7.
10.0.2627	Prevents the original release of Outlook 2002 clients from accessing the store.
-5.2818.0	Prevents any clients prior to Outlook 2000 from accessing the store.
4.993.3 - 5.1457.3	Prevents Exchange 4, 5, and original Outlook 97 clients from accessing the store.

> **WARNING** Avoid restricting clients whose MAPI version begins with 6.*Y.Z*, because you may restrict an Exchange 2000 component. If you restrict values 4.0 through 7.0, you will restrict the Exchange server components.

Once this feature is in place, clients will get a "The attempt to log on to the Microsoft Exchange Server computer has failed" message if they try to access the Exchange server from a client whose MAPI version you are blocking. One of the most common problems with this feature is administrators deploy an update to a client, but forget the feature is enabled. The update introduces a new MAPI version, which may be blocked at the server.

Applying Policies

Exchange 2000 introduces the use of system policies. Do not confuse Exchange 2000 system policies with Windows 2000 group policies. Exchange 2000 policies are designed to allow an administrator to apply the same settings consistently throughout the entire organization but only setting the policies in one place. Further, this person may be an organization-wide administrator, and local administrators may not have the ability to override these policies. However, using ADSIEDIT, an administrator can change any of the attributes of an object to which they have proper permissions.

For example, the organization-wide Exchange administrator can create a system policy that sets the mailbox storage limits. The administrator can create a mailbox store policy that sets these limits and apply these limits to all mailbox stores without having to set the limits individually for each mailbox store.

Operations

PART 2

Exchange 2000 affects three different types of server objects: server policies, mailbox store policies, and public folder store policies. Once a system policy is applied to an Exchange server, mailbox store, or public folder store, the configuration change has to replicate to the domain controller that the affected Exchange server is using. Then the RUS applies the policy to the affected object.

> **NOTE** Don't confuse system policies with recipient polices. Recipient policies (discussed in Chapter 2) affect the proxy addresses (SMTP, X.400, etc.) of mail-enabled objects.

Permissions to Assign Policies

Before reviewing how to create policies, let's see how a large organization might implement policies so that an administrator who is not authorized to assign policies could not override them. To do this, you will need to create an administrative group for the system policies, and then deny administrators in other containers the right to create system policies.

Let's look at an example. Somorita Surfboards has a single group of organization-wide administrators called Exchange Global Admins, which has been given the Exchange Full Administrator role to the organization object. These administrators need to be able to apply policies to all servers, mailbox stores, and public folder stores in the entire organization.

Their first step involves creating a new group called System Policies Administration. When delegating permissions to this new administrative group, Somorita's full Exchange administrator makes sure that the other Exchange administrator groups have only the Exchange View Only Administrator role. This creates a group (shown in Figure 4.2) that only the policy administrators will be able to access.

Figure 4.2   System Policies Administration group

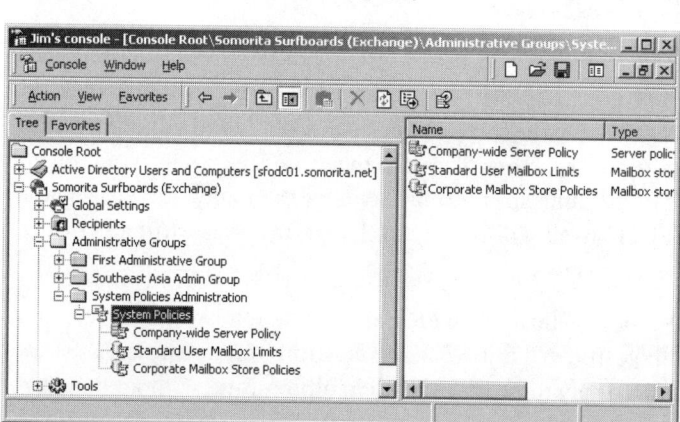

Next, the Exchange Global Admins group will need a minimum of the write permission to any object to which they will be assigning a policy. If the default permissions have been inherited from the organization object, then the Exchange Global Admins group will have full permissions to all administrative groups. However, if these permissions have been blocked, then the Exchange Global Admins group will need the write permission assigned.

Once the Exchange Global Admins group has the correct permissions, then Somorita's full Exchange administrator needs to make sure that the administrators of the other administrative groups cannot create (and assign!) their own system policies. If they could, they could override the ones that were applied. This is a little tricky, since it will involve editing the advanced permissions using the ADSIEDIT tool.

Somorita Surfboards has another administrative group called Southeast Asia Admin Group to which the group Southeast Asia Exchange Admins has been delegated the Exchange Administrator role. This role includes the ability to create and delete policies, and thus, you were relegated to block it. To do so, follow these steps:

1. Locate the Southeast Asia Admin Group in the configuration container of ADSIEDIT, display the properties, and select the Security tab.

2. Click the Advanced button to see the advanced permissions, and click the Add button.

3. Add the Southeast Asia Exchange Admins group. You will be presented with a detailed list of permissions like the one shown in Figure 4.3. (I'll bet you did not realize there were so many permissions!) Scroll down until you find the Create Exchange Policies Objects and Delete Exchange Policies objects; click the Deny check boxes for both of these permissions, and then click OK.

Figure 4.3   Denying permissions to create or delete system policies.

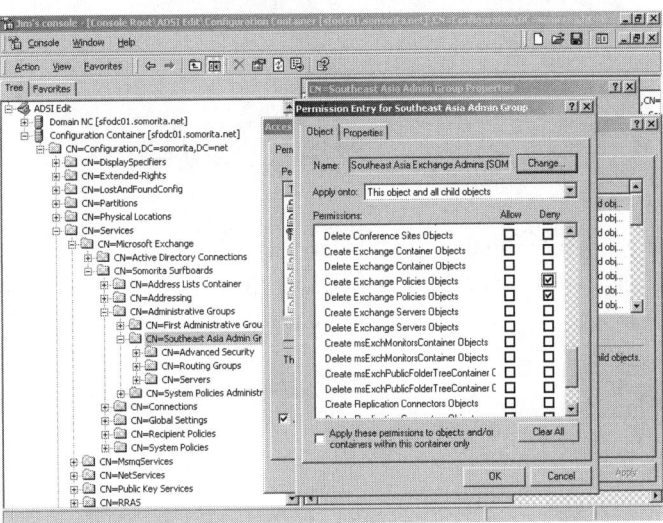

You will now see in the advanced permissions list where the Southeast Asia Exchange Admins group has been denied the permission to create or delete system policies.

To prevent other administrators from creating additional administrative groups, make sure that no administrators other than the Exchange View Only Admin role are assigned at the organization level. You can also restrict the ability to create administrative groups by assigning the other administrative groups only the read permission to the Administrative Groups parent container.

Server Policies

Server policies are the simplest of the Exchange 2000 system policies. A server policy consists of a single property tab, General, as shown in Figure 4.4.

Figure 4.4   General property tab of a server policy

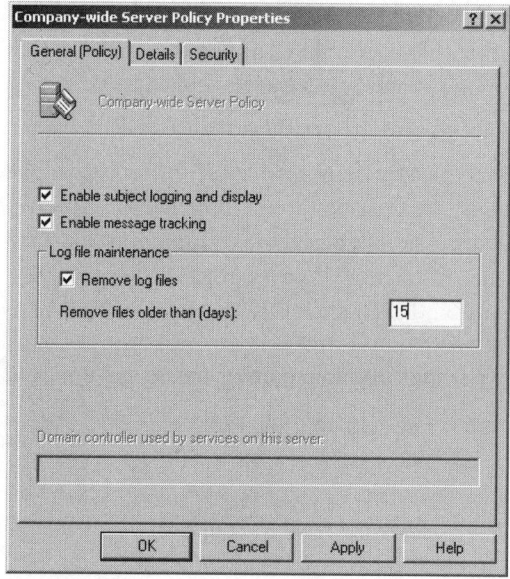

The General property tab allows you to do the following:

- Enable subject logging and display, which allows the message subject to be included in message tracking logs and to be shown in the SMTP queues.
- Enable message tracking.
- Specify how long message tracking files are kept before the System Attendant purges the old files.

Once the policy is created, it can be associated with one or more Exchange 2000 servers anywhere in the organization by right-clicking the server policy and choosing Add Server. The administrator who is adding a server to the policy must have at least write permissions to the server object.

To remove a server so that it is no longer affected by a system policy, right-click the server in the list of servers that are affected by the policy and choose Remove From Policy. If changes are made to the policy after it is created and assigned to servers, then you must right-click the changed server policy and choose Apply Now. This forces the Exchange System Manager to make the appropriate changes to all the affected server objects in Active Directory.

Figure 4.5 shows the General property page from server SFOEX001. Notice that the choices for Enable Subject Logging And Display, Enable Message Tracking, and the Log File Maintenance choices are grayed out. This is because these settings are now controlled by a server policy. An administrator cannot change these settings without removing the policy.

Figure 4.5   General property page under the influence of a server policy

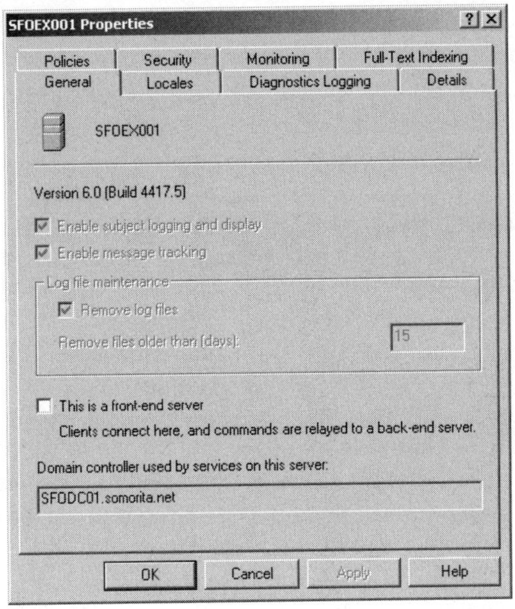

Notice also in Figure 4.5 that the choice This Is A Front-End Server is still available. This is because this choice is not controlled by a server policy and can be applied individually to the server. On the Policies property tab of the server's properties, you can see which policies are affecting each property tab.

Mailbox Store Policies

I find mailbox store policies to be the most useful of the three. Most organizations have a standard that they want their users to adhere to with respect to mailbox storage limits. Without mailbox storage limits, an administrator will have to apply these storage limits to each mailbox store in the organization.

When you create a new system policy, Exchange System Manager asks you which property pages you want to include in that policy.

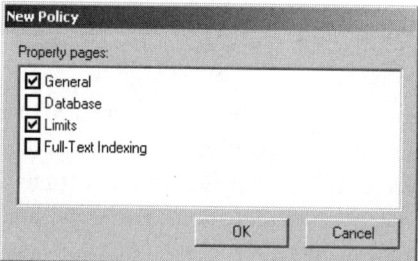

When creating a mailbox store policy, you can include the General, Database, Limits, and Full-Text Indexing tabs. However, if you decide to include an additional page or remove a property page later, simply right-click the policy and choose Change Property Pages. Table 4.4 describes the options you can set from each of the policy's property pages.

Table 4.4 Mailbox Store Policy Settings

Page	Policy Setting	Description
General	Default public store	For the mailboxes on the affected mailbox stores, this specifies which public folder store the MAPI users will connect to for public folders.
General	Offline Address Book	For the mailboxes on the affected mailbox stores, this specifies which Offline Address Book (OAB) will be downloaded to MAPI clients.
General	Archive all messages sent or received by mailboxes on this store	Specifies that messages sent or received by mailboxes on the affected stores will have a copy of each message sent to the specified mailbox.
General	Clients support S/MIME signatures	Provides support for clients to include S/MIME signatures in messages.

Table 4.4   Mailbox Store Policy Settings *(continued)*

Page	Policy Setting	Description
General	Display plaintext messages in a fixed-sized font	Messages that are formatted as plaintext, such as messages from the Internet, will be displayed in a fixed-size font such as Courier 10pt. Select this if you want to make sure that plain-text formatting is preserved on plain-text messages.
Database	Maintenance interval	Allows the time interval to be specified for online maintenance. The default time is 1:00 A.M. to 5:00 A.M.
Limits	Issue warning at	Issues a warning in the form of an e-mail message informing the user that their mailbox has exceeded the specified limit.
Limits	Prohibit send at	Prohibits MAPI clients from sending or replying to a message if their mailbox exceeds this limit.
Limits	Prohibit send and receive at	Causes the mailbox to reject incoming messages if the mailbox exceeds the specified limit.
Limits	Warning message interval	Specifies when a warning message will be generated for mailboxes that are over their Issue Warning limit. The default is midnight; be careful if creating a custom schedule because warning messages will be sent four times per hour if you select an entire hour block.
Limits	Keep deleted items for	Specifies how many days to keep mail items once a user has emptied them from their Deleted Items folder. The default is zero days. I recommend setting this value to at least 15 days; many administrators configure this value as high as 30 days.

Operations

PART 2

Table 4.4   Mailbox Store Policy Settings *(continued)*

Page	Policy Setting	Description
Limits	Keep deleted mailboxes for	Specifies how many days to keep mailboxes that no longer have an associated Active Directory account. The default is 30 days.
Limits	Do not permanently delete mailboxes and items until store has been permanently backed up	Once a mailbox or mail item is eligible for deletion, it won't be removed until after the next normal backup has completed.
Directory Access	Show	Select whether to display domain controllers, Global Catalog servers, or the configuration domain controller.
Directory Access	Add and Remove buttons	Manually add or remove domain controllers, Global Catalog servers, or the configuration domain controller.
Directory Access	Automatically discover servers	Specifies whether Exchange discovers servers through DNS queries (automatically) or by reading the registry.
Mailbox Manager	Start mailbox management process, Reporting Administrator	Mailbox Manager settings are discussed in more detail in the "Using Mailbox Manager" section, later in this chapter.
Full-Text Indexing	Update interval	Specifies how often the Microsoft Search indexing process will check for new items that need to be included in the index.
Full-Text Indexing	Rebuild interval	Specifies how long the Microsoft Search indexing process waits before it rebuilds the index.

Individually Assigning Offline Address Books

Offline Address Books (OABs) can be assigned through an Exchange system policy or directly to the users of a mailbox store. However, since OABs are associated with users based on the mailbox store to which their mailbox is assigned, this may not provide you with the greatest degree of flexibility. If you have a few users on a mailbox store who need a different OAB, there is a workaround. This procedure is a bit of a pain in the neck, so if you have very many users needing a specific OAB, you may be better off assigning all of those users to their own mailbox store and assigning the mailbox store to use that OAB. The downside to adding additional mailbox stores is the additional overhead that they cause the server to incur.

To perform the workaround, first create an OAB that contains only the address lists that need to be assigned to your special group of users. Then determine the distinguished name of that OAB; for example, an OAB that I created called Executives OAB has a distinguished name of CN=Executives OAB,CN=Offline Address Lists,CN=Address Lists Container,CN=Somorita Surfboards,CN=Microsoft Exchange,CN=Services,CN=Configuration,DC=somorita,DC=net.

Next, using ADSIEDIT or some other tool to manipulate the directory, assign the OAB's distinguished name to the user's msExchUseOAB attribute. This user will now download the individually assigned OAB.

Public Folder Store Policies

Public folder store policies allow the administrator to centrally set the configuration options for one or more public folder stores; these options are found on the General, Database, Replication, Limits, and Full-Text Indexing property pages. Table 4.5 describes the properties that can be set through public folder store polices. Creating, applying, and removing public store policies are exactly the same as for mailbox stores.

Table 4.5   Public Folder Store Policy Settings

Page	Policy Setting	Description
General	Clients support S/MIME signatures	Provides support for clients to include S/MIME signatures in messages.
General	Display plaintext messages in a fixed-sized font	Messages that are formatted as plaintext, such as messages from the Internet, will be displayed in a fixed size font such as Courier 10pt.
Database	Maintenance interval	Allows the time interval to be specified for online maintenance. The default time is 1:00 A.M. to 5:00 A.M.

Table 4.5 Public Folder Store Policy Settings *(continued)*

Page	Policy Setting	Description
Replication	Replication interval	Specifies the default time frame that public folder replication can occur for public folders on all affected public folder stores. The default is set to Always Run.
Replication	Replication interval for always	Specifies the time interval that is used when the replication interval is set to Always Run. The default is 15 minutes.
Replication	Replication message size limit	Specifies the message size limit for putting more than one update into a single message. If five 100KB replication messages need to be replicated to another server, three of them will be sent via a 300KB message, and the other two messages will be sent via a 200KB message. This does not affect the maximum replication message size. The default is 300KB. There is generally not a reason to change this value.
Limits	Issue warning at	Instructs the information store to issue a warning to the folder owner and designated folder contacts if the folder exceeds this limit.
Limits	Prohibit post at	Instructs the information store to stop accepting messages to any folder that exceeds this limit.
Limits	Maximum item size	Specifies the maximum item size that can be posted to affect public folder stores.
Limits	Warning message interval	Specifies when warnings are generated for public folders that are over their Issue Warning limit.

Table 4.5 Public Folder Store Policy Settings *(continued)*

Page	Policy Setting	Description
Limits	Keep deleted items for	Specifies how many days to keep mail items once a user has emptied them from their Deleted Items folder. The default is zero days. I recommend setting this value somewhere between 15 and 30 days. Once set, the owner of the public folder can undelete items that have been deleted.
Limits	Do not permanently delete mailboxes and items until store has been permanently backed up	Once a mailbox or mail item is eligible for deletion, it won't be removed until after the next normal backup has completed.
Limits	Age limits	Specifies the default age limit for items in public folders on the affected store.
Full-Text Indexing	Update interval	Specifies how often the Microsoft Search indexing process will check for new items that need to be included in the index.
Full-Text Indexing	Rebuild interval	Specifies how long the Microsoft Search indexing process waits before it rebuilds the index.

System Policies FAQ

Rather than write several pages on the ins and outs of system policies, I compiled a list of questions that are asked frequently by system administrators and students.

Can you apply more than one policy to a single object? Yes, as long as the two policies do not affect the same property page.

What happens if I remove a policy? Do the settings remain or do they revert back to their original settings before the policy was applied? Even though the policy has been removed, the policy settings that were enforced remain in effect on the object. However, once the policy is removed, any of the settings may be changed.

Why don't system policies always take effect immediately? Like all Exchange 2000 configuration data, the system policy settings are stored on domain controllers in the configuration partition. The changes must be replicated to the domain controller that each server is using as its configuration domain controller. Once the system policies have replicated to a server's configuration domain controller, the Recipient Update Service will update the policies within a minute or two.

Can mailbox store policy limits applied to a mailbox store be overridden at the mailbox store level? No, however they can be overridden on a per mailbox level.

Can public store limits applied to a public folder store be overridden at the public store level? No, but the limits can be overridden on a folder-by-folder basis.

Can I set the policy to affect only some of the items on a property page, but not others? For example, I want to set deleted mailbox retention time on a per–mailbox store basis, but I want to set mailbox storage through a mailbox policy. No, you cannot do this. In this case, you would have to set each mailbox store separately or create separate policies.

Database Technology, Storage Groups, and Stores

At the heart of message storage is the database technology that maintains the databases, and at the heart of Exchange 2000 scalability is the fact that we can have more than one mailbox store or public folder store on a single server. This section covers information about the Exchange database technology, including the use of transaction log files. Also covered in this section is information about storage groups and stores and how to manage stores and storage groups.

Exchange Database Technology

Exchange Server uses a database technology that Microsoft calls *ESE (Extensible Storage Engine)*; this technology is a modified version of the JET (Joint Engine Technology) database engine. Currently, Exchange uses ESE version ESE98; the Windows 2000 Active Directory database uses ESE97. Ultimately, the current Exchange database technology is a *very* distant cousin of the technology used by Microsoft Access. In reality, it is much more similar to modern database technologies such as SQL Server. However, the Exchange 2000 database is neither an Access database (oh, the horror!) nor a SQL database. ESE is highly optimized for the storage of hierarchical data such as folders, messages, message properties, and attachments. It's is also optimized for storage of data that does not fit a typical data set model; each item in a table may have a completely different properties, unlike an SQL table in which each row is made up of the exact same properties.

In order to ensure that the database files are available and correct, the Exchange technology borrows concepts from the minicomputer and mainframe database world. This includes the use of log files to record all transactions prior to the transaction being committed to the database file. In the 1970s, database transaction technology was defined and measured by the database ACID (Atomicity, Consistency, Isolation, and Durability) test. In order for a database to pass the ACID test, it must have the following characteristics:

- All operations on an Exchange Server database are *atomic*, meaning all transaction data are either committed to the database or rolled back. Exchange Server log files record data in the form of transactions and commit these transactions to the database once complete.

- In order to ensure *consistency*, the database is always transformed from one known, valid state to another. The atomicity of the transactions and the use of the transaction log ensure that the databases always stay in a valid state.

- All transactions are serialized and *isolated*. This prevents simultaneous activity from interfering with any specific transaction.

- Transaction results are *durable*; they are permanent and capable of surviving system failures.

Operations

PART 2

Exchange@Work: Much Ado About Transactions and Logs

A *transaction* is a sequence of operations that are treated as a single unit. In order for the transaction to be considered finished, all operations have to be completed.

For example, let's say that your bank has a database with two tables of data: checking data and savings data. You call the bank's customer service and ask that $100 be transferred from your checking account to your savings account. The transaction will consist of two operations: subtracting $100 from your checking account and adding $100 to your savings account.

What if the system fails right in the middle of the transaction? Did it finish, or are you out $100?

In the database world, both operations are recorded to a *transaction log* first. Once all the operations that make up the transaction are complete, the operation work is performed on the database. If the system fails in the middle of performing the "subtract" step on the database, when the system restarts, the database software detects an incomplete transaction. If all the information required to complete the transaction is located in the transaction log files, the transaction is "rolled forward." If not, the transaction is "rolled back"; in other words, the database is returned to a valid state.

Log Operations

To better understand what happens when a transaction occurs on the Exchange server, let's review a little bit about how log files are incorporated into the operation of Exchange.

The sum total of all data on the Exchange server is considered to be all the data in the mailbox stores plus the uncommitted data in the transaction log files. Prior to a normal shutdown, all data in the transaction log files are committed to the database. That brings the database to a *consistent* state; there is no uncommitted data in the transaction logs. However, during normal Exchange operations, at any given time there may be a few seconds (or even minutes) worth of data in the transaction logs that have not yet been committed.

The transaction logs are critical to the operation of Exchange server. Figure 4.6 illustrates the use of these logs in a somewhat simplified fashion on a single transaction—a user sending a new e-mail message. However, a transaction could also be a folder creation, message deletion, or moving a message from one folder to another.

Figure 4.6 Exchange data and transaction log files

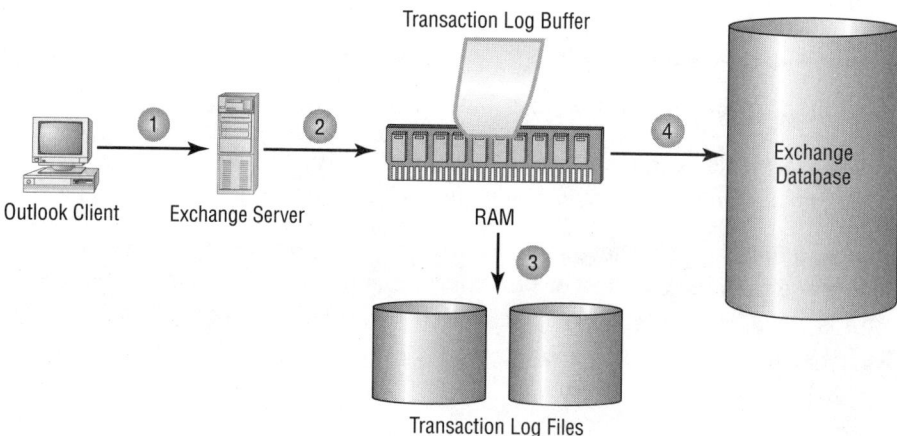

The process shown in Figure 4.6 illustrates a basic view of how transactions are treated with the ESE database engine:

1. A message arrives at the Exchange server from a client.

2. As the message arrives, it is placed in pages in RAM known as the transaction log buffer area.

3. Immediately after the transaction is committed to memory, it is committed to the transaction logs. The pages in memory are considered *dirty* because they need to be committed to the database.

4. Once all operations are completed for the transaction and they are all committed to the transaction log files, the data is read from memory and written to the correct database file.

This is an oversimplified explanation, but it gives you an idea of the importance of the transaction logs. For Exchange Server to have better performance or to improve scalability, one of the major bottlenecks is the need to commit data to the transaction logs. Writes to the transaction logs are synchronous. A single thread is responsible for transaction log writes; the thread is blocked from performing any other work until the action is completed. Reads from and writes to the database are asynchronous, the system can continue performing other operations while waiting for disk operations to complete. If the disk channel has read/write operations from other components queuing, this may mean that ESE may be delayed in writing data to the log files. For this reason, transaction logs should always be on their own separate physical disk drives. Separation of the transaction log files on separate spindles is not always enough. Attention should be given to the disk architecture; RAID 0 and RAID 1 drive arrays are as much as four times faster than RAID 5 for log file operations.

> **NOTE** Exchange uses write-ahead logging. This means that all data is committed to transaction logs first, as is all information that Exchange would need to reverse the transaction, if necessary.

Circular Logging

Circular logging is a feature designed to minimize the amount of space consumed by the transaction log files. Exchange will keep a small window of transaction logs (usually four or five) and delete the oldest transaction logs. In Exchange 5.5, the circular logging feature was enabled by default. However, if it was enabled, you couldn't perform incremental or differential backups, nor could you get up-to-the-minute recovery in the event of database corruption.

Exchange 2000 disables circular logging by default. The feature is enabled or disabled on a per storage group basis.

In an Exchange 2000 environment, if you can answer "yes" to all of the following questions, then you can probably enable circular logging:

- Are you going to perform a normal (full) backup every night?

- Are incremental or differential backups unnecessary?
- Are the log files and the database files on the same disk drive?

If you answered "no" to any of these questions, you probably need to keep circular logging disabled.

When circular logging is disabled, Exchange Server will keep all old log files until an online normal or incremental backup is done; the Windows 2000 backup or an Exchange-aware third-party backup utility must perform this backup process. However, the major advantage to the fact that you have all those log files on the hard disk is that you can perform an up-to-the minute recovery using the last normal backup.

I would enable circular logging under the following situations:

- On a front-end server that has an SMTP Connector or other messaging gateway.
- On a storage group that hosted a public folder store that received data from a Usenet newsfeed and the data could easily be re-replicated, if necessary.
- Temporarily enable circular logging on a server where I am migrating, importing, or moving a large number of mailboxes on to the server in a short period of time. Just don't forget to disable circular logging when you are finished moving mailboxes.

Exchange Database Files

Now that you have an idea of the Exchange database technology, let's review the files that you will find when you are examining Exchange data directories.

Exchange 2000 Stores   Sometimes I wonder if anyone really knows the difference between a store and a database—or if there really is an official difference. (This terminology is a common source of confusion amongst Exchange administrators.) Exchange 2000 has two types of stores: mailbox stores and public folder stores. Each type of Exchange 2000 store consists of two database files, the rich-text database (EDB) file and the native content database (STM) file.

The *rich-text database (EDB)* is the database we are used to seeing in previous versions of Exchange. This database is also called the MAPI database or property store because all of the data that is stored in here is stored with MAPI properties in a proprietary format called Microsoft Database Encapsulated Format (MDBEF).

The *native content database (STM),* or streaming database, is new to Exchange 2000. This file contains message content that has arrived on the server from clients other than MAPI clients; messages that arrive from any SMTP source (except for other Exchange 2000 servers in the same organization), the Exchange Installable File System (ExIFS), and Outlook Web Access (OWA) clients would be stored here. The STM file is not encrypted or encoded.

If the store is dismounted, you can actually view the native content in a text editor (shown in Figure 4.7).

Figure 4.7 STM file shown in Notepad

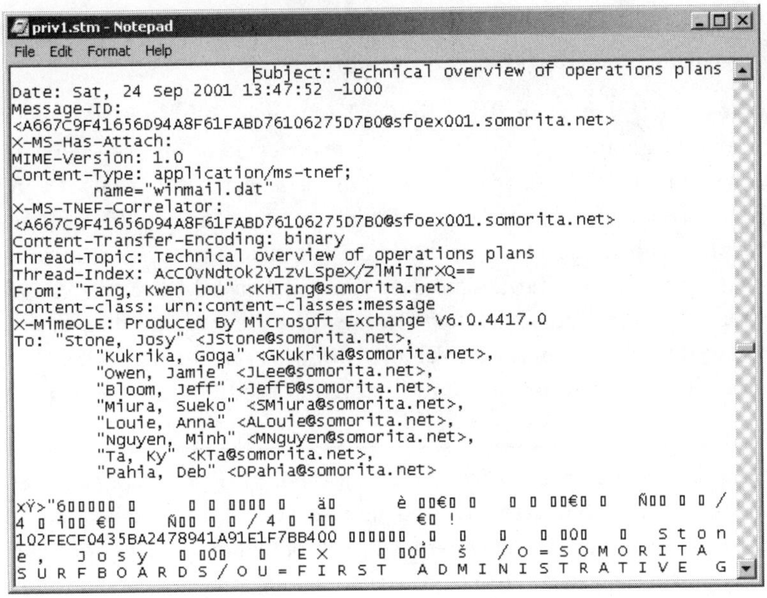

Collectively, these two database files are also referred to as a *store*. These database files must be backed up and restored together, and any type of offline maintenance is performed on both files. All content in the native content database has an associated set of MAPI properties in the rich-text database. When a message arrives in the information store from a non-MAPI client, the message itself is streamed into the native content database with no conversion. However, the message's header information (To, Cc, From, Subject, etc.) is promoted to MAPI properties and is stored in the rich-text database.

> **NOTE** The EDB and STM files are treated as a single store; the fact that there are two message database files rather than one is transparent to the end user.

Content Conversion Message content may be stored in either MAPI format or native format, depending on which client sent (or stored) the message. If a MAPI client retrieves a message that was sent from the Internet, the Microsoft Exchange Information Store service will convert the content "on demand." The content is not actually converted in the store database files, but rather in memory. The information store runs a process called IMAIL, which is responsible for all content conversion. Content conversion is transparent to the end user.

On-demand content conversion occurs in the following situations:

- A MAPI client retrieves a message that was sent by an SMTP or HTTP client.
- A POP3, IMAP4, NNTP, or HTTP client retrieves a message that was sent by an Outlook (MAPI) client.

If a MAPI client retrieves *and* modifies a message that was sent from an Internet client, the message is then saved to the rich-text store.

You might surmise that since all routing in Exchange 2000 is based on SMTP that even messages that originate in Outlook might be transferred to other servers and then stored in the STM database files. In reality, Exchange is smarter than that. If a message being sent to another server is stored in the EDB file, it contains an MS-TNEF (Microsoft Transport Neutral Encapsulation Format) body part. If this is the case, the message body is not converted to the default outgoing message type, such as S/MIME; instead, the message is transmitted in compressed TNEF format, meaning there are no non-TNEF body parts. When received by the destination Exchange 2000 server, the message is immediately recognized as being a MAPI message and is stored in the EDB file.

> **NOTE** In Exchange 5.5, anytime a POP3, IMAP4, HTTP, or NNTP client retrieved a message, the IMAIL process converted the message. Microsoft developers estimate that by not converting inbound Internet e-mail content to MAPI, performance will be improved, especially as more and more customers begin to depend on Internet-type clients and less on MAPI clients. Even if you have mostly MAPI clients, this architecture prevents inbound messages from being converted until necessary.

Transaction Log Files   As discussed earlier in this chapter, transaction logs are critical to the operation of Exchange Server. There will be a unique set of transaction logs for each storage group, and each set of transaction logs should be located on a separate physical hard disk.

The log files are always 5120KB in size; if you find a log file that is a different size, it is either not an Exchange transaction log or it is corrupted. Each storage group has an assigned log file prefix. The first storage group uses E00, the second storage group uses E01, and so on. The active log file in the first storage group transaction log file directory is E00.LOG. When this file fills up, it is renamed to e0000001.log, and a new E00.log is created. When the newly created log file fills up, it is renamed to e0000002.log, and another new E00.log is created. If you view either of these directories, you will see a collection of these old log files.

> **NOTE** All subsequent examples use the prefix E00. If you are managing more than one storage group, you may have a log file prefix of E01, E02, or E03.

When circular logging is disabled (the default), transaction logs will accumulate until a normal or incremental backup is run. On an Exchange 2000 server supporting 1500+ active mailboxes, I have seen a single storage group generate 2000 transaction logs in less than 48 hours. Regular backups must be run to ensure that the transaction log file disk does not run out of disk space!

> **NOTE** Never delete transaction logs manually unless instructed to do so by Microsoft Product Support Services (PSS).

Each transaction log file directory has two reserved log files, `res1.log` and `res2.log`. Reserved logs are used in case Exchange runs out of disk space when it tries to create a new `E00.log` file. If this occurs, the reserved files are used instead; any transactions in memory are flushed to the reserved log files, and Exchange will shut down the affected services. You must correct the disk space problems before you can restart Exchange.

If you have more than 10MB of transactions in memory that must be saved to transaction logs, then there will be data loss.

Patch Files   During an online backup, you will see *patch files* created. Each database that is being backed up has its own PAT file: `priv1.pat` or `pub1.pat`, for example. During an online backup, transactions can still be committed to the database files. However, if the transaction is committed to a part of the database that has already been backed up, the transaction is also written to the corresponding PAT file. When the database is completely backed up, the PAT file is backed up and then deleted.

> **NOTE** If you see a PAT file in any of the database directories, this indicates that the server is currently undergoing an online backup. If this file grows extremely large (more than a few hundred megabytes), make sure that there is not a backup running that has hung up or is waiting for an additional tape.

You do not need to delete the PAT files; Exchange will clean up the PAT files as necessary.

Checkpoint Files   In the Exchange storage group's system path location (the location of the storage group's working path), you will find the *checkpoint file*, `E00.chk`. This file is always 8KB in size.

A checkpoint is a place marker; it points to a location in the log files. All transactions before the checkpoint have been committed to the database; at least some of the transactions after the checkpoint have not yet been committed to the database. The checkpoint is stored in the `E00.chk` file.

Other Files   During normal operation of Exchange 2000, you may notice additional files being created in which the directories that the Exchange data and log files are stored. These files include:

- TMP files are created when the store process needs to create temporary storage or create a new log file. These files are created and deleted as necessary. If you find files with the .tmp extension, they will be deleted the next time the store service restarts.

- STF files are temporary files created by the IMAIL process during content conversion. These files will be cleaned up by the information store service.

- IFS files are temporary files created by the ExIFS. These files contain cached directory lists of the ExIFS and are deleted automatically by the information store service.

Storage Groups

An Exchange 2000 *storage group* is a collection of mailbox or public stores that share a common set of transaction log files, storage group configuration properties, and an instance of the ESE database engine. The first database in a storage group that is mounted causes a new instance of ESE.DLL to be loaded.

> **NOTE**   The first database mounted requires about 130MB of virtual memory. Subsequent databases mounted within the storage group require only an additional 25MB of virtual memory plus 10MB of RAM. A good practice is to fill out the first storage group with stores before creating additional storage groups.

The default storage group created is called First Storage Group. It automatically contains a mailbox store and a public folder store, though either of these can be deleted if necessary. The list below outlines some of the facts surrounding the creation of additional storage groups:

- Each storage group has a unique set of transaction log files. For best performance, each storage group's transaction log files should be on a separate physical hard disk. Even if circular logging is required only for a single store in the storage group, all stores in the storage group must share the same configuration.

- The first database mounted in a storage group will consume approximately 130MB of additional virtual memory due to the fact that it starts a separate instance of the ESE database engine.

- If any store in a storage group is undergoing an online backup, online maintenance will be suspended on the other stores in the storage group.

- If any database in a storage group suffers a catastrophic failure (disk failure or database corruption), the information store will dismount *all* stores in the storage group, mark the failed store as bad and then remount the good stores. This can interfere with normal operations for users whose mailbox or public folder is on a good store in the same storage group.

- Only one database can be backed up or restored at a time in a single storage group; this is true even if you select the entire storage group. Only a single store is backed up at a time, but you can back up all storage groups simultaneously. However, multiple backups or restores can occur across storage groups. If you are going to perform simultaneous restores, you cannot perform more than five minus the number of storage groups. In other words, if you have four storage groups, you can only run one restore. If you have three storage groups, you can run two simultaneous restore operations.

- A maximum of four storage groups can be created on any Exchange 2000 server. This limit is enforced due the fact that current hardware platforms cannot adequately support the RAM requirements that more than four storage groups would place on the hardware.

> **WARNING**   Backing up a single store in a storage group halts online maintenance on all stores in the storage group.

For most Exchange servers supporting fewer than 1500 to 2000 mailboxes, there will not be a need to create additional storage groups. You may need to create additional storage groups if:

- You have five stores in the first storage group and need more.

- You have a store, such as a public folder store, that requires circular logging.

- You have a service level agreement (SLA) that may require that certain mailbox data from different stores be backed up or restored simultaneously or on different schedules.

- You need to create a store that will not be affected by the possible failure of another store in a storage group.

Creating Storage Groups

Any administrator with the Exchange Administrator role can create additional storage groups. Simply right-click the server name on which you want to create a new storage group, choose New ➢ Storage Group, and enter the name of the storage group. In Figure 4.8, you can see a newly created storage group called Third Storage Group. The System Path Location will contain the checkpoint file (in this case, E02.CHK); the System Path Location took the default path (using the default Exchange location and the full storage group name). I modified the Transaction Log Location to demonstrate that it is probably simpler to choose your own directory names.

Figure 4.8 A newly created storage group

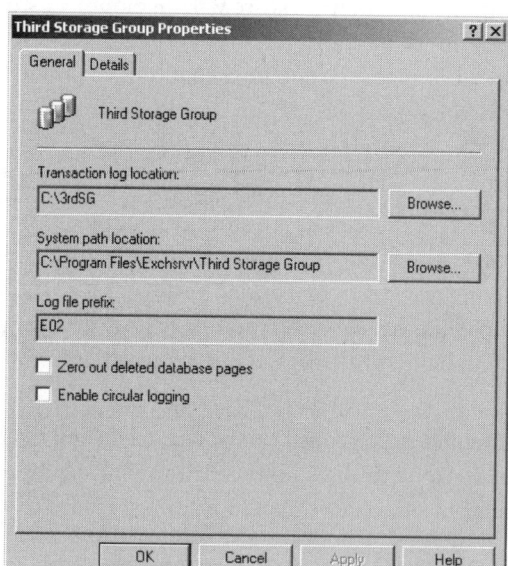

Also shown in Figure 4.8 are the check boxes to control whether or not to zero out deleted pages in the database files and if circular logging is enabled. If Zero Out Deleted Database Pages is checked, then the information store will zero out pages that the messages occupied once they are deleted during nightly the maintenance interval. If any data remains in the page, the page will not be zeroed out; this may leave some deleted information in the page until the page has been defragmented or new data takes its place. While this helps to ensure that even a data recovery expert cannot retrieve the data, it does add overhead to the server.

Moving Storage Group Files

The best way to move database files in Exchange 5.5 was to use the PerfWiz (Exchange Performance Optimizer). Moving storage group log files and the checkpoint file on Exchange 2000 is performed through the Exchange System Manager and is very simple. Simply display the properties of the storage group (as shown in Figure 4.8) and click the Browse button next to either the Transaction Log Location or System Path Location selections, and then select a new location. However, once you click OK, *all* stores in the storage group will be dismounted while the files are moved.

WARNING Transaction log locations and system path locations are easily moved, but all stores in the storage group are dismounted, and the users are disconnected while the files are being moved—without any warning.

Stores

Exchange 5.5 was limited to one private and one public information store, and administrators screamed for more scalability from Exchange 2000. This restriction was due to the fact that if administrators let a private or public information store grow too large, the backup times could exceed a reasonable backup window, restore times could exceed the time specified by an SLA, and hosting multiple organizations on the same Exchange server was more difficult.

Exchange 2000 introduced the concept of multiple stores on a single server. An Exchange 2000 server can support up to 20 stores (four storage groups with five stores in each). These stores can be any combination of mailbox and public folder stores.

> **NOTE** If using Exchange 2000 Server, the maximum size of a store is 16GB, and it only supports a single mailbox store; multiple public folder stores are supported using Exchange 2000 Server. Using Exchange 2000 Enterprise, the maximum store size is 16TB.

Servers supporting fewer than 1000 mailboxes may not need additional stores. The following is a list of things that may indicate that you need an additional store:

- The server is supporting many mailboxes, and the size of a single mailbox store cannot be quickly backed up or restored.
- An SLA specifies a maximum restore time for any single mailbox restore.
- You want to isolate VIP users such as managers and executives to their own, smaller mailbox stores.
- The Exchange server is supporting multiple organizations, and each organization needs to have its own mailbox store.
- Certain mailboxes or folders require full-text indexing, but not all of the information in the store.
- You are installing Microsoft SharePoint Portal Server, which requires an additional public folder store, or you need the server to host an additional public folder tree. In order to integrate SharePoint Portal Server, you must be using Exchange 2000 Server SP1, not Exchange 2000 Enterprise Server.
- You need to apply mailbox policies to different users to enforce mailbox limits and message size restrictions, or to utilize message archival.
- You need special store event sinks to run for everyone in a particular mailbox store.

You should be aware that creating an additional store initially requires approximately 10MB of RAM for the store to be mounted and approximately 25MB of virtual memory; as ESE dynamic buffer allocation (DBA) begins to allocate memory for caching, the memory will have to be split between all the mounted stores. Plus, single instance store is *not* preserved between the stores; thus if you choose to break up the mailboxes on a server into two separate mailbox stores, plan to group the mailboxes together based on which groups of people work together.

NOTE Single instance storage is not preserved between stores.

There are two default stores on a newly installed Exchange 2000 server. For a server called SFOEX001, the mailbox store is called `Mailbox Store (SFOEX001)`; the database files are `priv1.edb` and `priv1.stm`. The public folder store on the same server is called Public Folder Store (SFOEX001); the database files are `pub1.edb` and `pub1.stm`.

Creating a Store

Creating additional stores is simple. Simply highlight a storage group that currently has fewer than five stores, right-click, and choose New ≻ Mailbox Store or New ≻ Public Store. Most of the properties of the mailbox and public stores are well documented in the online documentation, so I will just cover the important points and spare you the details that you can easily learn within the Exchange 2000 interface.

Creating a Mailbox Store   When creating a mailbox store, all you have to provide is the store name. This is also referred to as the logical name, because the logical name shown in the Exchange System Manager hierarchy will not always match the actual names of the database files. A newly created mailbox store and the Exchange System Manager hierarchy are shown in Figure 4.9.

Figure 4.9   New mailbox store and the Exchange System Manager hierarchy

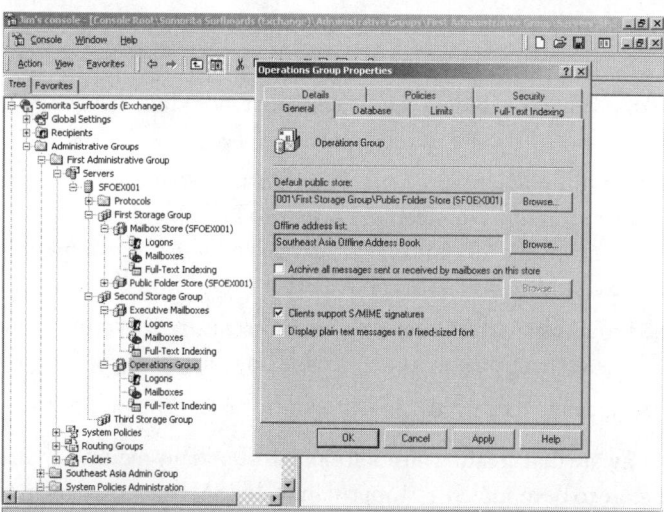

Properties that you assign to a particular mailbox store affect all of the mailboxes that are hosted on that particular store. Properties on the General property page include:

Property	Description
Default public store	If you have a dedicated public folder store for mailboxes that are using a particular store, don't forget to assign the default public folder store.
Offline address list	Assigning an offline address list if one other than the default will be used. Address lists must be created in the Recipients ➢ Offline Address Lists container. Offline address books can be assigned individually for a few users; OABs alone is not a good reason to create multiple mailbox stores.
Archive all messages sent or received by mailboxes on this store	This is the equivalent of the Exchange 5.5 message journaling feature, except that in Exchange 2000 this feature can be turned on or off for each mailbox store as opposed to for each server with Exchange 5.5.
Clients support S/MIME signatures	Specifies that this mailbox store will allow S/MIME signatures. If this check box is cleared, then the S/MIME signature is stripped from the message. This is turned on by default.
Display plain text messages in a fixed-sized font	Converts the font for plaintext messages to a fixed width font. This is turned off by default.

On the Database property page, you can specify the following configuration options:

Property	Description
Exchange database	Specifies the location of the rich-text store (EDB) database file.
Exchange streaming database	Specifies the location of the native content (STM) database file.
Maintenance interval	Specifies the interval during which online maintenance is performed.
Do not mount this store at start-up	Prevents this particular store from being mounted when the information store service is started.
This database can be overwritten by a restore	Prevents the information store from mounting the database if it detects that the store was restored from an offline restore. This setting has no effect on online restores.

Operations

PART 2

NOTE On a server that has many mailbox or public folder stores, try to stagger the online maintenance intervals of the individual stores so that they do not all occur simultaneously. The default is between 1 A.M. and 5 A.M. for all stores. But also be aware that none of the online maintenance intervals can intersect the backup of the store or any individual database. Once an online backup commences, any online maintenance that was occurring within the storage group is halted.

The Limits property page is by far the most useful of the lot. Figure 4.10 includes the defaults that I recommend for most organizations. The storage limits and deleted item retention can be overridden on a per-mailbox basis. Management of information resources is important, but storage limits need to be carefully thought out so that they provide the correct level of service for your users. An important goal of IT is to provide users with an adequate place for all the necessary data to be stored, not to prevent people from storing data. Carefully consider any limits you put in place to make sure they meet your business needs. Failing to apply limits has a cost associated with it (e.g., disk usage growing unchecked), but applying limits also has a cost (e.g., forcing users to delete data that they may need to do their jobs effectively). The question to ask yourself is, which cost is *least* costly for the entire company, not for the IT department.

Figure 4.10 Mailbox store Limits property page

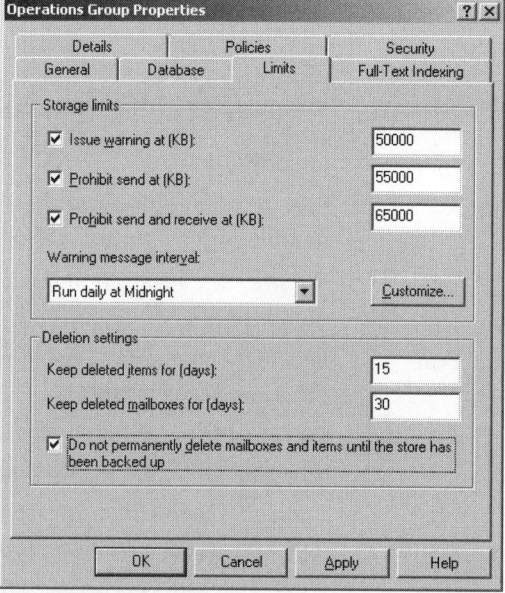

Limits that can be configured on the Limits property page include:

Property	Description
Issue warning at	Issues a warning stating that the mailbox has exceeded its storage limit.
Prohibit send at	Prohibits MAPI clients from sending or replying to messages if the mailbox exceeds this limit. This limit is not enforced for POP3 or IMAP4 clients. POP3 and IMAP4 clients' Send limits must be controlled through the SMTP virtual server they use to send mail.
Prohibit send and receive at	Causes the mailbox to reject messages until the user removes some of their messages.
Warning message interval	Specifies when a warning message is generated. The default is every night at midnight. If you use a custom schedule, set the interval to a single 15-minute period. Selecting an entire hour causes the warning to be generated every 15 minutes.
Keep deleted items for	Specifies how long (in days) to keep a mail message once the user has emptied it from their Deleted Items folder. The default is not to keep deleted items, but I recommend keeping them between 7 and 15 days. This may increase the size of your information store by as much as 10%, but it will reduce the likelihood of having to restore someone's important message that they accidentally deleted. Setting this value is a key component of your best practices.
Keep deleted mailboxes for	Specifies how long (in days) to keep a mailbox after the association between that mailbox and the Active Directory user account is deleted. The default is 30 days; during this time, the mailbox can be reconnected to any AD user account that does not have a mailbox.

Operations

PART 2

NOTE Message storage limits are in KB, not MB.

NOTE The default warning message that is issued when a mailbox is full cannot be customized easily. Most messages automatically generated by the Exchange 2000 are stored in the MDBSZ.DLL file. If you have a very specific need to customize these messages, contact Microsoft Consulting Services or Microsoft PSS.

The Full-Text Indexing property page is only active if a full-text index has been created for this particular mailbox store. Full-text indexing, which is discussed in more detail later in this chapter, can dramatically decrease the time it takes to search for a message in a public folder or mailbox folder. Settings on this property page include:

Property	Description
Update interval	Specifies how often to update the documents in the index.
Rebuild interval	Specifies how often to completely refresh the index. For a large information store, this process is very time consuming and processor intensive.

The Policies property page indicates which mailbox store policies affect each property page. The Details property page allows you to put in an administrative note.

Creating a Public Store   Creating a public folder store is similar to creating a mailbox store. However, prior to creating a public folder store, there must be an available public folder tree that can be assigned to this public store. Figure 4.11 shows a newly created public folder store called Web Folders Public Store that is associated with a public folder tree called Web Folders.

Figure 4.11   A newly created public folder store

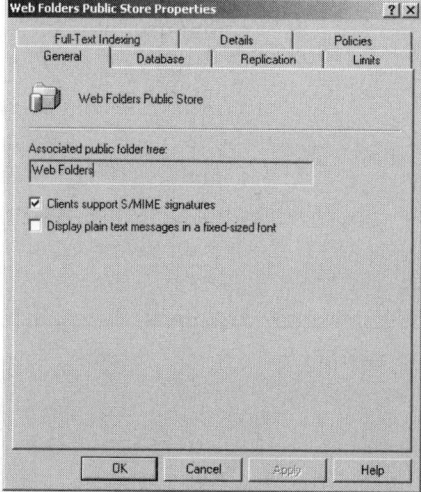

Options that can be set from the General, Full-Text Indexing, Database Policies, and Details property pages are the same as those for mailbox stores. However, unlike mailbox stores, public folder stores have no need for message archival, associated public folder stores, or offline address lists.

The Replication property page allows the following options to be configured:

Property	Description
Replication interval	Specifies the default replication interval for folders on this store. The default replication interval is set to Always Run. The always interval is specified in the Replication interval for always on this property page.
Replication interval for always	Specifies the replication interval used when Always Run is specified. The default is 15 minutes.
Replication message size limit	Specifies the message size limit for replication messages. Unless specified otherwise, the minimum size is 300KB. This specifies that messages smaller than 300KB will be batched and sent together.

NOTE The Replication Message Size limit is the minimum size of a replication message, not a maximum. See Microsoft Knowledge Base Q222833 for more information.

The Limits property page for a public folder store and the configuration options I recommend are shown in Figure 4.12. The storage, age limits, and deleted items limits can be overridden on a per-folder basis.

Options that can be configured from this property page include:

Property	Description
Issue warning at	Specifies the default maximum amount of storage folders on this store can take up before a warning limit message will be generated. This message is sent to the folder owners and the folder contacts. This limit can be overridden per folder.
Prohibit post at	Specifies the default maximum amount of storage folders on this store can take up before the folder will no longer accept new messages. This limit can be overridden per folder.

Operations

PART 2

Property	Description
Maximum item size	Specifies the largest message that will be accepted by the folders on this store. This limit can be overridden per folder.
Warning message interval	Specifies when the information store should generate warning messages for folders on this store that are over their quota.
Keep deleted items for	Specifies how long (in days) to keep deleted items and deleted folders before the disk space is reused. This limit can be overridden per folder.
Age limit for all folders in this store	Specifies the default maximum number of days a message will be kept. This is useful for transient data such as newsgroups and mailing lists. If you configure this setting for the entire public folder store, don't forget to configure the override settings for folders that need to keep their data longer than the default number of days such as Contact- and Calendar-type public folders.

Figure 4.12   Public folder store Limits property page and recommended values

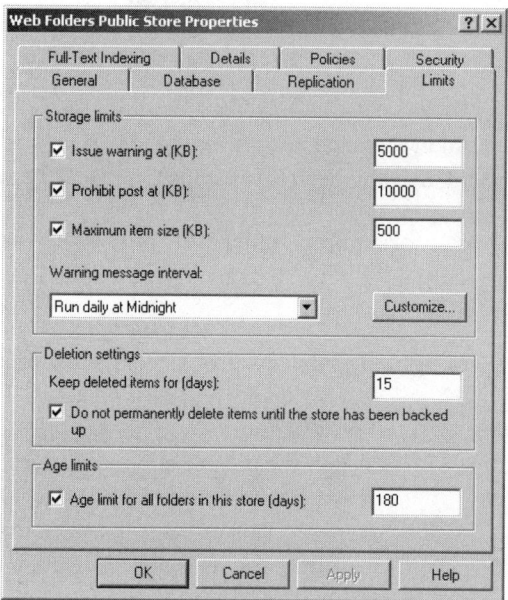

NOTE Public folders and public folder trees are discussed in more detail in Chapter 9.

Managing and Moving Stores

Once a mailbox or public store is created, there is generally not a lot of management that must be performed on the store itself. From a mailbox store's right-click menu, you can dismount (or mount) the store, or manage full-text indexing:

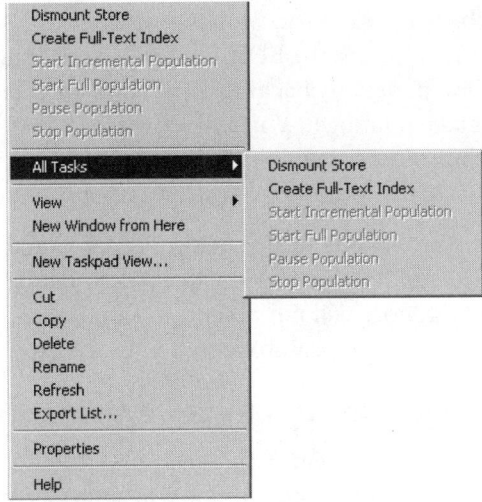

If you need to move a mailbox or public folder store's database files, you can do this from the Database property page of the store's properties. Simply click the browse button next to either the Exchange Database or Exchange Streaming Database selections and specify a new location for the files. Moving the database files will cause the store to be dismounted; users who are connected to this store will not be given any warning.

Deleting a Store   A store can be deleted if it is no longer in use. To delete a mailbox store, all mailboxes must be moved off of that store. If the Exchange Key Manager is using the store, you must also reconfigure the Key Manager to use another store. If there are any SMTP messages queued up in that particular store, they will be lost.

To delete a public folder store, the store must not contain the only copy of a public folder tree. Further, the store must not be the default public folder store (specified on per mailbox store). All public folders must be replicated to another public folder store first, and the public folder store you are deleting cannot be designated as the home server for any system folders. For information about rehoming public folders, see Microsoft Knowledge Base article Q288150.

WARNING   If you are going to remove a store, remove it while it is online. If you delete the database files while it is dismounted without first making sure that the database files are consistent, you may not be able to remount the other stores in the storage group.

Creating New Database Files   If you want to start over with new, empty database files, locate the directory that contains the EDB and STM files, dismount the database, delete the EDB and STM files (preferably backing them up to another location first!), and then right-click the store and mounting it. You will see the message "At least one of this store's database files is missing. Mounting the store will force the creation of an empty database. Do not take this action if you intend to restore an earlier backup." Select Yes to continue.

Though you will see some errors in the Event Viewer (9519 and 9547), new database files will be created. If you simply restart the information store, the "missing" databases will not be recreated, and the store will not mount. You must mount the store manually the first time in order for the missing databases to be re-created.

Accessing Storage through Exchange Installable File System

The Exchange Installable File System (ExIFS) was first introduced in Chapter 1, but now I want to delve in to more depth on the subject. When the information store service loads, it interfaces with the Exchange Installable File System (ExIFS) and creates an M: drive on the Exchange server. This drive is accessible only from the server console unless it is shared. Figure 4.13 shows Explorer on an Exchange server. Notice that the M: drive is available and that there is a folder in it called SOMORITA.NET.

The SOMORITA.NET name shown in Figure 4.13 is the default organization name, which is taken from the recipient policy's default policy. The SMTP domain that is checked as the default SMTP address is used in the M: drive. The Outlook Web Access virtual directories subsequently use this domain name; if the domain name is changed, the virtual directories are changed automatically.

Though the domain name says SOMORITA.NET, the only mailboxes that appear in the directory listing are the ones located on that specific server. The mailboxes are not sorted by storage group or mailbox store.

Figure 4.13   The M: drive supplied by the ExIFS

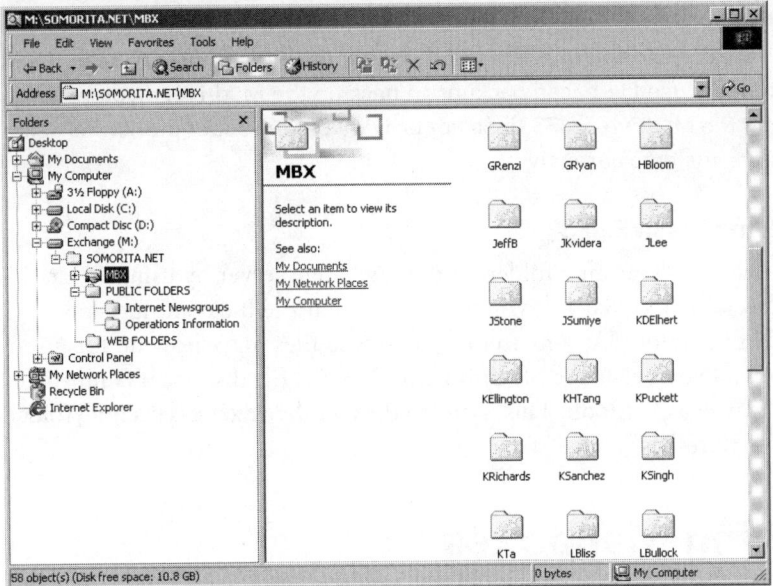

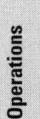

Notice also in Figure 4.13 that the M:\SOMORITA.NET\MBX folder is shared. In Exchange 2000 RTM, the shared folder symbol does not appear, and you have to re-create the shared folders each time the server reboots. This was fixed in Exchange 2000 SP1.

Figure 4.13 also shows the public folders that are on this server. The public folders that appear in the directory listing represent all of the public folder trees on this particular server.

Using Another Drive Letter

ExIFS can use a drive letter other than M:. The M: drive was probably picked either because it is easy to associate it with "mail" or "messaging," but it could be because some twisted person misses Microsoft Mail. (Though if the M: drive is in use when Exchange 2000 is installed, it will select the next letter available in the alphabet automatically.)

To change the drive letter, you must edit the Registry. Locate the following Registry key:

```
HKLM\SYSTEM\CurrentControlSet\Services\EXIFS\Parameters
```

Add a new value whose name is DriveLetter of a type REG_SZ. In the data field, enter the letter of the drive you want to use. Windows 2000 will need to be restarted for this change to take effect.

> ***WARNING*** I will mention this several times in this book, but it bears repeating. Never, never, *never* use file-based virus scanning software to scan the M: drive, and never use file-based backups to back up the M: drive. If you back up files using the M: drive, ExIFS does not provide the full set of properties necessary to restore the data correctly.

Phantom Files in ExIFS

If you delete a file from a folder on the Exchange server by using Outlook and immediately check the ExIFS drive, you may notice that the file continues to show up in the list of files in the folder. As a matter of fact, those files may show up for up to 30 minutes. However, if you delete the file through ExIFS, the file disappears immediately from both ExIFS as well as Outlook. This is due to the fact that ExIFS is caching folder information and only refreshes it once every 30 minutes.

Managing Mailboxes

If you are an administrator responsible for the health and well being of one or more Exchange servers, you probably spend a lot of your time worrying about mailboxes. Specifically, you probably worry about the evil that your users are plotting against your Exchange server. This evil may be in the form of a barrage of messages to a large distribution list, exceeding the size of their mailbox's allocated storage, or opening a message with a virus. Even worse still, you or one of your fellow administrators may be perpetuating the evil (by accidentally deleting a user account, for example).

Controlling Mailbox Storage

One of the most critical things that Exchange administrators must do is make sure that the amount of storage is not exceeded. This is essential to keeping the Exchange server available to all users. If a server runs out of disk space, the stores are dismounted.

Educating Users

As part of training for the Exchange system, users should be taught some important tasks about mailbox management, including:

- Message signatures are great, but don't go overboard with the graphics or too much text.
- Outlook HTML stationary makes a message look really spiffy, but it sure does increase the default size!

- Don't forget to clean up old messages in the Sent Items folder.

- Empty the Deleted Items folder periodically or configure Outlook to automatically clean it up.

- Don't send message attachments to internal distribution lists; send shortcuts to the attachment instead.

- Use WinZip or other compression software to compress attachments before sending them outside of the organization.

- Teach users never to create rules that will forward messages outside of the organization and possibly create a message loop. Accidentally setting up a message loop is far easier to do than you might think.

- Do not use the company e-mail address when filling out *any* form on the Internet.

- How to recognize spam, virus hoaxes, and chain letters and give them orders not to forward such things.

> **NOTE** I know a number of people who have made good use of message signatures, including one woman whose signature is 20 lines! Another fellow puts his picture into his signature, and still others include their company or departmental logo. These are all fine, but users should be careful just how big the signature or graphics images become. In most cases, a simple message with a picture in it will go from 1KB to 30KB or more once the picture is included!

Assigning Storage Limits

You can assign one of three storage limits that will affect mailboxes in one of three places. Limits can be assigned through a mailbox system policy, directly on each mailbox store, or individually on each mailbox. Settings that are applied directly to the mailbox will override mailbox store policies or storage limits applied to the mailbox store. To apply individual mailbox storage limits, on the Exchange General property page click the Storage Limits button; the Storage Limits box opens (shown in Figure 4.14). Applying mailbox system policies or storage limits to a mailbox store is discussed earlier in this chapter.

All storage limits are configured in KB; this is a common point of confusion as administrators often enter 50 assuming they're entering a limit of 50MB. The Issue Warning At limit issues a storage warning to the user if they exceed their allocated storage. This does not prevent the user from sending or receiving mail.

Figure 4.14 Storage limits per user

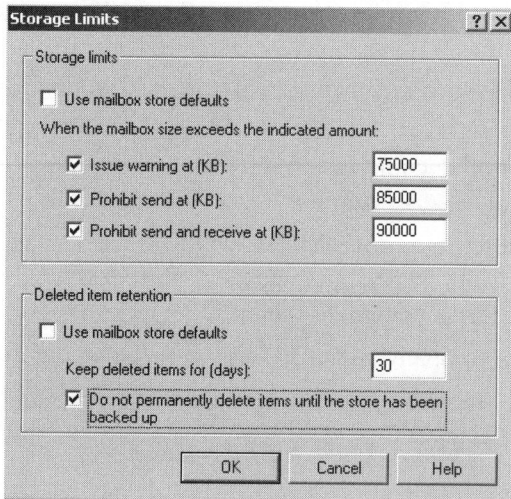

The Prohibit Send At limit prevents the user from sending or replying to messages until they delete enough messages to bring the mailbox storage space below the Prohibit Send At limit. This limit only applies to MAPI and HTTP clients.

The Prohibit Send And Receive At limit causes the mailbox to reject mail when the limit is exceeded. I highly recommend setting this limit, even if it is configured to a really high amount like 500MB. This will prevent a single mailbox from consuming massive amounts of disk space and possibly forcing the server to shut down.

Exchange@Work: Message Looping Forces Server Shutdown

Company WYZ was hesitant about placing storage limits on their Exchange mailboxes. The company managers did not want to "restrain" their users by imposing limits, even if that limit was particularly high. They set limits anyway, and sure enough, shortly after they brought Exchange online and migrated their mailboxes, a user decided that he wanted to forward all of his mail to his ISP's mailbox. Just to make sure he did not miss anything, he also forwarded all of his mail on his ISP mailbox to his Exchange mailbox.

The result? You guessed it. The first message that came along created a looping message. In two days, the Exchange server's disk reached capacity and shut down.

Exchange@Work: Message Looping Forces Server Shutdown *(continued)*

Solving this problem actually took several hours because the administrators had to locate the mailbox, delete all of the messages, and run an offline compaction of the mailbox store.

Preventing the problem would have been much simpler. WYZ could have applied a Prohibit Send And Receive At limit on the mailbox store. Even a very high limit (like 500MB) would have prevented this problem from happening. The other option that the administrators had was to configure the SMTP Connector to prevent auto-replies and auto-forwards to the Internet.

Reporting on Users Who Have Exceeded Storage Limits

Viewing the users who have exceeded their storage limits is simple. Locate the mailbox store in Exchange System Manager and select the Mailboxes folder. Figure 4.15 shows a slightly modified view of the mailboxes on this mailbox store; when creating this view, I included the Storage Limits column (View ➤ Choose Columns), which will allow me to quickly zero in on the users who are either over their limit or have disabled mailboxes.

Figure 4.15   Mailbox storage report

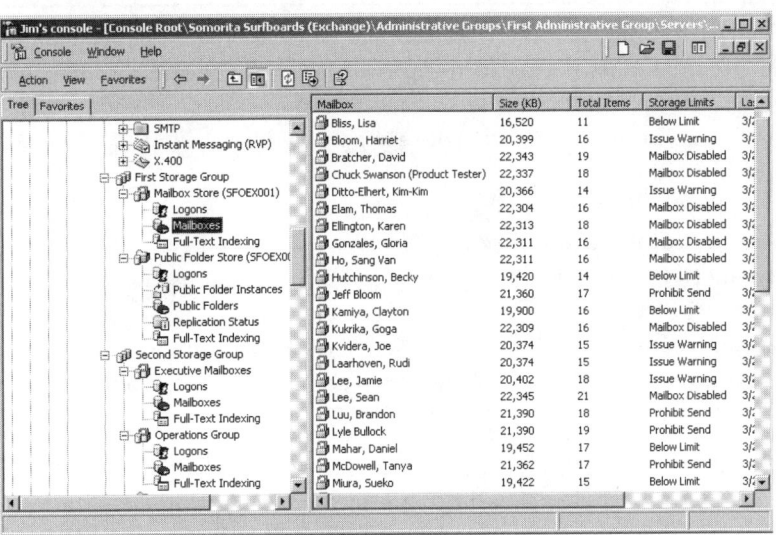

If the Storage Limits column is displayed, you will see one of four possible status lists:

- Below Limit indicates that no limits have been exceeded.
- Issue Warning indicates that the mailbox has exceeded the Issue Warning At limit.
- Prohibit Send indicates that the mailbox has exceeded the Prohibit Send At limit.
- Mailbox Disabled indicates that the mailbox has exceeded the Prohibit Send And Receive At limit.

You can save the listing in Figure 4.15 by right-clicking the Mailboxes container and selecting Export List. You can export the list to a tab-separated or comma-separated value file, which can be imported into Microsoft Excel.

You can also use the Windows NT Event Viewer to retrieve a list of mailboxes that have exceeded their limits. You can do this by locating the Exchange server in Exchange System Manager and displaying the server's properties. Select the Diagnostics Logging property page, highlight Storage Limits, and select a logging level of Maximum. When the mailbox store issues storage warnings to users, three events will be logged:

- Event ID 1077 will list the mailboxes that are over their Issue Warning At limit.
- Event ID 1078 will list the mailboxes that are over their Prohibit Send At limit.
- Event ID 1218 will list the mailboxes that are over their Prohibit Send And Receive At limit.

TIP   Make sure that you are reviewing the event logs regularly. Often Warning and Error messages get lost in the flurry of daily activity, and important events get overwritten or pushed out of the log. You can purchase third-party event log management software, or you can write a simple script that exports important events and mails them to you.

Why Aren't Storage Limits Taking Effect?   When Exchange 2000 was first released, I was convinced that storage limits were not working, because I would create a storage limit for a mailbox or an entire mailbox store, and it would not take effect. This is because mailbox and store limits are stored in Active Directory, and we must wait for Active Directory to replicate to the Exchange server's configuration domain controller.

Additionally, the information store only refreshes these limits (re-reads them) once every hour. So the change could appear to take effect very quickly, or it could take over an hour. You can adjust this by changing the frequency at which the information store updates the individual user mailbox limits and the mailbox store or public store limits. To do either, start by locating the HKLM\SYSTEM\CurrentControlSet\Services\MSExchangeIS\ ParametersSystem Registry key. To change the mailbox store or public store quota refresh times, add a new value of type REG_DWORD called `Reread IS Quotas Interval`, and specify a value in seconds (don't forget to click the Decimal button before entering a value, otherwise your value will be in hexadecimal). To change the interval for individual mailbox storage quota limits, add a new value of type REG_DWORD called `Reread Logon Quotas Interval`, and specify a value in seconds (again, don't forget to change the radio button to seconds).

Cleaning Mailboxes

Let's face it, sometimes even storage limits will not force a user to clean up their mailbox. Though enforcing mailbox storage limits is the most effective step toward keeping your server's disk space in check, reducing backup times, and reducing the clutter in mailboxes and folders, you may still be forced to do some house cleaning.

> **NOTE** If you right-click any mailbox store's Mailboxes folder, one of the menu options is Run Cleanup Agent. This menu choice does *not* have anything to do with cleaning up messages in mailboxes; it is used if you want to view immediately any mailboxes that have been deleted.

Using Mailbox Manager

The Exchange 2000 Mailbox Manager feature can trace some of its roots to Exchange Server 4 (the Clean Mailbox feature found in Exchange Administrator) and the BackOffice Resource Kit (the Mailbox Cleanup Agent). These two features were upgraded and improved over the years. Surprisingly, Exchange 2000 did not ship with any mailbox-cleanup features at all; the Mailbox Manager is only available once you have installed Exchange 2000 SP1. Following are some of the Mailbox Manager features:

- Allows you to archive messages based on folder, message age, and/or message size.

- Allows you to specify whether the messages are deleted immediately, moved to the Deleted Items folder, or moved to a special folder hierarchy called System Cleanup folders. Moving the messages to the System Cleanup folders allows users to recover messages easily that they may not want deleted.

- Sends a report to the user and the administrator regarding messages that are cleaned.

- Allows you to specify mailboxes to be managed by using the scope of existing recipient policies, or you can create your own recipient policies.

- Allows you to exclude certain types of messages, such as Contact objects.

Configuring Mailbox Manager

Configuring Mailbox Manager involves two steps. A recipient policy must be created that includes Mailbox Manager settings, and each server on which you want to the policy to be executed must be configured. You must configure a recipient policy that includes the user's mailboxes that will be managed by Mailbox Manager.

Configuring a Mailbox Manager Recipient Policy   You define the mailboxes that will be affected by Mailbox Manager using recipient policies, which cover the scope of users the policy will affect. While not a requirement, I recommend that you keep the number of recipient policies to a minimum so that they are not terribly complicated. You can either add the Mailbox Manager Settings (Policy) property tab (shown in Figure 4.16) to an existing recipient policy, or you can create a new policy that contains only the Mailbox Manager Settings (Policy) tab. To add the property page to an existing recipient policy, right-click the policy, choose Change Property Pages, select the Mailbox Managers Settings check box, and click OK.

Figure 4.16   Mailbox Manager Settings property tab

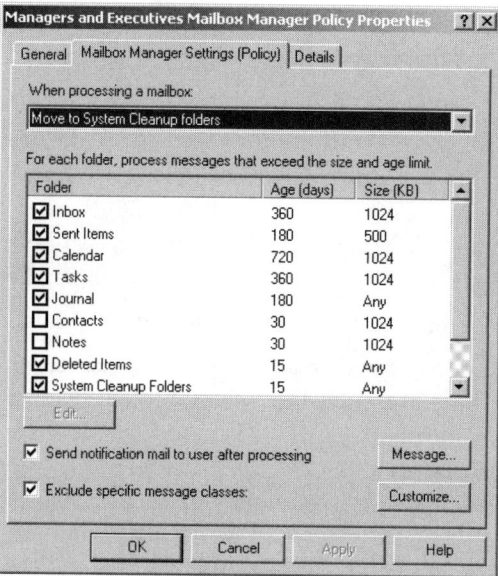

On the Mailbox Manager Settings (Policy) property page, the When Processing A Mailbox drop-down list box has four choices of what the Mailbox Manager should do when it processes mailboxes:

Generate report only   Sends an e-mail message to the user and informs them of how many messages are over the limit.

Move to Deleted Items folder   Moves any messages that meet the age or size limits to the Deleted Items folder. If users are emptying their Deleted Items folders frequently (such as when they exit Outlook), they may empty the folder and not realize that they have purged a recently deleted message.

Move to System Cleanup folders   Moves any messages or items to a corresponding folder in the mailbox called System Cleanup. For example, if messages in the Inbox are ready to be deleted, they will be moved to the System Cleanup folder \Inbox folder. Once the items in the System Cleanup folder are eligible for deletion, they will be permanently deleted. When the Mailbox Manager runs, messages are moved to the System Cleanup folder (if selected to be used when processing a mailbox). The messages are kept there until the age limit is reached for that folder structure, after which the messages will be *permanently* deleted.

Delete Immediately   Deletes any messages that are eligible for processing.

I recommend using the Move To System Cleanup Folders option; this will allow users to recover a message that they might still want to keep by browsing the folders under the System Cleanup folder. These folders under System Cleanup will match the folder names from the mailbox from which mail messages were deleted.

When you configure the Mailbox Manager Settings (Policy) property page, you must specify the maximum age limit and the maximum message size. For example, if you click the Edit box for the Sent Items folder and specify an age limit of 180 days and a message size of 500KB (as shown in Figure 4.17), only messages larger than 500KB *and* older than 180 days will be processed. If you want all messages to be processed, clear the Message Size check box. Conversely, you can also clear the Age Limits box and delete *any* message over the specified size.

Figure 4.17   Folder Retention Settings dialog box

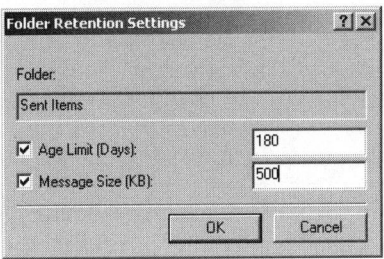

The age limit for a message is calculated by making sure that all three of the message's dates (message submission, message received, and message modified) indicate the message is at least as old as the age limit.

Operations

PART 2

NOTE When Mailbox Manager scans a message's age threshold, the submission, received, and modified dates must all be older than the age threshold; otherwise the message will not qualify for deletion.

When you set up a policy for managing mailboxes, simplicity is important. While you may want to set up several policies that affect different users, try to keep the number of policies at a minimum. Here is a list of suggestions for creating Mailbox Manager policies:

- The default setting for all folders is an age limit of 30 days and a minimum message size of 1024KB. This means that only messages older than 30 days *and* larger than 1024KB will be processed.

- Uncheck the option to process Contacts and Notes. Further, to ensure that these types of messages are not processed, exclude those message classes.

- Configure the Mailbox Manager to deliver a report to the user when mailbox cleanup has occurred. Do this by clicking the Send Notification Mail To User After Processing check box. Customize this report by clicking the Message button; make sure that you click the Insert The Number Of Messages Processed button on the Notification Message dialog box.

Each Mailbox Manager policy that you create allows you to exclude certain types of messages. Clicking the Exclude Specific Message Classes check box enables the Customize button, which allows you to enter message classes that will be excluded by this policy. Table 4.6 includes some of the common message classes you will encounter. If you have created any of your own custom forms, you will need to determine what the message class is for that form.

Table 4.6 Message Classes

Message Class	Description
IPM.Note	E-mail message (X.400 P2/P22 message)
IPM.Replication	Public folder replication message
IPM.Note.DRA	Exchange 5.5 directory replication message
IPM.Appointment	Calendar entry or meeting request
IPM.Contact	Contact item

Table 4.6   Message Classes *(continued)*

Message Class	Description
IPM.Post	Public folder posting
IPM.Task	Task entry
IPM.DistList	Distribution list entry in a Contact folder
IPM.Activity	Message Journaling entry
IPM.StickyNote	Notes folder note entry
Report.IPM.Note.IPNRN	Read recipient or recipient notification
Report IPM.Note.NPNNRN	Non-read recipient
IPM.Note.P772	Military message (DMS* X.400 P772 message)
Report.IPM.Note.P772.IPNRN	Military message read recipient
Report IPM.Note.P772.IPNNRN	Military message non-read recipient
IPM.Note.MSP	Military message (DMS P42 encrypted - MSP v3)
IPM.Note.MSP.Signed	Military message (DMS P42 signed and encrypted - MSP v3)
IPM.Note.MSP.IPNRN	Military message signed recipient notification
IPM.Note.MSP4	Military message (DMS P42 encrypted - MSP v4)
IPM.Note.MSP4.Signed	Military message (DMS P42 signed and encrypted - MSP v4)
IPM.Note.MSP4.IPNRN	Military message signed recipient notification (MSP v4)

*DMS = United States Department of Defense's Defense Messaging System

Enabling Mailbox Manager on a Server   Once you have configured a Mailbox Manager policy for your organization, you still must configure each server to run the Mailbox Manager process. Once Exchange 2000 SP1 is installed on an Exchange server, you will notice an additional property page, called Mailbox Management, on each server's properties (see Figure 4.18).

Figure 4.18   Mailbox Management properties tab

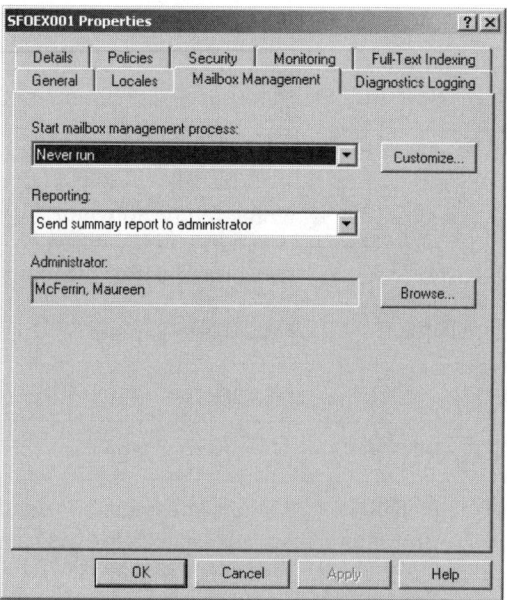

From each server, you must configure the schedule for which server will run the Mailbox Manager process, the reporting options, and the Mailbox Manager administrator for that server.

The most important option on the Mailbox Management property page is the Start Mailbox Management Process drop-down list box. You can select to start the process Saturday at midnight, Sunday at midnight, on a custom schedule, or never. I recommend running the process no more than once a week, yet you should make sure that it runs consistently so that users always knows when to expect that their mailboxes will be processed. Further, the cleanup process will cause a performance hit, so you should schedule it to run during off-hours.

The Use Custom Schedule option in the drop-down list box allows you to specify exactly when you want the mailbox management process to run. Be *very* careful when selecting a custom schedule, since the Customize button allows you to select the time interval in 15-minute intervals.

WARNING If you select an entire hour, the mailbox management process will run four times that hour! This also means that the users will get four mail messages an hour telling them that their mailbox was processed by the Mailbox Manager.

NOTE You can also run the Mailbox Manager manually by right-clicking the Exchange server in Exchange System Manager and choosing Start Mailbox Management Process.

Also on the Mailbox Management property tab of the Exchange server's properties, you will find the Reporting drop-down list box and the Administrator box. The Administrator box allows you to specify which mailbox the reports are delivered to once the processing. The Reporting drop-down list box allows you to specify the following reporting options:

Send summary report to administrator~MSSends a single mail message to the administrator designated in the Administrator box. This reporting option is my choice. This report contains a summary of information processed and looks like this:

```
The Microsoft Exchange Server Mailbox Manager has completed
processing mailboxes
Started at:          Tuesday, December 25 2001 10:23:49 AM
Completed at:        Tuesday, December 25, 2001 10:45:09 AM
Mailboxes processed:  148
Messages moved:       851
Size of moved messages:   1301.00 KB
Deleted messages:         622
Size of deleted messages: 8592.00 KB
```

Send detail report to administrator   Sends the same information as the summary report, but also includes a plaintext attachment that has the mailbox names and folder names of each mailbox processed, including the number (and size) of messages that were processed in a single folder. In my opinion, this report generates more information than is really worth keeping.

None   Generates no report for the administrator.

> **TIP** If you are debugging problems with Mailbox Manager policies and you cannot figure out which policy affects a specific user, turn on the Send Detail Report To Administrator option. In the text file that is attached to the message, it includes the name of the Mailbox Manager policy for which this report is being generated.

Defining Mailbox Manager Scopes   When you are defining Mailbox Manager scopes, you use the filter rules found on the General property page to define to which mailboxes the policy applies. In a small organization, you may actually be able to get away with a single Mailbox Manager policy that affects all users.

In most organizations, however, I usually end up with *special* users who are not constrained by the normal limits that I have to place on the bulk of the user community. I'll just call these folks VIPs, for lack of a more specific term. VIPs require special storage limits that allow them to store more data on the server and to have large message size limits. These are the same users for whom you will have to put in exceptions in the Mailbox Manager policies, since they will probably be allowed to have a longer message lifetime than the typical user.

The simplest way to do this is to create an additional mailbox store on the server (called VIP Mailboxes, for example) and move the VIPs' mailboxes to the additional mailbox store. When defining Mailbox Manager policies, use the mailbox store as the filter criteria for the policy. You can easily specify this on the General property page of the policy by clicking the Modify button, selecting the Storage property page of the Find Exchange Recipients dialog box, and choosing the mailboxes that you want this policy to affect.

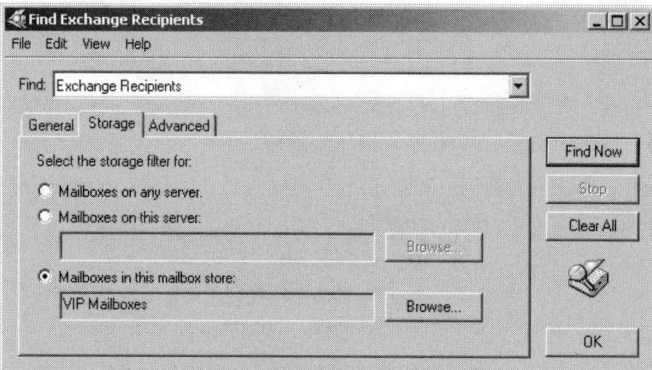

Mailbox Manager Best Practices Here are some best practices that I have found when using Mailbox Manager:

- Establish a schedule on which mailbox cleanup is performed, and stick with it. The user community will not be happy with automatic cleanup of their mailboxes, but if it is performed consistently, they will at least know when to expect it.

- Keep the policies as simple as possible; define only the policies that you need. If a mailbox is affected by more than one policy, then the highest policy (by priority) in the list will be the one that affects that mailbox.

- Clearly define to your user community what the criteria for cleanup actually is.

Automatic Message Archival

Outlook provides a tool called AutoArchive, which automatically moves messages from a server-based mailbox to a PST file. This feature is enabled at each Outlook client, or you can create a system policy to enable it for all of your users.

> **WARNING** Many Exchange administrators will tell you that PST = BAD. If information is important enough to be kept, it is important enough to be kept on the Exchange server where it can be managed and backed up. PSTs are corrupted easily, and it's often difficult to recover data from them once they're corrupted. A PST file that is nearing 2GB in size is a recipe for disaster (and corruption). I recommend adding more Exchange servers, more disk space, additional stores, and faster backup systems to a PST file in lieu of asking users to archive data that they may need to use in the future.

AutoArchive is enabled slightly differently for Outlook 97, 98, 2000 and 2002, but the basic idea is the same. It has to be enabled prior to configuring the folders for automatic archiving. To enable AutoArchive, choose Tools ➢ Options ➢ Advanced ➢ AutoArchive; the AutoArchive dialog box shown in Figure 4.19 appears.

Figure 4.19 The Outlook AutoArchive dialog box

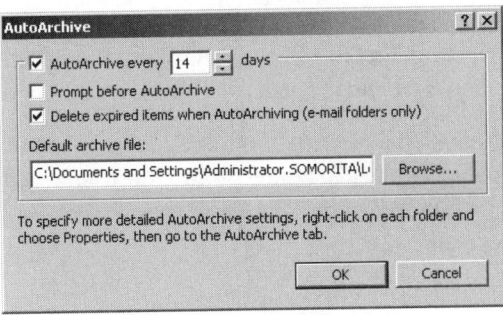

Operations

PART 2

From this dialog box, you control how often AutoArchive will run (the default is every 14 days), whether the user is prompted to run AutoArchive, if items that are expired can be deleted, and the name of the default PST file. The directory that the `Archive.pst` file is placed in appears by default. Some administrators specify a path on the local hard disk (in the user's profile directory) while others specify the user's home directory on a shared file server.

Once you have enabled automatic archiving for a mailbox, you should set the properties for each folder that you want AutoArchive to process. Figure 4.20 shows the AutoArchive properties for my Calendar folder.

Figure 4.20 The Calendar folder's AutoArchive properties

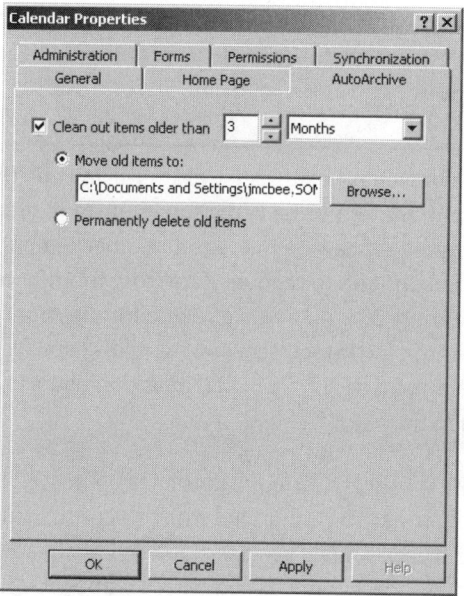

Figure 4.20 shows that all items older than three months will be moved to the archive file. The archive file path is too long to be entirely visible in the text box, but the default is to store it in the user's profile directory (in the `Application Data\Outlook` folder). The alternative to archive old calendar entries is to delete them permanently.

Some of the default folders in your mailbox have default AutoArchive properties already set up; these are listed in Table 4.7. Folders that your users create themselves do not have AutoArchive defaults. Once automatic archiving is enabled, folders will adhere to their individual archiving properties.

Table 4.7 Standard Outlook 2000 Folders and Their Default AutoArchive Actions

Folder Name	AutoArchive Enabled?	Default Action
Calendar	Y	Archives items older than six months.
Contacts*	N	
Deleted Items	Y	Archives items older than three months.
Drafts	N	
Inbox	N	
Journal	Y	Archives items older than three months.
Notes	N	
Outbox	N	
Sent Items	Y	Archives items older than three months.
Tasks	Y	Archives items older than three months.

*Contacts folders do not have the archive option.

Message items that are moved to an archive file are recoverable from the Deleted Item cache if you have enabled the `DumpsterAlwaysOn` Registry key. This key is discussed in Chapter 7 and in Microsoft KB article Q246153.

Local Delivery

Outlook clients do have the option of automatically pulling down all messages to a PST file as soon as the messages are delivered to their mailboxes on the server. After pulling the message off the server, the client deletes it from the server. This dramatically reduces the amount of storage that the server requires. Though I do not personally like storing active messages this way, I know administrators who use this feature and find it to be quite acceptable.

This feature is enabled in the messaging profile. From Outlook, choose Tools ➢ Services; choose Control Panel ➢ Mail (or Mail And Fax). Create a PST file if it has not previously been created to store the messages. Select the Delivery tab, and in the Deliver New Mail To The Following Location drop-down box, select the personal folder name to which you want the messages delivered.

> **NOTE** See Chapter 1 for more information about using PST files as the primary message storage mechanism.

ExMerge

One of my favorite utilities of the last century is ExMerge. Though it was introduced several years ago, it has only recently entered widespread use with a lot of administrators. ExMerge (short for Exchange Merge) is found on the Exchange 2000 CD-ROM in the \Support\Utils\I386\Exmerge directory and in the same directory on with Exchange 2000 SP1. I recommend using the latest version you can find. The features and uses of this program are too numerous to mention, but following are a few of the common uses for this utility:

- Archiving some or all of a user's mailbox to a PST file.

- Making backup copies of a user's mailbox in lieu of using a brick-level backup (discussed in Chapter 7).

- Extracting certain messages based on subject or attachment from selected mailboxes on the server. This is useful for removing viruses from the mailbox stores, but it should not be used as your primary virus-protection mechanism.

- Moving mailbox data from one Exchange organization or administrative group to another.

> **TIP** In the directory with ExMerge is a detailed, informative 70-page document on the programExMerge in the same directory you find the ExMerge program.

For this chapter, we are concerned only with extracting messages from mailboxes for the purposes of archival. ExMerge may be a last resort if you are using it solely for archival purposes and you have not been able to convince your users to archive of their own accord. Also, you will probably need management support to open and clean up your users' mailboxes.

To install the ExMerge program, copy the executable program into the \Exchsrvr\Bin directory. Before you can access any mailbox, you will need the Full mailbox access permission. (Mailbox and administrative security are discussed in Chapter 11.) At this point, I will assume that you have the correct permissions to access the necessary mailboxes.

WARNING Earlier versions of ExMerge do not work with Exchange 2000, so make sure you have the latest version. The Exchange 2000 version of ExMerge does not work on Windows NT 4 computers, only on Windows 2000 computers. The PST files that are created are interoperable between all versions of Exchange.

When you run ExMerge, keep in mind that this is a powerful and versatile program. It has many uses, and not all the options you will see may be useful for purposes of message archival. The following steps illustrate how you can archive a selected group of mailboxes:

1. Run ExMerge to start the ExMerge Wizard, and click Next to move past the introduction screen.

2. Select the Extract Or Import (Two Step Procedure) radio button and click Next. (We don't actually do the second step in this example, since we are only concerned with extracting the mailbox data.)

3. Choose Step 1: Extract Data From An Exchange Server Mailbox and click Next.

4. Specify the name of the Exchange server and optionally the name of a nearby Windows 2000 domain controller. Then click the Options button.

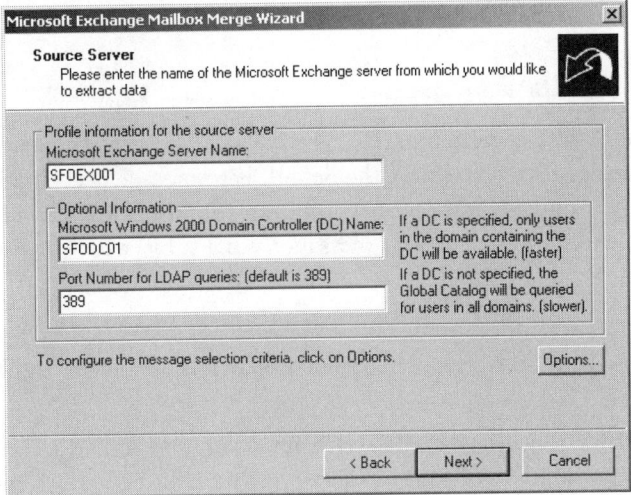

5. On the Data property tab, choose the User Messages And Folders radio button only. For this example, these are the only items we are interested in archiving.

6. Click the Import Procedure property tab and choose the Archive Data To Target Store radio button. The target store in this case is the PST file that will be created.

7. Click the Folders property tab. From this tab you can specify which folders to ignore or process. You can also specify whether or not to process subfolders. Notice below that I am excluding Calendar and Contacts since I probably don't want to archive these folders. If you click the Modify button, you can add other standard folders or enter custom folder names.

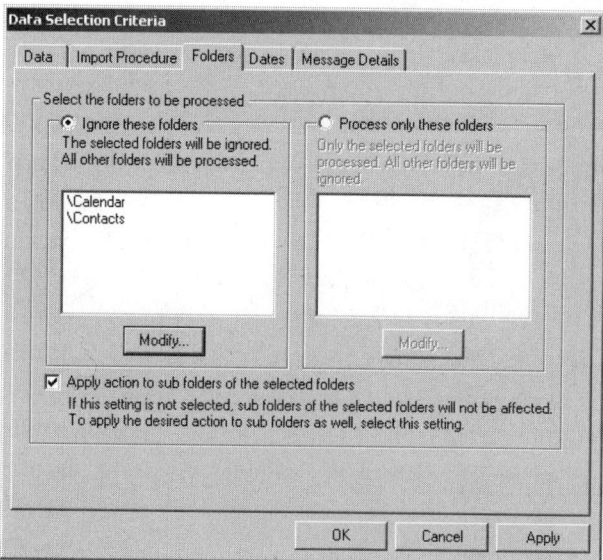

8. Click the Dates property tab. Here you will be able to select a date range for archival. If you don't specify anything, the default is to include everything! The Message Details tab is not relevant to message archival, but is interesting to know about in case you ever need to extract a message with a subject such as ILOVEYOU from all of your users.

9. Click OK to exit the Options box, and then click Next.

10. Select the mailbox store(s) from which you are going to be archiving messages and click Next.

11. Scroll through the list of mailboxes from which you will be archiving messages. You can select more than one mailbox by pressing Shift or Ctrl. When you are finished, click Next.

12. Select the default locale to specify which language should be used if a mailbox is being accessed for the first time. This controls which language the default folders are created in. While this is irrelevant for archival, you are still required to select it. When you are finished, click Next.

13. Specify the folder name in which the PST files will be created and click Next. On the Save Settings screen, you can specify if you want to save your configuration files for use later.

14. Click Next to start ExMerge.

When the ExMerge process is finished, you may wish to consult the ExMerge.log file that is created; ExMerge appends to this file after each processing run. You can find this file in the root of the C: drive. The PST files that are created are named using the user's Exchange alias.

NOTE The PST file that ExMerge creates often takes up far more disk space than the mailbox took before it was archived. This is a normal, expected behavior.

Exchange@Work: That Pesky Deleted Items Folder!

I recently monitored a customer's Deleted Items cache size using the Windows NT Performance Monitor (MSExchangeIS Mailbox object and the Total Size Of Recoverable Items counter). Their deleted item retention time was set to 30 days. I was quite surprised that a server supporting nearly 100 mailboxes would have a deleted items cache size of only about 50MB. The priv1.edb and priv1.stm files combined were nearly 3GB in size.

On a hunch, I sent an e-mail message asking that everyone choose Empty "Deleted Items" Folder from their Tools menu in Outlook. Within a few hours, the Deleted Items cache size had grown to nearly 400MB! Why did this happen? Users were diligent about keeping their mailboxes clean, but they were not emptying their Deleted Items folders.

The Deleted Items folder can be emptied manually (from the Tools menu) or automatically each time a user exits Outlook. To automatically empty the Deleted Items folder, from Outlook, choose Tools ➢ Options ➢ Other and click the Empty The Deleted Items Folder Upon Exiting button. This feature can also be turned on centrally through an Active Directory Group Policy Object.

Outlook Web Access users will have to click the Empty Deleted Items Folder icon next to the Delete icon on the OWA toolbar.

If you want to force the deletion of mail from mailboxes yourself, you can create a Mailbox Manager policy that purges only the Deleted Items folder. Once created, you can right-click the server name and choose Start Mailbox Management Process to clean up the Deleted Items folder immediately.

Operations

PART 2

Moving Mailboxes

Active Directory Users And Computers allows you to move mailboxes from one mailbox store to another. Simply select the user accounts for which you wish to move the mailboxes, right-click, and choose Exchange Tasks ➢ Move Mailboxes. Exchange 5.5 would only let you move mailboxes between servers in your own site, but now you can move mailboxes to any server to which you have connectivity and the appropriate administrative group permissions, whether the server is in your own administrative group or not. You will need the Exchange Administrator role to the administrative groups in which the source and destination stores are located. When moving mailboxes between servers, I recommend selecting only a few mailboxes (no more than 50) at a time. On a local area network, you will probably experience between 500MB and 1GB per hour of data transfer rates.

> **NOTE** When moving mailboxes to other servers, make sure that the transaction log disk does not fill up. To prevent this, you may want to run a full backup of the storage group periodically.

When you try to move mailboxes between Exchange 2000 servers, you may experience a couple of weird things. First, you may receive an error message in the application event log indicating that the attribute msExchUserAccountControl object could not be read. This attribute is required in Active Directory, but it might not be present if the server had recently been updated from Exchange 5.5. To make sure that this value is present and correct, using Exchange System Manager, force the RUS for the domain that contains the mailbox having the problem to perform a rebuild (not an update). See Microsoft KB article Q281607 for more information.

Second, mail might get caught in a loop or get lost when mailboxes are being moved. If you have to move more than a few mailboxes, consider pausing the SMTP service while you make the move.

Mailboxes that are moved to another store on the same server may take 15 minutes or more before users can access them. The information store caches the names of the mailboxes that are local to that store in a cache called MBI. The other option is to stop and restart the information store. If you are still running Exchange 2000 without the SP1 fixes, this interval could be up to two hours.

Moving Mailboxes and Servers between Administrative Groups

The fact that Exchange 2000 allows you to move mailboxes between mailbox stores in administrative groups allows you to rebuild your organization more easily. This is especially useful if you are unhappy with the site placement of your Exchange 5.5 servers. You can create new administrative groups with newly installed servers and move mailboxes to them. This brings up a question that I am asked quite frequently: "Can I move a server between administrative groups?"

Administrative groups are much like Exchange 5.5 sites; indeed, each mail-enabled object includes an attribute called legacyExchangeDN, which looks like an Exchange 5.5 site name, but maps to the object's Exchange administrative group. Each mailbox store and public folder store uses this legacy DN as well.

Active Directory Sites And Services is an Active Directory utility that moves the server object to a new container in Active Directory. However, it is not aware of Exchange 2000 objects, and it will *not* make all of the necessary changes to other objects in Active Directory or the stores. While this may appear to work, you run the risk of stores not being mounted and users not being able to access their mailboxes. Further, once you have made this change, moving the server back to the original administrative group may only cause further problems.

In all Microsoft technical documents and courseware, you are told that moving Exchange 2000 servers between administrative groups is not supported. However, some adventurous souls have found that you *can* move a server between one administrative group and another using the ADSS console. Microsoft PSS is aware that you can use ADSS to move the server, but they do not support its use. Don't expect much more than sympathy from them if you toast your server doing this. In the future, Exchange System Manager may be updated to perform this task, but until such time please do not try to use ADSS to move servers between administrative groups.

Controlling Mail-Enabled Groups

What is the most efficient way for a user to fill up the mailbox stores? Send a large message to the large mail-enabled group. Granted, if you have single mailbox store, the message is only stored a single time (single instance storage). But before the space in the information store can be reused, each recipient of that message must delete the message, *and* the sender must delete the message from their Sent Items folder.

While both of these suggestions were mentioned in Chapter 2, they are important enough that they bear repeating here. Mail-enabled groups with more than 100 members should have delivery restrictions placed on them. Figure 4.21 shows the Exchange General property page of the Singapore Users group. The maximum message size that can be sent to this list is 100KB. Only Singapore Users members, Asia Managers members, or user Minh Nguyen can address a message to this list.

Figure 4.21   Singapore Users mail-enabled group

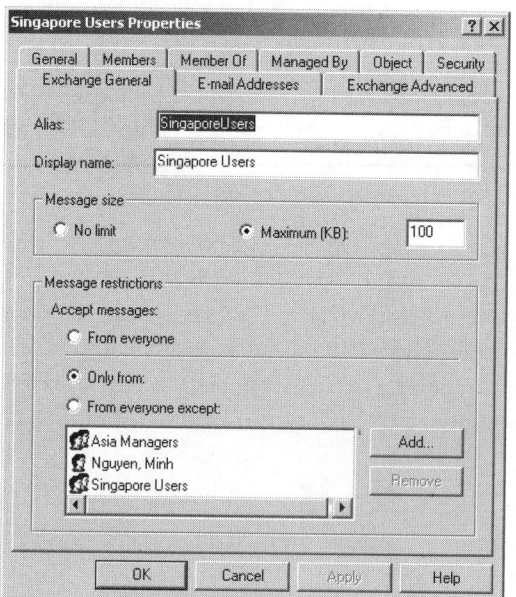

Restricting mail-enabled group usage will help prevent abuses of the mail system when someone decides to send a message selling their used car. Restricting who can use a mail-enabled group does not prevent them from selecting the entire global address list (GAL), but it does make it a little more difficult to send to a large number of mailboxes.

> **TIP** Users should be taught the difference between Reply and Reply To All! Microsoft PSS describes a problem that they call "Bedlam" in which someone sends a message (possibly a junk mail message) to a very large distribution list; inevitably, several people on the list select Reply To All with a message that says "I agree," "Leave me alone," or something similar. All these Reply To All messages also have to be processed by the SMTP message routing engine, which quickly becomes bogged down, processing nothing but these messages.

Limiting the Number of Recipients and Message Size

Now, you and I both know that users are not inherently evil—they may be uninformed, poorly trained, or at odds with practices that enhance productivity, but they're not evil. However, sometimes the devil does get the better of them, like when they fill up mailbox stores by selecting and sending messages to large numbers of users or by sending large messages. Two additional restrictions you can place on your user community involve the maximum message size they can send and the maximum number of recipients to which they can send a message. These limits can be configured globally or per user.

Only an administrator with Exchange Admin permission to the organization can configure the global limit. To do so, locate the Message Delivery properties under the Global Settings container and display its Defaults property tab (shown in Figure 4.22). The default is an unlimited size for incoming and outgoing messages and a maximum of 5000 recipients per message. In Figure 4.22, the maximum incoming and outgoing message size has been set to 5MB, and the maximum number of recipients has been restricted to 100. These limits have been used by a few of the organizations I have worked with, but may not necessarily work for you. Evaluate carefully what limits may be necessary in your organization to facilitate efficient message flow and to provide your user community with the necessary functionality to use the messaging system efficiently.

Figure 4.22   Global message delivery settings

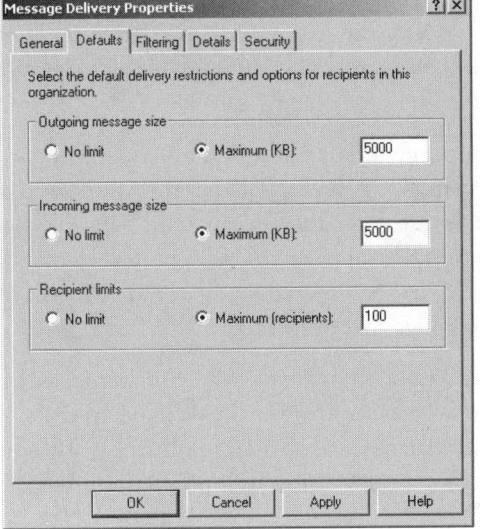

NOTE   The maximum number of recipients includes recipients in the To, Cc, and Bcc fields. All members of a mail-enabled group are included in this count. So if the maximum number of recipients is set to 100 and a group has 101 members, a user will not be able to mail to that group. This is different than in Exchange 5.5, which considered a distribution list to be a single recipient. If you have a Mixed-mode environment, the maximum number or recipients will not be enforced by distribution lists that are expanded on Exchange 5.5 servers.

These values can be overridden on a per-mailbox basis. The options are found on the Exchange General property page. Click the Delivery Options button to change the maximum number of recipients the owner of a mailbox can send, and click the Delivery Restrictions button to change the maximum incoming and outgoing message size.

NOTE Message limits are enforced by the message categorizer (PHATCAT.DLL).

Reconnecting and Purging Mailboxes

Accidents happen, and mailboxes get deleted when they shouldn't be. I know of one site that has an average of one mailbox accidentally deleted each month. This was a nightmare for the administrator when they were running Exchange 5.5, but Exchange 2000 introduces the ability to save mailboxes for a specified period of time and reconnect to that mailbox. The Keep Deleted Mailboxes For limit is set either through a mailbox store policy or directly to each mailbox store. The default limit is 30 days.

When a mailbox is deleted, the Active Directory user account's attributes that identify it as owning a mailbox are cleared. Of course, if you delete the user account, then all AD-related attributes will be deleted.

The Mailbox Cleanup Agent will run automatically during nightly information store maintenance, and the mailbox will be listed in the Mailboxes container with a red X over the mailbox icon. You can force the agent to run by right-clicking the Mailboxes container and choosing Run Cleanup Agent. Have patience; you may have to wait 15 minutes or more for the deleted mailbox icon to appear. Don't forget to refresh the container you are looking at in Exchange System Manager.

Once the deleted mailbox icon appears, you can right-click the deleted mailbox and choose Reconnect. then you can browse the Active Directory and locate an AD user who does not currently have an associated mailbox. After you reconnect the mailbox to a user account, make sure that the RUS runs and populates all of the necessary attributes that identify the object as mail-enabled.

If you don't want the mailbox to remain in the mailbox store any longer, you can right-click the mailbox and choose Purge. This will remove the mailbox immediately.

Reconnecting Many Mailboxes after Deleting AD Account

Even if the Active Directory user accounts were deleted, the mailboxes will remain in the store until the deleted mailbox retention period expires. You can reconnect many mailboxes back to AD user accounts using the mbconn.exe utility found on the Exchange 2000 CD-ROM in the \Support\Utils\I386 directory.

Simply run this utility (no installation necessary), and it will find mailboxes without associated AD accounts. Once it has found the mailboxes, you can preview them to make sure there are not any duplicates or users that appear to match more than one mailbox (collision). You can then create an LDIFDE file that can be used to create new AD user accounts or associate existing accounts with mailboxes.

> **NOTE**   For more information on the mbconn.exe utility, see Microsoft Knowledge Base article Q271886.

Dealing with the Recently Departed

One of my biggest pet peeves is users who subscribe to a hundred different mailing lists (list servers)—well, more specifically, those users who subscribe to a hundred different mailing lists and then leave the company. This unto itself is not a major hassle unless you have configured your SMTP virtual servers to forward all non-delivery reports to the postmaster's mailbox, which is what I recommend.

Consequently, the postmaster's mailbox is always full of mail destined for former employees. How should you deal with all this mail? One option is to not configure the SMTP virtual servers to forward NDRs to the postmaster. However, since this has other negative ramifications, there are other solutions, though they do require a bit more effort to configure and maintain. You can configure mailboxes of former users to auto-respond to senders or auto-forward messages to the person's new address. Another approach is to create a distribution list with no members; on the E-mail Addresses property page add the e-mail addresses of the departed users. The messages just disappear in to the ether. Or you can take steps to try and stop mail from being sent to users who no longer have mailboxes on your system.

Don't Delete That Mailbox!

Instead of deleting a mailbox, disable the AD account associated with this mailbox and assign the Administrator permission to the mailbox. This means, of course, that the messages will continue to arrive to that mailbox. As I see it, you now have two options.

First, you can use the forwarding address to specify that all messages that arrive to this mailbox are forwarded to another mail-enabled object in the AD. This is the same as the Alternate Recipient property in Exchange 5.5. Figure 4.23 shows a user account's Delivery Options dialog box (found on the Exchange General property page) forwarding all messages to Joe Kvidera. Note that the Deliver Messages To Both Forwarding Address And Mailbox check box is not checked. Unless someone was monitoring this mailbox, this would cause messages to accumulate.

NOTE   The alternate recipient specified in the Forward To box must be found in the Active Directory. This address can be any mail-enabled object in the AD including another mailbox-enabled user, a mail-enabled contact, a mail-enabled group, or a mail-enabled public folder.

Figure 4.23   Delivery Options dialog box

The other option is to use Outlook to create a server-based rule that automatically responds to each message. For example, let's say that Gloria Gonzales has left the company, and Ryan Tung is handling her customer accounts. I want to let folks who contact Gloria know that her e-mail address has changed (I'm such a nice guy!). To do this, I would create three rules: one that automatically forwards the message to Ryan, one that automatically replies with a preformatted message, and one that deletes the message. The preformatted reply message might look something like this:

```
Thanks for contacting the product testing department at Somorita
Surfboards. Gloria Gonzales is no longer with the company. Her
corporate accounts are being handled by Ryan Tung; your message has
been automatically forwarded to him. If you wish to contact Gloria,
she can be e-mailed at SurfBabe@BobsBoogieBoards.com. Thank you for
your time.
```

> **NOTE** If Gloria has gone to work for a competitor, I'm probably not going to be so charitable about letting everyone know her forwarding address. Automatically replying to every message sent to a user may raise the ire of some list server managers and the people subscribed to the mailing lists, as well.

You Can't Take It with You

Well, maybe you *can* take your mail with you, but only if someone in the IT department likes you. When someone leaves an organization, they often want all their mail forwarded to their new e-mail address. This is actually pretty simple to do; however, in a very large organization, I would not want to set a precedent for doing it every time someone left.

Let's take my previous example; user Gloria Gonzales has left the company. To automatically forward all of Gloria's mail to her new address, first I need to take note of her existing SMTP address, then I have to delete her mailbox. Next, I need to create a mail-enabled contact for her new Internet address. On the General property tab, Gloria's SMTP address would be `SurfBabe@BobsBoogieBoards.com`. However, on the E-mail Addresses tab, I will create an additional SMTP address that has her old SMTP address that she originally used (shown in Figure 4.24). Note that the default address (the one in bold) is still her new address.

Figure 4.24   An additional SMTP address for a contact object

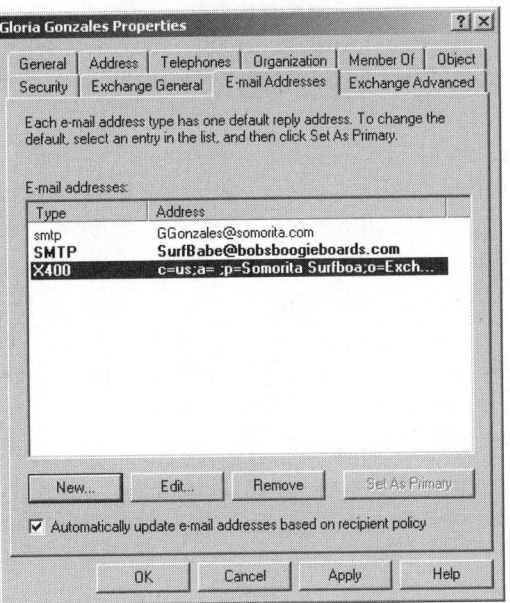

The SMTP message routing engine will accept the message going to Gloria's old address, but will turn the message around and deliver it to the BobsBoogieBoards.com domain. The Unix community does this with either an alias file or a .forward (dot forward) file.

Sending Everything to One Place

Another option for handling undeliverable inbound mail is to send everything to one place. In the past, I have created a single mailbox for former users' mail. Each time a user leaves the company, I delete that user's mailbox and then add that user's SMTP address to this user's E-mail Addresses tab. Then I create a server-based rule that automatically replies with a generic message like this:

```
Thank you for contacting Somorita Surfboards. The user you have sent this
e-mail message to is no longer at this company, and their e-mail account has
been deactivated. We have no forwarding address for this person on file. If
you have any questions, please contact postmaster@somorita.com.
```

I can then review this mailbox from time to time to see if anything important has arrived for any former users and purge the rest of the messages.

Yet another option is to create a mail-enabled public folder that has the e-mail addresses of the former users. This public folder can be reviewed by authorized users.

Stop Calling Here!

Every once in a great while, I finally decide to do something about all that extra NDR mail that is flooding my postmaster's mailbox. For me, this lasts the better part of a morning before I once again resign myself to filtering through all the garbage. But my brief inspiration toward a garbage-free postmaster mailbox involves trying to get some of the users off of some of the larger lists (the lists that generate the most traffic). I usually employ one of four tactics:

- Send an e-mail to the list manager or postmaster at the remote domain explaining that I am postmaster of my domain and would like to get one of my former users off of their mailing list. If those mailboxes are being answered, the list serve managers are usually more than willing to help out.

- Some list servers include instructions on the bottom of the message for how to unsubscribe. This usually entails sending a message *as that user* and asking to be removed. I use Outlook Express to do this rather than re-create the mailbox, though I could assign the former user's e-mail address to my postmaster's mailbox, set that address as the reply address, and send the messages as the postmaster.

- The really high-end list servers and mailing services have a web page you can usually connect to, enter the e-mail address to be removed, and Boom! Instant removal. Some list servers require a password to remove an e-mail address. If this is the case, you will probably need to contact the list owner to remove the e-mail address.

- Once I got tired of sending e-mail addresses to a particular domain asking to remove one of my users, so I just created a rule and forwarded everything from that domain to the mailbox's postmaster. I'm not sure, but I think they blocked my IP address from sending them anything else after that.

- If you just want to create a black hole for these messages, you can create a mail-enabled distribution group with no members. Then on the E-mail Addresses property page, add the SMTP addresses of the ex-employees. Then, on the Exchange Advanced property page, click the Hide Group From Exchange Address Lists check box. Messages will be accepted by SMTP, but they will be discarded.

Customizing Details Templates

As you can see, Exchange Server is highly customizable and extensible. A particularly cool Exchange feature is the ability to customize *details templates*, which are used by the Outlook client to display information found in the Active Directory. Figure 4.25 shows the User details template showing the details of a mailbox-enabled user account. An Outlook user can see this template whenever they locate a mail-enabled object in the directory and click the Properties button.

Figure 4.25   The User details template

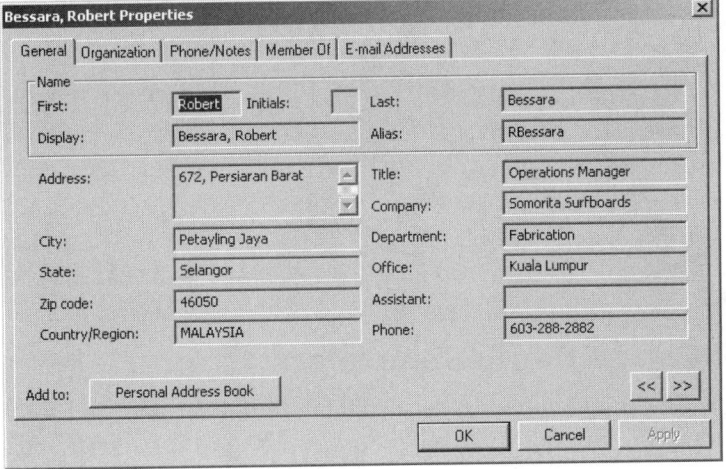

Details templates are stored in the configuration partition of the Active Directory. The template is not compiled, but rather consists of a series of instructors, fields, labels and coordinates that the client needs to build the template. When an Outlook client connects to the Exchange server, it downloads the detailed template information for the supported language.

For each supported language, Exchange Server has seven details templates that clients use to display and search for directory information.

Each template consists of edit fields (attribute data), field labels, and the coordinates necessary to display these fields and their corresponding labels in an organized fashion. This data is stored in the directory and is used by all Exchange servers in the organization; in Exchange 5.5 this data was site-specific. If you modify a details template for one site, it must be modified for all sites in order to be used throughout the organization.

In Figure 4.26, you will notice the User template for user Robert Bessara. The template is a little different that the one shown in Figure 4.25; this one has been customized with three additional fields: Job Code, Home Town, and Partner. The Outlook client used the information stored in the User details template to construct and display the mailbox data.

Figure 4.26   A customized User details template

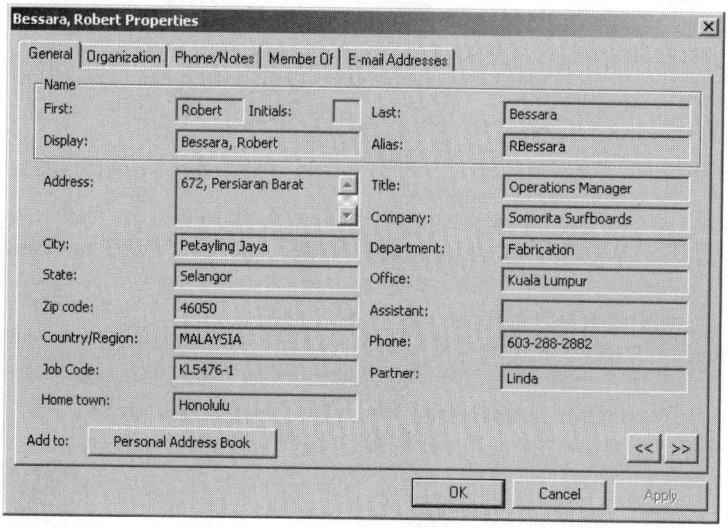

Customizing a Details Template

How difficult was it to customize the template? It took me about ten minutes, but I have had some practice. It's not hard, but it does require a little patience and some trial-and-error to get it right. I will walk you through the steps that I suggest for modifying a details template, using the User template as an example. To get started, follow these steps to view the User detail template:

1. First and most important, take a screen shot of the template you want to modify, and print it out.

2. On the printed template, jot down the coordinates of the existing labels and fields. This helps to better visualize the changes you are making to the layout and the coordinates of existing attributes.

3. Using Exchange System Manager, display the properties of the User template. To get to the details templates, navigate the Exchange hierarchy using Exchange System Manager; choose *Organization Name* ➤ Recipients ➤ Details Templates ➤ *Language*.

4. Select the User template in the contents pane and display its properties.

5. Click the Templates page (see Figure 4.27) to see the fields, labels, and controls that make up the details templates.

Figure 4.27 Templates page for the User details template

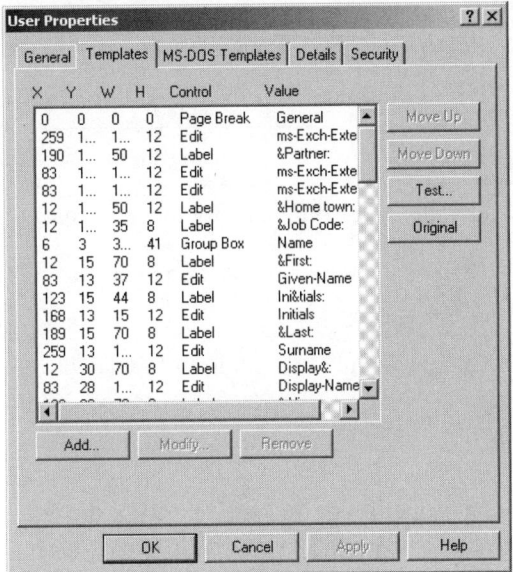

> *TIP* Notice the Test button in Figure 4.27? If you click this button, it will show you what the template looks like to the user. This will be very helpful when changing the details templates.

Figure 4.27 also shows the layout of the details template. Each label, edit box, group box, etc., is positioned based on X and Y coordinates and a width (W) and height (H). These numbers are in pixels.

The details template can contain a number of different types of controls; these are listed in Table 4.8. The most common controls are the Label, Edit, and Page Break controls, but the others come in handy on more complicated templates.

Table 4.8   Details Template Control Types

Control	Function
Label	Usually used for labeling edit fields or other controls, but can be placed anywhere in the template.
Edit	Any field that can be edited. These include mailbox properties and custom attributes.
Page Break	Defines a new property page.
Group Box	Defines a set of controls (fields) that are bound together by a box.
Check Box	Creates a check box control that can be either on or off.
List Box	Creates a box that has multiple choices.
Multi-Valued List Box Control	Creates a multi-valued list box control.
Multi-Valued Drop Down	Creates a multi-valued drop-down control.

Now that you have the properties of the User template, the next step in customizing the details template is to edit the existing labels for fields that you want to customize and to edit the labels for new fields that you created from Custom Attribute (extension Attributes) fields. To customize the User details template seen in Figure 4.26, follow these steps:

1. If you are changing any existing labels, locate and highlight each label field that you want to change, click the Edit button, and change of the label buttons that need to be customized. In my example, I did not change any of the existing field names.

> **NOTE**   Changing the values on the User template changes only the template seen by the clients; it does *not* change the User template seen in Active Directory Users And Computers.

2. Take your printed screen capture and locate an area near the bottom of the template where you want to add the new fields (in this example, Job Code, Partner, and Home Town). Jot down the coordinates of the fields near the bottom of the template; you'll need these to estimate the location of your new labels and edit fields. In our example, the Job Code is extensionAttribute1, Partner is extensionAttribute2, and Home Town is extensionAttribute3.

3. Through a little trial and error, locate the new Edit fields based on the coordinates, widths, and heights shown in Table 4.9. The Test button comes in really handy when you are figuring out the exact coordinates and measurements.

4. Click OK to close the Details Templates box; your changes will be saved. You can now test this template from an Outlook client, but Outlook should be closed and restarted first to make sure that the current template information is downloaded from the server.

> **TIP** For some templates, if you place an ampersand (&) character in front of a letter, it will underline that character on the template, making that character the hot key, which lets you use the Alt key and the corresponding letter to jump to that field. Be careful not to assign the hotkey character more than once per property page.

Table 4.9 Coordinates for the New Fields on the Mailbox Template

Control Type	Text/Field	X	Y	W	H
Label	&Job Code	12	140	35	12
Edit	ms-Exch-Extension-Attribute-3	83	140	100	12
Label	&Partner:	190	140	50	12
Edit	ms-Exch-Extension-Attribute-2	198	140	90	12
Label	&Home Town:	12	155	50	12
Edit	ms-Exch-Extension-Attribute-4	83	155	100	12

Does this all sound a little confusing? It is the first time you see it, but I guarantee that if you give this a try, preferably on a test server, you will become an old hand at it in no time—and you will be able to easily customize Exchange to meet your organization's needs. And here's some great news: If you really mess up your template, you can click the Original button, and it will revert to the default template.

Full-Text Indexing

One of the neatest new features of Exchange 2000 is *full-text indexing*. Not that we couldn't search for text in messages even with older versions of Exchange, but the search was slow, character-based, and did not include message attachments. Exchange 2000 full-text indexing incorporates the indexing and search service originally released as part of Microsoft's Site Server product. Following are some characteristics of Exchange 2000 full-text indexing:

- Is automatically integrated with all versions of Outlook using the Advanced Find menu choice from the Tools menu. No changes to the client side need to be made.
- Performs word-based searches rather than character-based searches.
- Searches attachments in addition to message bodies.
- Offers normalized searching, which permits searching of all verb stems. If you search for the word *jog*, the search will return *jogging* and *jogger*.
- Can customize "noise" words (words that you do not want indexed).
- Returns "filtered" results, so only documents the user has permission to see are shown.

By default, the search service can index the following attachment types: text (TXT), embedded MIME messages (EML), HTML messages (HTM, HTML, ASP), Word (DOC), Excel (XLS), and PowerPoint (PPT). Custom filters are available from third-party companies that provide the ability to index other file types.

Is Full-Text Indexing for You?

If all these features are so great, then should you enable full-text indexing? Not without understanding the downsides (and you knew there would be a few downsides, didn't you?), which include the following:

- Index data disk space usage can range between 10 and 40 percent of the size of the store that is being indexed.
- The indexing process is very CPU intensive. It is not unusual to see all server's CPUs running at 90 percent usage when an index is being refreshed.
- If the index is not updated frequently, it may become stale and return inaccurate search results.

Since not everyone may need the features of full-text indexing, it is configured on a per-store basis.

TIP You can put the public folders or mailboxes that require indexing on their own store and reduce the overhead by not indexing messages and documents that do not require indexing.

Indexing Architecture

The Exchange information store includes a query processor that performs property searches of data in the information store. While not very fast, this method does allow you to search for much of the data in a public folder or mailbox. If a full-text index is created for a public or mailbox store, the query processor in the information store then splits the query. Any type of word search is sent to the Microsoft Search service while queries based on MAPI properties (such as date or messages size) are handled by the query processor. Figure 4.28 shows the architecture of a search once a store has been indexed.

Figure 4.28   Full-text indexing architecture

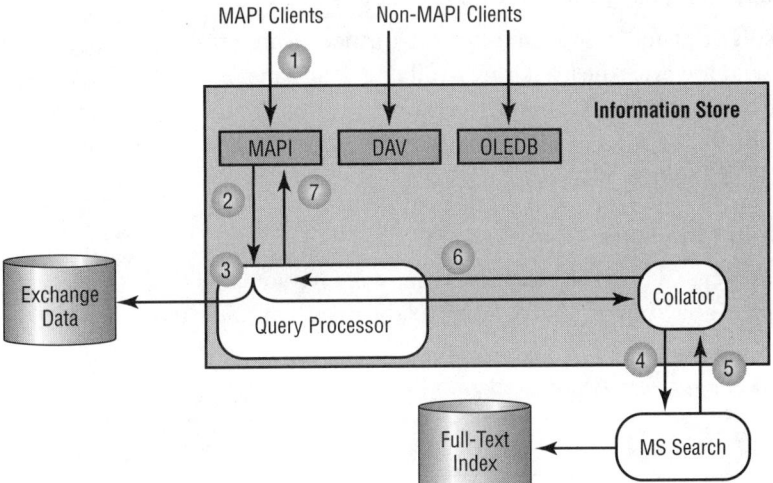

The process illustrated in Figure 4.28 goes something like this:

1. A MAPI client uses Advanced Find to send a query to the Exchange server; for example, seeking all documents that contain the word *surfboard* and are greater than 15KB.

2. The query is sent to the information store query processor.

3. If full-text indexing is enabled for the store that is being searched, the query is split into two parts: the MAPI properties (which include the size being greater than 15KB) and the word search (*surfboard*). The word search is sent to the search collator.

4. The collator forwards the search onto Microsoft Search, which runs as a separate process.

5. Microsoft Search queries the full-text index files for all documents that have the word *surfboard* in the folder that was queried. The results are returned back to the information store's query processor. The search service is also responsible for eliminating noise words from the query.

6. The query processor narrows down this list by keeping only documents whose size is greater than 15KB. Further, any messages or documents to which the person doing the query does not have permissions are eliminated from the list.

7. The query result set is returned to the user.

The MAPI properties that are indexed by the Microsoft Search service include: Sender (PR_SENDER_NAME), Sender's e-mail address (PR_SENDER_EMAIL_ADDRESS), Display name to (PR_DISPLAY_TO), Display name cc, (PR_DISPLAY_CC), Message subject (PR_SUBJECT), and Message body (PR_BODY).

Full-Text Searching through HTTP Clients

Microsoft does not include an interface for performing full-text searches through OWA currently. However, the hooks are available. You can create an ASP (Active Server Pages) file with VBS code and WebDAV methods into a public folder and use that code to search the public folder. Find instructions and some sample code in Microsoft Knowledge Base article Q259849.

Examining the Logs

There are several event log messages that will give you an idea of the progress of full-text indexing. Table 4.10 describes some of the common event IDs.

Table 4.10 Event IDs Associated with Full-Text Indexing

Event ID	Source	Description
7052	Microsoft Search	Search service has loaded a project (see event details for which project).
7000	Microsoft Search	Search service has started indexing the project specified in the event detail.
3019	Microsoft Search	Search service has begun a crawl on the project specified in the event detail.
3068	Microsoft Search	A specific language resource is not available for word breakers.

Table 4.10   Event IDs Associated with Full-Text Indexing *(continued)*

Event ID	Source	Description
3018	Microsoft Search	Project specified in the event detail has finished a complete crawl. Statistics on documents processed are found in the event details.
7049	Microsoft Search	The index build for the project specified in the details is complete.
4103	MssCi	Merge of new index information with existing information is complete.
7045	Microsoft Search	Catalog was not propagated after a crawl because there were no changes.
3042	Microsoft Search	Project crawl has been paused.
3044	Microsoft Search	Project crawl has been resumed.

When the indexing process runs, log files called *gather logs* are also created. These files are found, by default, in the \Program Files\Exchsrvr\ExchangeServer_servername\ GatherLogs. The default format of these log files is not very helpful; a few lines of this log file are shown here:

```
b0b323ef    1c0b6a4     4000001f    0    40d84
b1fec419    1c0b6a4     40000020    0    40d84
1235242d    1c0b6ad     4000001f    0    40d84
1442da1d    1c0b6ad     40000020    0    40d84
7409aaa7    1c0b6b5     4000001f    0    40d84
75dd4dfb    1c0b6b5     40000020    0    40d84
d5ed7965    1c0b6bd     4000001f    0    40d84
d7c11cb9    1c0b6bd     40000020    0    40d84
```

However, Exchange server ships with a VBS script that can open these files and interpret the results. This utility is found in the \Program Files\Common Files\System\MSSearch\ Bin directory and is called gthrlog.vbs. To run it, locate the log file you want to examine (my example uses pub50b51fe0.2.gthr) and type the following command:

```
cscript gthrlog.vbs pub50b51fe0.2.gthr
```

The output will be a little friendlier and look similar to this:

```
Microsoft (R) Windows Script Host Version 5.1 for Windows
Copyright (C) Microsoft Corporation 1996-1999. All rights reserved.
8/14/2001 12:00:04 AM        Add    Started Incremental    crawl
8/14/2001 12:00:06 AM        Add    Completed Incremental  crawl
8/14/2001 10:00:06 PM        Add    Started Incremental    crawl
8/14/2001 10:00:12 PM        Add    Completed Incremental  crawl
8/14/2001 10:08:54 PM        Add    Started Incremental    crawl
8/14/2001 10:08:56 PM        Add    Completed Incremental  crawl
8/14/2001 10:33:42 PM        Add    Started Incremental    crawl
8/14/2001 10:34:00 PM        Add    Completed Incremental  crawl
```

Errors that may be encountered with respect to permissions or documents that could not be indexed will be listed here.

Customizing Full-Text Indexing

One of the ways you can customize full-text indexing is to include your own *noise words*, words that should not be indexed. Noise words are configured for the entire server, not for each project. The default noise words files are found in the \Program Files\Exchsrvr\ ExchangeServer_*servername*\Config directory. The noise words (such as "and", "the", "or", and "what") file for English is noise.enu. Microsoft had to add "Microsoft" to their own noise words file since almost every document and message contained that word.

There is also a Search MMC console snap-in that allows you to make changes to Microsoft Search. Before you can use this console, you must register the MSSMMCISI.DLL for the snap-in. To register the DLL, type the following lines:

```
Regsvr32 "c:\Program files\common files\System\MSSearch\Bin\mssmmcsi.dll"
```

Now you can load the Search snap-in to a MMC console. If you have worked with Microsoft Site Server, you may recognize many of the configuration options. Indexes should continue to be created through the Exchange System Manager. Most administrators will never need this console, but one common problem that can be resolved through this console is time-out errors when the indexer is trying to open documents. These time-out values are the Wait For A Connection and Wait For A Request Acknowledgement values; both of these default to 120 seconds. If you are getting time-out messages, try raising these values to 180 seconds or higher.

To change these values from the Search console, go to *ServerName* ➤ ExchangeServer_ *servername* ➤ Catalog Build Server ➤ Properties ➤ Timing.

Creating Full-Text Indexes

Creating a full-index is simple. Right-click the mailbox or public folder store that you want to index and choose Create Full-Text Index. You will be prompted for location of the project files; the default is \Program Files\Exchsrvr\ExchangeServer_*servername*\ Projects, but you can select another drive and directory.

> **TIP** On a server that will have heavily used indexes, consider putting the indexes on their own RAID 5 volume. Keep in mind that the indexes files may consume 20 percent or more of the size of the store it is indexing.

Once you have created the index, you will need to plan how often you want the index to be updated and how often you want it to be rebuilt. These settings are found on the store's Full-Text Indexing tab (shown in Figure 4.29), or they can be applied through a mailbox or public store policy.

Figure 4.29   Full-Text Indexing properties

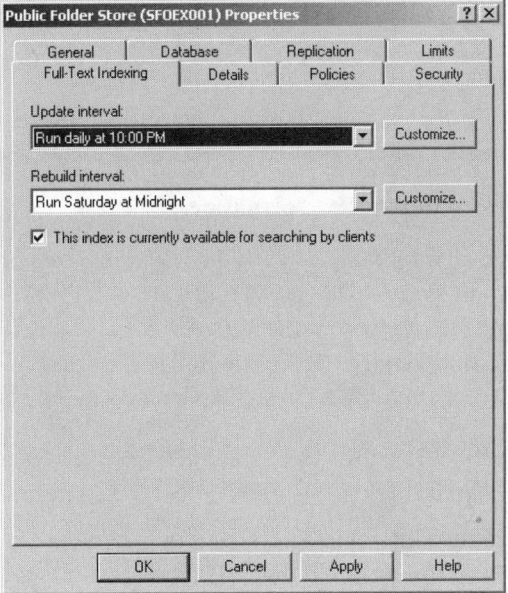

The first setting, Update Interval, is how often the index should be updated. During an update, the process that updates the index (known as a *crawl*) only indexes documents that have changed since the last indexing pass. The less frequently you run the crawl, the more stale the index will become. The more frequently you run the crawl, the more up-to-date the index will be, but the busier the server will be if it has to index many documents. For most installations, I recommend updating the index no more than once a day. However, messages and documents that have been added that day will not be searchable until the next day.

The other setting, Rebuild Interval, is how often to run a rebuild the index from scratch. I recommend doing this once a week at some off time of the day. The actual interval you do this on will be based partially on how long the data stays in the store. If it is purged infrequently, you can do rebuilds less frequently. Make sure that the full-text index rebuilds don't run at the same times that backups or online maintenance is running. Also make sure that they do not run during production hours.

Below the rebuild interval is a check box that asks if the index should be made available to users. If this check box is clear, the information store query processor will not direct queries to this index. This check box is supposed to automatically be updated when the first index pass is completed, but I have seen instances where it did not, so check it once the indexing is completed.

Right-clicking a store that has a full-text index gives you some additional menu choices. You can delete the index, start an incremental or full population, and pause or stop a pending population.

Exchange@Work: Indexing Performance

Here are some statistics for those of you who like hard-core numbers. These statistics were performed on a Pentium III 700 MHz system with 512MB of RAM. I selected to index a public folder store that contained approximately 30,000 messages. Out of these messages, approximately 500 of them had file attachments. The EDB file was approximately 310MB, and the STM file was approximately 307MB.

Prior to enabling full-text indexing, searching for the phrase *Outlook Web Access* took nearly six minutes. The search yielded 508 hits.

I enabled full-text indexing on this particular public folder store. The indexing process took 35 minutes to fully build the index the first time; the average CPU usage was 80 percent during this time. The index files in the projects folder took up 45MB.

Once the index was built, the same search took 15 seconds and yielded 570 hits. The number of hits is different after enabling full-text indexing, because the search is now word-based and includes results from message bodies, documents, spreadsheets, HTML files, and presentations.

Disaster Prevention Tips

Disaster prevention is one of my favorite subjects; I can spend hours discussing ways to make Exchange (and other BackOffice products) more stable and less susceptible to failure and downtime. Deep down, I believe that this has something to do with being inherently lazy; I hate being awakened in the middle of the night to come in and fix a down server or restore a database. Therefore, the more things I can do ahead of time to prevent disaster type situations from happening, the better off I am.

Preventing disasters and keeping Exchange Server up, running, and healthy are the primary reasons I am writing this book, and I'll bet they are the primary reasons you are reading it. One of the most useful activities I participate in is spending time with other administrators and system engineers, listening to them talk about their systems and the problems they have experienced and solved.

When I started working on this book, I talked to several dozen experienced Exchange administrators and asked them, "What tips can you pass on to other administrators to keep your Exchange servers running 24 hours a day, seven days a week? What types of things do you do to make your job easier?" Here is a list of tips from those who shared what they had learned (in no particular order of importance):

- Take training classes in Windows 2000, Active Directory, and Exchange Server early on in your Exchange deployment. Learn as much as you can these products.

- Confirm that deleted item recovery is enabled for all mailbox and public folder information stores. This will decrease the likelihood that you will have to restore data from tape if a user deletes something important from their mailbox or a public folder.

- Confirm that the feature that allows you to recover deleted mailboxes is enabled. This will dramatically decrease the likelihood that you will have to restore data from tape if an administrator accidentally deletes a user account or mailbox.

- Use a separate physical disk for each storage groups' transaction logs; this will both dramatically improve your chances for recovering data up-to-the-minute in case of a database failure as well as improve performance.

- Perform regular online backups, check your tape logs, and perform periodic trial restores.

- Standardize the tape backup hardware, software, tapes, and tape rotations you are using.

- Never run file-based virus scans or file-based backups on the ExIFS (M:) drive.

- Install a UPS and UPS monitoring software on your servers, hubs, and other network infrastructure devices such as switches and routers.

- Scan your event logs daily for critical errors.

- Never use NTFS file compression to compress Exchange databases and logs.
- Restrict mailbox disk space; especially the Prohibit Send And Receive limit.
- Have a disaster recovery plan and a disaster recovery kit. The kit should contain a written copy of the plan, system documentation, and all software required to rebuild any server in your site or organization. Practice disaster recovery and database restoration a few times a year.
- Restrict usage of large distribution lists.
- Run a Windows NT CHKDSK periodically and after any system upgrades.
- Install Exchange Server on member servers rather than on domain controllers.
- In an environment with more than two or three Exchange servers, create one Exchange server that acts as the communications hub (SMTP Connector, fax gateways, routing group bridgehead, etc.), and don't put any mailboxes on that server.
- Subscribe to Microsoft TechNet and use it whenever something comes up that you don't understand.
- Run Exchange database maintenance utilities to repair the database only as a last resort.
- Keep your user community informed.

You will find most of these tips explained in much more detail in this book; this list is just the "sound bites" version of them.

NOTE   Inevitably, disaster will strike when you least expect. Chapter 7 covers backup, disaster recovery and what to do when that fateful moment arrives.

5

Status Monitoring and Reporting

It is Tuesday morning, you have just finished your second cup of herbal tea (because I know you're trying to cut back on the coffee). Your boss storms into your office and tells you that the vice president of finance sent spreadsheets to the chief executive office yesterday afternoon, but the spreadsheets had not yet arrived as of this morning. The VP of finance called your boss directly and complained loudly.

There is nothing worse than having someone in a position of authority reporting problems to you, especially if these are problems that you should have been aware of to begin with.

The user community quickly diagnoses little interruptions of service, such as WAN link failures or virus outbreaks, as "e-mail system problems." Your user community will remember that five minutes of downtime six months ago, but they will quickly lose sight of the fact that the system has been available 24 hours a day, seven days a week since then. This is one of the most discouraging parts of my job, and I'm sure it is one of yours, too.

For this reason, it is important that you are proactive in monitoring the Exchange system and making absolutely sure that you know about problems before your user community reports them to you. Some of the types of information you will want to monitor or report on will include Exchange server and queue status, mailbox storage usage, protocol usage by client, and disk consumption.

To get to the point that you are aware of your system's usage and potential problems before the more influential members of your user community are, you have to implement a plan for monitoring your Exchange system's activities and consolidate that information into readable reports. Monitoring your system may also entail some sticky legal issues with your user community. Some of the topics in this chapter that may help you with this include:

- Using the Exchange System Manager Monitoring and Status Tools
- Customizing your own tools
- Message tracking and archiving
- Reporting
- Legal issues surrounding e-mail systems

Using the Monitoring and Status Tools

Once you have your Exchange 2000 server(s) up and running, the key to maintaining the system is preventative maintenance and monitoring. By monitoring the servers, you will be able to determine resource and reliability issues before they affect the performance of your servers and affect the end users. Exchange 2000 has a built-in feature to monitor physical and software resources and a way to notify administrators if these resources reach a warning state or a critical state; this feature is the Monitoring and Status Tools.

Warning State or Critical State?

What is a critical state or a warning state for a specific resource? That is going to depend on your individual environment. For some environments, anything less than one gigabyte of free hard disk space may indicate a critical state, but for other companies one gigabyte of free hard disk space may not even dictate a warning state.

For example, you might configure a warning state if the free disk space on the database disk drops below 1GB, but an alert state if the free disk space drops below 500MB. You could then create notifications that will notify the help desk for a warning state, but notify the system manager for an alert state.

To configure status monitors, first navigate through the Exchange 2000 System Manager to the Tools container and then to the Monitoring And Status container. Right-click the Status container and click New.

There are six categories of service monitoring that can be monitored for each server. These categories include:

- Windows 2000 services
- Available virtual memory
- CPU utilization
- Free disk space
- SMTP queue growth
- X.400 queue growth

Configuring Resource Status Monitors

To configure resource status monitors for an Exchange 2000 server, right-click the server name in the Status Container and choose Properties. This server's Monitoring property page opens, shown in Figure 5.1.

Figure 5.1   Monitoring properties of server SFOEX001

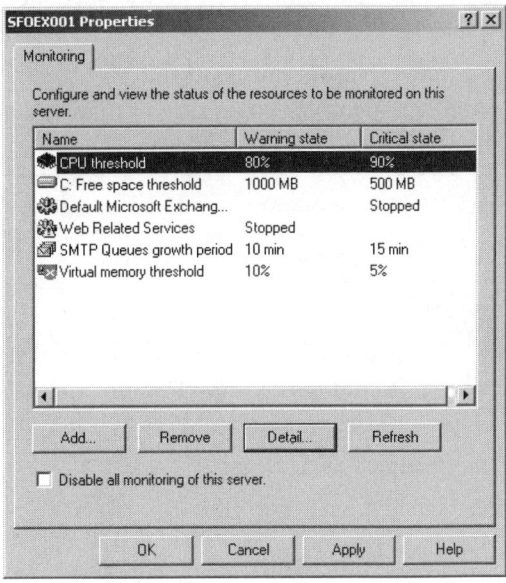

From the Monitoring properties dialog box, you can add additional resources that you want to monitor, remove resource monitors, or change the properties of a resource monitor. Notice that there is a small yellow triangle over the icon for Web Related Services; this indicates that the resource monitor is in a warning state. The Virtual Memory Threshold icon has a red and white X over it; this indicates that this resource monitor is in an alert state.

If you are planning to have a server or service offline for maintenance and you do not want to generate notifications, you can check the Disable All Monitoring Of This Server check box.

When you view the Status container located under the Monitoring And Status container, you will see a list of all the servers and connectors. The Status column will let you know the status of the server or connector. The following server and connector states are reported:

Available   All monitored services are responding normally on a server, or the connector is functioning normally.

Unavailable   The connector is not currently functioning properly. This may be due to a failed link.

Unreachable   Either a service is stopped, or the server cannot be contacted.

Critical/Warning   The current state is either warning or critical. This is followed by an explanation, such as Memory Usage or Service Not Running.

In Maintenance Mode   The administrator has disabled monitoring on this server because it is currently undergoing some type of maintenance.

NOTE   Exchange 2000 SP1 servers are monitored every 300 seconds (10 seconds for Exchange 2000 RTM).

Windows 2000 Services

The resource status monitor can monitor any Windows 2000 service, but by default, the only resource monitor that is configured is the Default Microsoft Exchange Services, which watches the following six services:

- Microsoft Exchange Information Store
- Microsoft Exchange MTA Stacks
- Microsoft Exchange Routing Engine
- Microsoft Exchange System Attendant
- Simple Mail Transport Protocol (SMTP)
- World Wide Web Publishing Service

The default is to change a service's state to critical if it is not running. You can add additional services to the Default Microsoft Exchange Services resource monitor from the resource monitor's properties box.

You may also want to monitor additional services, such as Microsoft Exchange IMAP4 and Microsoft Exchange POP3 services, but create your own resource monitor to do this rather than using the default service resource monitor. Further, you may want to include third-party tools in your service resource monitor.

For example, if the backup program is not running and properly backing up the transaction logs, they will fill up the drive and possibly cause the Exchange 2000 server to stop and not restart until the low disk space problem is corrected. With this in mind, if you are using a third-party backup utility on your Exchange 2000 server, you can monitor all of the services that it requires. For each of these services, you can specify that the monitor should send a warning or a critical alert message. Another service that you may want to monitor on your Exchange 2000 server would be a server-based fax solution.

Available Virtual Memory

Windows 2000 uses a virtual memory model and employs a page file (`pagefile.sys`) to swap physical memory with virtual memory stored on a hard disk. However, if the amount of available virtual memory is too low, Exchange may stop responding; at the very least, users will notice the server's diminished performance. The available virtual memory status will show you the percentage of virtual memory that is remaining.

Configure the available virtual memory status monitor by first specifying the duration (in minutes) that the thresholds must be met. If you set the duration to five minutes, the amount of available virtual memory must be below the values set for five minutes before the warning message will be sent.

> **WARNING**   Make sure to set a warning and critical state so you can be alerted before the server reaches an inoperable state. Also, know the patterns of your Exchange server; virtual memory may become low during activities such as online backup or full-text indexing.

In Figure 5.2, the virtual memory resource monitor has been configured to go to a warning state if the amount of virtual memory drops below 30 percent for 10 minutes. It will go to an alert state if the virtual memory drops below 20 percent available for 10 minutes, which indicates that your server probably needs more memory.

Figure 5.2 Virtual memory resource monitor

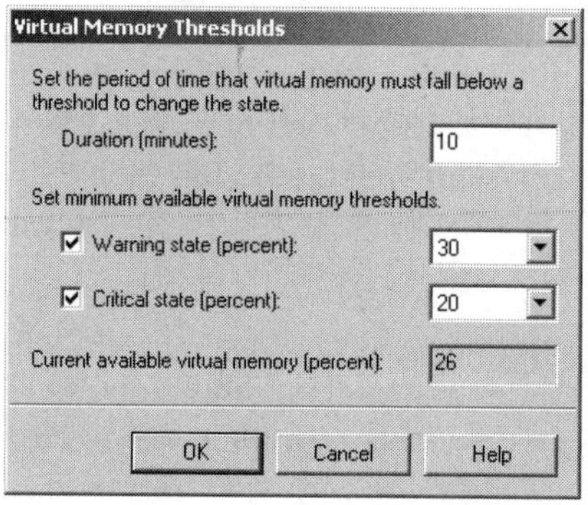

CPU Utilization

High CPU utilization can mean a couple of different things. First, the server may be overworked, and you should offload some of its responsibilities, such as moving mailboxes to another server that is not as heavily used. Second, a service or another application may be using the entire available CPU processing power. I have seen high CPU usage when a program encounters a bug or a condition it cannot resolve.

You monitor CPU utilization much like you monitor available virtual memory. You need to set the duration of how long the CPU needs to be above the specified thresholds as well as the warning and critical states.

In Figure 5.3, the CPU utilization threshold monitor is set to generate a warning state if the average CPU usage exceeds 80 percent for 30 minutes or more. If the CPU usage exceeds 90 percent for 30 minutes or more, the resource monitor will generate an alert state.

Figure 5.3 CPU resource monitor

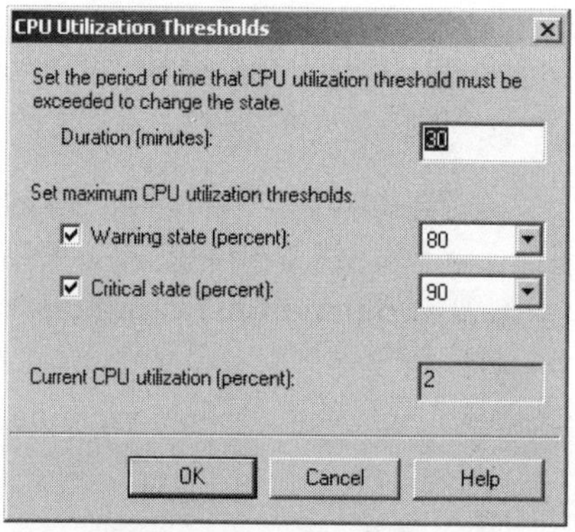

Free Disk Space

Free disk space is critical to an Exchange 2000 server. If your server runs low on free disk space, mailbox stores or entire storage groups will be dismounted. If the operating system drive runs out of disk space, the entire server will shut down, and it may not easily restart—if it restarts at all—until you resolve the disk space issue. With this in mind, it is easy to see why maintaining free disk space is so crucial to your Exchange server. The free disk space monitor is set per logical drive, not on a per physical disk basis.

In most Exchange 2000 systems, you will not want to have circular logging enabled in order to be able to recover the server up to the point of a system failure. A backup program designed to handle Exchange 2000 will clear the transaction logs after a successful full backup. If for some reason the backup program is not configured or is not working properly, the transaction logs may quickly fill up the partition defined for transaction logs. I see this happening in production systems several times a year merely because someone is not closely monitoring the backups and free disk space. Set a free disk space warning and critical state for *every* partition on your server.

Figure 5.4 shows a disk space threshold monitor for the C: drive. If the available disk space drops below 1GB, then the resource monitor generates a warning alert state. If the available disk space drops below 500MB, then the resource monitor will generate an alert. The exact values that you will enter in these fields will depend on your environment.

Figure 5.4   Disk space resource monitor

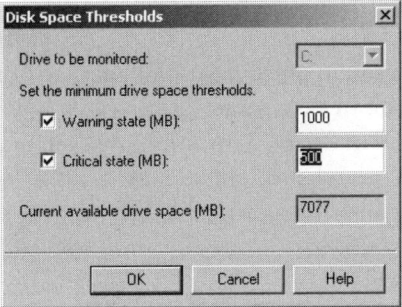

Operations

PART 2

NOTE   You will need to configure one disk space resource monitor for each logical disk on an Exchange 2000 server.

SMTP and X.400 Queue Growth

Exchange 2000 Server can monitor both the SMTP and X.400 queues. When you configure this setting, you indicate the number of minutes of continuous growth your queues should endure before the monitor sets off the critical and alert states. We monitor continuous growth, versus setting a message threshold, due to the potential number of messages that can flow through the queue. Some companies may only send 100 SMTP messages throughout an entire day, while other companies may send in excess of 1000 SMTP messages per hour. On an SMTP virtual server that is on an SMTP Connector bridgehead server, at any given time there may be dozens of messages in the queue waiting to be delivered. By defining a continuous growth in minutes, we are able to accommodate companies of all sizes.

When you configure the SMTP or X.400 queue growth resource monitor, you have to specify only two values. The first value is how many minutes to wait during a period of continual queue growth before entering a warning state. The second is the number of minutes to wait before entering an alert state.

Configuring Notifications

Now that you know what kind of resources you can monitor and how to configure the warning and critical states for each of these resources, let's talk about what to do with this information. After all, it isn't what information you know, it's what you *do* with the information to leverage it to your benefit. With Exchange 2000 Server, you can now take the statuses that you configured and set up notifications to alert the systems administrators of the problems that have arisen.

To configure a notification, in the System Manager, go to the Tools container and then to the Monitoring And Status container. Right-click Notifications, select New, and then choose either E-mail or Script. You configure each of the notifications based on the monitoring server and then when to run the notification, warning, or critical state. The Windows Management Instrumentation (WMI) service is responsible for generating these notifications.

TIP It's a good idea to have other servers monitor the monitoring servers and to set up multiple monitoring servers within your Exchange organization. If you configure the server to monitor only itself, and if the resource enters a critical state, your Exchange server may not be able to function—which means it won't be able to send out the notification e-mail.

Operations

PART 2

E-mail Notifications

An e-mail notification can be sent to anyone in the global address list and/or any SMTP address, and to one or multiple recipients. You can also Cc the message to others. It is always a good idea to send the message to more than one person or to a distribution group; in the case the primary recipient is unavailable to check their e-mail, at least one person receives the message.

> **TIP** For critical notifications, you may also want to set up a mail-enabled contact to send an alphanumeric page to some support personnel in case the servers enter a critical state after normal business hours.

When you configure an e-mail notification, you will need to specify a number of parameters, including the name of the monitoring server, whether to notify for critical or warning states, the To and Cc list, and the e-mail server. In addition, you have to specify the servers and connectors to monitor; your choices include:

- This server
- All servers
- Any server in the routing group (in which the monitoring server is located)
- All connectors
- Any connector in the routing group (in which the monitoring server is located)

You can also provide a custom list of servers and connectors if this suits your monitoring needs more precisely.

Figure 5.5 shows an e-mail notification configured to be sent to the Exchange Admins mail-enabled group ($ExchangeAdmins@somorita.net) and the Help Desk mail-enabled group ($HelpDesk@somorita.net). I find it very helpful to send the notifications via e-mail to the help desk, as well as to the server's administrators. This way, if the issue is large enough to affect users, the help desk will already be aware of the cause and be working toward a solution before getting inundated with calls.

You can also customize the message that is generated. By default, the message merely gives the status of the queues, drives, services, memory, and CPU.

When using notifications to monitor routing group connectors, you get a message when the routing group connector is marked as down. However, if no messages need to be sent between two routing groups, the connection will not be marked as down.

Figure 5.5 Notification e-mail

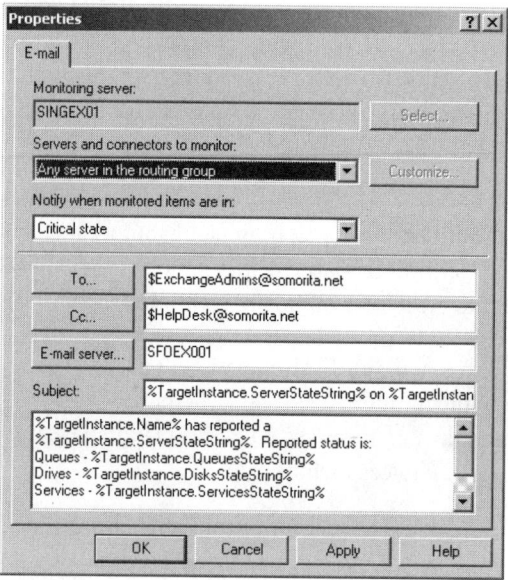

Script Notification

A script notification has more flexibility than an e-mail notification. Part of the script may actually be to send an e-mail message using a tool such as MAPIsend, as well as attempt to restart the services that have failed if the notification is for any of the Exchange 2000 services, or other Windows 2000 services. You can even have the script run an application, such as a paging application to send an alpha page to the server administrators. This type of notification would be a wise choice for some of the extremely critical monitors. You may use an e-mail notification for a warning and then use an e-mail and script notification for a critical notice.

Figure 5.6 shows the properties box for a simple notification that runs a script called RGCscript.vbs when any routing group connector in the server SFOEX001's routing group is marked as down.

NOTE Using automated e-mail tools, such as MAPIsend, is discussed in the "Reporting" section, later in this chapter.

Figure 5.6   Notification script

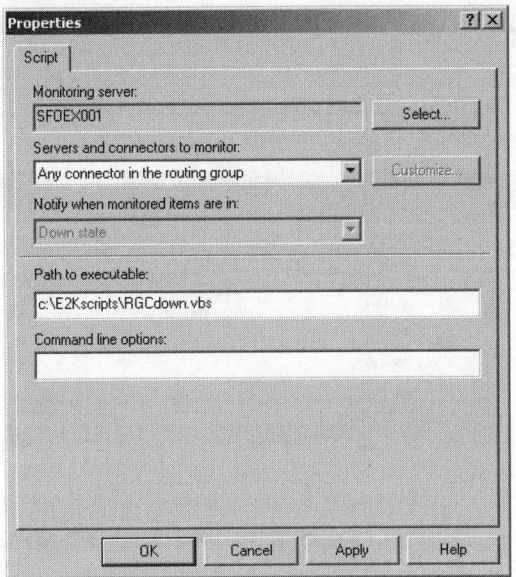

Customizing Your Own Tools

Exchange's built-in resource status monitoring and notification tools are great, but you may have a need for some additional tools that are not part of the Exchange System Manager. In this case, you'll need to rely on the Exchange 2000 Resource Kit or Windows 2000 tools to do the monitoring and reporting that you require.

Exchange 2000 Resource Kit Tools

The Exchange 2000 Resource Kit ships with a couple of tools that make life more interesting if you want to monitor your server status or mail queues, or to create a diagram of your Exchange 2000 organization. These include MailQ, Web Monitor, and the Topology Diagramming tool.

MailQ

Exchange 2000 Resource Kit's MailQ utility generates a summary of the status of each queue for a specified list of servers. This utility consists of a series of Visual Basic scripts that create an XML-based web page that reports the queue statistics. Figure 5.7 shows a sample web page generated using this utility.

Figure 5.7   Exchange queue lengths reported through a web page

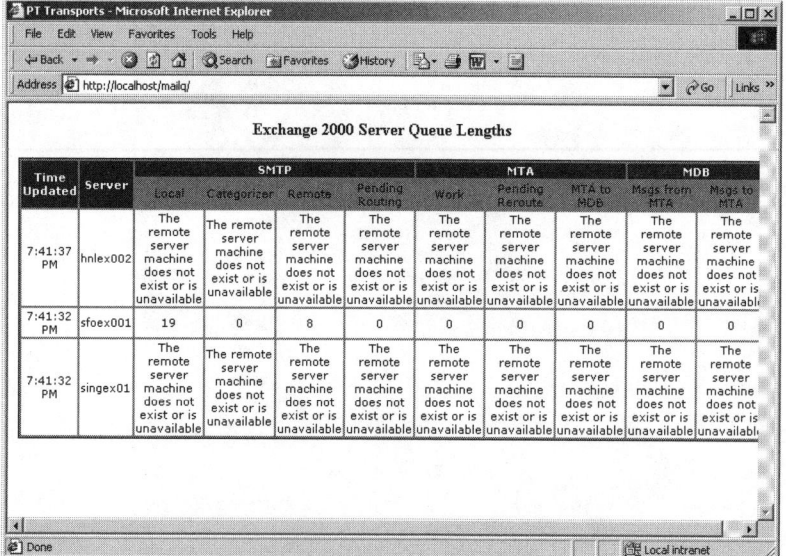

Time Updated	Server	SMTP				MTA			MDB	
		Local	Categorizer	Remote	Pending Routing	Work	Pending Reroute	MTA to MDB	Msgs from MTA	Msgs to MTA
7:41:37 PM	hnlex002	The remote server machine does not exist or is unavailable	The remote server machine does not exist or is unavailable	The remote server machine does not exist or is unavailable	The remote server machine does not exist or is unavailable	The remote server machine does not exist or is unavailable	The remote server machine does not exist or is unavailable	The remote server machine does not exist or is unavailable	The remote server machine does not exist or is unavailable	The remote server machine does not exist or is unavailable
7:41:32 PM	sfoex001	19	0	8	0	0	0	0	0	0
7:41:32 PM	singex01	The remote server machine does not exist or is unavailable	The remote server machine does not exist or is unavailable	The remote server machine does not exist or is unavailable	The remote server machine does not exist or is unavailable	The remote server machine does not exist or is unavailable	The remote server machine does not exist or is unavailable	The remote server machine does not exist or is unavailable	The remote server machine does not exist or is unavailable	The remote server machine does not exist or is unavailable

There are a couple of causes for concern in Figure 5.7. First, servers HNLEX002 and SINGEX01 are not responding, and second, the local delivery queues on server SFOEX001 are a bit high. This could indicate that a mailbox store has been dismounted.

The MailQ web page shows messages queued for the SMTP message transport as well as messages queued on the MTA. If a queue size exceeds 1000 messages, the cell will turn yellow; if the queue size exceeds 2000 messages, the cell will turn red. These values can be customized in the PtTransportPerf.VBS file; search for the string *strColor*.

Installing MailQ   To install MailQ, follow these steps:

1. Copy the \MailQ directory from the Exchange 2000 Resource Kit to a local directory on the server that will be handling the monitor. This example will use C:\MailQ.

2. Using Internet Services Manager, create a new virtual directory off of one of the websites that points to the C:\MailQ\Web directory. This virtual directory should allow for read and run scripts permissions.

3. In the C:\MailQ\Web\Globals.vbs file, change the variable *g_aServers* to list the servers you want monitored, and change the *g_strDataFolder* to point to the location for the data files, such as C:\MailQ. If you have scripting experience, you could even modify the scripts to automatically generate a list of servers using ADSI or LDAP queries.

To start the application, from the C:\MailQ\Crawler directory, type **cscript go.wsh.** The script will run every 60 seconds in a command prompt window, but you can install this script to run as a service using the Windows 2000 Resource Kit utility srvany.exe.

Web Monitor

If you like the capabilities that the MailQ utility provides for monitoring queue activity, then you'll love the Web Monitor tool. This utility creates a web page that provides status and monitoring information that can be set through status monitors (discussed earlier in this chapter). The tool consists of a series of ASP scripts that use WMI to poll for information about Exchange 2000 server resources.

The following steps are necessary to install the Web Monitor tool. Note that they follow closely the instructions provided with the Exchange 2000 Resource Kit.

1. Create a subdirectory called Monitor in the \Inetpub\Wwwroot directory.

2. Copy the files from the Exchange 2000 Resource Kit's \Tools\Admin\Webmon directory to this location.

3. Configure resource status monitors for each of the resources that you want to view in the web page. This includes queue growth, disks, CPU, virtual memory, and services. The web page will refresh every five seconds.

Figure 5.8 shows a simple example using Web Monitor. You can click the hyperlinks in the left frame to see more information about a resource in the right frame. Why are some of the resources on the SINGEX01 server showing as Unknown? Because there are no resource status monitors configured for them on the SINGEX01 server's properties in the Tools ÿ Status container of Exchange System Manager.

Figure 5.8   Web Monitoring tool output

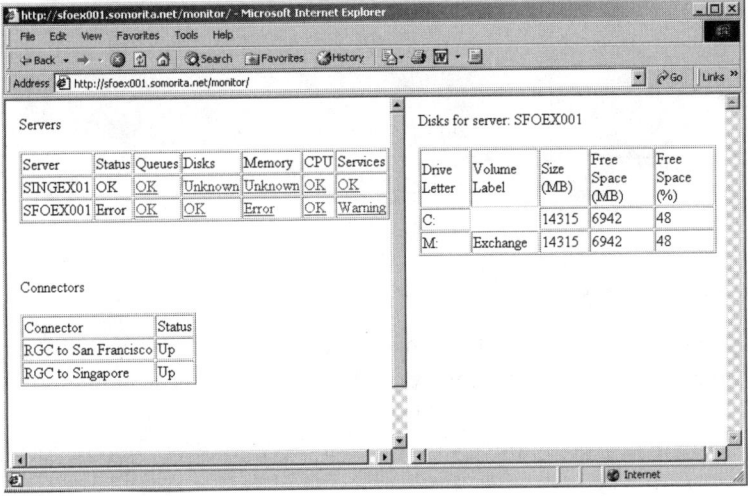

Topology Diagramming

While this does not really pertain to monitoring and reporting, a useful tool found on the Exchange 2000 Resource Kit is the Topology Diagrammer tool (ExMap), which works with Visio 2000 to read the Active Directory (AD) information about the Exchange 2000 topology and create a simple diagram that shows servers, routing groups, and connectors in the Exchange 2000 organization.

This tool requires access to an Exchange 2000 server and Microsoft Visio 2000. Once the Resource Kit is installed, the `exmap.exe` program can be found in the Kit's `\Tools\Admin\Exmap` directory. Make sure that Visio 2000 is installed, and then run `exmap.exe`. The first time the application runs, it will ask you for information about default directories and the name of a domain controller. Once you have set these properties, click Draw.

The output created by ExMap is a Visio drawing. Figure 5.9 shows both the drawing that was created for a very simple two-server, two–routing group network as well as the Visio stencil included with ExMap.

Figure 5.9   Visio drawing output from the ExMap program

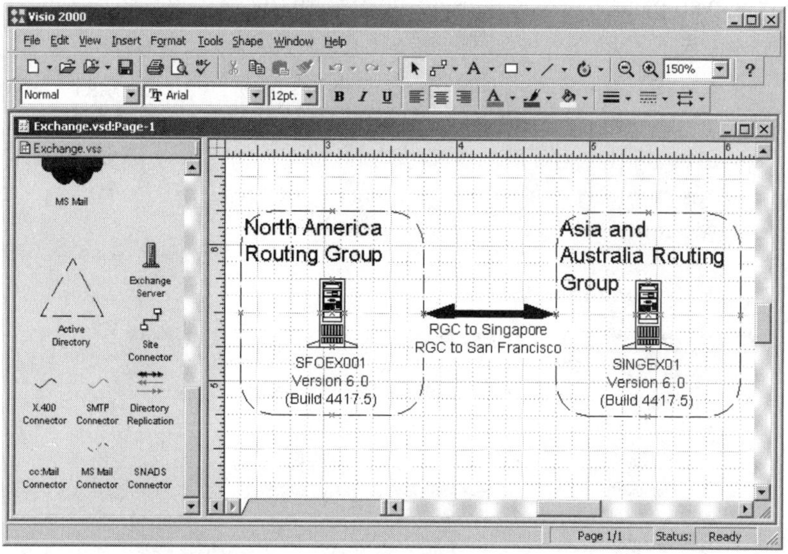

System Monitor

System Monitor in Windows 2000 behaves like the old Windows NT4 Performance Monitor. Its numerous performance counters allow you to monitor very specific services and processes within Windows 2000. Additionally, you can use Performance Management console to configure alerts to notify you if any of the Windows 2000 or Exchange 2000 counters stray too far from your specified norms.

Operations

PART 2

> **NOTE** See Chapter 6, "Performance Monitoring and Optimization," for more details on System Monitor counters used to monitor Windows 2000 and Exchange 2000 performance.

Status Monitoring with Counters

When Exchange 2000 and its associated components are installed, almost 1000 new performance counters are added that can be monitored. These counters are sorted into over 30 categories, some of which are shown in Figure 5.10. A few of these categories, as well as some of the more commonly used and more helpful counters, are discussed below.

Figure 5.10   System Monitor counters for Exchange 2000 Server

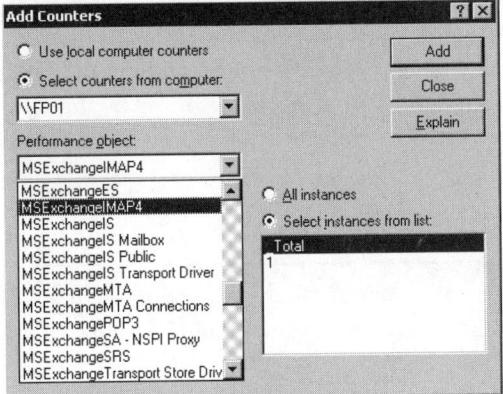

MAPI Client Counters   Outlook clients using the Exchange service use MAPI over RPCs (Remote Procedure Calls) to connect to the information store and directory services. For the majority of corporate and government Exchange 2000 installations, MAPI is still king of the store-access protocols, though I suspect this will change over time as more sophisticated IMAP4 and HTTP-DAV clients are released. Table 5.1 shows some of the more interesting counters that you can monitor to determine MAPI client connections. These counters can be found under the MSExchangeIS performance object.

Table 5.1   MAPI/RPC Client Counters Found in the MSExchangeIS Object

Counter	Explanation
User Count	The total number of unique user connections connected to the information store

Table 5.1   MAPI/RPC Client Counters Found in the MSExchangeIS Object *(continued)*

Counter	Explanation
Read Bytes RPC Clients/sec	The rate at which RPC clients read bytes of data from the information store per second
Write Bytes RPC Clients/sec	The rate at which RPC clients write bytes of data to the information store per second
RPC Operations/sec	The rate at which RPC operations are occurring per second
RPC Packets/sec	The rate at which RPC packets are processed per second
RPC Requests	The total number of RPC requests currently being processed
RPC Requests Peak	The maximum number of simultaneous RPC requests that were processed by the information store since the last time the store service was started

NOTE For information about other status counters that you may want to monitor, see the document called "Status Monitor Counters" at www.somorita.com.

Configuring Alerts

Once you have selected all of the objects that you want to monitor, you can configure System Monitor to send you an administrative alert. These alerts allow you to have a Windows 2000 Professional or Windows 2000 Server system running as a monitoring machine, checking all of the items you deem critical. You can then have the Windows 2000 monitoring machine send you a warning that one of the counters has hit a threshold.

To configure an administrative alert, follow these steps:

1. To start System Monitor, go to Start ÿ Run, and then type **perfmon.**
2. Navigate in the left pane to Performance Logs And Alerts ÿ Alerts.

3. Right-click the Alerts container and select New Alert Settings. Enter the name for your alert, and click OK. The New Alert dialog box appears:

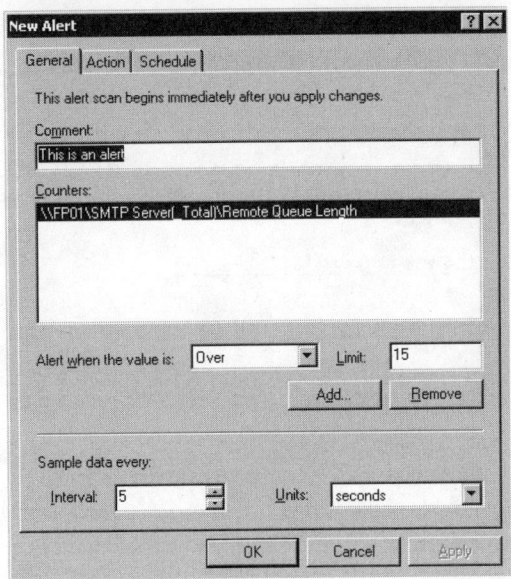

4. Add a counter by clicking the Add button. In the example dialog box above, I have added the SMTP Remote Queue Length counter. This object monitors how many outbound SMTP messages are in queues for remote servers. It has been configured to generate an alert if there are more than 15 items in the SMTP queues. The number 15 is just an example; some organizations may send 15 messages per minute to outside servers.

5. Click the Action tab to configure which actions you want this alert to take. For this example, I have configured my alert to perform multiple functions to ensure that someone receives this message. The Action tab shown below is configured to perform the following:

   ▫ Write an event to the application event log.

   ▫ Send a network message to the person responsible for the SMTP servers within the organization (user JRKvidera).

- Run a VB script that will actually send out an e-mail message as well as an alpha page to the SMTP administrators, notifying them that the server has reached a limit they should check.

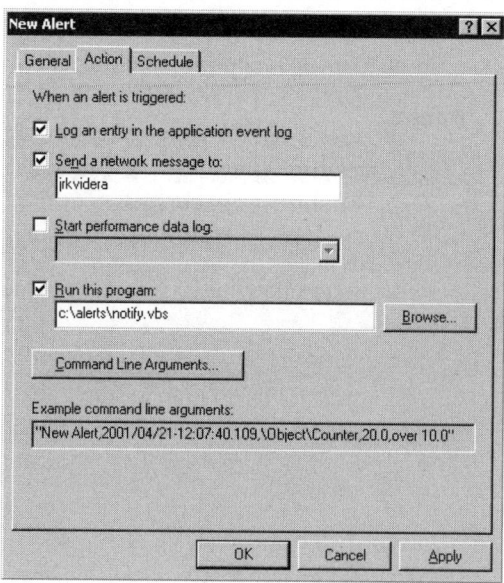

6. Click the Schedule tab and select when you want the alert to scan the counters that you have specified to monitor.

Below are some other counters that may be useful when creating alerts, as they notify you in the event of a system problem. Each of these is configured through the Performance console:

- You can monitor the Logical Disk object's %Disk Free counters to watch for low disk space.

- You can monitor whether each of your critical processes are running by monitoring the process's Instance found under the Process object. If a process's ID Process value is 0, the process has stopped.

- Each of X.400 queues and queues to Exchange 5.5 servers can be monitored through the MSExchange MTA Connections object. Monitor the Queue Length for each queue Instance. You will need to choose a threshold over which you should be notified.

- The Memory object's Available Mbytes counter is useful for monitoring if the amount of memory drops below a threshold. The threshold you specify will depend entirely on your server. Typically, you do not want a server to drop below about 5MB of available memory.

MADMAN MIB

Exchange 2000 Server includes a special SNMP management information base (MIB) that you can use to extend an SNMP-based management system with the capability for managing many Exchange 2000 Server functions. This MIB is based on the standard *Mail and Directory Management (MADMAN) MIB*, which is defined by RFC 1566. The Exchange 2000 MADMAN MIB works by mapping the System Monitor counters for the MTA and IMS objects to corresponding portions of the MADMAN MIB.

> **NOTE**   To learn more about the MADMAN MIB and how to use it along with other SNMP monitoring utilities, refer to the Windows 2000 Server Resource Kit.

E2KUptime Utility

If you want to generate a quick status report for your Exchange 2000 servers, I have just the utility for you. It's called E2KUptime, and it can be downloaded from www.exinternals.com. This utility is simply a VBS script (a 1100 line VBS script) that uses CDOEXM (Collaborative Data Objects for Exchange Management) to query information about Exchange server status. The report is displayed on the screen, but you can optionally send the data to a CSV file. To run a report, at the command prompt on an Exchange server, type **cscript e2kuptime.vbs** *servername*. The following is sample output:

```
C:\>cscript e2kuptime.vbs sfoex001

Microsoft (R) Windows Script Host Version 5.1 for Windows

Copyright (C) Microsoft Corporation 1996-1999. All rights reserved.


Exchange Server: SFOEX001

Version: Version 6.0 (Build 4712.7: Service Pack 1)

Total Mailboxes on this server: 61

Server has been running for: 8 days
```

Exchange Services Found Uptime	Mode	Status	Health	
Exchange Event Service	Manual	Stopped	N/A	N/A
IMAP4 Service	Auto	Running	OK	8
Information Store	Auto	Running	OK	8
Message Transfer Agent	Auto	Running	OK	8
POP3 Service	Auto	Running	OK	8

Routing Engine Service	Auto	Running	OK	8
Site Replication Service	Disable	Stopped	N/A	N/A
System Attendant	Auto	Running	OK	8
Search (Content Indexing)	Auto	Running	OK	8
Network News Transfer Protocol	Auto	Running	OK	8
Simple Mail Transfer Protocol	Auto	Running	OK	8

Storage Group: First Storage Group

Online	8 days	Mailbox Store (SFOEX001)
Online	8 days	Public Folder Store (SFOEX001)

Storage Group: Second Storage Group

Offline	- days	Designers
Online	8 days	Executive Mailboxes
Online	8 days	Operations Group
Online	8 days	Web Folders Public Store

Message Tracking

There are many reasons why you would want to track a message. You may simply need to confirm that a message was delivered. You may want to find where a message was stalled. You may need to monitor message activity between employees. Someone within your organization may feel that there is a threat to security from the content leaving your environment. You may want to determine which connectors are being used for inter-routing group messages, or which X.400 Connectors are being used to deliver to an X.400-based system.

Message tracking is configured through the Exchange System Manager via the Message Tracking Center snap-in. Message tracking in Exchange 2000 is enabled at the server level. To enable message tracking for a server, you must first allow messages to be tracked by setting this on the server's property sheet. Also here, if you check the Enable Subject Logging And Display check box, the subject for messages will be available for each message in the message tracking log, and the subject will be visible in the queue viewer. You can also specify how long you want a server to keep the message tracking logs; the default is 7 days.

Once message tracking is enabled, Exchange keeps a log of all messages transferred to and from that system. Log files are stored locally by default in the C:\Program Files\ Exchsrvr*server_name*.log directory and are automatically deleted by the System

Attendant service on each server. The message tracking log directory on each server is shared as *server_name**server_name*.log; for example on server SFOEX001, the directory is shared as \\SFOEX001\SFOEX001.LOG. The Message Tracking Center must be able to connect to this shared folder on each Exchange server through which a message passes.

> **NOTE** The default permissions for the message tracking log shared directory gives Everyone the Read permission, and local administrators and the local machine account get Full Control permissions. If you are concerned about security, you should remove the Everyone group's permissions to this shared folder.

The System Attendant creates a new log every day starting at midnight (GMT). The log files are named based on the year, month, and day. For example, the log for November 12, 2001, will be named 20011112.LOG.

Using the Message Tracking Center

To track a specific message, you first need to navigate to the Message Tracking Center with the Exchange System Manager. Then, to track a message, follow these steps:

1. Right-click the details pane and select Track Message. The Message Tracking Center dialog box opens.

2. Specify whom the message was from or to, as well as the server on which the message should be located. The example above shows all messages destined for Joe Kvidera.

3. Click Find Now; all of the messages sent to Joe Kvidera are listed.

4. To view the message history for a particular message, select the message you want to view and click Message History.

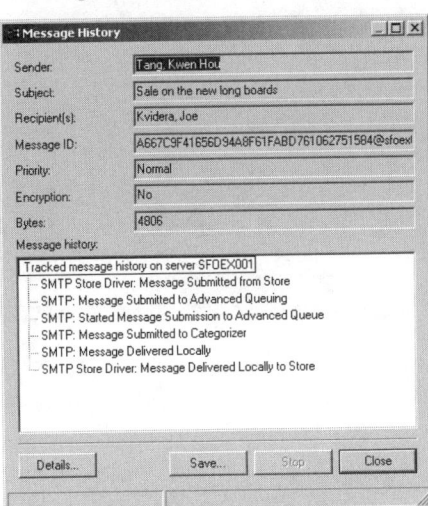

Operations

PART 2

Advanced Message Tracking Searches You can perform a more advanced search for messages by clicking either the Message Tracking Center's Date & Time tab or its Advanced tab. The Date & Time tab lets you specify a date or range of dates for which to search. You can also combine this criteria with information entered on the General and/or Advanced tabs.

The Advanced tab lets you search for a message using its message ID. Every message transferred by Exchange 2000 has a unique ID that includes the name of the originating server, the date, and a long series of digits. You can find the message ID for any message by viewing its properties in a mail client. Since you need access to the message and know where the message already is, this option will not be used for most messaging tracks that you perform, as you will typically not know the message ID.

> **TIP** It is best to use this option to track a message that you are using for testing purposes, such as testing to see how a message is being routed and delivered when you have access to the mailbox of either the sender or the recipient.

I have found the ability to search by message ID especially useful in environments where the message ID is often known, and the path that a message took must be ascertained. Figure 5.11 shows the Advanced tab and tracking by message ID. The message ID can be determined from a sent or received message by looking in Outlook under File ÿ Properties ÿ Message ID property page. The ID consists of the country, ADMD, and PRMD fields from the X.400 address plus a unique string that identifies the originating server, time (in UTC, GMT, or Zulu), and a unique message number.

Figure 5.11 Message tracking using the message ID

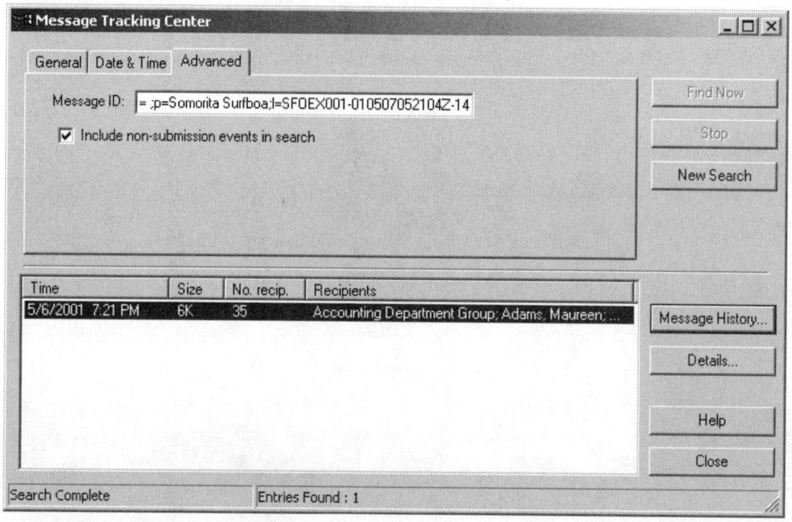

Should You Keep Old Message Tracking Logs?

As stated earlier, the default time to keep old message tracking logs is seven days, but this is configurable. On a server with a few thousand mailboxes, these logs may exceed 50MB per day, but they are text files and compress fairly well.

Should you keep these log files any longer than seven days? One of the nice things about having these logs is that you can run import them in to a third-party tool or run a script against them to do reports on the number of messages you are handling per day. Keeping log files (or at least keeping the data from the log files) can give you an idea of the number of messages you are processing per day and how your message use has grown over time.

Message Tracking Log Format

The message tracking log files are a simple-text format. These log files can be retrieved into any text editor, though I find them slightly easier to read in WordPad than Notepad. The data columns in the log file are separated by tabs; a sample of this log file is shown in Figure 5.12. The first two lines identify what the log file is and the version of System Attendant that created the files. The third line is the file header. A blank field in the file is represented by a hyphen (-); this means that no data for that particular action was necessary or available.

Figure 5.12   Message tracking log file

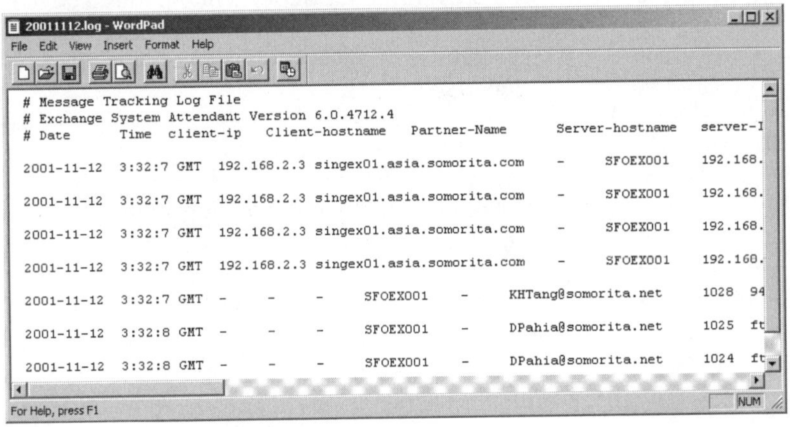

Each of the fields in the file provides information about the message. Table 5.2 lists the fields and their meanings. This message tracking log file format is different than the message tracking log files used by Exchange 5.5.

Table 5.2 Message Tracking Log File Headings

Field	Explanation
Date	Date of the event adjusted for GMT.
Time	Time of the event adjusted for GMT.
Client-IP	If the message originated from SMTP, this is the IP address of the client. If the message is local, this field will contain a hyphen (-).
Client-hostname	If the message originated from SMTP, this is the host name of the SMTP client. If the message is local, this field will contain a hyphen.
Partner-name	The name of the messaging service that handed this message to the current component. This field may contain SMTP, X.400, STORE, IMAP4, or POP3, or the field may be blank.
Server-hostname	The host name of the server that requested that this log entry be made. This is usually the local server's host name.
Server-IP	The IP address of the server that requested that this log entry be made. This is usually the local server's IP address.
Recipient-address	The SMTP or X.400 address of the message recipient.
Event-ID	The number of the event corresponding to the type of action logged.
MSGID	The message's message ID.
Priority	The priority of the message. A priority of 0 is normal, 1 is high, and 5 is low.
Recipient-report-status	This value is only used for delivery reports. It indicates the result of an attempt to deliver a report to the recipient. A value of 0 indicates the message was delivered, and a value 1 indicates that it was not delivered.
Total-bytes	The size of the message in bytes.

Table 5.2   Message Tracking Log File Headings *(continued)*

Field	Explanation
Number-recipients	Total number of recipients in the message.
Time-taken	The delivery time in seconds, calculated by determining the difference between the message timestamp and the time encoded in the message ID. This value will not be calculated for messages originating from outside the organization, and it will only be accurate if your organization's clocks are properly synchronized and the time zones on the servers are set correctly.
Origination-time	Time that the message originated in GMT. This value is blank for delivery recipients and NDRs.
Encryption	Specifies if the message body is encrypted. A value of 0 indicates the message is not encrypted. A value of 1 indicates that the message is signed. A value of 2 indicates that the message is encrypted. If the message is encrypted, you cannot determine if it is also signed.
Service-version	Version of the service making the log entry. You will see non–Exchange 2000 service versions making log entries here, such as the SMTP service.
Linked-MSGID	If there is a message ID generated by a different mail system (such as X.400), that message ID will be found here.
Message-subject	The first 256 bytes of the message's subject.
Sender-address	The SMTP, X.400, or distinguished name (DN) of the sender of the message. The DN is used if the user has been selected from the global address list. If you see a <>, this indicates that the message is a delivery status report.

To really make heads or tails of the logs, you will need to know the event IDs that can be generated by the various components that request that log entries be made; some of the common log entry event IDs are listed in Table 5.3. For more details on these event IDs, see Microsoft Knowledge Base article Q246959.

Operations

PART 2

Table 5.3   Common Message Tracking Log Event IDs

Event ID	Explanation
1019	Message is submitted to Advanced Queuing Engine.
1023	Message is designated for local delivery.
1020	Message transfer outbound via SMTP begins.
1025	Message processing begins.
1024	Message is submitted to categorizer.
1028	Message is delivered to local store by SMTP.
1027	Message is submitted to SMTP by local store.
1031	Message transfer outbound via SMTP is completed.

NOTE   For some basic scripts that parse and report on data found in the message tracking logs, visit www.swinc.com/resources/scripts.htm.

Message Archiving

Has someone within your organization ever asked you to check a user's mailbox for a message that may or may not exist? Or have you ever been asked to somehow monitor all messages sent to and from your Exchange server? To meet these needs, Microsoft incorporated a feature called *Message Archiving* into Exchange 2000. (In Exchange 5.5, this feature was called Message Journaling.) This feature is not for everyone; enabling the feature may require considerable disk space and administration. Organizations such as stockbrokers or banks that are required to keep records of all communication will find this feature useful.

Here are some facts regarding Message Archiving:

- Every message that is sent through a mailbox store has a copy sent to the selected mailbox. This mailbox should be used solely for archiving messages. This is different from Exchange 5.5, in which you had to enable message journaling for an entire site or an entire organization. Due to this limitation, minimizing the number of messages delivered to the journaling mailbox was fairly difficult. Now in Exchange 2000, you can enable this on a store-by-store basis. This allows you to archive messages sent to and from a very specific set of users. While this would require the creation of an additional mailbox store (and the overhead associated with that store), it does allow you to focus on which users you want to perform Message Archiving.

▪ Over time, the storage requirements of the archived messages will become a storage burden, and backing up the system that houses the archive mailbox will begin to take longer and longer. Thus you may want to consider using a dedicated server for Message Archiving. This server can be low-powered but with a lot of disk space; additionally, you can have it host multiple archive mailboxes for different mailbox stores so you can track and archive based on which group of users the messages were sent to or from. You may also want to establish a procedure of archiving these messages to a long-term storage media, such as a CD-ROM or DVD. This can be accomplished easily using ExMerge to archive the messages from the archive mailbox to a PST file, which you can then burn to CD-ROM or DVD. However, Outlook requires that the PST file be copied back to a read/writeable media if you ever need to read the PST in the future.

WARNING   Anyone who has Exchange Admin permissions within the AD can grant themselves permission to the archive mailbox. Then they can view all of the archived messages. One way to limit this is to remove the default AD permissions on the archive mailbox and limit access to the AD object to only the specific people who would need access to the data contained in each archive mailbox.

Enabling Message Archiving

In Exchange 5.5, in order to enable Message Archiving, you had to modify the Registry as well as use the Exchange 5.5 Admin tool in RAW mode in order to extract the DN of the message journaling mailbox. Thankfully in Exchange 2000, Microsoft has made this task much easier to perform. The following steps show how to enable Message Archiving for a mailbox store:

1. Create a mailbox-enabled Active Directory user account in the domain and as many mailbox-enabled archive accounts as needed.

2. After all of the message archiving accounts are created, open the Exchange 2000 System Manager and expand the list of servers within the appropriate administrative group.

3. Locate the mailbox store that you want to archive messages for, and open its properties.

Operations

PART 2

4. On the General tab, click the Archive All Messages Sent Or Received By Mailboxes On This Store check box, and then click Browse. This allows you to select the archive mailbox that you created in step 1.

5. Click Apply.

NOTE When creating the user account and mailbox for use with Message Archiving, make sure you create the mailboxes on a server that has sufficient storage space to accommodate all of the messages that you will be archiving. Again, using a dedicated archive server may be the best solution. Placing these user accounts in a separate OU will also allow you to limit the AD permissions to all of the archive mailboxes by placing permissions at the OU level. Further, by keeping these accounts separate, you can more easily ensure that no GPOs (group policy objects) will be applied to these accounts.

All messages that are sent to and from this mailbox store will now be archived to the mailbox that you have specified. What happens if you send a message to or receive a message from the archive mailbox? Will it create a continuous loop of messages as the archive mailbox sends or receives a message and then duplicates it? No, the system is designed to correctly handle this situation.

Managing Archived Mail Storage

Now that you have configured Message Archiving, you need to come up with a strategy for how to limit the amount of disk space the archive mailboxes will occupy. First and foremost, you need to make sure that you have sufficient disk space to store at least a few weeks of archives. By default, the mailbox you choose will assume the same storage limits as are specified for the mailbox store where it resides. I suggest that even if you do not place the archive mailboxes on a separate server, you should place them in their own mailbox store so that you can create a mailbox storage limit policy just for them. However, if you decide not to do this, you can override the limits on these mailboxes individually through Active Directory Users And Computers.

If you have placed storage limits on the mailboxes, you need to come up with a plan for how to manage the archive mailboxes. Message archival will stop if the mailbox exceeds is Prohibit send and receive limit. If you don't have a proactive approach to managing them, they may fill up your disk in a few weeks. If you have a separate server or a separate storage group for all of your archive mailboxes, you may want to enable circular logging so that your transaction log files do not occupy more space than necessary.

> **TIP** You may be tempted to put the archive mailbox in a storage group that has circular logging enabled. This may not be a good idea if you are required by law to keep the data in the archive mailbox. Enabling circular logging will make up-to-the-minute recovery of this mailbox impossible.

You will need to plan how to manage the size of the archive mailboxes; you want to be careful to make sure the archive mailboxes do not get too big. One of the best solutions would be to use ExMerge and export all of the mail messages to a PST file (provided you don't get near the 2GB limit for the PST file). You could automate this with a script and schedule a task to export these messages monthly. Then you could burn them to a CD or archive the PST files to a backup tape. Your strategy will depend on how long you'll need to have the messages available, as well as how quickly you will need access to the archived messages.

Reporting

Keeping an eye on your system's available storage, who is using the most space, and how your protocols are being used is important in your Exchange environment. Generating reports on system usage and providing that information in a readable fashion will make your job easier. This section covers reporting on storage usage, protocol usage, and sending e-mail from a command prompt. Also discussed in this section are a few of the many third-party utilities for monitoring Exchange 2000 and providing reports.

Storage Used

Exchange 2000 offers the ability to better manage user mailbox storage using multiple databases and storage groups. (See Chapter 7, "Backup and Disaster Recovery," to learn how to plan and deploy multiple mailbox databases and storage groups within Exchange 2000.) Once you have your database structure set up and configured, you can use System Manager to view the storage usage (shown in Figure 5.13). Simply navigate to the mailbox store and click Mailboxes. The right pane reports the storage space occupied by each user in this mailbox store. It shows the mailbox name, the size of the mailbox, the number of items in it, storage limits, and the last time it was accessed. The Storage Limits column lets you see which users have no limits (No Checking), are under their limits (Below Limit), are over their warning limit (Issue Warning), are over their send limit (Prohibit Send), and are over their send and receive limit (Mailbox Disabled).

Operations

PART 2

Figure 5.13 Mailbox store resources

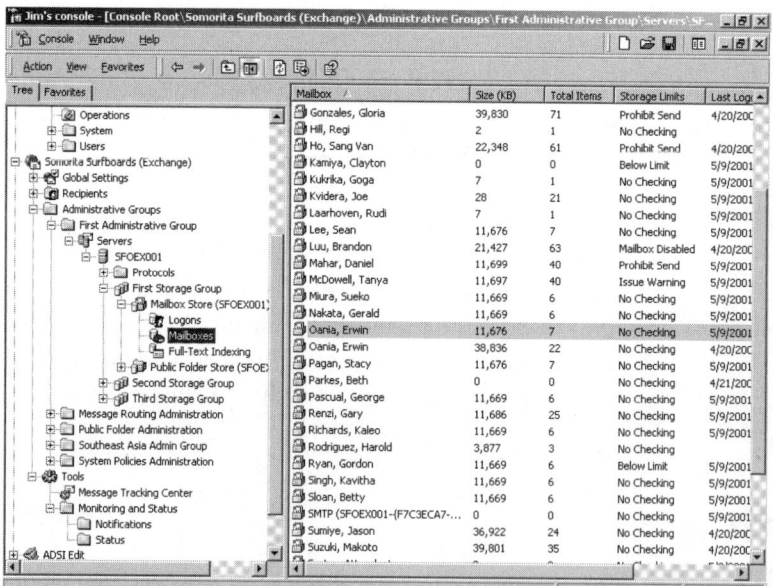

You cannot print the list in Figure 5.13, but you can export it to a text file. Simply right-click the Mailboxes container and choose Export List. You can then choose the file type (tab-separated or comma-separated) and export the data to a file. The file can then be read by a program such as Microsoft Excel, further manipulated, and printed.

Generating a Notice When Users Exceed Their Limits

We can automatically view the information of the users who are exceeding mailbox store policies. To configure reporting of which mailboxes are being sent warning messages about their storage space, follow these steps:

1. Start System Manager.

2. Navigate to the appropriate administrative group, right-click System Policies, click New, and click Mailbox Store Policy.

3. In the New Policy box, click Limits and then click OK.

4. In the Properties box's General tab, type a name for this policy, such as "Limit Notification".

5. On the Limits tab, indicate the storage limits that you want to configure for this mailbox store. Then set the warning message interval, which runs daily at midnight by default, and click OK.

6. Right-click the policy that you created (Limit Notification, in my example), click Add, and then add the mailbox store on which you want this policy's limits to enforce.

7. Under the Servers object, right-click the Exchange 2000 server that you want, and then click Properties.

8. Click the Diagnostics Logging tab, open MSExchangeIS, and then click Mailbox.

9. Click Storage Limits, and then set the logging level to Maximum. Click OK.

Once this is completed, you will see the following event IDs in the application log on the Exchange 2000 server that you are monitoring:

- Event ID 1077 indicates which mailboxes are over their storage warning limit.
- Event ID 1078 indicates which mailboxes are over their prohibit send limit.
- Event ID 1218 indicates which mailboxes are over their prohibit send and receive limit (mailbox disabled).

Protocol Usage

As an Exchange administrator, has someone ever asked you why they can't connect to a server using a different client such as Outlook Express or possibly using OWA over the Internet? These users want to be able to use the client software that is the most familiar and the most convenient for them. Yet once we do provide these types of access, how do we know that anyone is actually using them in order to connect to the Exchange 2000 server? Reporting mechanisms must be put in place in order to report on which protocols are being used and the ones that are the most popular.

> **NOTE**   Many of the protocol-related counters that can be monitored are discussed earlier in this chapter.

Why do I care how many people are using these new clients or if anyone at all is using them? I like to know which client is being used—and which ones are not—for support and security reasons. If users are only connecting using Outlook via MAPI, there's no sense in training my help desk and administrators on how to support POP3 or IMAP4 via Outlook Express or Office XP (Outlook 2002). Further, if users are not utilizing these other clients, then I will want to shut down the virtual servers and remove the inbound filters that I have placed on my firewalls to allow these protocols into the network. Any time I can limit the types of network traffic entering my network, I am creating a more secure environment.

You can use System Monitor to keep tabs on any client protocols you wish. For example, the server in Figure 5.14 has not had many POP3 or HTTP connections; most of them have been IMAP4. In this case, the report option of System Monitor was easier to read than the chart option would have been. To create a report in System Monitor, simply click the View Report button on the toolbar. For more information on creating reports and charts with System Monitor, see Chapter 6, "Performance Monitoring and Optimization."

Figure 5.14 Protocol usage report

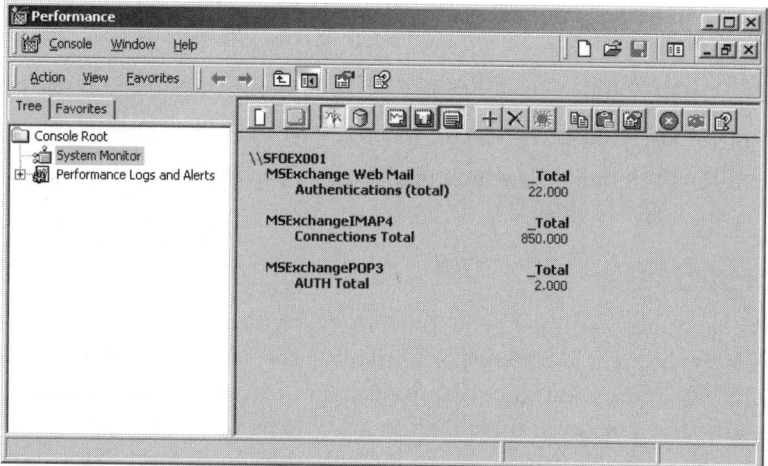

Exchange@Work: Pick a Client, Any Client!

While it is a very user-friendly policy to allow your users to dictate the client that they want to use, this can end up being a tremendous cost sink for your organization. Many organizations that have allowed their users to pick their clients end up going back to only the official standard clients.

One university environment that I worked with recently allowed their end users to pick any e-mail client they wished. Most of the office-based users picked Outlook 2000, some students picked OWA, and other students and faculty picked POP3 and IMAP4 clients, such as Outlook Express, Netscape Communicator, and Eudora.

Exchange@Work: Pick a Client, Any Client! *(continued)*

After a few months of time-consuming support issues surrounding this diverse group of clients, the university's IT department announced that they would only officially support Outlook 2000 for staff and faculty when they are in their offices and OWA for all remote, Unix, and Macintosh users, and for students with computers directly on the university network. They did leave POP3 and IMAP4 available, but with no official support from the IT department; this reduced overall support costs for the IT department. By cutting out layers of complexity, they could reduce their costs.

Automatically Sending E-mail from the Command Prompt

Do you have a message to send, but need to do it from the command prompt? Would you like to find a way to automatically e-mail a report or file to someone? If so, there are a couple of tools that you may find interesting including the MAPIsend command-line tool and Blat for Windows.

MAPIsend

The Exchange 2000 Resource Kit includes a utility called MAPIsend (`mapisend.exe`). This tool allows you to send messages and attachments from a command prompt or through a batch file from computers running Windows NT or Windows 2000.

You can create a batch file that creates and e-mails reports, such as disk space usage, tape backup logs, and other noteworthy system events. Then you can use the Windows NT Scheduler (if using Windows NT) or the Windows 2000 Task Scheduler to automate the batch file so that it runs periodically.

The downside to this tool is that it requires a MAPI profile to be configured. This can make sending mail from the command-line more complicated than necessary. Configuring a MAPI profile requires that Outlook be installed; I don't recommend installing Outlook directly on an Exchange server.

Installing and Using MAPIsend   Installing the MAPIsend program is simple. Copy the `mapisend.exe` file from the BackOffice Resource Kit (usually in \BORK\Exchange) or CD-ROM (\Exchange\Winnt\I386\Admin\MAPIsend), or from the Exchange 2000 Resource Kit (\exreskit\tools\admin\mapidsend), to a directory in the system's root, such as C:\winnt.

To use MAPIsend, you need to be aware of several command-line options:

Option	Explanation
-U	Contains the Exchange server name and mailbox name that MAPIsend will use.
-P	Specifies the password; MAPIsend requires a password to be specified, even if it is a dummy password.
-R	Specifies the recipient or recipients of the message MAPIsend is sending. Separate the multiple recipients with semicolons.
-C	Specifies Cc recipients. Separate multiple Cc recipients with semicolons.
-S	The message subject provided in quotes.
-M	The message body or text of the message in quotes.
-F	Specifies the file attachment, if any. Separate multiple attachments with semicolons.

When specifying command-line options, there must be a space between the command-line option and the parameter. A password must be provided, though it is not required if the currently logged-on user has ownership of Send As permissions to the mailbox. You can provide anything as a password, but there must be something in the password field. Also, make sure that the recipient specified in the -R option is unique. If it is ambiguous, MAPIsend will not send the message.

The best way to illustrate how to make MAPIsend work is to give an example of how I have used it. Every night, the Windows 2000 Backup program creates a log file in the C:\winnt directory called backup.log. I want to automatically e-mail this backup program to a mailbox whose alias is HelpDesk.

I already have a backup job that is scheduled to run every night that backs up the Exchange 2000 server. If I had not already done this, I would need to create a new Windows 2000 Active Directory account called BACKUP, and make it a member of the Account Operators.

Now I need to create a mailbox-enabled AD user account that will be used to send the nightly tape backup reports. I will give it a display name of something like Tape Backup System. The BackOffice Resource Kit documentation states that you can give the Domain Users group ownership permissions to this mailbox, because it does not matter who uses it, but I feel uncomfortable if everyone in the domain has permission to send messages as this mailbox. There is no point in asking for trouble.

Next, I need to log in at the server (or wherever the Task Scheduler service is running and where you will schedule it) as the BACKUP user and create a messaging profile. I'll call the profile BackupReport.

Finally, I am going to create another small batch file called `e-mailbackuplog.bat` and place the following command in it. This is the batch file that I will specify the Task Scheduler to run nightly.

```
MAPIsend -u BACKUP -p boguspw -r HelpDesk -s "Nightly tape backup
report" -m "Tape Backup Report is attached." -f c:\winnt\backup.log
```

> **NOTE**   This is just one example of how you can put this program to use. Please consult the Microsoft BackOffice Resource Kit or the Exchange 2000 Resource Kit for additional documentation and information.

Blat for Windows

Because the MAPIsend utility requires a MAPI profile to work properly, I am fonder of another utility, Blat for Windows. Blat is public-domain software for Windows NT that sends the contents of a file using SMTP. You can download Blat from www.interlog .com/~tcharron/blat.html. The download includes not only **blat.exe**, but also the source code.

To install Blat, copy `blat.exe` to a directory in your path such as the \winnt\system32 directory. You will now need to run Blat one time with some command-line options so that the default mail server and default From names can be set. For example, to configure the default SMTP mail server sfoex001.somorita.net and the default From e-mail address BackupOperations@somorita.net, type:

```
Blat -install sfoex001.Somorita.net BackupOperations@Somorita.net
```

Blat has many options that you can use from the command line; refer to the `readme.txt` file that accompanies the download for more information. Here are some of the basic options:

- `<filename>` indicates the filename to be used for the message body.
- `-to <recipients>` (multiple recipients must be separated by commas).
- `-subject <subject>` provides the message subject line.
- `-f <sender>` overrides the default sender name stored in the Registry.
- `-cc <recipients>` is the Cc recipient list.
- `-body <text>` allows you to specify the body of the message.
- `-r` requests a return receipt.

- -server *<server address>* allows you to override the default SMTP server stored in the Registry.

- -uuencode says to send the message using uuencode.

- -html says to send the message as an HTML message.

- -attach *<file>* specifies a binary file attachment.

- -attacht *<file>* specifies a text file attachment.

The following example sends a text file called BackupRpt.txt to user dbratcher@Somorita.net with a subject of "Backup Report".

```
Blat backuprpt.txt -subject "Backup Report" -to dbratcher@Somorita.net
```

NOTE Blat creator Tim Charron has created a utility called GetMail for Windows. This is a command-line tool that allows you to retrieve messages from a POP3 server and extract attachments. This may be useful for automatically processing mail. This program is shareware and free for non-commercial use. If you use it in your business, be nice and send him a registration fee to encourage him to keep the software up-to-date. It can be downloaded at www.interlog.com/~tcharron/getmail.html.

Third-Party Reporting and Monitoring Tools

Let's face it: Beyond the basic monitoring and reporting tools, Microsoft kind of leaves you out in the cold as far as the information for which you can easily generate reports. I like the new status and notifications features discussed earlier in this chapter, plus we can fairly easily report on mailbox space usage. However, more detailed reporting features are still sorely missing from Exchange 2000. That is where third-party vendors have come onto the scene and filled this need. There are many such tools on the market; this section discusses PromoDag Reports, Hypersoft OmniAnalyser, and NetIQ. Though I have reviewed a number of these tools and have customers who use them in production, I am neither endorsing nor recommending a specific tool.

PromoDag Reports

PromoDag Reports (www.promodag.com) measures the usage of Exchange from both an inside and outside perspective (internal messaging traffic as well as external message traffic) by summarizing data from the message tracking logs. This tool can analyze traffic patterns and generate color, 3D reports, and graphs. Reports include mailbox statistics, connector traffic, usage statistics (hourly, weekly, etc), average message delivery time, and message flow statistics. PromoDag has a free utility on their website called PromoDag StoreLog, which imports message tracking logs into an Access Database and provides some basic reports.

Hypersoft OmniAnalyser

Hypersoft's OmniAnalyser (formerly known as Exchange Analyser) is a tool for collecting usage statistics and creating reports for Microsoft Exchange and Lotus Domino. Reports include daily statistics, traffic reports, a service-level report, availability reports, mailbox statistics, server traffic reports, mailbox content reports, and server health reports. This product does require that an agent be installed on each Exchange server in your organization. This product provides specific reporting for Exchange rather than reports for many BackOffice components such as NetIQ. More information can be found on Hypersoft's website at www.hypersoft.com.

MicroData MELIA 2000

If you're looking for a tool to analyze your Exchange 2000 message tracking log files and provide you with usage reports, check out MicroData's MELIA (Microsoft Exchange Log Import Agent). This tool focuses on producing reports for the message tracking logs and does a good job with this task. You can find MicroData on the Internet at www.microdata.com.

NetIQ

NetIQ (www.netiq.com) is the granddaddy of all monitoring/reporting tools. This program includes comprehensive reporting tools not only for Exchange, but also for Windows NT, Windows 2000, and other Microsoft BackOffice products. If you are looking for a simple reporting solution for Exchange, then this product is overkill. If you are looking for a comprehensive tool for reporting and monitoring your enterprise, then NetIQ is a good place to start.

Mother Knows Best (Microsoft Operations Manager)

Microsoft has released their own enterprise management tools, collectively referred to as Microsoft Operations Manager (MOM). Based on older versions of NetIQ, MOM provides monitoring for not only Exchange Server, but also other products from the Microsoft BackOffice family. You can get more information about MOM from www.microsoft.com/mom.

Legal Issues Surrounding E-mail Systems

Messaging systems and the legalities surrounding e-mail are thorny issues at best. As e-mail becomes the standard communication method between companies, more potential legal issues may arise. E-mail messages are being sequestered in legal proceedings, employees are suing their employers for reading their e-mail, employees are being fired for what they are writing in e-mail messages, and companies are being sued for what employees are writing in e-mail messages.

What can you do to protect your company (and possibly yourself) from legal problems? First and foremost, you (and your company's principals) should develop a policy of acceptable use; this policy should outline what the e-mail system is and is not to be used for. If your Exchange administrators or the people up the food chain want to be able to open anyone's mailbox for *any* reason, this should be clearly stated in the policy.

A lawyer should review this policy to confirm that you making a good (and legal!) effort to control the use of your messaging system. Once the policy is developed and approved, each employee needs to read and understand that they are bound by this policy as long as they are using your organization's e-mail system.

> **NOTE** For a sample Acceptable Use Policy, see my website, www.somorita.com, and look under the Exchange 2000 link. If you use this document, a lawyer should tune it up. Another resource is a book called *E-Policy: How to Develop Computer, E-Policy, and Internet Guidelines to Protect Your Company and Its Assets,* by Michael R. Overly (Amacon, 1998).

Other organizations are taking other steps that are arguably not as effective. One popular approach has been with the use of a legal disclaimer appended to all outbound SMTP messages stating something that indicates that this e-mail may not represent the views of the organization as a whole. Now that disclaimers have been used for a while, the consensus is that they are not enforceable in a court of law, so this may not be the most effective use of your time and resources.

In order to configure an SMTP disclaimer to be appended to each of your outgoing SMTP messages, you can configure an *SMTP event sink*. Event sinks are actually COM-compatible program code, typically Visual Basic, VBScript, JavaScript, C, or C++. This code is then triggered by a defined event, such as all outgoing messages to an SMTP virtual server, and then it processes the rules you specified, such as adding a legal disclaimer to all outbound messages. Microsoft Knowledge Base article Q288098 contains a sample event sink that allows you to append a disclaimer to all messages. This sink is a sample and should not be considered ready for production.

Some organizations are using Message Archiving for purposes of auditing. For example, you may need to archive or audit your user's e-mail messages if you suspect employees within your company of sharing confidential information. In Exchange 2000, you can easily archive all messages sent internally, as discussed earlier in this chapter.

Additionally, more companies are using third-party tools to help them scan for information that may be confidential that should not be leaving the organization, as well as information that could be considered inappropriate for the workplace. Tools such as MIMESweeper, by Content Technologies (www.mimesweeper.com), or MMS (formerly known as World Secure), by Baltimore, can perform these functions.

These third-party tools, combined with an integrated antivirus solution, are a great way to protect your Exchange 2000 system from unwanted and potentially harmful e-mails. With these utilities installed, you will be able to monitor and scan all of your SMTP messages for very specific words and phrases and then either reject the messages or add a disclaimer to them. There is even an add-on for MIMESweeper called PornSweeper, which will scan all messages for imbedded or attached graphics and attempt to determine whether or not these pictures would be considered pornographic or offensive to some users. However, note that while these utilities are very helpful, they cannot guarantee that no harmful messages will be allowed through the system.

Exchange@Work: Destroying the Evidence

An organization (a law firm, ironically) that I recently worked with was concerned with the number of stories making news about their organization having their e-mail records subpoenaed and then used against them. Despite my own efforts and the efforts of the Exchange administrator to convince them otherwise, the firm's partnership made a decision to purge all e-mail older than one week (later extended to one month). Further, this decision included the requirement that the system should not be backed up so there would be no backup records of e-mail. They later reneged on this and let us keep a week's worth of backups as long as there were no tapes archived.

While this will certainly help keep the firm's potential liability at a minimum, they have succeeded in seriously limiting the functionality of their e-mail system. If I only had a week's worth of e-mail available to me, I would feel like I had my arm cut off.

Perhaps a better approach to this is not to try and bury evidence, but to train employees not to do anything illegal in the first place.

Operations

PART 2

6

Performance Monitoring and Optimization

As with any other software, providing good performance is one of the keys to a successful deployment of Exchange 2000. E-mail is the number one form of electronic communication in corporations today, and one of the most commonly used productivity applications used. So when performance on a server that supports mailboxes drops significantly (maybe it takes 10 seconds to open a mail message), what will your users report? And how will it affect their work? If one of your Exchange servers were to become unavailable, how many supports calls would your help desk receive in the first minute? What would happen if your entire Exchange organization became unavailable? Would you just have a prerecorded message at the help desk to handle all the calls that would be flooding in? Due to the amount of communication that flows through a mail system, people have become so dependant on their messaging environments that it is one of the most crucial services in an organization. In many cases, loss of messaging can stop business processes and interfere with the bottom line.

The key to ensuring that your mail systems stay up and running is making sure that both your Windows 2000 environment and your Exchange server are healthy. What is a healthy

Windows 2000 or Exchange server? Everyone will probably have a unique perspective on this, but my definition would include the following criteria:

- During the busiest times of the day, the Exchange server should be able to provide MAPI clients with the ability to open and display small messages (under 10K) in fewer than two seconds.

- The server should provide reasonable room for growth without adversely affecting users.

- Free/busy information should be current.

- Public folder content should be current and easily retrieved.

- External e-mail (to the Internet) should be available 99% of the time.

Once we have some context for overall performance monitoring, this chapter categorizes and discusses several Performance Monitor counters that may prove useful when performing system performance analysis. The categories include counters for monitoring basic Windows 2000 performance, counters for monitoring Exchange 2000 server objects, and counters that may provide useful information about your Exchange environment but that don't relate specifically to performance. The major topics covered in this chapter include:

- Taking a holistic approach to performance monitoring

- Monitoring Windows 2000 counters

- Monitoring Exchange 2000 counters

- Optimizing Exchange 2000 servers

The Holistic Approach to Performance Monitoring

I almost called this section of the book "Zen and the Art of Performance Monitoring." You would think that performance monitoring would be an exact science; either there is a performance problem or there isn't. I suppose given all of the variables that can be monitored, you could make performance monitoring an exact science, but that involves a *lot* of variables.

When you start monitoring a server, you have to take a holistic approach. You can't look at any single component of the system and decide that component is a bottleneck—you have to look at the system as a whole. Before we start discussing the basics of using the System Monitor tool, here are a few issues to keep in mind:

- Don't get monitoring tunnel vision! Don't monitor a specific resource and decide that resource is the bottleneck without taking a broader view of monitoring. For example, if the CPU looks over-tasked, check to make sure there is sufficient memory, as well. Consider third-party products that may be impacting performance, such as anti-virus applications, or other products that may be leaking memory.

- Make sure you know the scale that is being used when using the Performance Monitor chart view. Some values are percentages; naturally, the range goes from 0 to 100 percent. Other values, such as bytes free, RAM used, milliseconds, and so on, are actual measurements. Though they may be plotted on the graph from 0 to 100, a value near the top of the scale does not indicate that the resource is exhausted. This is very important to consider, especially when you are monitoring values of multiple resources on a single chart. Something at the bottom of the chart may actually indicate the problem due to the scale of the actual chart, so make sure to double-check the scale every time you work with Performance Monitor.

- Monitor activity during typical periods of activity. The system will definitely look under-used if you monitor these same resources at midnight. I do, however, recommend monitoring activity at midnight just to see how much of the major resources are actually being used when there is little to no activity on the server and to create an idle baseline.

- Don't sweat the peaks. Look for sustained activity throughout the life of your monitoring session. Spikes in activity such as CPU and disk usage are standard and nothing to be concerned about. It is normal for a CPU to spike to 100 percent occasionally.

- Establish a baseline for your system. Monitor your system when there are no active users to see how the system components such as memory, disk access, processor utilization, and network usage behave when the system is in an idle state. Then monitor your system as its load increases. Make sure to save the log files so that you can look at historical data and compare it with your projected system growth and system resource requirements.

- Maintain performance information over time to show growth impacts on the system and application availability.

Operations

PART 2

Monitoring Is Not a One-Time Occurrence

When you begin performance monitoring of any kind, you are concerned about averages, not spikes in activity. How do you get this average? By watching your systems over long periods of time. The performance data you gather from a single morning of monitoring may not be representative of your server's true behavior. The performance data you gather over a week may not even give you a true indication of the normal behavior of server performance. Only after taking samples for weeks at a time will you be able to get a better idea of average usage.

Monitoring Is Not a One-Time Occurrence *(continued)*

Taking a single look at an Exchange server and deciding from that single look that you have a certain type of bottleneck might yield accurate results. But then again, it may yield an incorrect solution based on incomplete information. You may spend thousands of dollars to fix a bottleneck that did not really exist in the first place. In the meantime, the real bottleneck goes on unresolved.

When you begin performance monitoring, have a long-term goal in mind. Learn to use analysis tools from something like Microsoft Excel. Or purchase a third-party package such as Tally System's Veranda (www.tallysystems.com) or NetIQ (www.netiq.com) that can help you to collect, store, and analyze Exchange performance data.

Performance Monitoring 101: Using System Monitor

When you begin monitoring Windows 2000 as well as how Exchange 2000 affects the server, keep in mind that any objects you monitor should include critical counters from the four main "sub-systems" within a Windows 2000 server: memory, processor, network, and disk. The counters that I always include in any monitoring session include the following:

Object	Instance	Counter
Memory		Available MBytes
Memory		Pages/sec
Processor	_Total	%Processor
Network Interface	Selected adapter	Bytes Total/sec
PhysicalDisk	_Total	%Disk Time
PhysicalDisk	_Total	Avg. Disk Queue Length

TIP Before monitoring any disk-related counters, you need to enable the disk performance counters by typing **DISKPERF –Y** at the command prompt and then rebooting. If you have a single array partitioned into multiple logical disks, use the LogicalDisk object to monitor performance on individual drives.

The tools that I use for performance monitoring are Windows 2000 System Monitor and the Performance Logs and Alerts console. Figure 6.1 shows a System Monitor chart that I have created. In this chart, I am interested in how a mailbox server that supports MAPI clients fares based on the number of clients. So I would plot not only the basic Windows 2000 counters, but also some counters relating to Exchange 2000, such as active users, messages sent per second, connector usage, and folders opened per second. When I am looking at the performance counters on this chart, I would consider, for example, how spikes in the messages sent per second might affect the memory, processor, network, and disk.

Figure 6.1   System Monitor chart plotting typical Windows 2000 counters and specific Exchange 2000 system counters

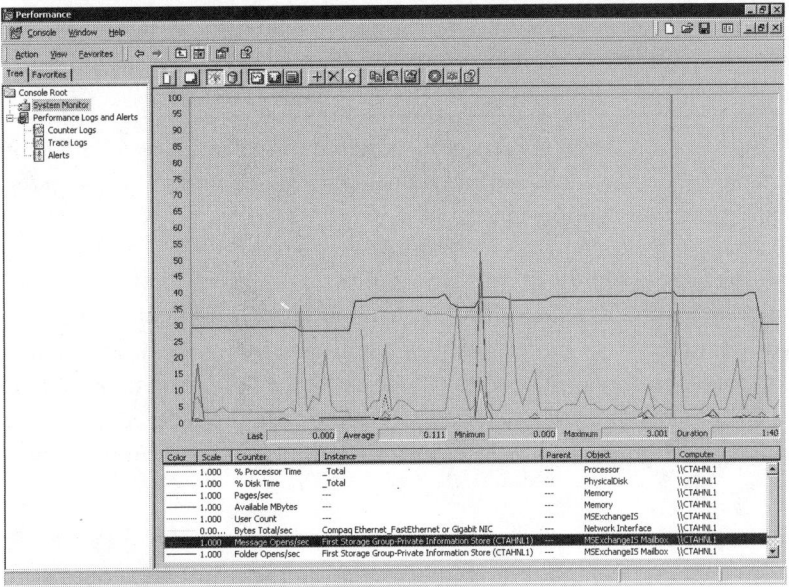

You can run System Monitor using the pre-built Performance console in the Start ➤ Programs ➤ Administrative Tools menu or you can create your own console. To create your own console, follow these steps:

1. Run the MMC utility by choosing Start ➤ Run ➤ MMC.

2. Add additional snap-ins and controls by selecting File ➤ Add/Remove Snap-in and clicking the Add button.

3. If you want to add System Monitor, select ActiveX Control, click Add, and click Next. Scroll down the Control Type list and find System Monitor Control, then click Next and click Finish.

4. If you want to add the ability to create log files and generate alerts, select Performance Logs and Alerts from the Add Standalone Snap-ins list.

5. Add additional snap-ins as desired to create in your custom console.

6. Click OK to go back to the consoles you have created. Don't forget to save this custom MMC in case you want to use it again.

Both System Monitor and the Performance Logs and Alerts console allow you to display, log, or generate alert information about counters on the Windows 2000 system. To use these features, you need to understand some of the information you will be prompted for when setting up monitoring.

On the Add Counters dialog box, you will be prompted for the server from which you want to choose counters. You are also asked to select *performance objects*; these are the major components of the Windows 2000 servers, such as memory, physical disks, processors, the web server, and an Exchange mailbox store.

TIP When monitoring servers, you should monitor the server from another machine on the network. This will reduce the impact of monitoring on the Exchange server's performance.

As mentioned above, *counters* are the actual performance statistics that you track. Each object has counters that gather different data about that particular object. For example, the Processor object has counters that track statistics such as total percentage of processor time, and total percentage of processor time by the CPU when in user mode versus kernel mode. The counters that the object supports are shown in the Select Counters From List box, which lists counters such as Messages Submitted, Messages Submitted/min, and Peak Client Logons.

Many objects will have multiple *instances*; such an object could be a processor in a multiprocessor system or a mailbox store in a server that has more than one mailbox store. If you have more than one mailbox store on a single Exchange 2000 server, that object will have an instance for each mailbox store.

Viewing Performance Data

What are your choices when reviewing data? Well, the System Monitor object has two options for presenting the data: chart view and report view. You can also view the data as a variation of a chart called a *histogram*. Back in Figure 6.1, you saw data presented in a chart; this is the default view. In some cases, such as when you're trying to find a bottleneck, data is more easily read and interpreted using a chart. A chart is also useful when you need to review data that you have previously captured in a log file and want to look for trends.

However, other data is more useful when viewed in a report format. This includes data containing average numbers from a log file or totals from monitoring queues. Figure 6.2 shows a sample report view. To switch the System Monitor control to report view, click the button on the toolbar that looks like a spiral notepad (left of the "+" button).

Figure 6.2   System Monitor showing a report view

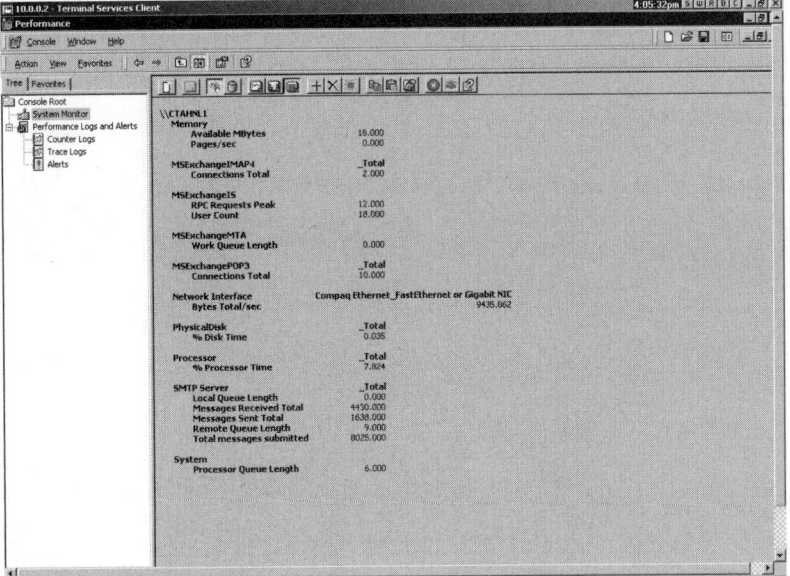

Don't be afraid of the report view! The chart view may be sexy and colorful and interesting looking, but the report may be a far better way to present raw data for interpretation.

Recording a Log

System Monitor allows you to view data either from current activity or from a previously recorded log file. The Performance Logs and Alerts console snap-in provides you with a useful tool for recording a log file. I have found this especially useful for recording a log file of system activity and reviewing it later.

Further, the Performance Logs and Alerts console allows you to specify a starting date and time and a duration for recording the log files. For example, let's say that I want to record activity on one of my servers from 8:30 A.M. until 11:30 A.M. on Monday; this is typically a busy time for most messaging servers. Here is the procedure to create and schedule the recording of this log file:

1. Launch the Performance console from the Administrative Tools menu.

2. Open the Performance Logs and Alerts container, right-click the Counter Logs container, and choose New Log Settings.

3. Enter the name of the Log you are creating and click OK.

4. On the General property page, specify counters you want to record and the sample interval.

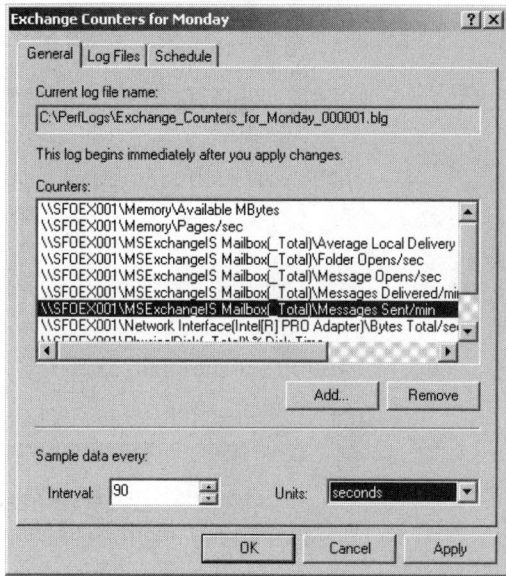

I'm recording this log file for three hours and am interested in averages, not spikes in activity, so I take a sample every 90 seconds. Be careful not to select too many counters or take samples too often, since this will dramatically increase the size of the log file.

5. If you need to change the default directory or the maximum size of the log file, this can be done on the Log Files property page. On this page you also can specify a directory to record this log in to as well as increment the log filename each time a new log file is created.

6. Specify a start date and time that the log should run. This is done on the Schedule tab (shown in Figure 6.3), where you can also set the log to run manually.

Once the log is complete, you can use System Monitor to review the log in either report or chart format. Only the counters you selected will be available to be viewed in System Monitor. Often the log data is imported into a database or spreadsheet for retention, comparison with historical data, and for projecting future resource needs.

Figure 6.3   Schedule property page of a counter log

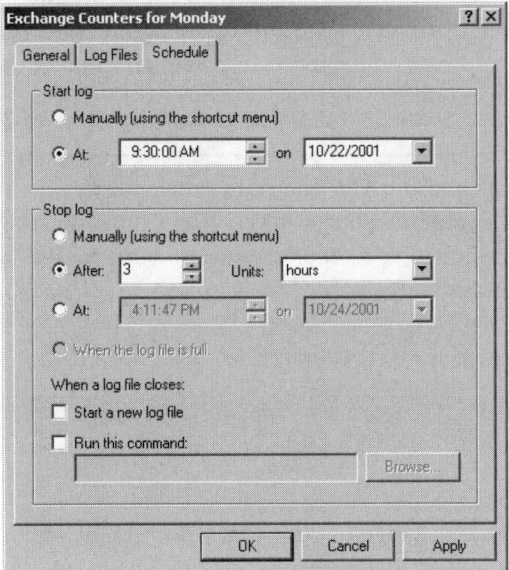

Disk Monitoring

If you are planning to monitor disk counters using System Monitor, you must make sure the correct counters are enabled. By default, only physical disk counters are enabled. If you want enable monitoring of the logical disk counters, at a command prompt use the diskperf command to enable and disable counters. The following are some command-line options that can be used to turn on and off disk counters. After these commands are typed, you must restart the system for them to take effect.

- Diskperf −y enables all disk counters.
- Diskperf −yv enables logical disk counters.
- Diskperf −yd enables physical disk counters.
- Diskperf −n disables all disk counters.
- Diskperf −nv disables the logical disk counters.
- Diskperf −nd disables the physical disk counters.

Establishing a Performance Baseline

Do you know what is normal for your system? If you start performance monitoring and notice that the percentage of disk time is running at an average of 30 percent, will you know if that is normal or not? The purpose of a baseline is to help you figure out what the system looks like under expected loads.

The first step toward calculating a baseline is to perform an analysis of typical performance counters when the system is not under a user load but all services are operating. Then, take another performance snapshot of the system when it is under a normal user load and operating as you would expect. Consider also taking snapshots of the system at peak loads, since these will be when users will most likely complain.

> **NOTE** The time for taking a baseline is *not* when the system begins to misbehave and you need to figure out what is wrong. You should do so when the system is installed and continue to take regular measurements for weeks after your system first starts operations.

When Should I Monitor?

Plan to perform system monitoring before and after any changes to your system, such as new hardware, new software, or additional users. New hardware and software may also affect your baseline.

If you have had a major change to your network infrastructure, you may also want to check a few of your network counters at this time. Even what may seem like a minor change may make a huge impact on your server's performance if that change is now causing routing issues with your SMTP messages.

As far as the time of day to monitor, unless you are taking a baseline measurement, you should monitor your system during typical periods of activity. For many Exchange 2000 environments, the first hour of the workday is the busiest, so you may want to isolate and analyze that part of the day from the rest of the business day. (The first hour is typically the busiest as employees log in during the early hours onto the network and immediately start to check their e-mail.) This allows you to know when your system is the busiest as well as what resources are the most used (or possibly when system bottlenecks appear) during this period.

Monitoring Windows 2000

How efficient can your Exchange 2000 server be if your Windows 2000 server isn't healthy? Can your Exchange 2000 server perform up to the required standards that your company has put in place if the Windows 2000 server has a hard enough time just booting? Ever had a supervisor or a client ask you to configure an existing server as an Exchange server even though you knew the system couldn't handle the additional load? After explaining this to them, they ask you to do it anyway. Then when it is up and running, they want to know why it is so slow and then ask you to fix it. There are just too many people in the world who are afraid to spend a little more money upfront to have a successful implementation.

In order to make sure that your Exchange 2000 server can perform up to standards, you need to make sure that the Windows 2000 server is healthy and capable of delivering high availability and acceptable response times for your environment. To determine this, the tool that will allow you to view charts, create logs, and view reports from previously logged data is the Performance console (which includes System Monitor).

If your Exchange 2000 server isn't performing up to your standards, what is wrong with it? Does it need more RAM? A faster CPU, or maybe an additional CPU? Is your disk subsystem too slow? Most users and administrators always think that their systems are too slow, and they will tell you that it is slower than it was last week or last month.

You can track this information using the Performance console. Create reports and charts that compare older statistics with current usage. There is nothing better than solid evidence in the form of numbers to quantify the fact that you need additional hardware in order to improve your system's response times.

Useful Windows 2000 Performance Monitor Counters

Before you start monitoring Exchange-specific counters, you need to look at counters that will let you know if your basic system resources are over-tasked. These counters are your first clue that you need more hardware resources or that your software configuration needs to be changed. Table 6.1 shows a list of Windows 2000 counters that you should monitor, which values to watch for, and how to improve each of these counters if the need arises.

Table 6.1   Basic Counters for Monitoring Windows 2000 Performance

Object ➤ Counter	Explanation	Desired Values	How to Improve
Processor ➤ % Total Processor Time	Total real work being performed by all system CPUs.	Less than a 70% sustained value.	Add an additional CPU or get a faster CPU.
System ➤ Processor Queue Length	The total number of threads in the queue waiting for a processor.	If this value is consistently more than 2, this may indicate a CPU bottleneck.	Add an additional CPU or get a faster CPU.

Table 6.1   Basic Counters for Monitoring Windows 2000 Performance *(continued)*

Object ➤ Counter	Explanation	Desired Values	How to Improve
Memory ➤ Pages/sec	The number of 4k pages written to or read from the paging file.	Fewer than 5–15 pages per second. Sustained larger values can indicate a low available memory situation.	Add more RAM or remove the demand for additional memory by reallocating resources.
Memory ➤ Mbytes	Amount of memory available after all process and caching memory have been allocated.	If this number is consistently below 15MB, consider adding RAM. This number should never drop below 4MB.	Add more RAM.
Paging File ➤ % Usage (_Total instance)	Total percentage of usage of the paging file.	If this value is greater than 75 percent, the page file is being heavily used.	Increase the initial size of the page file. Look at other memory-related counters to determine if there is a memory bottleneck.
Network ➤ Bytes Total/sec	Total number of bytes transferred to the network per second.	Should not approach the limits of the technology (such as 1.2MB/s for 10BaseT Ethernet or 12MB/s for 100BaseT).	Move to a switched network technology or segment the network into smaller pieces.
Physical Disk ➤ % Disk Time	Percentage of time that a logical disk is used for both reads and writes.	Should be less than 60% on a sustained basis.	Add additonal physical disks, faster disks, or faster disk controllers.

Table 6.1　Basic Counters for Monitoring Windows 2000 Performance *(continued)*

Object ➢ Counter	Explanation	Desired Values	How to Improve
Physical Disk ➢ Average Disk Queue Length	The average number of pending read and write requests for a specific disk.	Should be less than the number of spindles plus 2.	Add additional physical disks, faster disks, or faster disk controllers.
TCP ➢ Segments Retransmitted/sec	The number of TCP segments restransmitted per second as a result of network problems.	In a perfect world, should be zero, but in reality, it should be less than 5% of the TCP ➢ Segments Sent/sec counter.	You have a network problem. Your network is too busy or there is an unreliable link. Look at your network infrastructure to see if you can improve this.
Network Segment ➢ % Network Utilization	The percentage of network bandwidth used on this segment.	The ideal value for this counter will vary from nework type to network type, but should be below 30–40% on an Ethernet network. I have seen healthy switched networks run much higher.	Break your network into small pieces or implement switching technology.
Network Interface ➢ Output Queue Length	The length of the queue for packets waiting to be transmitted.	Values higher than 2 indicate a possible network bandwidth problem.	Break the network into smaller pieces or implement switching. Also consider getting a faster network adapter, looking at the network adapter settings, or updating the device driver.

Operations

PART 2

Table 6.1   Basic Counters for Monitoring Windows 2000 Performance *(continued)*

Object ➤ Counter	Explanation	Desired Values	How to Improve
Process ➤ % Process Time (lsass instance)	Percentage of processor time that the local security authority is using. If this is a domain controller, this is the Active Directory process.	On a domain controller, you can always expect to see this process using some CPU time. If it is sharing a server with Exchange, it should not use more than about 15%.	If it is exceeding the amount you expect, add an additional processor or move some tasks to another server.
System ➤ Context Switches/sec	The combined rate at which all processors on the computer are switched from one thread to another.	Context switches over 4000/sec might be cause for concern.	If it is exceeding the amount you expect, add an additional processor, or move some tasks to another server.

The counters in Table 6.1 are only a few of the many that are available to any Windows 2000 installation. However, they are the ones that I consider critical to locating system bottlenecks and determining if a single resource is overburdened. The desired values are my own, derived from a combination of a dozen books and white papers I have read, as well as personal experiences. These counters and desired values can apply to any Windows 2000 system, including those running Exchange 2000 server services.

Monitoring Exchange 2000

Once you've established that your Windows 2000 server is running, you can move on to monitoring your Exchange 2000 components. Now, how do you know if your Exchange server is healthy or not? Is it okay so long as your end users don't complain about slow access times to their mailbox? Or maybe your Exchange server is doing fine as long as you are able to send and receive Internet e-mail messages. While these may be factors in helping you determine whether or not the Exchange server is healthy, you shouldn't be using these as guides to determine the performance and health of your Exchange 2000 server.

Instead, use the Performance console and System Monitor, which allow you to track and view trends of your Exchange 2000 servers and the usage of the specific services and protocols that are enabled for the Exchange 2000 environment. Found that there is a bottleneck on the system and you would like to ascertain which Exchange 2000 component is causing the most system resource usage? Again, it's time to use System Monitor.

Exchange 2000 Performance Monitor Objects

When Exchange 2000 is installed onto a Windows 2000 server, over 30 additional performance monitor objects are installed and almost 1000 additional counters. You may use some of these objects only in rare circumstances (or never), while others may prove useful to you on a regular basis. Some of the objects included in Windows 2000 may also be useful when monitoring Exchange-specific technologies such as the SMTP counters. These objects include the following:

Database   Counters relate to overall database performance such as cache hits, log writes, and pages converted per second.

Database => Instances   Counters relate to performance for each instance (storage group) that is created for the information store.

Epoxy   There are instances under this object for DAV (HTTP), IMAP, NNTP, POP3, and SMTP. Counters include information about queuing of requests between IIS and the store for each of the instance types.

Microsoft Gatherer   Counters relate to the indexing service as a whole.

Microsoft Gatherer Projects   Counters relate to the process of creating the index for each project (each store that has a full-text index).

Microsoft Search Indexer Catalogs   Counters provide statistics for the contents of each catalog, such as the number of documents, wordlists, and index size.

MSExchange Oledb Events   Counters provide stats on the number of ExOLEDB events completed and the rate at which they are completed.

MSExchange Oledb Resource   Counters offer information on the ExOLEDB active data and transactions.

MSExchange Web Mail   This object has information for either IE5 and later browsers or non-IE5 browsers including counters on the deletion, creation, and updates of appointment items, attachments, posts, and messages.

MSExchangeAL   Counters provide information on reach Recipient Update Service (RUS), including LDAP queries and modifications.

MSExchangeDSAccess Caches   Counters provide statistics about the use, effectiveness, and size of the DSAccess cache.

MSExchangeDSAccess Contexts   Counters provide statistics about the use of the DSAccess cache for each process (you will have to find the process id in the context list and match this to the process ID using Task Manager in order to know which process is which in the instances list).

MSExchangeES   Counters report usage of the Exchange Event Service.

MSExchangeIM   Counters relate to the use of Instant Messaging (IM).

MSExchangeIM Virtual Servers   Counters provide an instance of each IM virtual server, including usage of all HTTP DAV methods used by IM.

MSExchangeIMAP4   Counters for the IMAP4 service.

MSExchangeIS   Counters for the entire information store service, such as total active users and RPC operations.

MSExchangeIS Mailbox   Counters offer statistics for each mailbox store including messages processed, store queue sizes, delete item cache size, single instance ratio, and delivery time.

MSExchangeIS Public   Counters provide statistics for each public folder store including store queue sizes, delivery time, replication statistics, and messages processed.

MSExchangeIS Transport Driver   Counters for use with the Exchange transport driver, including total MAPI messages submitted, total messages submitted via transport driver, total messages delivered locally on this server, and total messages transferred to the MTA.

MSExchangeMTA   Counters track total number and size of messages that the MTA has processed. These statistics reflect delivery to X.400 systems as well as Exchange 5.5 servers in the same administrative group.

MSExchangeMTA Connections   Counters are provided for each separate instance (X.400 connection objects and Exchange 5.5 servers) that indicate number and size of messages processed, queued messages, current associations, and message transfer statistics. Each X.400 and Exchange 5.5 connection is a separate instance under this object.

MSExchangePOP3   Counters specify POP3 usage, including number of authentications, connections, and statistics for each of the basic POP3 commands.

MSExchangeSA - NSPI Proxy   Counters track the usage of the DSProxy process that handles MAPI client directory service lookups for pre–Outlook 2000 clients and referrals generated for Outlook 2000 and Outlook XP clients.

MSExchangeSRS   Counters provide Site Replication Service (SRS) statistics related to the use of replication with Exchange 5.5 directory databases, including Exchange 5.5 directory service reads and writes, replication statistics, and LDAP searches.

MSExchangeTransport Store Driver   Counters indicate usage of the store driver for messages submitted via IIS services, such as SMTP.

SMTP NTFS Store Driver   Counters monitor inbound messages that are currently being stored on the file system for each SMTP virtual server.

SMTP Server   Counters track messages flowing through the SMTP protocol and Advanced Queuing Engine including, queues, categorizer statistics, message transport statistics, bad mail statistics, connection errors, and DNS lookups. You can look at the counters for either all SMTP virtual servers or individual SMTP virtual servers.

Useful Exchange 2000 Performance Monitor Counters

Earlier in the chapter, we looked at the basics of monitoring your Windows 2000 system counters. Now you can expand upon your knowledge of what your server is doing on the Exchange side by monitoring some of the Exchange-specific System Monitor counters. Table 6.2 lists several counters (but not all of them—remember there are almost 1000 of them added when Exchange 2000 is installed!) that are useful when monitoring Exchange 2000 server performance and response times.

Table 6.2   Exchange-Specific Counters for Monitoring Performance and Response Times

Object ➢ Counter	Explanation
Process ➢ %Process Time (store instance)	Percentage of the processor time that the information store is using. On a dedicated Exchange server, this will usually use more processor time than other the other processes on the system.
Process ➢ %Process Time (inetinfo instance)	Percentage of processor time that the services managed by the Internet Information Server is using (HTTP, IMAP4, POP3, NNTP, SMTP, and Instant Messaging).
Process ➢ %Process Time (mad instance)	Percentage of processor time that the System Attendant is using for processes such as DSProxy, DSAccess, DS2MB, and other tasks.
MSExchangeIS ➢ User Count	Total number of users connected to all mailbox and public folder stores on this server.

Operations

PART 2

Table 6.2 Exchange-Specific Counters for Monitoring Performance and Response Times *(continued)*

Object ➢ Counter	Explanation
MSExchangeIS ➢ RPC Requests	The current number of RPC requests being processed by the information store. This figure should usually be small; higher numbers indicate more activity from MAPI clients. If this number is consistently above 25, then your server is not keeping up with the MAPI client requests.
MSExchangeIS Mailbox ➢ Average Time for Delivery	Average time (in milliseconds) that the last ten messages waited before being delivered to the Advanced Queuing Engine. (High values could indicate the server is operating too slowly.) I don't like to see this value climb above 1500 milliseconds.
MSExchangeIS Mailbox ➢ Average Local Delivery Time	Average time (in milliseconds) that the last ten messages waited before being delivered to recipients on the same server (local delivery). High values could indicate the information store service is very busy. I don't like to see this value climb above 1000 milliseconds.
MSExchangeIS Mailbox ➢ Send Queue Size MSExchangeIS Public ➢ Send Queue Size	There will be one of these counters for each instance of public or mailbox stores. This is the number of messages waiting to be delivered by the information store. During busy times, this value may spike, but on average it should be very near zero. Non-zero values indicate the information store service is not keeping up with the load that has been placed on it.
Database > Database Cache % Hit	The percentage of database file page requests that were serviced by the database cache rather than having to go to the disk. If this value is below 75%, then consider adding more RAM to the server.

Table 6.2   Exchange-Specific Counters for Monitoring Performance and Response Times *(continued)*

Object ➤ Counter	Explanation
MSExchangeDSAccess Caches ➤ Cache Hits/sec MSExchangeDSAccess Caches ➤ Cache Misses/sec	The number of times that DSAccess is resolving entries from cache and the number of times that DSAccess is having to perform domain controller/ Global Catalog server lookups per second. Compare the number of cache hits per second with the number of cache misses per second. The number of cache hits per second should be at least twice what the number of cache misses per second is. If not, you should allocate additional memory to the DSAccess cache.
SMTP Server ➤ Messages Pending Routing	The number of messages that have been categorized but not routed. Seeing more than a few dozen messages pending indicates that the SMTP server is not able to keep up with the number of messages being forwarded to it. This could indicate a processor bottleneck or not enough server RAM.
SMTP Server ➤ Categorizer Queue Length	The number of messages in the Messages Awaiting Directory Lookup (Pre-Cat) queue. Consistently seeing items queued up here may mean that the categorizer cannot keep up with the message demands, or that there is a problem with an event sink.
SMTP Server ➤ Avg Retries/msg Delivered SMTP Server ➤ Avg Retries/ msg Sent	Ratios of the number of retries per message being transmitted outbound (msg Sent) or delivered internally (msg Delivered). Ideally, this number should be very small (less than .01). If the number approaches 1, that means that almost every message being delivered is being retried, which may be the result of network problems or a dismounted mailbox store.

Operations

PART 2

Table 6.2 Exchange-Specific Counters for Monitoring Performance and Response Times *(continued)*

Object ➢ Counter	Explanation
MSExchangeIS ➢ Virus Scan Queue Length	The current number of messages waiting for virus scanning. If this number is consistently above 1 or 2, the virus-scanning software is not able to keep up with the demand for messages to be scanned. Look for CPU or memory bottlenecks.
MSExchangeMTA ➢ Messages/sec	The number of message that the MTA sends and receives each second. Lower values are desired.
MSExchangeIS ➢ VM Largest Block Size	The largest block of free virtual memory available on the server. If this number drops below 16MB, you may not be able to mount additional stores or storage groups. This is critical for clustered servers, because it may prevent failover from occurring. In this case, schedule the information store on the server to be restarted. If this server is in an Exchange 2000 cluster, schedule all servers to be restarted. See Microsoft Knowledge Base article Q296073 for more information.

Table 6.3 lists some other counters that provide useful and interesting insight into an Exchange 2000 server, particularly when watching trends. These are not directly related to performance optimization, but they are useful when correlating activity to other variables, such as the number of users connected. The MSExchangeIS Mailbox and the MSExchangeIS Public objects have instances for each mailbox or public folder store on the server. The SMTP Server object has an instance for each SMTP virtual server.

Table 6.3 Additional System Monitor Counters

Object ➢ Counter	Explanation
MSExchangeIS ➢ User Count	The total number of connected client sessions.
MSExchangeIS ➢ Active User Count	The total number of users who have generated any activity within the previous ten minutes.

Table 6.3   Additional System Monitor Counters *(continued)*

Object ➤ Counter	Explanation
MSExchangeIS Mailbox ➤ Message Submitted/Min MSExchangeIS Public ➤ Messages Submitted/Min	The number of messages that have been submitted to the private (or public) information store. This does not include the total number of recipients per message.
MSExchangeIS Mailbox ➤ Total Size of Recoverable Items MSExchangeIS Public ➤ Total Size of Recoverable Items	The amount of space used by deleted items in the private (or public) information store database.
MSExchangeIS Mailbox ➤ Total Count of Recoverable Items MSExchangeIS Public ➤ Total Count of Recoverable Items	The number of messages used by deleted items in the private (or public) information store database.
MSExchangeIS Mailbox ➤ Single Instance Ratio	The average ratio of mailbox "pointers" to each message in the store. Many organizations consider themselves lucky if this value is above 1.8. This value will change over time as the users delete copies of messages with several recipients. A very low value may indicate that most of the messages sent and received are coming from and going to points beyond the Exchange server. This number is maintained on a store-by-store basis. So if your Exchange 2000 server has five mailbox stores, you will have five different ratios. This is not a server-by-server number!
MSExchangeIS Private ➤ Messages Submitted MSExchangeIS Public ➤ Messages Submitted	The total number of messages submitted to the private (or public) information store databases since the information store service was started.
SMTP Server ➤ Messages Received	The total number of messages received from the specified SMTP virtual server.
SMTP Server ➤ Store/ MSExchangeMTA Submits	The total number of messages received by the message transport driver from the mailbox stores and the MTA.

Table 6.3   Additional System Monitor Counters *(continued)*

Object ➢ Counter	Explanation
MSExchangeMTA ➢ Message Bytes/sec	The number of message bytes being processed by the MTA every second. Divide this value by the Messages/sec counter to get the average message size.
MSExchangeMTA ➢ Outbound Message Total	The total number of messages the MTA has delivered off the server since the service was started.
MSExchangeMTA ➢ Inbound Message Total	The total number of messages the MTA has received sine the MTA service was started.
MSExchangeIS ➢ Virus Scan Messages Processed	The total number of messages that have been scanned by the virus API since the information store was started.

SMTP Protocol and Advanced Queuing Engine Counters

You may also be interested in watching statistics about how many messages your system sends and receives and the amount of data that is being transferred. Table 6.4 shows some counters that are useful to watch if you are interested in the number of messages being processed by the SMTP protocol and the Advanced Queuing Engine.

Table 6.4   Useful SMTP Message Transport Counters

Object ➢ Counter	Explanation
SMTP Server ➢ %Recipients Local SMTP Server ➢ %Recipients Remote	The percentage of mail recipients that are delivered either locally or to a remote server. This will give you an idea of where the majority of your messages are going.
SMTP Server ➢ Messages Received Total SMTP Server ➢ Messages Sent Total	The total number of messages accepted/sent by an SMTP virtual server.

Table 6.4 Useful SMTP Message Transport Counters *(continued)*

Object ➤ Counter	Explanation
SMTP Server ➤ Refused for Size	Messages that were rejected because they exceeded size limitations.
SMTP Server ➤ DNS Queries/sec	The number of DNS queries per second.
SMTP Server ➤ Connection Errors/sec	The number of errors per second that are being generated by SMTP connections. This number should be low. More than one or two errors per second may indicate a network connection problem.
SMTP Server ➤ Cat: LDAP Searches/sec	Total number of LDAP searches that the categorizer submits per second.
SMTP Server ➤ Remote Queue Length	The number of messages queued to be delivered remotely.
SMTP Server ➤ Outbound Connections Refused	The number of connections this SMTP virtual server has initiated but remote servers have refused. A high number may indicate that your server is on a black-hole list or that your users are sending messages frequently that are too large for a receiving domain.
SMTP NTFS Store Driver ➤ Messages in the Queue Directory	Total number of messages stored in the queue directory for a particular SMTP virtual server. This indicates inbound messages.

NOTE Microsoft Knowledge Base article Q231734 has a complete list of the SMTP server counters that are used to monitor the Advanced Queuing Engine's message categorizer (PHATCAT.DLL).

NOTE For information on Microsoft Exchange Message Transfer Agent counters see the document titled "MTA Performance Counters" at www .somorita.com.

Operations

PART 2

Optimizing Exchange

As an Exchange administrator and consultant, I have seen Exchange servers set up so badly that I shake my head and wonder "what were they thinking?" I'm sure many of you have too. Once you have the Exchange server set up and running doesn't mean that you are done with your job. The key to maintaining the performance and even increasing the performance of your Exchange 2000 server is to make sure that you have it optimized.

Have you installed Exchange 2000 only to watch the performance degrade to the point of no return? One day everything seems to be running great, and the next day your hard drive is full and you cannot mount your databases. Take heart: There are a couple of things that you can do in order to protect your servers from this, including making a few modifications that will actually increase the performance of your system.

Exchange 2000 does not include a Performance Optimizer utility like the one included in Exchange 5.5. There are a number of reasons for this; the most prevalent is that Exchange 2000 and the ESE database engine are much more self-tuning than in past versions. Since we can move transaction logs and store databases through Exchange System Manager now, that feature of the Performance Optimizer is no longer necessary. If you are running an Exchange 2000 server with fewer than 1000 mailboxes, it is entirely possible that your servers are already running optimally for your environment. Still, there are parameters and options that you can tweak to improve the performance on heavily used servers.

When you set out to optimize an Exchange 2000 server, there are many areas on which you can focus. It is always tempting to think that faster hardware will provide you with better performance, but it may not if you have a poor design. The following is a list of things to consider when optimizing Exchange servers:

- Areas to look at improving performance include memory availability, CPU load, disk I/O, and network utilization. Make sure that the server has sufficient memory, fast disks, and a fast network adapter.

- Confirm that your Exchange servers are properly load-balanced so that resources are being used effectively. If not, move mailboxes, public folders, or connectors to other Exchange servers that are under utilized.

- Confirm that the network adapters are operating in the fastest mode possible given the hub or switch to which they are plugged. I have seen many Exchange servers that had 100Mbps network adapters, but the adapter was not automatically sensing that it was plugged in to a 100BaseT hub. If your hubs are capable of operating in full-duplex mode, don't forget to check and see if the adapter card is in full-duplex mode. An improperly configured NIC/hub combination can cause terrible network performance.

- Run Exchange 2000 on a member server rather than a domain controller. Exchange 2000 performance can suffer due to domain controller replication and authentication of users. The local security authority subsystem (LSASS), which actually runs Active Directory (AD), can place a significant demand on RAM and disk I/O.

- Switched networks and switched network backbones will provide far better performance than standard Ethernet networks.

- If a server has more than 1GB of RAM and it is running Windows 2000 Advanced Server or Windows 2000 Datacenter, confirm that the server's BOOT.INI file has the /3GB switch.

- Place the transaction log files on separate physical disk drives from the database files.

- On servers that are making heavy use of full-text indexing, place the index files on a separate physical disk drive from the database and the transaction logs.

- If you are using TLS/SSL technologies, offload the overhead of these to a front-end server or purchase co-processor network cards that offload the encryption processes.

- Ensure that each Exchange server has a domain controller and Global Catalog server "nearby" on the network. Exchange should never have to connect over a WAN connection to a Global Catalog server or domain controller.

- Schedule incremental and full-text indexing rebuilds for off hours.

- Schedule backups for off hours—and make sure that they do not conflict with online maintenance!

- Schedule virus scans of the stores for off hours.

- On heavily used servers (more than 1000 mailboxes), provide separate stores to create smaller databases (easier to back up and restore) and separate storage groups for more transaction logs to improve processing speeds of logging.

Optimizing Active Directory Access

One of the key causes of weird problems and server failures with Exchange 2000 is the fact that the server will lose contact with its Active Directory domain controllers and Global Catalog servers. If this occurs, the Exchange server will not be able to read the configuration partition of the directory, nor will it be able to route messages. Active Directory availability is critical to the operation of Exchange 2000. For this reason, each location that contains an Exchange 2000 server with more than 1000 mailboxes should contain at least two Windows 2000 domain controllers, one of which should be a Global Catalog server.

Tuning Active Directory LDAP Queries

Active Directory domain controllers are configured to support a maximum of 20 simultaneous LDAP queries. In an environment where there are more than four or five Exchange servers generating LDAP queries to a single domain controller (plus all of the normal load that a domain controller must undergo), the domain controller may notify the client (Exchange 2000) that the maximum number of LDAP queries have been exceeded. You change this value using the Windows 2000 NTDSUTIL tool. For example, to raise the limit from 20 to 30, follow these steps (one of the domain controller names is sfodc01.somorita.net):

1. Open a command prompt window on the domain controller, type **NTDSUTIL**, and press Enter.
2. Type **ldap policies** and press Enter.
3. Type **connections** and press Enter.
4. Type **connect to server sfodc01.somorita.net** and press Enter.
5. Type **q** and press Enter.
6. Type **show values** and press Enter. Note the current MaxActiveQueries value.
7. Type **set MaxActiveQueries to 30** and press Enter.
8. Type **commit changes** and press Enter.
9. Type **q**, press Enter, type **q** again, and press Enter.

This maximum number of simultaneous queries is set for all domain controllers in the forest. If you have a domain controller that is being overworked, it may be time to add an additional domain controller rather than changing a configuration item that affects all domain controllers. Take a close look at the domain controllers that are rejecting queries to see if they are overworked (examine their CPU, disk, network, and memory usage as discussed earlier in this chapter).

Tuning DSAccess

In larger AD sites and domains (more than a few thousand users), the Active Directory domain controller that is functioning as the PDC emulator operations master may also become inundated with requests, such as during Windows NT 4 domain controller synchronization and pre–Windows 2000 client password changes. The Exchange 2000 DSAccess component picks the PDC emulator as for Active Directory requests, but this may not be the best use of your domain controller resources, since this can cause degraded performance on the domain controller and on the Exchange server.

There is a Registry setting that allows you to specify a minimum number of Windows 2000 domain controllers that need to be detected in the same site and domain name before the PDC emulator is excluded from the list of domain controllers it uses. To enable this feature, create a Registry key on each Exchange 2000 server called `MinUserDc` of type REG_DWORD in the `\HKLM\System\CurrentControlSet\Services\MSExchangeDSAccess\Profiles\Default` key. Enter a value for this key that sets the minimum number of domain controllers that must be detected. If you set it to three, for example, DSAccess must detect at least three domain controllers before it will not include the PDC emulator.

> **TIP** The list of domain controllers that an Exchange server is using can be viewed using the DSADiag tool, discussed in Chapter 2, "Active Directory for Exchange 2000 Administrators."

DSAccess picks a list of domain controllers to use and then tries to determine which domain controllers are the closest based on the response times. Domain controllers that respond to LDAP queries within two seconds are considered "fast," and Exchange 2000 will attempt to use those domain controllers first. Domain controllers that take longer than two seconds (five seconds prior to SP1) are marked as "slow" and will only be used if there are no fast domain controllers responding.

Rather than just allowing DSAccess to pick a list of servers automatically, you may want to configure Exchange 2000 to use a specific set of domain controllers and Global Catalog servers. You can do this through the Registry on each Exchange 2000 server. The following example sets two domain controllers and two Global Catalog servers to be used by an Exchange server. Further, it manually configures the configuration domain controller. The following is a list of the domain controllers and Global Catalog servers available:

`sfodc01.somorita.net`	Domain controller
`sfodc02.somorita.net`	Domain controller
`sfodc03.somorita.net`	Global Catalog server
`sfodc04.somorita.net`	Global Catalog server

To configure the two domain controllers to be used by an Exchange server, you need to create two new Registry subkeys (not values) called `UserDC1` and `UserDC2` in the `\HKLM\System\CurrentControlSet\Services\MSExchangeDSAccess\Profiles\Default` key. In each of these new subkeys, create the following values:

Subkey	Value	Type	Data
UserDC1	IsGC	REG_DWORD	0x0
UserDC1	HostName	REG_SZ	sfodc01.somorita.net
UserDC1	PortNumber	REG_DWORD	0x185 (or 389 decimal)

Operations

PART 2

Subkey	Value	Type	Data
UserDC2	IsGC	REG_DWORD	0x1
UserDC2	HostName	REG_SZ	sfodc02.somorita.net
UserDC2	PortNumber	REG_DWORD	0x185 (or 389 decimal)

Next, you need to statically assign the Global Catalog servers. To do this, create two new Registry subkeys called UserGC1 and UserGC2. These keys should be created in the \HKLM\ System\CurrentControlSet\Services\MSExchangeDSAccess\Profiles\Default key. In each of these new keys, create the following values:

Subkey	Value	Type	Data
UserGC1	IsGC	REG_DWORD	0x1
UserGC1	HostName	REG_SZ	sfodc03.somorita.net
UserGC1	PortNumber	REG_DWORD	0xcc4 (or 3268 decimal)
UserGC2	IsGC	REG_DWORD	0x1
UserGC2	HostName	REG_SZ	sfodc04.somorita.net
UserGC2	PortNumber	REG_DWORD	0xcc4 (or 3268 decimal)

If you need more than two predefined domain controllers or Global Catalog servers, create additional subkeys such as UserDC3, UserDC4, etc.

WARNING   If you make errors manually configuring domain controllers or Global Catalog servers, Exchange will *not* automatically select alternate servers.

To manually select a preferred domain controller to be used for reading the configuration partition, open the \HKLM\System\CurrentControlSet\Services\MSExchangeDSAccess\ Instance0 key and create the following Registry values:

Value	Type	Data
ConfigDCHostName	REG_SZ	sfodc01.somorita.net
ConfigDCPortNumber	REG_DWORD	0x185 (or 389 decimal)

Unlike the preferred domain controllers and Global Catalog servers, Exchange will automatically select an alternate configuration domain controller if the preferred domain controller is not available.

TIP   Starting with Exchange 2000 SP2, the preferred domain controllers, Global Catalog servers, and configuration domain controller can be viewed and configured through the Directory Access property page of each Exchange server.

> **NOTE** For more information on how Exchange 2000 uses domain controllers and Global Catalog servers, see Microsoft Knowledge Base article Q250570.

Optimizing Database Performance

Quite simply, though Exchange 2000 has many components for handling message transport, essentially it acts like a database server. Every message that travels through the Exchange system is treated as a transaction or series of transactions; this includes instructions for moving, deleting, or modifying messages. As soon as the transaction occurs, it must immediately be written to the database transaction log files. Once the transaction has been successfully logged, it can be committed to the database file. Using these transaction logs, we can get up-to-the-minute recovery in the event of a failure.

> **NOTE** Several places in this section of the chapter recommend RAID 5 disk drives. I highly recommend hardware-based RAID 5 solutions over software-based solutions because RAID 5 provides the best cost/performance breakpoint. You can achieve better disk performance from other solutions such as RAID 1 + 0, but those solutions are more costly.

Optimizing Transaction Logs

The transaction logs are important to the recoverability of an Exchange server, but in order for Exchange to perform optimally, write operations to the transaction logs should be optimized. This means that the disk(s) on which the transaction logs are must be optimized. On servers that are supporting only 50 or 100 mailboxes, optimizing the log file locations probably won't buy you a lot of performance, but for servers that support larger numbers of mailboxes, you will begin to see performance gains. If you have a server with 50–100 mailboxes and you are experiencing performance problems, moving the transaction logs is not going to help. Here are a couple of recommendations for locating transaction logs on servers supporting more than a few hundred mailboxes:

- Place each storage group's transaction logs on separate physical disk drives.
- Nothing else should be on the transaction log disks (operating system, page files, software, database files, etc.).
- The transaction log disks will perform better on mirrored volumes that use hardware RAID 1 rather than software RAID 1. Further, RAID 1 will provide better write performance than RAID 5. Write performance is much more important than read performance because the transaction log files are only usually written to. For the best performance on transaction log disks, use hardware-based RAID 1 + 0;

you get the performance of multi-spindle writes and you get the protection of mirroring without the cost of parity generation. The cost of this performance is increased hardware expense.

- If you can configure your transaction log disk controller separately from the database disk controller, you can tweak out additional performance by setting the controller to 100 percent write-caching. Transaction log reads occur only if there has been a failure of some sort and the information store needs to initiate a recovery. Do this only if the controller supports battery backup.

- Do not put two storage group's transaction logs on the same disk.

WARNING   If you are using disk controllers that perform caching, do not enable write caching unless the controller has battery backup and can commit any data remaining in cache to disk when the system's power returns. Without battery backup, a power failure can cause significant data loss or file corruption. If you change the read/write caching ratios, make sure that you consider all types of data that the controller is servicing. You can hurt performance by turning off read caching on a controller that supports Exchange databases.

Optimizing Transaction Log Buffers   The Exchange database engine uses log buffers to store transactions in memory until the data can be written to the disk. Normally this happens almost instantly, but if the transaction log disk is busy, writes may be delayed. Further, there is only a limited number of buffers available for log buffers, so writes to the transaction log disk may be inefficient in an environment with more than 500 simultaneous users or where large messages are being sent. To improve performance for transaction log writes, you can increase the size of the transaction log buffers.

The default is 84 buffers, but Microsoft recommends that this value be increased to 9000 on all servers that are functioning as back-end servers. The number of log buffers is set for an entire storage group. To do this, you must use ADSIEDIT and navigate through the configuration partition to find the storage group object that you wish to configure. Display the properties of the storage group, locate the msExchESEParamLogBuffers attribute, and set this value to 9000.

Optimizing Database Access

The information store databases should be placed on their own set of physical disk drives. RAID 5–based disks are going to give you the best performance given the costs. RAID 1 + 0 can provide better performance, but at a significantly higher cost. Write performance on the database disk drives does not have to be quite as fast as it does on the transaction log disks, since the database writes are "lazy" writes, and most active data is read from

RAM cache. Again, this hardware-based RAID 5 set should contain only the database files. With these disks only containing the information store database files, we are able to provide the best access to these databases.

TIP When configuring RAID 5 volumes for use with Exchange, configure the stripe size to 64KB.

So, now that we know where to place the transaction logs and the database files, how do we get them to where we want them? In Exchange 5.5, we used to run the Performance Optimizer and it would recommend where we should put the files; we typically decided for ourselves where to place them and then had the Performance Optimizer run the application to automatically move these files for us based on drive letters.

Exchange 2000 does not have the Performance Optimizer, so it is up to you to figure out optimal disk locations for the database and transaction log files. Database files are moved using the properties of the mailbox or public folder store; transaction log files are moved using the properties of the storage group. Chapter 4, "Maintenance and Management," has more detailed information on how to manage storage groups and stores.

NOTE Moving a database may take some time, depending on its size. Make sure that you do this during off hours, otherwise your users could be without mail for a long time.

Increasing the Information Store Cache Size The Exchange 2000 information store cache size defaults to a maximum size of 900MB. On servers with large amounts of memory (over 2GB), increasing this value may improve performance. However, you should exercise caution if you want to change the amount of memory that is allocated for the information store cache. This value should *never* be set above 1200MB. Before you begin to set this value to anything other than the default, follow these steps.

First, let your server run for several weeks of normal operation. This will let the memory usage stabilize so that when you monitor memory usage you are getting values that reflect normal operation rather than what the system looks like when it has just restarted. After several days of operation, using the System Monitor, watch the Process object Virtual Bytes counter for the STORE.EXE instance. On Windows 2000 Advanced servers or Datacenter servers that have more than 1GB of RAM and have the /3GB switch in the BOOT.INI file, this value should be 2.7GB. On servers with 1GB of RAM or those that do not have the /3GB switch in the BOOT.INI, this value should not be over 1.7GB. If the Virtual Bytes counter is lower than these values, you can safely change the cache size to 1200MB, but if this counter is higher than those values, you could accidentally push the store over the maximum amount of addressable memory space (3GB) and cause the system to become unstable.

To change this value, use ADSIEDIT and browse the Active Directory configuration container. Locate the CN=InformationStore object in the configuration partition (CN=Configuration,CN=Services,CN=Microsoft Exchange,CN=*ExchangeOrgName*, CN=Administrative Groups,CN=*AdminGroupName*,CN=Servers,CN=*ServerName*, CN=InformationStore), where *ExchangeOrgName* represents the Exchange organization name, *AdminGroupName* represents the administrative group, and *ServerName* represents the name of the Exchange server on which you are increasing the cache size. Display the properties of the InformationStore object, and set the msExchESEParamCacheSizeMax value to 307200 (the default value is 230400 buffers, but this will not be shown in the interface). Make sure that you click Set and restart the information store service on that server.

NOTE   See Microsoft Knowledge Base article Q266096 for more information on increasing the store cache sizes.

Reducing Database File Fragmentation

The EDB and STM files grow in 1MB increments. Unless each of these files is on its own partition, significant file fragmentation can occur. This fragmentation can hurt read performance and slow down backup times.

Exchange 2000 SP1 introduced a new feature that allows the database files to grow in chunks of 16MB, regardless of how much storage is actually required. This must be configured for each storage group on a server, and it must be configured through ADSIEDIT or some other tool for modifying the Active Directory Configuration container. I highly recommend that you adjust this parameter to help reduce the amount of file fragmentation.

To change a storage group's database growth interval, follow these steps:

1. Using ADSIEDIT, open the Configuration partition and browse through the hierarchy until you find the storage group that you wish to change.

2. Locate the msExchESEParamDbExtensionSize attribute.

3. In the Edit Attribute box, enter **4096**, and click the Set button (the default is 256).

4. Click OK and exit ADSIEDIT (or change the other storage groups on the server).

5. Stop and restart the Exchange information store service.

The EDB and STM files will now allocate additional space at a rate of 16MB rather than 1MB. For more information, see Microsoft Knowledge Base article Q283691.

If you believe that your server is experiencing poor performance due to disk-level fragmentation, you should perform a complete backup of the system and do one of the following things:

- Run the ESEUTIL utility with the /D option to defragment database files; however, if the disk is badly fragmented, this may only make the problem worse.
- Move the EDB and STM files off the disk and then move them back onto the disk.
- Run the Windows 2000 Disk Defragmenter.

NOTE Running ESEUTIL or moving the ESB and STM files off the disk may only be partially successful if there are other files on the disk or if the disk is badly fragmented.

Operations

PART 2

Optimizing an SMTP Bridgehead Server

All inbound SMTP messages are first written to the NTFS file system in the Queue directory of the SMTP virtual server that accepted the message. For example, on a server with only one SMTP virtual server, mail is first stored in the \Exchsrvr\Mailroot\vsi 1\ Queue directory. On a server that is acting as an SMTP bridgehead server, you can improve performance by moving the SMTP virtual directories to another disk. Ideally, this disk should be on a RAID 5 volume with many physical disks; the more physical disks in the RAID 5 array, the better the read performance.

Each SMTP virtual server's directories must be moved individually by editing the Active Directory's configuration partition. To do this, you will need the ADSIEDIT tool from the Windows 2000 Resource Kit or the Windows 2000 Support Tools. To move the directories, follow these steps:

1. Stop the Simple Mail Transport Protocol (SMTP) service.

2. Copy the SMTP virtual server directory to the new location, and rename the old directory as a precaution (instead of deleting it).

3. Load a management console with ADSIEDIT. Open the Configuration Container partition until you get to the server on which you want to move the virtual server directories. In my example, the container would be CN=1;CN=SMTP,CN=Protocols;CN=SFOEX001,CN=Servers,CN=First Administrative Group,CN=Administrative Groups,CN=Somorita Surfboards,CN=Microsoft Exchange,CN=Services, CN=Configuration,DC=Somorita,DC=net.

4. Right-click the CN=1 container (this denotes SMTP virtual server 1) and display its properties.

5. Locate the property msExchSmtpBadMailDirectory, enter the new path in the Edit Attribute box, and click Set.

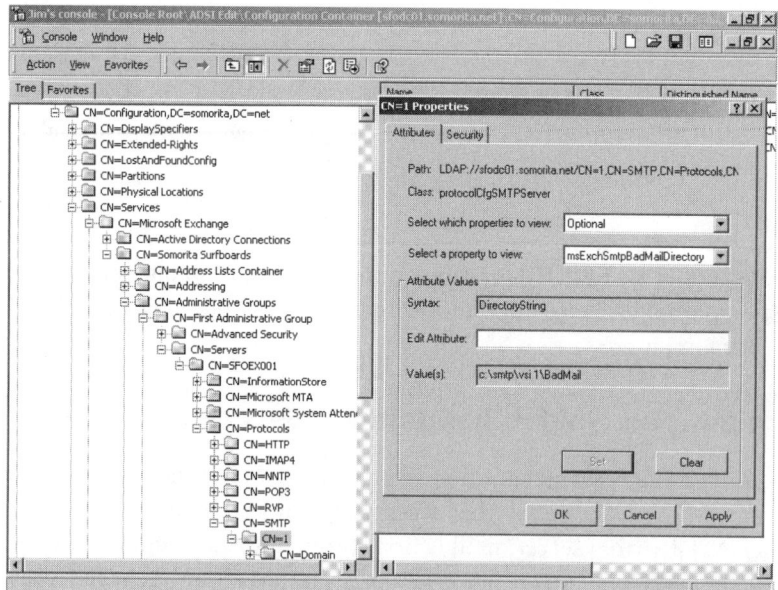

6. Repeat step 5 for the msExchSmtpPickupDirectory and msExchSmtpBadMail-Directory properties.

7. Allow time for Active Directory replication, and restart SMTP. If the changes have not taken effect, the System Attendant may not have run the Metabase update process, or the directory may not have completely replicated.

NOTE   The Windows 2000 Resource Kit contains a utility called MetaEdit that allows you to edit the IIS Metabase. Any configuration items relating to Exchange virtual servers and stored in the Active Directory configuration partition are considered the master configuration items. If you use the MetaEdit tool to make changes such as these, they will be overwritten.

If the hardware RAID 5 controller's read/write cache can be adjusted, then configure this controller to use 100 percent write cache. This ensures that when messages arrive, they are "committed" to the disk as quickly as possible; this in turn ensures that an acknowledgement for the message will be sent as soon as possible. If you are using RAID controllers with write caching enabled, ensure that those controllers have battery backup. Otherwise the controller may lose data in the event of a power failure.

NOTE For information on tuning SMTP parameters, see the document Tuning SMTP Parameters' located at www.somorita.com.

Optimizing Outlook Web Access

Providing web-based e-mail access has been a huge addition to Exchange that more and more companies are requiring. Users want to have access to their e-mail no matter where they are and no matter when it is. In today's world of high-speed Internet access, users don't want to be burdened with dialing up to gain access to their e-mail via a modem line and remote access services. Plus, supporting remote Outlook 2000 clients or remote POP3/IMAP4 clients places more burden on your support resources. You pretty much can't go anywhere now without seeing web terminals providing free browsing. Airports, malls, and everywhere else you go offers a way to access the Internet. With this in mind, what better way to let users gain access to their e-mail than via a web page?

When Outlook Web Access (OWA) was first introduced in Exchange 5, it wasn't very user-friendly for the installer or the end user, so not many people used it. Yet after the release of Exchange 5.5, more and more organizations were providing access to users' Exchange mailboxes via OWA. As this happened, one of the challenges that Exchange administrators had to solve was how to manage the loads that these servers were bearing. Exchange 5.5 OWA did not scale particularly well past a few hundred simultaneous users.

In Exchange 2000, you don't even have an option to "install" OWA—it is done automatically during the installation portion of Exchange 2000. However, in Exchange 2000, we have many new ways that we are able to optimize and load-balance between many Exchange 2000 servers providing the access to Exchange mailboxes via OWA.

Improving OWA Performance for Low-Speed Connections

If you have dialed in to a remote access connection over a low-speed connection, you may have noticed that each page you connect to initially takes a painfully long time to load. As a matter of fact, for the main Inbox screen, you may download up to 250KB of data before you see your messages list. This is because each of the OWA files (such as GIF files, tool bars, and controls) all expire after one day. So each day the remote user must download these files again.

You can improve the performance for these users by increasing the cache timeout period for the image files and the controls. To do so, follow these steps:

1. Using the Internet Services Manager, browse to the website that hosts your OWA virtual directories.

Operations

PART 2

2. Locate the Exchweb virtual directory and open it. Right-click the controls directory.

3. Click the HTTP Headers property page and change the Expire After value to be set to something higher than one day. I recommend setting it to 30 days.

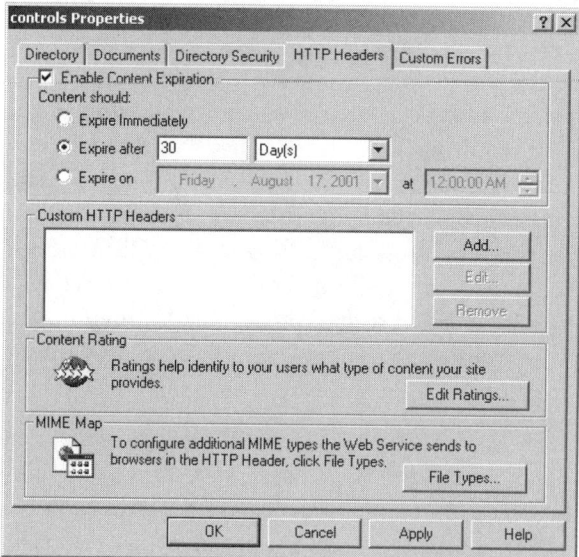

4. Repeat steps 2 and 3 for the img directory under the Exchweb virtual directory.

Even if the files change due to a service pack, the browser will detect that the images or controls have been modified and will download the newer versions.

Front-End Servers, Back-End Servers, and OWA

Exchange 2000 has a new capability that allows "protocol" services such as HTTP, POP, and IMAP to be partitioned onto front-end servers. These servers are responsible for handling the client load while the back-end servers are simply responsible for storing user mailboxes.

To configure an Exchange 2000 server as a front-end server, navigate to the server in the Exchange System Manager. Right-click the server that you want to configure as the front-end server, go to properties, and check the This Is A Front-End Server box. A reboot is now required. Once the server has been switched to a front-end server, mailboxes on the front-end server will not longer be accessible.

If the front-end server is not going to host an SMTP virtual server, then you can disable the information store, since it will not be used on the front-end servers.

Front-end servers also allow you to load-balance the front-end servers. You can use the Windows 2000 Load Balancing System to implement load balancing on the Exchange 2000 front-end servers. If you do not have Windows 2000 Advanced Server, then you can also do a form of load balancing by using round-robin DNS to the multiple Exchange 2000 front-end servers. By performing load balancing on the front-end servers, you can further off-set client load to multiple machines while still only having to provide your clients a single URL to connect to for their OWA site. This way, if a single server becomes unavailable, your users will still be able to function as well as have increased performance by off-setting the front-end load to multiple servers.

NOTE   Front-end and back-end servers are discussed at length in Chapter 15, "Internet Client Connectivity." For more information on tuning front-end servers, see the Microsoft white paper "Exchange 2000 Front-end and Back-end Topology," which can be found on the Microsoft website at www.microsoft.com/exchange/ techinfo/e2kfrontback.htm. For more information on tuning Exchange 2000, see the Exchange 2000 Internals Quick Tuning Guide at www.exinternals.com.

Operations

PART 2

7

Backup and Disaster Recovery

My theory is that if you are well prepared for an event, it probably won't happen. Unfortunately, most small to medium-sized organizations (fewer than 2000 mailboxes) don't have a good disaster recovery plan in place. Often, organizations don't even have a clear backup strategy, much less a recovery strategy.

A good disaster recovery plan is complemented by solid daily operations. Chapters 4, 5, and 6 provided you with the basics of maintenance, monitoring, and performance optimization to help you to avoid potential problems and give you knowledge necessary to employ disaster prevention measures. Yet despite the best preventive measures, sometimes an event occurs over which you have no control, and you'll have to focus your energy and resourcefulness on recovering from it. Thus this chapter reviews some of the more common Exchange disasters and how you can recover from them. These topics include:

- Performing regular backups
- Understanding the basics of disaster recovery
- Running an occasional fire drill to make sure you know exactly what you need to do in the event of a server or disk failure
- Preparing a disaster recovery kit that contains everything you need to recover from a catastrophic event

- Recovering from the accidental deletion of a single (important) mailbox
- Recovering from a complete Windows NT systems failure
- Recovering from the failure of the disk that contains the database files or a corrupted database file
- Recovering using offline backups
- Repairing a damaged store

Disaster Recovery Information Everywhere!

Since the initial release of Exchange 2000, there have been a number of white papers and guides to backup and disaster recovery. In my opinion, none of these guides provides a real complete guide to Exchange 2000 backup and disaster recovery, but they all contain good information.

- The white paper "Disaster Recovery for Microsoft Exchange 2000 Server" is available on the Internet at www.microsoft.com/exchange/techinfo/deployment/2000/E2KRecovery.doc. It serves as an introduction to Exchange 2000 disaster recovery, covering basic concepts and terms that all administrators need to be aware of.

- The "Exchange 2000 Server Database Recovery" white paper, written by Microsoft Consulting Services' Mike Lee, is probably the most comprehensive guide available. This paper is available at support.microsoft.com/support/exch2000/whitepapers/e2kdbrecovery.doc and includes information about backing up and restoring mailbox and public folder stores as well as about restoring the Site Replication Service (SRS) and Key Management Service (KMS) databases. Also included is a good reference on how to mount a database created in one administrative group to another administrative group.

- The "Mailbox Recovery for Microsoft Exchange 2000 Server" white paper is a good guide for learning how to protect your mission-critical and VIP mailboxes. This paper, on the Internet at www.microsoft.com/exchange/techinfo/deployment/2000/MailboxRecovery.doc, has some overlap with the aforementioned "Disaster Recovery for Microsoft Exchange 2000 Server" white paper, but it is good information nonetheless.

Operations

PART 2

Disaster Recovery Information Everywhere! *(continued)*

- The Compaq white paper "Exchange 2000 Disaster Recovery for Service Providers" is available at activeanswers.compaq.com/aa_downloads/6/100/225/1/42317.pdf. It covers basic Exchange 2000 disaster recovery information and it introduces a concept that Compaq calls Rapid Online, Phased Recovery (ROPR), which includes getting a failed Exchange server up and running as quickly as possible and restoring old mail data later.

- Chapter 5 of the "Exchange 2000 Server Operations Guide" has basic information about backing up and restoring Exchange 2000. This guide can be downloaded from Microsoft at www.microsoft.com/technet/prodtechnol/exchange/maintain/operate/opsguide/e2kopall.exe.

- The "MS Exchange Disaster Recovery" white paper was developed for Exchange 5.5, and its information mostly applies to Exchange 5.5. However, you may find some discussions in this white paper that will prove useful when managing Exchange 2000. This paper is available at www.microsoft.com/technet/treeview/default.asp?url=/TechNet/prodtechnol/exchange/support/edrv3p1.asp.

Backing Up Exchange

Neither RAID 5 drive arrays, clustered servers, nor mirrored disks are fault tolerant enough to get you out of performing daily Exchange backups. And if you do happen to skip backups for a while, you will eventually run out of disk space on the transaction log file disks since the log files will not be purged. There are too many things that can go wrong with both your hardware and software.

Putting together a good Exchange 2000 backup plan requires a good understanding of a number of different topics. These topics include:

- Understanding the capabilities and limitations of your tape backup hardware and software
- Knowing why online backups are so important
- Differentiating between the different types of Exchange 2000 backups and when to use each
- Understanding the effect that backup operations has on Exchange 2000

Backup Hardware and Software

The first step in a successful backup plan is to get quality backup media and software. I am approaching this from the traditional tape backup perspective, though there are many in the Exchange community who feel that other forms of backup (such as optical) and "snapshot" technology are coming of age.

Purchase a tape drive system that is easily and quickly capable of backing up your entire messaging system. In a smaller environment (one or two Exchange 2000 servers), I prefer to locate the tape drive hardware on the same machine that hosts the Exchange server. The costs are generally a little more, but the backups run quickly. When purchasing tape backup hardware, I also purchase the same tape drive type for all servers. This allows my tapes and my tape hardware to be more easily interchangeable. In a larger Exchange 2000 environment, budgetary and operation concerns are probably going to drive you toward centralized backup solutions. The advantage of centralized systems is that you can usually afford to purchase backup systems with considerable backup capacity and performance.

When you install Exchange 2000, the Windows 2000 Backup program is extended so that it can perform online backups of Exchange 2000 databases. The Windows 2000 Backup program does have its limitations, but it's free and is significantly improved over the Windows NT 4 Backup program. I prefer one of the third-party backup programs available, such as Veritas' Backup Exec, BEI International's UltraBac, or Computer Associates' ArcServe. These utilities have more flexible job scheduling, tape management, and better cataloging—not to mention that the third-party tools are faster than Windows 2000 Backup.

> **NOTE** When purchasing tape backup software and Exchange agents, you must purchase software that will work with Exchange 2000; backup software designed for Exchange 5.5 will not work. The Exchange agent is required for backing up Exchange while it is online.

> **NOTE** If you need to back up Exchange 2000 across the network, you can "extend" the Windows 2000 Backup program without installing the Exchange 2000 administrative tools. See Microsoft Knowledge Base article Q275876 for the procedure on extending the Backup program to back up Exchange 2000.

I Feel the Need for Speed

A big determination in how many users and how much data you can fit onto a single Exchange server is how long it takes to back up that data. I have seen vendors talking about backup rates of 35GB per hour. I can assure you that a typical production system backup utility cannot accomplish such a speed; this type of backup rate is only achievable with very specialized backup hardware (RAID 5 tape arrays and special tape array controllers).

Recent backup and restore rates that I have been able to achieve range from 2.5GB per hour (with an HP SureStore 5000 DAT tape drive) to 10GB per hour (with a Compaq 7000 DLT tape drive) to nearly 25GB per hour using storage area network (SAN) attached DLT tape drives. All of these systems were on Pentium III or better systems with PCI SCSI adapters, ample memory, Veritas Backup Exec, and no active users.

Backing Up to Other Storage

Microsoft introduced a snazzy new feature with the Windows 2000 Backup program: the ability to back up to a file rather than to a tape. This feature has proven to be tremendously useful to me, especially in environments where the tape drive is not functioning yet or is busy. I can select the data I want to back up, specify that I want to back up to a file on a disk drive, and start the backup. Figure 7.1 shows the Windows 2000 Backup program with the storage groups and the system state selected; the destination of the backup is a file rather than a tape device.

Figure 7.1 Performing a backup to a file

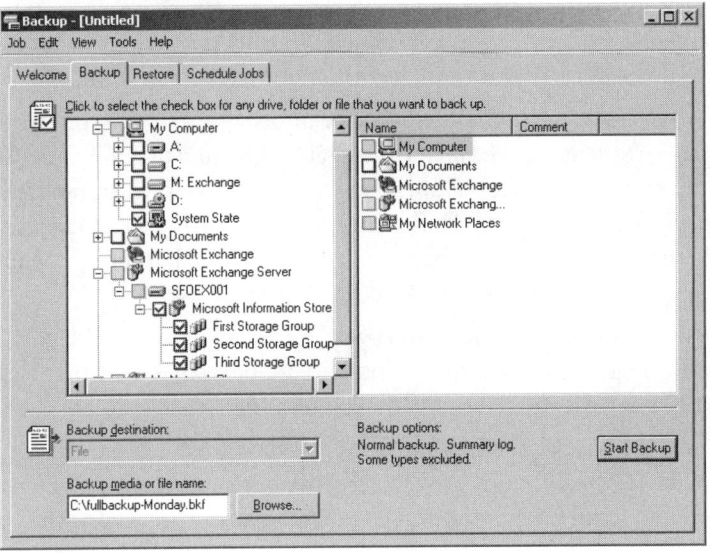

Online Backups Versus Offline Backups

Should you use the Exchange Server online backup feature? Yes, absolutely, certainly, for sure! Though many of us feel comfortable with the old, tried and true file-level backup, online backups are much better for Exchange. There are a number of reasons why you should perform online backups of Exchange, including:

- The online backups allows you to back up the database even if it is in use and are much easier to schedule than offline backups, because the stores do not have to be dismounted. Since the stores do not have to be dismounted, the user community does not have to be interrupted.

- Online backups back up the database files "page by page." As the page is transferred to tape, Exchange Server does a cyclic redundancy check (CRC) on the data to make sure that it is valid. If there are problems with the page of data, the backup stops, and an event is logged to the Event Viewer application log. If you were performing offline backups, you would not be aware of this.

- Online backups permit the use of incremental and differential backups (backing up only the log files), which occur much more quickly than normal backups.

Exchange Backup Options

Software that is capable of backing up Exchange has three backups it can perform: normal, incremental, and differential. You need to fully understand what each of these options are doing so that you can select the right backup type for your organization.

A *normal backup* will back up the entire information store or directory database. The normal backup then backs up the transaction logs and the PAT files. When the log files and the PAT files are backed up, all log files that have been committed to the database are purged from the disk. The patch files keep track of all changes to the database while the online backup is being performed. See Chapter 4, "Maintenance and Management," for more on patch (PAT) files.

An *incremental backup* selects and backs up only the Exchange server transaction logs. Once the logs are backed up, the log files are purged. A tape that had incremental backups put on it will have only the log files since the last full or incremental backup.

A *differential backup* selects and backs up only the Exchange server transaction log files. The log files are not purged after the backup, meaning they will continue to accumulate until an incremental or normal backup is performed.

NOTE In order to recover a database up to the moment of a failure, circular logging must be disabled. This ensures that there are log files to back up and recover. In Exchange 2000, circular logging is disabled by default, so there should be no action required here. However, if you are taking over administration of a system from another person, or if the system was upgraded from a previous version of Exchange, it is important to check this setting.

Circular Logging, Transaction Log Files, and Backups

With circular logging disabled, the transaction logs will accumulate until either an online normal backup or an online incremental backup occurs. Online differential and offline backups do not purge transaction logs. Here is what happens during a normal backup:

1. The backup program selects and starts backing up the specified store. During this process, any transactions that are written to parts of the database that have already been backed up are also written to the patch file.

2. After the store has been backed up, the patch file is backed up.

3. The patch file is purged from the system.

4. The checkpoint file is consulted, and any log files that were completely committed to the database and/or patch file are purged. These files are not necessary, since the transactions in these files have already been committed to the database.

During an incremental backup, only the log files are backed up. Based on information in the checkpoint file, transaction log files completely committed to the database and/or patch file are purged.

Performing a Server Backup

For me, a nightly backup consists of the mailbox stores and public folder stores. In addition, I want to make sure that there is a good backup of the Windows 2000 system state, which includes the Windows Registry, IIS Metabase, and the Active Directory database.

For me to feel warm and fuzzy about a backup, I set it to perform a verification pass when it is finished. I don't like doing file-based backups of the Exchange server directories; the data files in these directories will automatically raise errors on verification passes, because they change often. Performing backups of the Windows NT server's file system can extend the backup time and may not necessarily be useful during a restore. Further, I check the backup log files each day. However, the ultimate backup feeling comes from periodically performing trial restores to a standby server. This guarantees not only that the tape really contains the data, but it also helps keep me familiar with my disaster recovery procedures. Verification passes will double the amount of time required and thus may only be useful in an environment where you can easily back up everything in a short period of time. For the ultimate warm and fuzzy feeling, perform periodic restores to an isolated, test system.

The Exchange Server Key Management Service database and the Site Replication Service can also be backed up online, but the Exchange Server Directory Synchronization (used for MS Mail, PROFS directory sharing) databases do not get backed up during an online backup. In order to back up the Directory Synchronization database, you need to shut down the Microsoft Exchange Directory Synchronization service and back up the \Exchsrvr\DXAdata directory offline. I am not terribly concerned about backing up the Directory Synchronization database, since it is easy to re-create by simply reestablishing directory sync, but the Key Management Service database should be backed up nightly.

There may be other things on your server that you need to back up. For example, you may have event sinks registered on your server. Make sure that the DLLs or scripts that these sinks used are backed up. Any other scripts that you have installed on the server for administrative purposes should also be backed up. If the server is in a cluster, make sure that you back up the cluster quorum disk.

Here are some other tips for implementing a successful Exchange server backup plan:

- Rotate your tapes; don't use the same tape every night, and don't use a tape longer than the manufacturer recommends.

- Protect your tapes. Store them in a location that cannot be accessed by just anyone. Always keep a copy of a recent backup stored in a location other than near your computer room. In the event of a disaster that destroys the primary tape storage location, you will have a copy of your data elsewhere.

- Examine your backup log files and application log daily to ensure that the backups are running and that there are no errors.

- Clean your tape drives according to the schedule recommended by the tape manufacturer.

- Perform a trial restore of your standby server periodically.

- Make sure that the Exchange 2000 server does not lose contact with its domain controllers during a backup or restore operation. This can cause the backup to terminate.

- Exchange System Manager must be installed on the machine that is performing the backup in order for the online backup choices to be available. There is a workaround for this detailed in Microsoft Knowledge Base article Q251904.

Performing an Online Backup

An online backup of the Exchange 2000 data runs while the store is mounted and in operation. This is possible using backup software that supports the Exchange backup APIs. To perform an online Exchange 2000 server backup using the Windows 2000 Backup program, follow these steps:

1. Run the Windows 2000 Backup program and click the Backup tab. Select the storage groups or mailbox stores you wish to back up.

2. Select the destination and enter the media name (or filename if backing up to a file). A sample screen is shown back in Figure 7.1. Click the Start button.

3. The next screen is the Backup Job Information dialog box, which allows you to specify the backup description, whether the media should be replaced or appended, the media label, and whether or not the backup data should be restricted to the owner or Administrator. From here you can also set the job to run on a schedule and view the advanced properties of the backup job.

4. Click the Advanced button if you want to access the Advanced Backup Options (see Figure 7.2). Here you can change the backup type; the default is a Normal backup.

5. Click the Start Backup button on the Backup Job Information screen when you are ready for the backup to proceed.

Figure 7.2   Various Windows 2000 Backup options

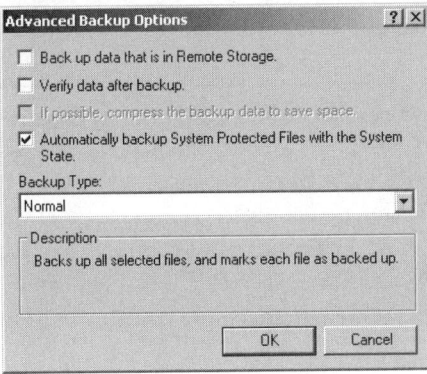

TIP   The best way to ensure that all transaction logs are purged is to back up the entire storage group rather than backing up individual stores.

Online Maintenance Schedules and Exchange 2000 Backups   By default, each morning from 1:00 A.M. until 6:00 A.M., the Exchange 2000 Information Store Service runs scheduled maintenance. This includes removing deleted messages, removing deleted mailboxes, online defragmentation, cleaning up indexes, expiring old messages from public folders, and making sure that space formerly taken up by deleted messages is returned to the pool of available space. This scheduled maintenance should run at least once per day for both the public and private information stores. The default online maintenance interval can be changed for each mailbox and public folder store on the Database tab of the store's properties.

WARNING   The online defragmentation process will not run if the tape backup is running on any database in the storage group. Make sure that the tape backup *does not* overlap the IS maintenance schedule. Each morning, sometime between 1:00 A.M. and 6:00 A.M., you should see an event ID 180 generated by ESE97 for both the mailbox and public information stores. If you are not confirming that database maintenance is completing during the week, it may be necessary to schedule longer windows of online maintenance on the weekends.

Performing an Offline Backup

An offline backup is performed when you dismount the stores and make backup copies of the database files. I recommend that you perform online backups using Exchange 2000–aware backup software. Only under very rare circumstances will I recommend performing an offline backup. In many cases, administrators will supplement regular online backups with an occasional offline backup as part of a disaster recovery process. To perform an offline backup, simply dismount the store that you wish to back up.

WARNING   Offline backups do *not* purge the transaction logs.

If you want to perform offline backups, there are a few things you should do to guarantee that the data you are backing up is indeed good. First, make sure that the database is consistent (all transactions have been committed); to do this, run ESEUTIL /MH *edb_file_name* and look for the words State: Consistent in the output. Second, run the ESEFILE utility on the EDB file to confirm that the file has no corruption; this is handled automatically during online backups.

Once you have dismounted all stores in the storage group, verified that all databases are consistent, and having verified that there is no database that has any corruption, you can delete the old log files. I recommend keeping the last hour or two of log files even though everything may look good.

Backing Up Other Messaging-Related Data

Even though you may be performing a normal backup of your Exchange server data, the system state, and Exchange server software, there may still be other messaging-related data that you should consider when making backup plans.

Does your user community have PAB files (personal address books), PST files (personal folders), SCD files (Schedule+ data), and other data that is related to the messaging system? Outlook offers a useful feature called AutoArchive that will automatically archive older message data to an `archive.pst` personal folder file. By default, this file is on the user's local hard disk; it is stored as part of their personal profile. Be sure it is being backed up.

The sheer difficulty of backing up this personal data is one of the reasons why administrators in large organizations will not take responsibility for backing up data such as PST files (especially if they are stored locally rather than as part of a server-based profile or Windows 2000 Group Policy Object redirected folder) and may make the usefulness of the AutoArchive feature more trouble than it is worth. Overall, it may be cheaper and less complicated to allocate more storage for users on the Exchange server.

Backing Up the System State

Windows 2000–aware backup programs provide you with the option of backing up the *system state*. Figure 7.3 shows the system state backup selection in the Windows 2000 Backup program. Backing up the system state is critical if you ever have to perform a disaster recovery on the Active Directory.

The system state backup includes the following:

- Windows 2000 operating system (parts of the \Winnt directory) and the boot files (NTLDR, BOOT.INI, etc.)
- The Registry
- COM+ class registration database

- Cluster service resource registry checkpoints and the quorum resource recovery log, if running on a cluster
- Certificate services database, if installed
- The SYSVOL directory, if on a domain controller
- The Active Directory database, if on a domain controller

Figure 7.3   Backing up the system state

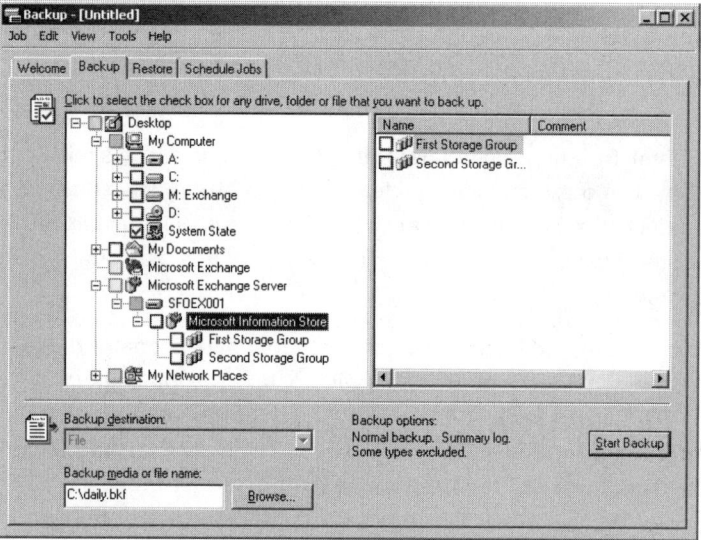

Backing Up the IIS Metabase

The Internet Information Server (IIS) Metabase contains the complete configuration for all components managed by IIS. While much of the Exchange related configuration data for IIS is handled by Exchange System Manager and stored primarily in the Active Directory Configuration partition, there may still be customizations that you have performed to IIS.

Consequently, it is a good idea to have a backup of the IIS Metabase. The Metabase is automatically backed up when the system state backup is run, and that backup can be used for purposes of disaster recovery. However, you can back up the Metabase separately if you need to undo a configuration change that went horribly wrong. To do this, launch the Internet Services Manager console, right-click the server name, and choose Backup/Restore Configuration. You will see a dialog box like the one shown in Figure 7.4. Click the Create Backup button. This creates a backup file of the IIS Metabase, which can be found in the \Winnt\System32\Inetsrv\MetaBack directory.

Figure 7.4   Backing up the IIS Metabase

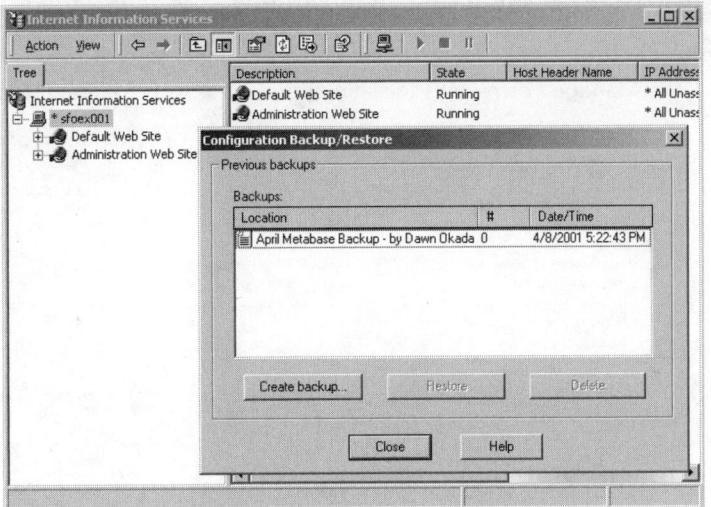

Exchange@Work: Backing Up Organization Forms

One of my customers recently had to rebuild their site folders. In the process of doing this, they accidentally lost the Organization Forms library, which is created in the System Folders container of the default public folder structure. In Exchange System Manager, connect to Folders ➤ Public Folders, right-click the Public Folders container, and choose View System Folders. The Organization Forms libraries are stored in the EFORMS Registry folder; there will be one Organization Forms library per language supported.

Ordinarily, to provide redundancy for this folder you would create a replica of the folder on a public folder store or in another routing group. Any backup of this public folder store will automatically include the EFORMS Registry folders. However, you can use Outlook to back up the forms that are in this folder. To do so, follow these steps:

1. From any version of Outlook, create a PST file.

2. Open the PST file and create a folder, calling it something like Forms Backup.

Exchange@Work: Backing Up Organization Forms *(continued)*

3. Right-click the Forms Backup folder, choose Properties, click the Forms tab, and click the Manage Forms button. This opens the Forms Manager dialog box:

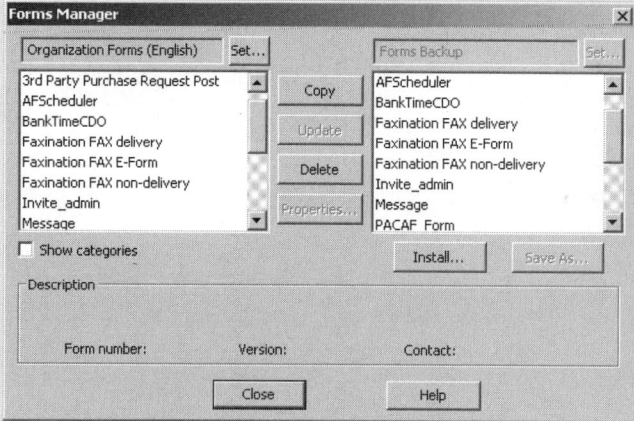

4. The list on the left-hand side should be the Organization Forms library for the language you are using; the list on the right side should be the folder in the PST file (Forms Backup). If not, click the Set button to browse other forms libraries.

5. Highlight the forms in the Organization Forms library and click the Copy button to make a copy of them to the PST file.

6. Repeat these steps for each language you support.

Snapshot Backups and Exchange 2000

Call me old fashioned, but I prefer antiquated tape technology to newfangled backup methods. However, I will be the first to admit that tape backups have their flaws, to which I have fallen victim several times. In an effort to be open minded, let's talk about a newer approach that is now emerging in many local area networks and that a number of vendors have been supporting for some time. It is called *snapshot technology*, and it uses several methods (disk sector-by-sector or even the Exchange backup APIs) of backing up Exchange data to another disk drive, not to tape.

> **NOTE** The Windows 2000 Backup program now supports performing backups directly to disk drives, just like some of the snapshot systems.

Snapshot technology has become popular for two reasons. First is the advent of increasingly large amounts of disk storage that are available via storage area networks (SANs) or network-attached storage (NAS). The second reason is that due to the speed at which SAN and NAS technology can operate, backups are extremely fast.

I know one organization in particular that is using this technology, and they are pleased with the results. Their Exchange server is connected to the NAS, and the vendor's backup software is used. With the vendor's Exchange-aware backup running, this organization is reporting throughputs nearing 75GB per hour. They keep the daily snapshot backups on the NAS disk for a few days and then archive them off to tape.

WARNING   SAN technologies have only recently been endorsed by Microsoft and thus supported by PSS. I am not aware of any NAS technologies that are currently approved by Microsoft and that will be supported in the event of a call to Exchange 2000 PSS. While any new, high-speed, high-capacity storage technology will look really cool sitting in your computer room, you must address the issue of supportability. Before purchasing any of these solutions, get your vendor to confirm (in writing) that Microsoft will support them. There is nothing worse than calling PSS and having them tell you to "remove component X from the system, and let's troubleshoot the problem," since you may not be able to remove component X quite so easily. While I am impressed with the performance of these new-fangled technologies, I would not want any unapproved devices on a server that I had to support.

Restoration is equally fast, and since the product uses the Exchange backup APIs, the data can be restored, and the outstanding transaction logs can be committed.

Is It Really a Snapshot Backup?

Vendors have frequently blurred the lines of their products to the point that you cannot tell if they are talking about a snapshot backup, an image backup, or an official Exchange API-based backup.

An *Exchange API-based backup* uses the API set that Microsoft provided to perform a page-by-page backup of the database files. As each page is backed up, the checksum of that page is checked to confirm that the page of the database is not corrupted. Most administrators refer to this type of backup as an online backup. This backup type may back up data to a tape device or directly to a disk drive (located on a SAN or NAS device).

Operations

PART 2

Is It Really a Snapshot Backup? *(continued)*

An *image backup* requires that the server be shut down. While the server is shut down, the backup software makes a sector-by-sector copy of the file system to a tape device or a file system. These types of backups are reliable and may even be faster for backups and restores, but they do require that the server be shut down during the backup and thus are not desirable for most production environments.

A *snapshot-based backup* involves some type of shim or file-system marker that maintains a change table and a page cache. Accesses to the snapshot are checked for any pages in the change table and, if present, are replaced by the data in the page cache when it is returned to the application. The problem is that Exchange is writing not only to the database files, but also to the transaction logs, and so there is a risk that at the time the snapshot is taken, the files are not in a consistent state. Further, I question the reliability of these backups, since they do not have a way to checksum the pages in the database Some vendors now include the ESEFILE utility with their product to verify the integrity of the backed up database pages. Microsoft is working on improvements to the Exchange backup APIs that will improve the capabilities and reliability of snapshot backups, but these changes have not yet been implemented.

Sample Backup Rotations

I prefer to do normal backups and to use a separate tape for each backup. I have had too many incidents where I was unable to get something off of a tape for one reason or another. I have developed a mistrust of tape systems in general, though PC-based tape systems are generally much more reliable today than they were 10 years ago. However, I also recognize that many organizations don't have the luxury of performing a full (normal) backup every night.

You may actually be performing an online Exchange backup to a disk or NAS device instead of directly to tape, but backup scheduling and procedures remain the same. If you are backing up to disk, you may also have the additional overhead of backing up the backup files from disk to tape. Here are examples of both daily and weekly backup rotations; choose one that is suitable for your situation.

Daily Rotation

The daily rotation—my personal preference—requires a normal backup each day. I put together a rotation of tapes that will enable me to have two weeks' worth of backups, plus a month of Friday backups. I label my tapes as follows:

Tape Label	Used On
Monday – Even	Monday the 2nd, 16th, etc.
Monday – Odd	Monday the 9th, 23rd, etc.
Tuesday – Even	Tuesday the 10th, 24th, etc.
Tuesday – Odd	Tuesday the 3rd, 17th, etc.
Wednesday – Even	Wednesday the 4th, 18th, etc.
Wednesday – Odd	Wednesday the 11th, 25th, etc.
Thursday – Even	Thursday the 12th, 26th, etc.
Thursday – Odd	Thursday the 5th, 19th, etc.
Friday – First	First Friday of the month
Friday – Second	Second Friday of the month
Friday – Third	Third Friday of the month
Friday – Fourth	Fourth Friday of the month
Friday – Fifth	Fifth Friday of the month

This rotation strategy can be extended to include a Saturday and Sunday backup as well. You should consider performing weekend backups if you have staff working on the weekend or if you have a tape autoloader system. If you have many users who send and receive mail on the weekends, you should definitely perform weekend backups. In many situations, I also include a monthly or bimonthly tape backup that is archived for an entire year.

For each day of the week, I schedule a backup to start at some point in the evening after the majority of my users are gone. The backup type is normal, so the entire information store and directory service should be on each tape.

Exchange@Work: Backup Paranoia

Those who are extra paranoid about their Exchange server backups perform more than just a normal backup each night. Additionally, every two hours during the day, they run a differential backup and append a backup of the transaction log files to the end of the normal backup tape.

Exchange@Work: Backup Paranoia *(continued)*

Though their log files are on a separate physical disk from the database files, this still protects them in the event of a catastrophic server failure. If the server experiences a catastrophe where all hard drives fail, the most data they will lose is two hours' worth.

If your organization is paranoid about backup and optimizing restore times, there are a number of high-availability solutions from vendors such as Compaq that keep a point-in-time backup of the databases and almost up-to-the-minute backups of all log files. These can be used to bring a system back online very quickly and with virtually no data loss.

Weekly Rotation

Though I much prefer running a normal backup each night, I don't always have that option due to time constraints, database size, or capacity of the tape drive hardware. In such cases, I revert to differential backups. The schedule consists of a normal backup one day a week and differential backups on the remaining days. Here is a sample set of tapes for a weekly backup:

Tape Label	Used On
Normal – 1	1st Friday of the month
Normal – 2	2nd Friday of the month
Normal – 3	3rd Friday of the month
Normal – 4	4th Friday of the month
Normal – 5	5th Friday of the month
Differential – Monday	Monday night
Differential – Tuesday	Tuesday night
Differential – Wednesday	Wednesday night
Differential – Thursday	Thursday night

If you choose to do a weekly rotation, I recommend scheduling a normal backup for Friday night and having a different Friday tape for each week. Since each Friday tape will have a complete backup of the server, there's not much need in having even/odd tapes for the weekly differentials; however, you may decide that you want to put those into your rotation.

When you need to restore a server, restore the most recent normal backup tape first, and then restore the most recent differential tape. The differential tape will contain all the log files created since the last normal backup.

WARNING The differential backup does not purge the log files. Watch the disk space on your transaction log drive to make sure that the log files do not accumulate and exhaust all available disk space.

TIP When planning for online storage capacity for transaction log files, plan for enough disk capacity to keep at least two weeks of transaction log files.

Brick-Level Backup

Many Exchange 4 and 5 administrators have cried mournfully, "I hate restoring a single mailbox!" The principal reason a single mailbox has to be restored is that a user deleted some important message(s) or folder(s). Microsoft has responded to the "oops, I deleted a really important message" statement with the deleted item recovery feature introduced in Exchange 5.5.

However, deleted item recovery will not help you if the entire mailbox gets deleted. Yet with Exchange 2000, Microsoft introduced the *recover mailbox procedure*. If an Active Directory user account gets deleted, the mailbox will not be removed for 30 days (the default). The administrator can simply recreate the AD user account (but not create a new mailbox), then use System Manager to reconnect the deleted mailbox to the new (or existing) user account.

Even with the ability to recover a deleted mailbox, some administrators insist on backing up mailboxes individually. Third-party vendors such as Veritas (`www.veritas.com`) and Computer Associates (formerly Cheyenne; `www.cheyenne.com`) have addressed this with a feature called *brick-level backups* (a.k.a. single mailbox backup and restore). While normal backups back up the information store databases a page at a time, a brick-level backup opens each mailbox separately and backs up the folders and messages.

The advantage of this feature is that you can now restore a single mailbox or even a single folder within a mailbox. The *dis*advantage is the amount of time that the backup takes to run and the space required on the tape. The backup program uses MAPI functions to open each mailbox and back it up message by message. By some estimates, the backup can take up to ten times longer than a standard backup.

TIP Avoid brick-level backups if at all possible. Never rely on brick-level backups in lieu of regular, online backups. Use these only to supplement your online backups, perhaps then backing up only VIP mailboxes. Brick-level backups are slow and at times unreliable.

Exchange@Work: Is a Brick-Level Backup Useful?

With Exchange 4 and 5, I primarily had to restore entire Exchange servers in order to recover a few items that were accidentally deleted from a person's mailbox. (Normally, the person carried a certain amount of weight with the IT department.) Since the release of Exchange Server 5.5 and the advent of deleted item recovery, I have not had to restore a single Exchange server due to accidentally deleted messages.

The main use now for a brick-level backup would be to restore a mailbox that was accidentally deleted. Though I think this is a good feature, the brick-level backups I have tested take anywhere from four to ten times longer to perform than a regular Exchange backup and usually take up considerably more tape space. Further, restoring a mailbox that was backed up using a brick-level backup will not restore the mailbox exactly as it was before. Here are some steps that some Exchange administrators have taken to eliminate the need to do a brick-level backup and restore:

- Implement deleted item recovery with enough time for people to recover any items they deleted. Recommendations range from 10 to 30 days. The longer you retain deleted items, the larger the information store must be—but most Exchange administrators believe the increase is worth it.

- Make use of deleted mailbox recovery. This feature is enabled by default; mailboxes can be recovered for up to 30 days after deletion.

- Implement a policy of not deleting user accounts and mailboxes right away. Use Active Directory Users And Computers to disable the user account rather than deleting it. Once the user has been gone for a respectable amount of time (60 to 90 days), then delete the account and the mailbox.

- Take advantage of the reconnect feature that allows you to reconnect a mailbox to a user who does not have a mailbox.

ExMerge As a Backup Tool

Several times in this book, I have extolled the virtues of the ExMerge program. Once again, I would like to take a moment and rave about its capabilities. I have a few customers who are using ExMerge to complement their backups. Rather than perform a brick-level backup of VIP mailboxes, they use the ExMerge program to back up VIP mailboxes.

NOTE   You can find good documentation for all of ExMerge's features on the Exchange 2000 CD-ROM in the \Support\Utils\I386\Exmerge\Exmerge.doc file.

This process does require a good amount of disk space if you are backing up more than one or two mailboxes, but it also allows you immediate access to backed up data through PST files. To use ExMerge to back up mailboxes, you must have permissions to open each mailbox. These permissions are discussed in Chapter 11, "Security within the Network." The ExMerge tool is found on the Exchange 2000 CD-ROM or the service pack in the `\Support\Utils\I386\Exmerge` directory. Simply copy the `exmerge.exe` and `exmerge .ini` files into the `\Exchsrvr\Bin` directory. To use ExMerge to back up mailboxes, follow these steps:

1. Run ExMerge and click Next to move past the introduction screen.

2. Choose the Extract Or Import (Two Step Procedure) radio button and click Next.

3. Choose the Step 1: Extract Data From An Exchange Server Mailbox radio button and click Next.

4. Specify the name of the Exchange server, Windows 2000 domain controller, and the LDAP port number, and then click Options to get the Data Selection criteria dialog box.

5. On the Data Selection Criteria dialog box Data tab, choose User Messages And Folders, Associated Folder Messages, and Folder Permissions.

6. Choose the Import Procedure tab and specify Merge Data Into Target Store. You can skip the other property tabs unless you want to export a specific data range, message subject, or exclude specific folders. Click OK, and then click Next.

7. On the Database Selection property tab, select the mailbox stores that contain the mailboxes you want to export.

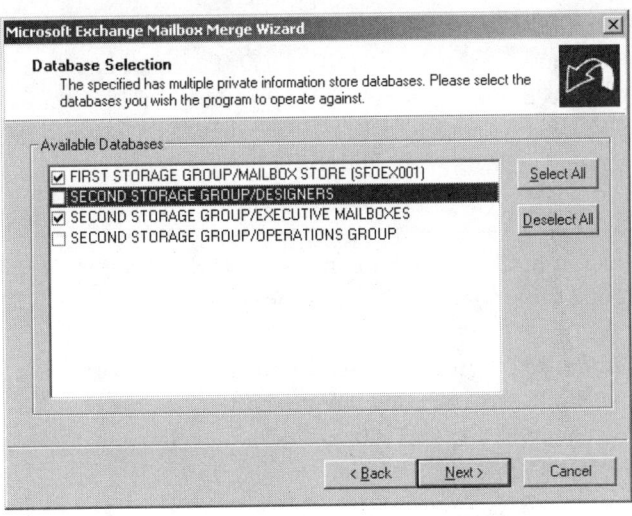

Operations

PART 2

8. You are now presented with a list of mailboxes that you can export to a PST file.

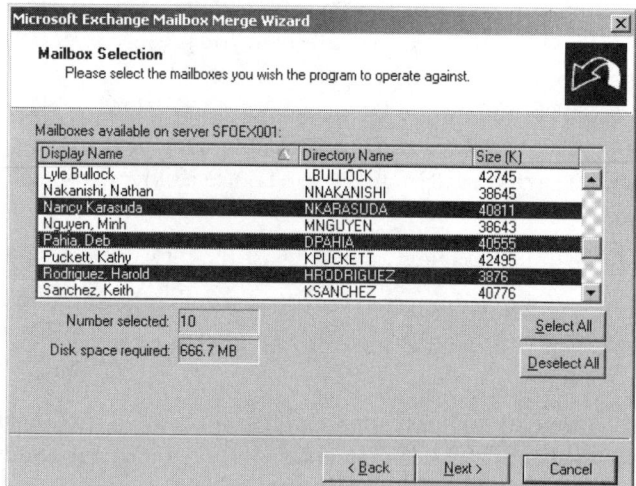

Select the mailboxes that you wish to export. Notice that the interface reports the total number of mailboxes selected and an *estimated* amount of disk space required. In my experience, this is a *maximum* amount of space required. Click Next when you have finished selecting the necessary mailboxes.

9. Select the default locale that the program should use to create the default folders and click Next.

10. Specify the folder name in which the PST files will be created. Remember that the disk drive must support up to the amount of disk space determined in step 8. Click Next.

11. You can now save the settings to INI and TXT files for later use. Click Next to begin the export procedure. Once the export procedure starts, you will see a progress screen indicating the current mailbox that is being processed. When the export is complete, simply click Finish.

TIP The export procedure will run much more quickly if it is run from the Exchange 2000 server on which the mailboxes exist.

Automating ExMerge   You can run the ExMerge from a batch file instead of running it and selecting the mailboxes each time. However, the list of mailboxes you want to export must be specified in a text file (MAILBOXES.TXT). Plus, you must have your configuration settings written to the EXMERGE.INI file.

In the previous step-by-step instructions, step 8 indicates the screen that you can select to specify the filenames. So to run ExMerge from a batch file, run the utility manually, make all the selections you want to make, then in step 8, save the settings to files so that you can then use them from the command prompt. The most important of these files are the MAILBOXES.INI and the EXMERGE.INI files, because those are the ones that you used during the mailbox export procedure. However, depending on the options you have selected, you may require other filenames. The list of ExMerge files and their default paths are shown in Figure 7.5. Make sure when you set up ExMerge that you save these files to retain your settings.

Figure 7.5   ExMerge file list

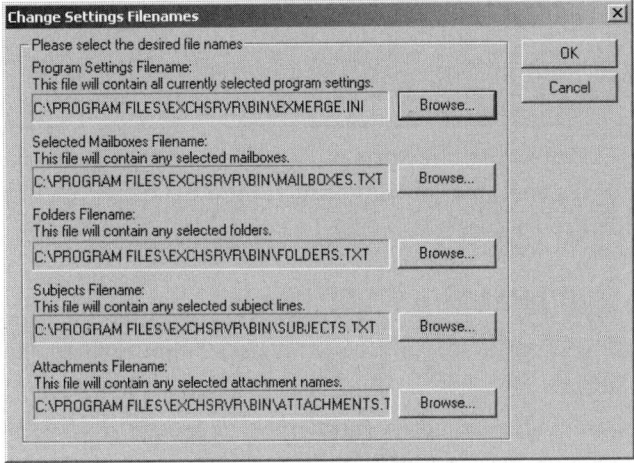

Once you have the files saved, you can run ExMerge from the command prompt and select a specific INI file. To do so, type:

```
exmerge -b -d -f c:\exmergesettings\exmerge.ini
```

The -d option tells ExMerge to display the Export Progress dialog box. If you are running this program as a service or on a schedule, then the -d option is not necessary. However, if you are at the server console and you have kicked off this command, you probably want to see the dialog box.

The list of mailboxes that are extracted is stored (by default) in a file called MAILBOXES.TXT. This file is shown in Figure 7.6. Once you have the files created, you can easily modify this file. Note that the mailbox names use the legacyExchangeDN name.

Figure 7.6   The MAILBOXES.TXT file used by ExMerge in batch mode

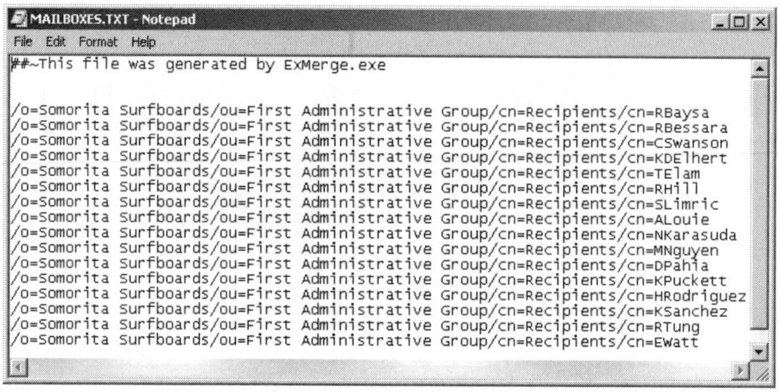

```
MAILBOXES.TXT - Notepad                                        _ □ ×
File  Edit  Format  Help
##~This file was generated by ExMerge.exe

/o=Somorita Surfboards/ou=First Administrative Group/cn=Recipients/cn=RBaysa
/o=Somorita Surfboards/ou=First Administrative Group/cn=Recipients/cn=RBessara
/o=Somorita Surfboards/ou=First Administrative Group/cn=Recipients/cn=CSwanson
/o=Somorita Surfboards/ou=First Administrative Group/cn=Recipients/cn=KDElhert
/o=Somorita Surfboards/ou=First Administrative Group/cn=Recipients/cn=TElam
/o=Somorita Surfboards/ou=First Administrative Group/cn=Recipients/cn=RHill
/o=Somorita Surfboards/ou=First Administrative Group/cn=Recipients/cn=SLimric
/o=Somorita Surfboards/ou=First Administrative Group/cn=Recipients/cn=ALouie
/o=Somorita Surfboards/ou=First Administrative Group/cn=Recipients/cn=NKarasuda
/o=Somorita Surfboards/ou=First Administrative Group/cn=Recipients/cn=MNguyen
/o=Somorita Surfboards/ou=First Administrative Group/cn=Recipients/cn=DPahia
/o=Somorita Surfboards/ou=First Administrative Group/cn=Recipients/cn=KPuckett
/o=Somorita Surfboards/ou=First Administrative Group/cn=Recipients/cn=HRodriguez
/o=Somorita Surfboards/ou=First Administrative Group/cn=Recipients/cn=KSanchez
/o=Somorita Surfboards/ou=First Administrative Group/cn=Recipients/cn=RTung
/o=Somorita Surfboards/ou=First Administrative Group/cn=Recipients/cn=EWatt
```

WARNING   Protect the directory into which these mailboxes are exported. These mailboxes probably contain sensitive information and should be protected from unauthorized access.

Exchange 2000 Backup FAQ

This is a list of questions that I am frequently asked about when planning backup strategies for Exchange 2000:

Should I back up the Exchange Installable File System (ExIFS) or the M: drive? No, under no circumstances should you back up this way. Back up Exchange using an Exchange-aware backup program. Backing up Exchange through the M: drive will not back up all the message properties and may actually corrupt messages and attachments.

How often should I perform a system state backup? Daily for domain controllers, probably no more than weekly for member servers whose system state will not change that often.

How often should I perform an IIS Metabase backup? This data does not change very often. I recommend backing it up immediately after any customizations or new virtual servers, and also about every two weeks. The IIS Metabase backups are not useful for disaster recovery, but they are useful if you have to roll back a configuration. For disaster recovery purposes, the system state backup includes the IIS Metabase.

Will the software that backed up my Exchange 5.5 server work with Exchange 2000? If the software was shipped prior to the release of Exchange 2000 in the fall of 2000, probably not. Confirm with the vendor whether or not your version will work.

Do you have a specific recommendation for backup software? For many people, the Windows 2000 Backup program will work just fine. You can even easily schedule backups with the Windows 2000 version. However, if you are requiring more advanced features, specialized tape drives, autoloaders, SAN-based backups, or other features, a third-party backup is going to be in your future. Don't forget to purchase the additional options necessary to take advantage of those features!

Disaster Recovery 101

Rule number one: "Don't panic!" When disaster strikes, keep your wits about you. To successfully recover from any sort of significant failure, you must have a plan and be familiar with what you need to do each step of the way. Here are some tips that will help your disaster recovery go more smoothly:

- Keep your system's standards and design document handy so that you can quickly refresh your memory on the standards that your organization is using.
- Document the hardware and software configuration of all Windows NT servers and any customizations that have been made to Exchange Server. Included in this documentation should be information on the Exchange 2000 configuration and the legacyExchangeDN attribute for each administrative group.
- Make sure that you know the Exchange organization name and each of the Exchange administrative group names. Documenting the logical (display) names of the storage groups and stores is also important.
- Have a written disaster recovery plan.
- Keep a disaster recovery kit that includes your system documentation, software CD-ROMs, and service packs.

Here are some steps to take to help recover from any type of disaster:

1. Identify the cause of the failure (disk, CPU, power supply, corrupted file, etc.).
2. Determine your course of action (restore from tape, rebuild server, run database utilities, etc.).
3. Estimate the time needed to complete the recovery action, and inform management and your user community of when service will be restored. (You might want to give yourself a cushion here, just in case of complications during repair.)
4. If the system is currently online, make an offline backup of it prior to going any further.
5. Perform the actual recovery.
6. Test to ensure that your recovery was successful.

TIP As soon as a problem strikes, create an outline based on these general disaster recovery steps. You should be able to refer back to this outline as the recovery progresses. During the recovery process, a lot of people are going to be asking questions, making suggestions, and screaming about downtime. If you get distracted by the commotion, you need to be able to easily pick up where you left off.

Exchange@Work: Image Backups of Basic Servers

One of my customers makes an image backup of the basic configuration of any server they deploy. When deploying Exchange 2000, they get the server completely configured and then make an image backup (using Symantec's Ghost software) of the server prior to installing Exchange 2000. This backup can then save them an hour or two of restoration if they ever have to rebuild the server from scratch.

Since Exchange 2000 is so tightly tied to Active Directory, I don't recommend making or relying on image backups for disaster recovery of the Exchange 2000 data. This might work—but it might not.

What Do You Want to Recover Today?

With any Exchange installation that I work on, I assist that organization in developing a recovery plan, which is based on the type of data that they actually have the ability to recover. When polling the company and IT management about what they would like to recover in the event of some type of catastrophic failure, they inevitably say "everything up to the moment of failure." The problem with that approach is the amount of overhead involved in making sure you can actually do that. "Everything" means that you have to be making just about constant backups of your transaction logs.

When you start making plans for disaster recovery, ask yourself what exactly you will *need* to recover. And ask yourself, in a worst-case scenario, what is an acceptable amount of data loss? Here are some common situations that your disaster recovery plan should cover:

- What is the maximum amount of time that the system can be down before at least some functionality can be restored?

- What procedures will need to be performed to recover a single mailbox, mailbox/public folder store, or an entire server?

- How much data loss is acceptable? An hour? An entire day?

We Don't Need No Stinkin' Plans!

If you think you don't need a disaster recovery plan, just wait until you have a significant problem, and watch your team running around not knowing what to do next. I can't stress it enough: *Have a disaster recovery plan in place*. It doesn't matter if you are supporting 100 users or 100,000. You and your co-workers must know what to do next. In the middle of a major problem is not the time to be figuring out the next step.

For large organizations, a disaster recovery plan may consist of many hundreds of pages and include contingencies such as off-site recovery, earthquakes, hurricanes, alien invasions, and the release of the next Star Wars movie. But for many of us, this plan will not be quite so detailed and may include only more likely scenarios. Here is a list of things that should be included in any disaster recovery plan:

- A current phone contact list, which should include:
  - Information Systems employees' information including home, pager, and cellular phone numbers. Special notes should be made for employees who have critical passwords such as the Administrator account password and the Exchange site services account, and the Active Directory Connector service account if backward compatibility with Exchange 5.5 is required.
  - Contact names and account numbers for vendors and support organizations. Don't forget phone numbers and circuit numbers used to report problems with WAN links.
  - Physical and environment contact information for power, air conditioning, and electricity providers.
  - Contact information for department heads and management along with who should be notified in the event of major outages.
  - Contact information and procedures for retrieving off-site backup information.
- A job responsibilities list that outlines what areas of the network and the software each IS employee is responsible for, and who each person's backup is.
- Procedures for retrieving backup data from off-site storage.
- Location of and person responsible for spare hardware, such as cold standby servers, extra disk drives, and so on.
- A printed copy of the MS Exchange Disaster Recovery documents.
- Instructions for common disaster-type events that may occur, including:
  - Failure of environmental services such as power or air conditioning.

Operations

PART 2

- The occurrence or prediction of a natural disaster such as an earthquake, hurricane, tornado, blizzard, flood, tsunami, volcanic eruption, and so on.

- Detection of a hacker break-in in progress.

- On the Exchange side, the failure of your bridgehead server, a server that supports mailboxes, or a server that supports critical public folders.

What Would *You* Do?

What would you do if you walked into your computer room and found that the racks supporting the 40-file server, print server, gateways, and backup systems that run your network had collapsed, and all the components had crashed to the floor? Computer cases were open, pieces of monitors and network hardware littered the entire room, and chaos reigned.

This is exactly what I asked myself minutes after the 1989 San Francisco earthquake. Our LAN computer room was almost completely destroyed. The rocking motion of the building (we were on the 22nd floor) was too much for the metal racks, and when they collapsed forward, all our components were sent crashing to the floor.

The steps that we went through to recover from this disaster could fill a book—we were not prepared. Do you have a plan that would dictate what to do in the event of the complete destruction of your computer room?

Does Anyone Know Where the Exchange Server CD-ROM Is?

How many times have you set out to install something, only to find that you spend most of your time looking for software, service packs, and system documentation? Twice in the past two months I have been called in to the middle of someone else's disaster. Both times I spent the better part of a day tracking down things like an Exchange CD-ROM, Windows NT CD-ROM, and device drivers for a SCSI controller—not to mention the countless phone calls I made to find out things like IP addresses, disk configurations, and system passwords. Why? Because the customers did not have the software and information close at hand when it was needed most.

To avoid wasting precious time in a crisis situation, I create a *disaster recovery kit* that contains everything I need to rebuild a server from the ground up (well, except for the actual hardware). My disaster recovery kit contains:

- A printed copy of the disaster recovery plan along with all the important phone numbers and service account numbers.

- System documentation for the Windows server and the Exchange server software configuration. This should be updated as necessary.
- CD-ROMs necessary to re-create the system including Windows Server, Exchange Server, Exchange Server service packs, Windows service packs, third-party software that is installed on the server, and hot fixes that have been applied.
- CD-ROMs and floppy disks provided by the manufacturer of the server hardware, including device drivers and supporting software for the server hardware.
- A backup that includes the Windows 2000 system state backup.

NOTE   System state backups are discussed earlier in this chapter.

As your software versions are upgraded and service packs are applied, make sure that you update your disaster recovery kit.

TIP   Once you have created a disaster recovery kit, don't loan out pieces of it such as CD-ROMs and floppy disks. Loaned items tend to disappear—and you won't realize that they're gone until you need them.

Practice Makes Perfect

I am a strong proponent of having an additional piece of hardware that is configured identically to your production Exchange servers with respect to disk space, disk controllers, and RAM. This is used as a *cold standby server* (cold meaning that it is not running in production all the time). I am also a strong advocate of performing periodic Exchange Server restores to your standby server.

Every few months, randomly pick one of your servers, pretend that it has had a catastrophic failure, and conduct a fire drill. How? Start your stopwatch. Then follow this checklist of steps you may have to take to rebuild your server in a disaster recovery, many of which are described in more detail later in the chapter:

- Separate the standby server hardware onto an isolated network and begin the restoration process. You will probably have to build the Windows 2000 server and apply all the necessary service packs.
- If the machine is a Windows 2000 domain controller, you will need to restore an updated copy of the Active Directory database to it; if not, then you will need an Active Directory domain controller in your isolated network.

Operations

PART 2

- Reinstall the Exchange Server software and service packs.

- Re-create the storage groups and store names based on the documentation you have of this server.

- Restore the Exchange databases.

- Confirm and/or match the legacyExchangeDN attribute of the databases with the administrative groups.

- Reconfigure the Exchange connectors that this server supported (you probably won't be able to confirm that the connectors are working since this server is on an isolated segment). Do anything else necessary to prepare the server to allow users to log back in.

- If you did not restore Active Directory from your production environment and you are planning to access the mailboxes on this test server, manually reconnect the mailboxes to existing Active Directory accounts using Exchange System Manager or automatically using the MBConn utility from the \Support\Tools\I386 folder of the Exchange 2000 CD-ROM or service packs.

Stop your stopwatch.

How long did it take? Granted a lot of the time was probably spent watching software installation screens or tape restore progress indicators. Yet the time that it took is important, because it can be used in service level agreements (SLAs) and, in the case of a real emergency, it can be used to inform your users of approximately how long it will take to restore the system to a usable state. (I usually add an additional 30 to 50 percent on to my test restoration times to cut myself a little slack.)

Evaluate your own performance during the test restoration. Was there anything that you could have done to make the restoration go faster? (Yes, we would all like faster hardware and tape drives.) Did you have all the software and documentation you needed nearby?

WARNING Restoration of an Exchange server is a complex process. Doing it for the first time is not something that you want to try while 1000 users are waiting. It is absolutely critical that you become familiar with the backup and restore procedures *before* you need to know them. I cannot emphasize enough the importance of thoroughly understanding the restoration process.

Exchange@Work: Practicing Disaster Recovery and Verifying Database Integrity

The management at GHI Corporation expects their messaging system to be available 24 hours per day. Their Exchange administrator is responsible for two Exchange servers that support almost 850 mailboxes. She has one maintenance window of six hours per month that she uses to restart the servers, apply service packs, and perform a bimonthly offline backup. Her Exchange servers have circular logging disabled, and she performs a normal backup at 11:00 P.M. each night followed by two differential backups, one at 10:30 A.M. and one at 3:00 P.M. Each server's normal backup takes approximately three hours, and the differential backups take an average of about 10 minutes.

During the design phase of her Exchange organization, the administrator was able to convince her superiors to purchase a third server identical to her two production servers. She uses this server as a cold standby and for practicing disaster recovery. Every three months, she picks one of the two servers and builds a recovery server on an isolated network. She then restores the server with the normal backup tape from the evening before and the most recent differential tape. Her time to restore the larger of her two servers (approximately 500 mailboxes and about 20GB of data) is just under four hours.

When the restoration process is finished and she is comfortable with the fact that the users could go back to work if necessary, she takes this recovery a step further. To further verify that a database is free of corruption, she performs an offline compaction/defragmentation. So on the *recovery* server, the administrator dismounts the mailbox store and runs ESEUTIL /D <*database_name*> so that the database is truly free of corruption. This is merely done for the sake of restoration practice, testing, and quality assurance; these recovered databases are never put back into production.

Though this process is time consuming, GHI Corp's administrator is assured that her Exchange databases are corruption free, and she has an excellent understanding of the recovery process.

Disaster Recovery Tips

No amount of tips and hints is going to make your disaster recovery a positive and joyful experience. Each time you have to recover from some type of system failure, you are going to learn a lot more. However, some things that may prove helpful in making the disaster recovery go a little smoother include:

- Keep your user community informed of how long you expect to be offline. You will be surprised how cooperative they can be if you just give them a straightforward, honest answer.

- Keep your boss and the help desk apprised of your progress. Your boss is your first line of defense against management pressures, and the help desk is your first line of defense against angry end users. If there are major problems, your boss and the help desk are going to find out anyway; it is best if you let them know rather than waiting until they ask. If you *are* the help desk, change your outgoing message on your voice-mail to give your users an update to the current situation.

- If you are trying to solve a database corruption problem, know when to quit and do a restore from tape. Restoring from tape is the preferred way to recover from database failures. The database repair tools (ESEUTIL and ISINTEG) should be considered viable options only if you have no recent backup.

- Ask for at least two separate phones in your computer room. One of these should have a hands-free headset, which should either be cordless or have enough cord so that you can access the consoles of all your servers.

- Prior to starting a disaster recovery, re-read the relevant parts of the Microsoft Disaster Recovery document.

Speeding Up Disaster Recovery

How can you decrease the amount of time spent recovering from server failures, database corruption, or other disasters? Here are some pointers:

- Practice disaster recovery until you know the steps by heart.

- Have all Exchange 2000 and AD documentation accurate, up-to-date, and easily accessible. This is not the time to discover that your documentation is "on the server."

- Make sure that all software you require is nearby.

- Create additional mailbox stores and distribute the mailboxes across multiple stores so that any one store is not too large.

- Purchase faster tape drives. Faster tape drives mean faster restore times.

Practicing Disaster Recovery

As I mentioned earlier, practice makes perfect. One of the best things that you can do to prepare for recovering data is to actually practice. Many sites I work on have a cold standby server sitting beside their production systems. However, if you do not have an identical system, the first step toward restoring an Exchange server is getting the recovery server built.

> **NOTE** If you have an identically configured standby server and a production server fails (memory, CPU, power supply, disk controllers), the first thing the IS team should do is move the drive arrays over to the cold standby system and attempt to bring the disks back up on new hardware.

Most of the skills required are going to be drawn from the Windows 2000 Active Directory side of your brain rather than the Exchange side. There are two types of rebuilds, and you should base your choice on the result you want to achieve. Are you attempting to recover a mailbox or test your disaster recovery procedures? Or are you attempting to restore your Windows 2000 system after a complete Windows 2000 server failure?

If you are attempting to restore a mailbox store to a recovery server or to test your disaster recovery procedures, then you will need to rebuild your Exchange 2000 server as well as a new Active Directory forest. If you are attempting to rebuild the entire system after a complete failure, you will need to reinstall the Exchange 2000 forest in disaster recovery mode.

Testing Complete Server Failure

If your busiest Exchange 2000 server failed right now, what would you do? What is the first step you would have to take toward getting back online? Do you have hardware that you can put into place? Not being sure if you're prepared for a disaster is why I recommend practicing this exercise prior to ever having to face the actual event.

Here is a basic outline of the steps I would want to be able to do quickly and easily. In this example, I will rebuild an Exchange 2000 system and simulate putting it back into production. This should take place on an isolated segment and *not* on the production network. I am assuming that the Active Directory domain controller and Exchange 2000 server are on different server hardware.

1. Build two Windows 2000 servers capable of supporting Exchange 2000 and an Active Directory domain controller. Confirm that the correct version of Windows 2000 is installed and that all necessary service packs and hot fixes are restored. The server names should match the server names on the production network.

2. On the Active Directory server, restore the system state and the AD, and confirm that AD is working properly. You will probably need to change some things such as which DNS server is being used, since this test AD server is on an isolated network.

3. On the Exchange 2000 server, follow the steps found in the "Recovering an Entire Server" section later in this chapter for performing a reinstallation of Exchange 2000.

4. Test mailbox access from Outlook and Internet clients.

For steps one through three, time the reinstallation process. How long did it take to get that server back into production? Can you live with that restoration time in production? What can you do to reduce the restoration time?

Disaster Recovery Scenarios

Earlier in the chapter, I mentioned a couple of common disaster scenarios from which you might have to recover. This section talks about recovering from these disasters. As I mentioned in the previous section in this chapter, you should have an accurate idea of how much time each of these steps will take to perform.

Recovering a Deleted Item, Deleted Folder, or Deleted Mailbox

Administrators don't usually consider the deletion of a single message—or maybe even an entire folder—a disaster. However, the user to whom the message or folder belongs may.

Exchange 5.5's deleted item recovery feature allowed the user to "undelete" the message even after the message had been emptied from the deleted items folder. Like Exchange 5.5, this feature can be enabled for mailbox stores and public folder stores. In addition, Exchange 2000 introduced the ability to undelete a mailbox. Figure 7.7 shows both the Keep Deleted Items and Keep Deleted Mailboxes settings. I *strongly* urge you to configure these for each mailbox store on every server or to use a mailbox store policy to enforce this setting for many mailbox stores.

Figure 7.7   Deleted item and deleted mailbox settings

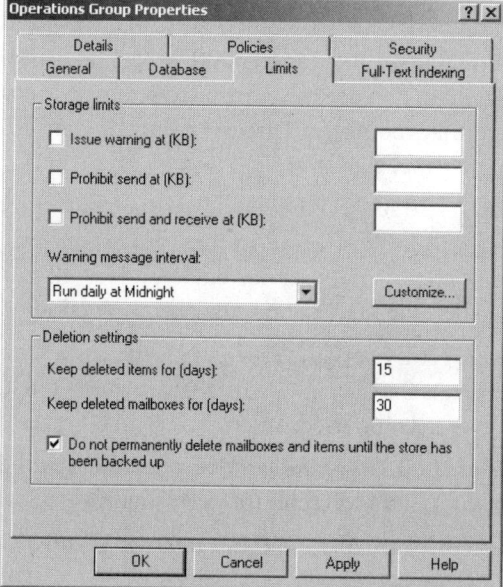

Recovering a Deleted Item or Deleted Folder

If you have configured all of your information stores to retain deleted items for a respectable number of days, users deleting items should not be a concern. The default Keep Deleted Items setting is blank, which means that deleted items are *not* available after they are deleted. I recommend setting this to 15 days (as shown back in Figure 7.7), but I see administrators setting this value between three and 30 days.

> **NOTE** Exchange 2000 does not keep deleted items by default; the administrator must enable this feature.

When a user deletes something accidentally from their mailbox (and subsequently purges their Deleted Items folder), they can use Outlook 97 (v8.03 or later), 98, 2000, or XP to recover the item. The Outlook Tools menu has a Recover Deleted Items choice, which is available when you have the Deleted Items folder highlighted. This feature is not currently implemented in Outlook Web Access.

When an Outlook 97, 98, 2000, XP, or Outlook Web Access client deletes a message, the message is moved to the Deleted Items folder. However, the client can do a *hard delete*, or *in-place deletion*, which bypasses the Deleted Items folder altogether. To hard-delete a message, highlight it and press the Shift+Delete keys.

> **NOTE** POP3 and IMAP4 clients perform a hard delete of messages.

Outlook 2000 and XP also transfer other deleted elements—such as calendar entries, contact items, notes, journal entries, and tasks—to the Deleted Items folder. Outlook 97 and 98 perform hard deletes of these items.

Entries that have been hard deleted are still recoverable, but you may have to edit the client's Registry. Add the value DumpsterAlwaysOn (data type is REG_DWORD) to the \HKLM\Software\Microsoft\Exchange\Client\Options Registry key. Enter a value of 1 to turn on the Recover Deleted Items menu choice for all folders, or enter 0 to turn it off.

> **NOTE** If a client's Recover Deleted Items From list is empty, the Keep Deleted Items setting is probably not enabled for their mailbox or public store.

Recovering a Deleted Mailbox

Exchange administrators everywhere are dancing on the tables thanks to the ability to recover a deleted mailbox. This is a feature that is sorely overdue in the Exchange world due in part to the difficulty of restoring a single mailbox in Exchange 5.5. I have seen this problem time and time again: A mailbox gets deleted accidentally, or the mailbox is intentionally deleted because the administrator believes the user has left the organization when they haven't.

Many Exchange 5.5 organizations have put procedures in place whereby the Windows NT account is disabled, the mailbox has its SMTP addresses removed, and the mailbox is hidden. Then, only after a respectable amount of time (usually 30 days), the mailbox and account are deleted.

I believe this is still a good procedure with Exchange 2000, but it is less necessary since a mailbox can be recovered. The default setting for each mailbox store is 30 days for new servers (shown back in Figure 7.7), and I recommend keeping this setting at this configured interval. If the server was upgraded from Exchange 5.5, this setting is 0 days.

Once a mailbox or user account is deleted, the Mailbox Cleanup Agent will run and mark this mailbox as being deleted. Figure 7.8 shows some deleted mailboxes in the default mailbox store on server SFOEX001. You can highlight a deleted mailbox and right-click it to get the choice to reconnect the mailbox to an existing Active Directory user account that does not currently have a mailbox associated with it.

Figure 7.8 Deleted mailboxes

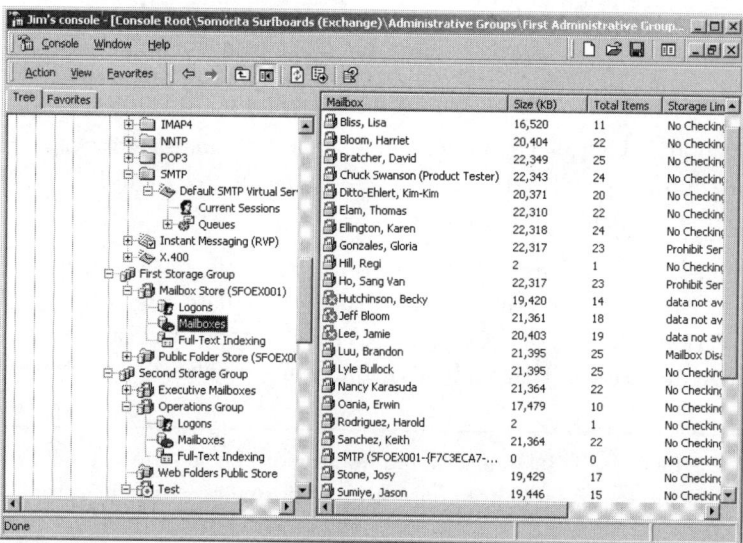

Additionally, you can choose Purge, which will purge the deleted mailbox immediately. You can accelerate the Mailbox Cleanup Agent by right-clicking the Mailboxes container and choosing Run Cleanup Agent.

Restoring Service Now and Data Later

Some months ago, I was called to an Exchange 2000 site that had a database corruption problem. The database was over 45GB in size, and the first attempt to restore it had failed due partially to the inexperience of the person doing the restore. The database took nearly 14 hours to restore the first time, and the user community was planning to burn an effigy of the IT director if the system they could not start sending and receiving messages soon.

We made a decision to restore the Exchange server to service with new, empty databases. To wipe the databases out, we made sure that the mailbox store files (the EDB and the STM files) were deleted from the server; then we remounted the store. A message appeared reminding us that there are no mailbox store data files so the files will be re-created.

Once the empty database files were created and mounted, the users could go back to work, but they had none of their old messages, calendar entries, or contacts. So now that the users can now send and receive message with the rest of the world, we were faced with the task of getting the data from the old server merged back into the production server. The advantage to this approach is that we could now work at a slightly more leisurely pace since messaging service (albeit minimal) had been restored.

NOTE   Compaq actually has a name for this process: ROPR (Rapid Online, Phased Recovery).

The first task at hand was to restore the mailbox store to a recovery server. (This task is described in more detail later in this chapter.) Once the recovery server was built and the data restored to the recovery server, our next task was to reconnect users and get access to their old mailbox data. To do this, we used the ExMerge utility to extract data out of the mailbox stores and into PST files. This process is detailed previously in this chapter, in the section titled "ExMerge As a Backup Tool," but in this case we had to export all of the mailboxes out of the server, not just the VIPs as described earlier.

Once the export process begins, patience becomes a virtue, because the export process can take hours or even days depending on the number of mailboxes you have selected. A single PST file will represent each mailbox exported and will be named using the user's alias. For example, the PST file for mailbox alias MEstrada will be named `mestrada.pst`. A mailbox with approximately 1300 messages (35MB reported in System Manager) took almost five minutes to export. The resulting PST file was almost 50MB; this is due to the fact that for each message extracted to a PST file, the message body is stored twice. The resulting PST file will always be larger than the amount of storage reported by System Manager.

TIP Monitoring available disk space on the disk that holds the PST files is important. You may want to export all of your managers and VIP users first and get those users' mailboxes imported to the production server before you export the majority of the user community.

In this particular export process, we had almost 700 mailboxes to export, so we broke them up into groups of about 150. After each group of mailboxes was exported, we copied the PST files to the production Exchange server and imported them. Then we ran the ExMerge import procedure directly on the production Exchange server. The entire process took nearly a whole weekend (we started on a Friday afternoon and it did not complete until late Sunday night).

An interesting note about this import is that the resulting EDB database file was 88GB in size. Why is this since the original store (EDB and STM files) was only 45GB total? First of all, we lost single instance storage when we exported the mail and reimported it. Second, ExMerge is a MAPI application and thus, when importing data back into the store, it will all be imported into the rich-text store (the EDB file).

Recovering a Corrupted Information Store

If you are getting messages in the Windows Event Viewer indicating that the database is corrupted, or if the database will not mount, the most expeditious thing you can do is immediately perform a restore from your last normal backup. In my experience, if you have a recent backup and you have up-to-date transaction logs, recovery will be much more quick and reliable than if you try to recover using the database utilities. There are two ways that you can restore a backup: from an online backup or from an offline backup.

Restoring from an Online Backup

If you performed an online backup, restoration is simple. There are many backup programs that may use slightly different steps to do this restore. The following steps use the Windows 2000 Backup program. If you have a database that is corrupted or will not mount, always make an offline backup of it and all the available log files before proceeding.

If the store you are restoring is currently mounted, make sure to dismount it before following these steps. (This is contrary to what the Windows 2000 backup program may indicate.) I am assuming that there are two backup sets, one that contains a normal (full) backup and a later differential backup set that contains more recent transaction logs. This example restores the mailbox store called Operations Group.

1. Start Windows 2000 Backup and select the media set that you are restoring from.

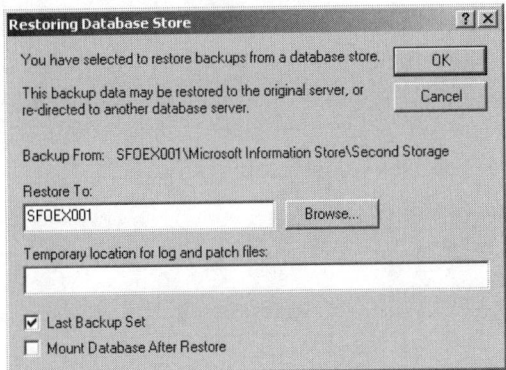

2. Expand the media set, and in the right-hand pane select the mailbox or public store you wish to restore.

3. Click the Start Restore button to see the Restoring Database Store dialog box.

4. Confirm that the correct server is listed in the Restore To field, and specify a temporary location for log and patch files. Click OK.

5. If you are restoring from a file, you will be asked which BKF file you need to select to restore this store. Once the file is selected, continue with the restore. The full backups must be restored first so that the `restore.env` file is created.

6. To restore the transaction log files, select the media set that contains the transaction log files and make sure that the Log Files folder is selected. Click the Start Restore button.

Operations

PART 2

7. On the Restoring Database Store dialog box, make sure that the correct server is listed in the Restore To dialog box, and make sure that the temporary location for log and patch files is entered. This *must* be the same directory that you specified in step 3. If this is the last backup set that will be restored, select the Last Backup Set check box. If you want the store to be mounted when finished, click the Mount Database After Restore check box. When ready to proceed, click OK.

8. If you are restoring from a file, you will have to select the BKF file that contains the transaction log files. The restore process should now begin. This may be time consuming depending on the amount of data you are restoring. If you have selected the Mount Database After Restore check box, once the restoration process has completed the database will remount and any outstanding transactions will be committed. If you did not check that box, then you will need to mount the database manually.

Temporary Location for Log and Patch Files The temporary directory that must be provided is the location to which the transaction logs, the PAT file, and the restore.env file are restored. This directory must be the same for all restore operations for a particular store or storage group (if you are restoring more than one storage group at a time). The restore steps from above created the temporary directory shown in Figure 7.9. I specified the directory called C:\TempRestore; the restore process created the \Second Storage Group subdirectory.

TIP Microsoft recommends restoring only one storage group at a time. However, if you specify separate temporary locations for each storage group that is being restored, you can restore two databases or entire storage groups simultaneously.

Figure 7.9 Temporary directory used during a restore

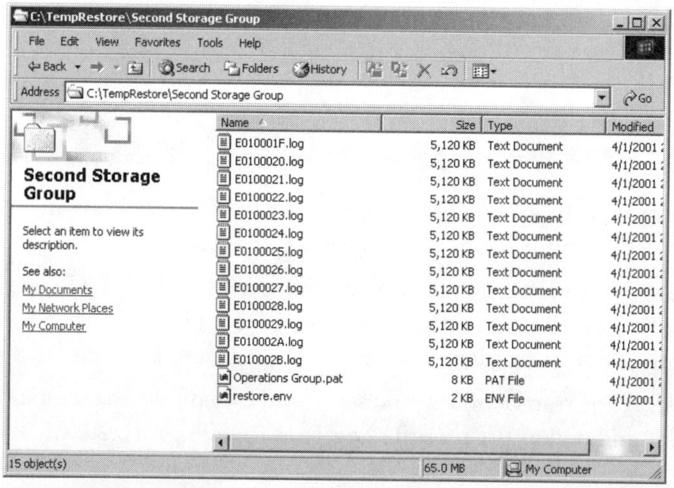

The PAT file (`Operations Group.pat` in Figure 7.9) is created during an online backup and contains all of the transactions that were committed to the portions of the database during the online backup that had already been backed up.

Exchange 5.5 had a Registry key called `RestoreInProgress` that let the information store know that a restore was currently happening. This key no longer exists in Exchange 2000; the `restore.env` file has replaced it. This file contains a record of which databases are being restored and which transaction logs have been restored. It is used by the ESE database engine store process to bring the database back into a consistent state. You can view the contents of the `restore.env` file by typing **eseutil /cm** *<path_to_restore.env_file>*. A sample file is shown in Figure 7.10.

Figure 7.10 Sample `restore.env` file

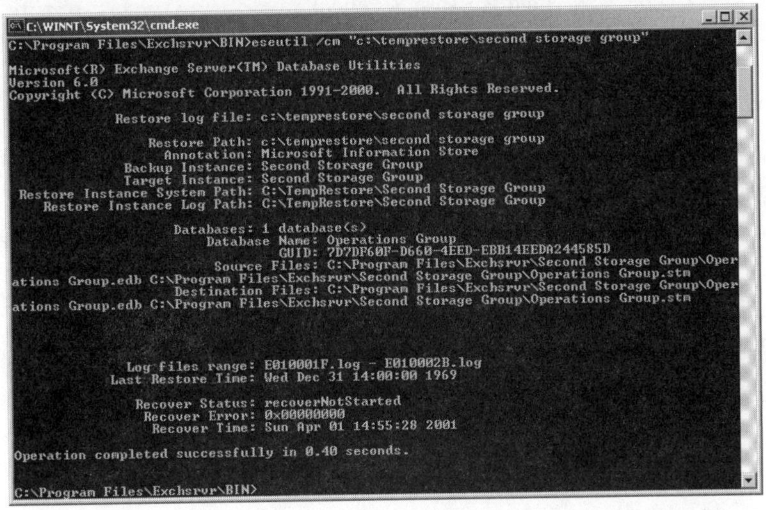

The `restore.env` file contains key information that will be needed to bring the database or databases to a consistent state. This information includes:

- The name of the storage group that contains the database or databases
- The path to the database or databases being restored
- The path to the transaction logs
- The path to the directory that contains the transaction log files
- The range of the transaction log names that will be used

NOTE For more information about the `restore.env` file, consult Microsoft Knowledge Base article Q253914.

Last Restore Set   The Restoring Database Store dialog box has a check box asking if this is the Last Backup Set. Check this box during the last restore that you are doing so that the database can then be brought back into a consistent state. In Exchange 5.5, this occurred automatically if the RestoreInProgress Registry key existed.

NOTE   The process of bringing the database back to a consistent state after a restore from backup is called a *hard recovery*. A *soft recovery* is the process of bringing the database back to a consistent state after an abrupt database shut-down (a crash). Bringing the database to a consistent state involves scanning the transaction logs (and PAT file if the database was restored) and committing any transaction not found in the database file.

If you forget to check the Last Restore Set check box during the last restore, you will not be able to mount the store. You will probably receive a message stating that an internal processing error has occurred. You will also see ESE98 error 619 and MSExchangeIS error 9519 in the application event log.

You must force the database to be brought into a consistent state with the ESEUTIL utility; otherwise you cannot mount the database. Do not run this process until you are sure that all the log files have been restored. To perform a hard recovery, type **eseutil /cc** *<path_to_restore.env_file>*.

NOTE   The eseutil /cc option may not work if the server is in a cluster. See Microsoft Knowledge Base article Q266689 for more information.

ESE takes the log files in the temporary directory and commits the transactions to the database if necessary; this is called *playing forward* the logs. If there are any production transaction logs in the actual log file directory, the ESE database engine then plays those forward. ESE does check the log file sequence to make sure that all the log files are present and to make sure that the log files match the backup set. If there are log files missing or that don't match the backup set, ESE only replays the log files from the backup tape. However, if it skips the production backup logs, any data created since the log file backup was run will not be committed to the database.

If you did not click the Last Restore Set check box, you can tell ESE to skip playing forward the transaction logs by using the eseutil /cc /t *<path_to_restore.env_file>* command-line switch. You can also tell ESE to preserve the log files used to recover the database file with the eseutil /cc /k *<path_to_restore.env_file>* switch. While this is not something that the typical administrator would ever need to do, these switches are useful if you did not check the Last Restore Set button during restore and you want to control how ESE commits the transaction logs to the database.

Exchange@Work: Is Everything Restored?

Due to a Jupiter-sized "whoops!" at ABC Corp (someone plugged an external SCSI system into a live Exchange server), they experienced database corruption in both the default mailbox and public stores. Transaction log files were on another disk controller altogether. The most recent normal backup was two days before.

The administrator started a restore job, selected the Last Restore Set check box, and restored the public and mailbox stores. She was surprised to find that all of her users' messages had been restored, including the past two days worth. While she was quite happy with the fact that everything had been restored, why was everything up-to-date (and not two days old)?

The answer is simple: When she restored the data, the database was restored to its original location, and the transaction logs from the tape were restored to the temporary location, but the existing transaction logs were not overwritten. Therefore, the transaction logs from the restore were committed to the database file, and then the transaction logs from the active storage group were committed.

Restoring from an Offline Backup

Offline backups occur when you dismount a store or shut down the information store service in order to back up the files. I do not recommend offline backups for a few reasons. The first of these reasons is that dismounting a store affects your uptime. Second, doing this is a manual process and thus requires an operator. Finally, online backups of the store include confirming that the checksum for each block of data in the store is good.

> **NOTE** All transactions are committed to the store when it is dismounted, so the store is considered to be consistent. Bringing the store back to a consistent state is not necessary, and transaction logs will not be replayed. Additionally, any transactions in transaction logs that are not in the store will not be committed to a database that is restored from an offline backup.

If you were performing a disaster recovery and chose to do an offline backup, you will need to perform a slightly different restoration process. To restore a store from an offline backup, follow these steps:

1. Dismount the store that you plan to restore.
2. Restore the EDB and STM files from the offline backup.

3. Display the store's properties and go to the Database tab.

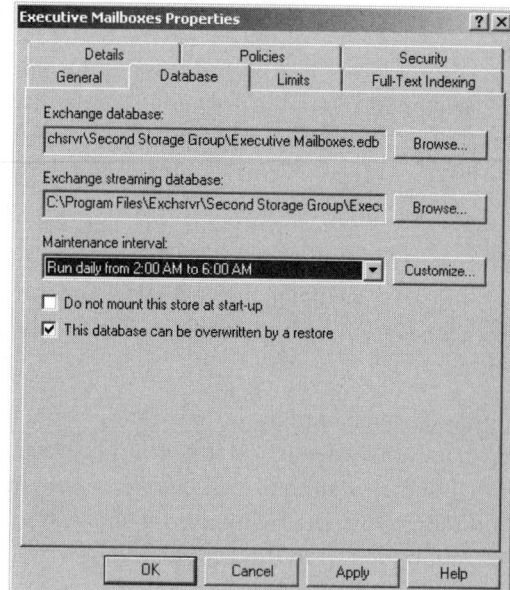

Click the This Database Can Be Overwritten By A Restore check box and click OK.

4. Right-click the store and choose Mount Store.

Recovering an Entire Server

Rebuilding an entire server and restoring all of the data to that server is not as lofty a task as it might initially seem. First of all, unlike Exchange 5.5, all is not lost when you lose the Exchange server. Much of the Exchange 2000 configuration is stored in the Configuration partition of Active Directory.

WARNING If you are planning to restore a server back into service, do *not* delete the references to the server from Active Directory.

Restoring Exchange 2000 from scratch consists of several major tasks. Assuming that your Exchange 2000 server is a member server and that Active Directory is accessible on a separate domain controller, these steps include:

- Reinstalling Windows 2000, service packs, hot fixes, and any additional software (resource kits, system tools), assuming that this information is not backed up
- Restoring the Windows 2000 system state backup

- Restoring the most recent IIS Metabase information
- Confirming that Active Directory connectivity is working properly
- Installing Exchange 2000 in disaster recovery mode
- Configuring names of Exchange objects to match the intended recovery objects
- Restoring the Exchange 2000 data and logs

Preparing Windows 2000 for Exchange 2000

Prior to even reinstalling Exchange 2000, you will be faced with several tasks that you must perform correctly, or else the data will be inaccessible. Here are the steps necessary to get to the point where you can reinstall Exchange 2000, assuming that Exchange 2000 is running on a Windows 2000 member server, rather than a domain controller:

1. Rebuild the server hardware using the same hardware (or hardware that is as close as possible to the hardware) that was used.

2. Reinstall the same version of Windows 2000 (Server, Advanced Server, or Data Center) that you were using previously, as well as any Windows 2000 service packs or hot fixes. Make sure you use the same version of Windows 2000 that you were using originally.

3. Restore the full backup of applications and other data on the hard disk drive. This may not be necessary if you had few applications installed on the computer to begin with and you prefer to reinstall them separately.

4. Restore the system state. If the hardware configuration is different, you may have to reboot in Safe Boot mode a few times to get all of the device drivers working properly again.

5. Confirm connectivity to Active Directory. Chapter 2, "Active Directory for Exchange 2000 Administrators," has some suggestions for using the NLTEST utility that will confirm that the server can contact domain controllers and global catalog servers, and see its own site properly.

6. Run the Exchange 2000 setup program with the /disasterrecovery switch. Make sure that you restore all of the software options that were installed on the server in the first place. If the system state restoration was successful, you may not be able to use the /disasterrecovery option, but if you can't, then you can use the /reinstall option.

7. Apply all Exchange 2000 service packs and hot fixes.

8. Restart the server. All of the necessary services will start, except none of the stores will mount since there will be no database files on the disk.

9. Restore each of the storage groups separately using the single store restoration procedure documented earlier in this chapter. The full backups need to be restored first, then the transaction log backups (if any). When you are ready to restore the last tape, confirm that the Last Backup Set option is checked.

10. Confirm that the stores mounted correctly.

11. Restore the SRS and KMS databases.

12. Confirm that the connectors that were hosted on that server are functioning correctly.

Restoring to a Recovery Server

A few times I have found it necessary to recover data to a recovery server rather than the production server. This includes the time mentioned earlier in this chapter where we had to recover a mailbox store from backup and then ExMerge the mailbox data to PST files. Also, if someone deletes an important mailbox or message, and if deleted item recovery or deleted mailbox recovery is not enabled, then this procedure may have to be run.

To restore data to a recovery server, you are going to require a few basics, including the following:

- Server hardware that will support Exchange 2000 and Active Directory running simultaneously. The hardware will also have to support the largest database size you might restore to it.

- The Exchange 2000 organization name, which can be found in the root of the Exchange System Manager console.

- The name of the administrative group to which the store belongs and the legacy Exchange distinguished name (legacyExchangeDN) for the administrative group.

- The name of the storage group that contains the store.

- The logical name of the store, which is the name found in the hierarchy in Exchange System Manager.

The most difficult information to gather will be the legacyExchangeDN. (For details about the legacyExchangeDN, see Chapter 2.) If the administrative group that the store is located in is the First Administrative Group, then you don't need to worry about this value. Otherwise, you will need to find it using a utility such as ADSIEDIT, LDIFDE, or LDP. Figure 7.11 shows the ADSIEDIT MMC and the legacyExchangeDN property of the First Administrative Group. To find this, I opened the Configuration partition in ADSIEDIT and browsed down through Services ➤ Microsoft Exchange ➤ Somorita Surfboards ➤ Administrative Groups ➤ Southeast Asia Admin Group.

Figure 7.11 ADSIEDIT showing the `legacyExchangeDN`

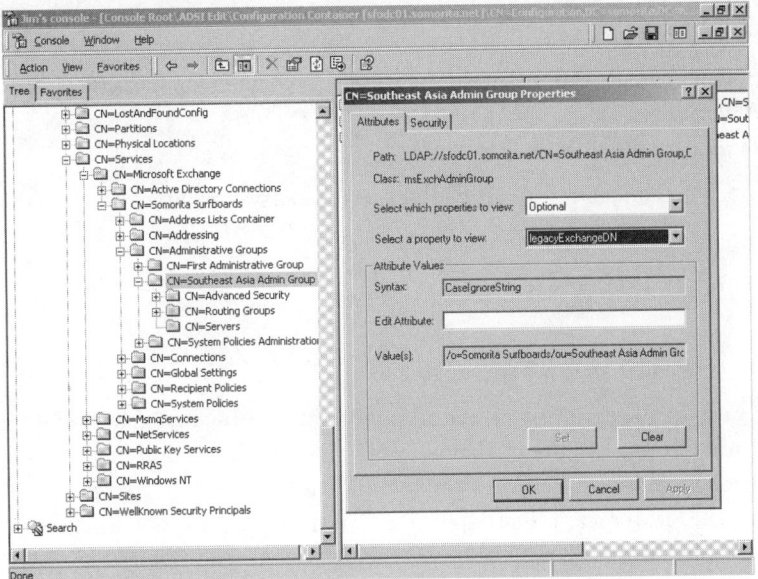

NOTE The `legacyExchangeDN` is required in order to create the correct administrative group name. The administrative group name used in the recovery site must have the same `legacyExchangeDN` as the administrative group in which the database originated.

Another way to get this information would be to use the LDIFDE command and specify the object that you want to view (with the –D option) and the properties to display (the –L option). The –P Base option tells LDIFDE to output only the specified object and not all objects in the subtree under the object. Following is an example of using LDIFDE; the portion in bold is the command that is actually typed:

```
C:\>ldifde -F CON -d "cn=southeast asia admin group,cn=administrative
groups,cn=somorita surfboards,cn=Microsoft Exchange,cn=services,cn=
configuration,dc=somorita,dc=net" -L legacy

ExchangeDN -P Base

Connecting to "sfodc01.somorita.net"

Logging in as current user using SSPI

Exporting directory to file CON
```

```
Searching for entries...

Writing out entries.dn: cn=southeast asia admin group,cn=administrative
groups,cn=somorita

 surfboards,cn=Microsoft Exchange,cn=services,cn=configuration,dc=
somorita,dc=net

changetype: add

legacyExchangeDN: /o=Somorita Surfboards/ou=Southeast Asia Admin Group


1 entries exported


The command has completed successfully
```

In this example, the administrative group we want the legacyExchangeDN for is Southeast Asia Admin Group, and the Exchange 2000 organization is Somorita Surfboards. The legacyExchangeDN of the administrative group that contains the database is stamped in the database when it is created. The database will not mount if the database legacyExchangeDN and the administrative group legacyExchangeDN values do not match. Microsoft Knowledge Base article Q273863 has more information on this problem.

Exchange@Work: Changing the legacyExchangeDN Attribute on a Recovery Server

If you are building a recovery server and you want to restore mailbox stores to it and then recover the data, you may end up with quite a bit of work each time you want to restore data if you have more than one administrative group. This is because the legacyExchangeDN of the administrative group has to match the one stamped on the database. Microsoft Knowledge Base article Q273863 describes a process you can perform using LDIFDE that allows you to change the legacyExchangeDN values for all of the necessary objects under the administrative group. Apparently this procedure was in big demand, because Microsoft has released a utility with Exchange 2000 SP1 and SP2 called LEGACYDN.EXE to help you automate this process. This utility is found in the \Support\Utils\i386\LegacyDn directory of the service pack, as is a detailed readme file, Readme4legacydn.txt.

Exchange@Work: Changing the legacyExchangeDN Attribute on a Recovery Server *(continued)*

LegacyDN is extremely useful if you need to restore databases from different administrative groups to your recovery server. It allows you to quickly change the `legacyExchangeDN` value on all of the appropriate objects under an administrative group without having to reinstall Exchange 2000. Not only can you change the `legacyExchangeDN` value, but you can also change the organization name and the administrative group name.

This utility is really helpful, but it cannot read the database to determine which `legacyExchangeDN` is stamped to the database; you must have that information documented prior to running LegacyDN. However, if you don't have that information available, restore the database to the recovery server and attempt to mount the database anyway. Then scan the application event log for event ID 1088 from the MSExchangeIS source; this event contains the `legacyExchangeDN` (referred to in the messages as the distinguished name).

Run this utility only on your recovery servers, *never* on your production servers.

Operations

PART 2

The logical name of the storage group and the store is a little bit easier to get. This is the name found in Exchange System Manager under the storage group. Figure 7.12 shows the mailbox store Executive Mailboxes in the Second Storage Group. Both of these names will be necessary when you create the Exchange 2000 recovery server.

Figure 7.12   Logical name of a storage group and store

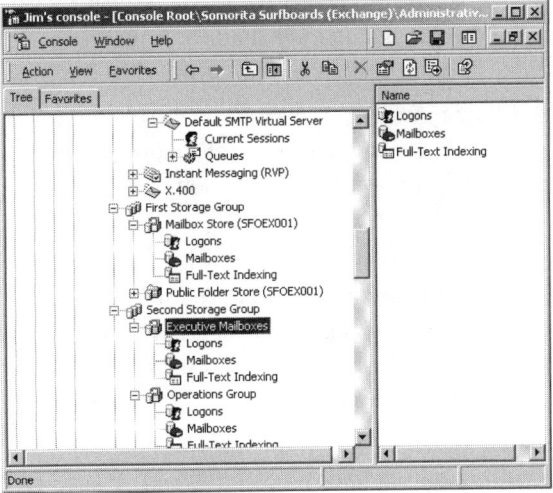

Since the recovery server will only be used to recover data from mailboxes or for practice recovery, many of the steps involved in reinstalling a server are not necessary, such as restoring Active Directory, the system state, and the IIS Metabase. In the following example, I'm going to install Active Directory and Exchange 2000 on the same machine. Follow these steps if you want to restore a mailbox store to a recovery server:

1. Install server hardware that will be capable of supporting the store databases that you need to restore. This server does not need to be on an isolated network.

2. Install Windows 2000 and any service packs and hot fixes. The Windows 2000 edition (Server, Advanced Server, or Datacenter) does not need to be the same edition as your production server is running. Install the DNS service on this machine and configure it to use itself as a DNS. The server name will have to be unique if you are installing it onto the same network.

3. Configure the disk drives to support the store database and transaction logs that you will be restoring.

4. Run the DCPromo utility and create a new Active Directory forest. The forest and domain names on the recovery server do not have to be the same name as the production forest. When asked about DNS, confirm that you want the DNS to be configured on this machine.

5. Run the Exchange 2000 Setup program in forest prep mode (`setup /forestprep`) to create the necessary classes and objects in Active Directory.

6. Run the Exchange 2000 Setup program again, choose a custom installation, and install *only* the Exchange System Management Tools component.

7. Run the Exchange System Manager and create an Exchange 2000 administrative group name that matches *exactly* the `legacyExchangeDN` name of the storage group where the mailbox store lives on the production server. You can skip this step if the store you are going to restore is in the First Administrative Group.

8. Run Exchange Setup yet again, and install Exchange 2000 Messaging and Collaboration Services. Install the Exchange server into this newly created administrative group. Apply any necessary Exchange 2000 service packs and hot fixes.

9. Run Exchange System Manager and create a storage group that matches exactly the name of the storage group on the production server. You can skip this step if the storage group name is First Storage Group.

10. Create a mailbox store that matches exactly the logical name of the mailbox store on the production system including the server name portion that is in parentheses. This step will be necessary unless the server name matches exactly the name of the production system. If the server name matches the production system, the default mailbox store will be the same as the recovery server.

11. Follow the steps outlined in this chapter's "Restoring from an Online Backup" section to restore the store databases.

12. Once the store is restored to the recovery server, ensure that the store is mounted.

13. Highlight the store's Mailboxes container, right-click, and choose Run Cleanup Agent. The mailboxes should now be listed with the X over the mailbox icon.

The mailbox data can now be recovered.

Recovering Mailbox Data from a Recovery Server

Once you complete the process of recovering a mailbox store to a recovery server, the mailbox data now exists on the server. However, it is not accessible by any clients because the mailboxes are not associated with user accounts in your new Active Directory forest.

If you have only a few mailboxes from which you need to recover data, then the simplest approach is to use Active Directory Users And Computers to create new Active Directory user accounts. Do not create mailboxes for the user accounts you are creating. Once you have the necessary user accounts created, use Exchange System Manager to display the mailboxes for the mailbox store you restored.

Once you see the list of mailboxes in the mailbox store, you will need to reconnect the mailboxes from which you need to recover data to user accounts. To reconnect mailboxes, right-click the mailbox you want to recover and choose Reconnect. Browse Active Directory until you find the user account you want to associate with this mailbox. Once the mailbox has been associated with the user account, give the Recipient Update Service (RUS) a few minutes to populate the necessary attributes for the user account, then you can open the mailbox and recover the necessary messages to a PST file.

Recovering Mailboxes in Bulk   If you have to recover more than a few mailboxes, creating each of the user accounts and reconnecting the mailboxes may be a tedious process. In this case, you can use the Mailbox Reconnect Tool (MBConn) utility provided with the Exchange 2000 CD-ROM; it is found in the \Support\Utils\I386\mbconn.exe directory. There is also an MBConn help file in this directory called mbconn.chm; additionally, you can find updated information on MBConn in Microsoft Knowledge Base article Q271886.

This utility lets you locate mailboxes that have no Active Directory user account (called *orphaned mailboxes*) and reconnect them to user accounts. The MBConn utility can also create an LDF file that can be used to create user accounts.

The first step is to use MBConn to generate a list of mailboxes that do not have Active Directory accounts and to use LDIFDE to create those accounts. To do this, follow these steps:

1. Run the MBConn utility, click Next, and enter the name of the recovery server and the domain controller. In a situation where you are doing a mailbox recovery, the recovery server and the domain controller may be the same machine.

2. Select the mailbox store with which you wish to work, and click Finish. You will be presented with a list of all the orphaned mailboxes located on that particular mailbox store; an example is shown here:

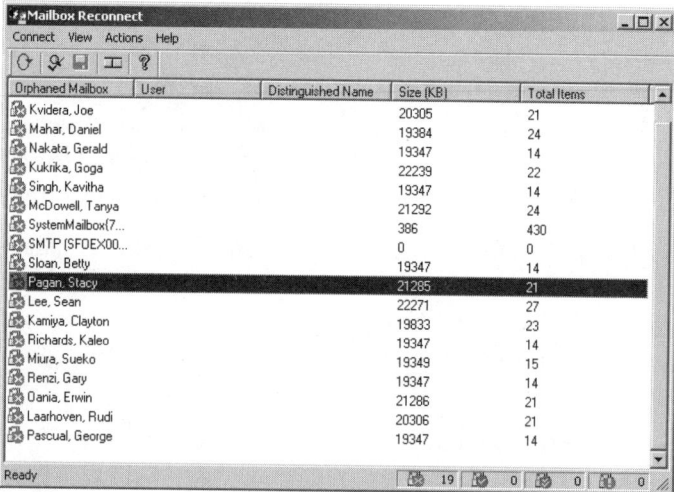

3. From the Actions menu, choose Export Users to create an LDIF file that can be used to create the user accounts.

4. Run the LDIFDE command (e.g., `ldifde -i -f ldf_file.ldf`) to create the Active Directory accounts necessary to which you will reconnect the mailboxes.

Once you have created the user accounts, you can now reconnect the mailboxes to the Active Directory accounts you have just created. If you have to reconnect only one or two mailboxes, it may be simpler to use Exchange System Manager. But if you have more than three or four accounts, you can use the MBConn tool. To connect the mailboxes to the user accounts you just created, follow these steps:

1. Run the MBConn utility, click Next, and enter the names of the recovery server, the domain controller, and the database to which you want to connect.

2. Select Actions ➤ Preview All.

3. Select the Active Directory container that holds the user accounts you just created, and confirm that a green check mark is displayed next to each mailbox. This indicates that MBConn has been able to match up a mailbox with an Active Directory user account.

4. To connect the accounts select Actions ➤ Apply.

The mailboxes are now reconnected to Active Directory accounts. You can use Outlook or ExMerge to extract the data in these mailboxes out to a PST file.

Restoration and Disaster Recovery FAQ

Following is a list of frequently asked questions that about disaster recovery and restoration. Often, restoration is a complex and time-consuming process; unfortunately, most administrators are not intimately familiar with this process, so a lot of questions about restoration arise. While I have tried to address many of these in the text of the chapter, some of these deserve to make their way to the FAQ.

One of my users has lost something in their mailbox, and it looks like I'm going to have to restore data from backup. Should I do a restore or not? Requests to restore data through a recovery server are not to be taken lightly. You should already have a good estimate of how long such a recovery will take (because you regularly practice disaster recovery, right?). Since restoration may take a considerable amount of your resources, requests for restoration should probably come through the user's manager to your manager. In some cases, it may simply be a matter of good customer relations to perform the recovery. On the bright side, if you have not practiced a disaster recovery recently, this is your big chance.

What type of hardware should I have for my recovery server? Your recovery server should be as close as possible in configuration to your production servers. This is especially true if you restore a production server's system state to a recovery server.

Under what circumstances should I build empty databases, bring a server online immediately, and then restore that data via a recovery server later? If your user community needs to go back to work immediately, this is the right approach. However, the downside to this process is that your mailbox stores may grow significantly due to the loss of single-instance storage.

How often should I perform a disaster recovery drill? You should perform such a drill at least once a month until you are very comfortable with the process. Once you have the procedure down, perform the drill once every two to three months in order to confirm that your backups are good and your restoration skills are intact.

Test restores are taking longer than I expected. Is there anything I can do to speed up restoration times? Well, new hardware comes to mind. Actually, there may be a couple of things you can do. Breaking one large mailbox store into several smaller stores will reduce the amount of time it takes to restore any single volume, but the price is more RAM overhead on the server to mount the additional mailbox stores. If the tape device is not local to the Exchange server, confirm that the server and the backup/restore computer are operating at the highest network speed possible.

Repairing a Damaged Store

If you have a store database file that has become corrupted for one reason or another, you have the option of trying to recover that file. However, if you call Microsoft Product Support Services (PSS) and tell them you have a corrupted database, one of the first things they will ask you is "When was your most recent backup?"

Why is this a common question? Because using database utilities to rescue a damaged store database file is a gamble. I have seen database files that could not be rescued no matter how many times I attempted to run a repair utility. Second, the rich-text store (EDB file) is broken up into blocks of information, and the blocks are organized in a tree structure (a B-tree). If a block of the file is damaged, it is quite possible that the entire branch of the tree below that block will not be recoverable.

Two utilities, eseutil.exe and isinteg.exe, can be used to rescue store databases. The store must be dismounted before either of these utilities can be run, but the Microsoft Exchange Information Store service must be running.

NOTE   ESEUTIL and ISINTEG require the presence of both the EDB and STM database files.

WARNING   The first rule of data recovery is "do no further harm." Prior to running *any* database utilities, you should perform a full, complete (normal) backup of all Exchange databases. If you cannot perform an online backup, run an offline backup. ESEUTIL and ISINTEG may actually make the problems worse, so you want to make sure that you have got a complete backup of your data. Microsoft recommends running the ESEUTIL and ISINTEG utilities only when advised by Microsoft Product Support Services.

The ESEUTIL Program

The eseutil.exe command-line tool is located in the \Program Files\Exchsrvr\Bin directory. This database repair utility understands the structure of the Exchange databases and blocks of data; it repairs, checks, and compacts Exchange database files. It also understands the underlying structure of the database, tables, indexes, and records, but it does not understand the Exchange data that is placed in those tables and records. In short, it is a database tool for database file errors.

You may find it necessary to run ESEUTIL if you are experiencing errors such as -1018, -1019, and -1022 error messages that appear in the Event Viewer. These messages indicate that there is damage to the database file.

You must dismount the store in order to run this utility. Table 7.1 lists some of the common command-line options for the ESEUTIL program.

Table 7.1   Common Command-Line Options for ESEUTIL

Option	Function
/?	Displays ESEUTIL options.
/d	Performs offline defragmentation/compaction on the selected database.
/g	Performs an integrity check on the selected database.
/p	Performs repair operations on the selected database. Used for a damaged database file. Data may be lost.
/r	Performs a forced soft recovery, bringing specified database into a consistent state.
/m	Performs a header dump of database files, log files, or the checkpoint file.
/c	Used with restore operations to view the header file or to bring a store to a consistent state.

TIP   Command-line switch order is important. You should always put the switch that is setting up the type operation first, e.g., /R, /D, /G, /M, and /P.

Using the ESEUTIL program to perform an offline compaction/defragmentation is discussed in Chapter 4. Using ESEUTIL with restore operations is discussed earlier in this chapter. The following three sections give some examples of using ESEUTIL to fix database file problems.

NOTE   If you used ESEUTIL with Exchange 5.5, you will notice that the /ISPRIV, /ISPUB, and /DS command options are no longer valid. You now have to specify the full path to the EDB database file.

ESEUTIL and Database Recovery

If the Exchange server has crashed or stores have been taken offline unexpectedly (such as if a disk drive fails), all stores in the storage group are temporarily dismounted. When

Operations

PART 2

the store is remounted, the ESE database engine automatically tries to bring the store to a consistent state (a soft recovery).

If for some reason the store cannot be brought into a consistent state, the database mount will fail. You can use ESEUTIL /R to attempt to bring all the stores in a storage group to a consistent state. ESEUTIL /R includes several additional command-line options you can specify:

/l log_path	Path to the transaction logs; the current directory is assumed.
/s system_path	Path to the system log directory; the current directory is assumed.
/i	Tells ESE to ignore missing files.

Imagine, for example, that a store will not mount, and you assume that the database will not mount because it is inconsistent. The following command will perform the /R option on all stores in a storage group.

```
Eseutil /r /l d:\E2Kdata /s c:\E2Kdata E01
```

The log files are on the D:\E2Klogs directory, and the checkpoint file is on the C:\E2Kdata directory. The E01 is the log file prefix for the storage group I am trying to make consistent.

Is a Database Consistent?

The /M option dumps information about the database files, log files, and checkpoint files. You can use the ESEUTIL program with the /M option to determine if a database is consistent or not. The following is a list of options that can be used with the ESEUTIL /M command.

H	Dumps the header of the specified database file.
H	Dumps the specified checkpoint file's header.
L	Dumps the specified log file's header.
M	Dumps the specified file's meta data.
S	Dumps the specified file's space usage.
/v	Sets the ESEUTIL to verbose mode.
/s stm_name	Sets name and path of the STM file. The default is the same directory as the EDB file.
/t table_name	Dumps information only for a specified table.

The following example dumps the header information for the E:\E2Kdata\managers.edb database file:

```
Eseutil /mh e:\e2kdata\managers.edb
```

ESEUTIL and Database Repair

When all else fails and you cannot mount the database under any circumstances, there comes a time that you will have to use the /P option. I want to stress again that restoring from backup is still a better option as long as you have a backup from which to restore.

The ESEUTIL /P option is your last ditch effort to save the database file. ESEUTIL /P goes through the database block by block building a new database file; due to this you will need enough free space to recreate the files. ESEUTIL /P has several command-line switches that can be used including:

/t temp_db	Specifies the name and path to the temporary database.
/s stm_file	Specifies the name of the native content database file.
/f prefix	Specifies the prefix used to create log files.
/I	Ignores signature mismatches between EDB and STM files. Before using this switch, confirm that you have the correct EDB and STM files; if you use this switch against databases you have accidentally mismatched, then you will lose data.

> **TIP** ESEUTIL /P creates a temporary database in the current folder. You can run ESEUTIL from another disk if there is not enough disk space on the partition containing the original database. Alternatively, you can use the /t parameter to direct the temporary database to a location with enough free space.

To repair the database and direct the temp database to the C: drive, type:

```
ESEUTIL /p /t c:\Temp\TempDB.edb e:\E2Kdata\managers.edb
```

In this example, the managers.edb database file was nearly 7GB, and the managers.stm file was over 3GB. The entire ESEUTIL process took almost 50 minutes to perform on a database that had no errors using a Pentium III 500MHz with 512MB of RAM. Once the process is completed successfully, a backup should immediately be run. The repair process changes the database signature, so the previous log files will be of no use.

Operations

PART 2

NOTE Exchange 2000 SP1's version of ESEUTIL introduces a new command-line switch, `/createstm`, that creates a new STM file if the existing STM file is unrecoverable. This command-line switch is used in conjunction with the /p switch. Make no mistake; you *will* lose data if you use this command-line switch! You should use it only if the EDB file is available, but there is no way you can retrieve the STM file.

Exchange@Work: To Repair or Not to Repair?

Microsoft asserts that you *never* run the ESEUTIL /P option unless at the recommendation of a Microsoft PSS engineer. Despite this warning, I have had a few problems where I did indeed need to run this utility, and it fixed my problems, but some messages were lost. If you have a database that you cannot use, try this method (but *only* if you are comfortable with self-medicating!):

- First rule of data recovery: Do no further harm. Or, at the very least, make sure you can get back to the point you were when the problem started. This means making a full, offline backup.

- Research any error messages you are receiving with the Microsoft TechNet and Knowledge Base.

- Run ESEUTIL with the /MH option to make sure the database is consistent.

- Run ESEUTIL with the /R option to see if you can bring the store to a consistent state. If this succeeds, try and start the information store or directory service.

- Run ESEUTIL with the /P option and perform the repair.

- Delete the log files and checkpoint file.

- Open a technical support incident with Microsoft PSS; they may have some additional tricks up their sleeves.

This method has worked for me in the past. If you are the slightest bit uncomfortable with these procedures, you should probably skip to the big finish and get Microsoft on the phone as soon as possible. Experimenting with these utilities can lead to worse problems than you are currently experiencing—which can cost you far more than a call to Microsoft PSS!

The ISINTEG Program

In contrast to ESEUTIL, which understands generic database files, the information store integrity checker (ISINTEG) knows all about Exchange messages, attachments, Access Control Lists (ACLs), folders, rules, deleted items, and so on. The `isinteg.exe` utility understands the data in the store, and it fixes problems where users cannot access messages or folders. ISINTEG should also be run if you have had to repair a database using ESEUTIL. ISINTEG is found in the `\Program Files\Exchsrvr\Bin` directory.

This utility generates a small temporary database when it is analyzing the selected database. (I have never seen this database grow to more than 10 percent of the total size of the database being fixed.) It can take a few minutes or many hours to run, depending on the number of tests that you select. If I have to run the entire battery of tests on a database, I plan for about 1 to 3 hours per GB.

Table 7.2 lists ISINTEG command-line options of which you should be aware.

Table 7.2   Command-Line Options Available for ISINTEG

Option	Operation
-?	Displays online help.
-s	Specifies the server name.
-fix	Fixes problems if they are found. The default is to check for problems and report them. Microsoft recommends running this option only on the advice of Microsoft PSS.
-verbose	Outputs in verbose mode.
-test	Specifies test name(s).
-l *<log filename>*	Specifies an alternative log filename and location. The log files are text files; their default names are `isinteg.pub` and `isinteg.pri`.
-t *<temp database location>*	Specifies the location of the temporary database that ISINTEG uses when checking the public or private information store database. The database it creates is called `refer.mdb`. Specifying another disk drive can improve performance, but specifying a network drive will hinder performance.

> **NOTE** The Exchange 5.5 ISINTEG utility included a -PATCH option that patched the globally unique identifiers (GUIDs) so that the Registry, information store, and directory service were in agreement. This option is not valid in Exchange 2000 because this function happens automatically when a store is mounted.

Below is an example for running ISINTEG to repair a store. Note that you do not have to specify the name of the store; you will be prompted for the store on which you want to run ISINTEG. This example redirects the temporary file that ISINTEG creates to another disk and specifies a log called Monday-ISINTEG.TXT on a server called SFOEX001.

```
isinteg -s SFOEX001 -fix -t c:\temp -l c:\Monday-ISINTEG.TXT
```

The output is shown here:

```
C:\Program Files\Exchsrvr\BIN>isinteg -s sfoex001 -fix -t c:\temp -l
c:\Monday.txt -test alltestsDatabases for server sfoex001:

Only databases marked as Offline can be checked


Index   Status        Database-Name
Storage Group Name: First Storage Group
  1     Online        Mailbox Store (SFOEX001)
  2     Online        Public Folder Store (SFOEX001)
Storage Group Name: Second Storage Group
  3     Offline       Designers
  4     Offline       Executive Mailboxes
  5     Offline       Operations Group
  6     Offline       Web Folders Public Store
Enter a number to select a database or press Return to exit.
5
You have selected Second Storage Group / Operations Group.
Continue?(Y/N)
```

At this point, you must answer Y to begin the tests. Store names are cached by DSAcess, so it may take up to 10 minutes before a newly created store appears in the list of stores that can be repaired. ISINTEG must be run manually, though through some creative scripting you might be able to automate its use.

NOTE You cannot run parallel instances of ISINTEG; you must run them one at a time. Further, the store must be dismounted, and the Microsoft Exchange Information Store Service must be running.

Which ISINTEG Tests Should You Run?

There are 29 separate tests that ISINTEG can perform individually or in three groupings. The Exchange 2000 databases are hierarchical, so data exists many tables. ISINTEG scans through these tables and confirms that references to data in one table actually exist in another table. You must specify a test or tests that you want ISINTEG to perform on the ISINTEG command line. Here are some examples that run a single mailbox test, all tests, and the message and folder tests.

```
isinteg -fix -verbose -test mailbox

isinteg -fix -verbose -test alltests

isinteg -fix -verbose -test message,folders
```

Sample output from the last example is as follows:

```
C:\Program Files\Exchsrvr\BIN>isinteg -s sfoex001 -fix -t c:\temp -l
c:\Monday.txt -test message,folder

Databases for server sfoex001:

Only databases marked as Offline can be checked


Index   Status      Database-Name
Storage Group Name: First Storage Group
  1     Online      Mailbox Store (SFOEX001)
  2     Online      Public Folder Store (SFOEX001)
Storage Group Name: Second Storage Group
  3     Offline     Designers
  4     Offline     Executive Mailboxes
  5     Offline     Operations Group
  6     Offline     Web Folders Public Store
Enter a number to select a database or press Return to exit.

5

You have selected Second Storage Group / Operations Group.
```

```
Continue?(Y/N)y
```

Test reference table construction result: 0 error(s); 0 warning(s); 0 fix(es); 0 row(s); time: 0h:0m:0s

Test Folder result: 0 error(s); 0 warning(s); 0 fix(es); 309 row(s); time: 0h:0m:1s

Test Message result: 0 error(s); 0 warning(s); 0 fix(es); 616 row(s); time: 0h:0m:1s

Now in test   4(reference count verification) of total   4 tests; 100% complete.

Note that even though only two actual test names were specified, ISINTEG includes the creation of the reference table (the temporary file) as a test and then the verification of that reference table as another test. There are 29 tests in total; some are relevant only for mailbox stores, while some are relevant only for public folder stores. Some of the more useful tests are listed in Table 7.3. Some of these tests are performing reference tests and thus check more than one table.

Table 7.3   ISINTEG Tests

Test Option	Description/Operation
folder	Folders table
message	Messages table
aclitem	ACL on message items
delfld	Deleted messages
timedev	Timed events
rowcounts	Row counts in folders, deleted messages, and dumpster count
attach	Attachment table
morefld	Categorization table, restriction table, and search folder links
searchq	Replication schedule
dlvrto	Delivered to references
peruser	Per user read/unread

Table 7.3   ISINTEG Tests *(continued)*

Test Option	Description/Operation
Search	Folder reference verification
dumpsterprops	Folder, deleted messages, attachments, and dumpster count verification
msgref	Folder, deleted messages, and attachment verification
Msgsoftref	Folder and deleted messages
Attachref	Attachment-to-message reference verification
Acllistref	ACL reference verification
Aclitemref	ACL item verification
fldsub	Folder reference count verification
Dumpsterref	Folder, deleted messages, attachments, and dumpster count verification
mailbox	Folder, deleted messages, and mailbox verification; mailbox stores only
Ooflist	Mailbox stores only
Fldrcv	Folders, mailboxes, sites, and special folders reference count verification; mailbox stores only
Artidx	Public folder article index table; public stores only

If you are having problems and you can't accurately pinpoint whether they're related to messages, folders, attachments, or ACLs, then you can run more than one test. ISINTEG includes three group tests:

alltests	Runs 21 common tests for mailbox stores and 18 common tests for public folder tests. The alltests option does not include the ACL tests, out of office list test, or dumpster properties test.
allfoldertests	Runs tests related to folders.
allacltests	Runs tests related to ACLs.

If I have to run ISINTEG, I typically will pick the `alltests` option, even though it's more time consuming. Watching the application event log for reports of specific problems may also give you a hint as to which tests to run to fix a problem.

TIP   If ISINTEG finds and corrects errors, run the test(s) again until it is no longer reporting errors.

Corrupted Messages

While not necessarily a disaster, corrupt messages can make you wish that you had just lost the entire mailbox store. I have seen a couple of corrupt message scenarios that always end up being a hassle to fix.

The first of these happened to a number of people within my own company, including me. I had a message that I had previously opened and then deleted. The message returned and was marked as unread. I could neither open nor delete this message. Further, the fact that this message existed in my Inbox broke my ability to synchronize to an OST file.

Numerous passes of ISINTEG and even ESEUTIL did not fix this problem. We installed another server and attempted to move my mailbox to the other server. The mailbox would not move to the other server either.

Finally, we managed to export my entire mailbox to a PST file, delete the mailbox, re-create the mailbox, and re-import the mail. My theory regarding this problem is that there was a MAPI property that was corrupted, but it was not one that was checked or fixed by ISINTEG.

The second problem with message corruption actually deals with some type of corrupt character in the message body or the message attachment. One of my customers had an outbreak of this type of corruption recently, but we never figured out why. The only reason we found this is because this customer was running a Veritas Backup Exec mailbox-level (brick-level) backup, which was reporting errors on certain messages in some users' mailboxes. We found that Backup Exec was hanging for as much as an hour when it attempted to back up a specific message.

We attributed one of these errors to a corrupted attachment. We tried running ISINTEG and ESEUTIL on the database, but this did not fix the problem. Once we removed the attachment from the message, the problem was solved. The other messages did not have attachments, so we had to delete the actual message to solve the problem.

> **_TIP_** If users are complaining that they cannot open messages, try shutting down the server's anti-virus software and ask them to try it again. Some antivirus software packages are notorious for making attachments appear corrupted when the attachment is a ZIP file or an encrypted ZIP file.

Database Utilities FAQ

Below are some frequently asked questions about running the database file utilities:

How often should I run an offline defragmentation/compaction (ESEUTIL /D)? This operation will shrink the database size if there is a large amount of empty space in the file. However, I would only run this if I have recently moved or deleted several mailboxes from the server. Event ID 1221 (generated during online maintenance) will tell you how much empty space is in the database files. I would not consider running it unless it would regain at least 30 percent of the database file size.

Should I run an offline integrity check periodically (ESEUTIL /G)? This is not necessary. Online backups should provide all the integrity checking necessary during normal operations.

Does it hurt to run the repair utilities on a database (ESEUTIL /P)? Do not run this option of the ESEUTIL utility unless you are absolutely sure you need it. You may actually damage a good database.

Why do I need to run a backup immediately after running ESEUTIL? The ESEUTIL utility rebuilds the database and resets the database signature. The previous transaction logs will become useless after this, and thus you should start a new generation of backups.

Does it help to run ISINTEG on a regular basis? Don't run this utility unless you have a specific reason to run it. I know administrators who run it against their databases every few months. While this may give them a warm and fuzzy feeling to know that there are no errors, it is not necessary.

How do I know which ISINTEG utility to run? If the users are reporting problems opening messages, folders, or attachments, check the application event log. Often these errors are reported along with a suggested course of action. If all else fails, run the `-test alltests` option.

8

Clustering Exchange 2000

Though I am not at all surprised, much of the information technology community has been surprised that messaging has become such a business-critical system. Over the years I have heard the expression "It's only e-mail" used time and time again. As new applications have been incorporated into Exchange, executives, managers, sales people, and others are finding that Exchange is more than just e-mail. It is their calendar, contacts list, to do list, customer communication system, document storage, expense reporting system, faxing system, workflow system, and more.

The first time an organization loses their Exchange server for any length of time, or if they lose any messaging data, the user community begins screaming for more fault tolerance. And Exchange servers are not the only BackOffice products from which users are demanding more uptime. One possible answer to this dilemma is to introduce *clustering* to your Windows 2000 platform.

Windows 2000 clustering provides support for an Active/Active clustering platform, which means that each cluster node (two if Windows 2000 Advanced Server is used and four if Windows 2000 Datacenter Server is used) is capable of running Exchange simultaneously. This can increase your fault tolerance by providing redundant hardware platforms and automatic failover if a server fails. The downside to installing clusters is that they require additional (and often specialized) hardware as well as additional administrator/operator training. Clusters also require "cluster-aware" software in order to provide fault tolerance for that software.

Before starting down the cluster path, it is important to understand the basics of deploying and operating a Windows 2000 cluster. Further, it helps to know that Windows 2000 clusters maintain only a single copy of the Exchange data; the Exchange data is not mirrored to a separate server. So the Windows 2000 cluster does not protect against corruption of data; it protects against the hardware failure. This chapter includes:

- Basics of clustering
- Hardware requirements
- The necessity of clustering
- Installing a cluster
- Moving to an Exchange 2000 cluster
- Cluster operations

Before I jump into clustering, I want to make a couple of points clear. By installing a cluster, you are not waving a magic wand that is going to give your operation better uptime and availability. Highly available systems are a combination of many things: Technology is only one element, and training and good operational practices are just as important. Equally important is having a good relationship with an organization that has successfully installed other clusters.

Further, Exchange 2000 clustering has limitations that may not be immediately apparent. With Exchange 2000 RTM (release-to-manufacturing, or the initial release), the maximum recommended number of simultaneous users is about 1000. Due to improvements in memory management introduced by Exchange 2000 SP1, that number has been raised to about 1500. Exchange 2000 SP2 has improved ESE memory management capabilities, but since SP2 has just been released, I don't have recommendations at this time on the maximum number of simultaneous users that an Exchange 2000 SP2 cluster can support.

> **NOTE** Products such as NSI Software's Double-Take provide similar capabilities as Windows 2000's Cluster Services; Double-Take also provides data mirroring. Find more information at www.nsisoftware.com. Many of the third-party products that provide Exchange fault-tolerance solutions are not on the Microsoft "approved list," and thus getting support from Microsoft may prove difficult.

Clustering 101

Clustering technology is a method of grouping two or more computers together so that they appear as one computer to the rest of the network. Understanding the basics of Windows 2000 clustering along with its limitations with respect to Exchange 2000 will help you to decide if clustering is for you and to operate a cluster more effectively.

Each node in the cluster is given access to the same physical external storage devices and has a network connection to a private cluster network. Each node in the cluster has its own local disks and operating system, but the shared data or cluster-aware applications are installed on the external storage devices. The shared data is accessible by any node of the cluster and made available on the network. Figure 8.1 shows a two-node cluster. Internal to the cluster is the ability for one node to pick up another node's processes in the case of the first node failing. This failover ability is what allows clusters to provide "high availability" for applications and services that can be failed over from one node to another.

Figure 8.1   Typical two-node Windows 2000 cluster

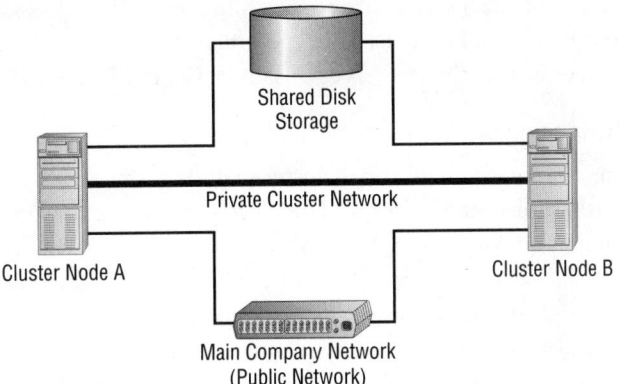

There are two different approaches to how cluster technology deals with accessing the external cluster resources. One way is that each node can have full access to all resources at all times, this can allow for load balancing across the cluster nodes. This type of cluster architecture is called a *shared-all architecture*. The other approach, and the one supported by Windows 2000 Cluster Services, is called a *shared-nothing architecture*, in which only one cluster node can access (own) any given cluster resource at a time.

The ability to cluster Exchange has been available since the introduction of Microsoft Windows NT 4 Enterprise Edition and Exchange 5.5 Enterprise Edition. In the Windows NT 4 timeframe, the service was called Microsoft Cluster Services (MSCS), but was often referred to by its code name "Wolfpack."

In these early days, it was possible only to configure an Exchange cluster in an Active/Passive fashion. This meant that if Exchange were the only cluster-aware application in the cluster, that cluster node A would be running Exchange and cluster Node B would sit there idle, waiting for node A to fail so it could assume its duties. Some companies found it difficult to cost-justify clustering, as half of the hardware resources was just burning CPU cycles.

With the release of Windows 2000 Cluster Services and Exchange 2000, Microsoft built in the ability to configure Exchange 2000 in an Active/Active fashion. Furthermore, a single cluster node is not limited to running just one instance of Exchange 2000. In any size cluster, two nodes or four nodes, up to four Exchange 2000 virtual servers can be supported.

> **NOTE** For general information on clustering from a generic perspective, an excellent book is *In Search of Clusters: The Ongoing Battle in Lowly Parallel Computing* by Gregory F. Pfister (Prentice Hall, 1998).

Components of a Windows 2000 Cluster

A cluster makes use of specialized hardware to support the Windows 2000 Clustering Services and cluster-aware applications. The types of hardware that can be used to implement a cluster are varied, but all clusters have the same basic hardware and logical components.

Hardware Components

Hardware components that make up a cluster include the nodes of the cluster, the cluster (private) network, and shared storage. The *cluster nodes* are the Windows 2000 servers on which you load and configure Cluster Services. Typically, these servers are configured identically with respect to processor, memory, and internal drive configuration, though these could vary slightly with little effect on the cluster's performance. However, there are a number of components that should be identical across all nodes; these are the internal drive configuration and the logical layout of the directories, the SCSI controllers, and the NICs (network interface cards) and fiber cards. By having these components be identical across all nodes, you can eliminate the potential issue of driver incompatibility, and troubleshooting is much easier.

> **TIP** Cluster designers recommend that all hardware on all cluster nodes match as closely as possible. All hardware used in a cluster should be on the hardware compatibility list (HCL) and supported by the hardware vendor.

Figure 8.2 shows the Exchange 2000 Cluster Administrator console. This cluster has two nodes, CLUSTERNODE1 and CLUSTERNODE2, both of which are online.

Each cluster node is going to have two network interface cards, one for communication to the public network and one for the private cluster network to provide communication to the other nodes in the cluster (shown previously in Figure 8.1). In order to establish proper routing of packets through the correct interfaces, it is necessary to have each set of NICs on different IP networks.

Figure 8.2   Windows 2000 Cluster Administrator console

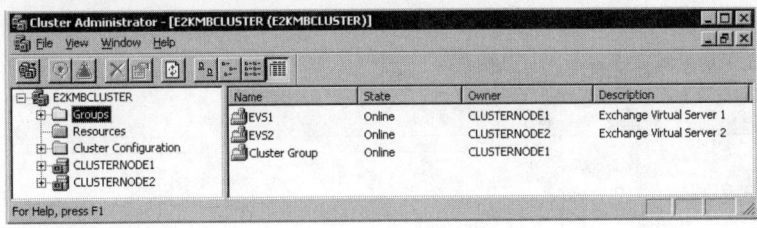

> **WARNING**   Keep in mind that the cluster NICs should have statically assigned IP addresses. Don't allow your cluster nodes to be DHCP clients!

Selecting the IP address for the cluster nodes and services is easy; the public interfaces should be IP addresses that are legal on your company's network. The IP subnet that you use for the internal cluster communication can be anything, as long as it is on a different IP subnet from the public network; consider picking a private address space that does not exist anywhere else on your network. You can configure each network to be available to the cluster and what communications it can be used for in the cluster. Here is a summary of the NICs in a clustered server:

Public network interface   Each cluster node communicates to the rest of the world through this interface.

Private network interface   Each cluster node communicates to the other cluster nodes through this interface to send and receive an 'I'm alive!' heartbeat signal. In a two-node cluster, a crossover cable usually connects these two cards. The private network is also called the cluster network.

The private network is configured to send a heartbeat signal between the nodes in the cluster. This heartbeat is used to determine if any node in the cluster has failed. Figure 8.3 shows the Cluster Administrator console showing the public and private (labeled Heart-beat) network adapters. On the property page of any of these network adapters, you can configure it as being available for use with the cluster, and you can rename it.

SCSI controllers or fiber channel connectors usually handle connectivity to the shared storage system. These are the interfaces through which each node will communicate with the external storage unit. Typically, communication with the external storage unit is through some type of SCSI or fiber channel hub or switch; if you're lucky, you have connectivity through an arbitrated fiber switch.

Operations

PART 2

Figure 8.3 Cluster Administrator console showing the configured public and private networks

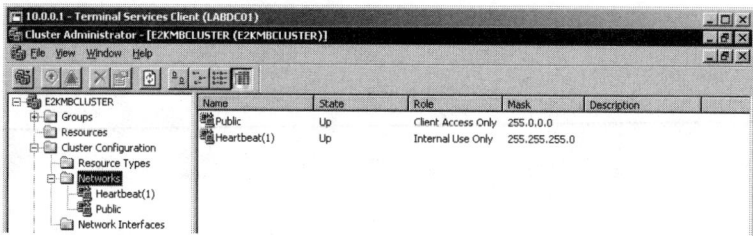

The *external shared storage unit* is some type of external disk subsystem. This can be as simple as a stand-alone drive chassis with a dozen or so disk drives or a storage area network (SAN) with hundreds of drives and terabytes of space. The crucial feature of the external storage unit is that all the nodes are connected to it and can communicate with it.

Logical Components

A cluster also has some logical components that are provided by or configured through the Windows 2000 Cluster Administrator console. *Cluster Services* is the Windows 2000 component that is loaded after the initial OS load. Windows 2000 Cluster Services manages all the cluster resources and applications, failover and fail back (discussed in the next section), and communication both inside the cluster and between the cluster and the outside world.

Cluster Services needs to keep track of which cluster node "owns" a cluster resource at any given time; it does so on a logical drive on the shared external drive array called the *quorum drive.* Typically, the quorum drive is given the drive label Q:, so in Disk Administrator and Windows Explorer, it appears as the Q: drive. While this disk does not require more than about 500MB, you should go ahead and give it a dedicated physical disk (mirrored or duplexed).

Cluster resources are logical and physical objects that, when combined in a resource group, define a unit of failover within the cluster. For example, the cluster itself is comprised of a network name (NetBIOS) to which network calls are made, an IP address that maps to the network name, and the quorum drive. Figure 8.4 shows some of the resources that are found on a Windows 2000 cluster that is supporting Exchange 2000 in Active/Active mode. This is a two-node cluster and thus has two Exchange virtual servers (EVSs): EVS1 and EVS2.

Figure 8.4   Cluster resources on an Exchange 2000 server

Name	State	Owner	Group
EVS1 IP Address	Online	CLUSTERNODE1	EVS1
EVS1 Network Name	Online	CLUSTERNODE1	EVS1
Disk G:	Online	CLUSTERNODE1	EVS1
Disk I:	Online	CLUSTERNODE1	EVS1
EVS1 SA	Online	CLUSTERNODE1	EVS1
Exchange Message Transfer Agent Instance - (EVS1)	Online	CLUSTERNODE1	EVS1
Exchange Information Store Instance - (EVS1)	Online	CLUSTERNODE1	EVS1
Exchange Routing Service Instance - (EVS1)	Online	CLUSTERNODE1	EVS1
SMTP Virtual Server Instance - (EVS1)	Online	CLUSTERNODE1	EVS1
Exchange IMAP4 Virtual Server Instance - (EVS1)	Online	CLUSTERNODE1	EVS1
Exchange POP3 Virtual Server Instance - (EVS1)	Online	CLUSTERNODE1	EVS1
Exchange HTTP Virtual Server Instance - (EVS1)	Online	CLUSTERNODE1	EVS1
Exchange MS Search Instance - (EVS1)	Online	CLUSTERNODE1	EVS1
EVS2 IP Address	Online	CLUSTERNODE2	EVS2
EVS 2 Network Name	Online	CLUSTERNODE2	EVS2
Disk H:	Online	CLUSTERNODE2	EVS2
Disk J:	Online	CLUSTERNODE2	EVS2
EVS2 SA	Online	CLUSTERNODE2	EVS2
Exchange Information Store Instance - (EVS2)	Online	CLUSTERNODE2	EVS2
Exchange Routing Service Instance - (EVS2)	Online	CLUSTERNODE2	EVS2
SMTP Virtual Server Instance - (EVS2)	Online	CLUSTERNODE2	EVS2
Exchange IMAP4 Virtual Server Instance - (EVS2)	Online	CLUSTERNODE2	EVS2
Exchange POP3 Virtual Server Instance - (EVS2)	Online	CLUSTERNODE2	EVS2
Exchange HTTP Virtual Server Instance - (EVS2)	Online	CLUSTERNODE2	EVS2
Exchange MS Search Instance - (EVS2)	Online	CLUSTERNODE2	EVS2
Cluster IP Address	Online	CLUSTERNODE1	Cluster Gr

Exchange Virtual Servers   An *Exchange virtual server (EVS)* is a collection of resources and services that are required to provide all the functionality of an Exchange server. There are a few resources that must be defined manually through the Cluster Administrator console:

- The cluster group name
- The IP address for the EVS (not the IP address of the computer)
- The network name for the EVS (not the name of the network name computer)
- The drives in the shared array that the EVS will use for databases, transaction logs, and working directories
- The EVS System Attendant service

After the System Attendant is created and brought online, it will proceed to create all the other required services.

Exchange 2000 Cluster Basics

The most important part of getting an Exchange 2000 cluster operational is to make sure that you have planned the server configuration properly. Planning Exchange 2000 clusters starts with deciding how many Exchange virtual servers are going to be supported in the cluster. As previously mentioned, there can be anywhere from one to four EVSs in a cluster depending on two things: disk groups and total number of storage groups required.

Disk groups   A disk group is initially defined when the drive arrays are created in the external storage unit. Typically, a number of drives are placed into an array, and these then appear as a physical disk to the operating system. Because any given EVS can run only on one node at a time, and because any given disk resource can be owned by only one node at a time, it follows that each EVS must have at least one disk group assigned to it. These disk resources are added to the EVS cluster group resource and are owned by that EVS.

Storage groups   There is a hard-coded limit in Exchange 2000 that no more than four storage groups can run on a single server at a time. This has significant implications on how Exchange 2000 is configured in any cluster. Remember that any single node in a cluster must be able to support all the other nodes resources in case of a failover and since any single server can only support up to four storage groups, this means that there can be no more than four storage groups in any cluster.

Exchange 2000 Cluster Limitations

If you are introducing Exchange 2000 into an existing Exchange 5.5 organization, there must be a stand-alone Exchange 2000 server already in the Exchange 5.5 site in which you plan on putting the cluster. The Exchange 2000 cluster server cannot be the first Exchange 2000 server in an Exchange 5.5 site. This has to do with the fact that the Exchange 2000 cluster supports the Site Replication Service (SRS). The SRS is an Exchange 2000 service that imitates the Exchange 5.5 directory service and allows an Exchange 2000 server to appear as an Exchange 5.5 server to other Exchange 5.5 servers from the perspective of directory communications. The following shows the Exchange 2000 services that are supported in a cluster and in which configuration:

Service	Not Supported	Active/ Passive	Active/ Active
Exchange/IIS HTTP (Outlook Web Access)			✓
Exchange/IIS NNTP virtual server	✓		
Exchange/IIS SMTP virtual server			✓
Exchange/Windows 2000 Active Directory Connector	✓		
Exchange cc:Mail Connector	✓		
Exchange Chat Server		✓	

Service	Not Supported	Active/ Passive	Active/ Active
Exchange Conferencing Server	✓		
Exchange GroupWise Connector	✓		
Exchange Information Store			✓
Exchange Instant Messaging	✓		
Exchange Key Management Service	✓		
Exchange Lotus Notes Connector	✓		
Exchange Message Transfer Agent		✓	
Exchange POP3 and IMAP4 virtual servers			✓
Exchange Routing Engine			✓
Exchange Routing Group Connector			✓
Exchange Site Replication Service	✓		
Exchange SMTP Connector			✓
Exchange System Attendant			✓

NOTE Though IIS services such as Outlook Web Access (OWA) and SMTP are supported in clustered configuration, these services (like POP3 and IMAP4) are better suited to a front-end/back-end configuration using Windows Load Balancing Service (WLBS) to provide redundancy.

Failover and Failback

The terms failover and failback get to the heart of what clustering is all about: the moving of cluster resource groups from running on one cluster node to another (failover), and then moving them back once the original cluster node is back online (failback).

Operations

PART 2

NOTE Cluster administrators must understand that failover and failback are *not* instantaneous. On a heavily loaded Exchange 2000 server, failover for an Exchange 2000 virtual server could take 10 minutes or more due to the fact that transaction logs may have to be committed to the database when a new cluster node takes over ownership of a cluster group. As a result of this time delay, users may notice a disruption in service.

Failover

Failover is actually a multi-step process. In the case of a hardware failure of one of the nodes, the heartbeat signal from the failed node stops. The working node detects this due to the absence of the other node's heartbeat. At that point, the Cluster Services will take all the resource groups and the contained resources offline and transfer ownership to the working node. This transfer of ownership is logged on the quorum drive, and the resource group is brought back online on the working node. The services supplied by the resource group are made available again to the network.

There are two parameters that influence the behavior of failover: the threshold and the period. Together these two parameters control how many times a resource group is allowed to failover (*threshold*) over a certain time interval (*period*). The default values for these are 10 failovers of a resource group in six hours. By having these configured, a resource group will not 'ping-pong' endlessly back and forth between two nodes. Figure 8.5 shows the Failover property page of an Exchange 2000 virtual server, EVS1.

Figure 8.5   Exchange virtual server threshold and period configuration

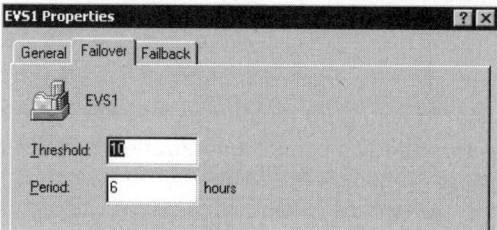

Failback

When Cluster Services detects that the heartbeat from the previously failed node is restored, *failback* can begin. This process goes through the same steps as failover and differs only in that it signifies the return of ownership of the cluster group that had failed over to the original cluster node.

Similar to failover, failback is configurable—it can be allowed or prevented. If it is allowed, it can happen immediately upon the detection of the restored heartbeat or only during certain hours. By default, this parameter is set to Prevent Failback. It is advisable to leave this setting as is; this allows the administrator time to diagnose and fix whatever hardware or software failure caused the resource group to failover in the first place. Also, the failback process may disrupt users. Figure 8.6 shows the Failback property page of an Exchange 2000 virtual server.

Figure 8.6   Failback settings of an Exchange 2000 virtual server

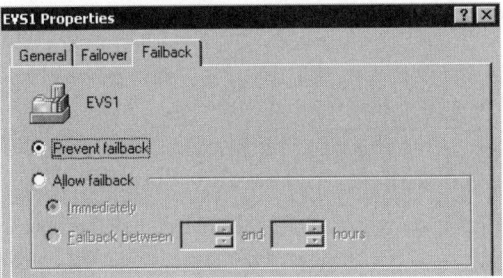

Hardware Requirements

The hardware required to implement cluster technology is expensive. When determining if you must implement clustering, you should determine if the cost of doing so is greater than the cost of operating without the application that you are planning to cluster. In other words, if you are going to invest in hardware for clustering, don't be afraid to purchase the best hardware you can given your budget. Remember, one of your design goals should be that once the cluster is built and functioning, you shouldn't have to touch the hardware for two to three years; the load on Exchange is only going to increase from whatever your present load is.

Critical to the choice of hardware for the nodes and the external storage units is that they must be on the supported HCL from Microsoft. In fact, during the cluster installation, there is a screen that requires you to confirm that the hardware that you are using is on the HCL. If you are running a Windows 2000 cluster on non-supported hardware, don't expect much sympathy from Microsoft PSS or your hardware vendor if you have problems.

Cluster Server Hardware Scalability

Chapter 15 of the Exchange 2000 Resource Kit is dedicated to server hardware sizing for stand-alone servers. This chapter of the Resource Kit is a good place to start for calculating hardware requirements for a stand-alone server, but for clustered servers, practical experience advises otherwise. The hardware that you pick for clustered servers must be able to support the load of both nodes in the cluster in the event of a failover.

There are a few questions that must be answered in order to develop a working hardware specification. These questions include:

- How many EVS and storage groups will be supported for each cluster node?

- In case of a failover, is degraded performance acceptable, or must the single node be able to support all messaging functions for all EVSs with no noticeable degradation in performance?

- How many users will be hosted on each EVS?

There are also some assumptions that will be made here with respect to figuring out the right amount of hardware for the cluster nodes:

- There will be no other cluster applications running on the cluster nodes except for cluster-aware virus scanning and backup software.

- The cluster will not be supporting other network infrastructure services such as domain controllers, DNS servers, DHCP servers, RIS servers, etc.

- The mailbox size limit is small (say 10–20MB).

- The number of mailboxes listed is the total number of mailboxes in the cluster, not in the node. In case of failover, a single node must be able to support all mailboxes with no degradation in performance.

NOTE   For more information on cluster sizing and recommended hardware for different sized clusters, see the Cluster Hardware document at www.somorita.com.

Should You Cluster?

Clustering technology developed from the need to have higher availability of applications and services to a network. It specifically addresses the issue of how the services that a server was supporting can continue to function in the event of the failure of the server they were running on.

High availability needs to be contrasted with another term, *fault tolerance*. Defining fault tolerance exactly is difficult, because there are varying degrees of fault tolerance in most high-end servers. Fault tolerance typically refers to specialized hardware redundancy built into a system that allows for the fastest possible recovery from a single component failing. Typically, these types of systems are significantly more expensive than high availability systems because there is complete redundancy at every level of hardware, and there is special software required to make the system work. For example, the most common type of fault tolerance is multiple disks in a RAID configuration; if configured correctly, the system can tolerate the failure of a physical disk drive. Another example is a system with multiple power supplies provides some fault tolerance. The system can tolerate the failure of a power supply. As you add additional layers of fault tolerance to any system, the potential downtime goes down as the overall cost goes up.

A good example of a fault-tolerant system would be Marathon Systems servers, where one server is in lock-step with all the processes that are running on the other node and can fully assume the other server's functions with split-second delays.

When looking to clustering as a technology solution, only two issues should be addressed:

- Planned outages/rolling upgrades: A company must support very high levels of availability of Exchange 2000, but they also need to perform maintenance that requires server downtime at planned intervals.

- Unplanned outages/server failure: A company demands that Exchange 2000 messaging services are available to a higher degree than they are with the pre-existing stand-alone machines. That is to say that the company is experiencing an unacceptable number of messaging system outages due to hardware failure of the servers and is looking to remedy this situation. However, clustering only protects you against a specific set of hardware failures such as RAM and system back-planes. Power supplies, NICs, SCSI controllers, and disks can all be made redundant without clustering.

WARNING   If a company is considering clustering for any other reasons, they will not find that the solution they purchased will meet their needs. There is often the misperception that clustering will protect from data corruption and that is certainly not the case with Windows 2000 clustering. Further, unless you purchase far more capacity than you really need, if a node in the cluster fails, the node on which the services failed over to will suffer from performance problems.

Here are some numbers to consider when deciding what the percentage level of uptime means in real time per year:

99%	3 days, 15 hours, 21 minutes
99.9%	8 hours, 44 minutes
99.99%	52 minutes
99.999% ("5 nines")	5 minutes

Even sites that experience a major hardware-related problem once a year can still advertise 99 percent uptime. In my opinion, it is very difficult to achieve 99.9 percent uptime due to the frequency of service packs, hot fixes, and security fix releases. Just two scheduled shutdowns per year will quickly eat up those eight hours and 44 minutes you have each year if you are trying to maintain 99.9 percent uptime.

Clustering and Server Roles

The services that Exchange 2000 provides can be spread out across several different physical servers, each performing a specific role in the messaging infrastructure. There are front-end servers for handling Internet client (HTTP, IMAP4, POP3, STMP, and NNTP) requests, back-end servers for hosting mailboxes or public folders, bridgehead servers for hosting connectors, Exchange 2000 Conferencing Services servers, Instant Messaging servers, and chat servers. All of these are Exchange 2000 servers, which can be clustered, but not all of these Exchange server roles are suitable for clustering. In fact, the only Exchange 2000 server role that is well suited to clustering is the mailbox server.

Following are several disadvantages of clustering some of the other servers:

Public folder servers   There can be only one MAPI-based public folder hierarchy in the entire cluster, and that is specific to one EVS in the cluster. Thus having a public folder server clustered is much like running a cluster in an Active/Passive mode: One node is hosting the public folder hierarchy, and the other is waiting for it to failover. Public folders are already made resilient by the fact that you can have multiple replicas on separate systems.

Connector servers   Only the basic connectors—the Routing Group Connector (RGC) and the SMTP Connector—are supported on cluster servers. Most third-party connectors such as fax servers and voicemail servers are usually supported on clusters. Even the MTA is not supported on an Exchange 2000 cluster. This means you will still have to have a non-clustered system to support the MTA, third-party connectors, and the Site Replication Service (SRS).

Front-end servers   Front-end servers can take advantage of a different type of clustering, Windows Load Balancing Service (WLBS). WLBS allows many front-end servers to respond to a single namespace (e.g., `owa.somorita.com`) and thus the load is divided up between multiple servers. Because front-end servers are well suited to WLBS clustering, they are not optimized for Cluster Services.

Instant Messaging server   Instant Messaging is not supported on clusters.

Chat server   The Chat service is supported, but only in Active/Passive mode.

Installing a Cluster

When preparing to install a Windows 2000 cluster, the most important steps are to get the certified hardware configured and to get Windows 2000 configured on the cluster. This section focuses on getting Windows 2000 and Exchange 2000 configured to run in a cluster. The basic steps for installing a cluster, which are discussed in depth in the following pages, are as follows:

1. Install certified cluster server hardware and shared storage.

2. Install Windows 2000 Advanced Server or Windows 2000 Datacenter on all nodes of the cluster. Confirm that you are running the latest service packs and hot fixes. You should run at least Windows 2000 SP2.

3. Install and configure Cluster Services on the first node in the cluster.

4. Install and configure Cluster Services on the additional nodes in the cluster.

5. Assign disk drives to each of the cluster resource groups.

6. Install Exchange 2000 Enterprise on the first node in the cluster. Don't forget to install Exchange 2000 SP1 or later.

7. Configure the Exchange virtual server on the first node. This entails configuring the IP address, cluster name, and the System Attendant.

8. Start the Exchange 2000 System Attendant, and the remainder of the Exchange 2000 services will automatically be configured in the cluster resource group.

Prerequisites

Make sure that you have met the hardware requirements necessary to implement a Windows 2000 cluster.

Hardware Prerequisites

The hardware requirements for a cluster are fairly straightforward; you must adhere to them, or you may get, at best, a cluster that runs that Microsoft won't support, or the cluster may not be functioning at all. Here are the necessary components:

Cluster server node   Hardware that is on the Windows 2000 Advanced Server HCL and the cluster HCL. If you are working with Windows 2000 Datacenter Server, your hardware will come preloaded with Datacenter, so you can be sure that your hardware is on the HCLs.

Disk controllers and shared disks   Two separate array controllers are required, one for the internal disks that will have the Windows boot and system partitions on it and one for accessing the drives in the external storage unit. The external disk storage unit should be listed on the Windows 2000 HCL and the Windows 2000 cluster HCL. You will need connectivity in the form of the fiber or SCSI cables necessary to connect the cluster nodes to the hubs or switches and then to connect them to the external storage. All shared disks should be visible from both nodes; take care in configuring this, and make sure to follow your hardware vendor's instructions. Each drive array must be formatted as NTFS and be a basic disk, not a dynamic disk.

Network adapters   A minimum of two network adapters is required. At least one NIC is required for the public network and one for the private (cluster heartbeat) network. These NICS should operate at least 100Mbps.

Logical Prerequisites

Before you start to load Windows 2000 Cluster Services, be prepared with the following items (for a two-node cluster):

- A unique NetBIOS network name for the cluster; this is the name that the cluster will respond to on the network.
- Five static IP addresses: two for the public NICs, two for the private NICs (remember, configure the public and private networks to be totally separate for purposes of routing), and one for Cluster Services itself (this address will be associated with the network name that has been assigned to the cluster). Do not use DHCP for assigning IP address to the cluster nodes. For the private (cluster) network, use private IP addresses that do not exist anywhere on your network.
- All cluster nodes must also be members of a Windows 2000 Active Directory domain.

Permissions

Prior to loading Cluster Services or Exchange 2000, there are some tasks that you will want to accomplish and some things you'll need to know. Some of these tasks will require administrative permissions either to the local domain or to the entire forest.

TIP   I strongly recommend that the schema extensions (Exchange 2000 CD \setup\i386\setup /Forestprep) that Exchange 2000 requires and the creation of machine groups (Exchange 2000 CD \setup\i386\setup /Domainprep) be performed prior to the installation of the first Exchange 2000 server in the organization.

In order to perform the forest prep process, you must use an account that has Schema Admin, Enterprise Admin and Domain Admin rights. During the forest prep step, whatever account you use is assigned permissions to delegate authority to other accounts over the Exchange 2000 organization. The /Domainprep option must be run by someone with a minimum of Domain Admins permissions in the domain you are preparing. For a detailed discussion of permissions required to install Exchange 2000, see Chapter 11, "Security within the Network."

Installing a Windows 2000 Cluster

Once you have the entire cluster hardware configured and Windows 2000 Advanced Server loaded (Windows 2000 Datacenter is loaded by the hardware vendor), it is time to load Cluster Services. One of the most important things to remember is that, whatever account you use to load Cluster Services, you must be logged on as that account when you install Exchange 2000 into the cluster. In general, it is best not to use the Domain Administrator account. If you haven't already done so, take a moment and create an account (for example, Installer) that you can use to install Cluster Services and Exchange 2000.

Installing the First Node in the Cluster

The first step toward getting your Exchange 2000 cluster up and running is to get Windows 2000 Cluster Services installed on the first node. This process assumes that all the necessary hardware is installed, Windows 2000 Advanced Server is installed, required service packs and hot fixes are installed, and the device drivers are loaded.

1. Start the Cluster Services installation process by shutting down and powering off one of the nodes (I'll call the first server Node A and the second Node B).

2. Log on as the Installer account (for example) to Node A and start the Windows 2000 Add/Remove Programs applet.

3. Select Add/Remove Windows Components and select the Cluster Service component.

4. Now you must certify that you understand that Microsoft does not support cluster hardware that is not on the Windows 2000 cluster HCL. Once you click the I Understand button, you are prompted to create a new cluster or join an existing cluster. Since Node A is the first node in the cluster, select The First Node In The Cluster.

5. You are prompted for the network name of the cluster and the security account on which to run Cluster Services. The network name is the name as which the cluster appears to the users. For the security account, use the Installer account that you are currently logged on as.

6. Identify which disks are going to be available for Cluster Services to manage. Select all the disks in the external array, as shown here. This list must include the disk that you are going to use as the cluster quorum disk.

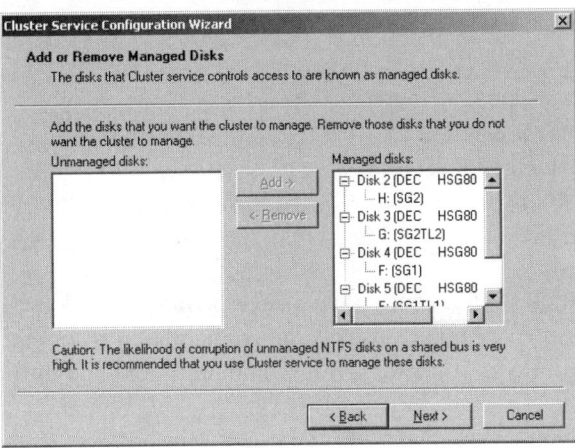

7. Out of the drives that have just been identified, select which disk will be the Quorum (Q) disk. Typically the Q: drive is a hardware-level mirrored pair that is separate from the drive arrays that will be used for the Exchange 2000 transaction logs and storage groups. The following shows the dialog box that prompts you to select the quorum disk (the dialog box refers to it as the Cluster File Storage disk).

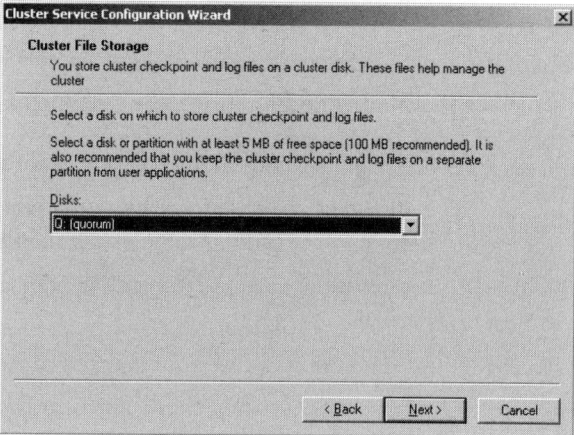

The last step in configuring the first node in the cluster is to set up the networks. You should have a very clear picture before configuring your networks as to which network will be used for which type of communication. One of the dialog boxes that you will see during the installation of Cluster Services could not make this any clearer:

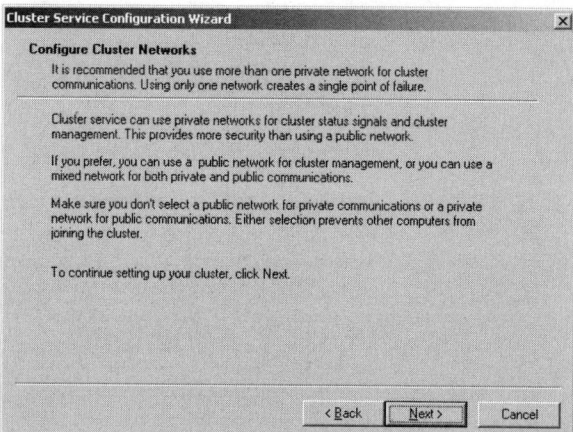

For practical purposes, while configuring a single private network with a crossover cable does represent a single point of failure, usually this configuration is extremely reliable, and the private network is configured only for private communications and the public network only for public communications. If redundancy is required for the private network, configure the public network for mixed communications. Realize, however, that if a failure does occur with the private network and internal cluster communications failover to the public network, the cluster will continue to function, but you may not be aware that the private network has failed.

Figure 8.7 shows the configuration dialog box for configuring the public network adapter.

Figure 8.7   Configuring an adapter for a public network

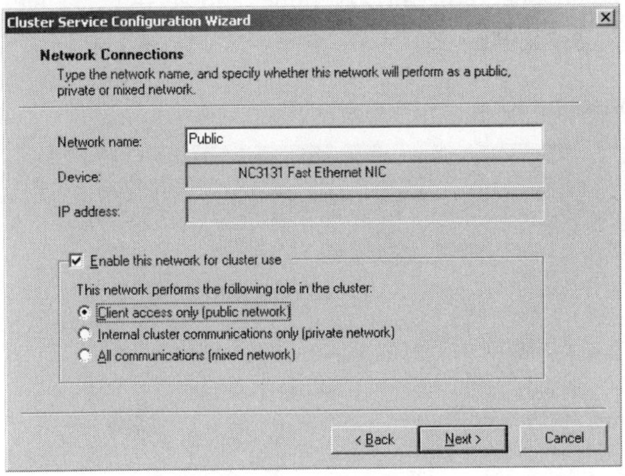

Once you have configured the network adapters for the public and private networks, you must enter the IP address for the Cluster Service. This is the IP address that has been identified to be linked with the network name for the cluster, and all nodes in the cluster share it. This IP address is input in the IP Address box shown in Figure 8.8.

Figure 8.8   Configuring an IP address for the cluster

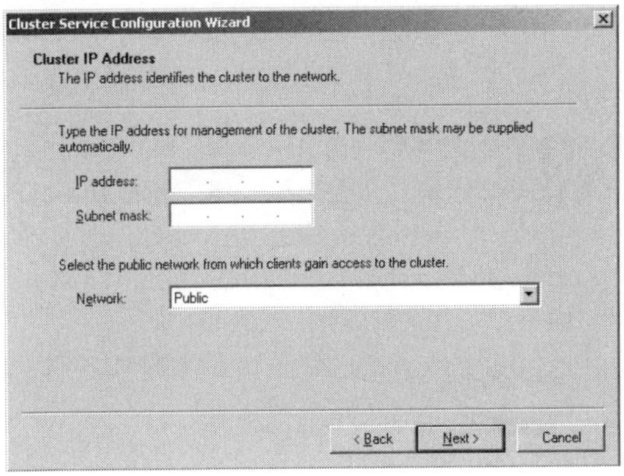

Installing Additional Cluster Nodes

Installing the second node into the cluster is much like the first with a few minor changes. To start make, sure that the first node in the cluster is up and running, then power on Node B. Start the same procedure as you followed for Node A; go to Control Panel ➤ Add/Remove Programs and install the Cluster Service. When you reach the screen where you are presented with the choice to join a cluster or create a cluster, choose to join the existing cluster. Next, you will be prompted for the cluster name (the network name that was established when installing the first node) and account credentials to connect to the cluster, as shown in Figure 8.9.

Figure 8.9 Connecting to an existing cluster

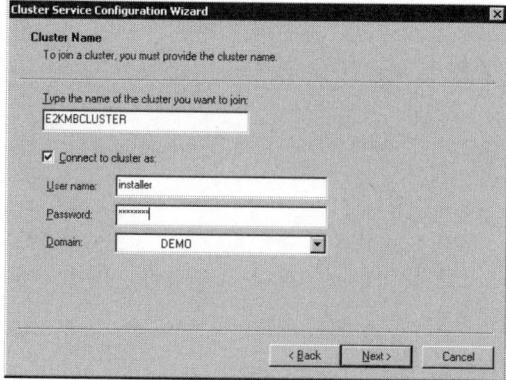

Once you have specified the cluster that Node B must join, continue to configure the cluster resource groups. To do this, open the Cluster Administrator console and select the cluster group resource. Right-click and select Move Group. This will take the cluster group resources offline, move them to the other node, and then bring them back online. This is a controlled and orderly failover, and it proves that your cluster is up and working properly.

Removing Unnecessary Services

The fewer services the server is running, the better off it will be, so remove or disable any unnecessary services on the clustered nodes. This includes services that may have been installed by accident and services that are automatically installed but are not necessary, such as:

- Distributed Link Tracking Client
- Distributed Link Tracking Server
- Distributed File System

- Remote Access Connection Manager
- Print Spooler Service
- License Logging Services
- Computer Browser

Installing Exchange 2000 into a Cluster

Now that Windows 2000 Cluster Services is installed and a move of a cluster resource has been successful, you can move on to installing Exchange 2000 Enterprise. The standard edition of Exchange 2000 does not support clustering; you must have Exchange 2000 Enterprise. As when you were preparing to install and configure the Cluster Service, there are several items you should prepare before beginning your Exchange 2000 installation.

- All the disk arrays in the external storage unit should have been configured already, and you should know which array (disk group in the cluster administrator) will be used for each Exchange virtual server. For example, say you are planning on having two EVSs, and you wisely choose to separate the transaction logs from the databases. Further, you have chosen to place the transaction logs on a mirrored pair and the databases on a RAID 1 + 0 array. Take a moment and write out the drive letters, and record their assignment to Exchange and EVS.

- Make certain that you are logged on as the exact same account that was used to install Cluster Services. The install will fail if you are not.

- Ensure that the drive letters and directory paths on the internal node drives are identical. The Exchange binaries should be placed on the same drive letter and in the same directories on both nodes.

- Ensure that both nodes can see all the external arrays and that they see them with the identical drive letter assignments. For example, you can't have one node seeing drives E:, F:, G:, and H:, and the other seeing L:, M:, N:, and O: assigned to the same physical drives.

- Have the IP addresses and network names for the EVSs documented and available. Know which disk group is going to be assigned to which EVS.

- Take a few moments and look through the installation documentation first; for the uninitiated it can be a little confusing the first time.

- Make sure you have the required service packs, hot fixes, and security fixes necessary to support Exchange 2000 in a cluster.

- Paul Bowden's document "Exchange 2000 Service Pack 1 Clustering Guide" contains updated information about clustering Exchange 2000 and is quite helpful. It is available on the Web at www.exinternals.com.

> **NOTE** When assigning volume labels to the shared storage partitions, it may be helpful to assign the logical drive label to be the same or similar to the disk drive letter.

After you are logged on as the Installer account, open the Cluster Administrator console and be sure that the node that you are loading owns the shared disk resources that will belong to the EVS that will be preferably homed on the node. Then launch the Exchange 2000 Setup program. Select Exchange Server Setup, proceed through the welcome screen, and select I Agree on the EULA screen. Depending on the type of installation media you have (from a Select or Enterprise Agreement or purchased individually), you may need to enter the CD key.

Next, select the installation directory for the Exchange 2000 binaries. If you have prepared a partition on the local drive that is separate from the OS, consider installing the Exchange 2000 binaries there. One item to be aware of is that if you do choose an alternate installation path from the default, you must be sure to create the directory structure that you want beforehand.

When you reach the Component Selection screen, you will notice that, so far, it is no different than a typical installation of Exchange 2000.

When choosing the components to install, you should accept the default of a Typical installation with Microsoft Exchange Messaging and Collaboration Services and Microsoft Exchange System Management tools. There is not much point to installing the connectors, Key Management Service, or the Chat server, because they are not supported in a cluster. Note that if you are installing the Exchange binaries to a location other than the default, the path must be changed here.

Once you have selected the components for installation and agree to the license agreement for per-seat licensing, review the component summary, and then click Next; the installation proceeds. You may begin to wonder if you are actually installing Exchange 2000 in a standard server mode, but almost at once, the Exchange installation program will prompt you with a pop-up windows stating that "Setup shall install the cluster-aware version of Microsoft Exchange." Click OK, and feel good that the correct version of Exchange is being installed on the node.

Setup then completes and requires an immediate reboot. This is different from installing Exchange on a non-clustered server, and it is required in order for the Cluster Administrator console to recognize the Exchange 2000 extensions that have been added. This gives the MMC the ability to create and control cluster resources that are needed for Exchange. Examples are the System Attendant resource and information store resources.

It is now necessary to install Exchange 2000 on the second node prior to configuring any EVSs. The installation procedures are identical to the first node.

Configuring an Exchange Virtual Server

Now both cluster nodes have the necessary files to support one or more EVSs, but the EVSs have not been configured yet. Upon completion of the following steps, if you look in the Exchange System Manger, you will see the EVS that has been created looking just like an Exchange server that is not on a cluster.

To configure an EVS, follow these steps:

1. On the node that you want to be the preferred owner of the EVS, open the Cluster Administrator console, and make sure that the node owns the disk resources that will be added. Confirm this by opening Windows Explorer and checking to see if the drives are there and accessible.

2. In the Cluster Administrator console, right-click the Groups object in the left-hand pane, and select Create A New Group. You are prompted for the name of the group and a description. Provide this information, and then click Next.

3. Select the preferred owner of the EVS (being sure to list only one node as the preferred owner), and click Next. The cluster group for EVS1 is created.

4. Right-click the new EVS1 group to create the Exchange resources that will support EVS1. The first cluster resource to be created is the IP address that the EVS will use. Enter the appropriate information and click Next.

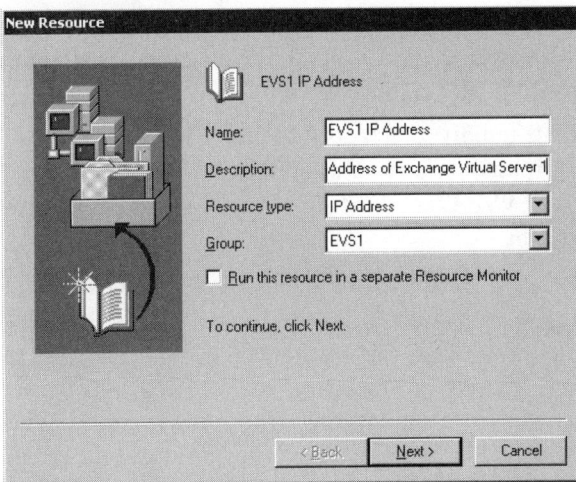

5. To select the possible owners of this resource, accept the default, which should be both nodes; if it's not, add both nodes to the right-hand pane. This is necessary since either node may need to own this resource during a failover.

6. The next parameter to be configured is the other cluster resources that must be up before this resource can be brought online. These are the same types of dependencies that are encountered when other Windows 2000 services are started. For the IP address however, there are no dependencies, so you can simply click Next to skip past this screen.

7. Enter the actual IP address that you want the EVS to use. This process will yield an IP address cluster resource in the EVS1 cluster group.

8. The next resource to be created is the network name. The following steps are necessary to create a network name resource.

   1. Right-click the EVS1 group, and select Create A New Network Name. This is the Exchange server name that will be configured as the Exchange server in Outlook profile.

   2. Configure the name of the resource object. This process is almost identical to creating an IP address resource, except on the New Resource screen, choose Network Name in the Resource Type drop-down list box.

   3. Select the dependency for the network name. This will probably be a simple choice, as there will be no other resources configured in this resource group; select the IP address resource you previously configured. Both nodes must be possible owners of the network name resource just like the IP address.

   4. Enter the network name parameter. This is the name that will be visible to the network clients.

9. The next set of resources to be added to the EVS1 cluster group are the disk groups. Add these by dragging and dropping the disk resources from the right-hand pane into the desired cluster resource group (EVS1).

10. After you drag and drop each disk into the EVS1 resource container, you are asked to confirm that this is what you want to do. Click Yes to confirm that the disk should be assigned to EVS1. Once the disks are assigned, the EVS1 network name container will look like this:

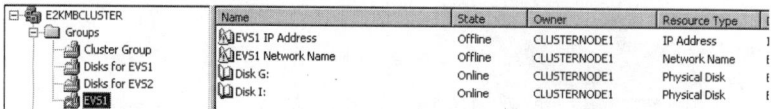

11. Right-click the EVS1 group and select to bring it online. When this is completed successfully, the white X in the red circle on the cluster group disappears.

12. You are now ready to create the Exchange System Attendant resource for EVS1, the last resource that will be created manually. Once the EVS System Attendant is brought online, it will create all the remaining necessary Exchange cluster resources.

    1. Right-click the EVS1 group and create a new System Attendant resource. The Resource Type drop-down box should contain a type of Microsoft Exchange System Attendant.

    2. Configure both nodes as possible owners, and select all resources as dependencies. Note that because the network name is dependant on the IP address, it is not required that the IP address be listed as a dependency, only the network name. However, it is more consistent to list all the group resources as dependencies for the SA.

    3. You are prompted for a directory for the EVS1 databases and transaction logs. Ensure that this points to one of the disk groups that have been assigned to the EVS1 group. In this EVS, the transaction logs will be placed on drive G: and the databases on drive I:. However, all Exchange data resources will initially be placed on the G: drive, and the databases will be moved to drive I after the EVS is fully created and online.

13. Select to bring the EVS1 group fully online. This starts the System Attendant, which then creates all the other Exchange services in the resource group. When this process completes, the Cluster Administrator console should so something similar to this:

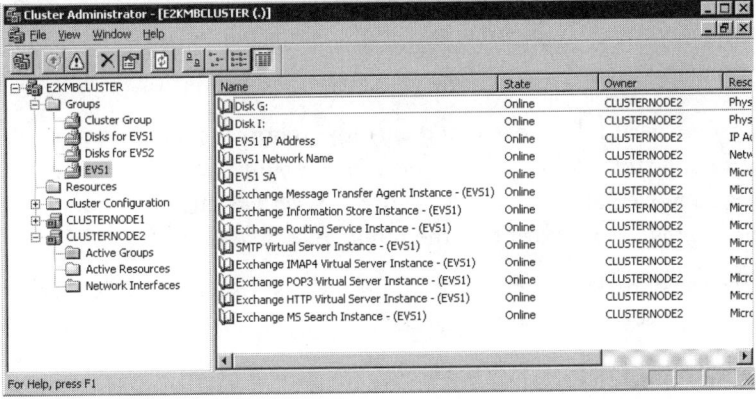

14. Open the Exchange System Administrator (ESM); you should see the newly created EVS1 under the appropriate Administrative Group ➤ Servers object.

15. Expand the server object to navigate to the mailbox store object, bring up its properties, and go to the Databases tab. The default drive that I selected earlier is the G: drive (when I configured the System Attendant cluster resource), so now I need to move the database drives to the I: drive. Figure 8.10 shows the default database paths for the default mailbox store on EVS1.

Figure 8.10 Default database paths on EVS1

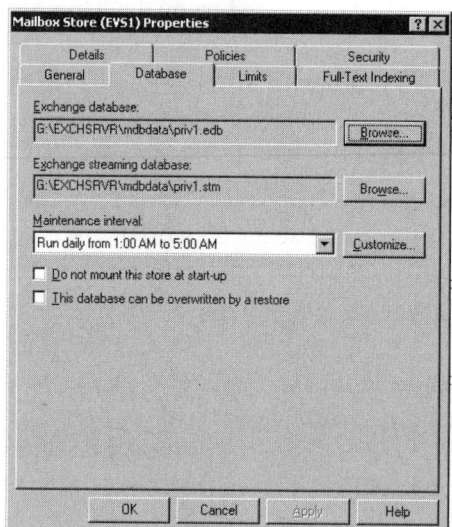

TIP Moving databases (and log files) is exactly the same for a cluster server as it is for moving databases and log files on a stand-alone server. See Chapter 4, "Maintenance and Management," for more information on moving databases and transaction logs.

EVS1 has now been fully created and is ready to host mailboxes and public folders as desired. If public folders are going to be homed on an EVS, it is recommended that these databases be moved also to a database drive. Use the same procedure that was used to move the mailbox store except on the public folder store.

Once the procedure has been completed for the first Exchange 2000 server in the cluster, repeat the process for additional servers.

Preventing Possible Problems

There are some common problems that you may encounter when operating an Exchange 2000 cluster. Here are some things that you can do to catch or prevent these problems:

- As mentioned earlier, in a mixed environment, you will have to have at least one non-clustered server to support the services that are not supported on a cluster (site replication service, NNTP, instant messaging, etc.).

- Ensure that none of the Internet protocol virtual servers (IMAP4, POP3, or HTTP) are set to use TLS/SSL exclusively. Cluster Services checks with the standard ports, and if they don't respond, it will initiate a failover. If clients require TLS/SSL (and they should!), use front-end servers.

- Make sure you move the SMTP \Mailroot directory to a shared disk, not to the local hard disk of the clustered node. These can be moved using ADSIEDIT; see Chapter 6, "Performance Monitoring and Optimization," and Chapter 2, "Active Directory for Exchange 2000 Administrators."

- Make sure that any hard-coded Registry settings that you make on one node of the cluster (such as DSProxy and DSAccess settings) are made to the other nodes in the cluster.

Moving to an Exchange 2000 Cluster

How you move to a new Exchange 2000 clustered server depends a lot on your current configuration. If you have a brand new Exchange 2000 installation, then this is a no-brainer because you are starting from scratch. If you are currently running Exchange 5.5 or Exchange 2000 but not in a clustered configuration, then you are probably going to want to use the "move mailbox" method (discussed in Chapter 3, "Exchange 2000 Migration and Upgrades") to move mailboxes to the clustered servers a few at a time.

If you have an NT 4 Enterprise Edition cluster installed, there are a number of different ways to upgrade to Windows 2000. Which one you use depends on what additional hardware resources are available, what is running on the cluster, the amount of allowed downtime, and the level of risk that you are willing to accept.

> **TIP** I always view upgrade time as a time to get new hardware, so I recommend installing new cluster hardware and moving the mailboxes from the existing Exchange 5.5 cluster to the Exchange 2000 servers. This provides the minimum disruption to users.

Rolling Upgrades on the Cluster

Earlier in this chapter, I stated that one of the valid reasons for a company to implement a cluster was to take advantage of rolling upgrades and planned outages for maintenance without losing availability of the services provided by the cluster. What this means is that if a procedure needs to be performed on one (or both) nodes that requires a reboot or shutdown, all the services on that node would be failed over to the other node, and the first node would be taken down, worked on, and then brought back up. Then the services would be moved from the second node to the first, and the process repeated. This works just fine for service pack installations and hardware upgrades.

NOTE Microsoft supports this method of upgrade from an NT 4 cluster to a Windows 2000 two-node Advanced server cluster—with some caveats.

Requirements for performing a rolling upgrade to Windows 2000 Cluster Services include:

- Both of the cluster nodes must be running Internet Information Server (IIS) 4 and Windows NT 4 SP4 or later. The service pack must have been applied after the installation of Windows NT 4 Cluster Services.

- All the cluster resources must be able to support running in a Mixed-mode cluster. A cluster is considered as being in a Mixed-mode state when one node is running one version (NT 4) of Cluster Services and the other is running a different version (Windows 2000). If there are any cluster resources that cannot run in a Mixed-mode cluster, a rolling upgrade is not possible. Consult Chapter 5 of the "Windows 2000 Advanced Server Getting Started Guide."

At a high level, the procedure for performing a rolling upgrade would be to move all services off of Node A, pause Node A, run the OS upgrade on Node A, and restart Node A. Once Node A is back online, the cluster is in Mixed mode. Then proceed to move all the resources off Node B to Node A and repeat the OS upgrade process.

If Exchange 5.5 is running on the cluster that you have upgraded, remember that once you get the cluster upgraded to Windows 2000 Cluster Services, you would still have to upgrade to Exchange 2000 to take advantage of multiple EVS. This means that you would need to perform the rolling upgrade procedure again to get from Exchange 5.5 to Exchange 2000.

As with any upgrade procedure, there are some pros and cons. The primary advantage of performing a rolling OS upgrade with all the services remaining online is that the only interruption of Cluster Services to the end users is during the resource move. The largest risk involved is that of the rolling upgrade process on either node failing. You may be left in a position where one node is working and the other not. In this case, the only option would be to eject the non-functional node from the cluster and rebuild it from the OS level. The rebuild would require that the high-availability services be left running on just one node for an extended period of time, thereby increasing the odds that the service may become unavailable due to failure of the functioning node.

Alternatives to the Rolling Upgrade

If it is acceptable to have complete downtime for some of the services on the cluster, you can simply stop those services that are not capable of running in a Mixed-mode cluster, then perform the rolling upgrade process. If it is acceptable to have the entire Cluster

Service unavailable, then you are free to perform the OS upgrade after all the Cluster Services have been stopped. These alternatives still have the disadvantages of 1) Some or all Cluster Services will not be available during the upgrade, and 2) If the upgrade does not complete successfully, you will have to reload from the OS level.

Swing Server Upgrade   The swing upgrade method is probably the one most favored by administrators who prefer not to roll the dice with their server upgrades. When these procedures are applied to moving from Exchange 5.5 to Exchange 2000, this is typically called a *migration* rather than an upgrade. Essentially, the swing method involves having other servers assume the functions of the cluster servers (e.g., implement additional WINS servers and move all the Exchange 5.5 mailboxes to a different Exchange server in the Exchange 5.5 site). Once the cluster has been depopulated of services, you are then free to wipe clean the cluster down to the hardware level and rebuild with a fresh install of the OS. After the cluster has been rebuilt, move the desired services back.

The downsides to the swing method include:

- Obviously, in order to perform this type of upgrade, there must be sufficient server-class hardware available to assume the functions of the cluster.

- This type of upgrade requires more planning and more time than simply moving to new hardware, as it involves multiple servers and multiple moves of services between servers.

- When high-availability services are running on stand-alone servers, the exposure to service failure is increased.

Some of the advantages to the swing method of upgrading include:

- Reduced downtime of services during the upgrade. If planned properly, replacement services that perform the same functions as those on the cluster can be brought online in the network in parallel with the Cluster Services. This means that there will be no interruption of services to the clients.

- When moving mailboxes between servers, it is recommended (but not required) that the users be logged out of their mailboxes during the move. Therefore, only the users who are being moved—not all users on the server—may experience an interruption of messaging services, as in the case of a failover of the entire EVS from one node to another.

- As you have seen, Exchange 2000 can take advantage of multiple EVSs, each of which requires its own disk resources. With the option available to completely erase the cluster, the disk arrays can be rebuilt to support multiple disk groups and therefore multiple EVSs in the cluster.

- There is no risk of promoting any abnormalities that may have existed in the NT 4 cluster into the Windows 2000 cluster; the same applies to the Exchange 5.5 EVS that was running on the NT 4 cluster.

- Because all the services that were on the cluster are being supported by other servers, there is more time available for performing hardware and software upgrades to the cluster's physical resources.

Cluster Operations

The methodologies and tools that are employed in managing and maintaining a cluster and its resources are the same ones that the administrator uses every day on non-clustered servers with the addition of the Cluster Administrator console. For example, the administrator should still examine event logs daily, perform daily backups, ensure that the server does not run out of disk space, check the queues, and configure performance monitor counters on critical server objects.

The only major shift in management methods are that all Windows services that are running on the cluster should be managed (stopped, started, and restarted) only from the Cluster Administrator console, not from the individual nodes.

Forced Failovers

There are two different schools of thought about performing regular controlled failover tests on the cluster. One is that failovers should be performed in order to verify that the failover/failback occurs as expected and is successful. If the test does not complete successfully, you must take steps to fix the problem before an uncontrolled failover/failback occurs. I would recommend performing a test like this after the cluster is put into production but before there are large numbers of users who depend on the cluster for services.

The other school of thought is not to perform tests like this, the reason being that the Cluster Services are online, being used, and stable. If a failover is purposely introduced, change is put into an otherwise stable system. With the introduction of change into the system comes instability; this is unavoidable as the system changes from one static stable state to another. Many administrators avoid this altogether and have formulated extensive change-control policies to minimize the effects of change on their networks and server environments.

TIP   Avoid putting the cluster through test failovers once it has a significant load.

Monitoring Cluster Performance

Monitoring cluster performance-monitor counters from the cluster nodes themselves is generally not recommended, as there can be problems with the counters' ability to continue recording information in the event of a failover. The generally accepted best practice is to monitor performance across the network from a workstation.

> **WARNING**   Do not monitor system performance using System Monitor directly from a cluster node.

In the System Monitor control, only one process is added that is specific to Cluster Services: clussvc under the Process object's %Processor time. All the typically expected System Monitor counters are present for an Exchange server in a cluster. Chapter 6 discusses many Windows 2000– and Exchange 2000–specific counters that you may want to monitor.

Best Practices

While operating a cluster is not too terribly different from operating stand-alone servers, here are some suggestions that you may find useful.

- Install *only* the services necessary to run Windows 2000, Cluster Services, and Exchange 2000 on the cluster nodes. Introducing unnecessary services to clustered nodes increases the likelihood of the node or the entire cluster to become unstable.

- Always verify that the third-party applications (virus scanning and backup) that are necessary for your Exchange 2000 servers are cluster-aware and are capable of running in Active/Active mode.

- Make sure that your cluster nodes and resources are documented thoroughly.

- Always make sure that your backups include the system state of both nodes of the cluster and the quorum disk.

- Though these numbers will change with later service packs, try not to exceed more than 1500 simultaneous users on any node of the cluster.

- Monitor drive space usage for the external unit. Just because it's large doesn't mean it can't be filled.

- Configure a Performance Monitor alert to be sent out in case of any unplanned failover. Failovers occur because something has gone wrong—you need to know about it and fix it before failing back to the original node. See Chapter 6, "Performance Monitoring and Optimization" for more information on tuning Exchange 2000 and monitoring memory usage.

- Take some time to get trained on the hardware that your cluster will run on. Remember that clustering primarily protects against hardware failures, so you should know your hardware inside and out so you can affect rapid repairs.

- Getting trained on Exchange 2000 is a must. To effectively take advantage of the benefits of multiple storage groups and mailbox stores, you need to understand them and the limitations of implementing them in a clustered environment.

- Clustering/high availability is great technology that will increase service uptime, but it is only a tool, and it is only as good as how it is managed. Don't allow yourself to lapse into a false sense of security that clustering will protect you from everything!

9

Public Folders

Up until now, you have been focused on satifying users on an individual basis. Yet if you want to share information more easily with your collective, you can use public folders. Essentially, these are centralized repositories for e-mail messages, customized forms, spreadsheets, presentations, documentents, multimedia clips, and more. The beauty of public folders is that they are accessible to just about anyone with Outlook 2000, Internet mail clients, newsreaders, a web browser, Microsoft Windows Explorer, Office 2000, Office XP, or even standard Windows programs. However, not all features (such as custom forms) will be available to all users due to the fact that not all applications will be able to read all of the data types stored in a public folder.

You might be wondering how Exchange 2000 Server can make access to data so simple? It's easy, thanks a number of features that combine together to create the Web storage system. These featues include MAPI access to public folders, NNTP access, IMAP4 access, HTTP access, and a new feature called the Exchange Installable File System (ExIFS), which makes public folders as accessible as any folder sitting on your hard disk.

Exchange 2000 provides a number of new features to enhance the use and administration of Exchange 2000 Server public folders. For example, you'll love multiple store support, integration with Microsoft Windows 2000 security groups, and public folder connection agreements (CAs). In addition, there's also web exposure, a new way to configure public folder affinity, and full-text indexing.

NOTE If you're upgrading public folders from Exchange 5.5 to Exchange 2000, you will have to take additional steps to reconfigure public folder affinity, which is not upgraded by default. In addition, you'll also have some challenges with multiple store support, setting permissions due to integration with Windows 2000 groups, and public folder CAs.

Here's a quick rundown of some other public folder features and capabilities:

Mail-enabled public folders   Send messages to folders using the folder's e-mail address (stored in Active Directory) instead of having to post them directly.

Multiple public folder trees   Enables you to have more than one public folder hierarchy.

Secure items in public folders   Assign permissions individually to items in public folders using the Exchange Installable File System (ExIFS).

Accessibility from the Web   Use a web browser to gain access to public folders by specifying a URL to the folder.

Accessibility from the file system   Use EXIFS to share public folders and allow users to access public folders through Windows Explorer.

Full-text indexing capabilities for public folders   Offers the same Find or Advanced Find functionality users already know in the Microsoft Outlook clients.

Referrals enabled by default   Gain access to any folder in the organization. Exchange 2000 enables referrals by default between routing groups.

Although public folders are primarily managed using Exchange System Manager, users can create public folders with Outlook 2000, Internet clients, web browsers, or Windows Explorer. In addition, they can set permissions and configure several other options with these applications. If you decide to create a public folder, you should be ready to own it, because the creator becomes the owner and is responsible for manging folder permissions and rules using Outlook 2000.

TIP   One strategic decision you should make is whether or not other users can serve as owners of the public folder.

What's New with Exchange 2000

As with most Microsoft products, they improve with time and future releases; Exchange 2000 is no exception. Exchange 2000 Server offers many things that were not available in Exchange 5.5 Server including a number of new features that affect public folders. Exchange 2000 also improves some of the Exchange 5.5 public folder features. Below is a list of features and differences for Exchange 2000 public folders:

- Microsoft Office 2000 and custom applications can also access Exchange public folder stores. You can open and save documents directly in the public folder stores using Web folders.

- Exchange 2000 offers public folder CAs to provide interoperability with Exchange 5.5.

- In Exchange Server 5.5, public folders were placed in the directory by default, but not displayed in the global address list (GAL). For backward compatibility, MAPI public folders in an Exchange 2000 Mixed-mode environment are always mail-enabled and cannot be mail-disabled.

- In previous versions of Exchange, each administrator had all of the rights assigned to the administrator group. Exchange 2000 permits much more granular control of public folder rights and permissions; this feature will be useful in large organizations with decentralized administration.

- Previous versions of Exchange did not support item and property permissions, but Exchange 2000 supports both item-level and property-level permissions.

Managing Public Folders

Management of public folders is done largely by the Exchange System Manager console or from the Outlook client. By sharing or delegating the responsibility of managing public folders to others, an administrator can reduce the burden of certain tasks on the IT team within her organization. For example, the best person to manage client permissions is likely the user who creates or owns the public folder, because he knows the individuals within the organization who should have permissions to it; the user can accomplish this through Outlook.

If public folders are mail enabled, then an object in Active Directory (AD) also represents the public folder. This is similar to how public folders were created in Exchange 5.5. The mail-enabled public folders are created in the Microsoft Exchange System Objects container. If the folder is mail-enabled, it will have an Active Directory Discretionary Access Control List (DACL).

Although there are many management tasks relating to public folders, controlling rights and permissions, replication, and managing disk space used are important; the most crucial is ensuring that there is a standardized structure for your public folder trees. This structure will make finding and using public folders much easier on your user community. Setting rights and permissions, as well as replication, are discussed later in this chapter.

Designing Public Folder Structure and Hierarchy

A well-defined public folder structure is essential for any Exchange server implementation, because it allows delegation of administrative tasks and quicker retrieval of information. Tasks such as adding permissions and adding and removing folders can be performed by users or delegated to a group administrator.

When you begin designing a public folder structure, you have to make a couple of major architectural decisions, including the hierarchy of the public folders in any given tree, and whether or not to replicate public folders. Public-folder replication and some of the things that may affect your decision to replicate or not to replicate are discussed in the Public-Folder Replication section.

When managing the default MAPI public folder tree or an application public folder tree, you need to decide what hierarchy of folders to use for your organization. The hierarchy of public folders in a public folder tree helps organize public folders into collections of information that are easy to browse. Typically, public folder hierarchies reflect a company's internal organizational structure. Figure 9.1 shows hierarchy based on Somorita Surfboard's locations; it includes a Company Wide folder that incorporates information of interest to everyone in the company.

> **NOTE** I strongly recommend removing the Create Top-Level Public Folder permission from the Everyone group. This should be removed at the Exchange organization object at the top of the Exchange System Manager hierarchy. This will prevent users from creating their own folders in the root of the hierarchy. When you are setting up new organizations, confirm that this right has been removed.

When you install Exchange 2000, a default public folder tree is created. All MAPI clients, such as Microsoft Outlook, can access this public folder hierarchy to read messages and store documents. This tree will exist (by default) on each Exchange 2000 server installed into the forest. In addition to this default hierarchy, you can create alternate public folder hierarchies for applications or web browsers to access. There are different methods to access the default public folder hierarchy and to access alternate hierarchies that you create. The means of accessing a particular hierarchy is based on its intended use. Outlook Web Access (OWA) users, for example, access their dedicated public folder hierarchy through Hypertext Transfer Protocol (HTTP). Other groups might find Network News Transfer Protocol (NNTP) more suitable.

> **NOTE** If you want tight control over public folder administration, create an administrative group and move the default Folders container into it.

Figure 9.1   Folder hierarchy based on company locations

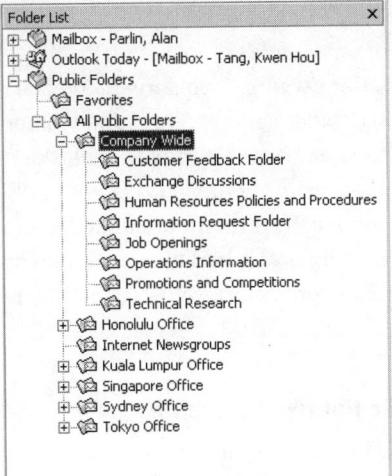

Dedicated Public Folder Servers

Many organizations with more than two or three Exchange servers decide to dedicate one or two servers in each routing group exclusively to public folders. This reduces the overall resource load on mailbox servers. If you decide to do this, first replicate all of the routing groups to the dedicated public folder servers. Don't forget to replicate the system folders such as the EFORMS REGISTRY, Events Root, OFFLINE ADDRESS BOOK, etc.

Once the folders have had a chance to completely replicate (this could take days if you are replicating more than a few gigabytes), then remove the replicas from the public stores in the routing group. Once you have done this, you can remove the public folder stores from the servers that will not support public folders.

Exchange@Work: Creating Dedicated Public Folder Servers

Company XYZ has nearly 300 Exchange servers placed around the world. They noticed that even though they had very few public folders configured for replication, they were still generating tens of thousands of public-folder replication messages every day. These messages were the result of public folder hierarchy replication and public-folder replication status messages.

Exchange@Work: Creating Dedicated Public Folder Servers *(continued)*

To reduce the amount of public-folder replication traffic, XYZ's administrators reduced the number of public folder servers. Two servers in each routing group were designated as dedicated public folder servers. The public folders that were relevant to each routing group were replicated to each server in that routing group in order to provide redundancy. By reducing the number of servers with public folders in their organization, they were able to reduce the amount of public folder replication traffic and status messages. Since each routing group had two dedicated public folder servers, Outlook clients were always able to connect to a close copy of a public folder replica.

OWA Clients and Public Folder Hierarchies

The Outlook Web Access client provides users with access to public folders, e-mail, personal calendars, group scheduling, and collaboration applications through a web browser. The version of Outlook Web Access that you are using will determine which public folders you can access through HTTP.

If clients run Exchange 5.5 OWA, they can access all folders in the MAPI public folder hierarchies. OWA 5.5 clients can see all folders on Exchange 5.5 servers and any folders in the default public folder (MAPI) tree on Exchange 2000 servers. However, OWA 5.5 clients cannot see the alternate public (general purpose) folder hierarchies created on Exchange 2000 servers.

If clients run Exchange 2000 OWA, they can access all folders on Exchange 2000 servers. Unlike Outlook 2000 clients, Exchange 2000 OWA clients can use both the default and the alternate public folder hierarchies. OWA 2000 clients cannot see any public folders on Exchange 5.5 servers unless the Exchange 5.5 folder content is replicated on the Exchange 2000 server.

For users to access all public folders on either Exchange 5.5 or Exchange 2000 servers, a replica of all folders must exist on an Exchange 2000 server. After the replica is in place, the default public store setting on the mailbox store properties should point to an Exchange 2000 server.

Creating a Public Folder

Just about anyone—administrators or everyday users—can create a public folder, provided they have the correct permissions. The difference is that administrators use Exchange System Manager, and users typically use a MAPI client such as Outlook. The administrator does have a bit more power: Once the base-level folders have been established, the administrator sets permissions and configures items as needed, and then "opens the flood gates" to allow users to add subfolders to the hierarchy and provide the contents.

As an administrator, you'll want to use Exchange System Manager to create generic public folders. To do this:

1. Open Exchange System Manager.

2. Open the appropriate administrative group, locate the Folders container, and locate the public folder tree to which you want to add a public folder.

3. Right-click the public folder tree and choose New ➤ Public Folder.

4. When prompted, type a name for the new public folder.

If you want to create a public folder that contains any type of item other than a mail message item (IPM.Note) or a public folder post message (IPM.Post), you must create the public folder with Outlook. When you do, the Create New Folder dialog box prompts not only for the name, but also for the type of item the folder contains. You can select the Folder Contains drop-down list box and choose Appointment Items, Contact Items, Journal Items, Mail Items, Note Items, or Task Items; the default is Mail Items. Once the folder is created, this cannot be changed.

Mail-Enabling Public Folders   If your Exchange 2000 organization is in Native mode, then all public folders you create will *not* be mail enabled. This means that they will not have an object in AD, and you will not be able to address messages to the folder. Folders are automatically mail enabled only if the organization is in Mixed mode (to maintain compatibility with Exchange 5.5).

To mail-enable a public folder, using Exchange System Manager, right-click the folder name, and choose All Tasks ➤ Mail Enable. Once this is done, you can then view the Exchange properties of the folder by right-clicking and displaying the folder's properties. The Exchange property pages include E-mail Addresses, Exchange General, and Exchange Advanced. You can add custom e-mail addresses to the E-mail Addresses property tab (see Figure 9.2).

If you do not want the folder to be visible to the address lists, be sure to check the Hide From Exchange Address Lists button on the Exchange Advanced property tab. You can right-click a mail-enabled folder and disable the e-mail features by choosing All Tasks ➤ Mail Disable.

Figure 9.2 A mail-enabled public folder's E-mail Addresses property tab

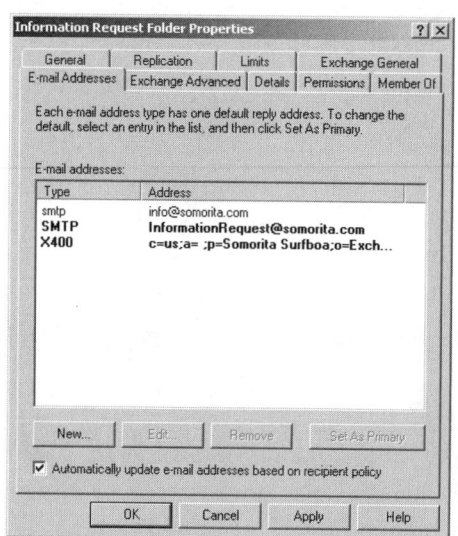

Public Folder Stores and Trees

Public folders are maintained in public stores. Each store consists of a rich-text database file, which holds items in MAPI format, and a native content (streaming) database for items in Internet-based formats. The Exchange System Manager allows you to create these stores, check the location of the databases, and move the database files.

One or more storage groups and public stores may be created on a particular server. It is also possible to remove all public stores from a server to create dedicated mailbox servers. However, at least one server holding the default public tree (the MAPI-based public folder tree) must exist within an administrative group. This is due to the fact that each administrative group must have access to the system folders such as the Offline Address Book, Event Services, etc.

The Exchange System Manager enables you to administer public folders by

- Viewing all available public folder trees within an administrative group and the folders contained in each tree.

- Creating and configuring folders.

- Mail-enabling a public folder that adds an e-mail proxy for the folder to Active Directory.

- Configuring the security settings for a public folder or public folder tree root and propagating them down the hierarchy.

In addition to the default public folder tree that is created when the first Exchange 2000 server is installed, you can create additional public folder stores and associate them with other public folder trees. Multiple public folder trees (top-level hierarchies) provide administrators with greater control and flexibility to manage public folders. For example, you can create a separate public folder tree to collaborate with external users and keep that content separate from the default public folder tree. Or you might want to create an additional tree at a remote location to make it easy for "local" users to access relevant data.

Each public folder tree stores its data in a single public folder store. You can't have two stores on a single server sharing the same tree. However, you can replicate specific folders in the tree to every server in the company that has a public folder store associated with that public folder tree.

You can view the properties on the public folder root in Exchange System Manager to determine the type of folder hierarchy you are currently working with. To do this, locate the desired public folder tree using Exchange System Manager, right-click and display its properties, select the General tab, and look in the Folder Tree Type field to determine which clients can access a public folder tree.

> **NOTE** If "MAPI Clients" is displayed in the Folder Tree Type box, clients such as Outlook can access the hierarchy, in addition to applications, web browsers, and IFS shares. If "General Purpose" is displayed, MAPI clients cannot see the hierarchy, but applications, web browsers, NNTP, and IFS shares can access the public folder hierarchy. Although one server can have multiple public folder stores, only one public folder store contains the default public folder hierarchy.

Default Trees and General Purpose Trees

The All Public Folders hierarchy is the default public folder tree (the MAPI tree). If you're looking for it in Exchange System Manager, you'll find it listed as Public Folders. The default store is associated with every mailbox store on a server to ensure that all MAPI, IMAP4, NNTP, and HTTP clients can access the All Public Folders hierarchy.

All folders that exist beneath public folder trees other than the Folders ➤ Public Folders tree are called general-purpose public folder trees. These are top-level hierarchies and are accessible from Microsoft Windows applications in which the folders in the hierarchies are mapped as network drives using Installable File System (IFS), web clients (through WebDAV, a.k.a. Web Distributed Authoring and Versioning), and NNTP clients. Users cannot access these via MAPI clients, such as Outlook 2000 (unless viewed on a web page hosted in Outlook 2000).

General-purpose public folder trees are ideal for department, group, or project file repositories. The Microsoft SharePoint Portal Server can also use general-purpose public folder trees. Although there can be only one MAPI folder tree per server, there can be several general-purpose folder trees per server. Administrators can create and use these additional trees. You can also use general-purpose public folder trees for collaboration with browsers and applications, such as Office 2000, that can use HTTP to access the store.

Before supporting multiple public folder trees, consider the following:

- Because the default public folder tree is created on every public folder server, and its list of folders is always replicated, additional public folder trees affect only the servers on which they are configured. This means that you can create a set of departmental or local folders on one server or on a subset of servers. You do not have to replicate these additional public folder trees to every public folder server.

- Additional public folder trees allow you to minimize the overall size of the default public folder tree (simplifying navigation) and to reduce the cost of replicating the hierarchy of the default tree.

- MAPI top-level hierarchy client permissions are the traditional MAPI permissions (Editor, Owner, etc). General-purpose, top-level hierarchy client permissions are based on the Active Directory security architecture.

- There can only be one MAPI top-level hierarchy per organization. However, you can have multiple general-purpose, top-level hierarchies per organization.

- Each public folder tree that you create can be stored only once on each Exchange 2000 server.

- MAPI top-level hierarchy does not support deep traversal searches (the ability to search the entire tree), while general-purpose trees do.

- In Mixed mode, MAPI top-level hierarchy folders are mail-enabled by default; general-purpose, top-level hierarchy folders are not. In Native mode, both types of folders are mail-disabled by default.

Creating a Public Folder Tree

To create and begin using a general-purpose public folder tree, you must first create the tree and then create a public folder store to which you assign the tree.

To create an additional public folder tree, follow these steps:

1. Open Exchange System Manager.

2. Locate the Folders container in the appropriate administrative group and right-click the Folders object.

3. Choose New ➢ Public Folder Tree.

4. You are prompted for the name of the tree. You will notice that the Folder Tree Type field is automatically set as General Purpose, which indicates that the folder is available only for non-MAPI clients.

Now that the tree is created, you will need to create a public folder store on each server that will host the tree and associate the store with the tree.

1. Open Exchange System Manager.

2. Locate the server onto which you want to create the public store. Open the storage group that will contain the new store.

3. Right-click the storage group and click New ➢ Public Store.

4. In the Properties box (shown in Figure 9.3), enter a name for the new public folder store. Click Browse to select a public folder tree to associate to your store. If all public folder trees have been assigned to public stores on this server, you will not be able to create a new public folder store.

Figure 9.3   Creating a new public folder store

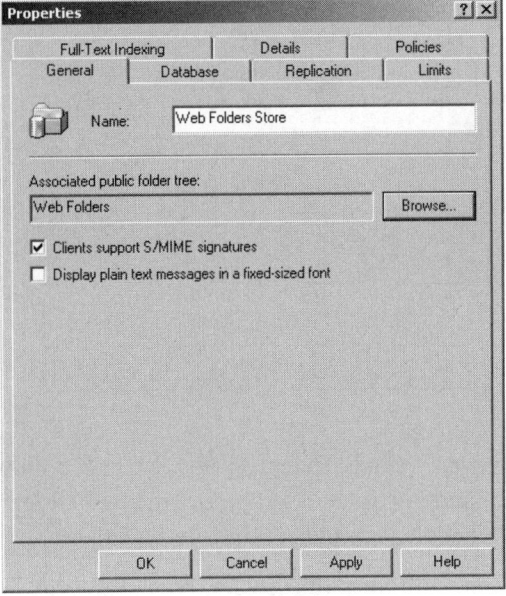

After you configure and mount the store, you can add new folders in the public folder tree.

NOTE If no unassociated public folder tree exists, you receive the following error message when you attempt to create a new public folder store: "All the public folder trees already have an associated public store on this server. You will need to create a new public folder tree before creating this new public store."

To verify what public store is associated with a public folder tree, under the Folders container, right-click the Public Folder Tree, click Properties, and view the General tab. Figure 9.4 shows a public folder tree called Web Folders that is associated with a public folder store called Web Folders Public Store in the Second Storage Group on server SFOEX001.

Figure 9.4 Web Folders public folder tree

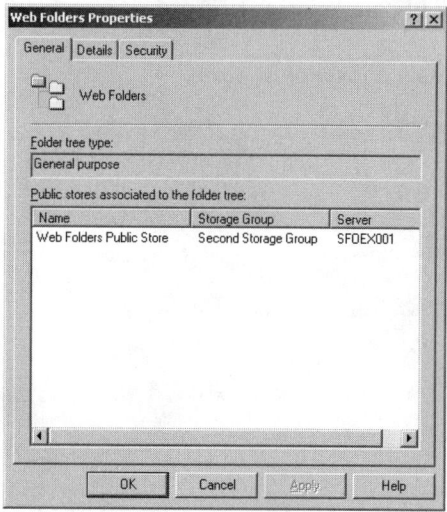

Public Folder Properties The Exchange System Manager allows you to configure public folder properties. A public folder's Properties dialog box lets you configure settings such as replication schedule, age and storage limits, and more.

The following tabs make up the public folder store properties:

- The General tab provides a description of the folder and controls how the folder name will appear in the address list. You can use this tab to enable read/unread information to speed up clients.

- The Replication tab specifies the servers within the organization that contain replicas. You can use this tab to indicate the times at which this public folder will replicate to other replicas of the folder that exist throughout the Exchange organization, and to establish replication message priority.
- The Limits tab specifies age/store limits and deleted item retention length.
- The Details tab provides an administrative description of the public folder.
- The Permissions tab specifies who can access and administer the folder. It also indicates who can administer the proxy object for the folder in Active Directory on a mail-enabled folder.

NOTE For more information on public folder store properties, consult Chapter 4, "Maintenance and Management."

Operations

PART 2

Publishing Additional Public Folder Trees Using OWA

You can publish any of the public trees you have created so that Exchange 2000 Outlook Web Access users can view them. Public folder trees are published on each OWA server using the HTTP virtual server object. To publish a new public folder tree, follow these steps:

1. Locate and open the server's HTTP virtual server container.
2. Highlight the Exchange virtual server (or other HTTP virtual server), right-click, and choose New ➤ Virtual Directory. The Virtual Server properties dialog box appears.
3. Enter the name of the virtual server. This is the name that you will use in the URL path in the web browser.
4. Select the Public Folder radio button and click Modify.
5. Select the public folder tree or the specific public folder that you wish to publish. Click OK twice.

Full-Text Indexing and OWA

In Exchange 2000, you can greatly improve search performance by applying full-text searching to a public folder store. Full-text indexing is enabled per public folder store and is discussed in more detail in Chapter 4. I regularly use and recommend indexing public folders, but keep in mind that a full-text index of your public folders could consume additional 20 to 40 percent of the disk space used by the public folder store. Full-text indexing indexes the message body and message properties as well as the message attachments.

By default, Exchange 2000 Outlook Web Access does not allow you to search a public folder using the full-text indexes. However, with some creativity and an Active Server Page (ASP) script, you can enable WebDAV using CONTAINS or FREETEXT in a WHERE clause of a SQL query.

NOTE See Microsoft Knowledge Base article Q259849 for more information on performing index searches through HTTP and a copy of the script.

Setting Limits

Any experienced Exchange administrator will tell you that Exchange data, left unchecked, will grow to meet the limits of your available storage. Even a small user community can quickly fill up a disk drive if you do not place boundaries on their storage usage. Placing storage limits includes placing reasonable limits on the usage of public folders. Public folder storage limits can be set in one of three ways:

- Through an Exchange system policy to affect a group of public folder stores
- Individually to each public folder store that will affect all folders that store
- On an individual folder's properties

I recommend placing blanket limits through Exchange system policies to ensure that all folders have at least some basic restrictions such as maximum message size, prohibit post limits, issue warning limits, deleted item retention limits, and age limits. However, you will probably need to fine-tune these settings for some folders. For example, some folders—such as a data from a news feed, company announcements, or a For Sale folder—may need to be posted for only a few days or weeks. Figure 9.5 shows the Limits property tab of a public folder called Job Openings.

Figure 9.5 Job Openings public folder Limits property tab

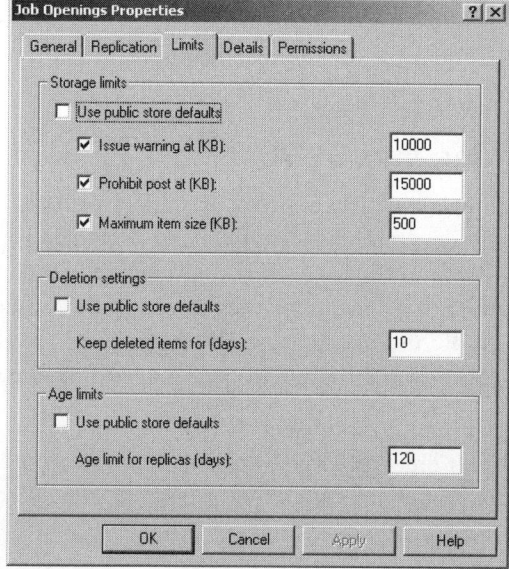

In Figure 9.5, the limits set by the public store and the limits that may have been set by a public folder store policy have been overridden. The Age Limits property configures this folder to keep items for 120 days, after which the item will be "expired" and the item will no longer appear in the folder. Age limits for a particular store can be overridden if you want to keep items on a specific public folder store for longer than the default interval for that server. To override a specific age limit for a folder, use Exchange System Manager and open the Public Folder Instances container on the public folder store whose age limit you want to change. Right-click the desired public folder and choose Replica Properties. This displays the Limits property page for this particular replica of the folder. From here you can either extend the limits longer than the default for the folder or reduce the number of days that items are kept in this replica of the folder.

MAPI Client Connections to Public Folders

When an Outlook client selects a public folder from the folder list, the client has to be directed to which server it should connect. The mailbox store on which the user's mailbox is located directs the user to their default public folder server (on the General properties tab of the mailbox store properties). The default public folder server provides a list of servers that contain a replica of that folder. The client attempts to connect to any replica in order to present the requested data to the user. Here are the steps that occur to get this list and connect to a replica of the public folder:

1. A call is made into the default public folder server. The default public folder server returns a list of all Exchange servers in that organization that have a copy of the requested public folder.

2. The information store then makes a call into the Microsoft Exchange Routing Engine API, commonly referred to as the routing service. The routing service returns the cost associated with the routes to public folders that are not in the same routing group.

> **NOTE** The store will cache the cost for each server that has the requested public folder for one hour. This is done to prevent repeated calls into the routing service. You can purge this cache by restarting MSExchangeIS.

3. The default public folder server sorts this list and returns it to the Outlook client. The client attempts to connect to the public folder replicas starting at the top of the list. This list is created based on the following criteria:

   - If the default public folder server has a replica of the folder, this server is at the top of the list.

- Public folder servers that have a replica of the folder in the local routing group are considered next.

- Public folder servers from remote routing groups (on which the public folder referrals option is enabled) are sorted by the cost of the connector.

- If there are no local replicas and no replicas in routing groups to which this routing group has a referral, the client will not be able to view the contents of the public folder.

Public Folder Referrals

You can route public folder requests to specific folders via the public folder referrals feature of Exchange 2000 messaging connectors. Public folder referrals can be routed to servers in another routing group by implementing and configuring an RGC between the two routing groups. Public folder referrals can be configured for the routing group going in each direction. This task requires two instances to be configured for bi-directional traffic, since the RGC is unidirectional.

NOTE Routing group and messaging connectors are discussed in detail in Chapter 14, "Connectivity within Your Organization."

As the administrator, you can specify whether to allow or deny public folder referrals for each individual connector; to do so, open the properties of a connector using Exchange System Manager. The Do Not Allow Public Folder Referrals check box is not selected by default, thereby allowing public folder referrals to pass through this connector. Figure 9.6 shows an RGC's General property page.

Public folder referrals between routing groups are transitive and allow all referrals over the connection when enabled. For example, if Routing Group A allows public folder referrals to Routing Group B, and Routing Group B allows public folder referrals to Routing Group C, this means that Routing Group A allows public folder referrals to Routing Group C, and vice versa.

If you do not want to allow public folder referrals between specific routing groups, simply check the aforementioned check box.

Figure 9.6 A routing group connector's General property page

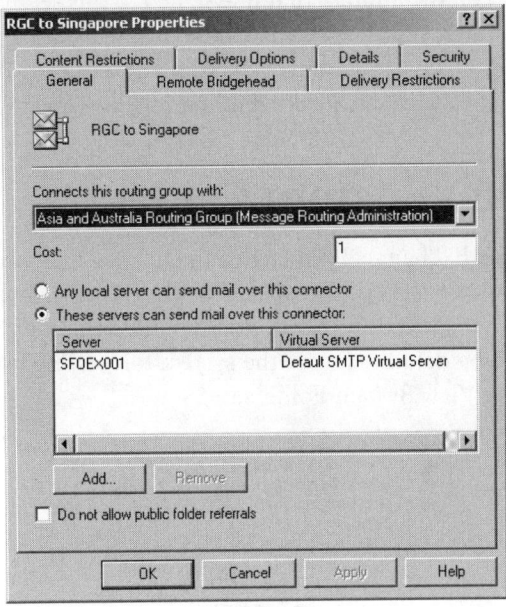

Cost and Load Distribution

To optimize message flow, you must consider cost and load distribution. For instance, the cost associated with each Exchange 2000 connector, including SMTP, X.400, or RGC, could be a value between 1 and 100. If Connector A has a cost of 30 and Connector B has a cost of 90, Exchange 2000 will route messages through Connector A, because it has the lowest cost. If two or more routes are available with the same cost, Exchange 2000 distributes the load as equally as possible between them. This cost also factors in to determining the route the client will use to access public folders on remote servers (via public folder referrals).

> **NOTE** Any route with an infinite cost will be discarded by the information store. An infinite cost indicates that, for an available route to the public folder, one or more connectors have the Do Not Allow Public Folder Referrals check box selected.

Multiple Servers in the Same Routing Group

If multiple servers in the same routing group have a replica of the requested public folder contents, the public folder server will return a list of these servers from which the client software can choose. The client then randomly selects one server and assigns a corresponding number associated with that server. This process is transparent to the end user.

For all future attempts to access this public folder, the client will first try the server initially selected (based on the number that it assigned to this server). Each client will select its own random number, so the number will be different for each client. The process where the public folder store randomly selects one server provides some degree of load balancing among the various clients contending for the same public folder.

Exchange 2000 System Folders

When designing your Exchange 2000 environment, you may need to create additional replicas of system folders to control your network traffic or simply to meet the needs of your user community. System folders are stored in the default public store tree (the MAPI tree) and are hidden by default. To see the system folders, right-click the Public Folders folder tree and select View System Folders:

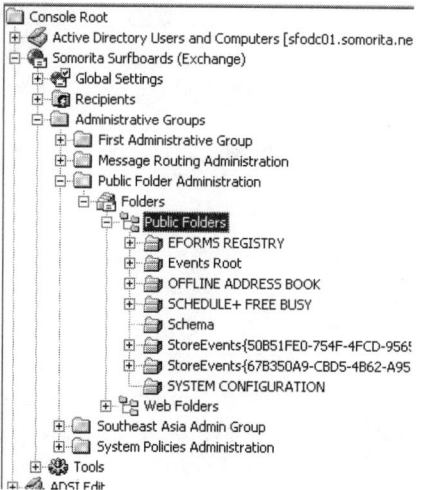

The following lists common system folders that are automatically created on a server when it is installed as the first server in an administrative group:

EFORMS REGISTRY   Storage for forms saved to the Organizational Forms library.

Events Root   Contains scripts for the Exchange Server 5.5–compatible Event Service.

OFFLINE ADDRESS BOOK   Stores offline address books for MAPI clients to download.

SCHEDULE+ FREE BUSY   Stores schedule information for users. Outlook uses this to determine meeting availability.

Schema   Defines properties for objects kept in the public folder store.

StoreEvents   Contains Exchange 2000 event sink code for a specific server. There will be one of these folders for each public folder store.

SYSTEM CONFIGURATION   Contains public folder expiry information.

Creating Organizational Forms Libraries

The Organizational Forms library contains forms that are available to all Outlook users. You can have one Organizational Forms library for each language that you support. To create an Organizational Forms library, follow these steps:

1. Right-click the Public Folders public folder tree and choose View System Folders.
2. Right-click the EFORMS REGISTRY folder and choose New ➤ Organizational Form.
3. Enter the name of the forms library.
4. Choose the language in the E-forms Language drop-down box with which the forms in this library will be used. Click OK.
5. Right-click your newly created library and choose Properties.
6. Select the Permissions property tab and click the Client permissions button. Assign the Author role to the user who must publish forms. (Users of these forms need only the Reviewer role, which is the default.) Click OK twice.

Solving Problems with System Folders

If there is more than one instance of the EventConfig_*servername* public folder for an Exchange 2000 server, the following event may be logged in the Windows 2000 application event log when you attempt to start the Microsoft Exchange 2000 Event Service:

```
Event ID : 5
Source : MSExchangeES
Type : Error
Category : General
Description : An unexpected MAPI error occurred. Error returned was [0x80004005]
```

To resolve this issue, you need to delete both instances of the EventConfig_*servername* folder, and then restart the Event Service. To do this:

1. Ensure that the Events.exe process is not running in Task Manager.
2. In Exchange 2000 System Manager, view system folders.

3. Rename one of the instances so that both can be deleted. If you try to delete one while a duplicate exists, you will get a warning informing you that you must rename one of the folders.

4. Delete both instances of the EventConfig_*servername* folder.

5. Restart the Event Service. This re-creates a single instance of the EventConfig_*servername*.

When you follow these steps, all assigned rights and client permissions to the EventConfig public folder will be lost, and any scripts will be removed from the server.

Security and Public Folders

In Windows 2000, mail-enabled groups in Active Directory provide the functionality of distribution lists in Exchange 5.5. Although different Windows 2000 group types can provide access control and mail routing, each type can behave differently for Exchange. Because Exchange 2000 relies entirely on Windows 2000 for both security and mail distribution groups, it is important to understand the group types to determine which group to use.

Further, if migrating from an existing Exchange 5.5 organization, you should be aware of the ramifications of migrating public folders. Save yourself a lot of problems and make sure that you have cleaned up the public folder ACLs (Access Control Lists). This includes users and groups that no longer exist, but may still have permissions to a public folder. You can largely clean up the public folder using the Exchange 5.5 DS/IS Consistency Adjuster.

When you begin to migrate public folders, the first step is to create an Active Directory Connector (ADC) public folder connection agreement (CA). This will replicate the public folders to Active Directory. Any public folders that have Exchange 5.5 distribution lists assigned permissions will need those permissions matched to an Exchange 2000 security group.

Exchange 2000 converts the Exchange 5.5 ACLs to Exchange 2000 ACLs, which map directly to Active Directory security principals (users and security groups). When the Exchange 2000 information store makes this conversion, it copies the ACL into memory and goes through each of the ACEs (access control entries) trying to match them to an Active Directory security principal. If it encounters an ACE that cannot be resolved to an AD security principal, only the owner's ACE entry is added to the ACL for the public folder on the Exchange 2000 server. This means that only the owner will be able to access the public folder—which in turn will mean lots of support calls.

TIP Check the application event log for problems related to bogus ACEs on public folders or Universal distribution groups that have been assigned permissions.

WARNING Don't adjust public folder permissions through ExIFS using Windows Explorer. This can mess up public folder permissions and make the folders inaccessible to Outlook and other mail clients.

The bottom line on public folder permissions is that the sooner you can get all of your public folders moved over to Exchange 2000 servers, the better off you will be.

Security via Groups

Windows 2000 supports both types of Microsoft Windows NT 4 groups—Domain Local and Global. *Domain Local* membership in Mixed-mode domains contains user accounts and global groups from any domain. In Native-mode domains, Domain Local contains user accounts, Global groups, and Universal groups from any domain in the forest. In addition, it also handles Domain Local groups from the same domain. Permissions for Domain Local groups apply only to objects in the domain in which they exist, and folder access is available to public folders in the same domain only.

In Mixed-mode domains, *Global groups* contains user accounts from the same domain. In Native-mode domains, however, Global groups contain user accounts from the same domain and Global groups from the same domain. Permissions apply for all domains in the forest, even if they reside in another location from the Global group. Users with Global membership are able to access all public folders in all domains.

In Mixed-mode domains, *Universal distribution groups* can be created. These groups can contain user accounts and Global groups from any domain. Once the domain is converted to Native mode, you can create Universal security groups. Universal groups are a lot like Exchange 5.5 distribution lists in that the membership is replicated to the entire forest (the membership is stored in the Global Catalog). Thus Universal security groups can be assigned permissions to any resource in the forest. Any mail-enabled Universal group can be used for mail distribution anywhere in the Exchange organization.

In addition, Active Directory provides e-mail functionality for these groups. A major change in Windows 2000 group design is that groups can function as one of the following:

Security groups This type of membership can assign permissions to resources, including public folders.

Distribution groups This type of membership is mail-enabled—they cannot assign permissions to resources.

Security is implemented in Exchange 2000 based on the following:

- The same type of permission is applied for a folder, or items in it. Then, these are assigned to a user account or security group in Windows 2000.
- The Discretionary Access Control List (DACL) uses security identifiers (SIDs) of Windows 2000 users and groups. Exchange 2000 assigns the Anonymous access permissions to the special ANONYMOUS LOGON account and the Default access permissions to the Everyone group.
- When determining access to a resource in Windows 2000, all entries in the DACL are processed until:
  - An entry denies permission.
  - All of the requested permissions are granted.
  - The end of the list is reached without all permissions granted.
  - If permissions are not explicitly granted or denied, the user has no access to the folder.

Setting Permissions

Setting permissions is a big part of managing Exchange public folders. If user sophistication allows, it is something best assigned to users, which will make the administrator's life much easier.

Public folder permissions can be configured in the client and from the Exchange System Manager console. The difference between the two is that the Exchange System Manager has a feature that allows the same properties to be propagated to all subfolders. This is handy, because public folder trees can grow very long, and managing public folders on a per-folder basis can become tedious. However, propagating permissions from a parent folder to all child folders requires Exchange System Manager. The possible utility of this function, however, is not enough to justify giving end users and supervisors the ability to run the Exchange System Manager console. There is no easy way to limit their access to only public folder administration.

Exchange@Work: Propagating Permissions

Company XYZ's user community makes heavy use of their public folders, and originally, not a lot of thought was given to public folder permissions. Departments created public folders and began to create their own child folders. Then the engineering department complained that users outside of their department were reading and posting items to their folders. The administrator removed the default permission from the Engineering top-level folder, but others were still accessing some of these folders. It turns out that some users outside of engineering had put the Engineering child folders into their public folder Favorites.

If a user has created a public folder Favorite (similar to a Microsoft Internet Explorer Favorite) and is locked out at the parent level, the user can bypass the tree and gain direct access to the public folder. This is what happened to many of the engineering department's child folders. However, by restricting or setting permissions using the Exchange System Manager without propagating the change down the entire Engineering folder hierarchy, the users were prevented from jumping directly to a particular folder in the tree. However, the problem was that permissions had been reset at the parent folder, not at the subfolder level.

A better solution would have been to initially give more thought to public folder permissions and make sure that the departmental folders were locked down to begin with. Users don't like to have something and then have it taken away.

Operations

PART 2

TIP You can assign client permissions to mailbox-enabled users and mail-enabled security groups only. If you assign permissions to a mail-enabled Universal distribution group, it will be converted to a Universal security group automatically.

Parent Folders

A *parent folder* is a folder that has at least one child folder; the parent can be at the top-level folder in a public folder tree or somewhere down in the hierarchy. Permissions can be assigned to this folder and then propagated to all subfolders in that tree. To configure permissions for a public folder tree, open the folder's Properties dialog box and click Security. A newly created folder will inherit permissions from folders above it in the administrative hierarchy, including the administrative group permissions and organization permissions.

To propagate folder properties, including permissions, to subfolders, use Exchange System Manager. Locate the folder you want to propagate the settings on, right-click that parent folder, and select All Tasks ➢ Propagate Settings. You will see the Propagate Folder Settings dialog box:

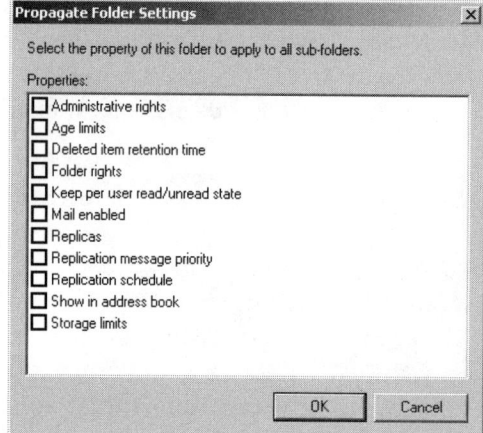

A summary of the properties you propagate to child folders include the following properties:

- Administrative permissions and folder rights.
- Replicas, replication message importance, and replication schedules.
- Age, storage, and deleted item retention time limits.
- Keep read/unread information on a per-user basis.
- Directory settings such as Mail-enabled and Show In Address Book.

Assigning Access Permissions

When you create a public folder, Exchange 2000 assigns a set of permissions that specify the individuals with the right to perform designated activity in that folder. You can assign permissions to folders, items, and properties. Permissions can be inherited from higher-level objects, such as the public folder tree and administrative group.

The permissions for public folders in Exchange 2000 are divided into four separate categories:

- Folder rights (a.k.a. client permissions) enable you to control the permissions of users accessing the folder. For example, you can control who has read/write permission on a public folder.
- Message rights enable you to decide which users can gain access to messages sent or posted to a mail-enabled public folder. These permissions cannot be set through Outlook, but you can set them through the ExIFS.
- Directory rights enable you to control which users can manipulate the object that is created in AD when mail-enabling a public folder.
- Administrator rights enable you to assign specific rights to specific administrators.

> **NOTE** Subfolders only inherit parent folder settings when you create them. If you make changes to the parent folder at a later date, the existing subfolders do not automatically inherit the changes. And, if you've made changes to the subfolder and later choose to propagate settings from the parent folder, the subfolder settings will be modified.

Public folders use individual accounts or distribution lists to define custom security for users. All objects stored in a public folder inherit the permissions. For instance, if there is a Microsoft Word document stored in a folder, then Microsoft Office enforces the permissions that are assigned to the user on the public folder. This capability allows the maintenance of the security of documents from application to application.

Using Outlook, you can only assign client permissions (folder rights). If the Permissions property page is not visible, then you are not logged in as a user who has the Owner role to that public folder.

Using Exchange System Manager, you can set the client permissions, Active Directory object rights, and the folder administrator rights. Right-click the public folder in Exchange System Manager and select the Permissions property tab (shown in Figure 9.7).

Figure 9.7 Public folder Permissions property tab

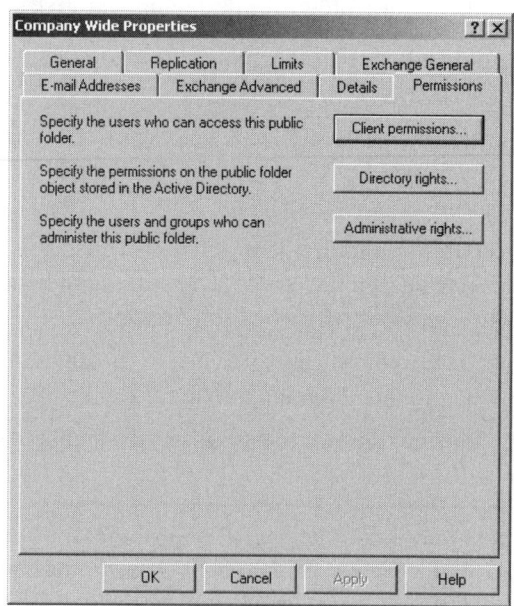

Administrative Rights

An administrator can apply access control to a folder or any resource. These rights allow you to specify the types of things an administrator can do to this folder. Some of the rights that affect public folder administration are shown in Table 9.1.

Table 9.1 Public Folder Administrative Rights

Administrative Right	Meaning
Modify Public Folder ACL	Assign or change the client permissions.
Modify Public Folder Admin ACL	Assign or change the administrative rights.
Modify Public Folder Deleted Item Retention	Change how long deleted items are retained.
Modify Public Folder Expiry	Change the age limits.
Modify Public Folder Quotas	Change warning limit, prohibit post size, and maximum item size.
Modify Public Folder Replica List	Configure folder replication.

I recommend setting the administrative rights at the administrative group level, the top of the hierarchy, or at the tree level, and then making changes only for any exceptions.

Active Directory Rights

Active Directory in Windows 2000 is used to enforce security on Exchange 2000 resources. The operating system manages and enforces permissions that are specific to Exchange 2000 AD. This option is available only if the public folder is mail-enabled.

Client Permissions (or Folder Rights)

You can set public folder permissions using a client application such as Outlook 2000, or through Exchange System Manager. A public folder's Security Settings dialog box (viewed through Outlook 2000) displays the Roles And Permissions page. The role you assign to a user will determine the level of permission he will have. When you assign one of Outlook's predefined roles to a user, she automatically has the permissions associated with the role. When you configure public folder permissions by using Outlook, which displays the legacy roles, Exchange 2000 automatically configures the corresponding Windows 2000 permissions. Figure 9.8 shows the Client Permissions dialog box that is accessible from the folder properties under both Exchange System Manager and Outlook.

Figure 9.8   Client Permissions dialog box

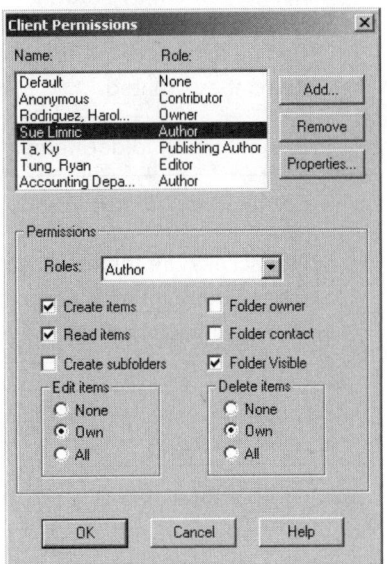

Table 9.2 outlines the predefined roles available in Outlook and describes the permissions associated with each.

Table 9.2 Roles and Client Permissions

Assigning This Role	Gives the User Permission to...
Owner	Read existing folder items, create new items, create subfolders, edit or delete all items, and change access permissions to the folder for other users.
Publishing Editor	Read existing folder items, create new items (including subfolders), and edit or delete all items.
Editor	Read existing folder items, create new items, and edit or delete all items.
Publishing Author	Read existing folder items, create new items (including subfolders), and edit or delete items they created.
Author	Read existing folder items, create new items, and edit or delete items they created.
Non-Editing Author	Read existing folder items, create new items, and delete items they created.
Reviewer	Read existing folder items.
Contributor	Create new folder items.
None	Not access the folder. This is a good default permission when you want to limit the folder audience to only those you specifically add to the Name/Role box.

NOTE On any other public folder information store, or on non-MAPI folder trees, these roles are not displayed when you set permissions on folders using Exchange System Manager. The permissions that are displayed are the same permissions that are displayed in Windows 2000.

WARNING When you press Ctrl and click the Client Permissions button in Exchange System Manager, you will see the Windows 2000 permissions. Do not use this option to set Windows 2000–style permissions on a MAPI folder; use it only to view permissions. If you make changes to a MAPI folder by using Windows 2000 permissions, the folder's permissions are fixed permanently and cannot be modified.

Item-Level Permissions

You use item-level permissions to specify what a user can do with a specific item, such as a message. You can set these permissions by accessing a public folder through the ExIFS. You can also configure standard file-system permissions. Unless you specify permissions for an item, the item automatically inherits the permissions of its parent folder.

A new feature of Exchange 2000 is the ability to support property-level permissions for the MAPI properties. For example, this would allow you to set permissions so that a message item could be read, but the user could not modify its subject line.

NOTE Programmatic configuration is necessary for property-level permissions.

Public-Folder Replication

One of the management decisions you will be faced with when managing public folders is whether or not to replicate the content of your public folders. There are two types of replication with respect to public folders: hierarchy replication and content replication. The Microsoft Exchange Information Store Service is responsible for both types of replication; replication is message-based, meaning that replication information is e-mailed to other public folder stores.

Hierarchy replication is the process of replicating the public folder tree (folder names and properties) to public folder servers. The hierarchy replicates to all public folder stores that have a copy of a particular public folder tree. The information store checks for changes to the hierarchy (new folders, deleted folders, folder property changes) and replicates these once a minute. A hierarchy replication message will be sent to all other servers in the forest that have a copy of that particular public folder tree. You have no control over the replication of the hierarchy.

Content replication is configured on a folder-by-folder basis. The message headers, message body, and any attachments make up content. When a single item in a folder changes, that item is replicated to all servers that have a replica of that folder. You can distribute multiple instances of a public folder to different Exchange 2000 servers and keep them synchronized through public-folder replication.

A public folder can exist in an organization as a single copy or as multiple copies. If multiple copies exist, they are called *replicas*, which are all equal, allowing you to distribute user load on servers, increase fault tolerance through redundancy, distribute public folders based on geography, and back up public folder data. A replica copied from one server to another is a separate instance of a public folder and its contents. There is no master replica. *Public-folder replication* (content and hierarchy) is a mail-based process that relies on SMTP as the replication transport mechanism.

There are a couple of ways to configure public-folder replicas using Exchange System Manager. They can be configured through the Public Folder Instances object or via the Replication tab for a specified folder. Additionally, you can propagate replication settings to subfolders or replicate system folders between servers. Once configured, public-folder replication is automatic.

Different components of public-folder replication are controlled by different services. For instance:

- Active Directory handles the replication of mail-enabled public folder directory objects.

- The Exchange 2000 store takes responsibility for the replication of public folder hierarchies.

- The Exchange 2000 administrator controls the replication of the public folder contents.

NOTE   When you create a public folder, only one copy of the public folder exists within the organization.

Picking a Replication Design

It's best to begin with a simple replication design that includes a single copy of a public folder, because it is likely that the structure of your public folder hierarchy will change often. However, a single-copy public folder design has advantages and disadvantages. Thousands of users attempting to access to a single public folder location will likely create a serious bottleneck. Imagine that your human resources department places the company handbook on the public folder to be shared. Okay, a single-copy public folder design won't take too big of a hit, but what if there's news of a company stock-split and all the employees attempt to access the details regarding their new fortunes? Look out for a lot of frustrated users who can't access the information due to a bottleneck. Another disadvantage is the lack of fault-tolerance for the contents of the public folder.

So you've heard the bad news. Now what's good about a single-copy public folder design?

- Simpler administration
- Lack of concern about bandwidth considerations in terms of replicating the contents of the public folders around the organization

You may be wondering if there are other alternatives. Sure, you could choose to have multiple replicas of a public folder. This design is where the contents of a public folder are located on multiple servers. Multiple replicas offer fault tolerance and load balancing, but at the cost of overhead and increased hardware costs.

Monitoring Modifications and Replication Conflicts

Public-folder replicas provide multiple, redundant information points and load balancing for accessing data. It is important that you understand the concepts and processes of replication so that users can access data without taxing your server or your network loads.

To keep track of replication progress and to determine whether a public folder is synchronized, the public folder store uses:

- Change numbers
- Time stamps
- Predecessor change lists

When more than one instance of a public folder is configured, an information store process called the Public-Folder Replication Agent (PFRA) monitors changes, additions, and deletions. The PRFA also sends change messages to other information stores on which replicated instances are located.

Change Numbers

The *change number* is a globally unique information store identifier and a server-specific change counter. Change numbers are information store–specific, but they also reflect sequential changes. The change counter is not sequential for a single message or folder, but is sequential across all messages and folders on that information store.

When a user makes a change, such as an addition, modification, or deletion, to any message in any public folder located on a particular server, the change counter is incremented to reflect that the contents have been modified. It is the job of the PFRA for that information store to assign a new change number to the message.

Time Stamps

When a message arrives in a public folder, the PFRA on the information store assigns a *time stamp* to the message. If a user modifies the message instance, the PFRA for that information store assigns a new time stamp based on the greater of either the current system time or the old time stamp.

Predecessor Change List

The *predecessor change list* for a message is a list of the information stores that have made changes to the message and the last change number made by each information store. The receiving store checks the information and compares it with its predecessor change list—the key to replication. If the information in the two predecessor change lists matches, the replicated server will update it with the new information.

How It All Works

When a change is made to an instance of a message in a replicated public folder (the *original message*) on a particular information store (the *originating information store*), the PFRA for that information store updates the state information for that message. The PFRA then sends a replication message and all of its attachments to all other information stores that have been configured to maintain a replica of the public folder in which the message resides.

Transit time and the nature of the data needs to be taken into account in estimating replicated changes and updates. Changes replicated over the Internet will not happen as quickly as changes replicated over a dial-up connection. And stores such as stock-market data will be checked and changed much more frequently than policies and procedures manuals. Because multiple people accessing the same message on multiple stores at the same time will lead to conflicting information, it is probably not wise to replicate frequently modified information. If change A happens before change B but doesn't reach the changed record first due to a slow network connection or long replication cycles, the updates will be replicated out of sequence, resulting in a conflict.

At this point, the folder owner and the message originators will get a message revealing that a folder conflict has occurred. Either the originators or the owner will receive both messages, and need to choose which one to apply.

> **NOTE** If two people approve different versions of a saved message, a conflict will occur.

For data that changes rapidly, the number of replicas happening in the organization may need to be minimized unless they are one-way. For one-way replication, such as stock-market data, a *push process* is happening: Only one group is changing the data and distributing it to many different servers and users. For this type of information update, replication is fine. When two or more different groups are modifying folder information, this method is not recommended. Potential conflicts should be considered when deciding to replicate or to use a referral to another routing group.

To view the list of public folder servers maintaining replicas, look at the public folder's Replication tab (Figure 9.9).

Figure 9.9   Public stores that have a replica of the Company Wide public folder

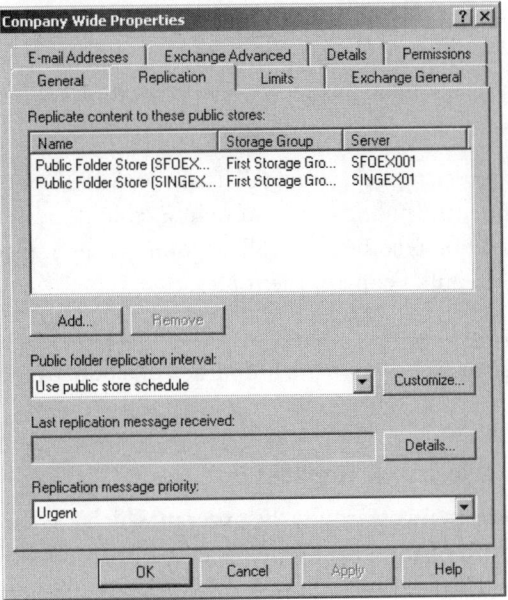

Receiving Messages   When a replication message is received by a public folder store, the new message contained in the replication message is used to replace the existing message. This occurs only if the modification that caused the replication was made against the same message or a later version of the message. Keeping the PFRA in mind, if the change number of the local message is included in the predecessor change list of the update message, then the change is made.

Updating Messages   If the predecessor change list of the update message does not include the change number of the local message, it indicates that the original message was not the same as the local message. This indicates that the original message is older than the local message. If this occurs, a conflict results because the change was made to a version of the message that had not incorporated some previous change on some other information store.

Creating a Public Folder Replica

The Information Store Service replicates the public folder hierarchy to every server using system messages during public-folder replication. However, the contents are not replicated unless an administrator has set up replicas for a particular server. When a user creates a public folder, its location in the hierarchy is replicated to every server. The contents of the new folder are located on the user's default public folder server.

During replication, the information store sends changes made to items in a replica to all other replicas of the public folder throughout the organization. The information store replicates changes made to the folder, the folder's properties, or the public folder hierarchy to all servers. When you no longer want a public folder replica, you can delete it from its database.

To create a public folder replica, select All Tasks ≻ Add Replica from the Public Folder Instances object under the public folder store in Exchange System Manager. This type of replication configuration is sometimes called a *pull process*, since you are configuring the public folder store to pull a copy of the folder.

> **NOTE**   You can also configure the properties of a public folder by using the Replication tab.

Setting Message Priority for Replication

Message priority properties determine the order in which Exchange 2000 sends messages. You can set the priority for replication messages sent by a public folder. Those with an Urgent priority are delivered first, and Normal priority messages are sent after Urgent ones, but before Not Urgent messages. These are delivered last.

To set a priority for replication messages using Exchange System Manager, follow these steps:

1. Expand the Administrative Groups/Administrative Group/Folders container and locate the folder you want to modify.

2. Right-click a folder, click Properties, and then click the Replication tab (shown previously in Figure 9.9).

3. In Replication Message Priority, select Not Urgent, Normal, or Urgent; click OK.

NOTE If there is a significant amount of public folder replication, changing the replication message priority may cause delays in the delivery of end-user e-mail. Increase the priority of a public folder's replication messages *only* if it is critical that replication messages get delivered as soon as possible. Decrease the priority of a public folder's replication messages if the folder's content does not need to interfere with the delivery of normal messages.

Replicating Public Folder Content from Exchange 5.5

Your recently installed Exchange 2000 server will have a default public folder store, but the one thing it won't have is content. To add some, first you must configure the server to replicate with Exchange 5.5 servers. You do not have to replicate the content of all your existing public folders; however, if you are migrating to Exchange 2000, it's wise to replicate your public folder content to Exchange 2000 servers as quickly as possible. You get to determine which public folders will replicate content to the new server. The result of this process is that content that was stored on Exchange 5.5 servers is replicated to Exchange 2000 public stores.

Replicating the Content

If you upgrade an Exchange 5.5 server that is configured to replicate with other Exchange 5.5 servers, the upgraded server retains its Exchange 5.5 content and continues to replicate that content based on settings prior to the upgrade.

To replicate public folder content from Exchange 5.5 servers, follow these steps:

1. Run Exchange System Manager.
2. Expand the administrative groups and locate the one that has the public folder container.
3. In the console tree, expand Folders, and then expand the folder tree that contains the folder you want.
4. Right-click a folder, and then click Properties.
5. On the Replication tab, view the list of servers in Replicate Content To These Public Stores.
6. To add an Exchange 5.5 server, click Add.
7. Select the server from which you want to replicate content.
8. On the Replication tab, you can also decide to use the store's replication schedule, or you can customize a new schedule.

To upgrade an Exchange 5.5 server that has never replicated with other Exchange 5.5 servers, or to add Exchange 5.5 public folders to an Exchange 2000 server, you must:

- Replicate public folder objects to Active Directory.
- Wait for the public folder hierarchy to replicate to the Exchange 2000 server.
- Replicate the content to the server.

Replicating entire public folder trees enables you to configure replication without having to configure the replica server list in a folder's replication properties. To replicate any public folder in the associated public folder tree to the public store that you are administering, follow these steps:

1. Right-click the Public Folder Instances object.
2. Select All Tasks.
3. Click Add Replica.

Mixed versus Native Mode

When you install the first Exchange 2000 server in an Exchange 5.5 site, you create a Mixed-mode environment. For your Exchange 5.5 and Exchange 2000 public folders to function properly in a Mixed-mode environment, the public folder objects must exist in the Windows 2000 Active Directory directory service. Exchange 5.5 public folder information is replicated to AD through an ADC's public folder connection agreement.

If you are upgrading an Exchange 5.5 server that was previously configured to replicate public folders with other Exchange 5.5 servers in your organization, it already contains the hierarchy and the content in the database. Before you upgrade the server to Exchange 2000, you must upgrade the directory objects in Active Directory—but you do not need to create the hierarchy or replicate the content into Exchange 2000 databases.

Public Folder Connection Agreements

Public folder connection agreements (CAs) replicate public folder names between the Exchange Server 5.5 directory and Active Directory. To manage public folder CAs, you use the ADC on a computer running Windows 2000. After domain prep runs in the domain in which you are installing the first Exchange 2000 server, you can create a public folder CA for each of your Exchange 5.5 sites. Then the ADC creates the public folder objects in AD from the Exchange 5.5 directory service. After this, you can verify or set permissions on the folder containers.

Public folder CAs function in the following ways:

- They always use two-way replication.
- Public folders are the only objects you can replicate in a public folder CA. To replicate other objects, you must create different types of CAs.

- For public folder CAs, ADC automatically selects the Windows organizational unit, the Exchange container, and the default destination containers for Windows and Exchange. You cannot change these containers.

- They are always primary CAs from Exchange, and this cannot be changed. This is beneficial because a primary CA can create new objects, whereas all other types of CAs replicate information to existing objects only.

- They cannot be CAs between organizations.

Monitoring Public-Folder Replication

Monitoring public folders is important, especially when using replication. To ensure that public folders are replicating properly, you can view the status of public-folder replication for each folder or for each store.

To view the status of a specific public folder:

1. Right-click the public folder, and then select Properties.

2. From the folder's Properties dialog box, click the Replication tab (shown back in Figure 9.9).

3. On the Last Replication Message Received tab, select the Details button to view the folder's replication status (see Figure 9.10).

NOTE Take what the Replication Details dialog box tells you with a grain of salt. In both Exchange 5.5 and Exchange 2000, I have noticed that this dialog box is not always completely accurate.

Figure 9.10   Replication details

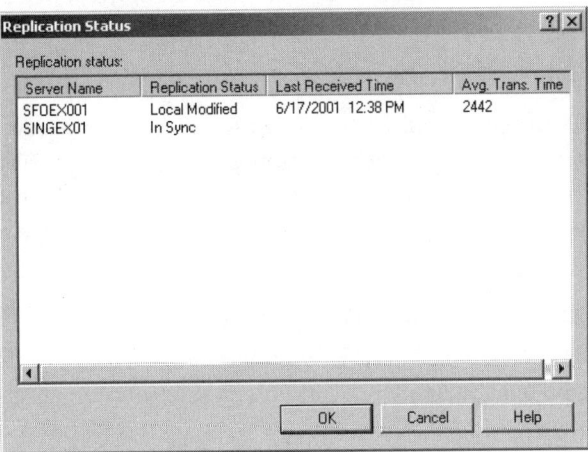

To view the status of all instances of public folders in a particular public folder store:

1. Double-click the public folder store to expand the subcontainers.

2. Select Replication Status from the subcontainers. The status appears in the details pane.

Exceeding Maximum SMTP Message Size

During monitoring, you may discover that public-folder replication messages are exceeding the size limits for message delivery. This is probably happening because users are posting large items to public folders. To allow for replication between public folders, you may need to increase the size limit allowed on inbound SMTP connections. Alternatively, you can restrict the maximum posting size for public folders. If the replication is occurring between routing groups, you can also create an additional connector that permits large messages, but only transports system messages.

Diagnostic Logging for Public Folders

With the use of diagnostic logging, an administrator can take note of replication-related problems and public folder store logons in the Microsoft Exchange environment. The Server Properties ➢ Diagnostics Logging tab enables administrators to set up diagnostic logging. This tab, which you can access by expanding the Information Store Service (MSExchangeIS) and selecting Public Folder, has properties for logging specific to public folders.

The Event Viewer Application Log displays events generated by diagnostic logging. For each category, you can select None, Minimum, Medium, or Maximum logging levels. With each successive level, more information is reported to the application log.

> **WARNING** Take care when turning on diagnostics logging, especially if you turn the logging level to Medium or Maximum on more than a few categories. This will negatively impact performance and produce event logs that are large and difficult to review.

Several event IDs are produced when you set logging to Maximum in the Replication Incoming Messages and Replication Outgoing Messages categories. The event IDs note that replication messages have been either sent or received. If you discover that replication messages are being sent out but not received, try enabling message tracking on the server that is sending the updates.

Replication messages being sent from the public information store are sent from an alias that looks similar to the following (in this example, the server name is SFOEX001):

```
SFOEX001-IS@somorita.net
```

To track public folder replication messages, open Exchange System Manager and then navigate to the Tools ➢ Message Tracking Center container. Then, track messages being sent from SFOEX001-IS@somorita.net (substitute your own server and domain name). This message path will help you to determine where the messages are getting lost. Figure 9.11 shows the message tracking center and a message that was sent from the SFOEX001-IS to SINGEX01-IS.

Figure 9.11 Tracking a public-folder replication message

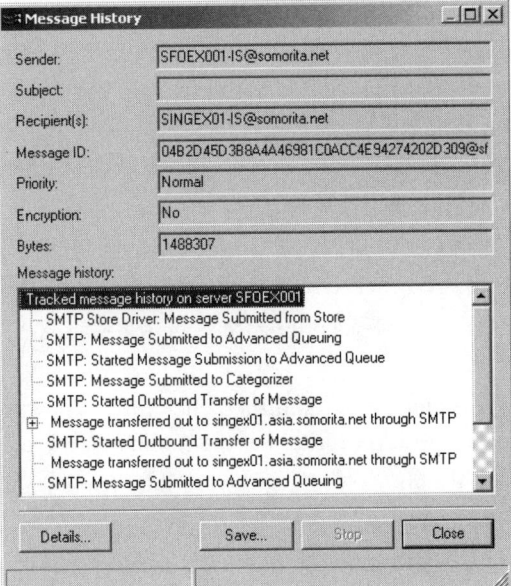

Out of Sync Public Folders and Backfill

Public folders sometimes become out of sync and need to be resynchronized. This can occur for many reasons. For instance, perhaps a change is posted to one information store, but it is lost before it can be replicated to other information stores. Whether it got lost because there was a bad network connection, an administrator mistakenly cleared a queue, or the server was down for maintenance and missed a replication message, the result is the same: The information store is out of sync.

Don't consider this a lost cause. Occasionally—about every three hours—an information store sends out a status message, which is basically a snapshot of the store's present view of the world. Another information store receives the status message, reads it, and realizes that its view is not the same as the information store that sent the message.

This second information store sends a backfill request; *backfill* is the process of re-synchronizing missing information. This request is a plea to have the original information store resend the replicated information. The two public folder stores avoid a knock-down, drag-out fight but must negotiate to determine whose information is out of sync. The winner sends out the updated information.

Assigning a Public Folder a New Home

You may find that you need to rehome public folders from one server to another in Exchange 2000. This may be necessary if you are creating a dedicated public folder server, removing a public folder store, or are about to shut down an older public folder server. To do this:

1. Start Exchange System Manager, click Folders, and then click Public Folders.

2. Right-click a top-level public folder, and then click Properties.

3. Click the Replication tab, click Add, and then add a replica to the target server where you want the folder rehomed.

4. Click Apply, and then click OK.

5. Right-click the same top-level public folder, click All Tasks, and then click Propagate Settings.

6. Select the Replicas check box, and then click OK. When you complete this step, all subfolders of that top-level folder have a replica on the target server.

7. Repeat steps 1 through 6 for all top-level folders and subfolders that you want to rehome.

8. After replicas have been made to the target server, repeat steps 1 through 6, but in step 3, click Remove instead of Add to remove the replicas from the source server.

Offline Replication Capabilities

Exchange 2000 Server and Outlook natively support the ability to replicate public folders—their contents, views, and forms—all offline. This replication allows an user to work with public folders while disconnected from the network, and to synchronize the changes to the offline copy back to the Exchange server. A part of this replication is the ability to filter the items to be replicated offline so that users do not have to replicate large amounts of content to their offline replica. Instead, users can replicate only filtered information from the public folder.

In order for to use the Outlook synchronization features with public folders, the user must first add each public folder to be synchronized to their Favorites list (there is no ability to synchronize multiple public folders at once; each folder must be added to the Favorites list and marked for offline access independently). Once this is done, the user can right-click a folder, choose the Synchronization property page, and click the When Offline Or

Online radio button. Once this is configured, the Outlook client will synchronize the public folders when the rest of the mailbox is synchronized.

Removing a Replica

You can remove a replica using Exchange System Manager by locating the public folder store properties and clicking Public Folder Instances, right-clicking the folder containing the replica that you want to remove, selecting All Tasks, and then clicking Remove Replica.

Public Folder Best Practices

There are some basic things you can do to make creating and managing public folders easier. For instance, you should:

- Develop a public folder strategy before deployment—and make sure all administrators stick to it!
- Restrict who can create top-level public folders to prevent too many root folders.
- Move the Folders container into a separate administrative group.
- Use the Administrator program to propagate permissions and other attributes to large folder trees.
- Focus client connectivity by using server locations, replication, and affinity.
- Review domain trusts for complete client access.
- Deploy public folders with the consideration of providing users with the ability to create collaborative solutions.
- Carefully consider to whom you give administrative rights.
- Fully understand replication, including the fact that the hierarchy replicates to all servers that have a copy of the particular tree.
- Remember that you must have at least one public folder server per site, and you must have at least one public folder store per administration group.

10

Automating Tasks

Automating tasks is a great thing, especially if it helps to lighten your already heavy administrative load. Using scripting, you can automate tasks and schedule them to run. Exchange 2000 already has a number of automated tasks that occur nightly. The most resource-intensive of these tasks occur at night, but there are some that may also occur throughout the day if you are not careful about when you schedule them to run. If you are managing servers that handle many users on a "non-traditional" business day, such as servers that support 24-hour operations or users in many different time zones, then knowledge of these tasks is vital. Some of the automated tasks include information store maintenance, rebuilding offline address books (OABs), and performing full-text indexing. You can write your own automated tasks to run reports, import message tracking logs, or manage user accounts and mailboxes.

Exchange 2000 and Windows 2000 also provide developers with many opportunities for automating tasks using scripts and Exchange 2000 event sinks. Knowledge of these features can help you to further automate the operation of your Exchange servers, develop workflow applications, or optimize performance of your servers. This chapter includes discussions of the following:

- Regularly scheduled maintenance
- Exchange 2000 event sinks
- Scripting and Exchange 2000
- The Microsoft Exchange Event Services
- Client automation

Things That Go Bump in the Night

There are several scheduled processes that run on a scheduled basis on the Exchange server. Most of these operations run at night so that they do not interfere with typical operations. These tasks include information store maintenance, and System Attendant functions such as the DS2MB (Directory Service to Metabase) process, generating storage warnings, OAB generation, and the Recipient Update Service (RUS).

NOTE   The full-text indexing process also runs based on schedules defined for each mailbox or public folder store, if enabled. This process can be very CPU-intensive. Indexing and scheduling indexing are discussed in Chapter 4, "Maintenance and Management."

Information Store Maintenance

Online maintenance is an essential part of keeping an Exchange server running optimally, and fortunately it requires no intervention on the part of administrators. Each Exchange server runs daily maintenance on its mailbox and public folder stores. By default, this maintenance runs between 1:00 A.M. and 5:00 A.M. (local time) each day. This value is configurable for each store on the server.

WARNING   If *any* store in a storage group is undergoing an online backup, any online maintenance that is occurring during that time will halt and will not resume until the backup has completed. If the backup completes before the online maintenance interval ends, then online maintenance will resume and run until it completes. For this reason, it is critical that online backup and online maintenance schedules complement one another.

Online maintenance tasks on the information stores include:

- Generating an LDAP query against an Active Directory (AD) Global Catalog server for each mailbox in the store to confirm that the user account still has a mailbox associated with it. This will generate one query for *each* mailbox; for example, 2000 mailboxes means 2000 LDAP queries generated.

- Performing a hard delete of any mailbox that has been deleted longer than the Keep Deleted Mailboxes For (Days) interval.

- Performing a hard delete of any messages that have exceeded the Keep Deleted Items For (Days) interval.

- Performing an online defragmentation of the stores; the stores remain mounted and in use while the defragmentation occurs.

- Purging folder view indexes that have not been used recently. Eight days is the default.

- Expiring public folder messages that have exceeded the time limit specified on the public folder age limits.

- Removing tombstone information used by public folder replication.

- Expiring newsgroup articles.

Of these tasks, the online defragmentation, purging of deleted messages, and purging of deleted mailboxes are the most system-intensive from the Exchange server's perspective; the Exchange server's disk is the most utilized resource during this process. Performing LDAP queries for each mailbox to confirm that the mailbox is still linked to the AD account is not intensive for the Exchange server, but it can generate quite a load on the AD Global Catalog server.

Recommended Schedules

If your server has a single mailbox store and public folder store, then you probably do not need to worry about staggering the online maintenance intervals. Just keep in mind that the backup process should either not start until you are confident that online maintenance has completed or be completed before the online maintenance interval window starts.

For more complex server arrangements, plan some sort of staggering of the maintenance windows for each store. As an example, Table 10.1 shows an Exchange 2000 server, SFOEX001, with multiple storage groups and stores.

Table 10.1   TSFOEX001 Storage Groups and Stores

Storage Group	Store Name	Users	Estimated Size
First Storage Group	Mailbox Store (SFOEX001)	30	2GB
First Storage Group	Public Folder Store (SFOEX001)	N/A	15GB
First Storage Group	San Francisco Users	600	35GB
VIP Users SG	Executives and Managers	35	10GB
VIP Users SG	Account Managers	50	5GB

Nightly backups should be performed to ensure that the data is recoverable, but the backups should not interfere with the online maintenance, and much of this server's user community works as late as 9:00 P.M. each night. Online backups for this server generally run at about 22GB per hour. The public folders and the Account Managers stores need to be full-text indexed once per day, and this process is very CPU-intensive. Further, online maintenance should be staggered such that each store completes in an optimal amount of time. All that said, here are the recommended backup and online maintenance intervals:

8:00 P.M.: Backup of First Storage Group

11:00 P.M.: Backup of VIP Users SG

12:00 A.M.: Full-text indexing of public folder store

12:30 A.M.: Full-text indexing of Account Managers mailbox store

1:00 P.M. to 2:00 A.M.: Executives and Managers store maintenance interval

2:00 A.M. to 3:00 A.M.: Account Managers store maintenance interval

3:00 A.M. to 4:00 A.M.: Mailbox Store (SFOEX001) maintenance interval

4:00 A.M. to 5:00 A.M.: Public Folder Store (SFOEX001) maintenance interval

5:00 A.M. to 6:00 A.M.: San Francisco Users maintenance interval

In this example, I have staggered the start times of each store's maintenance interval so that it will start at some point after the other stores. I saved the largest store (San Francisco Users) until last. By that time, all backups and other stores' maintenance intervals will be completed.

NOTE Online maintenance begins at the scheduled time and runs until completed or interrupted, even if the maintenance process continues past the maintenance window. The maintenance window does not have to be long enough to allow maintenance to complete each unless you expect a backup process to interrupt the online maintenance. If the maintenance window is still valid, the online maintenance process will resume once the backup is finished if the current time is still within the maintenance interval. If maintenance completes quickly, the maintenance operations may restart later during the interval; however, the subsequent passes will complete much more quickly.

Online maintenance can be scheduled per store or using mailbox or public store policies. I recommend scheduling them per store. To do so, display the store properties and click the Database property tab. You can pick a pre-built schedule (such as 11:00 P.M. until 3:00 A.M., midnight until 4:00 A.M., 1:00 A.M. until 5:00 A.M., or 2:00 A.M. to 6:00 A.M.) or you can create a custom schedule by clicking the Customize button.

Each selection period on the Customize window is an interval of time during which online maintenance can start. If you select several different grid blocks, online maintenance may complete and start again later, provided the maintenance process is still in effect.

Is Online Maintenance Complete?

How do you know if the online maintenance interval has completed? A quick scan of the Windows 2000 application event log will give you that answer. Start looking at the approximate times that online maintenance is supposed to start. The following event IDs will tell you that a particular phase of the maintenance is complete:

Event ID	Source	Description
701	ESE98	Online defragmentation is complete for specified store.
1207	MSExchangeIS Public, MSExchangeIS Mailbox	Cleanup of items past retention date is complete.
9535	MSExchangeIS Mailbox	Cleanup of mailboxes past retention date is complete.

Message expiration and index aging are not logged unless you specify that they should be enabled. (Index aging occurs when folder view indexes have not been used in 30 days.) To turn on event logging for index aging in the public folder or mailbox stores, display the properties of the server and choose the Diagnostics logging tab. For the MSExchangeIS ➢ Mailbox and MSExchangeIS ➢ Public Folder options, set logging to minimum for the Views category.

To enable event logging for public folder message expirations, set the MSExchangeIS ➢ Public Folder Replication Expiry category to minimum.

> **NOTE** Relevant Microsoft Knowledge Base articles relating to online maintenance include Q159196, Q159306, and Q271222.

The System Attendant

The System Attendant performs certain maintenance operations throughout the day and night. Some of these run as needed (such as the RUS and the DS2MB update service), others occur at regular intervals (such as cleaning up message tracking logs), and still others operate on a schedule (such as sending storage warnings and rebuilding OABs). Many of the tasks that the System Attendant performs require queries to an Active Directory domain controller or Global Catalog server. Understanding when and how often these tasks occur can help you to plan for the number and locations of the Global Catalog servers on your network.

Storage Warnings

The System Attendant issues warning messages, following a schedule set forth on the Limits property page of each mailbox or public folder store. The default is to run this daily at midnight, but you can create a custom schedule. Generally I recommend leaving the schedule alone or even reducing it to generating warnings fewer times per week (like Sunday night, Tuesday night, and Thursday night).

NOTE An interesting point about Schedule dialog boxes that have a Detail View choice of 1 hour or 15 minutes: If you select an entire hour, the process you are scheduling will run every 15 minutes! Make sure that if you want the task to run only once during an hour, first change the view using the 15-minute radio button.

Replying to Storage Warning Messages   Many people have asked me how a user can reply to a message sent by the System Attendant that indicates that the mailbox is full. The message originates from the System Administrator, but there is no mailbox by that name. To create an alias that will allow a user to reply to these messages, select the user who will receive the replies. Using Active Directory Users And Computers, display the user's properties and click the E-mail Addresses tab. Add a new Custom Address whose e-mail address is System Administrator and whose E-mail type is SYSTEM:

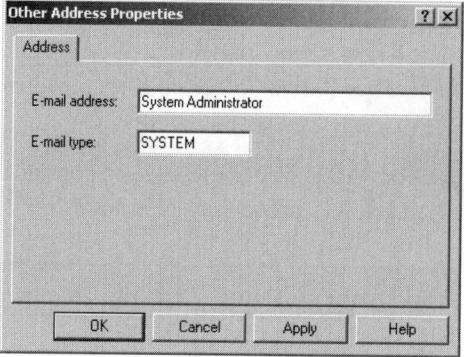

Directory Service to Metabase

The System Attendant runs the DS2MB (directory service to Metabase) process to keep changes relating to the Internet Information Server Metabase synchronized with the Active Directory configuration partition. This is a one-way synchronization (AD to Metabase). Events relating to this process show up in the Event Viewer from a source called MSExchangeMU.

The DS2MB process copies entire subtrees of data from the Active Directory configuration partition and writes the properties to the local Metabase. There is no conversion of the data since it is stored in AD in the same form as in the Metabase. The relative distinguished names of the objects in the AD map directly to the key names in the Metabase.

This process queries the domain controller designated as the configuration domain controller every 15 minutes for updates to the configuration partition. When Exchange 2000 selects a configuration domain controller, it tries to select a domain controller that is not a Global Catalog server; you can view the configuration domain controller on the Exchange 2000 server's General property tab and on the Directory Access property page, or using the DSADiag utility. Note that an administrator may make a change to a different domain controller, so it may take 15 minutes or more for the configuration change to be replicated to the Exchange server's configuration domain controller.

Recipient Update Service

The System Attendant runs a process called the Recipient Update Service (RUS) that is responsible for updating address lists and proxy addresses. Events relating to the RUS appear in the Event Viewer as being from a source called MSExchangeAL. The configuration for the RUS can be found in Exchange System Manager under the Recipients ➤ Recipient Update Service container. Here you will find a RUS object for each domain in your organization (each domain that contains users that will have mailboxes). There is also a RUS (Enterprise Configuration) object, which is responsible for updating address information for objects found in the Active Directory configuration partition.

Each RUS object can be scheduled to run at specific intervals by editing the properties of the object (shown in Figure 10.1). You can configure the RUS to always run, to never run, to run every hour, every two hours, every four hours, or on a custom schedule. The default is Always Run, which means that the RUS checks Active Directory every minute for changes that would require an update, such as new mailboxes or new address lists. If you change the RUS update interval to a longer time, new users will take longer to appear in the address lists and will not get their proxy addresses generated as quickly.

When the RUS runs, you will notice LDAP queries and responses from the Exchange server to a domain controller in the domain for which the RUS is configured to service.

NOTE   For more on the Recipient Update Service, see Chapter 2, "Active Directory for Exchange 2000 Administrations."

Figure 10.1 Recipient Update Service properties

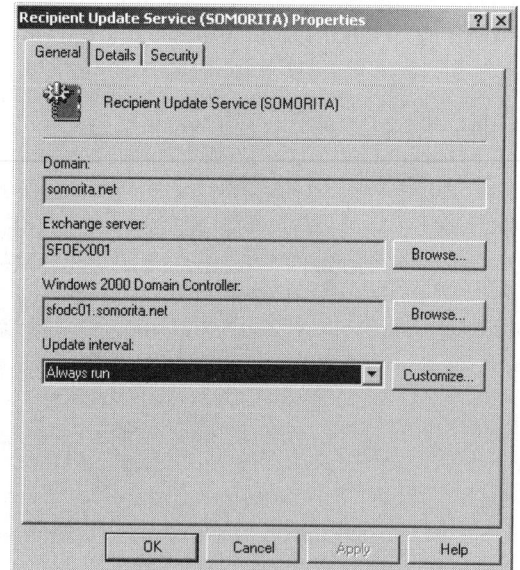

Offline Address Book Generation

The System Attendant is responsible for building the offline address books that you have created. By default, the System Attendant rebuilds these address books at 5:00 A.M., but this interval can be scheduled on each OAB's General property page.

The resources that the regeneration of each OAB consumes will depend on the address book's size. Even an OAB that consists of only a few hundred names can generate thousands of frames and megabytes of network traffic. An OAB with more than 10,000 names could take 45 minutes or longer to generate. For this reason, you may want to schedule different update intervals for different OABs to prevent the system from being overwhelmed at any given point.

> **WARNING** If you set a custom schedule for the offline address book update interval, make sure you are selecting the times in 15-minute intervals. If you select an entire hour, the OAB will be regenerated four times that hour!

You can turn on diagnostics logging for OAB generation on the Exchange server properties (in Exchange System Manager). Simply click the Diagnostics Logging property page, locate the MSExchangeSA service, and enable logging for the OAB Generator.

Exchange 2000 Event Sinks

A fascinating improvement to Exchange 2000 is the addition of event sinks. An *event sink* is nothing more than a bit of script or compiled code that is called when a specified event occurs. Event are fired when the message is saved to the information store or when it is submitted to the SMTP routing engine. Even if you are programmatically impaired (such as I am), it's easy to recognize the enormous potential of event sinks to automate some types of operations that occur within Exchange.

Microsoft even incorporates the use of store and transport event sinks into the day-to-day operations of Exchange 2000. Content indexing, workflow, unified messaging, and message routing all use event sinks to accomplish their particular tasks. Even Active Directory uses SMTP event sinks when using SMTP-based directory replication between sites.

Don't confuse event sinks with the Event Service that originated with Exchange 5.5 (and continues to be supported for backward compatibility in Exchange 2000). Event Service scripts are registered for a single folder, whereas Exchange 2000 event sinks can be registered for the entire information store or the entire message transport. Event sinks can run either asynchronously or synchronously depending on the particular event; this means that they can react to an event not only after they occur, but before they are finished. All Exchange 5.5 events ran as asynchronous events. Essentially, the developers have given us a way to alter the behavior of Exchange to better suit a specific business model.

Event sinks can be broken down into three categories:

Store events take place in the information store. You will see these events referred to as *Web storage system events* in the Microsoft Exchange Software Development Kit. Store events allow you to manipulate messages in the store when they are saved, deleted, or changed, or at a specific time. The store also has events that are triggered by the startup or shutdown of a store; while these are messaging related, they may be useful for administrative tasks.

Transport events take place within the STMP Message Transport system. They allow you to change the behavior of how messages are processed in the Advanced Queuing Engine.

Protocol events allow you to change the behavior of the SMTP or NNTP protocols. For example, you could change the behavior of the SMTP "Mail From" command verb so that it immediately checks to see if the recipient is valid in Active Directory and rejects the message if it is not.

Operations

PART 2

WARNING Any event sink that you implement in Exchange 2000 should be tested carefully before being put into production. An improperly implemented event sink or an event sink that fires on every message the Exchange server processes can quickly destroy server performance.

Exchange@Work: Processing Forms Using an Event Sink

Company FGH has salespeople all over the world. They needed a method whereby their remote salespeople could enter sales statistics and orders. Creating a web page seemed to be the ideal way to do this, but a pilot project indicated that this method didn't work as well as everyone thought it would because of the amount of time that it took to enter the data. This was compounded by the fact that many times throughout the remote salesperson's day, they were not near a telephone line.

To solve the problem, a custom form was developed using Outlook 2000 that allowed the remote salespeople to enter their sales data directly into a mail message. This data could be saved and edited until they were ready to transmit it at the end of the day.

The messages using the custom forms were all sent to a specific mailbox on the Exchange server; when the message arrived, an event sink script fired, opened the message, extracted the data, and imported it into an SQL database.

This solution worked great for Company FGH because the salespeople could enter data periodically throughout the day, but remain offline. The solution was not only easy to use, but it saved a substantial amount of money in long-distance phone charges.

Types of Store Events

There are three types of store events: synchronous, asynchronous, and system. An application that uses a *synchronous event* can modify the item before it's saved to the store, prevent it from being saved to the store, or, in the case of a delete event, prevent it from being deleted from the store. Because the application is called before the item is saved, the application has an opportunity to modify the item before any client can access it or is even aware that it is there. Generally, synchronous events are not available to scripting languages; since synchronous events block threads in the store service, great care must be taken when implementing them. Code that executes within a synchronous event must complete before the item can be saved to the store, so it is important to ensure that synchronous event sink code does not delay the saving of the item more than is necessary.

One application that might be useful for synchronous events is content inspection. Below are the two of the synchronous event sink methods:

- OnSyncSave events execute when a message is saved to the store, but they execute before the message is actually committed.

- OnSyncDelete events execute when a message is deleted from the store, but they execute before the message is actually deleted.

Asynchronous event sinks fire after the item has been saved to the store. They should be used as a notification or when it is not necessary to modify the item before it is saved. Asynchronous event sinks are not guaranteed to fire in a particular order, nor are they certain to have access to the item that caused the event to fire. Useful applications of asynchronous events include automated processing of messages such as messages delivering data to another application. There are two asynchronous event sink methods:

- OnSave events are called when a message is saved to the store, but only after the message is completed committed to the store.

- OnDelete events are called when a message is deleted from the store, but only after the message has been deleted.

The *system events* available are not related to operations on message items in the store, but rather to the operation of the Exchange server and the store itself. Useful applications for system events include running scripts when a specific store is mounted or dismounted (which, of course, includes when the server is shut down) and running a script based on a clock timer. Here are three system event sink methods:

- OnTimer events are called based on a schedule or a time interval. For example, an OnTimer event might be used to check the aging time of items in a folder used for problem submissions, and then send an escalation e-mail to a manager for each item more than an hour old.

- OnMDBStartUp events are called when an information store is mounted. These events might be used to restore share folders within the web store when a store is restarted.

- OnMDBShutdown events are called when an information store is dismounted. These events might be used to save information that needs to be used when a store restarts, such as saving shared folder information within the web store.

Operations

PART 2

NOTE   For more information on store (or Web storage system) events, download the Exchange 2000 Software Development Kit (SDK) from msdn.microsoft.com/exchange. Documentation for the Exchange 2000 SDK and Web storage system events can be found at msdn.microsoft.com/library/default.asp; browse down through Enterprise Development, .NET Enterprise Servers, and Microsoft Exchange Server to get to the documentation.

Transport and Protocol Events

Exchange 2000 is built on the Windows 2000 SMTP transport event architecture. There are two main categories of SMTP service events: protocol events and transport events. As mentioned earlier, protocol events affect the SMTP communication between the SMTP client and the SMTP server by modifying inbound and outbound command verbs and responses to those commands. Transport events occur when messages flow through the SMTP core transport system, whether the message is sent to another machine or delivered locally. Transport event sinks can be fired at a number of places as a message passes through the Advanced Queuing Engine. Figure 10.2 shows the message transport architecture and some of the places event sinks can be executed. The most common privately developed sinks will either be OnSubmissionEvent or CDO_OnArrivalEvent, since these events are fired when a message enters the Advanced Queuing Engine.

Figure 10.2   Advancing queuing and event sinks

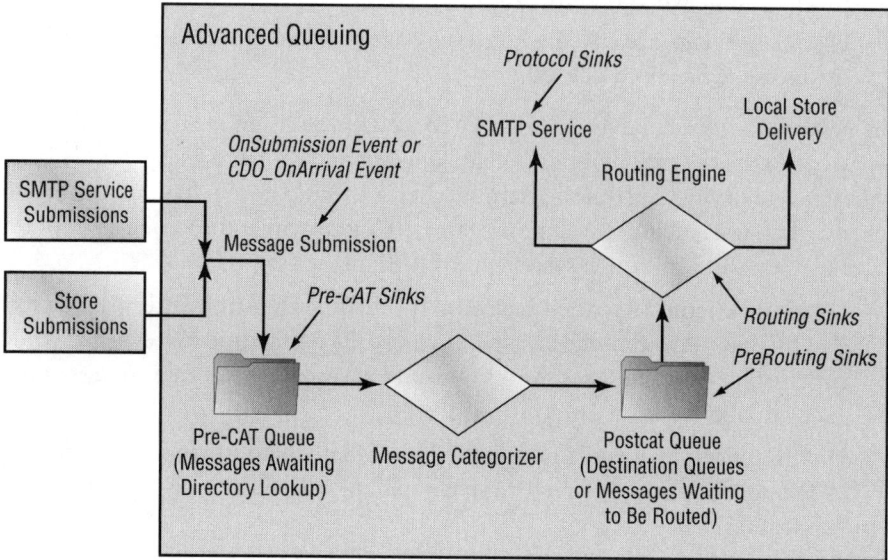

> **NOTE**   Much of the message routing and message categorizer architecture that enhances the Windows 2000 SMTP service is using "in process" event sinks, or event sinks that run as part of the Advanced Queuing Engine. Third-party and privately developed sinks run "out of process." Running a sink "out of process" prevents the sink from crashing the SMTP service.

The event sink architecture in Figure 10.2 allows you to customize message flow and add custom actions as messages flow between servers. Additionally, protocol events can be used to modify the SMTP protocol to add new Extended SMTP (ESMTP) commands or even to change the action of existing ones.

With protocol events, you could perform billing and charge-back computations based on the number and length of connections, or perhaps monitor systems through SMTP by implementing new ESMTP commands. Transport events can do much more than protocol events. You can use them to:

- Forward all mail for a domain to a mailbox.
- Add a disclaimer to the end of each message that leaves your network.
- Scan all incoming mail from the Internet for keywords, subjects, and attachment filenames that might be used for applications that check for spam, viruses, or other types of content inspection.

Transport and protocol events are run every time a message enters or leaves the server, so the code behind them needs to be fast. For production servers, these sinks should be developed using C or C++.

Operations

PART 2

Want More Details?

For more information about transport and protocol event sinks and scripting, check out the following:

- See the CDO (Collaborative Data Objects) for Windows 2000 and SMTP server events for Windows 2000 sections of MSDN on the Web at msdn.microsoft.com.

- CDO guru Siegfried Weber has two excellent websites devoted to development using CDO: www.cdolive.com and www.cdolive.net.

- Technical Editor Andy Webb also has a growing archive of scripts on the Simpler-Webb web site at www.swinc.com/resource/scripts.htm.

- For information on MSDN, remember to look under Windows 2000 for information on developing transport and protocol events, since these are basically features that support the Windows 2000 SMTP service and are not specific to Exchange 2000.

- Mindy Martin's book *Programming Collaborative Web Applications with Microsoft Exchange 2000 Server* (Microsoft Press, 2000) comes highly recommended by developers working with Exchange 2000.

Want More Details? *(continued)*

- Another useful book is *Programming Microsoft Outlook and Microsoft Exchange* by Thomas Rizzo (Microsoft Press, 2000).

- Consider taking Microsoft Official Curriculum course #2019—Building Solutions in Microsoft Exchange 2000 with the Web Storage System.

Developing Event Sinks

The event architecture is based on Microsoft's Component Object Model (COM), and the event sinks are simply COM objects that take advantage of the appropriate COM interfaces. An event sink can be developed in a language as simple as VBScript or JavaScript using Collaborative Data Objects (CDO); however, not all of the event interfaces are exposed through CDO, and so the capabilities of event sinks developed in VBScript or JavaScript will be limited. And since VBScript and JavaScript scripts are interpreted rather than executed as a compiled application, performance may be poor. For event sinks that have the potential to fire on every message that the server processes, a higher performance language such as C or C++ should be used. All of the event interfaces are available to languages such as C or C++.

Event sink developers have a couple of development libraries at their disposal including Active Data Objects (ADO), Collaborative Data Objects (CDO), and Collaborative Data Objects for Exchange Management (CDOEXM). These libraries access the Exchange OLEDB layer to interact with the Exchange server. Accessing ADO libraries directly can prove complex and requires the use of, Visual Basic, C, or C++. However, ADO-based applications may provide an application whose performance is better than an application based on CDO. The choice of a library will depend entirely on the application you are developing. ADO applications are much more efficient at traversing a folder or folder hierarchy, and its query and recordset handling is much better. However, developing an application that creates a meeting or sends a message will be much simpler with CDO.

The CDO library has proven to be extremely popular with developers, because the CDO library provides an easy way to create, manipulate, and send Internet messages. The new version of CDO provides an easy-to-use interface to ADO 2.5. CDO can be accessed from VBScript, Visual Basic, JavaScript, C, or C++. There are a couple of different flavors of CDO:

- CDO 1.2x provides a wrapper for MAPI functions and is used primarily with Exchange 5.5.

- CDO 2.0 provides access to Windows 2000 SMTP messaging functionality, but no Exchange-specific features.

- CDO 3.0 provides a wrapper for Exchange 2000 OLEDB and HTTP/DAV. Though CDO 1.2x will work with Exchange 2000, CDO 3.0 provides better performance and access to much more of the Exchange 2000 functionality.

Newly introduced with Exchange 2000 is CDOEXM, which is yet another collection of COM objects and interfaces aggregated from CDO and Active Directory Services Interface (ADSI) objects. With CDOEXM you can programmatically manage Microsoft Exchange 2000 Server, items in the stores, and store recipients (users). You can create, move, copy, reconfigure, monitor, or delete these items.

CDOEXM encapsulates and simplifies many programmatic tasks that are specific to managing Exchange 2000 Server. It is useful for system administrators who need to do such things as archive stores every week, monitor the stores, set storage limits, set proxy addresses, create mailboxes and recipients, move and delete mailboxes, mail-enable public folders, create mailbox and public stores, or manage the server remotely. You can also use CDOEXM for server tasks typically used in Internet applications, such as automatic provisioning of users and e-mail management.

Sample Event Sinks

To give you an idea of how to install an event sink, let's take a very simple VBScript script and register it as a store event sink. The code for this script (NewItemAlert.VBS) can be downloaded from `www.somorita.com`. This script was developed by Siegfried Weber of CDOLive (`www.cdolive.net`) to monitor a public folder and notify a recipient (`Everyone@domain.com`) if a new item is posted to this folder. The folder is specified when the script is registered, not in the script itself. For this example, I will call this script `NewItemAlert.VBS` and put it in C:.

Registering a Store Event

Before you register the script, you need to get Exchange 2000 configured to properly execute script-based store events. To do this, you will need to follow these steps to register a new COM+ application on the Exchange server:

1. Run the Component Services console (Start ➤ Programs ➤ Administrative Tools ➤ Component Services).
2. Open the Component Services ➤ Computers ➤ My Computer ➤ COM+ Applications container.
3. Right-click COM+ Applications and choose New ➤ Application.
4. Click Next, and then choose the Create An Empty Application button.
5. Enter a name for your application such as ScriptEventSink.
6. Confirm that the Server Application radio button is selected, and then click Next.

7. Select a user who will have owner permissions to the application you are creating, or choose the current user by selecting the Interactive User—The Current Logged On User radio button.

8. Click Next, and then click Finish.

9. Open the newly created COM+ Applications folder, right-click the Components subfolder, and choose New ➢ Component.

10. Click Next, then choose Install New Component(s).

11. Click Add, browse the file system, and select \Exchsrvr\Bin\EXODBESH.DLL. Then click Next and Finish.

12. You need to register two DLL files that are found in the \Exchsrver\Bin directory. At the command prompt, change to that directory and type **regsvr32 exodbesh.dll** and then type **regsvr32 exodbprx.dll**.

13. Either restart the Exchange server or right-click My Computer under Component Services ➢ Computers and select Refresh All Components.

Now that store-based scripts have been configured to execute property, you can write your application and register the event to fire for a specific folder. In the previous example, I called the script NewItemAlert.VBS and placed the script in the C: directory. To register the event, type this command at the command prompt:

```
cscript RegEvent.vbs Add "OnSave" ExOleDB.ScriptEventSink.1
↳"file://./backofficestorage/yourdomain.com/public
↳ folders/YourFolder/NewItemAlert" -f c:\NewItemAlert.vbs WHERE
↳ "DAV:ishidden" = FALSE
```

This will register this event sink for the folder called YourFolder. The script is now ready to run.

Registering a Transport Event

If you need to register a transport event rather than a store event, the procedure is a little different. You need to use SMTPREG.VBS to register this script and set its properties. The SMTPREG.VBS script can be found on the Exchange 2000 SDK. This example shows how to register a script called C:\SubjectFilter.vbs on the Exchange 2000 server. First, type

```
cscript smtpreg.vbs /add 1 onarrival SMTPSubjectFilter
↳CDO.SS_SMTPOnArrivalSink "mail from=*"
```

Now set the properties on the script so that the Advanced Queuing Engine actually knows where to find the script file. To do this, type

```
cscript smtpreg.vbs /setprop 1 onarrival SMTPSubjectFilter Sink
ScriptName c:\SubjectFilter.vbs
```

Event sinks are registered with the IIS Metabase. In the input above, SMTPSubjectFilter is the name of the script as it will be registered with the IIS Metabase.

> **NOTE** On Exchange 2000 RTM servers, you may have to reboot the server to get the scripts to begin processing.

> **NOTE** For sample scripts and information about event sinks, visit Siegfried Weber's website at www.cdolive.net. Compaq has two white papers that are also helpful for learning scripting relating to Exchange 2000; these are "Part 1: Introduction to the Use of Exchange 2000 with Windows Script Host" and "Part 2: Managing Exchange with Scripts, Advanced Topics." Links to both of these documents can be found at www.exinternals.com in the white papers section.

Determining What Event Sinks Are Installed

Whether you are looking for transport events or store events will determine what event sinks are installed. If the event sink is a store event, you can use the Web Storage System Explorer or the REGEVENT.VBS script to find registered store events. You can also search for events programmatically by searching for any property DAV:contentclass with values storeeventreg or workflowprocessdefinition.

Searching for transport event sinks is a bit easier. You can use the transport event sink registration that is included with the Exchange Software Development Kit. Simply type **cscript smtpreg.vbs /enum** to list the events.

There is also a tool on the www.exinternals.com website called the Transport Event Sink Registration Wizard that clearly and easily shows which event sinks are registered and active. However, this tool requires that Visual Basic 6 be installed on the server.

Scripting and Exchange 2000

There are many ways to automate and ease your administrative tasks using scripts in Windows 2000. Library functions from ADSI and CDOEXM allow you to access Active Directory and Exchange 2000 easily. The following section discusses a couple of sample scripts that I have found useful.

> **WARNING** I have tested each of the following scripts, but I am neither a developer nor a scripting wizard, so please don't contact me for technical support. You can download these scripts from my website at www.somorita.com, and if you have scripts that you would like to share with the rest of the Exchange community, feel free to forward them to me.

One of the most common questions that Exchange administrators ask is how to change the display name in Active Directory without having to do this automatically. You can find a script that does this on the web site www.somorita.com.

NOTE You can find additional information about Active Directory and Windows scripting in Charles Opperman's book *Microsoft Windows 2000 Active Directory Programming* (Microsoft Press, 2001) or Jeffrey Honeyman's *Scripting Windows 2000* (McGraw-Hill, 2000).

Creating a User and Mailbox Object

Another useful script feature is the ability to create user accounts and assign mailboxes from a script. The following script creates a user account and assigns it a mailbox; if you use this script, make sure that you adjust all of the LDAP parameters to fit your own organization. The line that starts with Set ou = GetObject sets the appropriate container in Active Directory to create the object. The line that starts with objMailbox.CreateMailbox is long; it sets the configuration container that contains the mailbox stores.

```
SG="Mailbox Store (SFOEX001),cn=First Storage Group"


Set ou = GetObject("LDAP://ou=Finance,dc=somorita,dc=net")
Set usr = ou.Create("user", "cn=MEstrada")
usr.Put "samAccountName", "MEstrada"
usr.givenName = "Manfred"
usr.sn = "Estrada"
usr.displayName = "Estrada, Manfred"
usr.title = "Executive Director"
usr.telephonenumber = "(415) 555-1228"
usr.l = "San Francisco"
usr.st = "California"
usr.postalCode = "94119"
usr.department = "Operations"
usr.Company = "Somorita Surfboards"
usr.SetInfo


Set objMailbox = usr
```

```
objMailbox.CreateMailbox ("LDAP://sfodc01.somorita.net/CN=" + SG +
⤷",cn=InformationStore,CN=SFOEX001,

⤷cn=Servers,CN=First Administrative Group,cn=Administrative
⤷Groups,cn=Somorita Surfboards,cn=Microsoft

⤷Exchange,cn=Services,cn=configuration,dc=somorita,dc=net")


objMailbox.EnableStoreDefaults = FALSE

objMailbox.StoreQuota = 10000


usr.setPassword "password"

usr.AccountDisabled = False

usr.SetInfo


wscript.echo "User and mailbox created"
```

Event Services

Exchange Server 5.5 introduced an Event Service as one of the options that can be installed with the standard Exchange services. It is also included with Exchange 2000 for backward compatibility, and is now called the Microsoft Exchange Event Service. This service is set to start manually, so don't forget to start it and set it to Automatic if you plan to use it.

The Event Service watches public folders and folders in mailboxes that have an agent associated with them. Agents are triggered when:

- A new message is created.
- An item is changed in the folder.
- An item is deleted.
- A scheduled event occurs.

When the agent is triggered, it runs the script associated with the folder that performs whatever action the script writer intended. It should be noted that there are some limitations in the Event Service that are addressed by Exchange 2000 store event sinks. Event Service events run asynchronously. A newly arrived message may not be processed before an Event Service script has an opportunity to run the script.

Enabling Event Agents and Permissions

Even though the Event Service is installed and you have started it, it's not enabled within Exchange or accessible by the clients. Two different actions must be taken to make the services function as required. First, the Microsoft Exchange Event Service must be enabled within the Exchange Administrator. Second, the Outlook client must be enabled to see the Agents tab.

To configure the Event Service, access the Exchange System Manager, open the Public Folders hierarchy, right-click, and choose View System Folders. Once the system folders are visible, you'll find the Events Root folder; it is here that permissions are granted for users that need to publish scripts. A separate folder is created under the Events Root for each Exchange server within the organization that has the Event Service started (such as this sample folder EventConfig_SFOEX001). If you do not see any folders in the Events Root folder, it is because the Microsoft Exchange Event Service has not been started on any servers.

> **NOTE** Ensure that the Event Service is enabled on the server where the scripting needs to be processed. The best place for the event scripting service to be enabled is on a public folder server. In some cases, you may have an event scripting service on private folders to support collaborative solutions for resource booking or company calendars.

To enable management of the Event Service, event managers must be granted permission to use them. Only those users with the Owner role to the EventConfig_*ServerName* folder will have the capability to install agent scripts on the folders. Once agent scripts are installed, those users who are granted Editor permissions within the EventConfig_*ServerName* folder can modify the scripts or the schedules installed. These permissions do not override the permissions that are granted to the users on the folders; they just define the users' roles for the generation of events.

Users will not see the Agents tab for the folders until they have installed the scripting agent add-in. To enable this capability, the user selects Tools ➢ Options, chooses the Other tab, and then selects Advanced Options ➢ Add-In Manager. The dialog box that opens lists the add-ins available to the client. Checking the Server Scripting selection enables and displays the Agents tab on all folder property displays.

> **NOTE** If Server Scripting is not a displayed option, click the Install button in the Add-In Manager dialog box and select the scrptxtn.ecf file to install it. This file is found in the \Program Files\Microsoft Office\Office\Addins directory.

Creating Event Agents

Once the Event Service is enabled and the Outlook client can see the Agents tab, Outlook can be used to create scripts to perform functions based upon events that happen within this folder. Those events occur when an item in the folder is created, changed, deleted, or based upon a scheduled event.

The best way to explain the usage of scripts and how to create and install an agent is to use a common example. You may have noticed using Outlook's group scheduling features that when you want to see if a user is available, you can select the Attendee Availability tab of the meeting request (see Figure 10.3). From this property page, you can click the Invite Others button and invite Required and Optional attendees. The Attendee Availability page will show you whether or not the person you select is available.

Figure 10.3   Scheduling a meeting using attendee availability information

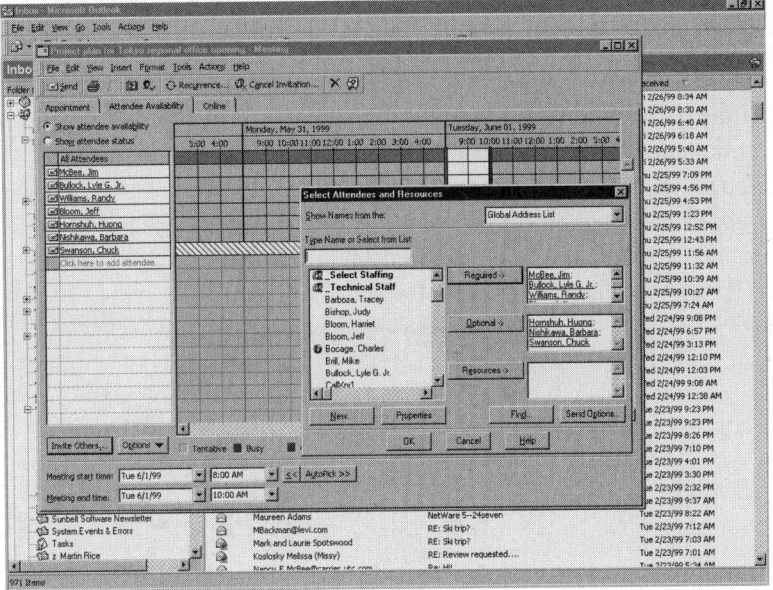

Notice also in Figure 10.3 that the Select Attendees And Resources dialog box is open in the foreground; you get this dialog box by clicking the Invite Others button. From here, you can also select resources such as conference rooms, overhead projectors, and so on. The problem with selecting resources such as conference rooms is that there has to be a copy of Outlook running with that mailbox open somewhere. Otherwise, the meeting never gets booked for the conference room. If you use the Event Service, a script could be developed to automatically accept meeting requests for times when the resource is available.

Exchange@Work: Automatically Accepting Conference Room Bookings

Company JWM uses many conference rooms and resources. They did not want to leave a copy of Outlook open to automatically schedule these resources; they had to find a way to get resources to automatically be booked. Here is the process they went through.

First, the resources had to be created. They began by creating a mailbox for each resource. (You may recall from Chapter 2 that I recommended creating a separate recipient container called Resources just for this purpose.) For example, they created a mailbox with the display name !HNL 3rd Floor Conference Room (they put an exclamation mark in front of all of their shared resources so that they sort to the top of the global address list, and they include the location of the resource as part of its name).

Next, they made sure that the event scripting service was running and enabled as described earlier. To do so, they needed to open this resource mailbox from within Outlook, create a messaging profile, and log on to the mailbox.

Once they got the mailbox open, they highlighted the Inbox for their conference room resources and right-clicked to display the properties of the Inbox. Then they selected the Agents property page and clicked the New button to see the New Agents dialog box. In the Agent Name box, they entered Automatically Accept Appointments and clicked the A New Item Is Posted In This Folder check box. Now any time a new item is posted to this folder, the script will run.

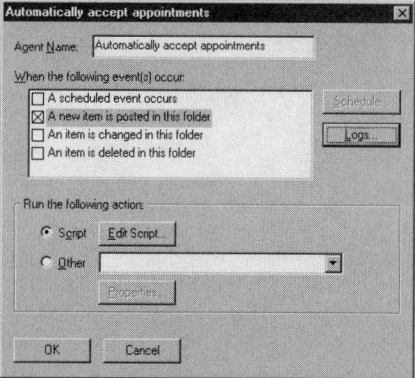

To edit the script, they clicked the Edit Script button and opened Notepad with a VBScript program in it—well, at least the shell of the script. Here is where they would write their script to automatically accept appointments. There is an Auto Accept script that can be downloaded from www.exchangecode.com, but as of this writing, it is recommended only for Exchange 5.5.

Client Automation

No one wants to individually "visit" every workstation on their network each time new software has to be installed or a user needs to create a new profile. Yet that is exactly what many administrators do, and these visits are time consuming. Visiting each workstation over and over again is a thing of the past; there are a number of ways that you can automatically deploy software, including Windows 2000 Group Policy Objects and Microsoft Systems Management Server, to the desktop in an automated or semi-automated way.

Microsoft provides some tools for automating the distribution of Outlook, automatically creating messaging profiles, and making changes to the user's environment. While this book does not go into depth on any of these tools, they include the following:

- Outlook 97 deployments can be made simpler and more automated with the Office 97 Network Installation Wizard.

- Outlook 98 installation and configuration can be automated with the Outlook 98 Deployment Kit.

- Outlook 2000 deployment and configuration can be automated using the Custom Installation Wizard found on the Office 2000 Resource Kit (you can download this from www.microsoft.com/Office). An updated version of this software that you can download will support Outlook 2002 and Office XP.

- You can automatically create Exchange profiles with the automated profile generator utility (PROFGEN).

Your Windows NT network should include the use of logon scripts and server-based home directories. Any utility that is going to automatically install software must be initiated somehow. One of the more reliable ways to do this is through the logon scripts.

Automatically Creating Profiles

The messaging profile contains a user's preferences regarding which Exchange server their mailbox is located on, the mailbox name, the personal folders that they use, and more. This profile is created in one of three ways:

- By the user the first time they launch Outlook
- By the administrator using the Mail (or Mail and Fax) Control Panel application
- By some type of automated process

When Outlook is launched, it looks for the default messaging profile. If this profile does not exist, a program called NEWPROF is run to create it. NEWPROF can be found in the \Program Files\Windows Messaging\ directory. NEWPROF searches the Registry and the local hard drive for a profile definition file (PRF), which contains the preferences of a user's messaging profile. It first looks in the following Registry key for default profile information (for Outlook 2000):

\HKLM\Software\Microsoft\Office\9.0\Outlook\Setup\PRF

If NEWPROF does not find the required profile information in the Registry, then it looks for the OUTLOOK.PRF file in the \Program Files\Microsoft Office\Office directory. If no PRF configuration information exists on the machine, the Outlook Setup Wizard is launched. The Outlook Setup Wizard asks the user which information services should be used, the server name, and the mailbox name; from this information a profile is created.

NOTE Outlook 2002 includes tools to automatically create an Exchange profile.

The Roving-User Profile Generator (PROFGEN)

Creating profiles using the NEWPROF utility is tedious at best. This is mainly because NEWPROF is not very good at determining the correct mailbox name to use. Microsoft introduced a program with the Exchange 2000 Resource Kit called PROFGEN (Profile Generator), which improves on NEWPROF's capabilities; PROFGEN require the presence of NEWPROF.

The purpose of PROFGEN was to automatically create profiles for users who work at more than one desktop and for users who have mandatory profiles (a profile that they share with many people and cannot change). PROFGEN can also be used to greatly simplify deployment of new clients.

When PROFGEN runs, it searches for a valid OUTLOOK.PRF file, obtains the Windows NT domain user ID, modifies the MailboxName= entry in the OUTLOOK.PRF file, and, when the process is completed, renames the OUTLOOK.PRF file to OUTLOOK.PR~. Table 10.2 lists the switches available for the PROFGEN program.

Table 10.2   PROFGEN Command-Line Switches

Switch	Function
-U	Substitutes the current Windows NT domain account name in the MailboxName= line in the PRF file.
-P *path*\OUTLOOK.PRF	Determines the path and name of the PRF file to be used.
-N	Uses the current Windows NT domain account name as the name of the profile.

Table 10.2   PROFGEN Command-Line Switches *(continued)*

Switch	Function
-I *login_ID*	Uses the specified login ID instead of the current user.
-J	In any place in the PRF file that has a $USERNAME$, substitutes for the current login ID.
-L	Creates a log file named C:\PROFGEN.LOG.
-R	Does not rename the PRF file when finished.
-T *path*	Specifies the path to the temporary file created when PROFGEN runs. If nothing is specified, the default is C:.
-X	Runs the NEWPROF program with the –X option so that it starts automatically. Must be used with the –P option.

The PROFGEN utility can be further customized using the PROFGEN.INI file. A sample of the PROFGEN.INI file can be found in the \BORK\Exchange directory of the BackOffice Resource Kit.

> **NOTE**   The PROFGEN utility documentation can be found in the PROFGEN.DOC file in the BackOffice Resource Kit \BORK\Exchange directory.

Using the PROFGEN Utility

Using the PROFGEN utility is a little tricky only because you must provide the path to the correct NEWPROF.EXE. There is a Windows NT/2000 and a Windows 95/98 NEWPROF utility. Here is an example of how to keep things straight:

1. In a shared directory, create a subdirectory called \WinNT and a subdirectory called \Win95.
2. Create a shared directory in each site called Outlook.
3. Copy the NEWPROF.EXE from each operating system into its respective directory.
4. Copy the PROFGEN.EXE utility and the OUTLOOK.PRF file to the Outlook shared folder. Make sure that you have modified the OUTLOOK.PRF file so that the line that has the HomeServer= statement in it contains the name of one of the servers in your site.

In the logon script, you are going to have to determine which operating system is running the logon script before you can execute the PROFGEN utility. There are a lot of better ways to do this, but in this example, I am just checking for the existence of certain operating system–specific files. Here is a simple example taken from a logon script:

```
@Net use i: \\sfofp001\outlook /y
@if exist c:\winnt\system32\ntoskrnl.exe goto WINNT
@if exist c:\windows\command\chkdsk.exe goto WIN95
@goto end
:WINNT
@I:
@Profgen y:\winnt\newprof.exe -P Y:\default.prf -N -R
@Goto end
:WIN95
@Profgen y:\win95\newprof.exe -P Y:\default.prf -N -R
:end
c:
net use I: /delete /y
```

There are a lot of ways to handle launching PROFGEN, and there are utilities for detecting what type of operating system is running the logon script. See the Windows 2000 Resource Kit utility GETTYPE.EXE.

Profile Maker

While PROFGEN and NEWPROF are free, you will get what you paid for. They will work in most cases, but automating creation of profiles can still cause you headaches. A favorite tool of many Exchange administrators is AutoProf's Profile Maker (www.autoprof.com). This tool allows you configure virtually all settings in Outlook centrally and all of the Outlook client services I have ever heard of including Exchange server, PST files, PAB files, OAB, Microsoft Mail, Microsoft LDAP directory provider, cc:Mail, and others. This tool works with all versions of Windows 95/98/NT/2000 and provides profiles for all versions of Outlook as well as the old Exchange client (from Exchange 4).

Part 3

Security

Topics Covered:

- Administrative Security
- Client Authentication
- Communication between Exchange 2000 Servers
- Message Vulnerability and Security
- Encryption Basics
- The Key Management Service
- Enabling Advanced Security on the Client Side
- Protecting Your Exchange Servers from Outside Compromise
- Protecting against Viruses
- SMTP Mail and Security
- Exchange, Firewalls, and Proxy Servers
- Microsoft ISA Server Basics

11

Security within the Network

E-mail systems have become business-critical components of many of the organizations in the world today. With this increased responsibility in the corporate eye comes increased vulnerability to both external and internal threats. Not a week goes by that I don't hear a story of an unauthorized user reading another user's e-mail. This may be the result of permissions being applied incorrectly, a user's password being compromised, or it may simply be a matter of a desktop or printout left unsecured.

One of the most pervasive problems I see in Exchange installations (Exchange 2000 as well as earlier versions) is that administrators have too much permission to the Exchange organization. Further, permissions are often assigned to individuals rather than to groups. The object's Access Control List (ACL) becomes large, and often it is easy for a user or group to "sneak by" with more permission that they should really have.

Exchange 5.5 blocked inherited permissions at several levels through the Exchange hierarchy, but that is not the case with Exchange 2000. Permissions granted at the top of the organization will propagate all the way down through the hierarchy. Exchange 2000 integration with Active Directory allows you to assign much more granular permissions than Exchange 5.5 did. However, there are many new individual permissions that can be assigned, and this can make Exchange 2000 permissions more difficult to manage. The granularity of control is a real double-edged sword. Thus, it is important to understand what the permissions are and how they propagate through the organization.

Administrative Security

Incorrectly applied administrative permissions are a bigger problem than most people realize. Recently a client called me and asked why he could open everyone's mailbox. Upon further investigation, we found that he didn't fully understand the ramifications of the permissions he had given himself. The complexity of the new Exchange 2000–specific Active Directory permissions reflects a common need for a better understanding of the administrative permissions and roles that many organizations are going to need to apply.

Further, many larger organizations are finding that taking advantage of the new granular permissions capabilities is much more complex than they originally thought it would be. Administrators providing specific permissions for tasks such as creating public folders often grant more rights than are necessary to do the job. Thus, specific task administrators such as help desk personnel actually get more permissions than they need. Some organizations are developing their own interfaces or scripts for their help desks to manage specific tasks, rather than giving them tools like Exchange System Manager. These interfaces and scripts can be more easily tailored to perform specific tasks and to provide better activity auditing than Exchange 2000 provides. Yet, regardless of how administration is handled, some high-level administrators are going to have to understand how permissions are applied and which permissions must be applied to specific task-oriented users.

Built-In Administrative Permissions

During the forest prep process or during the first Exchange 2000 server installation (if you did not perform a separate forest prep), the setup program prompts you for the name of the user or group that should be given full Exchange administrative permissions. The default is the user as whom you are currently logged in; for the sake of example, let's assume that user is Administrator.

The following list illustrates the default permissions that are assigned to the Exchange organization object after the installation of the first Exchange 2000 server. Figure 11.1 shows the Exchange organization object's Security property tab.

The following permissions are assigned by default:

- The Administrator user has all permissions except the ability to Receive As and Send As.

- The Authenticated Users group has the permission to read object properties and to list the object. These are viewed by clicking the Advanced button.

- The Domain Admins group has all permissions except Full Control, Receive As, and Send As.

- The Enterprise Admins group has all permissions except Receive As and Send As.
- The Everyone group has Create Top Level Public Folder, Create Public Folder, and Create Named Properties In The Information Store.
- The Exchange Domain Servers group has all permissions except Full Control, Write, Delete, Change Permissions, Take Ownership, Delete Children, Add/Remove Self, Write Properties, Delete Tree, and List Object. This group *does* have the Receive As and Send As permissions.

Figure 11.1   Exchange organization object's Security property tab

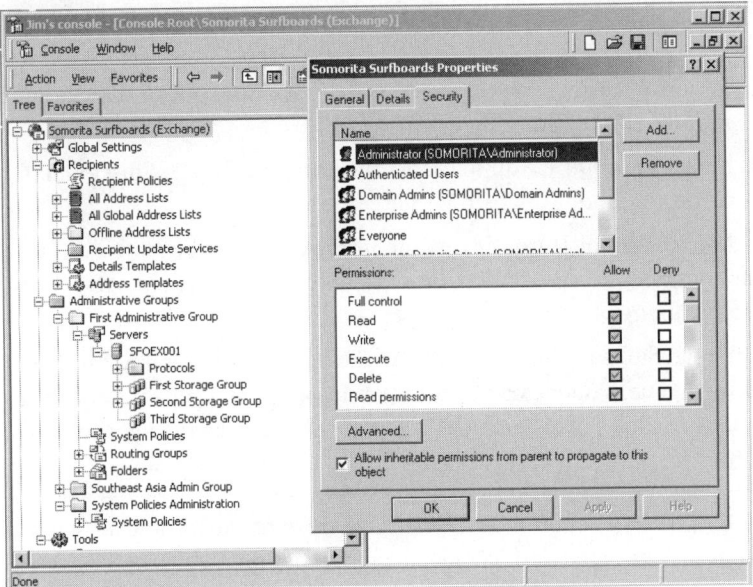

Security

PART 3

> **NOTE**   The Security property tab on your Exchange organization or administrative groups does not show up unless you edit the Registry. Make sure that Exchange System Manager has been opened at least once for your user account. Then create the Registry value ShowSecurityPage with the type of REG_DWORD. Set this value to 1 to enable the security page or 0 to disable it. The ShowSecurityPage value should be created in the \HKCU\Software\Microsoft\Exchange\ExAdmin key.

Several of these groups' permissions are applied at the CN=Services,CN=Microsoft Exchange level of the configuration container or above that container and simply inherited down through the organization.

If your organization consists of a single Active Directory (AD) domain and the domain administrator will be the Exchange administrator, then you probably don't need to worry about any special administrative permissions. The Domain Admins and Enterprise Admins groups are automatically full Exchange 2000 administrators.

Administrator Roles

The recommended way to grant administrator permissions to users or groups is to use the Delegation Wizard found in the Exchange System Manager. If you right-click either the organization object or any of the administrative groups, one of the menu choices is Delegate Control. This choice launches the Delegation Wizard; in order to use the wizard, you will need to have the Exchange Full Administrator role.

The Delegation Wizard gives you the choice of assigning one of three administrative roles to the container you have highlighted:

- Exchange View Only Admin grants the user or group permission to list and read the properties of all objects below that container.

- Exchange Administrator grants the user or group all permissions to objects below that container except for the ability to take ownership, change permissions, or open user mailboxes.

- Exchange Full Administrator grants the user or group all permissions to all objects below that container except for the ability to open user's mailboxes or impersonate a user's mailbox. This includes the permission to change permissions.

NOTE   The Delegation Wizard grants permissions to *all* objects in the container you have highlighted and *all* objects below that point.

When a role is assigned to the organization or an administrative group, those permissions are inherited by all objects below that container. If you give a user the Exchange Full Administrator role to the organization object, that user will have those permissions throughout the entire organization (all administrative groups) unless the inheritance is blocked. Inheritance can be blocked from the Security property tab (shown previously in Figure 11.1); however, care should be taken when blocking inheritance, as this can adversely affect a complex Exchange environment.

If you choose to block inheritance by clicking the Allow Inheritable Permissions From Parent To Propagate To This Object check box, you are presented with a dialog box that asks if you want to copy the inherited permissions or remove all but the explicitly assigned permissions. Perform this task only if you know *exactly* what you are doing. It is entirely possible that you could block the server's own permissions to operate Exchange 2000 or to communicate with other servers. This is very easy to do if you block permissions to administrative groups that have Exchange 2000 servers in them.

Assigning Roles

Since assigning administrator roles is the simplest way to assign administrative permissions, that is the path that I would recommend you follow. However, you need to make sure that you assign only the permissions that are necessary for the person to do their job. This may be difficult to do if your administrators have very specific tasks that they must perform; if this is the case, make sure that the user has the least amount of permissions possible to do their job. If you are the sole administrator in an Exchange organization, then you probably want to assign yourself the Exchange Full Administrators role at the organization level. The permissions this role assigns will propagate down to all objects in the entire organization.

However, your permissions needs may be a little more complicated. In this case, you should break down the permissions based on what types of administrators you need to have. The following are some basic roles that may need to be fulfilled:

- Organization-wide administrator capable of managing all administrative groups, recipient policies, address lists, and global settings
- Administrative group administrators who need to manage all objects, but not set permissions
- Administrative group administrators who need to manage all objects in an administrative group but not permissions

To better illustrate this, let's use a typical example. Somorita Surfboards has two administrative groups: Southeast Asia Admin Group and North America Admin Group. They create global or universal security groups: Somorita Exchange Full Admins, Southeast

Asia Exchange Admins, and North America Exchange Admins. The roles are assigned as follows:

Object	Group	Role
Somorita Surfboards	Somorita Exchange Full Admins	Exchange Full Administrator
	Southeast Asia Exchange Admins	Exchange View Only Administrator
	North America Exchange Admins	Exchange View Only Administrator
North America Admin Group	North America Exchange Admins	Exchange Administrator
Southeast Asia Admin Group	Southeast Asia Exchange Admins	Exchange Administrator

The permissions assigned at the organization level ensure that the Somorita Exchange Full Admins group has full administrator permissions to the entire hierarchy, and the Southeast Asia Exchange Admins and North America Exchange Admins group have view-only permission to the organization-level objects, but the Exchange Administrator role to their respective administrative groups.

Should the Exchange Full Administrator role have been assigned to the Exchange Admins groups instead? That would depend on whether those administrators needed to change permissions on those objects.

Was the Exchange View Only Administrator permissions necessary at the organization level for the Admins groups? The obvious answer is that permission is necessary so that the administrative group administrators can view the organization hierarchy. However, when the Delegation Wizard is used to delegate an administrative role to an administrative group, the wizard automatically assigns that group permissions to see the objects at the organization level. Note that you can only see these permissions using a utility such as ADSIEDIT, which is discussed in Chapter 2, "Active Directory for Exchange 2000 Administrators."

Segmenting and Customizing Administrative Roles

Let's suppose that you want to further segment the administrative responsibilities. You want administrators in each administrative group to manage their Exchange servers (including storage groups, stores, and protocols), but you want to maintain separate administrative responsibilities for things such as routing groups, public folders, and system policies.

First, create one or more administrative groups that will contain the objects you want to administer separately. The example in Figure 11.2 shows how administration of public folders, system policies, and routing groups can be separated from the other administrative functions.

Figure 11.2   Administrative groups for other administrative functions

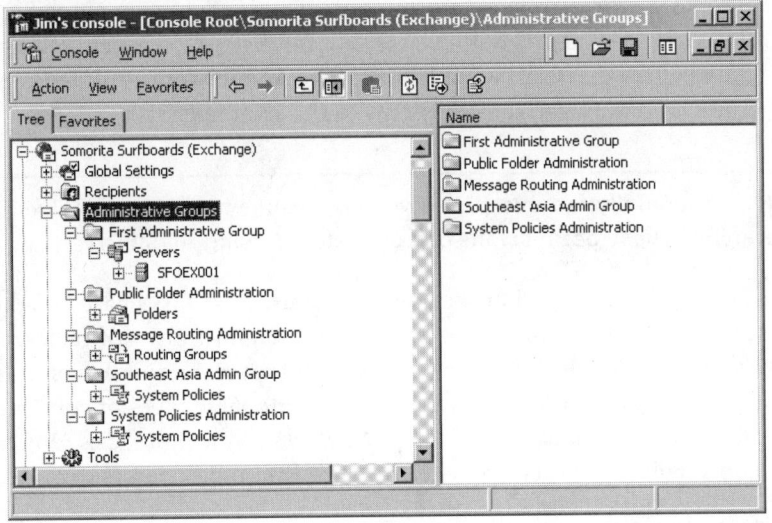

In the example shown in Figure 11.2, there are several additional administrative groups created. These include:

Public Folder Administration contains all of the organization's public folder hierarchies. Some organizations may actually need more than a single public folder administrative group since they may be running applications such as Microsoft Share Point Portal Server, which requires its own application public folder hierarchy. To create a folder, hold the public folder hierarchies, right-click the container, and choose New ➤ Public Folders Container. When assigning a role to this container, you may assign the Exchange Administrator or Exchange Full Administrator roles. The actual role you choose will depend on whether the user or group has to be able to assign permissions. Once created, you can move the public folder hierarchies from other administrative groups.

Message Routing Administration contains all of the organization's routing groups. Once created, you can use Exchange System Manager to create a routing groups container (right-click the container name and choose New ➤ Routing Groups Container) as long as the organization is in Exchange Native mode. If the organization is not in Exchange Native mode, a new routing group container cannot be created, nor can objects be moved into this container. Grant the users or groups that will be performing routing group and connector administration the Exchange Admin role to this container. The other routing group containers can (and should) be deleted from the other containers.

System Policies Administration contains the mailbox, public folder, and server policies for the organization. To create a system policies container in this administrative group, right-click and choose New ≻ System Policy Container, and assign the user or group. Once created, assign the Exchange Administrator role to the user or group that needs administrative permissions to this container.

TIP Accidentally remove your own permissions to manage the Exchange hierarchy? These permissions can be restored using ADSIEDIT.

In the example above where I broke up the administrative tasks based on different types of job responsibilities, I would want to block the administrators of each group from creating system policy, public folder, or routing group containers in each of the other administrative groups. You can deny permissions to create these types of containers using ADSIEDIT. These permissions include Create/Delete System Policies Objects, Create/ Delete Public Folder Objects, and Create/Delete Routing Group Objects.

Blocking or Assigning Specific Permissions

The Exchange Administrator and Exchange Full Administrator roles are fine if the administrator needs blanket permissions to the organization or an administrative group. However, you may need to get even more granular when you assign administrative responsibility to an administrative group.

You can view more detailed security information on the Security property page in Exchange System Manager (shown earlier in Figure 11.1). In this security list, you will find two types of permissions. The first permission type includes the standard Active Directory permissions listed in Table 11.1.

Table 11.1 Standard Active Directory Permissions

Permission	Function
Full Control	Grants full permissions to the object.
Read	Allows you to see the object in Exchange System Manager.
Write	Allows you to make changes to the object.
Execute	Has no effect on Exchange 2000 objects.

Table 11.1   Standard Active Directory Permissions *(continued)*

Permission	Function
Delete	Allows you to delete the object.
Read Permissions	Allows you to see the permissions assigned to the object.
Change Permissions	Allows you to change the permissions assigned to the object.
Take Ownership	Allows you to become the owner of the attribute.
Create Children	Allows you to create objects in this container.
Delete Children	Allows you to delete objects from this container.
List Contents	Allows you to view contents of a container.
Add/Remove Self	Has no effect on Exchange 2000 objects.
Read Properties	Allows you to view the properties of an object.
Write Properties	Allows you to modify the properties of an object.
Delete Tree	Has no effect on Exchange 2000 objects.
List Object	Allows you to view the objects in a container.

The second type of permissions includes those that specifically address things you can do to Exchange 2000 objects. These permissions were added when the forest prep process extended the AD schema. Some of these basic Exchange 2000 permissions are shown in Table 11.2.

Table 11.2   Exchange 2000–Specific Permissions

Permission	Function
Add PF To Admin Group	Allows creation of a public folder in an administrative group container.
Create Public Folder	Allows creation of a public folder.
Create Top Level Public Folder	Allows creation of a top-level public folder.
Modify Public Folder Admin ACL	Allows modification of the administrative permissions of public folders.

Security

PART 3

Table 11.2   Exchange 2000–Specific Permissions *(continued)*

Permission	Function
Modify Public Folder Deleted Item Retention	Allows modification of deleted item retention times for public folders.
Modify Public Folder Expiry	Allows modification of public folder age limits.
Modify Public Folder Quotas	Allows modification of public folder quotas.
Modify Public Folder Replica List	Allows modification of which servers contain replicas of a public folder.
Open Mail Send Queue	Allows the administrator to view mail queues.
Read Metabase Properties	Allows the administrator to view the properties of protocols and virtual servers.
Remove PF From Admin Group	Allows the removal of a public folder container from an administrative group container.
Administer Information Store	Allows administration of a mailbox or public folder store.
Create Named Properties In The Information Store	Allows a user to create new properties in a public folder store.
View Information Store Status	Allows the administrator to view store statistics such as folder and mailbox space usage.
Receive As	Allows mailboxes to be opened.
Send As	Allows the user to send mail as another mailbox.

ADSI Permissions

Do you need to get extremely detailed in the permissions that you grant or revoke? Using ADSIEDIT, you can access permissions that allow you to grant very specific management rights for Exchange objects. Some of these permissions include:

Create/Delete ADC Connection Agreement Objects

Create/Delete ADC Service Objects

Create/Delete Address List Objects

Create/Delete Addressing Policy Objects

Create/Delete Administrative Groups

Create/Delete Advanced Security Objects

Create/Delete Exchange Policies Objects

Create/Delete Exchange Server Policy Objects

Create/Delete Exchange Server Objects

Create/Delete Information Store Objects

Create/Delete Instant Messaging Global Settings Objects

Create/Delete Internet Message Formats Objects

Create/Delete Key Management Server Objects

Create/Delete Monitoring Link Configuration Objects

Create/Delete Monitoring Server Configuration

Create msExchMDB Objects

Create/Delete Offline Address List Objects

Create/Delete Private Information Store Objects

Create/Delete Private Information Store Policy Objects

Create/Delete Public Folder Objects

Create/Delete Public Folder Top Level Hierarchy Objects

Create/Delete Public Information Store Objects

Create/Delete Public Information Store Policy Objects

Create/Delete Recipient Policy Objects

Create/Delete Recipient Update Service Objects

Create/Delete Routing Group Objects

Create/Delete Routing Groups Objects

Create/Delete SMTP Connector Objects

Create/Delete SMTP Policy Objects

Create/Delete Storage Group Objects

Create/Delete System Policies Objects

Create/Delete x400Link Objects

In addition to these, there are individual permissions that allow you to specify who can create or delete virtual protocol server objects and different mail connectors. Figure 11.3 shows the Permission Entry dialog box for a group that has been assigned permissions to the Exchange organization. To view this dialog box, display the properties of an Exchange object in ADSIEDIT, select the Security tab, click the Advanced button, and then click Add or View/Edit to assign the permissions you want to grant.

Figure 11.3   Setting individual permissions through ADSIEDIT

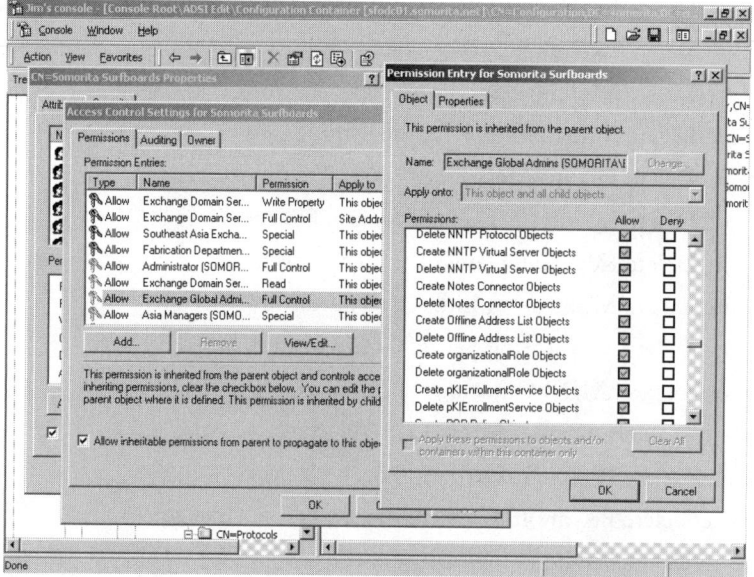

NOTE   Permissions that appear in a check box with a gray background are inherited from a higher container.

Many of the permissions found in ADSIEDIT are not specific to Exchange 2000, but rather are generic to AD.

WARNING   Use extreme care when using ADSIEDIT to assign specific detailed permissions. You can accidentally revoke or deny important permissions and toast your Exchange server.

Accessing Mailboxes

If you have the right Exchange permissions, you can give yourself permission to access other user's mailboxes. This section covers how to do this, but you have to promise to use your powers for good and not evil. Opening another user's mailbox is a serious act, especially if you have not been authorized to do so. I know of a few companies that have fired administrators for taking a stroll through other users' e-mail messages.

Single Mailbox Permissions

You can grant a user permission to open another user's mailbox through the AD Users And Computers console. Simply locate the user account, display its properties, select the Exchange Advanced property page, and click the Mailbox Rights button. The Permissions dialog box for a mailbox is shown in Figure 11.4.

Figure 11.4   Permissions dialog box for a mailbox

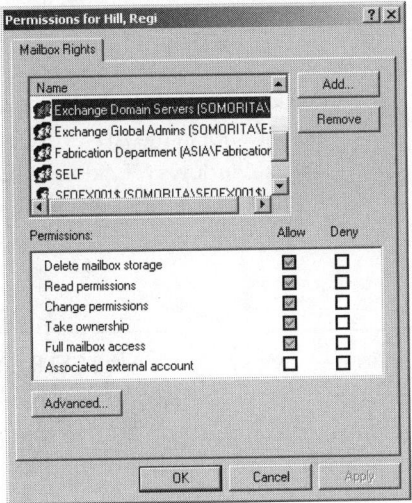

> **NOTE**   If the Exchange Advanced property page is not visible on the user object in AD Users And Computers, select View ➤ Advanced Features.

You may notice that the mailbox permissions list includes all of the permissions inherited by the mailbox from the organization. The Exchange Domain Servers group, the Exchange server's computer account, and the mailbox owner (SELF) have permissions to open the mailbox. Table 11.3 lists the permissions that can be assigned to an individual mailbox.

Table 11.3   Individual Mailbox Permissions

Permission	Description
Delete Mailbox Storage	Allows the user to purge the mailbox from the mailbox store.
Read Permissions	Allows the user to view the permissions on a mailbox.

Table 11.3   Individual Mailbox Permissions *(continued)*

Permission	Description
Change Permissions	Allows the user to change the permissions assigned to a mailbox.
Take Ownership	Makes the user the owner of the mailbox.
Full Mailbox Access	Allows the user to open the mailbox and send messages as the mailbox.
Associated External Account	Assigns a user permission to the mailbox for user accounts that are not in the AD forest (such as from a trusted AD forest or Windows NT 4 domain). See Knowledge Base article Q278888 for more information on this feature.

> **NOTE** The mailbox rights may only contain the SELF right because the mailbox has not yet been created in the store. Once the user has accessed their mailbox for the first time, or once a message is delivered to that mailbox, the Recipient Update Service (RUS) will calculate the mailbox rights.

The permission necessary to open the mailbox is either Full Mailbox Access or Associated External Account. Simply assign another AD user (or external account) one of these permissions in order to allow that user to open that mailbox.

There are also Send As and Receive As Active Directory permissions. These permissions are found on the Security property page of the user object in the AD. These permissions have no effect on Exchange 2000.

> **NOTE** Be patient when granting a user account permissions to another mailbox. You may have to wait 15 minutes or more before the user can actually open the mailbox due to replication latency.

Accessing All Mailboxes

By default, all administrators who are assigned an administrative role through the Delegation Wizard are explicitly denied the Send As and Receive As permissions at the CN=Services,CN=Microsoft Exchange,CN=<*organization name*> level of the configuration partition. This prevents any member of these groups from accessing mailboxes in *any* administrative group unless the permission is explicitly applied directly to the mailbox.

The Domain Admins group, Enterprise Admins, and the user who installed Exchange are explicitly denied the Send As and Receive As permissions at the organization level. Figure 11.5 shows the Security property tab of the Somorita Surfboards Exchange organization object. In this example, Domain Admins is highlighted; the allowed permissions have a gray background because they are inherited from the CN=Services,CN=Microsoft Exchange container of the configuration container. However, the Send As and Receive As permissions are explicitly denied at this level; these permissions will be inherited by all subcontainers unless inheritance is blocked.

Figure 11.5   Blocking Send As and Receive As permissions from the Domain Admins group

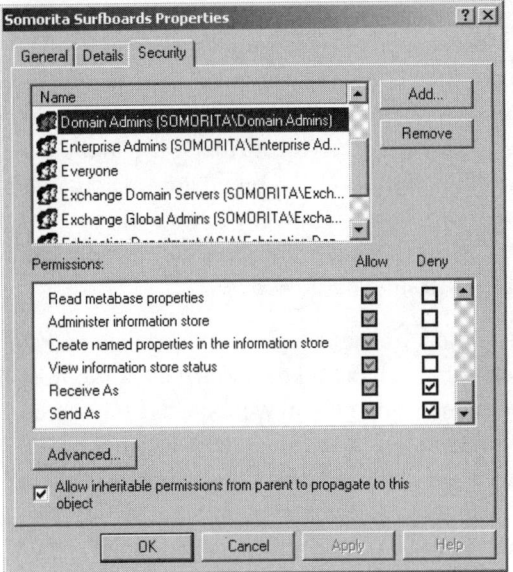

The simplest approach to granting permissions is to make the user account a member of the Exchange Domain Servers group in the local domain. That will give that user full access to the Exchange mailboxes; that is, permission to open any mailbox on any server in the organization provided that user account is not a member of the Domain Admins or Enterprise Admins groups (these groups are explicitly denied permission to open mailboxes).

Exchange@Work: Only Permissions Necessary to Do the Job at Hand

In the past, users with administrative permissions often had only a single user account; this was the user account that was granted the administrative permissions. The user would log on to this account to perform normal, day-to-day tasks (reading e-mail, preparing documents, etc.). Any security expert will tell you that this is a bad practice since it allows viruses to spread more easily and may be easy for an intruder to exploit.

Many organizations are now requiring that their administrative users have at least two user accounts, one for the day-to-day stuff and one for performing administrative tasks. The administrative account should *not* be mailbox-enabled. For example, I would have two user accounts: JMcBee and A-JMcBee. The latter account would be granted administrative permissions.

Windows 2000 makes using two separate user accounts much simpler to do with the advent of the Secondary Logon service (a.k.a. Run As). For example, I can stay logged on as my regular user account (JMcBee), but if I need to create a user or launch Exchange System Manager, I can locate that MMC in the Start menu, press and hold the Shift key, and then right-click the menu item. There will be a Run As selection on the context menu; selecting Run As prompts me for credentials. At this point, I would use the A-JMcBee user account. Only the window I launched using Run As will actually have administrative permissions.

For years I have felt this was a good practice because early in my networking career I saw a virus (Jerusalem-B) spread through 1000 computers because several of the administrators had gotten it and were always logged on as the administrative account. However, with the advent of e-mail–based viruses, I am afraid that some virus writer out there is writing a nasty little thing that checks to see if the currently logged on user account has administrative permissions. There is no telling what the virus could do if it found a user who was an administrator, but I'm sure the result would be anything but good.

Another approach is to create a group and assign it explicitly the permissions that are required directly to that group.

The third approach (and maybe least desirable) is to remove the Send As and Receive As Deny permissions from the Domain Admins and Enterprise Admins at the Exchange organization level. This will give all members of these groups permission to open any mailbox they wish. These permissions must be assigned or edited through Exchange System Manager or ADSIEDIT.

TIP Make sure you allow time for these permissions to replicate through your organization.

Exchange@Work: Allowing Access to Mailboxes

Many antivirus scanning programs, workflow applications, and gateway products require direct access to each user's mailbox. In the Exchange 5.5 days, we simply would have assigned the program that required this level of access to use the Exchange site services account, since that user already has such permissions.

With Exchange 2000, the approach I recommend is to create a special group or groups and assign the user the appropriate permissions. For example, let's say you have installed a virus-protection software package on a server in the North America Admin Group administrative group. Use the Delegation Wizard to assign permissions such as Exchange View Only Administrator. Then, from the Security property page of the administrative group, locate the Send As and Receive As permissions and make sure that those permissions are allowed. If the user or group you granted the permissions to has the Deny check box checked and it is grayed out, then they are inheriting permissions from a higher container. If you are using an antivirus software package that is certified for use with the Exchange 2000 SP1 VSAPI, then the software package may not need MAPI access to mailboxes.

NOTE For more in-depth information on Exchange 2000 permissions, visit www.exinternals.com and look for the Exchange 2000 Internals Permissions FAQ white paper.

What Permissions Do I Require?

The following is a list of common tasks that you may need to perform as an Exchange administrator and the permissions required to perform those tasks:

1. Install the first Exchange 2000 server in the organization.
    - Member of the root domain's Schema Admins, Enterprise Admins group
2. Run domain prep in a domain that has no Exchange 2000 servers.
    - Member of the domain's Domain Admins group

3. Install additional Exchange 2000 servers.
   - Exchange Administrator role at the organization level
   - Local administrator group on the server where you will be installing the server
4. Change global message formats, thresholds, and message filtering options.
   - Exchange Administrator role at the organization level
5. Create an administrative group.
   - Exchange Administrator role at the organization level
6. Create a routing group.
   - Exchange Administrator role in the administrative group that contains the routing group container
7. Create Address lists.
   - Exchange Administrator role at the organization level
8. Create mailbox-enabled users.
   - Exchange View Only Administrator role in the administrative group in which the server is located
   - Permissions to create a user object in the Active Directory or the specific organizational unit of the AD
9. Move mailboxes between mailbox stores, servers, or administrative groups.
   - Permissions to modify the AD user account (Domain Admins or Account Operators, or have these permissions delegated in Active Directory Users And Computers)
   - Exchange Administrator role in the administrative group that contains the source and destination servers
10. Delete mailboxes.
    - Exchange View Only Administrator role in the administrative group in which the server is located
    - Permissions to delete a user object in the AD or the specific organizational unit of the AD
11. Create public folders.
    - Exchange Administrator role in the administrative group that contains the public folder hierarchy or granted the permission to create public folders on the Security tab or in ADSIEDIT
    - Must be a mailbox-enabled user

12. View SMTP queues.

   - Exchange View Only Administrator role in the administrative group in which the server is located

   - Local administrator group on the server at whose queues you want to look

13. Delete SMTP queue messages.

   - Exchange Administrator role in the administrative group in which the server is located

   - Local administrator group on the server at whose queues you want to look

14. Enable a user account for instant messaging.

   - Permissions to modify the AD user account (Domain Admins, Account Operators, or have these permissions delegated in Active Directory Users And Computers)

   - Exchange View Only Administrator role in the administrative group that contains the Instant Messaging server

Exchange@Work: Permissions to Install New Servers

Company XYZ's central IT department was in a bit of a quandary over administrative rights. They had numerous administrative groups into which servers were going to be installed by the administrators in the remote locations. The central IT department did not want to grant the Exchange Administrator role to the entire organization for each of these remote administrators.

Their solution was to create a temporary group called Exchange Server Installation; this group was granted the Exchange Administrator role to the entire organization. Now, when the remote administrators need to install an Exchange server, they must first notify someone in the central IT department, who then adds the remote administrator's account to the Exchange Server Installation group. Once the installation is complete, the remote administrator's account is removed from this group.

While this solution works well for XYZ, another solution would be to create an "install" user account that has the correct permissions, then change the password after the remote administrator has used the account to install an Exchange server.

Client Authentication

As Exchange administrators, we need to understand how clients are authenticated and whether user passwords are transmitted over the network in a form that someone can decode. Client authentication can be broken down into two general categories: integrated Windows authentication and Internet client authentication.

Integrated Windows Authentication

Integrated Windows authentication is a general term that covers both Windows NT LAN Manager (NTLM) and Kerberos authentication. Both of these methods are used to authenticate users and to verify that the user's password does not fall into the wrong hands by preventing the client from having to pass the password over the network "in the clear," or visible to network analyzers.

Windows NT LAN Manager Authentication

All older clients such as Microsoft Windows NT, Windows 9*x*, Windows Me, and DOS authenticate using Windows NT LAN Manager (NTLM), a challenge/response authentication system. In other words, when the client attempts to log in, the server sends a challenge code of some sort, and the client encrypts that code with some commonly known key and sends back the encrypted code.

Figure 11.6 illustrates a typical logon session using Windows NT challenge/response. In step 1, a Windows client issues a logon request. In step 2, the authenticating server returns a challenge; the challenge is simply a 16-bit number. The Windows client takes the user's password and performs a function on it called a *one-way function (OWF)*, which is an irreversible hashing function. The result is known as the *OWF password*. In step 3, the Windows client encrypts the challenge using the OWF password and sends it back to the authenticating computer (such as domain controller).

Figure 11.6   Windows NT LAN Manager challenge/response

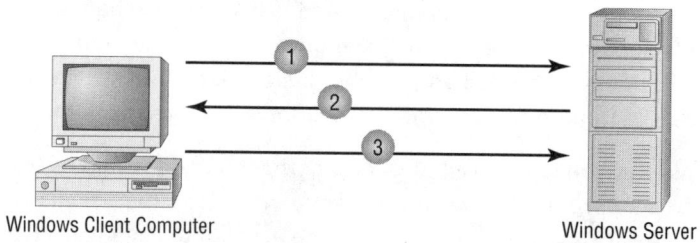

Windows Client Computer   Windows Server

The password on the authenticating computer is stored in the local security database as an OWF password also. Since the authenticating computer knows the OWF password and the unencrypted challenge string, it can calculate what the correct encrypted challenge should be. If in step 3 the client returns the encrypted challenge that matches the server's version of what the encrypted challenge should be, then it is confirmed that the client entered the correct password.

However, with NTLM there is no authentication that the server is really who it is supposed to be. The client could be logging in to a rogue server, plus those OWF passwords are often not too hard to crack using "brute" force methods such as L0phtcrack (www.10pht.com).

> **TIP** You can require strong passwords in Active Directory by using a group policy. For more information on strong passwords and how to encourage users to create and remember them, see the Strong Password Manifesto on my web site, www .somorita.com.

Outlook Authentication and Encryption When Outlook MAPI clients (Outlook 97, 98, 2000, and 2002) connect to an Exchange server, Outlook will query Windows for your current logon credentials (username, domain name, and password). If the user account you are logged on as is not the user account that owns or has permissions to the mailbox, you will be denied access.

However, Outlook can be configured to prompt you for a username, domain name, and password that *do* have permissions to access the mailbox via the following dialog box:

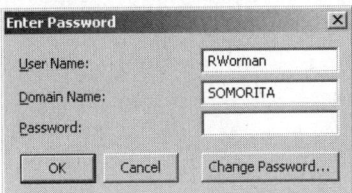

To configure Outlook to prompt you for a user account, edit the mail profile:

1. Go to Control Panel ➢ Mail.
2. Highlight the Microsoft Exchange Server service, and click Properties.
3. Click the Advanced property tab (shown in Figure 11.7).
4. Configure the Logon Network Security drop-down box to None; the default is to use NT Password Authentication and click OK.

Security

PART 3

Figure 11.7 Exchange Server service Advanced property tab

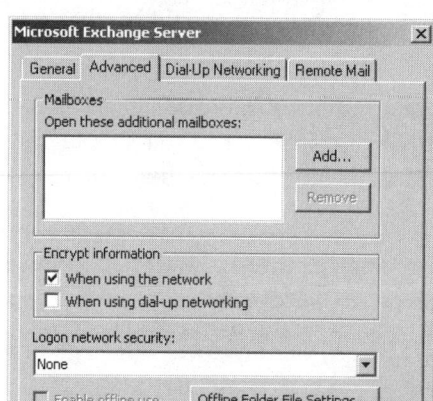

You can also enable encryption of messages between Outlook and the server. By default the messages are encoded, but not encrypted. In the Encrypt Information section of the dialog box in Figure 11.7, check the When Using The Network check box.

If the logon dialog box does not remember your username and domain name, you can create a Registry key called Exchange in the \HKCU\Software\Microsoft subkey so that the username and domain name are stored. The next time you launch Outlook and enter your username and password, Outlook will create values in this key called LogonDomain and UserName.

Kerberos Authentication

Kerberos is a network authentication system that provides secure authentication for client/server applications by using secret-key (symmetric) cryptography. However, unlike NTLM, not only does the client authenticate with the server, but the server may also authenticate with the client. This prevents "man in the middle" types of hacker attacks by ensuring that both the client and the server are authenticated.

> **NOTE** An in-depth discussion of Kerberos is beyond the scope of this chapter and this book. However, a basic understanding of the authentication process is useful for administrators who have to debug Windows 2000 authentication problems.

Microsoft introduced Kerberos V5 into the Windows family with the introduction of Windows 2000. Thus Kerberos authentication only works with Windows 2000 (and higher) computers, and those computers must be members of the AD forest. There are two different authentication operations that occur when using Kerberos and Windows 2000: the initial logon and requesting services.

A Kerberos initial logon phase is illustrated in Figure 11.8. When looking at it, understand that in a Kerberos environment, there is a computer known as the key distribution center (KDC) that is responsible for issuing *tickets*; The KDC issues the client a ticket-granting ticket (TGT) that is used for getting session tickets; the TGT is held in local cache. In Windows 2000, each Windows 2000 domain controller is a KDC.

Figure 11.8   Kerberos initial logon

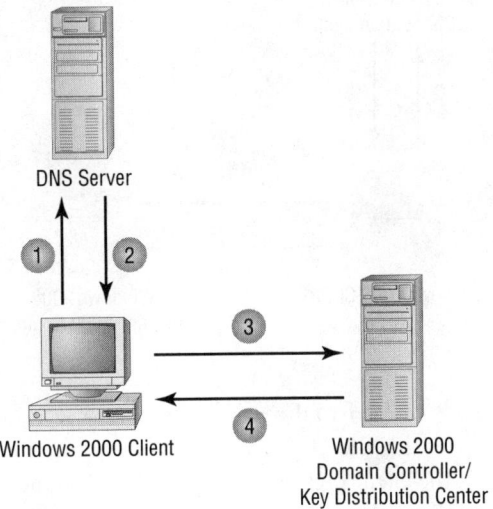

DNS Server

Windows 2000 Client

Windows 2000
Domain Controller/
Key Distribution Center

In step 1, the Windows 2000 client queries DNS for a service locator record to its DNS server. (You can also issue an NSLOOKUP query to find a list of KDC servers.)

In step 2, the DNS server returns a list of all the KDC servers for the domain queried. The client contacts the KDC in step 3 and authenticates to that server. In step 4, the KDC returns to the client an encrypted ticket-granting ticket (TGT). The TGT has a time stamp, authentication information about the user, and a service key for future communication with the KDC. Now the client has successfully authenticated and can access services on the network.

When the user gets ready to access a service, such as Exchange 2000, the client now has to get a session ticket (ST) that it will present to the Exchange 2000 server. To get a ST from the KDC, the client must use its TGT (getting to be a few too many acronyms, yes?). Figure 11.9 shows this process.

Security

PART 3

Figure 11.9   Kerberos session ticket process

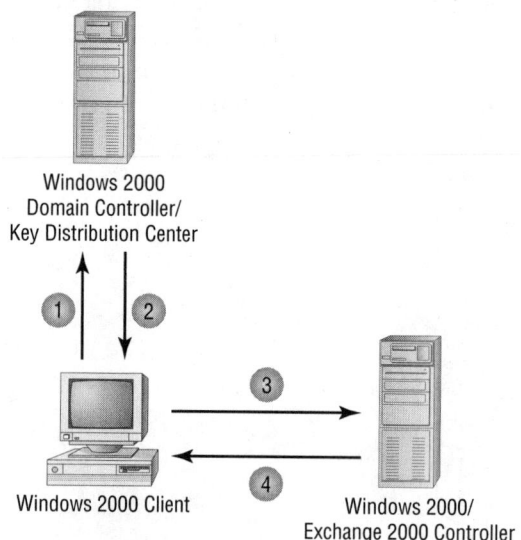

In step 1, the client sends its TGT to the KDC asking for a service ticket to contact a specific server. The KDC confirms that the TGT is valid and has not expired and sends an ST to the client in step 2. In step 3, the client presents the ST to the Exchange 2000 server, and in step 4 the Exchange server confirms that a session has been granted. The Exchange 2000 server may also request an ST for the client if mutual authentication is required.

Ticket-granting tickets and service tickets have expiration times that are set when the tickets are issued. The default TGT and ST lifetime is 10 hours; however, if the ticket time discrepancy between the KDC and the client is more than five minutes, the ticket is considered invalid. This means that time synchronization across the organization is very important. All of these options are configurable using security policies.

> **NOTE** You will find some great information about Kerberos at the Moron's Guide to Kerberos on the Web at www.isi.edu/gost/brian/security/kerberos.html. The author of this web page, Brian Tung, has also published a great book called *Kerberos: A Network Authentication System* (Addison-Wesley, 1999).

Internet Client Authentication

One of the biggest security problems with most Exchange Server installations is that administrators fail to consider that basic authentication is enabled for Internet clients. This means that any POP3, IMAP4, or NNTP client that authenticates to the Exchange Server sends their logon credentials *and* password over the network in cleartext.

The same weakness is true for Outlook Web Access (OWA) clients that are using a front-end server or that are using a client other than Internet Explorer. The username and password are sent over the wire in an unencrypted format.

Securing POP3, IMAP4, and NNTP Client Authentication

On the Exchange server virtual protocol servers for POP3, IMAP4, and NNTP protocol objects, the administrator can choose two types of authentication, basic and integrated Windows. To configure these authentication options, open the virtual server's properties, click the Access property tab, and click the Authentication button.

Outlook Express provides the user the option of choosing secure password authentication when configuring the Outlook Express client's account. When configuring the Outlook Express POP3, IMAP4, or NNTP accounts, on the Servers property tab (shown in Figure 11.10), choose Log On Using Secure Password Authentication.

Figure 11.10 Authentication options for Outlook Express

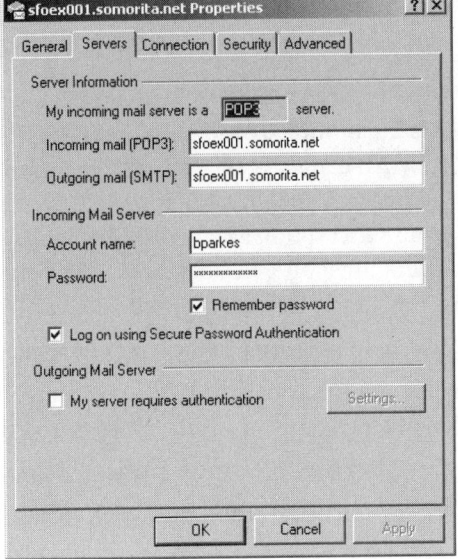

This option will protect the username and password provided the client is using Outlook Express to connect to an Exchange server. If the client is using some other client software, then the password is passed across the wire in the clear.

Below are two frames captured during a POP3 authentication between a client and a POP3 server. In the first frame, we can see that the user is authenticating as username BParkes.

```
00 03 47 1F 2E 62 00 10 4B 9C 19 B1 08 00 45 00    ..G..b..K....E.
00 36 34 44 40 00 80 06 41 2A C0 A8 02 01 C0 A8    .64D@...A*......
02 02 05 87 00 6E 94 9D 99 B8 6B A9 C7 9C 50 18    .....n....k...P.
44 15 6E 72 00 00 55 53 45 52 20 62 70 61 72 6B    D.nr..USER.bpark
65 73 0D 0A                                        es..
```

In the second frame, the client is sending the user's password to the server. Here you can clearly see that the password is Purity$Control.

```
00 03 47 1F 2E 62 00 10 4B 9C 19 B1 08 00 45 00    ..G..b..K....E.
00 3C 34 45 40 00 80 06 41 23 C0 A8 02 01 C0 A8    .<4E@...A#......
02 02 05 87 00 6E 94 9D 99 C6 6B A9 C7 A1 50 18    .....n....k...P.
44 10 02 4A 00 00 50 41 53 53 20 50 75 72 69 74    D..J..PASS.Purit
79 43 6F 6E 74 72 6F 6C 0D 0A                      y$Control.
```

It's a shame—another good password ruined by the fact that, by default, passwords are sent over the network in cleartext unless the administrator takes steps to block this. Not to mention that I can just as easily read the e-mail that the client retrieves using Network Monitor.

Adding Secure Sockets Layer for POP3, IMAP4, and NNTP   Adding Secure Sockets Layer (SSL) for POP3, IMAP4, and NNTP virtual servers is simple, but this process assumes that you have already installed a Microsoft Certificate Server into your Active Directory. (Certificates and encryption are discussed in more detail in Chapter 12, "Messaging Security)." To configure POP3, IMAP4, or NNTP virtual server to use SSL, follow these instructions. For this example, I am using the default POP3 virtual server.

1. Using Exchange System Manager, open the server on which you want to configure SSL.

2. Open the Protocols container, open the POP3 container, highlight the Default POP3 Virtual Server container, right-click, and choose Properties.

3. Click the Access property tab, click the Certificate button, and click Next.

4. Choose Create A New Certificate, and then click Next.

5. Choose Send The Request Immediately To An Online Certification Authority. This choice will not be available if the Certificate Authority (CA) is not visible in the AD. If you know that it has been installed, try logging out and then logging back in. Also make sure you allow time to replicate fully. Click Next.

6. Enter the name and the bit length of the certificate you are requesting. I typically choose a bit length of 1024; this makes the encryption much stronger, but it also slows performance a bit. Click Next.

7. Enter the organization and organization unit (department name). The organization name does not have to match the Exchange organization name. Click Next.

8. In the Common Name box, enter the fully qualified domain name (FQDN) of the server. This should be the name that the clients will be using to connect to this server. For example, if the server name given to the clients is POP3.SOMORITA.COM, then you would enter **POP3.SOMORITA.COM** in the Common Name box. Click Next.

9. Enter the country, state, and city information, and then click Next.

10. Choose the CA that you want to process your certificate request. If your organization has more than one CA, you need to click the drop-down list and select the appropriate one. Click Next.

11. Review and confirm the information you have provided, click Next, and then click Finish.

12. Click the Communication button to see the Security dialog box. Check Require Secure Channel if you want all clients to use SSL. For increased security, you can also click the Require 128-Bit Encryption button.

Once SSL is enabled, not only will authentication information be encrypted, but the entire conversation between the client and the server is encrypted.

SMTP Client Traffic and Security   If you have POP3 or IMAP4 clients, then one of your SMTP virtual servers must be configured to allow for relay. There are two basic ways that you can allow SMTP clients to relay through one of your SMTP virtual servers: configure the IP addresses or domain names that are allowed to relay through the SMTP virtual server, or require that the clients successfully authenticate. If you need to reconfigure your SMTP virtual server, relay restrictions are configured on the SMTP virtual server's Access property tab behind the Relay button. The Relay Restrictions property page is shown in Figure 11.11.

Figure 11.11 SMTP virtual server relay restrictions

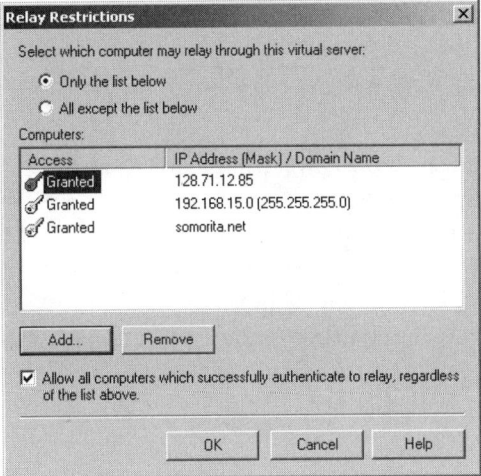

When configuring relay restrictions, the Relay Restrictions dialog box allows you to specify a list of restricted computers; you can specify Only The List Below or All Except The List Below radio buttons. The restricted relay list can be based on a single IP address, an IP subnet, or a specific domain name. If you select to restrict relay by domain name, each connection will require a reverse lookup and will slow performance. Further, each client that will relay must have a PTR record that identifies his or her IP address as being part of that domain.

The default is to allow clients that successfully authenticate to relay through the Exchange SMTP virtual server. The authentication options are nearly the same as they are for the other Internet mail clients except for a few additional features. Figure 11.12 shows the Authentication dialog box for an SMTP virtual server. Note that you can require TLS for Basic authentication. The Authentication option can be found behind the Authentication button on the SMTP virtual server's Access property tab.

Figure 11.12 SMTP virtual server authentication options

The client software must support SMTP authentication; the POP3 and IMAP4 services in Outlook Express support SMTP authentication on the server's property tab. On this tab, which is shown in the background of Figure 11.13, check the My Server Requires Authentication check box. You can customize the authentication settings by clicking the Settings button; this displays the Outgoing Mail Server dialog box shown in Figure 11.13. The default is to use the same authentication settings as the incoming mail server, but this can be overridden.

Figure 11.13 Outlook Express configured to authenticate to the SMTP virtual server

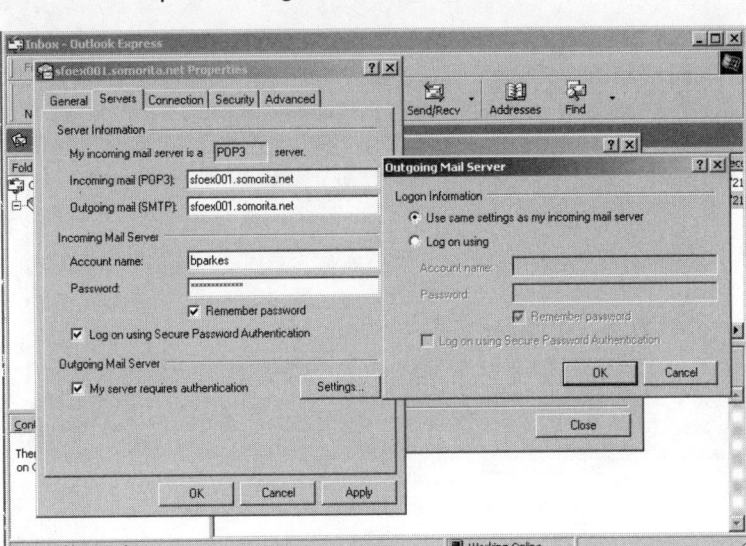

Securing Outlook Web Access Clients

Outlook Web Access clients using Internet Explorer connecting directly to an OWA server that is on a back-end Exchange 2000 server will use integrated Windows authentication (NTLM authentication). Using this method, the password is never sent over the network—only an encrypted challenge is. NTLM authentication is somewhat more secure than cleartext, but is also compromised easily by someone with the right tools.

However, if the OWA client is connecting to an Exchange 2000 front-end server, if the only authentication method specified is Basic, or if the browser client is using a browser other than Internet Explorer, then the password is sent over the wire in an encoded (but not encrypted) format. This is configured for each virtual directory. Figure 11.14 shows the Exchange virtual directory for the default Exchange virtual server. To get to the Authentication Methods dialog box shown in Figure 11.14, open the server's HTTP protocol container, open the Exchange Virtual Server container, right-click the Exchange virtual directory, display the properties of the virtual directory, choose the Access tab, and click the Authentication button.

> **WARNING** Basic authentication is the only method available to OWA running on an Exchange 2000 front-end server. SSL must be used between the client and the front-end server in order to protect the logon information and mail data. To protect the data between the front-end and back-end servers, a solution such as IP Security (IPSec) or some other type of protected connection must be implemented.

Security

PART 3

Figure 11.14 Authentication methods for OWA

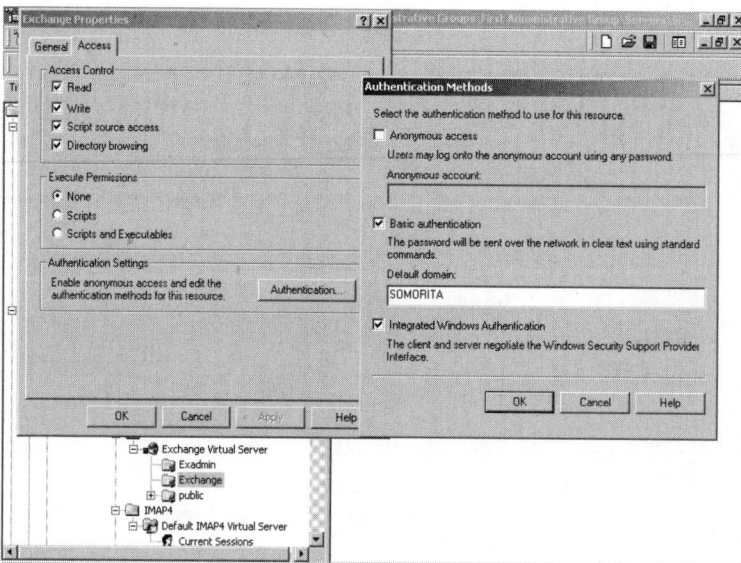

When the browser client connects to a web server, the browser client assumes that the server allows anonymous connections. If you watch this transaction take place using a tool such as Network Monitor, you will see the GET request for the \Exchange virtual directory. The server will respond with an HTTP/1.1 401 error message indicating that access is denied and a status code of Unauthorized.

The browser client then disconnects and immediately reconnects to the web server, except this time, the GET \Exchange request includes an authentication string. For example, the authentication request would look like this:

    HTTP: Authorization = Basic c29tb3JpdGFccmJlc3NhcmE6JGVjcmV0QDQy

The user and password are encoded using base 64 encoding; this data is not encrypted. Anyone with a program that will decode base 64 can decode this data. Below is the text from a decode session using a program I downloaded from the Internet called BASE64.EXE. The text that I typed is in bold; I inserted the encoded string from the authentication line.

C:\>**base64**

>> **decode c29tb3JpdGFccmJlc3NhcmE6JGVjcmV0QDQy**

somorita\rbessara:$ecret@42

decode succeeded

>>

The third line is the program output. The user's name is RBessara in the Somorita domain, and his password is $ecret@42. Regardless of how strong his password really is, I can still intercept it and decode it.

Adding Secure Sockets Layer for OWA   SSL is the solution you are looking for if you want to encrypt the user account and password information as well as all of the e-mail content. Enabling SSL on the server requires a server certificate; certificates are discussed in more detail in Chapter 12. SSL is enabled through the Internet Services Manager console, not Exchange System Manager.

> **NOTE**   SSL encrypts not only the authentication portion of the conversation, but all data transmitted.

To enable a server to use SSL, follow these steps, which assume that you have installed the Microsoft Windows 2000 Certificate Server into your AD hierarchy. If not, you will have to create the certificate request and have it processed by a CA.

1. Load the Internet Services Manager console and open the web site for which you wish to enable SSL.

2. Right-click the website's name and choose Properties.

3. Select the Directory Security property tab and click the Server Certificate button.

4. Click Next, select Create A New Certificate, and select Send The Request Immediately To An Online Certification Authority.

5. Enter a name for the certificate and choose the bit length. Typically I choose a key length of 1024. Click Next.

6. Specify an organization name and organizational unit such as the company and department name. This does not have to match your Exchange 2000 organization name. Click Next.

7. On the Common Name field, enter the server's fully qualified domain name that the users will use to connect to the server. This is not necessarily the same as the server's true host name. For example, the server's host name might be `SFOEX001.SOMORITA.COM`, but I may give the user community the name `OWA.SOMORITA.COM`. So, I would want to enter `OWA.SOMORITA.COM`. If this does not match correctly with the URL that the user types, the certificate will not match the host name, and the user will receive an error. Click Next.

8. Enter the Country, State, and City information and click Next.

9. Choose the CA name to which you will send the request. If there is more than one CA in your Active Directory, then the drop-down list will list all of these servers. Click Next.

10. Review the summary information for your request. If it is correct, click Next and then Finish. Otherwise, click Back to revise the incorrect information.

Once this is done, for users to use SSL, they must type in the https://owa.somorita.com URL instead of http://owa.somorita.com. You can require SSL by clicking the Edit box on the Directory Security tab. When you click Edit, the Secure Communications dialog box is shown (see Figure 11.15). Click the Require Secure Channel (SSL) check box. For increased security, you can also click the Require 128-Bit Encryption button, which requires that all browser clients support 128-bit encryption.

Figure 11.15 Requiring SSL for a website

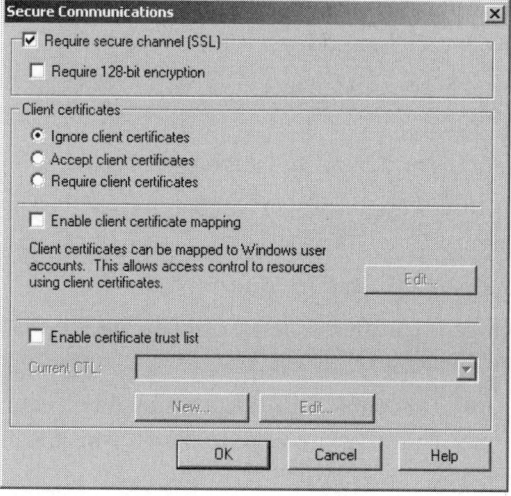

Another option is merely to tell the user to connect to the owa.somorita.com website and create a default web page that redirects the users to the secure site.

NOTE   Client-side certificates cannot be used for OWA authentication.

Communication between Exchange 2000 Servers

Within the same site, Exchange 5.5 administrators did not have to worry about encryption or authentication issues between Exchange 5.5 servers. Between servers in the same Exchange 5.5 site, all communication is handled using Remote Procedure Calls (RPCs); Windows NT and Windows 2000 include the ability to encrypt RPC traffic. Exchange's designers took advantage of this, and thus all communication between servers within the site was automatically encrypted. Authentication was handled using the Exchange site service account.

However, communication between sites was another story—it depended on which messaging connector was employed. If the site connector was used, the data was transferred using RPCs and thus encrypted. Using the X.400 connector required its own authentication mechanism, and data encoding; the data was not encrypted. Finally, using the Internet Mail Service as a site messaging connector, data was transferred in cleartext with no authentication by default.

Exchange 2000 uses SMTP as its native transport between routing groups as well as between servers in the same routing group. If there is an Exchange 5.5 server or site in the organization, RPCs are used, but you cannot configure Exchange to use RPCs between two Exchange 2000 servers.

NOTE   Authentication between Exchange 2000 servers is handled using Kerberos as discussed earlier in the chapter. This is true regardless of whether the server is in the same routing group or a different routing group.

Message Data Format between Exchange Servers

When a message leaves an Exchange 2000 server's SMTP virtual server, the message must be converted to an SMTP message, because that is now the native format for message transport. The SMTP virtual server determines the next hop for the message and bases the type of message it will request on the destination of the message. The SMTP virtual server requests that the information store service convert the message; the information store service's IMAIL service then converts (on the server where the message originated) the message to the requested format.

The SMTP message formats are as follows:

Summary Transport Neutral Encapsulation Format (Summary TNEF, or S-TNEF)   This format is used if the Exchange message is going to be transported to another Exchange 2000 server in the same routing group. This format contains the traditional SMTP To and From headers, but the rest of the message is essentially an 8-bit binary blob of data. Only other Exchange 2000 servers can understand this message format. This is the most efficient means of transporting an Exchange message from one Exchange 2000 server to another. Figure 11.16 shows part of a message that is being transmitted. You can see certain things in the text portion of the message, such as the sender (Tang, Kwen Hou), recipient, the message tracking ID (c=us;a=.;p=Somorita Surfboa;l=SFOEX001-010422220417Z-2), and message subject (Sales Projections for 2002). You can see this information if you look in the ASCII decode section on the bottom center portion of the protocol trace.

Transport Neutral Encapsulation Format (or TNEF)   This format is used if the message is going to be transported to another Exchange server in another routing group. This format is exactly the same format that is used by the Exchange 5.5 Internet Mail Service; it contains the traditional To and From headers as well as the plaintext part of the message and a base64-encoded blob of data. This allows the message to cross 7-bit mailers such as the Exchange 5.5 Internet Mail Service.

MIME or UUENCODE   These message formats are used if the message is going to be leaving the Exchange organization. The default message format is MIME, but this format can be overridden on a per-domain basis by creating a custom message format in Exchange System Manager using the Global Settings ➢ Internet Message Formats.

Figure 11.16 Message encoding Exchange 2000 server to Exchange 2000 server

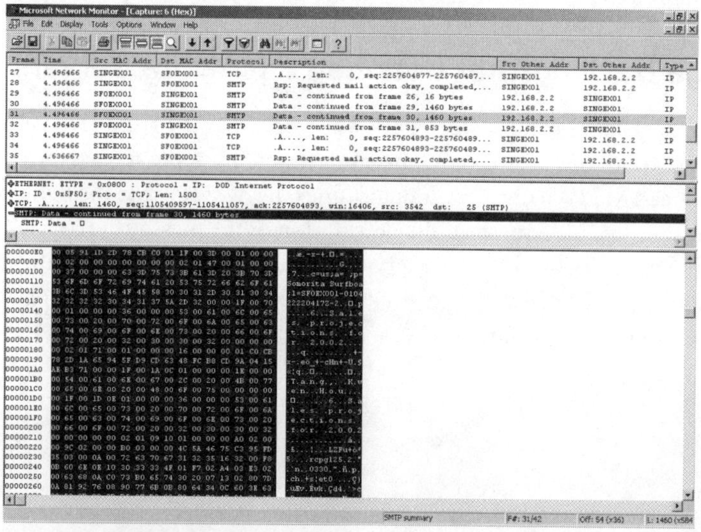

When an SMTP message leaves an Exchange 2000 server, it may be encoded; this prevents an amateur running Network Monitor from viewing the content of the message. However, someone with the right tools *will* be able to read it. If you are concerned about messages being intercepted between servers, you should implement IPSec. Across public networks to users who are not part of your organization, you will need to implement some type of message encryption technology such as S/MIME, which is discussed in Chapter 12.

LDAP Directory Queries

When an Exchange 2000 server has to perform a directory query to AD, it will contact either a domain controller or Global Catalog Server, depending on the type of data required. These queries are performed using LDAP on TCP port 389 (domain controller) or TCP port 3268 (global catalog server). These queries are neither encrypted nor encoded.

Securing Server-to-Server Communications

In the previous section, we looked at the server-to-server communication that anyone with a network analyzer can see on your network. Is this a concern? Does any part of your organization cross a public network? Is there a danger of unauthorized people running a network analyzer on your network?

If the answer to any of these questions is yes, then there are a couple of solutions that can improve the security of your server-to-server communications. These include implementing Transport Layer Security (TLS) and IP Security (IPSec). The advantage to implementing any encryption scheme between two servers is increased security, but naturally the cost is diminished performance.

Implementing SMTP Transport Layer Security

Each Exchange SMTP virtual server is capable of requiring secure communications. This is configured on each virtual server. To require secure communications between SMTP clients and SMTP servers, locate the SMTP virtual server on *each* Exchange server in your organization. Click the Access property tab, install an SSL server certificate on that server (described earlier in this chapter), and then click the Security property tab. On the Security tab, you can click Require Secure Channel.

Once you have done this step on each Exchange 2000 server in your organization, all SMTP mail will be transported using TLS. Is this a good thing? Sure, this is a great thing as long as no other SMTP servers out there in the world want to communicate with your Exchange 2000 servers.

WARNING   Requiring a secure channel will cause your Exchange 2000 SMTP virtual server to reject connections from SMTP clients that do not support TLS.

Most of us today do have SMTP connectivity to the outside world, so one of your virtual servers will probably have to allow cleartext communications. I recommend designating one (or possibly two, if you want a backup) of your Exchange 2000 servers to host the SMTP connector. On each of these servers, create an additional SMTP virtual server with a separate IP address that does not require secure communications. The DNS MX record for your organization will point to the non-secure SMTP virtual servers.

Is It TLS or SSL?

Many people, including myself, often use the terms TLS and SSL interchangeably. In fact, I often use these terms incorrectly, so let's try to set the record straight.

Transport Layer Security (TLS) is the Internet standard outlined in RFC 2246 for providing secure communications between two applications. TLS is based on an Application-layer encryption method developed by Netscape Communications called Secure Socket Layer (SSL). TLS is based on SSL v3.0; the differences are barely discernable to a non-crypto person, but enough so that the two are not natively interoperable. However, any application that is written to work with the TLS standard provides allowances for applications that only support SSL, and thus it is backward compatible.

SSL has become an industry standard due to its widespread use. A number of RFCs have been developed to encourage movement toward using standard TLS rather than simply SSL. These RFCs include 2712, 2487, and 2830. This move toward TLS will likely be eased by the fact that TLS will work with clients that only support SSL.

Exchange 2000 secure communications supports TLS and thus also supports SSL, though you will often see people referring to this as exclusively SSL.

IP Security and Exchange 2000

Requiring a secure connection for SMTP virtual servers will work if you only want to encrypt SMTP server-to-server traffic. However, TLS (and SSL) encrypt at the Application layer and are not terribly efficient. Any other server-to-server communication is still passed in its native format. Microsoft introduced IP Security (IPSec) integration with Windows 2000. IPSec encrypts data at the Network layer (layer 3) of the OSI model, rather than at the Application layer, and thus (almost) all communication between two IPSec enabled computers is encrypted.

Most of the white papers available today recommend the use of IPSec, not TLS, for securing server-to-server. However, even though implementing IPSec is not a terribly difficult task, implementing it in a fashion that is right for your organization is not simple. Certainly it is a topic beyond the scope of a small section of this chapter, so here I just cover the basics and make some simple recommendations on implementing IPSec to protect your Exchange 2000 servers.

IPSec 101   Before you implement any IPSec solution, you should understand the basics of IPSec and how it works. IPSec has initially proved to be popular providing enhanced security for remote access solutions as well as virtual private networks (VPNs). IPSec provides an additional layer of security using one of two protocols:

- The Authentication Headers (AH) protocol provides data integrity and authenticity, anti-replay protection, and anti-spoofing protection.
- The Encapsulating Security Payloads (ESP) protocol provides data encryption, authenticity, anti-replay protection, and anti-spoofing protection.

IPSec supports two separate modes of operation. These modes determine who is responsible for encryption and where you want the encryption to occur. These modes are as follows:

- Tunnel mode, which usually encrypts data between two points on a network such as a router, firewall, or other VPN device. Tunnel mode works best when only a portion of your network is unsecured. This allows the overhead of encryption to be off-loaded to another device.
- Transport mode, which provides end-to-end encryption. Transport mode works best when you want to encrypt all (or a certain type of) traffic between two computers. This is the mode that we're interested in for protecting Exchange servers.

If you are going to use IPSec between network nodes on opposite sides of the firewall, the firewall must be configured to allow IP protocol identifier 50 for the ESP protocol, or IP protocol identifier 51 for the AH protocol. The firewall must also be configured to allow UDP port 500 through the firewall. IPSec cannot be passed through a network address translator (NAT).

When you configure a Windows 2000 computer to use IPSec or you configure a policy that will affect many computers, you are presented with three IPSec policies:

- Secure Server (Require Security) requires that all traffic into or out of this node be secure. This is the most secure policy, but it will exclude communication with any client that does not support IPSec. This is not the best option for servers that must support client requests.

Security

PART 3

- Client (Respond Only) allows that the client use IPSec if the server requests the secure communications.

- Server (Request Security) is the mode that we are interested in for securing Exchange servers. This mode causes the computer to request secure communications for all incoming requests, but if a computer that does not support IPSec connects, communication will occur anyway.

Part of the security that IPSec provides is authentication. IPSec has three options for authentication, which are independent of the user who initiated the traffic:

- Kerberos version 5 authentication is the mode that we are interested in when using Windows 2000 computers.

- Certificate-based authentication requires that each computer that will use IPSec have exchanged public keys first. Certificate-based authentication can be used between a Windows 2000 computer and other platforms.

- Pre-shared key authentication requires that a password or passphrase be configured on both sides of the IPSec connection. Pre-shared key authentication can be used between a Windows 2000 computer and other platforms.

NOTE For more information on IPSec, consult the Windows 2000 Server Resource Kit's Internetworking Guide or the TCP/IP Core Networking Guide. Also, the IETF (Internet Engineering Task Force) has several white papers on IPSec at www.ietf.org/ids.by.wg/ipsec.html.

Enabling IPSec   This section gives a simple example of how to enable IPSec using a Group Policy Object (GPO). The first thing you want to do is to create an organizational unit in Active Directory Users And Computers that will contain all of your Exchange servers and move the Exchange 2000 servers to that organizational unit. If you want secure communications between domain controllers, apply an IPSec policy to those servers as well.

Once you have grouped all of your servers into a single organizational unit, create a policy that will configure IPSec on these computers. To do this, follow these steps:

1. Right-click the container that contains the Exchange 2000 servers, and choose Properties.

2. Click the Group Policy property tab.

3. Click New to create a new GPO, and assign the policy a name on the Group Policy property tab:

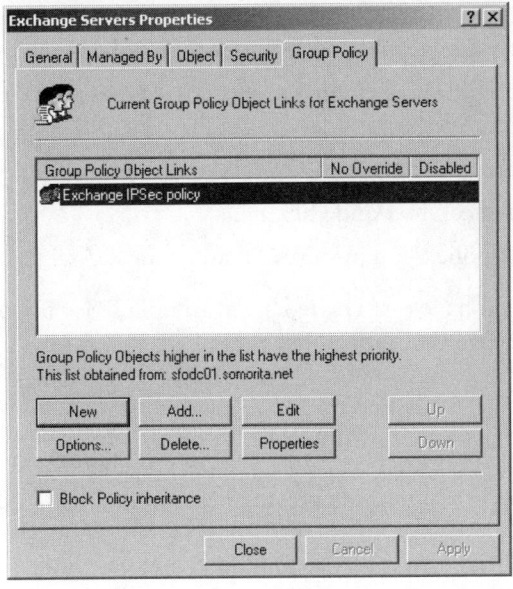

4. Highlight your newly created GPO, and click Properties. Put a check in the Disable User Configuration Settings check box. This will improve performance of this policy. Click OK.

5. Click the Edit button to edit the policy options for this GPO.

6. Go to Open Computer Configuration ➤ Windows Settings ➤ Security Settings ➤ IP Security Policies On Active Directory. This hierarchy is shown here:

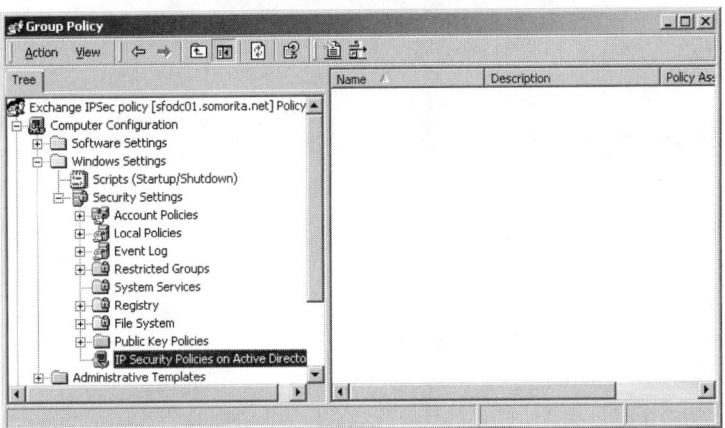

Security

PART 3

7. Right-click the IP Security Policies On Active Directory container and choose Create IP Security Policy. This launches the IP Security Policy Wizard. Click Next when it launches.

8. Type in a name and a brief description of the policy you are creating. Click Next.

9. Leave the Activate The Default Response Rule check box checked, and click Next.

10. Confirm that the Windows 2000 default (Kerberos V5 protocol) radio button is selected and click Next.

11. Clear the Edit check box and click Finish.

12. Right-click the policy you just created and choose Assign.

Congratulations, you have just created a very simple IPSec policy that affects your Exchange 2000 servers! Once the policy is applied, it may take between 60 and 120 minutes for the policy to actually take effect, possibly longer depending on AD replication.

You can further customize the policy to include only specific IP addresses or protocols by highlighting the policy you created, right-clicking, and choosing Properties. From the Rules tab shown in Figure 11.17, you can create filters for specific IP addresses or protocols.

Figure 11.17   IPSec Rules dialog box used for creating new filters

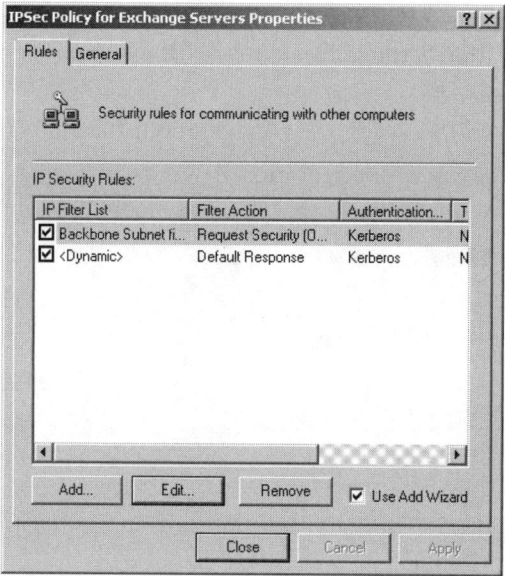

With some planning and additional work, you can create IPSec policies that affect only the specific servers between which you require encrypted communications.

12

Messaging Security

Five years ago, many companies used their e-mail systems simply to send phone messages and to ask "Do you want to grab lunch today?" Today, that use has broadened to include routing critical company information, expense reports, sales proposals, custom communication, purchase orders, and confidential client information both within their own organizations and with vendors and customers.

With the advent of e-mail's modern usage come common, resounding questions from e-mail users. "Is the e-mail I send safe?" "Is the message protected from prying eyes?" "Is there something that prevents someone from modifying my message after I have sent it?" Unless you have specifically done something to protect your messaging system, the answer to all three questions is "No!"

Many people are surprised to learn that an administrator with the proper permissions can give himself or herself permission to a mailbox and read any message in that mailbox. Further, that administrator can even send messages as another user!

Messaging security is not rocket science, but if you have not worked with encryption before, this chapter is going to introduce you to some new terms and concepts, including understanding e-mail vulnerability, configuring the Key Management Service (KMS), and enabling advanced security for clients. If you research encryption further, you will probably find enough mathematics to make a calculus professor cringe.

Message Vulnerability

Securing your messaging system requires an understanding of where messages are vulnerable and that they can be intercepted in a variety of places; consequently, a clever person can alter a message in transit or while it is being stored. This section reviews where a message can be viewed or changed, what types of risks a message is susceptible to, and the requirements you need to make sure that you have adequately secured your messaging system.

Implementing an organization-wide e-mail security system also introduces questions surrounding the usage of message encryption and key recovery. What messages should users encrypt? Who should have key recovery permissions, and under what circumstances should key recovery be used?

Message Capture on the Wire

In Chapter 11, I did several protocol traces using the Microsoft Network Monitor, a powerful tool that is included with Windows NT Server and Microsoft Systems Management Server (SMS). Network Monitor allows you to capture the network conversation between two computers; further, the tool can decode and display much of the information contained in that transmission.

Many messaging systems transmit an e-mail message across the network in cleartext ("in the clear") or simply encoded. Between Exchange servers, SMTP messages are in cleartext and can be captured by just about anyone with a network analyzer and access to the network traffic, and anyone can download simple network analyzer tools for Windows NT or Windows 95/98. The ability of someone to capture data using Network Monitor hinges on a couple of things. First, the Network Monitor user must be in the "path" of the message; in other words, the message must be on the same network segment as the Network Monitor user. Second, if the network implements switching technology, the Network Monitor user probably will not be able to capture information between another client and a server.

SMTP is one of many protocols that transfer messages over the wire in cleartext (though between Exchange servers the message is encoded). From the time the message leaves the SMTP client until the SMTP server receives it, the message can be read at any point along the way.

NOTE   I have several friends who refuse to give their credit card number via a website. However, these same friends don't give a second thought to e-mailing their credit card number across the Internet. Under most circumstances, e-mail messages are not secure and can be easily intercepted, while websites can be configured to require SSL (Secure Sockets Layer).

> **WARNING** Messaging clients that pass messages over the wire in cleartext have a much greater risk than is first apparent. These systems (in the case of POP3 and IMAP4) also pass the user ID and password in the clear. For Exchange-based systems, this is the Active Directory user account and password. If that is compromised, you have worse problems on your hands than just snoops reading your messages.

Exchange Messaging Connectors

The Exchange 2000 Routing Group Connector (RGC) uses SMTP to transfer messages to other Exchange 2000 routing groups—and thus, by default, is insecure. However, if the RGC or the Exchange 2000 message transfer agent is used to connect to an Exchange 5.5 server, it uses Remote Procedure Calls (RPCs) between Exchange servers; RPCs are encrypted with 40-bit RSA RC2 streaming encryption (except if you have the North American edition of Windows NT Service Pack 3 or later, in which case Windows NT uses 128-bit encryption). Windows 2000 provides the ability to use IPSec (IP security) between clients and servers as well as between servers. This is also a valid way to provide internal encryption.

The X.400 Connector provides no native encryption or security beyond basic encoding of the message data. Though the X.400 Connector is robust and flexible, it provides no network-level security.

Using the SMTP Connector to connect routing groups is not secure by default; all messages are exchanged using the standard SMTP format. However, the SMTP Connector provides the ability to use integrated Windows authentication and TLS encryption.

> **NOTE** A common misconception is that messages are secure as long as they do not leave your organization. People believe that as long as a message remains on their internal LAN or WAN, it is safe. Consequently, they only take steps to protect messages that leave the organization. I have demonstrated to a number of clients (with their permission) how easy it is to place a network analyzer on their network (also known as "internal espionage"). Keep in mind that messages should not only be secure outside of your network, but that messages can be intercepted from within your network, as well. One way to protect against this type of security breach is to provide strong physical security for your networking devices; another approach is to implement network switching, thereby ensuring that network data is not easily intercepted by a network analyzer.

Messages on a User's Local Hard Drive

Once a mail program has removed the message from the server, it has to be stored somewhere—usually on the user's local hard drive. If a technically adept, curious person can get access to the user's computer, chances are good the person can find that user's e-mail message files.

In the case of Outlook configured to store messages locally, all local messages are stored in a personal folder (or PST file). Even if the user's primary message storage location is on the server, the user may still have messages stored on their local hard disk in PST files. Users are often asked to make backup copies of important messages, to archive messages they want to keep, and to use the Outlook AutoArchive feature to put all messages on the local hard disk into a PST file.

If you study the PST file, as well as many other methods for local storage, you will find that either the files are encrypted or they can be password protected. However, this is not an obstruction for a tech-savvy person who is intent on reading your mail. The best way to secure such files is with a combination of NTFS permissions and the Windows 2000 Encrypting File System (EFS).

TIP   Though the Outlook program can set a password for the PST file, there are PST-cracking utilities available on the Web. Try www.lostpassword.com for a sampling of these tools, or search the Internet for words such as exchange, pst, file, and crack.

Messages in the Exchange Information Store

Messages that are stored in a user's private mailbox on the Exchange server are also vulnerable. An Exchange server mailbox cannot be opened by just anyone; the person must have an Active Directory user account. Though a mailbox is safe from the majority of people who have mailboxes on an Exchange server, an Exchange administrator who has the Exchange Full Administrator role can give themselves the Receive As permission through Exchange System Manager, or the Full Mailbox Access Right through Active Directory Users And Computers.

WARNING   Administrative and mailbox permissions are discussed in more detail in Chapter 11, "Security within the Network."

Catching Improper Mailbox Access   If you are watching your Windows NT application logs, you can scan for an event that will tell you if someone other than the mailbox owner is trying to access the mailbox. The event ID is 1016, and the source is MSExchangeIS Mailbox.

If you see this event in the application log (yes, the application log, not the security log), it means that someone other than the user assigned to the mailbox owner has access to the mailbox. Starting with Exchange 2000 SP1, you must turn up diagnostics logging in order to see the mailbox access events. The description of the event (shown in Figure 12.1) will tell you which Windows NT user account was used and which mailbox was accessed.

Figure 12.1   Mailbox access by someone other than the mailbox owner

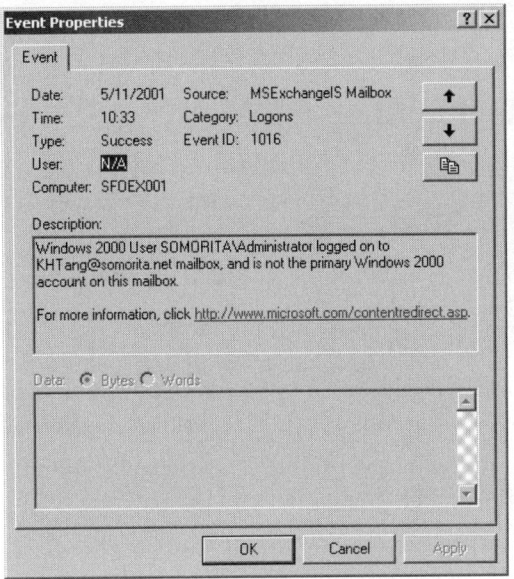

These messages also appear if the user has been given delegate access and is merely accessing a mailbox to which they have been given official permissions. Further, certain virus-scanning, voicemail integration, fax, and backup programs that perform brick-level backups also log this event. So before you jump to any conclusions when you see this message, think about why you might be seeing it.

Messages during Gateway Conversion

If a message is being routed to a system other than its native system, it is probably going to be converted to a text file before it is migrated into the destination system. In the Exchange world, message connectors extract messages from the Exchange server database and usually write them to disk in some sort of standardized file format.

While these messages are stored on the disk in temporary format, anyone could read them if they have the correct file and directory access to the directory in which the messages are stored. Usually these messages can be opened and clearly read (and possibly modified!) with a utility as simple as Notepad.

> **NOTE** Please refer to your connector's architecture information to determine the "conversion" working directory. You should secure this directory so only the Exchange site services account can access it. If necessary, you may need to add appropriate foreign mail system accounts so they can gain access.

Outbound SMTP messages are stored in the mailbox store where they originated until they are ready for delivery. Inbound SMTP mail messages are stored in the `\Program Files\Exchsrvr\Mailroot\<virtual server name>\Queue` directory.

Secure Messaging Should Be...

Now that you're scared of all the places that messages can be intercepted, read, and possibly modified to serve a Dogbert-like agenda, let's take a look at some goals you should have for securing your messaging system:

- Messages should be *private*. Only the sender and the intended recipients should be able to examine the content of a message during its journey through the messaging system or after it is stored.

- Message *integrity* should be verifiable. The receiver should be able to confirm that the message has not been modified since it was transmitted.

- Message *origin* should be verifiable. The receiver should be able to confirm that the person in the From field really did send the message.

- Messages should be subject to *non-repudiation*. The sender cannot come back later and say, "I did not send that message."

- Message encryption may need to be *recoverable*. The administrator of the mail system may need to recover the keys in order to decrypt a message. When implementing a secure messaging system, organizations should decide if this is one of the goals. If there are no key recovery capabilities in place, if a user leaves the company or simply loses their keys, their encrypted messages are lost forever.

Encryption Basics

We have come a long way from the days of the Cracker Jack secret decoder rings. Data encryption is a booming business, and there are a million confusing terms out there. So this section gives a little bit of background that you should be familiar with for most any type of system that takes advantage of encryption.

To truly secure your messaging system, you should lock all of your doors, never send a message to the outside world, and post armed guards at all computers. However, I suspect you are going to want to use a more flexible approach—a combination of message encryption (Microsoft calls this *sealing*) and message signing (*digital signatures*).

Have you heard but not quite understood terms such as secret keys, bulk encryption keys, public/private key pairs, PKI, hashing, and certificates? The next few sections define these and other encryption-related terms, discuss what all this means, and reveal how it applies to the messaging world.

Common Encryption Terms

A term that you hear quite often in the encryption world is *cipher*. A cipher is the algorithm (formula) that is used to encrypt and decrypt a piece of data by defining how a block of text is processed as it is being encrypted. The encrypted data is sometimes referred to as *ciphertext* or an *opaque item*, whereas the unencrypted data is sometimes referred to as *plaintext*. There are two types of ciphers that are commonly used:

- A *block cipher* takes a block of data (or even an entire file) and processes it a block at a time. The block cipher produces a ciphertext block for each plaintext block it is given.

- A *stream cipher* (a.k.a. *streaming encryption*) processes elements of a stream of data continuously. It is not uncommon for a stream cipher to encrypt data either one bit or one byte at a time.

Table 12.1 lists common cipher and hashing algorithms that are used with Microsoft products, including Exchange.

Table 12.1   Common Algorithms

Algorithm	Description
CAST	Carlisle Adams and Stafford Tavares developed this 64-bit symmetric block cipher. It is similar to DES (Data Encryption Standard). It supports keys between 40 bits to 128 bits.
DES	Data Encryption Standard, developed by IBM for the government, is a NIST (National Institute of Standards and Technology) data-encryption standard that uses 56-bit keys with a 64-bit symmetric block cipher. This is probably the best known and mostly widely used encryption in the world.
3DES	Triple DES has several different approaches to encrypting data, but all involve three separate encryption passes.
DH	Diffie-Hellman is a method for secret (symmetric) key exchange. This is discussed in the next section.
KEA	Key Exchange Algorithm is an improved version of Diffie-Hellman.

Security

PART 3

Table 12.1 Common Algorithms *(continued)*

Algorithm	Description
MD2	Message Digest is a hashing algorithm that creates a 128-bit hash value; it was developed by Ron Rivest of RSA.
MD4	An RSA hashing algorithm that creates a 128-bit hash value.
MD5	An improved version of the RSA MD4 that creates a 128-bit hash value.
RC2	An RSA 64-bit symmetric block cipher (RC stands for Rivest's Cipher or Ron's Cipher).
RC4	An RSA stream cipher that can use variable length keys. Microsoft commonly uses either a 40-bit or 128-bit key.
RSA	Very popular public/private key encryption scheme, developed at RSA, naturally.
SHA	Developed by NIST, Secure Hash Algorithm produces a 160-bit hash value. It is similar to MD5, but more secure (and slower).
Skipjack	An 80-bit symmetric block cipher used by the Clipper and Capstone chips.

Diffie-Hellman Key Exchange

Public/private key encryption is very secure and provides better (but slower) key management than symmetric secret keys. However, secret key encryption is more vulnerable to compromise. What's an encryption dude to do? Whitfield Diffie and Martin Hellman (hereafter known as Diffie-Hellman) asked the same question. (Diffie and Hellman are extraordinarily clever; when I mention their names, you have to stand, bow to the west, and chant thrice.)

Their answer was the development of a method of key exchange suitably known as *Diffie-Hellman key exchange*. In a nutshell, they combined the best of both the secret and public/private key worlds. Simply, if I (and my friend) have a program that is capable of using Diffie-Hellman key exchange, I run the encryption program and enter my friend's public key. The program randomly creates a secret key and uses some predefined method to encrypt the data; encryption methods to encrypt the data or message use some type of block cipher such as CAST or DES. This part of the encryption process is sometimes called the *bulk encryption algorithm*. Since the secret key (the bulk encryption key) is used to encrypt the data, the data is encrypted very quickly. This solves the problem of slow encryption.

The secret key is then encrypted with my friend's public key and attached to the end of the encrypted file. This solves the problem of how to deliver the symmetric (secret) key to my friend. When my friend receives the file, she opens it and uses her private key to begin decrypting the message. What really happens is that the private key is used to decrypt the encrypted secret key. The encryption program can now decrypt the entire file because it has the secret key, which was used to encrypt the file. Pretty spiffy, eh?

> **NOTE** When using S/MIME messaging, the encrypted symmetric key is placed into a virtual "lock box" attached to the message. It is considered a lock box because the strong encryption of the public/private key pair is used to secure it.

Key Strength

One of the jobs of the *cryptographer* is to perform *cryptanalysis*, the process of figuring out or reverse-engineering ciphertext. One approach is to attack the method of encryption itself; if the cipher is weak, adept cryptographers may be able to break the encryption. However, today's well-known ciphers are considered strong enough to resist most attempts to compromise them.

Many efforts at decryption focus on using a brute-force attack; that is, trying all possible combinations of the key. Key size is normally measured in bits. The more bits used in the key, the more possible combinations exist in the *key space*. The larger the key space, the longer the key—and the more difficult a brute-force attack is.

To really appreciate how hard it is to decrypt a specific key length, think about the total number of combinations for a specific key length:

Key Length	Number of Possible Keys in the Key Space
40-bit	1,099,511,627,776
56-bit	72,057,594,037,927,936
64-bit	18,446,744,073,709,551,616
128-bit	340,282,366,920,938,463,463,374,607,430,000,000,000

Actually, my calculator cannot even handle 2 to the 128th power, so I had to do some rounding for the 128-bit value.

Security

PART 3

With some effort, a very resourceful person and several very fast computers could break 40-bit encryption within a few days. Both DES 56-bit and RSA 64-bit encryption have been broken by the Distributed Project (`www.distributed.net`), a collection of people from all over the world taking a small piece of the key space and processing it. It took them many months to break both of these. A few years ago, I was running several computers as part of the Distributed Project trying to break RSA 64-bit encryption. My computers processed about 700,000 keys per second. At this rate, I will break the 64-bit encryption in about 580 years. Let's not even think about trying to break 128-bit encryption; it is still quite strong. However, if the private key is compromised because its owner is careless, the whole process breaks down, and all secured messages sent to that person are compromised.

> **NOTE**   As processor power improves and 64-bit computing platforms become more common, breaking keys that are 128 bits in length will become possible.

The Key to Encryption

A *key* is a set of characters of varying length that is used with the cipher (encryption formula) to generate encrypted data. There are many ways to define a key and many types of keys; for purposes of this book, I will stick to the two key types that are relevant to messaging: secret keys and public/private keys.

Secret Keys

A *secret key* is a secret password. For example, I make up a password, such as "$uper+=Pass123" and use this password to encrypt a Microsoft Word document. When I want to retrieve this document, I must enter **$uper+=Pass123** to gain access to the file. Basically, the same password that is used to encrypt the file is also used to decrypt it. Secret keys are also called *symmetric keys*, because there is only one key for both encryption and decryption. You may also hear secret keys referred to as a *bulk encryption* key.

The advantage of a secret key cipher is that it is generally very fast; a computer can encrypt a large amount of data in a very short time using a secret key cipher. However, if I want to send a password-protected file to someone else, I must somehow give her the password. I could put it on a Post-It note, I could e-mail it to her, or I could call her and give it to her over the phone. However, even if no one overhears my password, what if my friend gives it to someone else? My password is compromised and I can never use it again. How do I get my password (secret key) to her? I need a way to securely transmit it while ensuring that the secret key is not reused.

Public and Private Keys

A *public/private key pair* (also called *asymmetric keys)* is a special type of key relationship. This arrangement consists of two very large keys (typically 512 bits, 1024 bits, or longer) that are mathematically related to one another, but the mathematical relationship is virtually impossible to calculate. In this relationship, I have two keys; I can give one to anyone who wants it (hereafter known as the public key), and I alone have access to the other key (hereafter deemed the private key). Data encrypted with the public key must be decrypted with the private key.

If I wish to send a secret document to a friend, I ask her for her public key. Since the key is public, she doesn't care who has it. She can send it to me over unencrypted e-mail, give it to me over the phone (if I wanted to write down a 512-bit number!), write it down for me, or post it publicly on her home page.

Once I have my friend's public key, I run the encryption program on the data I wish to encrypt using *her* public key, not my own private key. I then transmit the encrypted data to her over any type of network. My friend runs the decryption program and uses her private key. Whether the data is sent over the network or stored it in a file, it doesn't matter if the data is intercepted because it is encrypted. Even if everyone on the network has my friend's public key, the *only* key that can decrypt the data is her private key.

The advantage to public/private key encryption is that the keys are much more secure since you alone control access to the private key. Also, since the key size is so large, the encrypted data is very hard to decrypt. However, large key size also makes encryption and decryption *very* time consuming and CPU intensive.

> **NOTE** You can find volumes of information on public/private keys on RSA's website, www.rsasecurity.com.

Public Key Infrastructure (PKI)

PKI is a generic term that encompasses all the technology required to build a public key infrastructure. PKI assumes the use of public key cryptography for authenticating a message sender or for encrypting a message. A PKI consists of a Certificate Authority (CA) for issuing and verifying digital certificates, a Registration Authority that verifies CAs, a directory where the public keys are held, and a system for managing certificates.

> **NOTE** For more information on Certificate Authorities, see that section later in this chapter.

Hashing (Message Digests)

Hashing is a mathematical function that is applied to a string of characters of any length, or to an entire file. The hashing function reduces any length of characters to a fixed length. Hashing is also sometimes called a *message digest* because the hashed value uniquely represents the original data. Even if you have the message digest and the formula that was used to produce the message digest, you cannot reverse-engineer it back to the original data. If you alter one single bit in the original data and run the hashing function again, the message digest will change.

Hashing functions are commonly used in message signing (digital signatures) to create a unique "signature" of the message in question. There are a number of algorithms that are used to create a message digest, including RSA's MD2, MD4, and MD5, which all create a 128-bit hash.

NOTE   Want to know more about hashing? One of my favorite websites, www
.whatis.com, has a good overview of hashing at whatis.techtarget.com/
definition/0,289893,sid9_gci212230,00.html. RSA has detailed technical
information at www.rsasecurity.com/rsalabs/faq/2-1-6.html.

Certificates

Suppose you send me a message and ask for my public key. In a few days, you receive a reply from me with my public key. That was pretty simple, wasn't it? You can now use the public key to encrypt messages and data for me; only my private key can decrypt the secret and confidential data you have sent me. Further, let's say that I send you a message that I have "signed" to guarantee its authenticity (I sign the message using my private key). I include with that message my public key so that you can verify that the message did indeed come from me and that the message has not been altered.

Do you see a possible hole here? Did I hand that public key over to you personally? Did you check my passport or driver's license? Do you know me personally? Do you know someone who can vouch for me? If not, how do you know that it was really my public key and not the work of a hacker intent on getting your secrets? Muahahahaha!

This is where certificates come into play. A *certificate* is a digital document that attests to the validity of a public key and thus establishes your digital credibility. The ITU (International Telecommunications Union) has developed a standard for digital certificates called X.590. There are two flavors of X.509: X.509v1 and X.509v3. X.509v3 certificates are the most widely accepted and used; the S/MIME standard uses X.509v3 certificates. The Windows 2000 Certificate Server (and thus the Exchange 2000 Key Management Service) issues

X.509v3 certificates. However, the Exchange 2000 KMS will issue X.509v1 certificates exclusively, if you still have a necessity for backward compatibility with older Exchange clients. If you are given a choice, you should choose to issue X.509v3 certificates.

> **NOTE**   The Key Management Service is discussed later in this chapter.

All versions of Outlook since Outlook 98 support S/MIME messages and use X.509v3 certificates. Figure 12.2, from an Outlook 2000 message, shows some of the typical fields found in an X.590v3 certificate.

Figure 12.2   X.509v3 certificate details as shown from Outlook 2000

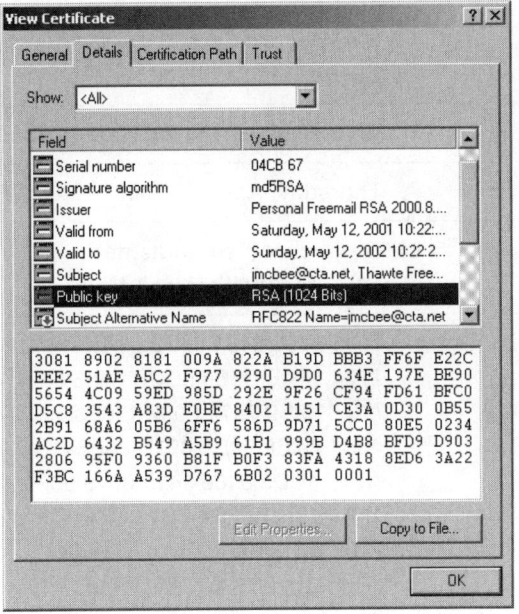

> **NOTE**   The Exchange 4, 5, and 5.5 KMS supports the issuance of X.509v1 certificates; however, the X.509v1 certificates that the KMS issues are only interoperable with other Exchange systems.

Table 12.2 lists the fields that are found in an X.509v3 certificate. I used my Thawte (www.thawte.com) Freemail certificate as an example.

Table 12.2   Fields in an X.509v3 Certificate

Field	Sample Value
Version	V3
Serial number	04AF 92
Signature algorithm	md5RSA
Issuer	CN = Personal Freemail RSA 2000.8.30 OU = Certificate Services O = Thawte L = Cape Town S = Western Cape C = ZA
Valid from	Wednesday, April 25, 2001 11:48:23 PM
Valid to	Thursday, April 25, 2002 11:48:23 PM
Subject	E = jmcbee@somorita.net CN = Thawte Freemail Member
Public key	3081 8902 8181 00D8 E1AB CA10 96F7 E2BF 35D8 E8F2 2704 8FAE D5B6 3DDB C4F5 9337 1A6B 0C22 9BB8 DB29 A246 82B9 7871 E992 128E 200B 4A08 A3BA 9988 7100 44B4 4ACF 5AE5 0F7D 40E8 E925 C72C D81E E24B 0E1E A71B 1CD3 9166 141E 0049 53F5 34E1 0C9B 468C 5089 19A9 7E6D AFEA FB79 C214 D516 E649 9602 7583 1084 8792 46B8 6A50 C430 0200 0B1B 7BE3 4502 0301 0001 (This is an RSA 1024-bit public key from the certificate.)
Subject alternative name	RFC822 Name=jmcbee@somorita.net
Key usage	Digital Signature, Non-repudiation, Key Encipherment, Data Encipherment, Key Agreement (F8)
Basic constraints	Subject Type=End Entity Path Length Constraint=None
Thumbprint algorithm	sha1
Thumbprint	6DB1 4C1B ACF6 2BC3 1296 BF77 CDA1 B367 1FC1 4633

Depending on the type of key and the issuer, a certificate may be kept in a central location so that anyone can easily get access to it. In the case of Exchange 2000, these certificates are stored in Active Directory. Note that the certificate does not contain a copy of the private key.

The private key (for Windows NT, Windows 2000, and Windows XP users) is stored as part of the Protected Storage system. This consists of a Windows service and the user's Windows profile. The Protected Storage service is responsible for encrypting and protecting the private keys.

Getting Your Own Certificate

Many of us do not work for an organization large enough to worry about putting a PKI in place. So how to do we get a certificate so that we can send signed messages and so people can send encrypted messages to us? Visit CA Thawte on the Web at www.thawte.com. In addition to providing reasonably priced web server certificates, they provide free secure e-mail certificates. Follow the link on their main page to Secure Your Email and enroll for your free certificate. It is very nice of the folks at Thawte to offer this service, and it should not be abused.

Security

PART 3

Certificate Authorities

A *Certificate Authority* (CA) issues keys and certificates and is responsible for managing security credentials for keys. The CA will not issue you a certificate until it can verify that you are who you say you are. Remember that the certificate is your digital ID. Would your country's government issue you a passport just because you asked for one? That is unlikely; you must prove that you are really you. Just like the government will stand behind you once they have issued you a passport, your CA will verify that your certificate is real and valid.

A CA is part of a PKI, which provides the ability for a root CA to allow subordinate CAs to issue keys. If a subordinate CA issues a key, the validity of the subordinate's signature can be confirmed by contacting the root CA. The Exchange 2000 KMS uses the Windows 2000 Certificate Authority as its source for certificates.

For example, lets say that I want to issue a digital certificate to all of my users so they can send S/MIME messages. I could pay a root authority to create and issue all my certificates, or I could become a subordinate authority to a well-known root. There are a number of trusted root authorities that can either create X.509v3 certificates for your users directly or that can trust your certificate server and allow you to create trusted X.509v3 certificates yourself.

NOTE Prior to Exchange 5.5 SP1, the Exchange 5.5 Key Management Service acted as its own CA and could only create X.509v1 certificates.

S/MIME? What's All the Fuss About?

MIME (Multipurpose Internet Mail Extensions—RFC 1521) describes how to organize an electronic mail message to be transmitted using SMTP (RFC 822, 2821, and 2822)). MIME formatting permits e-mail to include attachments such as documents, text, multimedia, and more in a standardized manner via MIME-compliant mail systems. However, MIME alone does not define any security capabilities.

S/MIME (Secure Multipurpose Internet Mail Extensions) is an extension to MIME that provides a way to send encrypted messages between two dissimilar clients. It extends the MIME capabilities by describing how to encrypt message data and attach digital certificates to the message. S/MIME follows a syntax described in the Public-Key Cryptography Standard (PKCS) format #7. (As of this writing, RSA has submitted S/MIME to the Internet Engineering Task Force for consideration as an Internet standard. See RFCs 2311 and 2633.) The PKCS standards were developed by RSA in cooperation with Apple, DEC, Lotus, Microsoft, MIT, and Sun. They include standards for RSA encryption, password-based encryption, extended certificate syntax, and cryptographic message syntax.

In order for an S/MIME client to be compatible with the proposed S/MIME standard, it must recognize and implement the following RSA standards:

- PKCS #1: RSA Encryption

- PKCS #7: Cryptographic Message Syntax

- PKCS #10: Certification Request Syntax

(For more information about PKCS #7, see ftp.rsasecurity.com/pub/pkcs/doc/pkcs-7.doc.)

You will see some additional MIME types when an e-mail message is an S/MIME message. These include:

- Application/pkcs7-mime (attachment type of .p7m)

- Application/pkcs7-signature (attachment type of .p7m)

- Multipart/signed

S/MIME? What's All the Fuss About? *(continued)*

Outlook 2000 SR1 introduced support for S/MIME v3 (RFC 2633) that adds additional support for stronger encryption. The software is installed but the user interface does not display the additional features. To use the additional features, you need to add a key to the Registry called `EnableSRFeatures` of type REG_DWORD; set this value to 1. This key should be created in `HKLM\Software\Microsoft\Office\9.0\Outlook\Security`. Two other Registry entries of interest that can be used in this key include `AlwaysSign` (1 is on, 0 is off) and `AlwaysEncrypt` (1 is on, 0 is off).

S/MIME has industry support from vendors such as Lotus, Novell, Microsoft, Veri-Sign, Qualcomm, and, of course, RSA. For more detailed information on S/MIME, check out `www.rsa.com/smime`.

Trusting Other Organizations

If you send mail often to another organization, you need the public keys for anyone to whom you are going to send mail in that organization. The users in the other organization need to send you their own certificates (which you store in your Personal Address Book or the Outlook Contacts folder).

But how do you know you can trust certificates generated by another organization? Trusted CAs are managed in two separate locations. The Windows client has a list of trusted authorities that is stored in Internet Explorer. All versions of Outlook after Outlook 98 as well as Outlook Express use this list of trusted CAs when verifying a certificate. You can view this list in Internet Explorer (5.*x*) by selecting Tools ➢ Internet Options, viewing the Content property tab, clicking the Certificates button, and clicking the Trusted Root Certificate Authorities property tab.

You can add your own authorities to this list by installing the CA's certificate on your own computer. For example, if you have a Microsoft Windows 2000 Certificate Server, you can connect to the page to retrieve a CA certificate or *certificate revocation list* (CRL, a list of all certificates that should no longer be considered valid); the virtual directory is /certsrv. The default, full path on my `sfodc01.somorita.net` server is `https://sfodc01.somorita.net/certserv/certcarc.asp`. This page is shown in Figure 12.3. Click the Download CA Certificate link to download this CA's certificate.

Figure 12.3   Retrieve the CA certificate or certificate revocation list.

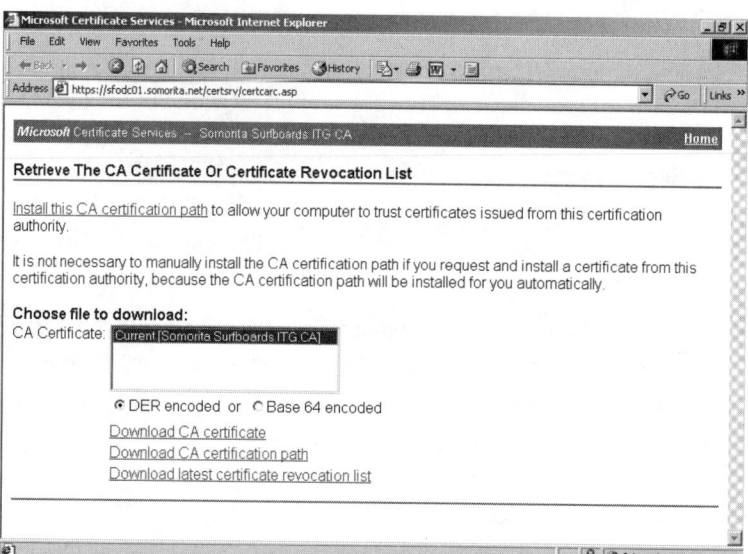

You can also get the .CRT or .CER file from the administrator of the CA and import it using Internet Explorer, or you can distribute it with the Internet Explorer Admin Kit. These files can contain the X.509 certificate of the server.

The Windows 2000 Certificate Server supports Exchange Server 5.5 with SP1 or later supports a feature called *certification trust lists (CTLs)*. A CTL gives an administrator the ability to publish a list of external entities that his organization trusts. Now your users will be able to automatically authenticate any signed messages accepted from a trusted company (a signed message includes a copy of the user's signing certificate). However, users will still need a copy of the remote user's public sealing (encryption) certificate.

What If My Private Key Is Compromised?

Suppose the bad guys get their hands on your private key. Is all lost? Not exactly, but different systems handle this in different ways. In the Exchange world, you could contact your Exchange security administrator as soon as you thought your private key had been compromised. The administrator would revoke your current keys and issue you a new set. Your old certificate number would then be placed on a CRL. The CRL is maintained by the Windows 2000 Certificate Authority, but you can use the Exchange 2000 KMS to add certificates to the CRL list or to take certificates off of the CRL. If a user has encrypted mail that was previously encrypted with a certificate that is now revoked, they will still be able to access that message. However, if a user's certificate is revoked for message signing, other users will not be able to verify the authenticity of messages signed with that certificate.

Certificate Expiration

Don't be surprised if your certificate has an expiration date. This is normal and important in ensuring that the validity of the certificate is maintained. Some certificates have a lifetime as short as one year, such as older versions of Microsoft Exchange's KMS certificates. I have seen certificates that are good for up to five years, but those are special situations, such as where an agreement has been reached with the CA for a certificate with a longer lifespan.

However, not to fear—as the life of your certificate approaches the end, you can renew the certificate, effectively extending its life.

The Key Management Service

The Exchange 2000 Key Management Service (KMS) interacts with a Windows 2000 Enterprise Certificate Authority to create, distribute, and manage certificates for Outlook clients. Other clients such as Outlook Express or Netscape Communicator must request their certificates directly from a CA such as the Windows 2000 Certificate Server.

Configuring the Windows 2000 Certificate Authority

Before you install the Exchange 2000 KMS, you must configure a Windows 2000 Enterprise Certificate Authority to support the KMS. The Windows 2000 Certificate Server can be installed on any Windows 2000 server in the domain. For large organizations, I recommend using a subordinate Enterprise CA to generate the Exchange certificates rather than using the root CA for all certificate activity in the domain.

Once the certificate server is installed, you must configure the CA to issue the correct certificates. To do this, launch the Certification Authority console on the certificate server. From that console, choose and right-click the Policy Settings folder, and choose New ➤ Certificate To Issue (See Figure 12.4). Make sure that you include the Enrollment Agent (Computer), Exchange User, and Exchange Signature Only certificate templates in the Policy Settings container.

Security

PART 3

Figure 12.4   Adding a new certificate template from the Certification Authority console

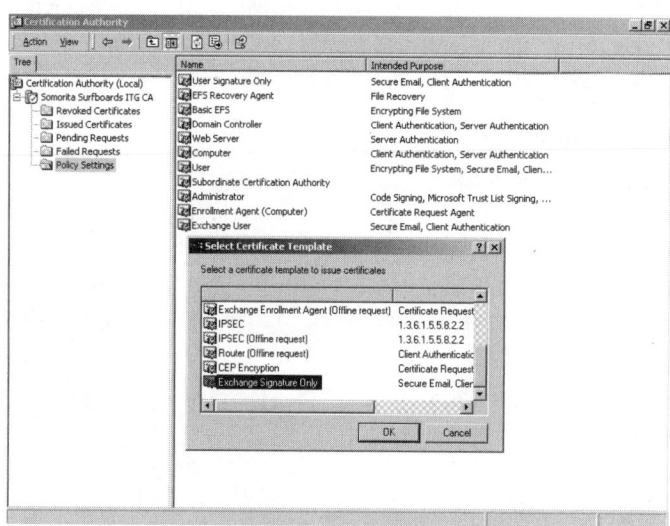

Installing the Key Management Service

To install the KMS, you use the Exchange 2000 Installation Wizard and include the Microsoft Exchange Key Management Service found under the Microsoft Exchange Messaging And Collaboration Services component. Here are some considerations to keep in mind when preparing to install the KMS:

- A Windows 2000 Enterprise CA must be installed. The authority cannot be a stand-alone CA. This CA must be configured to issue Enrollment Agent (Computer), Exchange User, and Exchange Signature Only certificates.

- The KMS is not cluster-aware and must be installed on a non-clustered Exchange 2000 server.

When you launch the Exchange 2000 Setup program and choose to install the KMS, you will be prompted to choose an administrative group in which the CA will be installed. If you break up administrative responsibilities by administrative group, you may want to install the KMS in an administrative group to which most administrators have limited authority.

Also, you will be asked whether you want to use a manual password entry or to read the password from a disk. This password is critical to the operation of your KMS and is required when the KMS service starts because it is necessary to decrypt the KMS database.

WARNING If you lose the KMS startup password, you will never be able to start the KMS service again! There is *no* back door.

If you choose Read Password From Disk, you must provide a floppy disk. Each time the KMS service is started, this floppy must be in the A: drive of the server. If you choose this option, make several copies of the floppy disk and store them in a safe place! The password is stored in cleartext in the `kmserver.pwd` file on the floppy disk. The disk must be in the floppy drive when the server starts or you restart the KMS; make sure you remove the floppy and store it in a secure location once the service is started.

If you choose Manual Password Entry, the password will be displayed one time in a pop-up box (see Figure 12.5). Write down this password and store it in a safe place; I take a screen capture of this dialog box so that I am sure I have correctly recorded the password.

Figure 12.5   The KMS startup password

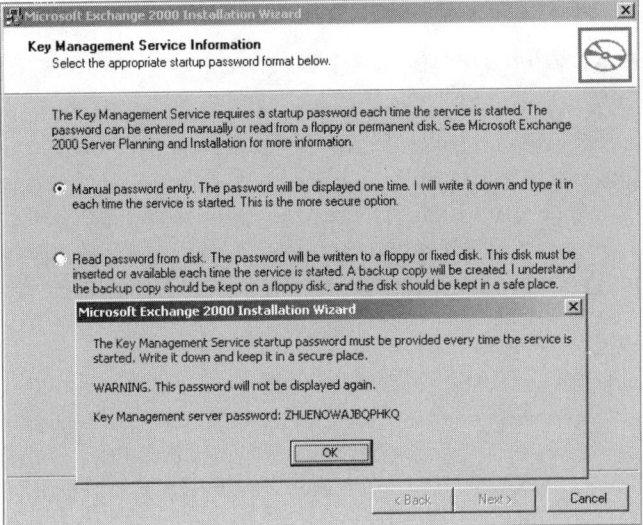

Starting the KMS

The KMS must be started manually, because the password must be provided for each startup. From the Services console, right-click the KMS service and choose Properties. On the Start Parameters line (shown in Figure 12.6), type the startup password you were provided. Note that the password is always uppercase letters.

Figure 12.6   Starting the KMS with the startup password

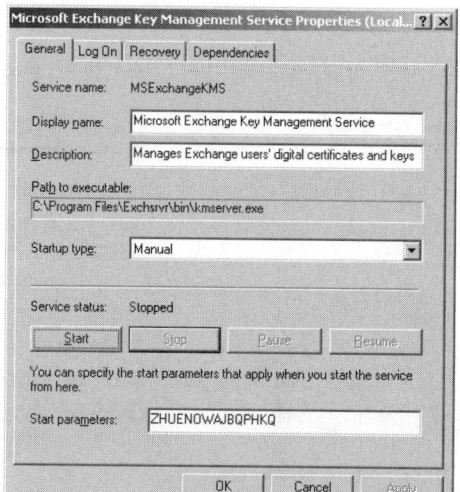

Using the Key Management Service

Once the KMS is installed, you can now load the Exchange Advanced Security console and manage advanced security settings. The Exchange Advanced Security console displays all of the administrative groups that have Exchange 2000 servers. The administrative group into which you installed the KMS will have two items: Key Manager and Encryption Configuration. All other administrative groups will have only the Encryption Configuration.

The Key Manager Object

The Key Manager object exists in each administrative group that contains an Exchange 2000 KMS. The first (and possibly most important) thing you need to be aware of with this object is that a separate password is required to manage it. By default, only the user who installed the KMS is allowed to manage the object; thus you should install the KMS only as an administrative user that should have permissions to manage the KMS object. It may be even better if you actually create a special KMS manager user account. The default password is *password*; this password is case sensitive.

NOTE When managing the Key Manager object, you may be prompted for your password several times. This is normal; currently there is no way to get the Exchange Advanced Security console to remember your password.

To manage the Key Manager object, right-click it and choose All Tasks. From this menu, you can:

- Start and stop the Microsoft Exchange Key Management Service.
- Enroll users.
- Revoke certificates.
- Recover keys.
- Export and import users.
- Save the KMS certificate so that you can distribute it to users.
- Change the KMS startup password.

NOTE Importing and exporting users allows you to move users between one KMS and another.

You can also manage the Key Manager object by right-clicking it and choosing Properties (you will be required to enter your KMS password). From the General property page, you can see a list of the known certificate servers and can view the certificates from each of them.

The object's Administrators property page (see Figure 12.7) allows you to designate other KMS administrators and to change their passwords. These passwords are *not* synchronized with the Active Directory passwords, and they are stored in the Key Management Service database, not in Active Directory.

The Passwords property page (see Figure 12.8) introduces a whole new concept that I like to call "missile key." Though you may not have been in a missile silo or a missile submarine, you have probably seen in the movies that no single person has the authority to launch a nuclear missile. At least two people have the keys and, of course, the keys have to be turned simultaneously.

Security

PART 3

Figure 12.7   Administrators property page of the Key Manager object

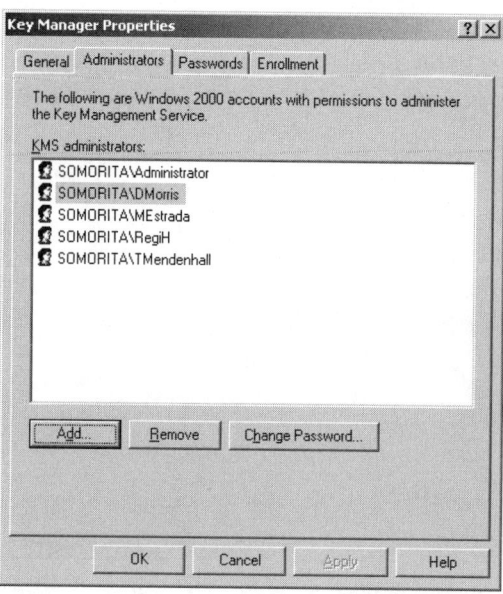

Figure 12.8   Passwords property page of the Key Manager object

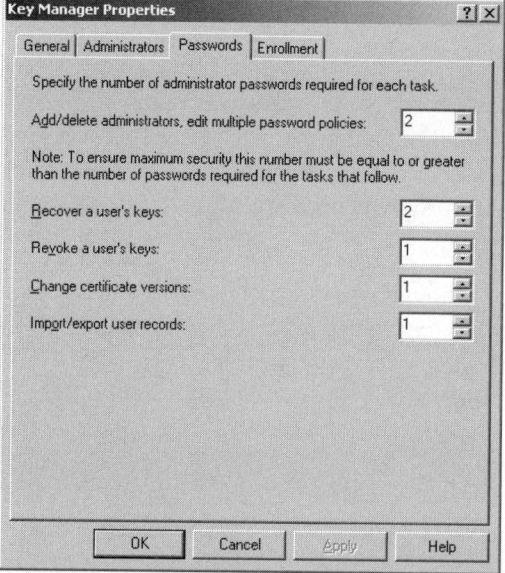

The Passwords property page allows you to configure how many administrators must enter their password before a particular action can be configured. The choices include requiring multiple passwords for the following:

- Adding and deleting administrators or changing the password policies
- Recovering a user's keys
- Revoking a user's keys
- Changing certificate versions
- Importing or exporting user records

In Figure 12.8, note that revoking users' keys, changing certificate versions or importing/exporting user records requires only one password (and thus a single administrator can perform these tasks). However, recovering a user's keys is a much more serious operation, since it could allow a single administrator to get access to a user's encrypted messages. For this reason, recovering keys requires two separate administrators.

The Enrollment properties page allows you to specify how the enabling token is distributed and whether or not X.509v1 certificates are required. X.509v1 certificates will only be required if you have Outlook 97 clients.

The Token Distribution is the most important part of the Enrollment property tab because this is where you specify how the enabling token is delivered to the user. By default, when you enable a mailbox, you are given a token. You must then give that token to the owner of the mailbox so that they can enable their mailbox for advanced security. All tokens generated are stored in the \Exchsrvr\KMSData\Enroll.log file, which should be protected against compromise. Figure 12.9 shows an example of this file after enabling a few users.

Figure 12.9   Enroll.log file containing all the tokens generated on a particular KMS

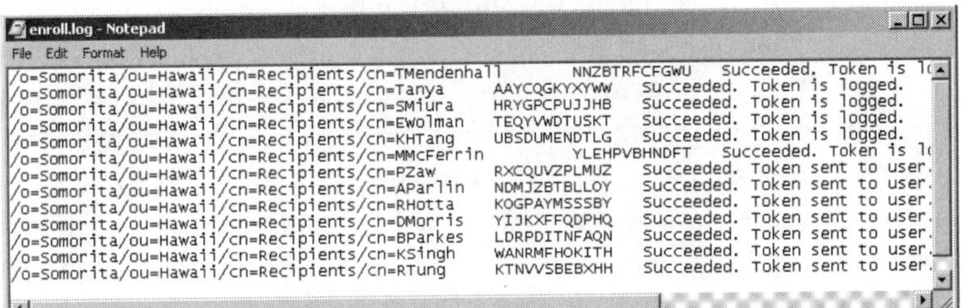

However, if you select the Send Token In An E-mail option, the user(s) you are enabling will receive an e-mail with the token and instructions for how to enable advanced security. Figure 12.10 shows this message; I have highlighted the token, which the message

Security

PART 3

calls the temporary key. You can customize this message by clicking the Customize button shown back in Figure 12.9.

Figure 12.10 E-mail message delivery of the token

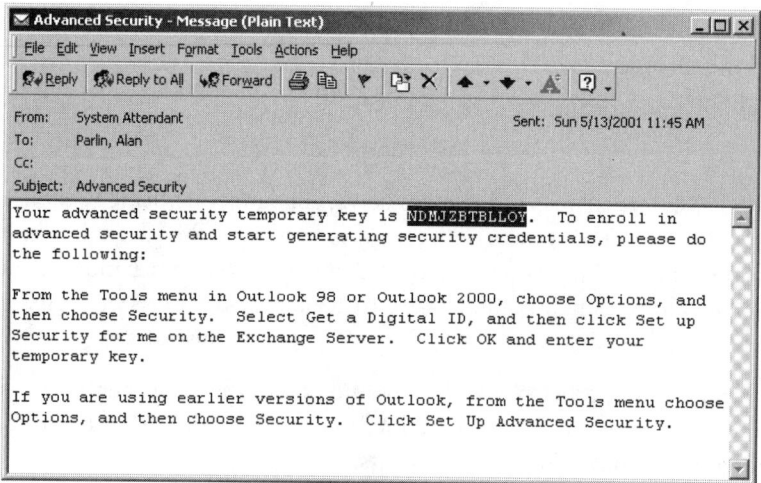

WARNING Users should be encouraged to immediately activate their advanced security features. If the enabling token was delivered via e-mail, the likelihood increases that someone else could access the message and enable the user's advanced security features.

Enrolling Users Once you have configured the Key Manager, you are ready to start enrolling users so that they can receive tokens and enable themselves to use advanced security. To enroll a user or group of users, right-click the Key Manager in the appropriate administrative group and choose All Tasks ➤ Enroll Users. You will then be required to enter your KMS password. Next, you can choose if you want to view users from the global address list (GAL) or to sort them based on mailbox store, Exchange server, or administrative group. I usually choose the GAL, but picking a specific store is much more useful in a large organization. Figure 12.11 shows the list of users from which you can pick to enroll users.

Figure 12.11 Enrolling users

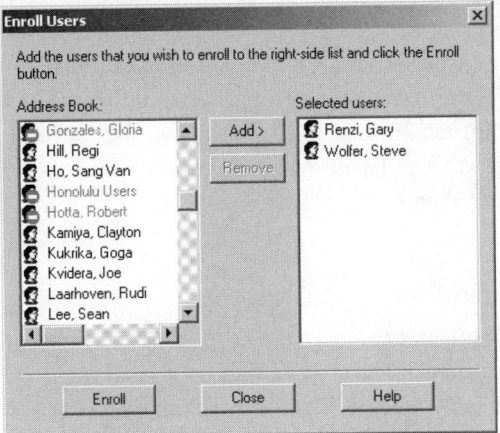

The list shown in Figure 12.11 contains all mail-enabled objects. Notice that several users are grayed out and have a red and white circle across their user icon. These objects are not enrolled in advanced security. There are a couple of reasons that an object may not be eligible, including:

- The mail-enabled object is already enabled.
- The mail-enabled object is from an administrative group that is not configured to use a KMS.
- The mail-enabled object is actually a mail-enabled group.

Once you highlight the users you wish to enroll, click Enroll. If configured, these users will receive an e-mail message similar to the one shown back in Figure 12.10.

Revoking Certificates At some point, you may be required to revoke a user's certificate. The user may have quit the company or they might be using the certificate in an improper manner. Whatever the reason, you are actually adding the user to the CRL, a list of certificates that a CA has issued but no longer considers valid. The CRL is maintained by the Exchange 2000 KMS, but it synchronizes the CRL to the Windows 2000 Certificate Server.

To revoke a user's certificate, highlight the Key Manager object, right-click, and choose All Tasks ➢ Revoke Certificates. Select the user whose certificate you wish to revoke and add that user to the Selected Users list, then click the Revoke button. You can only revoke a single user at a time.

Security

PART 3

Recovering Keys A user may lose access to their protected store certificates because their local hard disk crashed, or perhaps because the user password-protected their certificates and has forgotten the password. To recover the user's keys, right-click the Key Manager object, choose All Tasks ➤ Recover Users, provide your advanced security password, and select whether you want to look through the global address list for the user or a specific server or information store. Finally, add the user whose keys you wish to recover to the Selected Users list and click Recover. This process gives you a choice of displaying the enabling token or sending it to the user via e-mail; this token allows the user to recover the keys.

Encryption Configuration

Each administrative group that has servers in it has an Encryption object visible in the Exchange Advanced Security console. On the General property tab of the Encryption object's property page is the Key Management Service location option. If the administrative group has a KMS installed, then you cannot change this option; the servers in the administrative group must use that server. For administrative groups that do not have a KMS, you can designate which KMS in the organization will create certificates for these users in this administrative group.

The Algorithms property tab (shown in Figure 12.12) allows you to configure the encryption algorithms used for message encryption. You can also specify the default message security format (S/MIME or Exchange 4.0/5.0).

Figure 12.12 Encryption configuration options

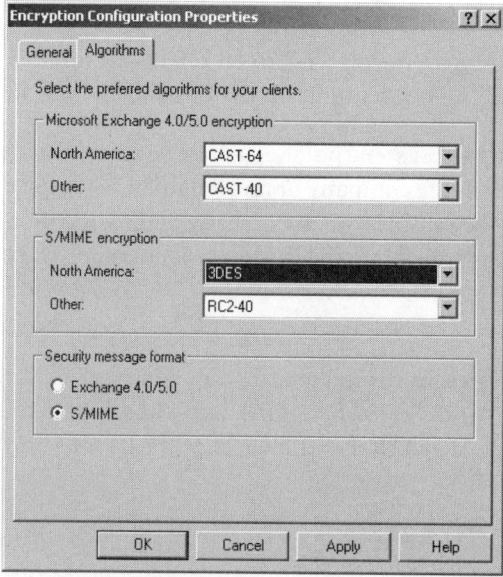

Enabling Advanced Security on the Client Side

Finally, after many pages of preparation (and many hours of work), you are at the point where you can enable a client to use advanced security. Advanced security was designed with the Outlook client in mind, and since all client revisions since Outlook 98 support S/MIME, I will stick to that scenario.

Once the keys and certificates are generated, advanced security is entirely a client-side function. It allows you to digitally *seal* (encrypt) and/or digitally *sign* a message. These actions allow message senders and recipients to ensure that privacy is maintained, that the integrity and the origin of the message can be verified, and that the sender cannot deny later on that he sent it. The Outlook/Exchange client, not the Exchange server, performs the signing and sealing functions.

Sealed messages are not only transferred across the network, but they are stored in the private information store or PST file as an encrypted message. Signed messages contain a digital signature that is protected by the sender's private key so that it cannot be altered.

> **NOTE** In a sealed message, the entire message body and attachments are encrypted. However, the To, From, CC, and Subject fields are not.

Enrolling the User

Earlier in this chapter, we discussed enrolling users. Now you need to set them up so that they can activate advanced security. To do so, follow these steps:

1. Open the Exchange Advanced Security console.

2. Open the administrative group that has the Key Management Server installed in it and right-click the Key Manager icon.

3. Choose All Tasks ➢ Enroll Users, and provide your KMS password.

4. Choose the method that you wish to use to locate the user, such as displaying the list from the GAL.

5. Highlight the user(s) you wish to enroll and add them to the Selected Users list.

6. Click the Enroll button.

7. If they keys are delivered using e-mail, the user will get a message with their advanced security enabling token. Otherwise, you can retrieve the enabling token for each of the users from the Enroll.log file in the KMSData directory.

Now each of the users has been enrolled in advanced security; the remainder of the work will be performed within the Outlook client.

Enabling Outlook for Advanced Security

Once you have enabled your user(s), it's time to enable Outlook for advanced security. If the enabling token is distributed using e-mail, the first step is to open the message with the subject of Advanced Security from the System Attendant. If the token is hand-carried to the user, they must have it to complete these steps:

1. From within Outlook, choose Tools ➤ Options, and click the Security property tab (shown in Figure 12.13).

2. Click the Get A Digital ID button and select the Set Up Security For Me On The Exchange Server option. Note that this option will not appear unless KMS is installed in the organization.

3. Provide a name for this digital ID and enter the enabling token into the Token text box. Click OK.

4. Provide a password that you will use when the digital ID is returned to you from the KMS, and click OK. This will cause the enabling request to be mailed to the KMS, which can take anywhere from 20 seconds to 15 minutes (or longer) depending on the location and the load of the KMS.

5. When you receive a reply from the System Attendant with the subject of Reply From Security Authority, open that message and provide the password that you entered in step 4. You may need to re-enter this password.

Figure 12.13 is from Outlook 2000 SR1, which supports S/MIME v3, so there are a few additional options that are not found in Outlook 98 or Outlook 2000.

Figure 12.13 Outlook 2000 SR1 security options

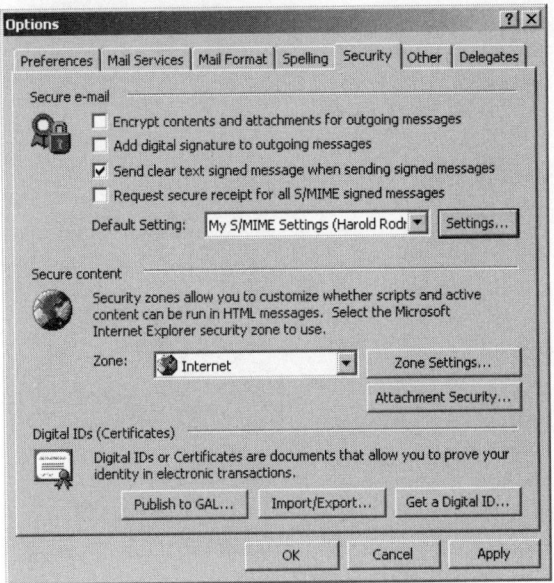

Another noteworthy item on the Security Options page is the Publish To GAL button. This button is newly added with Outlook 2000 SR1. While this feature is useless for certificates that you obtained from the Exchange 2000 KMS (they are automatically published to Active Directory by the Outlook client), this is especially useful if you have received your certificate from a third party such as Thawte.

> **NOTE** The Publish To GAL option allows you to publish third-party certificates to Active Directory.

Also of note is the Settings button, which allows you to configure the security settings for the current digital ID (see Figure 12.14). The settings you can change include which certificates and algorithms are used for signing and encryption as well as the default message format.

Security

PART 3

Figure 12.14 Changing security settings

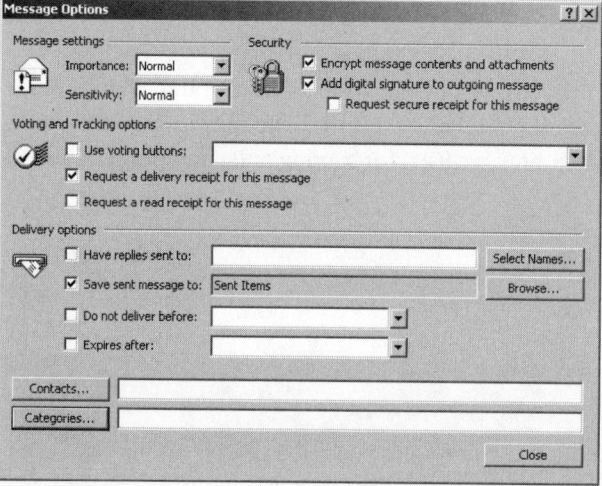

Using Outlook and Advanced Security

Once advanced security is enabled for a mailbox, the user can send encrypted messages and digitally sign messages. To sign or encrypt message contents, click the Options button when composing a message (see Figure 12.15). Click Encrypt Message Contents And Attachments to encrypt the data (the subject is *not* encrypted). Select the Add Digital Signature To Outgoing Message check box to digitally sign the message.

Figure 12.15 Digitally signing or encrypting a message

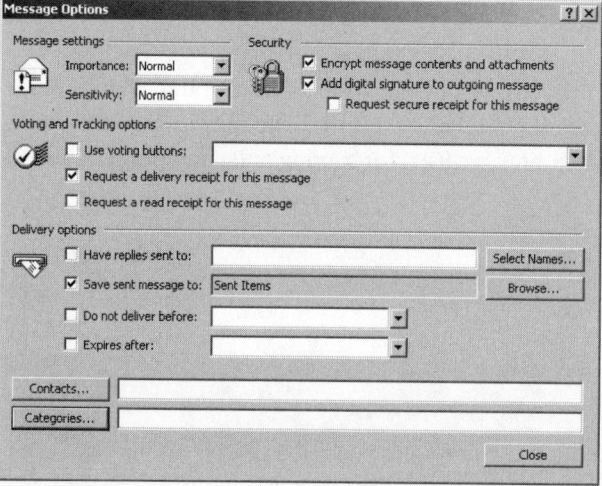

Once the user has selected that they want to sign or encrypt a message, when they click Send they will be prompted for the password that protects their protected store (and private keys). Then the Outlook client will query Active Directory to confirm that these users are indeed enabled for advanced security, download their certificates (and public keys), and update its own local certificate revocation list.

Signed messages can be sent to any user, even a user on the Internet, but if any of the recipients in the message are not capable of receiving an encrypted message, the user will be informed that the message cannot be sent.

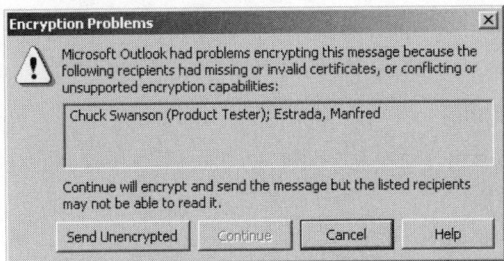

Usually the reason that you cannot send an encrypted message to another user is that they are not enrolled using KMS or that user has not sent you a certificate.

NOTE Currently, Outlook Web Access cannot send signed or encrypted messages. OWA can open digitally signed messages, but it cannot display the certificate or verify the signature.

NOTE Since decryption is handled by the client and not by the server, many handheld and wireless devices (such as the Blackberry) will not be able to read an encrypted message. Organizations that are deploying such wireless devices should consider this when planning a PKI environment.

Message Sealing

When a message is encrypted or sealed, the Outlook client is then responsible for sealing the message when the user clicks the Send button. The process goes something like this:

1. The Outlook client software checks the list of recipients to make sure it has a public sealing certificate for each of the users. The public certificates may be stored in Active Directory or in the user's private address book. If the intended recipient does not have a certificate, Outlook won't be able to send an encrypted message to the recipient.

2. Outlook randomly generates a secret (symmetric or bulk encryption) key between 40 and 128 bits in length (depending on your configuration and country) and encrypts the message using the secret key.

3. The secret key is then encrypted once for each message recipient (and once for the sender) using the recipient's public sealing key and placed in a lock box. This lock box is attached to the end of the message.

4. The message is transmitted and stored.

Remember Diffie-Hellman key exchange (discussed earlier in this chapter)? Well, this is where it is applied. A large message can be encrypted very efficiently with a secret key, and then the smaller secret key is encrypted and transmitted to the recipient.

Message Decryption

When the message arrives at the recipient's mailbox and the recipient opens it, the messages must be decrypted. That process goes something like this:

1. Outlook accesses the recipient's private signing key; the private keys are usually stored on the local hard disk or as part of the user's Windows profile. The recipient may be prompted for a password so that Outlook can retrieve the private key. Some third-party vendors incorporate other technologies, such as smart cards, that store keys and identities, but these are probably only used in high-security environments. The U.S. Department of Defense's Defense Messaging System uses hardware cards to store their users' credentials and private keys; this card is called a Fortezza card.

2. Outlook locates the recipient's lock box and decrypts the secret key using the private sealing key.

3. Once Outlook has the secret key, the message content can be quickly and efficiently decrypted.

Message Signing

To seal a message, an Outlook user clicks the Options button and chooses the Add Digital Signature To Outgoing Message check box in the Security section (shown back in Figure 12.15). The Outlook software takes care of creating the signature and attaching it to the message like this:

1. Outlook verifies that the sender has a signing certificate.

2. The Outlook software applies a hashing function to the message and its attachments. This reduces the entire message and attachments down to a 128-bit *message digest*. If one single bit in the message or any attachment were to change, the original message digest would no longer agree with the new message digest.

3. The Outlook client accesses the sender's private key; the user may be prompted for a password to allow Outlook to retrieve it.

4. Outlook then encrypts the message digest using the sender's private signing key (not their public key).

5. Outlook attaches a copy of the sender's signing certificate (which contains the public signing key) to the message and transmits it.

NOTE   Note that nowhere in the signing process was the message encrypted. Signing does not encrypt the message content; it merely allows the message to be verified.

When the signed message arrives, the user retrieves the message and will notice a new icon on the right-hand side; in Outlook 98, this looks like a little red and yellow certificate. If the user clicks this certificate, they will be given a dialog box that will verify the digital signature:

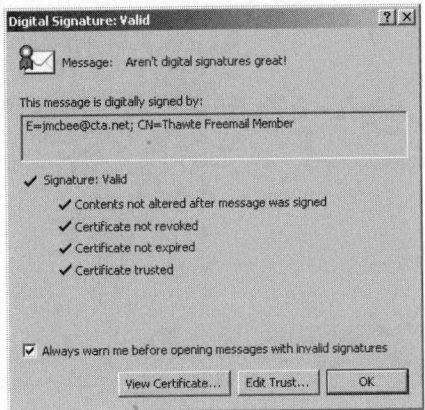

From this dialog box, the user can tell if the message was altered during transit, if the sender's certificate was revoked or expired, if the CA can be trusted, and whether the e-mail address on the certificate matches the sender's address. Further, the user can click the View Certificate button to see information about the certificate.

The Outlook client takes care of validating the digital signature in this way:

1. Outlook runs the message and attachments through the hashing formula and comes up with its own message digest.

2. The sender's public signing key is retrieved from the public signing certificate attached to the message. The attached, encrypted message digest is decrypted using the sender's private signing key.

3. The calculated message digest and the original message are compared. If they are identical, then the message has not been modified during or after transmission.

Receiving the Message

When a signed message arrives in a user's mailbox, it will have a small red seal on the message icon. If the message has been encrypted, or encrypted and signed, the icon will have a small blue lock on it. When you open the message, if it has been encrypted, you will be required to enter your protected store password (if you have not told Outlook to remember it).

When the message is opened, you will see one or two new icons on the message. Figure 12.16 shows a digitally signed and encrypted message; the blue lock in the message header indicates it was encrypted, and the red seal indicates it was signed.

Figure 12.16 Message received with signed and encrypted properties

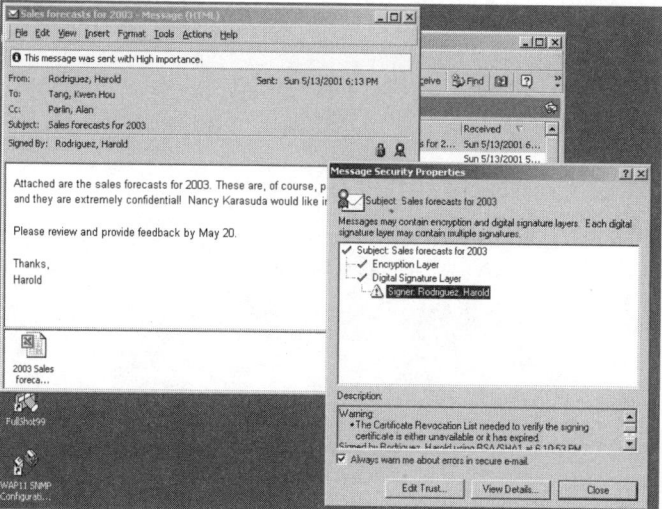

You can highlight either the encryption icon or the signature icon to verify the encryption or signature, respectively.

Getting Certificates from Outside Users

Suppose you want to send a signed or encrypted message to someone outside of your organization. How do you go about doing this? Well, if you simply want to send them a signed message, then just send the message. You do not need the recipient's certificate. However, if you want to send an encrypted message, you will need their encryption certificate.

The best way to get this certificate is to ask them to send you a signed message. Once you have received it, follow these steps so that you have a copy of this person's certificate in your Outlook Contacts folder:

1. Open the message so that you see the red seal in the messages header.

2. Click the message seal and display the properties of the digital signature (shown back in the Message Signing section).

3. Click the View Certificate button (if there is a verification problem with the sender's certificate, you may have to click View Details ➤ View Certificate), and display the Details property tab.

4. Click the Copy To File button and click Next.

5. Select the DER Encoded Binary X.509 (.CER) radio button and click Next.

6. Specify the filename that you want to create and click Next. Then click Finish and OK. You now have the certificate file exported to a standard format.

7. Create an Outlook Contact for the person who sent you this message, if one does not exist already. The e-mail address to which you are sending messages *must* match the SMTP address on the certificate.

8. Click the Certificates tab for the contact:

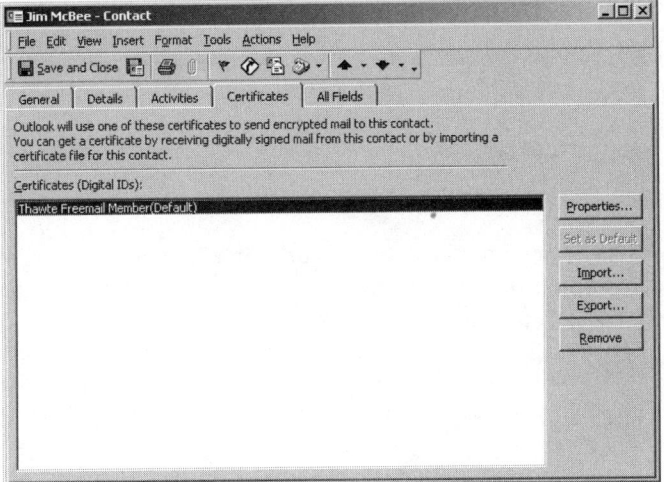

9. Click the Import button, and import the certificate file you just exported.

You can now send encrypted messages to this contact. In order for this person to send encrypted messages to you, you must send them a signed message (or export your CER file).

S/MIME Compatibility Problems

When the Outlook client sends a signed message, it includes both the signing and encrypting certificates to the recipient. The current implementation of S/MIME allows for only one key pair to be used when signing and encrypting messages, but the Microsoft implementation uses two key pairs (one for signing and one for encrypting).

There is currently a draft of a new S/MIME standard in front of the IETF that will permit multiple key pairs. Most modern S/MIME clients support this new draft of the standard including Outlook Express, Outlook 2000+, and Netscape Communicator. If external users report problems receiving certificates from your users, the best course of action is to suggest that they upgrade to a more recent version of the client.

> **NOTE** If you have clients other than Outlook MAPI clients and you wish to send and receive signed and encrypted messages, you can request a client certificate from the Web interface of the certificate server. The virtual directory you need to connect to is \CertSrv.

For Further Information

Did this chapter tell you everything you need to know about cryptography? Well, as a network administrator, I hope it did. But cryptography is a fascinating subject, and you might want to learn more. Here are two books that I commonly refer to:

- *Cryptography and Network Security Principals and Practices,* 2nd edition, by Williams Stallings (Prentice Hall, 1998).

- *Applied Cryptography,* 2nd edition, by Bruce Schneier (Wiley & Sons, 1996).

Some other resources that you may find enlightening can be found on the Web:

- Thawte is my favorite Certification Authority. They are easy to work with, widely accepted and trusted, and reasonably priced. Their website, www .thawte.com, is also a great resource.

- RSA Data Security is the public/private key expert. On their website, www.rsa.com, you will find many white papers and other reference materials on cryptography.

- VeriSign is probably the largest and best known CA. They have a lot of great reference material on their site, www.verisign.com.

- Consider visiting the Computer Emergency Response Team website, www.cert.org. (CERT Computation Center is a division of Carnegie Mellon University, so you will often see it referred to as CMU's CERT/CC.)

13

Securing Your Exchange Servers

The Internet can be a cold, hard place. Hackers may be lurking around every corner; even your own users may be moments away from accidentally (or deliberately!) compromising your systems and data. Just when you think you have tightened security to the point that you can relax, new security holes are found. Hard to believe? Intruders don't attack only high-profile organizations like the U.S. Internal Revenue Service, Microsoft, or the U.S. Department of Defense, you know.

Any server that is connected to a network outside of your own by way of a direct connection or dial-up connection is vulnerable. Network administrators often make the mistake of assuming that the danger only sits outside the front door; by some estimates as much as 80 percent of the data loss, data compromise, and denial-of-service (DoS) attacks are the result of internal breaches of security.

Whatever the risk, you must take steps to keep your servers running and available, and to protect the data from compromise. Some of the risks that your Exchange servers face include:

- Unauthorized mailbox or public folder access
- DoS attacks
- Forced shutdown of due to virus infection
- Defacement of websites

In the words of security expert Scott Collins, "you should be exactly as paranoid as it is cost effective to be." What does this mean to you? How do you determine how much time to devote to your internal and external data security? New security holes are found every week. Software updates, bug fixes, and patches arrive almost as frequently. What is a modern administrator to do?

Security is a huge topic, one that certainly cannot be covered in a single chapter of an Exchange 2000 book. That said, this chapter addresses some major issues, including protecting your Exchange servers from outside compromise and viruses, SMTP mail and security, firewalls and proxy servers, and Exchange 2000 and Microsoft ISA Server.

> **NOTE** Here are some links and resources that will help you with additional security information:
>
> Microsoft's security site: www.microsoft.com/security
>
> SecurityFocus.com (formerly NTBugTraq): www.securityfocus.com
>
> The SANS Institute: www.sans.org
>
> Windows Security Administrator newsletter: www.win2000mag.com

Protecting Your Exchange Server from Outside Compromise

The majority of server vulnerabilities exist not in Exchange 2000, but rather in Windows 2000 and Internet Information Server (IIS). Many of these vulnerabilities don't actually allow an intruder access to your data; they expose some weakness that allows a successful DoS attack to be mounted. However, there are vulnerabilities that can be particularly nasty and must be patched. Mind you, your definition of "nasty" may differ from mine. Any security hole that can provide an intruder with access to my data, such as many of the IIS bugs found during 2001, falls into the "must be patched right away" category. Security holes that pose an immediate threat to my system's uptime, such as the Code Red worm, also fall into this category. Other security holes that may fix DoS problems fall in to the "apply at the next scheduled outage" category.

The single most important facet of Exchange 2000 security is securing the Windows 2000 platform. If the platform is compromised in any way, the operation of the Exchange server is in jeopardy. Here is a list of things you can do to improve security of your Windows 2000 system:

- Implement strong passwords.
- Keep servers up-to-date with the latest service packs and security fixes.

- Implement a firewall or filtering routing to protect the NetBIOS ports (TCP and UDP ports 137, 138, and 139).

- Ensure that all file systems are formatted with NTFS.

- Remove all unnecessary Windows services, applications, samples, and IIS virtual directories.

- Move critical Windows command-line tools to a protected directory.

- Enable logging for IIS and SMTP, as well as message tracking and Windows 2000 auditing.

- If you enable the Telnet service, make sure that the rights to use it are restricted.

- Confirm that users don't have excessive rights or permissions.

- Be proactive about security! Spend an hour each week reviewing security bulletins and notices from sites mentioned in this chapter, and perform an internal audit periodically to ensure that no users have administrator permissions either in the domain or on member servers.

How can you be proactive about Windows security? Keep up-to-date on the latest vulnerabilities by clicking the Bulletins link on Microsoft's security web page at www.microsoft .com/security/; you can also subscribe to updates via e-mail from this page. Another excellent resource for security related information is www.securityfocus.com (formerly www.ntbugtraq.org).

Implementing Passwords

If a vendor were able to build the most secure operating system ever conceived, it would still probably be vulnerable to the most common security hole: weak—or should I say foolish?—passwords. I can't tell you how many of my clients' systems are accessed by logging in as "Administrator" and entering the password "password." Recently I was helping debug a bizarre Outlook client problem, and I sat down at the company president's desk. I told the administrator, "We need to get her to log in," and the IT guy said, "Oh, there is no password, she doesn't like having to remember one." Almost as bad as this are the users who use their children's or significant others' names as passwords.

To avoid leaving a system wide open, develop a security policy that includes requiring strong passwords for *all* user accounts, not only in the domain but also on the local workstations. This policy can be enforced using the Domain Controller Security Policy console found in the Administrative Tools folder. Figure 13.1 shows a domain controller security policy that I believe is acceptably secure for most corporate environments.

Figure 13.1   Domain controller security policy

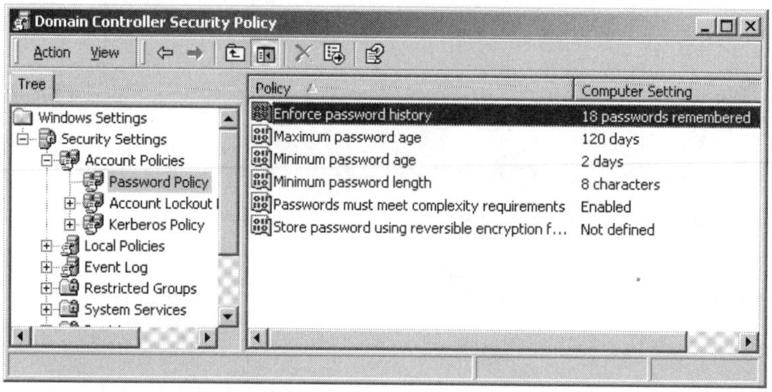

The policy shown in Figure 13.1 enforces password uniqueness, requires a password change every 120 days, requires that two days must pass before the user can change their password again, sets a minimum password length of eight characters, and requires complex (strong) passwords. A strong password consists of three out of four of these:

- Lowercase characters (a–z)
- Uppercase characters (A–Z)
- Numbers (0–9)
- Special characters (@, $, %, ^, &, *, +, =, {, \, ;, !)

Educate users on how to create strong passwords and the importance of protecting that password from compromise. Additionally, help users to create complex passwords that they can easily remember. For example, put a dollar sign or the letter Z in the password in place of an S. Using this scheme, the password $cullyRulz2 would easily be remembered, because what I am trying to say is Scully rules, too. (This is more of a passphrase than a simple password.)

> **NOTE**   For more information on helping users to remember strong passwords, see the Password Manifesto on my website at www.somorita.com.

Installing Service Packs and Security Fixes

Many of the vulnerabilities that make Windows 2000 susceptible can be fixed with service packs, hot fixes, and updates. Make absolutely sure that all of your servers and domain controllers are running Windows 2000 Service Pack 2 at a minimum. Consult with the Microsoft security website (www.microsoft.com/security) for information about vulnerabilities that have been discovered since SP2 was released. When searching the Microsoft Bulletins page, look not only for Windows 2000, but also Internet Information Server 5 and Exchange 2000 to confirm that you have found all of the vulnerabilities.

Don't be intimidated by bug reports that mention things such as "superfluous decoding operations" or "buffer overflows." I have a tendency to look at something like a superfluous decoding operation and think, "I don't know what this is, so it must not be too bad." This is not a good approach. Read the bug report and confirm that the vulnerability that it exposes does not affect you in any way. If there is any question about this, apply the fix for the patch.

> **NOTE** Many known Windows exploits continue to be used simply because administrators procrastinate about applying fixes. In 1996, the U.S. FBI website was hacked using sample CGI programs installed by default on the web server's hard disk. Similarly, the bug that allowed hackers in China to deface thousands of websites in 2001 had been documented and published for over six months!

Maintaining Physical Security

If I can get physical access to your Exchange servers, there is a very good chance I can compromise your data. At the very least, a malicious person can make sure that no one is going to read their mail for a while. Servers should be under lock and key at *all* times.

Removing Unnecessary Services and Software

Several Windows 2000 administrators I have worked with recently have needed to understand exactly which services are required for Exchange 2000. Some of their servers had almost every networking service that could be installed on a Windows 2000 server, including DNS, DHCP, and WINS, even though these services were not necessary. The following is a list of Windows 2000 and IIS services that are required for Exchange 2000; unless you have a specific need for another service, you should probably remove it from your Exchange server. These services are found in Control Panel ➢ Add/Remove Programs ➢ Add/Remove Windows Components.

- Internet Information Services ➢ Internet Information Services Snap-In
- Internet Information Services ➢ NNTP Service
- Internet Information Services ➢ SMTP Service
- Internet Information Services ➢ World Wide Web Server

Once Windows 2000 is installed, remove the following virtual directories from the default website using the Internet Services Manager:

- IISSamples
- IISHelp
- MSADC

NOTE Many operating systems have vulnerabilities with the Remote Procedure Call (RPC) ports, and thus many network managers are reluctant to open RPCs to the outside world. However, RPCs are required by MAPI clients (Outlook); if Outlook clients must connect from outside the firewall, consider implementing a virtual private network (VPN). A VPN provides remote Outlook users access to the Exchange server, but it provides far more security protection for RPC-based services.

Securing Command Tools

Due to a buffer overflow problem with IIS, in the spring of 2001 Chinese hackers were able to deface thousands of websites using HTTP. Below is a simple example of how I can use that same vulnerability to do a directory listing of the root of the C: drive on a server:

```
servername/scripts/..\../WINNT/system32/cmd.exe?/c+dir+c:\
```

If you put this command into your web browser and replace *servername* with your server's name, and if you get a directory listing, then you have not applied the latest security fixes.

The best way to prevent a non-administrative user from taking advantage of this security hole and possible future ones is to secure access to the command line tools so that only administrative users can use these tools. The following are a list of command-line tools that you should set the NTFS permissions on so that only the administrators can use them: CMD.EXE, FTP.EXE, NET.EXE, XCOPY.EXE, RSH.EXE, RCP.EXE, REXEC.EXE, WSCRIPT.EXE, CSRIPT.EXE, TELNET.EXE, PING.EXE, AT.EXE, FINGER.EXE, ARP.EXE, ROUTE.EXE, RUNONCE.EXE, SYSKEY.EXE, POSIX.EXE, EDLIN.EXE, FINGER.EXE, ATSVC.EXE, QBASIC.EXE, CACLS.EXE, IPCONFIG.EXE, SECFIXUP.EXE, NBTSTAT.EXE, RDISK.EXE, DEBUG.EXE, REGEDT32.EXE, REGEDIT.EXE, EDIT.COM, NETSTAT.EXE, TRACERT.EXE, and NSLOOKUP.EXE.

Enabling IIS Logging

The Internet Information Server can be configured to create logs of all activity. While these logs are useful for monitoring what content is being accessed on your web server, they are also useful for tracking unauthorized activity. Logging is configured for each website that you have created using the Internet Services Manager. To do so, display the properties of the website. On the Website property page, make sure that the Enable Logging check box is checked and that the Active Log Format is set to W3C Extended Log File Format. Click the Properties button to configure the log time period and the log file directory.

If you click the Extended Properties tab (see Figure 13.2), you can customize what data is included in the log file. You should include at a minimum the following ten logging categories:

Date	Time
Client IP Address (c-ip)	User Name (cs-username)
Server IP Address (s-ip)	Server Port (s-port)
Method (cs-method)	URI Stem (cs-uri-stem)
Protocol Status (sc-status)	Win32 Status (sc-win32-status)

Figure 13.2   IIS Extended logging properties

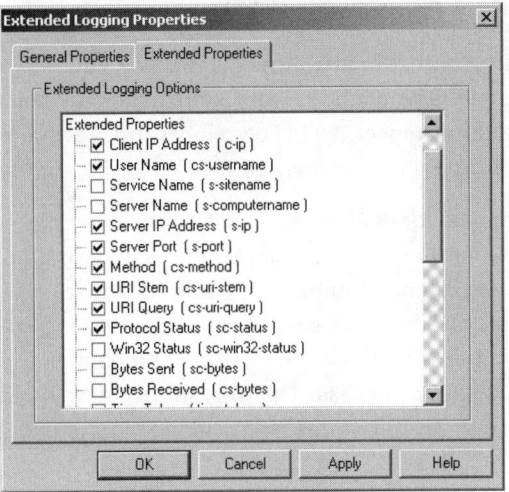

Other useful pieces of information that you can also include in the log include Bytes Sent, Bytes Received, and User Agent. The User Agent will tell you what type of web browser was used. The files that are created are ASCII text files; there are a number of programs, including Microsoft Site Server 3's Usage Analyst, that will read these logs and generate usage reports. If you do not have Site Server 3, consider using tools such as WebTrend (www .webtrends.com) or LiveStats (www.deepmetrix.com). The website www.davecentral.com has information about these and other network tools.

Securing Telnet

If you are planning to use the Telnet daemon included with Windows 2000 for remote administration via the command-line, you should restrict who has permissions to telnet into the server. By default, any authorized user can do this. To restrict this, create a local group (in the domain or on the local member server) called TelnetClients, and add the authorized users to this group.

WARNING When using Telnet, all information is passed over the network in cleartext unless you have implemented an IPSec policy. A popular alternative to Telnet is to use SSH (secure shell). An SSH solution works a lot like Telnet except that the sessions are encrypted. For more information on SSH, visit tech.erdelynet.com/ssh.asp or www.ssh.com/tech/archive/secsh/architecture.txt. Pragma (www.pragma.com) has an SSH solution for Windows 2000.

Exchange@Work: A Painful Lesson in the Importance of Logging

Company EFG's system administrators disabled all auditing and logging on their Exchange 2000 servers when the servers were installed. Their rationale was that this would improve performance. While I certainly cannot argue that disabling logging will improve performance, I don't agree with removing all forms of logging.

Their error became evident after their Exchange server had been in production for a few months. An employee was receiving threatening e-mail messages from an internal mailbox to which a number of users had access. The problem was that they could not ascertain which user had accessed that mailbox to send the message. They could not even tell if the mailbox had been accessed through Outlook or through Outlook Web Access. The only information available to the administrators was through the SMTP message headers, which were blank, indicating that the message had been sent locally.

In order to more properly track server administration, server access, and mailbox usage, EFG should have enabled the following logging:

- Windows 2000 Account Logon Events auditing (both Success and Failure) should be enabled in the domain as well as on the local member servers that host Exchange 2000.

- Windows 2000 Account Management auditing (both Success and Failure) should be enabled in the domain.

- Exchange 2000 diagnostics logging should have the MSExchangeIS ➢ Mailbox ➢ Logons category set to Minimum on all Exchange 2000 servers.

Exchange@Work: A Painful Lesson in the Importance of Logging *(continued)*

- Exchange 2000 message tracking should be enabled on all Exchange servers. Plan to keep at least 15 days worth of these logs.

- IIS should have logging enabled for any website that is used with Exchange. Plan to keep at least 30 days worth of these logs.

- SMTP logging should be enabled for the SMTP virtual servers that are handling e-mail connectivity to the Internet. Plan to keep at least 30 days worth of these logs.

If you enable logging, don't forget to increase the size of the Windows 2000 system and application event logs. On the typical server, make sure that the log files are large enough to hold at least two weeks' worth of events, or have an archive procedure in place whereby you archive logs and keep them. Also, make sure that you have sufficient disk space to hold the IIS and SMTP logs; these logs are not automatically purged, so make sure you have an archival procedure in place.

Additional Security Practices

Here are some other things that will be helpful when making sure that your Exchange server and its data are secure:

- Protect your backup tapes and ensure that unauthorized backups are not being performed.

- Format all file systems using NTFS. Protect the Exchange server data directories so that only the SYSTEM and Administrators have access to those directories. Some of the files stored in those directories are easily readable (the native content database is stored in cleartext).

- Implement a Windows 2000 auditing policy that includes logons and logoffs at a minimum.

- Review the IIS logs, security event log, and application event log on each Exchange 2000 server to look for unauthorized activity.

- Implement some type of intrusion-detection software to monitor for possible break-ins. Snort! is software that can be found at www.clark.net/~roesch/security .html#Whatsnort. Internet Security Systems has a similar tool called RealSecure; you can find more information at www.iss.net.

Security

PART 3

- Perform proactive scanning of your system to look for vulnerabilities. Internet Security Systems' Internet Scanner can perform these types of assessments; see more information at www.iss.net. Nessus, a free scanning tool, can be found at www.nessus .org/intro.html.

- Subscribe to a security newsletter, or monitor the security websites on a regular basis. Microsoft provides a security notification list at www.microsoft.com/ security. You may find a more balanced view on a list such as Russ Cooper's NTBugTraq list; subscribe at www.ntbugtraq.com. Another excellent source of security-and bug-related information is Carnegie Mellon's CERT Coordination Center website, www.cert.org.

TIP Be proactive. Just because your system is secure today does not mean that it will be secure next week.

Exchange@Work: Security through Message Size Limits

Company XYZ was reaching the limits of their Exchange 2000 server since the edition they purchased was limited to a single mailbox store of 16GB. One Monday morning, the employees arrived to find that the Exchange server was down. Upon further investigation, the administrator found that the mailbox store was at 16GB, though they knew that as of Friday the entire store was not more than 12GB. They managed to restart the server and discovered that many mailboxes had hundreds of megabytes of messages.

After much investigation, the company found that a disgruntled former employee had spent the prior weekend sending massive amounts of e-mail to the company in hopes of overloading their system. The former employee succeeded quite nicely through this simple DoS attack.

As a result of this incident, the company instituted maximum mailbox size limits and maximum message size limits to prevent the mailbox store from filling up and shutting down the server. This is an example of where developing tools to monitor your Exchange servers (such as those discussed in Chapter 5, "Status Monitoring and Reporting") or third-party tools such as NetIQ (www.netiq.com) can be very useful. You can set thresholds for various services such as usage levels, queue lengths, and disk space. If your system statistics moves outside of these thresholds, the software can notify of impending problems or attempt to take corrective actions such as shutting down services.

Protecting against Viruses

Over the last two years, I have observed more downtime, lost productivity, loss of service, administrative costs, and chatter in the newsgroups due to viruses than server crashes, database failures, or hardware problems combined. And e-mail viruses do not discriminate between Exchange 5.5 and Exchange 2000.

When viruses such as the ILOVEYOU, Melissa, Joke, Nimda and others appeared, many systems became so overwhelmed that the administrators stopped the SMTP services, the message transfer agent (MTA), and the Internet Mail Service (Exchange 5.5), or they shut down their servers all together in an effort to prevent further infection. Several military bases that I work on took to posting signs at the front gates during virus outbreaks informing their users not to open messages with specific subjects.

Virus detection and removal is an essential part of the operation of your Exchange servers. If you allow your user community to send and receive e-mail from the outside, you must form a strategy to fight e-mail viruses. Additionally, you must recognize the types of viruses that you may encounter. I break these into two categories:

- *Traditional viruses* infect a file such as a macro virus. These viruses are not e-mail aware—they are in an e-mail message because the sender is sending a file that is infected with the virus. From the e-mail system perspective, these viruses are not particularly dangerous.

- *E-mail–based viruses* contain a program or script and are e-mail-aware (usually Outlook-aware). These viruses will take your address books and address a copy of themselves to the recipients found in your personal address lists as well as the global address list. A large organization (such as the U.S. Air Force at 400,000+ mailboxes) will suffer greatly from a virus like this, because the messages generated clog mail queues, use server resources, and use large amounts of network bandwidth.

Security

PART 3

WARNING Some companies think they can use file-based virus scanning (such as Norton AntiVirus Corporate Edition) to protect their Exchange server. File-based virus scanners should *never* be used to scan Exchange server databases, log files, or queue directories. Further, they should *never, never* be used to scan the Exchange Installable File System (ExIFS) drive (typically the M: drive).

Are You for Real?

Virus hoaxes are another problem that plagues the e-mail world. These are often as much of a problem as the real thing because they put the user community into panic mode—which generates an influx of help desk phone calls. If you suspect a hoax, consult your antivirus software vendor's website.

Two other excellent resources for learning about virus hoaxes are www.vmyths.com and www.antivirus.com/vinfo/hoaxes/hoax.asp.

Restricting Attachments

I used to be an advocate of leaving attachments alone and letting the virus-scanning solution determine if the attachment was okay or not. Yet outbreaks such as Melissa and ILOVEYOU helped to change my mind due to the fact that all of the antivirus software vendors were several hours behind the outbreak in coming up with updated signatures.

I strongly advocate restricting the types of attachments that a user can send or receive. The following is a list of attachments that I automatically send to the quarantine or delete if they enter the mail system:

- VBS, WSH, WSC, WSF, SHS, and JS attachments that are scripts. These can be used with the Windows scripting host.

- REG files, which are used with the Registry Editor. A user could inadvertently make changes to their Registry by opening these files.

- BAT and CMD are Windows batch and command files. These can be used to run programs.

- EXE and COM files are command and executable programs. You may get some resistance from your users if you block these files, but it may also be necessary to prevent EXE-based viruses.

If you often distribute software updates via e-mail, then removing the EXE, BAT, or CMD file types may prevent you from doing this. Consider blocking these file types from entering your e-mail system, but allow them internally. To do this, you would need a mail gateway that scans inbound messages using one set of policies, but a separate scanning policy for internal mail. The only way that I know to do this is using two separate products: an Exchange-based scanning solution and an inbound e-mail scanner.

If your users truly need to send some of the above file types to one another, advise them to zip the attachments. Though it is possible for someone to send a virus through a zip file, the chance of another user actually executing the virus is greatly diminished. Messages that have zipped attachments will require far more user intervention to actually run a virus.

> **NOTE** Outlook 2002 has a feature that limits the types of attachments that can be opened and thus minimize the damage that a mail-based virus can actually do. If you are running Outlook 98 or 2000, you can update those clients by downloading the Outlook Email Security Update.

Content Inspection Gateways

One product that has gained a lot of acceptance in the past few years is a *content inspection gateway*, which sits on the network between the Internet and the Exchange server as shown in Figure 13.3. Inbound MX records point to the content inspection gateway, not the SMTP connector on the Exchange server. Optionally, outbound mail may also be redirected through this gateway.

Figure 13.3   A content inspection gateway

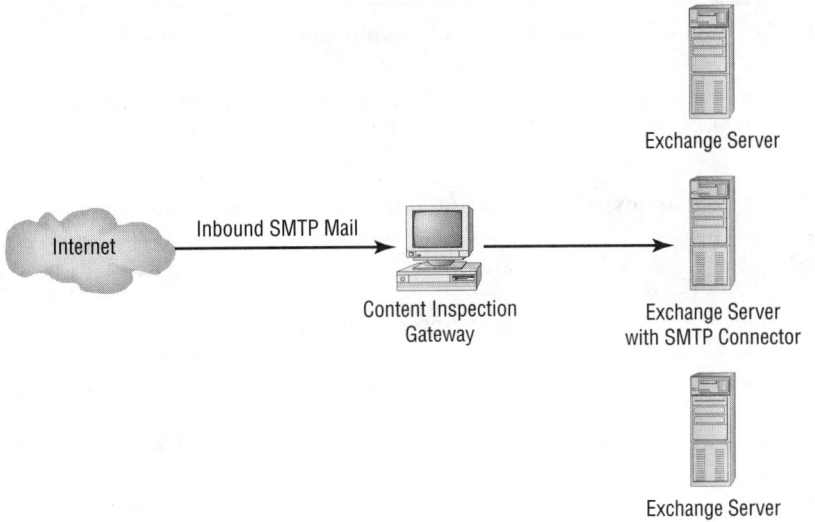

> **NOTE** The term content inspection is used rather loosely, yet there are many possible definitions. Some anti-virus vendors consider virus scanning or removing attachments to be content inspection, while other vendors consider it to be the process of opening a mail message or attachment and scanning for keywords (such as objectionable terms).

In a larger environment (supporting more than 500–1000 messages per hour), you might implement two of these gateways for redundancy and load balancing. In a smaller environment (fewer than 50 SMTP messages per hour), most of these products can be installed directly on the Exchange server, but the SMTP virtual server's TCP port must be changed to something other than port 25. Changing the inbound SMTP port is discussed in Chapter 14, "Connectivity within Your Organization."

Inbound messages pass through the gateway and are stored briefly. The content inspection system may be something as simple as inspecting the inbound and outbound messages for viruses or removing blocked attachments. In reality this type of gateway is simply an antivirus SMTP gateway. True content inspection gateways go even further by searching message content for prohibited words or phrases. Many of these products are designed to protect against users sending out confidential documents or receiving inbound spam mail. For example, you could block all inbound messages that mention the phrase "make money fast."

> **NOTE** Spam is also known as *unsolicited commercial e-mail* (UCE).

Some of the more popular vendors that make content inspection systems and antivirus gateways include those shown in Table 13.1.

Table 13.1 Content Inspection and Antivirus SMTP Gateway Vendors

Vendor	Product	URL
Symantec	Norton Antivirus for Gateways	www.Symantec.com
Trend Micro	InterScan VirusWall	www.trendmicro.com
Computer Mail Services	Praetor	www.cmsconnect.com
GFI	Mail Essentials	www.gfi.com
Elron	Internet Message Inspector	www.elronsw.com
Content Technologies	MIME Sweeper	www.mimesweeper.com

> **NOTE** Some of the vendors in Table 13.1 also make snap-in products for Microsoft Proxy 2 or Microsoft Internet Security and Acceleration (ISA) Server, both of which are mentioned later in this chapter.

Fighting Spam

I give up! The spammers are winning the spam war. I have been a good boy. I never put up my real e-mail address on Internet newsgroups. I never give my e-mail address to the Web sweepstakes sites. I don't register for the joke-of-the-day list. I have never subscribed to an online dating service. I have reported open relays until my fingers hurt from typing. Yet somehow I still get between 15 and 30 spam messages per day. I even have a Yahoo address that I have *never* given out, yet it still gets a couple of spam messages per week.

At any rate, I have given up fighting for now. Instead, I recently tested Praetor by Computer Mail Services (`www.cmsconnect.com`) and found it to be an interesting product. You can tweak the rules that they provide and customize it for your own environment. A number of vendors produce content inspection software like Praetor that looks for spam-like messages and blocks them by putting them into a queue until the administrator can look at them. I have tried a couple of these products and found them to be more trouble than they're worth. The users object to any of their inbound mail being "inspected," and even in a small organization, you may end up having to inspect a few hundred messages every day.

I have found that tools such as Praetor work best (and the users are the happiest) if I modify the rules to stamp "**Possible UCE message**" at the top of the messages and let the users deal with it.

So, what can you do to reduce the amount of spam that you receive? I recommend testing one of the anti-spam packages on the market. However, much of the problem boils down to end-user education. In order to keep these unscrupulous marketers from getting e-mail addresses, pass along these tips to your user community:

- Never give your or anyone else's e-mail address to a website run by a company that you do not know. If your users want to do this, ask them to create a Yahoo or Hotmail account for personal use.

- Never use your real e-mail address when posting to Usenet newsgroups or Web discussion groups. I always use something like `jmcbee@somorita.com.spambegone`. An Internet-savvy person will pick up on this and figure out what my real address is, but most of the 'bots that harvest addresses won't. However, even the e-mail 'bots are becoming more sophisticated and may figure out your obscured address anyway.

- Even on websites operated by companies you know, if you fill out an online form that includes your e-mail address, make sure that you can remove yourself from their mailing lists if you choose.

NOTE For more information about unsolicited commercial e-mail, visit the Coalition Against Unsolicited E-Mail at `www.cauce.org`.

Exchange Server–Based Virus Scanning

Over the last few years, the use of Exchange server–based virus scanners has exploded. These products are installed directly on the Exchange server and detect viruses in mailboxes located in the Exchange server's mailbox or public folder stores.

There are two approaches to scanning for viruses on an Exchanger server. The older approach uses MAPI to open mailboxes and scan messages. This approach, while slow, does manage to detect viruses found in Exchange store–based messages. However, on a busy server with many simultaneous users, MAPI scanning may not be sufficient since the antivirus software may not have time to scan the message before the user opens it.

In response to complaints from vendors and customers stating that virus-scanning software was missing some messages, Microsoft developed the *Antivirus Application Programming Interface (AVAPI, VSAPI, or VAPI)*, which allows an antivirus software vendor to scan the message as it is being stored, rather than by opening it in the mailbox. There are two major flavors of AVAPI: Version 1.0 works with Exchange 5.5 and Exchange 2000 RTM, while version 2.0 provides more features, faster scanning, and is available with Exchange 2000 SP1 and later. The advantage of using a virus scanner that supports AVAPI 1.0 is that messages are scanned much more quickly, but the disadvantage is that the virus-scanning software cannot report which message or user had the virus. AVAPI virus scanners that support AVAPI 2.0 can additionally provide the messages and users that have been infected.

> **NOTE**   There were some issues with the RTM (release to manufacturing) of Exchange 2000. You should be using Exchange 2000 SP1 in order to fix AVAPI-related problems and to get the maximum available features that your antivirus vendor can provide. To better understand the improvements with AVAPI 2.0 and how virus scanning affects your server, see Microsoft Knowledge Base article Q285667.

Most Exchange server–based antivirus software packages on the market today, some of which are listed in Table 13.2, support both MAPI as well as AVAPI. Once you are running Exchange 2000 SP1, you should limit the virus scanner to AVAPI mode only, since MAPI scanning is very processor-intensive.

> **NOTE**   The AVAPI 2.0 supports only one antivirus product running on an Exchange 2000 server; thus that you cannot run two products simultaneously.

Table 13.2 Exchange-Based Antivirus Software

Vendor	Product	URL
Symantec	Norton Antivirus for Microsoft Exchange	`www.symantec.com`
Trend Micro	ScanMail for Exchange	`www.trendmicro.com`
Sybari	Antigen for Microsoft Exchange	`www.sybari.com`
McAfee	Groupshield for Exchange	`www.mcafeeb2b.com`
Panda Software	Panda Antivirus for Exchange 2000	`www.pandasoftware.com`

Cleaning Up an Infection

There may come a time when you have to clean up a virus infection because your virus software does not yet have the signatures that will detect the virus. This is often the case with fast-moving viruses such as ILOVEYOU because vendors cannot get signature files out the door quickly enough.

> **NOTE** If you have a virus infection and have recently updated your signature files, check your antivirus software to see if there is an option to re-scan the mailbox and public folder stores after a signature update. I do not recommend keeping this option on all the time, but it can be useful when you already have infected messages and have received a signature file to detect them.

Removing the virus from the mailbox store is now your priority. There are a number of Microsoft utilities, such as ISScan and ExMerge, that can perform this task. ISScan is only available from Microsoft PSS, but the ExMerge utility (also discussed in Chapters 4 and 7) is found on the Exchange 2000 CD-ROM. Simply copy it from the `\Support\Utils\I386\ExMerge` directory to the `\Exchsrvr\Bin` directory. The ExMerge utility will allow you to specify a certain attachment or message subject that you want to remove from one or more mailbox stores.

The following example will step you through removing the Anna Kournikova virus. First, you have to determine what the subject of the virus is or what attachment it is carrying; in the case of this virus, we know that it is carrying a VBS scripted called `AnnaKournikova.jpg.vbs`.

1. Ensure that the user as whom you are logged on has the Receive As permission to all mailboxes you want to access (see Chapter 11).

2. Start the ExMerge utility and click Next.

3. Click Extract Or Import (Two Step Procedure) and click Next.

4. Click Step 1: Extract Data From Exchange Server Mailbox and click Next.

5. Specify the name of the Exchange 2000 server, the domain controller and the domain controller port used for LDAP queries. Then click the Options button; the Data Selection Criteria dialog box opens.

6. Click the Import Procedure property tab and select the Archive Data To Target Store radio button. This tells ExMerge to move any messages from the Exchange mailbox store to a PST file.

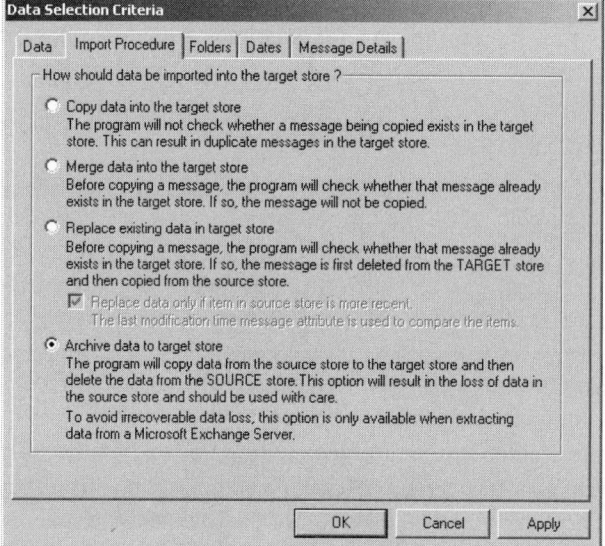

7. Now you have to specify exactly which messages qualify to be ExMerged. If you don't specify anything on the Folders, Dates, or Message Details property tabs, then *all* messages will be archived out to PST files. Click the Dates property page and specify a date range if you want to search for messages from a certain date range. This will help speed up the ExMerge process. You could also specify certain folders for ExMerge to search through, but if a user has rules on their folder, there is no telling where the message got moved to.

8. Click the Message Details property tab and type **AnnaKournikova.jpg.vbs** in the Enter New Attachment Name box. Click the Add button.

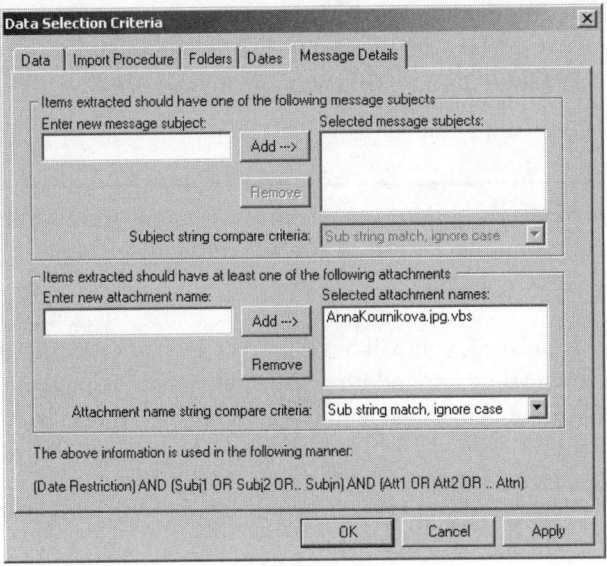

9. Click OK to save these changes, then click the Next button.

10. Click the check box next to the stores through which you want to search and click Next. If you are attempting to eradicate a widespread virus, typically you will select all of the mailbox stores. Click Next.

11. Select the mailboxes that you wish to search for the specified attachment. Typically you will select all of the mailboxes. Click Next.

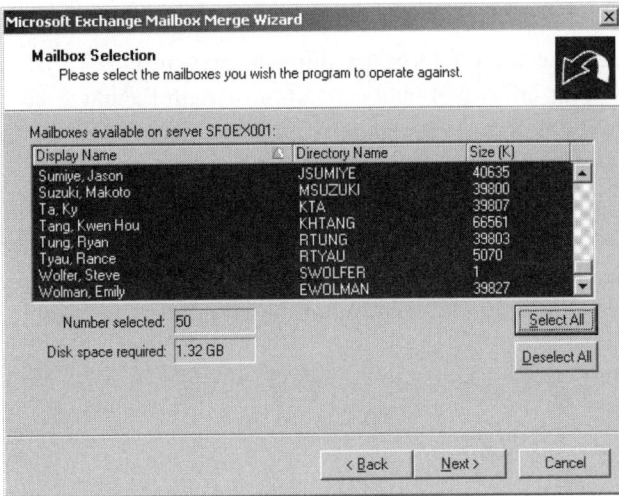

Security

PART 3

12. Select the default locale that will be used to define the default language for new mailboxes (if mailboxes have to be created). Then click Next.

13. Specify the location where the PST files will be created. The default directory is C:\ExMergeData. Make sure that this disk has enough disk space to accommodate all of the PST files; even a PST file with no messages in it will be 32KB in size. Click Next twice.

NOTE The above procedure extracts messages only from server-based message stores. If users have moved an infected message to a local PST file, they will have to remove it manually.

When ExMerge is finished, you will have a directory (C:\ExMergeData) full of PST files. I recommend keeping these around for a few days (or archiving them to tape) just in case someone had a legitimate message with the attachment name AnnaKournikova.jpg.vbs.

Virus-Protection Best Practices

Here is a list of ways to maximize performance of your virus-protection products:

- Keep your virus signatures up-to-date. Some vendors release new signatures every few days; recently one vendor released four new signature updates in one week!

- Use a combination of technologies. Implement Exchange server–based scanning as well as a content inspection system. Many administrators prefer to use two vendors for content inspection and scanning so that different virus-detection engines are used.

- Block scripting and executable attachments.

- If you use an antivirus client to scan for viruses on the Exchange server's hard disk, make absolutely sure that you are excluding the Exchange data directories.

- Set message size and mailbox size limits to prevent DoS attacks through "mail storms." Great inflows of mail can shut down an Exchange server, yet restricting maximum inbound message sizes to under 10MB can prevent this.

- Apply the Outlook Email Security Update patch for Outlook 98 or Outlook 2000, or apply Office 2000 SP2 to restrict the types of files that Outlook can transmit. These patches were designed to make it harder for a virus to spread itself. The fix is automatically implemented in Outlook 2002. See www.slipstick.com/outlook/esecup.htm for more information on these updates.

SMTP Mail and Security

SMTP mail is inherently insecure by its very nature. SMTP was originally developed when the Internet was one big happy family and the likelihood that it would be abused much less. When SMTP was developed, there were far fewer people on the Internet who would have taken advantage of open mail servers. Today, in order to effectively manage any SMTP-based mail server, you need to understand how to trace e-mail using SMTP headers, control SMTP relay, block unwanted SMTP traffic, and get off of black hole lists.

Understanding SMTP Headers

You may be called upon to view the headers of an SMTP message to determine if the message really originated in the location that you expected. The Outlook client can view the SMTP headers of a message by opening the message and choosing View ➢ Options (see Figure 13.4). The SMTP headers are shown as the Internet headers.

Figure 13.4   SMTP headers as shown from Outlook

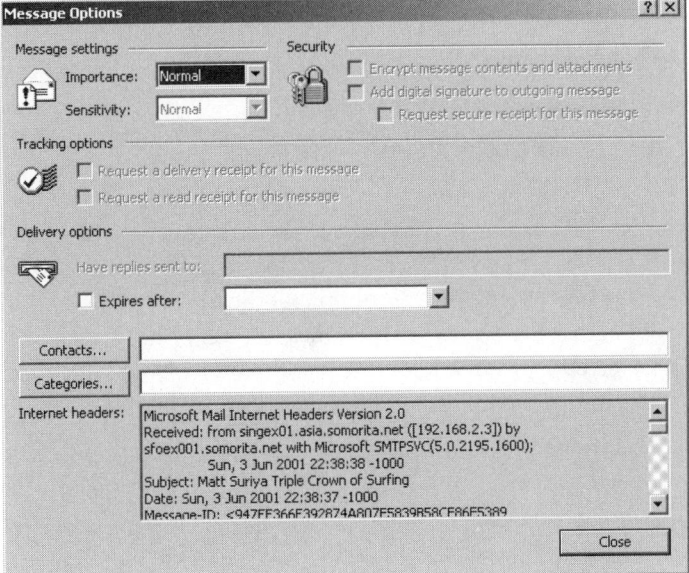

The SMTP headers show all of the SMTP servers through which this message was routed. This includes mail relays, antivirus/content inspections systems, and any internal Exchange 2000 servers that may have touched the message. SMTP headers also indicate where the message originated and what e-mail server or program was used to send it. In Figure 13.4, the message was sent internally to Somorita Surfboards. The message originated on a machine called singex01.asia.somorita.net and was received by sfoex001.somorita.net.

Below is example of a slightly more complicated SMTP header. This header has the message going across three SMTP systems.

```
Microsoft Mail Internet Headers Version 2.0

Received: from antivirus.cta.net ([66.32.164.4]) by hnlex001.cta.net
with Microsoft SMTPSVC(5.0.2195.1600);

Tue, 5 Jun 2001 20:20:50 -1000

Received: from hawaii.rr.com ([24.25.227.35) by antivirus.cta.net
(InterScan E-Mail VirusWall NT); Mon, 05 Jun 2001 20:20:14 -1000
(Hawaii Standard Time);

Received: from kalapana ([24.36.71.111]) by hawaii.rr.com with
Microsoft SMTPSVC(5.5.1877.517.51);

 Tue, 5 Jun 2001 20:18:38 -1000

Message-ID: <000a01c0ee50$86eae7f0$6f471f18@kalapana>

From: "Jim McBee" <mcbeej001@hawaii.rr.com>

To: <jmcbee@cta.net>

Subject: SMTP message header test

Date: Tue, 5 Jun 2001 20:18:39 -1000
```

To read this header, you have to start at the earliest Received label. The message originated from an SMTP client called kalapana and was transmitted to an SMTP server called hawaii.rr.com. The SMTP server hawaii.rr.com transmitted the message on to a server called antivirus.cta.net. From there, the message was transmitted to a server called hnlex001.cta.net. Note also the times in each of the Received lines; sometimes the time zone is given and sometimes it is just the offset from Greenwich Mean Time (minus 10 hours in my example).

The Windows 2000 SMTP service may also insert into the IP address field something that looks like ([66.32.164.4] unverified) or ([66.32.164.4] RDNS failed) if it cannot properly verify the sending SMTP host's fully qualified domain name (FQDN). You will see FQDNs or the word "unverified" in the header of SMTP messages only if the SMTP virtual server has reverse lookups enabled. These are not enabled by default, since it can increase the overhead on the Exchange server.

> **NOTE**   Much of the SMTP header can be spoofed (faked), so don't believe all of the hops that you see. Generally the last hop (the one where the message was accepted by your server) will be accurate, but the rest of the hops may be wrong.

Who Owns an IP Address?

If you see an IP address in the mail headers, there are two ways to determine who owns it. The less accurate of these ways is to use the NSLookup program. Here is a simple example to determine who owns the address 66.37.160.1:

```
nslookup -q=ptr 66.37.160.1
```

Using NSLookup assumes that the IP address has an associated reverse lookup PTR record. A more accurate way of seeing to whom the IP network is registered is to use one of the IP address databases on the Internet. Depending on where the IP address is located, you will have to use a different database:

- ARIN (American Registry for Internet Numbers; www.arin.net/whois/arinwhois .html) tracks IP addresses found in North, Central, and South America.

- APNIC (Asia Pacific Network Information Centre) (www.apnic.net) tracks IP addresses registered for networks in Asia and the South Pacific, including Australia and New Zealand.

- RIPE (Réseaux IP Européens; www.ripe.net/cgi-bin/whois) tracks IP addresses registered for European networks.

- U.S. Department of Defense addresses are tracked by the DoD NIC (www.nic .mil/dodnic).

- U.S. government IP addresses are tracked by the government's Network Information Center (www.nic.gov/cgi-bin/whois).

SMTP Relay

An *SMTP relay host* is an SMTP mail server that accepts mail from SMTP clients (clients could be Outlook Express users, Netscape Communicator users, other Exchange servers, or other SMTP servers) and forwards those messages to their destination. Relayed mail is sent to a domain other than the local domain. If you are supporting POP3 or IMAP4 clients, you must have a server configured to act as a relay server for those clients.

Unfortunately, if you have an improperly configured server that acts as an SMTP relay server, it will allow relay mail from anyone on the Internet. This means that an unscrupulous spammer (is there such a thing as a spammer with scruples?) can use your server to send thousands of e-mail messages to others. When the recipients view the SMTP messages, the message will appear to have come from your SMTP server. In addition to having your bandwidth and resources used (don't you feel kind of violated?), you can expect to get some nasty e-mail messages and even may be put on a black hole list (discussed in the next section). Exchange 2000 automatically blocks relay for all SMTP virtual servers except for users who authenticate to the SMTP virtual server. This is in stark contrast to the Exchange 5.5 IMS, which allowed relay by default. This resulted in many network administrators spending a few panic-stricken days trying to figure out how to get off of a black hole list or why their mail server was trying to deliver 100,000 messages.

The Exchange 5.5 Internet Mail Service (IMS) automatically allowed relay to any host that wanted to send SMTP messages through the IMS. All Exchange 2000 SMTP virtual servers automatically block relay for all SMTP hosts except for those that authenticate.

Figure 13.5 shows the Relay Restrictions dialog box for an SMTP virtual server (you can find this dialog box by clicking the Relay button on the SMTP virtual server's Access property page.) The default is that only computers that authenticate are allowed to relay; Exchange 2000 SMTP virtual servers will automatically authenticate to other Exchange 2000 servers in your organization. Outlook Express clients can also authenticate to the SMTP virtual server.

Figure 13.5   Relay restrictions for an SMTP virtual server

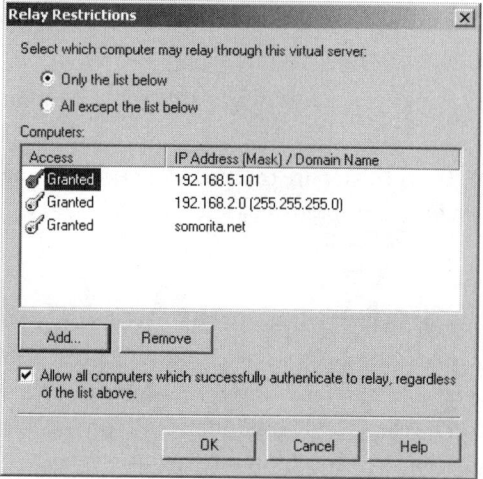

Note in Figure 13.5 that I have specified certain computers that are allowed to relay through this SMTP virtual server. I can specify one of three types of allowable computers:

- A specific IP address.

- An entire IP subnet using the subnet number and subnet mask.

- Any computer from a specific domain. This option requires that those computers have PTR records confirming that their IP address is part of that domain. This option also increases the processing load on the SMTP virtual server due to the reverse lookups.

Testing an Open Relay

There is a simple test (using Telnet) that you can perform to confirm that relay on your SMTP servers is open. In this example, my internal domain is somorita.net, but I will use Telnet to try and send a domain to SuekoM@bobsboogieboards.com. When you run Telnet, make sure that you turn on local echo so that you can see what you are typing. To do so, at the Microsoft Telnet prompt, type **set local_echo** and press Enter.

To initiate this SMTP conversation, at the command prompt connect to a SMTP server by typing **telnet sfoex001.somorita.net 25** (don't forget to include the 25 on the end of the command, which indicates to which port you are connecting). Below is a sample SMTP session using Telnet; the lines that I typed are in bold.

```
220 sfoex001.somorita.net Microsoft ESMTP MAIL Service, Version:
5.0.2195.1600 ready at Wed, 6 Jun 2001 22:25:08 -1000

ehlo spammer.spammeister.com

250-sfoex001.somorita.net Hello [127.0.0.1]

< ESMTP extension list

250 OK

mail from: <sneakyspammer@spammeister.com>

250 2.1.0 sneakyspammer@spammeister.com....Sender OK

rcpt to: <SuekoM@bobsboogieboards.com>

550 5.7.1 Unable to relay for SuekoM@bobsboogieboards.com
```

The first line is where the SMTP client introduces itself with either an EHLO (meaning it speaks enhanced SMTP) or a HELO (meaning that it speaks standard SMTP) command. I then specify in the mail from command the originator of the message, and with the rcpt to command I specify the recipient of the message. If relay is blocked, then I will get a message that indicates that the host is unable to relay. Different SMTP servers may generate slightly different messages.

If relay is open, when the rcpt to command is issued, the response will look something like this:

```
250 2.1.5 <SuekoM@bobsboogieboards.com>
```

Then the SMTP server will take responsibility for delivering the message.

Another (and more thorough) way to test if an SMTP relay is open is to use the service provided by the Network Abuse Clearinghouse (www.abuse.net/relay.html). You must register to use this service; all relay tests are logged, and they only permit a few relay tests per hour. The tests performed are common ways to get an SMTP server to relay a message. Here are the results of a relay test I ran from their web page:

```
<<< 220 sfoex001.somorita.net Microsoft ESMTP MAIL Service, Version:
5.0.2195.1600 ready at Wed, 6 Jun 2001 23:08:55 -1000
>>> HELO www.abuse.net
<<< 250 sfoex001.somorita.net Hello [208.31.42.77]
Relay test 1
>>> RSET
<<< 250 2.0.0 Resetting
>>> MAIL FROM:<spamtest@abuse.net>
<<< 250 2.1.0 spamtest@abuse.net....Sender OK
>>> RCPT TO:<SurfingGeek_2000@yahoo.com>
<<< 550 5.7.1 Unable to relay for SurfingGeek_2000@yahoo.com
Relay test 2
>>> RSET
<<< 250 2.0.0 Resetting
>>> MAIL FROM:<spamtest>
<<< 250 2.1.0 spamtest@somorita.net....Sender OK
>>> RCPT TO:<SurfingGeek_2000@yahoo.com>
<<< 550 5.7.1 Unable to relay for SurfingGeek_2000@yahoo.com
Relay test 3
>>> RSET
<<< 250 2.0.0 Resetting
>>> MAIL FROM:<>
<<< 250 2.1.0 <>....Sender OK
>>> RCPT TO:<SurfingGeek_2000@yahoo.com>
<<< 550 5.7.1 Unable to relay for SurfingGeek_2000@yahoo.com
Relay test 4
>>> RSET
<<< 250 2.0.0 Resetting
>>> MAIL FROM:<spamtest@[66.37.160.3]>
<<< 250 2.1.0 spamtest@[66.37.160.3]....Sender OK
```

```
>>> RCPT TO:<SurfingGeek_2000@yahoo.com>

<<< 550 5.7.1 Unable to relay for SurfingGeek_2000@yahoo.com

Relay test 5

>>> RSET

<<< 250 2.0.0 Resetting

>>> MAIL FROM:<spamtest@somorita.net>

<<< 250 2.1.0 spamtest@somorita.net....Sender OK

>>> RCPT TO:<SurfingGeek_2000@yahoo.com>

<<< 550 5.7.1 Unable to relay for SurfingGeek_2000@yahoo.com

Relay test 6

>>> RSET

<<< 250 2.0.0 Resetting

>>> MAIL FROM:<spamtest@[66.37.160.3]>

<<< 250 2.1.0 spamtest@[66.37.160.3]....Sender OK

>>> RCPT TO:<SurfingGeek_2000%yahoo.com@[66.37.160.3]>

<<< 550 5.7.1 Unable to relay for SurfingGeek_2000%yahoo.com@
↳[66.37.160.3]

Relay test 7

>>> RSET

<<< 250 2.0.0 Resetting

>>> MAIL FROM:<spamtest@[66.37.160.3]>

<<< 250 2.1.0 spamtest@[66.37.160.3]....Sender OK

>>> RCPT TO:<SurfingGeek_2000%yahoo.com@somorita.net>

<<< 250 2.1.5 SurfingGeek_2000%yahoo.com@somorita.net

>>> DATA

<<< 354 Start mail input; end with <CRLF>.<CRLF>

>>> (message body)

<<< 250 2.6.0 <rlytest-991904811-23502@abuse.net> Queued mail for
↳delivery
```

The last test (Relay test 7) appears to have worked; the Exchange 2000 SMTP virtual server accepted the message, but it will not deliver it. Using the % and the ! characters is described in RFC 1123. Many Unix-based systems will forward messages with the % and ! characters, but Exchange does not, so the messages are put in the \Badmail directory.

Security

PART 3

If any of these tests seem like they're working, then you should check the mailbox you specified when you started the test to see if the message was really relayed.

Black Hole Lists

A *black hole list,* also known as a *real-time black hole (RTB)* list, is a record of known open relays on the Internet. If your SMTP server is reported as having forwarded spam messages or being an open relay, it may end up on a black hole list. There are some SMTP server software packages that consult a database of IP addresses on this list before they will accept mail from anyone. If your SMTP server's IP address is on this list, the receiving SMTP system will not accept a connection from your server.

> **NOTE**   Mail Essentials (www.gfi.com) and Praetor (www.praetor.com) both provide options to check a black hole list before accepting a connection.

Exchange 2000 does not perform this check out of the box, but an event sink could be written that would integrate this functionality into the Exchange SMTP virtual server. In my own experience working with software that supports checking RTB lists, about 30 percent of the inbound messages that got blocked were from spammers, and the remaining 70 percent were from legitimate mail senders whose servers had accidentally gotten onto the RTB list.

You may not even realize it if your server ends up on one of the RTB lists. The postmaster alias at your domain may get a message indicating that you are on the list, but this is not a given, nor should you expect it. You can possibly discern this information from non-delivery reports (NDRs) and from the SMTP protocol logs.

> **NOTE**   The two most common RTB lists can be found at www.mail-abuse.org and www.abuse.net. On these sites are instructions for reporting someone or having your server removed (make sure you block relay first).

Blocking Unwanted SMTP Traffic

A particularly useful anti-spam feature of the SMTP virtual server is its ability to block inbound SMTP mail. Mail can be blocked based on the sender's e-mail address or domain name, an empty or null sender, or the IP address of the SMTP client.

Blocking messages based on the sender's domain or address is a two-part process. First, on the SMTP virtual server, you must enable the filter feature for each IP address that you want to filter. This is done on the General properties tab of each SMTP virtual server. Click the Advanced button and select All Unassigned or the specific address you wish to filter, and click Edit (see Figure 13.6). Click the Apply Filter check box to enable filtering for this selection.

Applying the filter merely specifies which IP address on the local server you want to be filtered. The other piece of this equation is that you must now specify what you want filtered. This setting is configured globally (all servers in the organization.) Locate the Message Delivery object under Global Settings in Exchange System Manager and display its properties. Click the Filtering tab to see the list of e-mail addresses and domains you can filter. In Figure 13.7, I am filtering all mail from the domains checkthisout.com, passthison.com, and smartbotpro.net as well as mail from the user friend@public .com. The Accept Messages Without Notifying Sender Of Filtering check box will cause the SMTP virtual server to accept the messages, but not notify the sender that we are not going to deliver their message.

Figure 13.6   Applying a filter to All Unassigned IP addresses on a virtual server

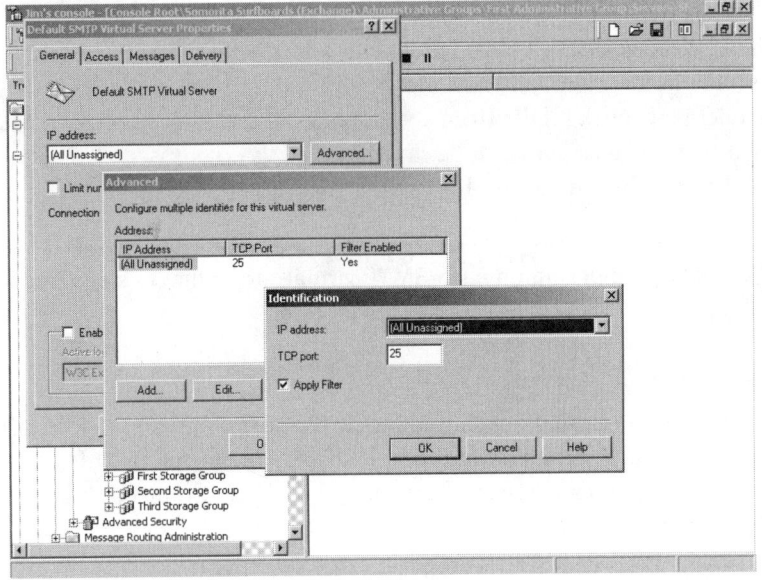

Figure 13.7   Filtering messages from specific users or domains

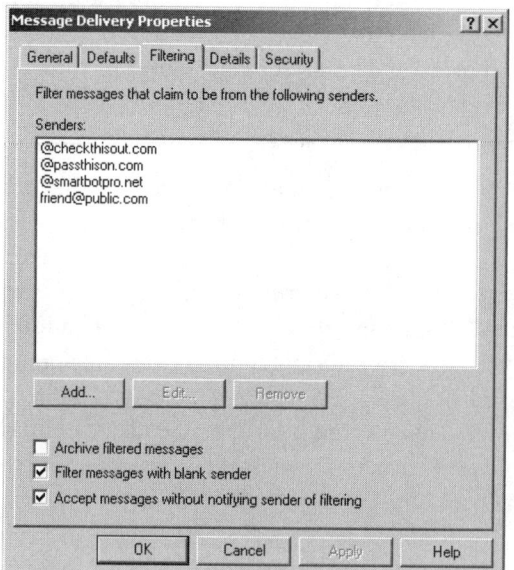

If the Filter Messages With Blank Sender check box is selected, any messages that do not have a sender in the From field will not be allowed. However, blocking messages with a blank sender may block NDRs from <> addresses. If the Archive Filtered Messages check box is selected, the messages will be saved to the \Mailroot\vsi 1\Filter directory (there will be a unique directory for each virtual server).

NOTE   Enable blocking on each SMTP virtual server that has an MX record pointing to it or that is connected to the Internet.

Blocking Mail by IP Address

You can also block inbound mail based on the IP address of the SMTP client. This feature is configured on each virtual server. Simply display the properties of an SMTP virtual server, choose the Access property button, and click the Connection button. The Connection dialog box opens.

There are two approaches to configuring the inbound connections restrictions on an SMTP virtual server; deny everything except those permitted (the Only The List Below radio button) or allow everything except a specified list (All Except The List Below).

When planning to block traffic, the latter is the most useful, because you can use it to block someone who is repeatedly sending you e-mail. Options for blocking include:

- The IP address of a specific SMTP client.
- An entire IP subnet.
- Any hosts whose reverse DNS lookup indicates that they are part of a specific domain. This option requires that the hosts you are blocking have PTR records.

Exchange, Firewalls, and Proxy Servers

Just a few years ago, protecting your network from the rest of the Internet was not necessary. The word *firewall* brought a confused look to the face of even the most savvy network administrator. Only the most visible companies or the ones that had the most at-risk data implemented firewalls. Today things have changed to the point that even the most obscure company with a connection to the Internet must have protection from the evils that lurk on the Internet. Today it is not uncommon for hackers to perform *port scans* on IP address ranges in order to determine if services such as NetBIOS (Microsoft file and print services) are available. Once available services are found, it is simply a matter of the hacker figuring out a way to exploit the service.

Vulnerabilities in software products along with poor security procedures have increased the need for network protection, and thus the need for people who specialize in firewall deployments and administration has emerged. In most medium-sized and large companies, the Exchange administrators are not responsible for design or configuration of firewalls. However, I have found that a knowledge of firewalls, and what may need to be configured, to be essential for Exchange gurus.

> **NOTE** Firewalls should not be seen as the ultimate solution to security. In the spring of 2001, a group of hackers (purportedly from China) exploited a weakness in IIS that defaced thousands of websites using nothing more than HTTP. Even more advanced firewalls could not have prevented this attack; only applying updated security fixes could prevent this particular vulnerability.

Firewalls 101

A *firewall* is a specialized network device that may be either a self-contained "black box" or simply a computer with two network interface cards. The firewall is placed between the internal portion of the network and the outside world—the Internet, a separate subsidiary, another business, or other offices. The firewall has a set of programs that inspect all inbound (and possibly outbound) IP network traffic and apply a set of security policies relating to the type of traffic that is permitted.

There are many possible configurations for firewall installations. Often (and foolishly) companies will place their web servers, Exchange 2000 front-end servers, and SMTP relay servers outside the firewall. This makes these servers significantly more vulnerable to attack.

Another approach (shown in Figure 13.8) puts everything behind the firewall including the front-end servers, web servers, and SMTP relay servers. While this configuration is certainly more secure than leaving the servers exposed, it requires that some traffic from the Internet be forwarded to servers on the internal network. One server may be compromised merely because a server that is accessible from the Internet is attacked.

Possibly a more secure approach is to create a perimeter network or DMZ (demilitarized zone) in which you locate servers that must be publicly accessible. While some organizations use two firewalls (often from separate vendors), many firewall solutions now come with three ports. Figure 13.9 shows a firewall with three ports: one to the external network, one to the perimeter network, and one to the internal network.

Figure 13.8   Putting everything behind the firewall

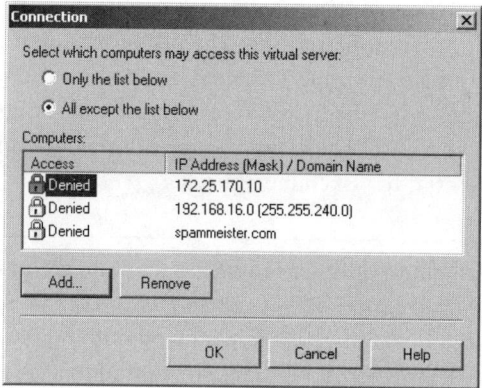

> **WARNING**   You should never place domain controllers in the perimeter network. Placing a domain controller on a network that has partial access from the Internet may expose your user account database.

Figure 13.9 Implementing a perimeter network (DMZ)

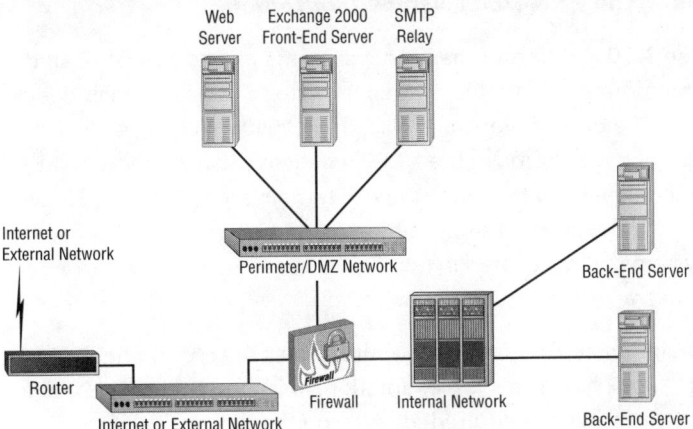

The firewall in Figure 13.9 is configured to allow only specific types of traffic through from the outside network to the servers in the DMZ. Further, the firewall is configured so that only specific types of access are permitted between the servers in the DMZ and the servers on the internal network.

A Chink in the Proverbial Armor

During the early beta period for Exchange 2000, the fact that Exchange 2000 supported a front-end/back-end configuration was frequently discussed. Many network administrators were excited by the prospect of putting their publicly available servers in their DMZ and keeping the domain controllers, mailbox servers, and public folder servers on the private network. Since I am a non-firewall kind of guy, I was among those who considered this a good idea.

The first DMZs that most organizations actually used were designed to allow *only* HTTP (either port 80 or 443) and possibly SMTP (port 25) through to the DMZ. But now, organizations are finding many uses for DMZs, including POP3, IMAP4, NNTP, FTP, LDAP, chat, media, and other services. Suddenly there are a slew of ports that must be opened between the Internet and the DMZ. With *each* additional service that you open up to the Internet, you increase the likelihood that a chink in the armor can be exploited. The reason that web servers were originally put in the DMZ was that these systems were not trusted to have access to the internal network.

A Chink in the Proverbial Armor *(continued)*

Exchange 2000 is different than most systems placed in a DMZ since it requires access to information on the internal network; this access includes domain controllers, Global Catalog servers, and Exchange 2000 mailbox/public folder servers. Any weakness of the systems in the DMZ increases the likelihood that Exchange 2000 servers could be used to compromise internal servers or data. This is not to say that making a DMZ secure is not possible—it just becomes more difficult with more and more systems being located in the DMZ. Great care must be taken to ensure that the internal network is adequately protected.

If you are interested in providing secure access to an Exchange 2000 OWA server for Internet clients, here is a simpler solution. Place the Exchange 2000 front-end server (if a front-end server is required) directly on the internal network. Open *only* port 443 to the front-end server's IP address. This is far simpler than a complex configuration for front-end and back-end communications through a firewall, and it doesn't open up any unnecessary ports to the internal server.

An additional security setting that you might use would be an IPSec policy on the front-end server that would further lock down what the front-end server is allowed to communicate.

Exchange 2000 TCP/UDP Port Usage

When you begin to configure a firewall to allow specific types of messaging or directory traffic to get to your Exchange 2000 servers, knowing which ports that Exchange uses is important. The common TCP/UDP port numbers that Exchange 2000 uses are listed in Table 13.3.

Table 13.3   Exchange 2000 TCP/UPD Port Usage

Port	Description
25	SMTP
53	DNS
80	HTTP (OWA, Instant Messaging)
88	Kerberos

Table 13.3 Exchange 2000 TCP/UPD Port Usage *(continued)*

Port	Description
102	X.400 message transfer agent (MTA)
110	POP3
119	NNTP
135	Remote procedure calls (RPCs)
143	IMAP4
379	LDAP for site replication service (SRS)
389	LDAP (domain controllers)
390	Microsoft-recommended port for LDAP on an Exchange 5.5 server running on a Windows 2000 domain controller
636	LDAP using Secure Sockets Layer (SSL)
443	HTTP using SSL
465	SMTP over SSL (Note that most current implementations of SMTP including Exchange 2000 use port 25 for TLS/SSL communications. Exchange 2000 does not currently use port 465.)
563	NNTP using SSL
691	Link-state updates within a routing group
636	LDAP using SSL
993	IMAP4 using SSL
995	POP3 using SSL
1503	T.120 data conferencing services (used with Exchange 2000 Conference Server)
1720	H.323 video conferencing services (used with Exchange 2000 Conference Server)
1731	Audio conferencing services (used with Exchange 2000 Conference Server)

Security

PART 3

Table 13.3 Exchange 2000 TCP/UPD Port Usage *(continued)*

Port	Description
3268	LDAP to Active Directory global catalog servers
3269	LDAP using SSL to global catalog servers
6667/7000	IRC and IRCX (Internet Relay Chat)

NOTE The Exchange MTA can be reconfigured to use another port other than 102 through the Registry. See Microsoft Knowledge Base article Q161931.

NOTE For more information on using enabling conferencing services and NetMeeting through a firewall, see Knowledge Base article Q158623. Other articles relevant to Exchange connectivity through firewalls can be found in Knowledge Base articles Q280132 and Q270836.

Outlook MAPI Clients outside the Firewall

If you are going to place your Outlook clients outside of a firewall and MAPI over RPC, then you must open additional ports. The problem with opening these ports is that the information store and directory service ports are dynamically assigned. These ports must be statically configured first before you can configure the firewall.

WARNING Opening RPC ports directly to the Internet will make your Exchange servers vulnerable to DoS attacks. While opening these ports is fairly simple, setting up a virtual private network (VPN) is almost as easy and is far more secure. For details, see the "Outlook Clients and a VPN" section, later in this chapter.

NOTE MAPI clients cannot connect to a front-end server.

To do this, you must modify the Registry and each Exchange server that has MAPI clients outside of the firewall. I have not heard of any specific compromises of Exchange servers using these open ports, but if you are concerned about opening up this type of access, consider putting in a VPN instead of opening up the ports. When using a VPN, you do not have to statically map any ports on the Exchange server.

To configure Exchange so that the directory service ports are statically mapped to a single port, you will need to statically map the directory service proxy (DSProxy) and referral interfaces (RFR). Using `regedt32.exe`, create a new Registry value called `TCP/IP NSPI port` of type REG_DWORD in the following key:

`HKLM\System\CurrentControlSet\Services\MSExchangeSA\Parameters`

In the data field, pick a port above 1500 (decimal). This sets the TCP/IP port for the RFR interface. Please note that this is opening up MAPI client access to the Global Catalog; while authentication is required, this does not mean that future vulnerabilities will not be found.

> **WARNING** When statically assigning ports, make sure that you are not assigning a port that another application is using.

Finally, you will need to statically map the information store service to a static port. Create a Registry value called `TCP/IP port` of type REG_DWORD in the following Registry key:

`HKLM\System\CurrentControlSEt\Services\MSExchangeIS\ParametersSystem`

In the data field, pick a port above 1500. Take note of all three static ports that you have configured. On the firewall, open port 135 and the three ports that you have statically configured. The Exchange Server System Attendant (and thus all other Exchange services) will have to be restarted after these Registry changes have been made.

> **NOTE** Static ports are not always configured for external firewalls. I have a couple of customers who maintain a "backbone" firewall and thus want to know all ports that are in use from the corporate network to the server backbone.

> **NOTE** For more information on configuring ports statically and opening firewall ports for Exchange, see Microsoft Knowledge Base articles Q280132 and Q270836.

Are New Mail Notifications Arriving Slowly? In some circumstances, your clients outside of the firewall may receive new mail notifications in batches. I see this in many situations where the firewall is blocking UDP ports above 1024. When the Outlook client initializes, it negotiates a port in the range of 1024 to 65535 that the Exchange server uses to push notifications of new e-mail. There is no way to statically map this port.

Security

PART 3

This problem can drive me nuts, because I will be using Outlook from home and will not be receiving new messages. In order to receive new messages, I need to force Outlook to contact the server by clicking a folder or creating a new message. My "automated" solution is to configure an offline folder and have my client synchronize every 30 minutes while I am online.

Outlook Clients and a VPN

If you are concerned about opening up RPC ports directly from the Internet to the Exchange server, you are not alone. The most secure solution is to set up a VPN through which your clients can access the internal network. Many third-party vendors on the market provide VPN solutions; even some firewall vendors provide VPN solutions. While complete coverage of installation of a VPN server is not possible in this text, I want to explain some of the basics of setting up a VPN using Windows 2000.

You can install a simple VPN by building a simple Windows 2000 server with two network interface cards (NICs). Attach one NIC to the public network and one to the internal network. Make sure that all of the latest service packs and hot fixes have been applied to this Windows 2000 server. This server should be a member of the Active Directory (AD) domain so that clients can be authenticated, but it should not be a domain controller. Follow these steps to set up this server as a VPN endpoint:

1. Log in as a user who has local administrator permissions on the VPN server.

2. Launch the Routing And Remote Access console found in the Programs ➤ Administrative Tools menu.

3. Right-click the server in the Routing And Remote Access tree, and choose Configure And Enable Routing And Remote Access. Click Next when the wizard starts.

4. Click the Virtual Private Network (VPN) Servers radio button and click Next.

5. Confirm that TCP/IP is in the protocols list, select Yes, All Of The Protocols Are On This List, and click Next. If TCP/IP is not selected, you will need to install it.

6. Highlight the network adapter that is connected to the public network when prompted for the Internet connections, and then click Next.

7. Choose the Automatically radio button and click Next.

8. Click No, I Don't Want To Set Up This Server To Use RADIUS Now, and click Next.

9. Click Finish.

Congratulations! You have just configured a simple VPN server that will support up to five simultaneous PPTP clients and five simultaneous L2TP clients. You can increase or decrease this number by right-clicking the server's Ports container, editing the WAN Miniport (PPTP) or WAN Miniport (L2TP) devices, and clicking Configure.

Next, you need to enable the appropriate users to have remote access. There are many ways to accomplish this through remote access profiles, but the simplest way is to display the user's properties in Active Directory Users And Computers, locate the Dial-In property tab, and click the Allow Access radio button.

Finally, you need to configure the VPN client. All Windows 9*x*, NT, 2000, and XP clients are capable of connecting to a VPN, however Windows 95 needs to have its dial-up networking software upgraded. Each of these clients has slightly different procedures for connecting to the VPN server, but each requires the IP address or FQDN of the VPN server's network interface. For Windows 2000, the following procedure applies:

1. Right-click the My Network Places desktop icon.

2. Run the Make New Connection Wizard. (If you have never run this wizard before, you may be required to set up your country, area code, number to dial for an outside line, and tone or pulse dialing.) Click Next.

3. Click the Connect To A Private Virtual Private Network Through The Internet radio button, and then click Next.

4. Enter the IP address or FQDN of the VPN server's public network interface.

5. Choose the Only For Myself radio button if you are the only person on this computer who will need this connection; otherwise, choose For All Users. Click Next twice.

6. If you want to add a shortcut to this connection, click the Add A Shortcut To My Desktop check box, and then click Finish.

The VPN connection is ready to use. The first time the user launches it, they will need to provide their AD domain name, username, and password.

The above procedure allows VPN clients to access *any* node on your internal network. An alternative is to set up the Exchange 2000 server as the VPN server. This will allow remote clients to connect only to the Exchange server. To do this, you must allow VPN traffic through your firewall to the Exchange 2000/VPN server. Here is some additional information you need to know about to open up VPN connections through a firewall:

- For PPTP VPN clients, you must open IP protocol 47 (generic routing encapsulation or GRE) and UDP port 1723.

- For L2TP clients, you must open IP protocol 115 and UDP port 1701. If IPSec is used with L2TP, you must open up IP ports 50 and 51 and UDP port 500.

Exchange 2000 and Microsoft Proxy 2

A *proxy server* is a software-based system that operates at the Application layer receiving requests from the inside network (usually a network using private IP address space) and sending the request out to the Internet on an official IP address. The proxy server keeps track of which sessions are generated by internal clients and can direct responses back to the clients appropriately.

A proxy server can also be used to restrict certain types of outbound traffic, IP addresses, and which users can use certain protocols. Some proxy servers can perform virus scanning and content inspection, and deny users certain types of Internet access during specific times of the day.

Microsoft Proxy Server 2 can perform many of these duties including allowing a single client inside the network to "acquire" certain ports on the proxy server and have all traffic inbound to those ports redirected to an internal client; for example, the Exchange 2000 server that is running the SMTP connector. Or you can redirect POP3 or IMAP4 requests to a mailbox server.

This example assumes that you are going to direct all SMTP, IMAP4, and POP3 traffic to the same Exchange 2000 server. If the proxy server is running on Exchange 2000, make sure that the IIS's SMTP service is not installed. To configure Exchange 2000 to use the proxy server, follow these steps:

1. Install the Winsock client on the Exchange 2000 server from the proxy server's Mspclnt share.

2. Confirm that your POP3, IMAP4, and SMTP virtual servers are configured and that the IP address fields are set to All Unassigned.

3. Create a file in the \WINNT\SYSTEM32\Inetsrv directory called Wspcfg.ini. The file should contain the following lines:

   ```
   [inetinfo]
   ServerBindTCPPorts=25,110,143,993,995
   ForceCredentials=1
   Persistent=1
   KillOldSession=1
   ```

4. Open a command prompt and change to the \Mspclnt directory (this is the proxy client software). Type the following command where *username* is a user who has permission to bind to the proxy server, *domainname* is the domain of that user, and *password* is the user's password.

   ```
   Credtool -w -n inetinfo -c username domain password
   ```

5. Restart the IIS Admin service.

The user whom you specified in step 4 must be given permissions on the proxy server to use SMTP.

Configuring Firewall Support for Exchange

Once a firewall is in place, there are several basic approaches to configuration. Let's take the example shown back in Figure 13.9. This is not recommended under any circumstances. The firewall will still have to be configured to allow front-end server traffic to the back-end servers, domain controllers and DNS. This configuration will be identical to the configuration between the servers in the DMZ and the back-end servers shown in Figure 13.11.

Table 13.4 lists the required and optional ports that must be opened between servers in the DMZ or servers outside the firewall and servers on the internal network. Some of these ports may not be required if you do not plan to use the services. Remember that you should open only required ports.

Table 13.4   Exchange Ports That May Be Required through the Firewall

Function	TCP Ports	Required?	Explanation
Domain controller	389/636/88 (TCP and UDP port 88)	Y	Used for server logon authentication using Kerberos, and Exchange configuration updates.
Global catalog	3268/3269	Y	Used for querying information about address lists, universal group memberships, and mail-enabled objects attributes.
DNS	53 (TCP and UDP)	Y	Used for DNS queries for domain controller, global catalog servers, AD sites, and Kerberos KDCs. Assumes the internal DNS is on the internal network.
RPCs	135/445 plus additional ports above 1024	Y	Used for Active Directory service discovery, client authentication, and MAPI client communications. Beginning with Exchange 2000 SP2, front-end servers in a DMZ do not require RPC connectivity to the internal network.

Security

PART 3

Table 13.4   Exchange Ports That May Be Required through the Firewall *(continued)*

Function	TCP Ports	Required?	Explanation
SMTP	80	N	Required between Exchange 2000 servers designated to send and receive outside SMTP mail (with an SMTP connector, for example). Not required between Exchange 2000 front-end servers that support only POP3, IMAP4, HTTP, or NNTP.
HTTP (OWA and Instant Messaging)	80	N	Used for HTTP between Exchange 2000 front-end and back-end servers. SSL is not used.
POP3	110	N	Used for POP3 between Exchange 2000 POP3 front-end virtual servers and back-end servers. SSL is not used.
IMAP4	143	N	Used for IMAP4 between Exchange 2000 IMAP4 front-end virtual servers and back-end servers. SSL is not used.
NNTP	119	N	Used for NNTP between Exchange 2000 NNTP front-end virtual server and back-end servers. SSL is not used.

TIP   TLS/SSL is not used between front-end and back-end servers. If you want to secure this type of traffic between the front-end and back-end servers, use IPSec.

What about Figure 13.8 in which all of the servers are inside the firewall, or Figure 13.9 in which all publicly accessible servers are in the DMZ? How does the firewall have to be configured to allow external traffic into these servers? Table 13.5 shows the ports that must be opened to allow various client types to access the front-end servers. I strongly urge you to consider using nothing but SSL-based clients rather than opening ports that will transmit data, usernames, and passwords in the clear. Data transmitted in the clear is easily intercepted by anyone with a network analyzer who happens to be sitting on the same non-switched network segment.

Table 13.5   Ports Possibly Required by Internet Clients through the Firewall

Function	TCP Ports	Required?	Explanation
SMTP	25	N	Used by messages inbound from the Internet and by POP3 and IMAP4 clients to send messages.
HTTP (OWA or Instant Messaging)	80/443 (SSL)	N	Used for OWA, Instant Messaging.
POP3	110/995 (SSL)	N	Used by POP3 mail clients to retrieve mail.
NNTP	119/563 (SSL)		Used by NNTP clients and NNTP servers for push newsfeeds.
IMAP4	143/993 (SSL)		Used by IMAP4 clients to retrieve mail and public folder contents.
LDAP querying domain controllers	389/636 (SSL)		Used by LDAP clients to query a Windows 2000 domain controller.
LDAP querying global catalog server	3268/3269 (SSL)		Used by LDAP clients when querying a Windows 2000 domain controller configured as a Global Catalog server.

Exchange 2000 and Microsoft ISA Server

If your environment uses a lot of Microsoft products, you are probably already aware of Microsoft's Internet Security and Acceleration Server (ISA Server). Your organization may even have this product implemented already. Understanding the basics of ISA Server and how it may be used in conjunction with Exchange is important for accurately communicating the Exchange server's firewall requirements to the administrator of the ISA server.

ISA Server Basics

ISA Server is a firewall and web-caching server that runs on top of Windows 2000. It has its roots in Microsoft Proxy Server 2, yet it is much different and more advanced. ISA Server has all the capabilities of Proxy Server 2, but has many new features and improvements, including:

- Scheduled content download (automatically downloads frequently used websites)
- Integration with Active Directory
- Web cache stored in RAM
- Policy-based inbound and outbound access control
- Easy to implement wizard-driven Web, server publishing, and VPN setup
- Smart application filters for complex protocols
- Built-in intrusion detection

ISA Server is certified by the ICSA (www.icsa.net), has received high praise for the performance of its web-caching engine, and has a number of third-party add-on products available for it. You can put ISA Server at the edge of the corporate network or in strategic positions at the edge of campus LANs to reduce the amount of traffic on the corporate backbone. ISA Server is the ideal firewall to place in front of Exchange 2000 because the two products share a common configuration interface and integrate tightly with Active Directory.

Requirements for ISA Server

Before you begin to deploy ISA Server, you need to decide which version of ISA you need as well as to make sure that you have sufficient hardware for the load you are going to place on the server. ISA Server comes in two versions:

ISA Server Standard can take advantage of Active Directory integration for assigning access to AD user accounts. It can provide web caching, but it cannot take advantage of a caching array. ISA Server Standard is limited to four processors per machine and a maximum of 8GB of RAM.

ISA Server Enterprise takes advantage not only of AD user accounts, but can participate a caching array. The array configuration is stored in AD in the same way that Exchange 2000's configuration is; AD integration provides a fault-tolerant configuration for ISA Server parameters and allows you to create a centralized access policy for the entire organization. ISA Server Enterprise supports as many processors as the underlying Windows platform will support.

Choosing the correct hardware platform for ISA Server is equally important. If you don't have sufficient hardware, access to resources outside of your network will be slow. Minimum installation requirements are the same for Standard and Enterprise versions; the requirements are:

- Pentium 300 MHz or better with 256MB RAM.
- A minimum of 20MB of disk space available for applications and 100MB available for web caching. The file system must be formatted with NTFS to support web caching. On systems supporting more than 100 to 200 users, you should separate the log files onto different physical disk drive from the web caching files.
- Windows 2000 Active Directory is required for ISA Server Enterprise, but ISA Server Standard will work with both Windows 2000 AD and Windows NT 4.

ISA Server Installation Modes

ISA Server can be installed in one of three modes: cache, firewall, or integrated. *Cache mode* should be used only when you need a web-caching solution. The feature is typically used by organizations that already have a firewall in place and do not need ISA Server to perform firewall duties. Cache mode installs the Web proxy service and allows internal clients to take advantage of the web cache. Cache mode also supports web server publishing.

WARNING   Cache mode should be used only for web caching and should not be placed on the edge of the network. ISA servers installed in cache mode do not support packet filtering or other inbound and outbound access control features that are provided by the firewall service.

Firewall mode is intended for servers placed on the edge of the network. A firewall-mode ISA server can protect the network from external attacks through the use of its packet-filtering features. Firewall mode does not install the web-caching feature.

Integrated mode includes the features of both cache and firewall modes. Install ISA Server in integrated mode if you want to take advantage of all the features available in ISA Server, as listed in Table 13.6.

Table 13.6   Features of ISA Server in Firewall and Cache Modes

Feature	Firewall Mode	Cache Mode
Web publishing	Yes	Yes
Server publishing	Yes	Limited to publishing web servers only

Security

PART 3

Table 13.6 Features of ISA Server in Firewall and Cache Modes *(continued)*

Feature	Firewall Mode	Cache Mode
Caching array	No	Yes
Enterprise access policies	Yes	Yes
Packet filtering	Yes	No
Smart application filters	Yes	No
Web filters	Yes	Yes
Real-time monitoring	Limited	Limited
Web protocol support (HTTP, HTTPS, FTP, Gopher)	Yes	Yes
Other Winsock Protocols (SMTP, NNTP, TELNET, POP3)	Yes	No
Alerts	Yes	Yes
Reports	Yes	Yes
VPN Wizards	Yes	No
Outbound PPTP	Yes	No

ISA Server Logic

ISA Server inbound and outbound access controls are policy driven. If there is a policy in place that allows a packet, the packet is passed. If there is no policy that allows the packet, or if a policy denies it, the packet is dropped. The default configuration of ISA Server is to disallow all inbound and outbound access. This is in contrast to Microsoft Proxy Server 2, which allowed outbound access for HTTP requests by default.

There are four ISA Server features that control inbound and outbound access: publishing rules, packet filters, policy elements, and access policies.

Publishing Rules   *Publishing rules* are used to control inbound access. External hosts can be allowed access to resources on the internal network by creating publishing rules. There are two types of publishing rules:

Web publishing rules are used to publish HTTP and FTP servers; they take advantage of the features provided by the Web proxy service. One major advantage of using Web publishing rules to publish Web and FTP servers is that you can publish multiple internal servers using a single IP address on the external interface of the ISA server. Multiple FQDNs can map to the same IP address, and ISA Server will examine the header information in the request and forward it to the appropriate internal web server. Web publishing rules allow the ISA Sever to cache the requests from external network visitors.

Server publishing rules can be used to publish any service but cannot take advantage of the features provided by the Web proxy service. The main advantage to using server publishing rules is that you can publish any service, not just HTTP and FTP. However, if you wish to publish the same server twice (such as two internal SMTP servers), you must bind each instance to a different IP address on the external interface of the ISA server.

NOTE   If you require that the source address for an HTTP request be stored in the published web server's log files, you must use server publishing rules. If you use Web publishing rules, the address on the internal interface of the ISA server will appear in the log files.

Packet Filters   *Packet filters* are used to control inbound access to the ISA server's external interface. If the server is configured in either firewall or integrated mode, you can enable packet filtering to close all ports on the external interface of the ISA server.

To open a port on the external interface of the ISA server, you can either create a publishing rule or a packet filter. Publishing rules are used to allow access to resources on the internal network, while packet filters are used to allow access to resources on the ISA server itself. Packet filters are also used to allow applications (such as mail client software) outbound access to external network resources.

NOTE   You do not need to create a packet filter for published services. For example, if you publish an internal SMTP server, the publishing rule will open TCP port 25 on the external interface automatically. You do not need to create a packet filter to allow inbound SMTP after the publishing rule is created.

Security

PART 3

Policy Elements   Before you can create Web publishing rules and outbound access policies, you must create *policy elements* to support the rules. The policy elements available in ISA Server include: schedules, bandwidth priorities, destination sets, client address sets, protocol definitions, content groups, and dial-up entries.

Policy elements that most impact configuring inbound and outbound access for Exchange Servers and clients include *destination sets* and *protocol definitions*. Destination sets typically include the FQDN of an internal or external resource. They can be used to control access to external sites, or they can be used in Web publishing. For example, if your internal site maps to the IP address of your external interface, you should create a destination set with the FQDN of your internal site. When you create multiple destination sets with FQDNs that map to the external interface of the ISA server, you can publish multiple internal websites with a single IP address on the external interface.

You use protocol definitions to control what protocols are allowed or denied. They can be used to allow access to external resource or be used in server publishing rules. For example, if you wanted to publish an internal SMTP server, you can use the SMTP Server Protocol Definition in the publishing rule. The SMTP Server Protocol Definition defines TCP port 25 inbound.

Access Policies   *Access policies* are used primarily to control outbound access. There are three types of access policies: site and content rules, protocol rules, and IP packet filters.

Site and content rules are used to allow or deny access to resources by location. For example, if you wanted to prevent users from accessing www.amazonsurferbabes.com, you can create a site and content rule that blocks access to this site. You can fine-tune site and content rules by applying them to selected users and groups.

Protocol rules are used to control outbound access by protocol. For example, if you want to allow outbound access to external SMTP servers, you will need to create a protocol rule. The protocol rules are based on the protocol definitions policy element. Protocol rules can be fine-tuned to allow access based on user, group, or IP address.

IP packet filters have limited utility in terms of outbound access for internal network clients. However, you do need to configure IP packet filters for outbound access when you need to allow non-TCP/UDP protocols access to external network resources. Protocol rules are used for only TCP/UDP-based protocols. For example, if you need outbound access to a PPTP VPN server, a packet filter must be in place to allow the clients access, because PPTP depends on the Generic Routing Encapsulation Protocol (GRE – IP Protocol 47).

Exchange behind ISA Server

ISA Server can be configured to allow external users access to an internal Exchange server, and to allow an Exchange server on the internal network to access external SMTP servers. It allows external users access to Exchange in the following ways:

- Secure Mail Server Publishing
- Web Publishing Outlook Web Access
- Server Publishing Outlook Web Access for SSL
- Inbound VPN connections
- Publishing terminal services

Using ISA Server's Secure Mail Server Publishing Wizard

The Secure Mail Server Publishing Wizard allows you to publish a variety of Exchange services with ease. For novices, this is the simplest way to publish services through the ISA server. Follow these steps to run the Secure Mail Publishing Wizard:

1. Using the ISA Management console, expand the Publishing node and right-click the Server Publishing node. Click the Secure Mail Server command. Click Next to continue past the wizard welcome screen. The Mail Services Selection dialog box appears.

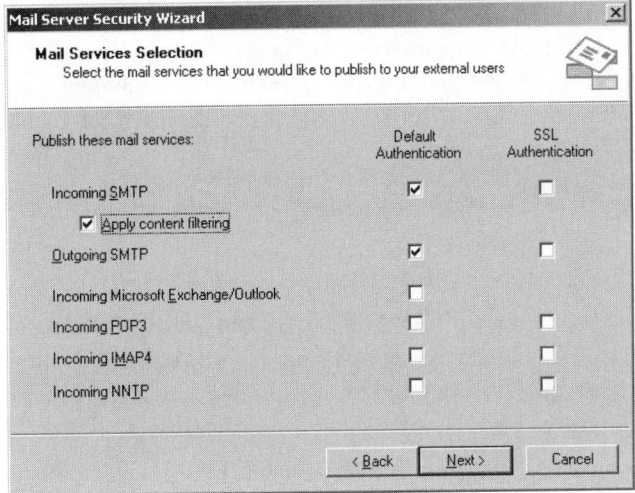

2. Select the protocols you wish to publish. Note that all protocols support SSL authentication except for incoming MAPI requests. ISA Server supports content filtering in tandem with the ISA Server *message screener*, an optional feature that can be used to examine the header and data information in SMTP messages. In this example, we'll choose Incoming SMTP and Outgoing SMTP by clicking the Apply Content Filtering check box and clicking Next.

3. In the ISA server's External IP Address dialog box, type in the IP address on the external interface that you want to accept inbound requests. If you want to publish multiple mail servers, you will need to bind multiple IP addresses to the external interface of the ISA server; only a single mail mapping per external physical interface is supported. Click Next.

4. On the Internal Mail Server page, type in the IP address of the internal mail server; this will be the internal IP address of the Exchange 2000 server. If a mail server is running on the ISA server itself, select the On The Local Host radio button. Click Next.

5. On the last page of the wizard, review your settings. The firewall service on the ISA server must be restarted before the publishing rule can take effect (because we selected the content filtering option). You can restart the service manually or allow the wizard to restart it for you. It is best to restart the service yourself because you have more control over when the rule takes effect. Click Finish.

After the firewall is started, the internal Exchange server will be able to receive mail from external clients and servers. Unlike Proxy Server 2, the Exchange server does not require any special configuration. All you need to do is configure the Exchange server with a default gateway that routes Internet-bound traffic to the internal interface of the ISA server. You should not install the firewall client (or Winsock Proxy client) software on the Exchange server.

Web Publishing Outlook Web Access

ISA Server supports Outlook Web Access by using Web publishing rules. You can use Basic or integrated Windows authentication to access the OWA site. However, if you wish to use integrated Windows authentication, you must use Internet Explorer 5.5 or above. There are three steps to publishing the OWA site:

- Configuring Incoming Web Requests Listener.
- Configuring the OWA destination set.
- Configuring the OWA Web publishing rule.

To configure the Incoming Web Requests Listener, perform the following steps:

1. Using the ISA Management console, right-click the server or array and click Properties.

2. Click the Incoming Web Requests tab and click the Configure Listeners Individually Per IP Address radio button:

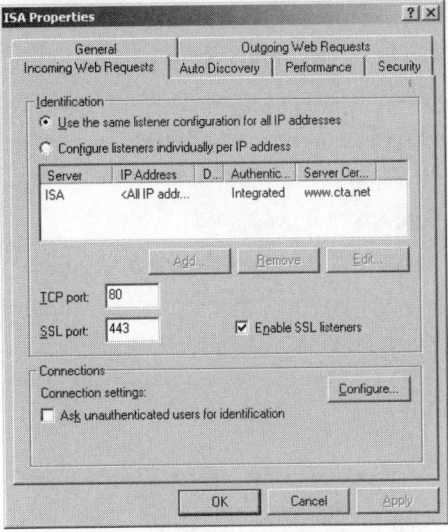

3. Click the Add button; the Add/Edit Listeners dialog box opens. Select your server name, the IP address of the external interface you wish the ISA server to listen on for inbound OWA requests, and a descriptive display name for this listener. Click OK.

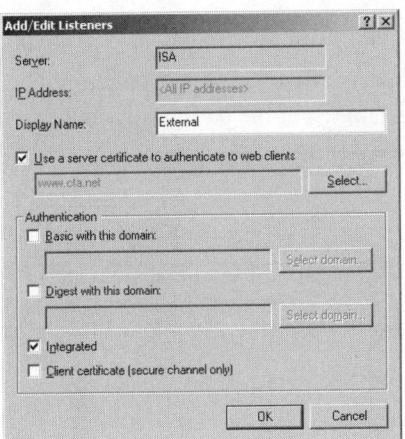

4. On the Incoming Web Requests property tab, click Apply. A Warning box opens that tells you that you must restart the Web proxy server. Select the option to restart the service manually and click OK.

Security

PART 3

The next step is to configure the Destination Set that will be used in the Outlook Web Access Web publishing rule. To do so, follow these steps:

1. Using the ISA Management console, expand Policy Elements and right-click the Destination Sets node. Then select New ➢ Set.

2. In the Name box, give the destination set a descriptive name like OWA, then click Add.

3. In the Destination text box, type in the FQDN or IP address of the external interface of the ISA server to which the external users will connect.

4. In the Path box, type **/exchange/***, and click OK.

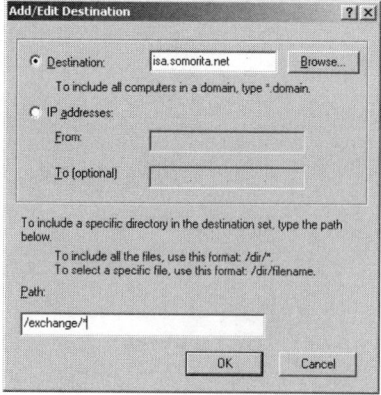

5. Repeat steps 2 through 4 for the /exchweb/* and /public/* virtual directories.

6. When you are finished, the destination set you created (in this case, called OWA) should list the FQDN host names and the path to the content. When finished, click OK.

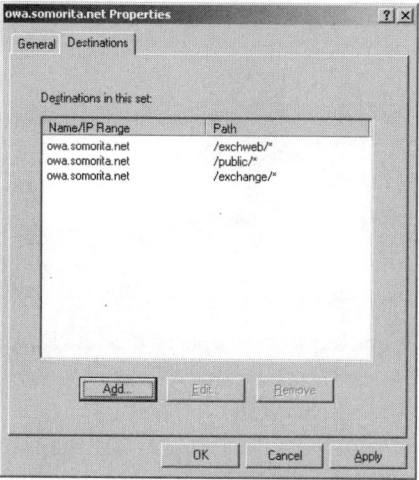

After the Incoming Web Requests Listener and the destination set are configured, you are ready for the last step: creating the Web publishing rule. Perform the following steps to publish the OWA site:

1. Using the ISA Management console, expand the Publishing Node and right-click the Web Publishing Rules node. Then Click New ➢ Rule.

2. On the Welcome page, type a name for the rule. In this example, I will call the rule OWA. Click Next.

3. On the Destination Sets page, select the Specified Destination Set option in the Apply This Rule To drop-down list. Click the Name drop-down list and select the OWA Destination Set you created previously.

4. On the Client Type property page, select the client type you wish to be able to access the site. You can select Any Request, Specific Computers (Client Address Sets), or Specific Users And Groups. In this example, I'm assuming you checked the Any Request radio button. Click Next.

5. On the Rule Action page, select the Redirect The Request To This Internal Web Server (Name Or IP Address) radio button and type the IP address or the name of the internal OWA server. Make sure to select the Send The Original Host Header... check box. Leave the other settings at their default values and click Next.

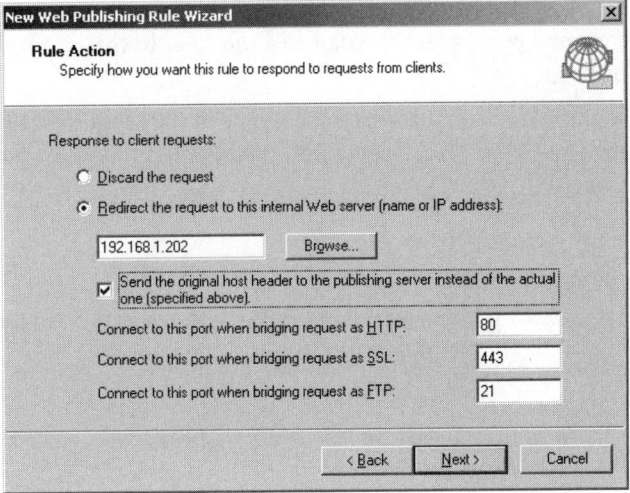

6. Confirm your settings and click Finish.

> **TIP** If the OWA site is on the ISA server, you must disable the IIS socket pooling feature. If you do not, IIS will listen on port 80 on all interfaces and the Web publishing rule will not work. Microsoft article Q238131, "How to Disable Socket Pooling," describes the procedure.

Using Server Publishing to Support OWA and SSL

ISA Server supports SSL connections to its external interface. It is possible to install a Web server's certificate into the ISA server's certificate store and have the ISA server impersonate the credentials of the internal web server. However, this does not work with OWA, because ISA Server cannot pass-through the SSL connection to the internal OWA site.

If you wish to create an SSL connection to the OWA site, you must use a server publishing rule. The drawback to this is that you can publish only one SSL site per IP address. If you use server publishing rules to publish multiple SSL sites, you must have an IP address bound to the external interface for each site.

To create the SSL server publishing rule, perform the following steps:

1. Using the ISA Management console, expand the Publishing node and right-click Server Publishing Rules. Then select New ➢ Rule.

2. On the Welcome page, enter the name of the rule. In this example, I'll call it OWA SSL. Click Next.

3. On the Address Mapping property page, type in the IP address of the internal server and the External IP address on the ISA Server. Click Next.

4. On the Protocol Settings page, click the drop-down list box, select the HTTPS Server protocol, and click Next.

5. On the Client Type page, select Any Request, and click Next.

6. On the last page of the wizard, review your settings and click Finish.

The ISA server is now ready to accept inbound connections to the site. You do not need to restart any services.

Allowing Inbound VPN Connections

Although ISA Server supports inbound MAPI connections directly to Exchange 2000 servers, this method of connecting to the Exchange server is considered an insecure method of accessing resources on the internal network since it opens up RPC and information store ports on the Exchange server. A far better alternative is to configure the ISA server to accept inbound VPN connections. After doing so, users can establish a VPN link to the ISA server and access the Exchange server on the internal network via its IP address or NetBIOS name.

ISA Server leverages the features of Windows 2000 RRAS to allow inbound VPN calls. To configure ISA Server to accept calls from VPN clients, perform the following steps:

1. Using the ISA Management console, right-click the Network Configuration node and click the Allow VPN Client Connections command.

2. The Virtual Private Network Configuration Wizard Welcome screen appears. Click Next.

3. The Completing The ISA VPN Server Configuration Wizard page appears. If you click the Details button, you will see the changes the wizard will make to your RRAS configuration. If RRAS is not running, the wizard will start the service and open the VPN ports on the external interface.

ISA Server creates packet filters to allow inbound PPTP and L2TP/IPSec connections to the external interface of the ISA server. You should configure the internal interface of the ISA server with the IP addresses of the WINS and DNS server you wish the VPN clients to be assigned. The default configuration uses DHCP to assign IP addresses to VPN clients. If you do not have a DHCP server, or do not wish to use the DHCP server to assign IP addressing information to the VPN clients, you should configure a static address pool in the RRAS MMC.

NOTE You are ready to accept inbound PPTP connections after configuring the addresses for name servers on the ISA server's internal interface. In order to allow inbound L2TP/IPSec calls, you must configure the ISA server with an IPSec certificate, and all clients using L2TP/IPSec must also be assigned an IPSec certificate. RRAS will configure an IPSec policy automatically if you do not have any IPSec policies configured.

Publishing Terminal Services

Users connecting to the VPN through an analog dial-up connection may be disappointed in the performance of the link. Outlook will refresh very slowly, which can frustrate users to the extent that they will use Outlook only as an SMTP/POP3 client.

You can significantly improve client-side performance by publishing a Windows 2000 terminal server located on the internal network. Users can connect to this server using the terminal services client included with Windows 2000, or they can connect to the Terminal Services Advanced Client web page and launch a terminal client session in their browsers.

Security

PART 3

There are three procedures you need to perform to publish an internal terminal server:

- If Terminal Services is running on the ISA server, you must remove it or configure it to listen only on the internal interface.
- Create a protocol definition that allows inbound RDP traffic on TCP port 3389.
- Create a server publishing rule to allow inbound connections to the internal network terminal server.

To configure the interface on the terminal server, perform the following steps:

1. From the Administrative Tools menu, open the Terminal Services Configuration MMC.
2. In the right pane of the Terminal Services Configuration MMC, right-click the RDP-Tcp entry and click Properties.
3. Click the Network Adapter property tab; in the Network Adapter drop-down list box, select an internal network adapter. The default setting is to allow Terminal Services to listen on all adapters. You do not want Terminal Services on the ISA server itself to listen on the external interface of the ISA server, because this will require you to change the listening port for the terminal server. Click Apply and then click OK.

The next step is to configure the protocol definition for inbound RDP connections. There is already a protocol definition included for outbound RDP connections, but you have to manually create one for inbound connections. Perform the following steps to create the *RDP Server* Protocol Definition:

1. Using the ISA Management console, expand the Policy Elements node and right-click the Protocol Definitions node. Select New ➤ Definition.
2. On the Welcome page, type the name of the protocol definition. In this example, we'll name it RDP Server. Click Next.
3. On the Primary Connection Information page, enter the port number, protocol type, and direction. Click Next.
4. On the Secondary Connections page, accept the default selection, which is No. Click Next.
5. Review your selections and click Finish.

The final step is to create the server publishing rule. To do so, follow these steps:

1. Using the ISA Management console, expand the Publishing node and right-click the Server Publishing node. Select New ➤ Rule.
2. On the Welcome page, type the name of the rule. In this example we'll call it Terminal Services. Click Next.
3. On the Addressing Mapping page, enter the IP address of the internal server and the external IP address on the ISA server that you want to listen for incoming RDP requests. Click Next.

4. On the Protocol Settings page, select the RDP Server Protocol Definition that you created earlier. Click Next.

5. On the Client Type page, select Any Request if you want any computer to be able to connect to the internal Terminal Server. You can select the Specific Computer (client address sets) option if you want to limit access to the terminal server. This requires that you have configured a client address set that includes the IP addresses of computers that you want to allow access. In this example, we'll select Any Request and click Next.

6. On the last page of the wizard, review your selections, and then click Finish.

The ISA server is now ready to accept connections to the internal terminal server.

> **NOTE** If you need more information on configuring ISA Server, a great starting place is Tom Shinder's ISA tutorial site, www.isaserver.org/shinder/tutorials.

ISA Server Best Practices

ISA Server, like any firewall, is a complex product. However, if you follow these best practices, you can keep yourself out of trouble:

- Make sure that you have the latest service packs and hot fixes for Windows 2000 and ISA Server.

- Make sure that your DNS infrastructure is in place to support name resolution for both local and Internet hosts. If the Exchange Server will be resolving Internet mail domain names by using an external DNS server, make sure that a protocol rule is configured to allow outbound access to TCP port 53 and UDP port 53.

- Create a protocol rule that allows outbound access to TCP port 25 to all Exchange servers that need to communicate with external mail servers.

- Use a *least privilege* model, and only allow outbound and inbound access to protocols that are required.

- Enable packet filtering on the external interface of the ISA server.

- Do not create packet filters for the same ports that are supported by publishing rules.

- Do not allow inbound MAPI connections to the ISA server; this is considered insecure and opens up potential vulnerabilities.

- Always use SSL server publishing when allowing external network clients access to Exchange via OWA.

- If you have problems with ISA Server setup or configuration, visit www.isaserver.org and check out their tutorials. You can also ask questions and find solutions on the message boards on that site.

Security

PART 3

Part 4

Connectivity

Topics Covered:

- Exchange 2000 and SMTP
- Customizing SMTP
- Designing Routing Groups
- X.400 Connectivity
- SMTP Connectivity
- POP3 and IMAP4 Virtual Servers
- Outlook Web Access
- Front-End and Back-End Servers
- Instant Messaging

14

Connectivity within Your Organization

Most often, Exchange 5.5–based organizations were designed around the geographical, connectivity infrastructure, and bandwidth constraints of the organization they served. This was irrespective of how the organization was really administered, because Exchange 5.5 servers have to be grouped together and managed as an Exchange 5.5 site. The Exchange 5.5 site is a collection of Exchange 5.5 servers separated by permanent, high-speed connectivity, and it serves as a boundary of administration, directory replication, and messaging connectivity. Connectivity between all servers within the site is handled using Remote Procedure Calls (RPCs), which are synchronous and thus do not tolerate low-speed connectivity. Connectivity within the site includes all server-to-server e-mail messages and Exchange 5.5 directory replication.

Unfortunately, the Exchange 5.5 site design proved to be too rigid for many large organizations wanting to separate their message routing needs from their server administration tasks. Thus the concept of administrative groups and routing groups was introduced. Administrative groups and routing groups ease administration and make Exchange 2000 more flexible.

Since Exchange 2000 does not have its own directory database (it relies on Active Directory), directory replication between Exchange 2000 servers is moot. Further, to make Exchange 2000 more tolerant of low-speed links and more standard, server-to-server message routing, it uses SMTP instead of RPCs. Exchange 2000 uses SMTP for connectivity between all Exchange servers in a Native-mode organization. However, Exchange 2000 does not provide the SMTP transport and queuing components; Windows 2000 Internet Information Server (IIS) provides these. Exchange 2000 merely extends the functionality of the Windows 2000 SMTP service by adding additional DLLs (dynamic link libraries).

SMTP Basics

There has been a lot of discussion in the messaging industry regarding Microsoft's decision to switch to native SMTP. There are good arguments on both sides of the fence for making the switch or not. X.400 is an internationally recognized standard of the International Telecommunications Union (ITU) and runs on many platforms and network protocols (e.g., TCP/IP and X.25). Historically, however, X.400 has been complex and difficult to implement. Further, there is no consensus for implementing security using X.400. (Standards documents for X.400 can be ordered through the ITU at www.itu.ch, though they are *not* cheap.)

SMTP is simple (hence the name "Simple" Mail Transfer Protocol), widely adopted, and fairly easily to employ. Most computing platforms in the world today support SMTP natively. Though natively insecure, security issues surrounding SMTP, such as message encryption and allowing SMTP through a firewall, are clearly defined and understood. Standards documents relating to SMTP are freely available on the Internet through www.ietf.org; look for RFC 2821 and 2822 for starters (these RFCs superseded RFCs 821 and 822).

SMTP is generally easier than X.400 to troubleshoot, and the message formats are much easier to understand. Most messages on the Internet today (including messages transmitted by Exchange servers) are formatted in the industry standard MIME format (Multipurpose Internet Mail Extensions). Many organizations feel—and Microsoft agrees—that there are "big picture" advantages to moving to a native SMTP transport.

It is important to note (and X.400 supporters will note this emphatically) that while there is little difference in the transmission of small messages, messages containing large binary attachments (50KB and above) can incur as much as 30 to 40 percent more overhead with SMTP. This additional overhead comes from the fact that SMTP is designed to transfer 7-bit ASCII text. Any 8-bit data (such as binary attachments or any modern e-mail message) must be encoded. This causes the conversion to take longer when the message is being transmitted, and it causes the amount of data transmitted to be larger than the actual file size.

SMTP: More Information

The constraints of this book don't permit an in-depth discussion of SMTP, so here are a number of links and sources where you can do your own research:

- If you are looking for detailed technical knowledge of the basics of SMTP, go to the source: RFCs (request for comments) 2821 and 2822. RFC 1869 defines the capability for SMTP to be extended so that additional functionality can be built on top of the existing SMTP standard. RFC 974 describes how SMTP systems use DNS and the use of MX records. These RFCs are freely available on the Web at www.ietf.org.

- The Connected: Internet Encyclopedia has a brief overview of SMTP located at freesoft.org/CIE/Topics/94.htm.

- The Internet Mail Consortium (www.imc.org) has many links and pages relating to SMTP mail and mail on the Internet.

NOTE If your organization is in Mixed mode and there are still Exchange 5.5 servers, messages destined for Exchange 5.5 servers are transferred to the Exchange 2000 message transfer agent (MTA) and sent to the Exchange 5.5 server using RPCs.

Exchange 2000 Message Transport Architecture

Collectively, the Exchange 2000 message transport operates as a series of processes running under the IIS Admin Service (INETINFO.EXE). These components process *all* messages transported by Exchange 2000. Though this was discussed in Chapter 2 in some detail, this section explores more deeply the components that make up the message transport system. The major components are the Advanced Queuing Engine (AQE), the Routing Engine, and the SMTP Service. Figure 14.1 shows the components and the queues that are found within the message transport and the path that a message flows through when it is processed by the AQE.

Connectivity

PART 4

Figure 14.1 Exchange 2000 message transport components

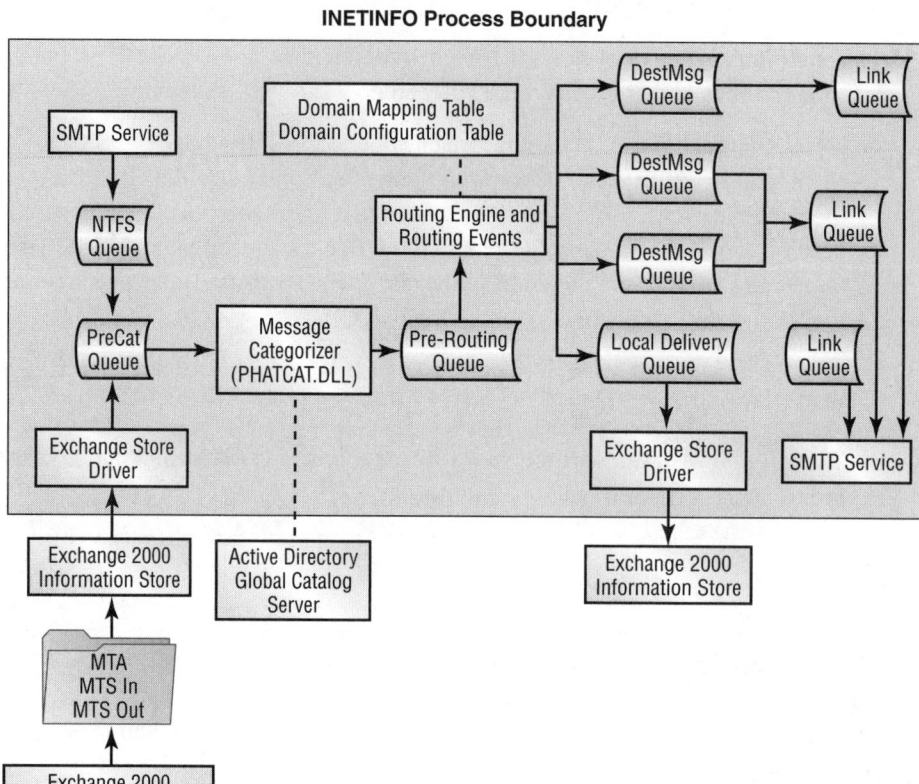

When a message is passed through the message transport, all that is really passed through the transport is a small memory object called an IMsg (a.k.a. MailMsg or IMailMsg). The body of the message and the message attachments remain in their originally stored location (a mailbox store or the SMTP NTFS queue). Here are some of the components that are involved in moving a message through the queue:

Advanced Queuing Engine The AQE manages all messages submitted to the Exchange 2000 message transport. The AQE is passed the IMsg object from the Exchange Store driver or the NTFS driver. AQE supervises the flow of messages through all of the queues and all of the message transport components.

Exchange Store driver The Exchange Store driver serves as an interface between the IIS message transport and the Exchange 2000 information store. This allows messages to be read from and written to the information store.

Pre-cat queue   This component is known by several names. The SMTP Queue Manager in Exchange System Manager refers to it as *Messages Awaiting Directory Lookup*, but you may see it referred to as the *inbound queue*. I prefer pre-cat queue because this is the queue messages wait in until the Message Categorizer can process them.

Message Categorizer   The Message Categorizer is responsible for querying a Global Catalog server to do mail-enabled group expansion, check limits, and check restrictions on mail-enabled objects. It determines if the recipient is local, remote within the routing group, remote in another routing group, or outside of the organization. The Message Categorizer may also *bifurcate* the message if it determines that different recipients need to receive the message in different formats. Bifurcation is the process of breaking the message into two uniquely formatted messages (e.g., a plaintext version and a MIME version). This occurs when a message has multiple recipients, each of which require different formats. The Windows 2000 IIS has a basic message categorizer (CAT.DLL), but it is not enabled by default. When Exchange 2000 is installed, a new message categorizer (PHATCAT.DLL) is installed and enabled, which has the additional capabilities that the AQE requires to work with Exchange 2000.

Pre-routing queue   Also known as the Categorized Message Queue (CatMsgQueue), this queue serves as an interface between the categorizer and the routing system. In Exchange System Manager, it is referred to as the *Messages Waiting To Be Routed* queue.

Routing Engine   In conjunction with routing event sinks, the Routing Engine determines the best next-hop for each message and places the messages into the appropriate destination message queues. The Routing Engine also consults the domain mapping tables and the domain configuration tables.

Domain Mapping Table (DMT)   The DMT resolves domain names to the destination message queues, which are associated with specific final destinations for the messages. A single destination queue may exist for a gateway such as the Microsoft Mail connector.

Domain Configuration Table (DCT)   The DCT maps a domain to a specification configuration for that domain. This information helps to determine if another domain uses ETRN, requires authentication, etc. This information is derived from SMTP Connector configurations and the Internet Message Formats; setting up different Internet Message Formats is discussed later in this chapter.

Destination message queue (DestMsgQueue)   The destination message queues are associated with logical remote destinations. They are also used for delivering messages based on size and are used for delay notifications of currently queued messages. Destination Message Queues are then grouped into link message queues.

Link message queue (LinkMsgQueue)   One of these queues may contain several destination message queues, which are associated with link queues based on routing information. Link queues represent the next hop for the messages in the queue. They are created and used by the Connection Manager to create SMTP connection objects.

Local delivery queue   This queue is used for messages that are to be delivered to a local mailbox or public folder store. Messages may queue in the local delivery queue if the destination store is dismounted or if there is an I/O bottleneck and the AQE cannot deliver messages to the destination server or store.

Connection Manager   The Connection Manager is used to determine which link queues should be used to satisfy a connection request. It makes this decision based on message size, message priority, connector schedule, and the number of messages.

SMTP protocol   The business end of the message transport, the SMTP protocol is used to deliver messages that have been placed in the link queues.

DSN Generator   The DSN (delivery status notification) Generator is used each time an IMsg object is acknowledged as being delivered. The DSN Generator is responsible for sending delivery receipts, non-delivery receipts, and delay notifications.

SMTP Extensions Supported

The Windows 2000 SMTP service supports most of the standard SMTP extensions specified in recent RFCs relating to SMTP. When Exchange 2000 is installed, some additional features are supported. Table 14.1 shows a list of the SMTP extensions that are supported through Windows 2000 and the Exchange 2000 extensions.

Table 14.1   Windows 2000 and Exchange 2000 SMTP Extensions

Extension	Windows 2000	Exchange 2000	Explanation
AUTH	✓	✓	Defines the ability for a remote client to authenticate an SMTP session to a remote server if the client and server both support the same authentication methods. This command uses SASL (Simple Authentication and Security Layer). See RFC 2554 for more information.

Table 14.1 Windows 2000 and Exchange 2000 SMTP Extensions *(continued)*

Extension	Windows 2000	Exchange 2000	Explanation
ATRN	✓	✓	Triggers the download of remotely queued messages with authentication. See RFC 2645 for more information.
TURN	✓	✓	Triggers the download of remotely queued messages with no authentication or verification of host name. Essentially, once the client issues the TURN command, the server becomes the client and the client becomes the server.
ETRN	✓	✓	Triggers the download of remotely queued messages. The remote server does a DNS lookup to determine the requesting domain's MX record and mail server IP address, and initiates a new connection to that IP address. See RFC 1985 for more information.
SIZE	✓	✓	Allows a remote server to advertise the maximum size message it will accept or allows the sender to send the estimated size of the message. See RFC 1870 for more information.

Connectivity

PART 4

Table 14.1   Windows 2000 and Exchange 2000 SMTP Extensions *(continued)*

Extension	Windows 2000	Exchange 2000	Explanation
PIPELINING	✓	✓	Designed to make SMTP more efficient by allowing the client to "pipeline" commands to the SMTP server. The client does not have to wait for the 250 OK message before transmitting the next SMTP command verb. See RFC 2197 for more information.
DSN	✓	✓	Allows SMTP to notify clients of delivery, delivery failure, or delivery delays in a standard fashion rather than relying on the vendor to implement delivery status mechanisms. See RFCs 1891, 1893, and 1894 for more information.
ENHANCED-STATUSCODES	✓	✓	Provides a way for the client and the server to Exchange more useful information about the reason a message was not delivered. See Chapter 1, "Client Troubleshooting," for more information or RFC 2034.
8bitmime	✓	✓	Defines a transport for transmitting MIME-encoded information using 8-bit rather than 7-bit data. Also known as 8bitMIMEtransport. See RFC 1652 for more information.

Table 14.1 Windows 2000 and Exchange 2000 SMTP Extensions *(continued)*

Extension	Windows 2000	Exchange 2000	Explanation
BINARYMIME	✓	✓	This command works with the BDAT command to allow for the transmission of binary data. See RFC 1830 for more information.
CHUNKING	✓	✓	Designed to make SMTP more efficient by notifying the SMTP server how much data the client intends to transmit. The SMTP client issues a BDAT command verb along with the number of bytes of data that will be transmitted rather than a DATA command verb. The DATA command is terminated only by a <CR><LF>.<CR><LF> transmission. See RFC 1830 for more information.
VRFY	✓	✓	Even though VRFY is listed as a supported command verb, it is not enabled in Exchange 2000. The intent of VRFY is to allow an SMTP client to verify that a user really exists before transmitting mail to that server, but this feature is often considered a security risk.
X-LINK2STATE		✓	The LINK2STATE command is specific to Microsoft Exchange and is used by the Routing Group Connector (RGC) to relay information about network link status changes.

Table 14.1   Windows 2000 and Exchange 2000 SMTP Extensions *(continued)*

Extension	Windows 2000	Exchange 2000	Explanation
XEXCH50		✓	Microsoft proprietary SMTP command that is used to transfer MAPI properties of a message between Exchange servers.
STARTTLS / TLS		✓	An extension to SMTP that allows an SMTP client and an SMTP server to use TLS (Transport Layer Security) to negotiate a secure, encrypted channel to transmit message data. For more information, see RFC 2487.

You can view the command verbs and SMTP extensions that any SMTP server supports by simply using Telnet. If you want to see the commands that you type, turn on local echo by running Telnet and then typing **SET LOCAL_ECHO**. Once local echo is enabled, you can open a connection to an SMTP server; if you need to, remove the local echo type **UNSET LOCAL_ECHO** at the Telnet prompt.

Also notice that the SIZE SMTP extension includes 5120000. This is because this particular SMTP virtual server has the Limit Message Size (KB) restriction set to 5000KB.

Establishing an SMTP Session

Now let's take a look at the particulars of establishing an SMTP session to another SMTP server. There are a couple of things that are useful for you to know if you have to debug problems with the SMTP server, including name resolution and the types of commands that are issued between a SMTP client and a SMTP server.

DNS Lookups

When an SMTP virtual server needs to initiate SMTP connectivity to another SMTP server, it must perform a DNS query in order to resolve the IP address of the destination host. The SMTP virtual server always does an MX record lookup first before resorting to a record (A). Figure 14.2 shows a filtered Network Monitor trace where the server sfoex001.somorita.net is sending an SMTP message to server singex01.asia .somorita.net; server SFODC01 is the DNS server.

Figure 14.2   Two DNS queries (Frame 27 MX record and Frame 29 A record)

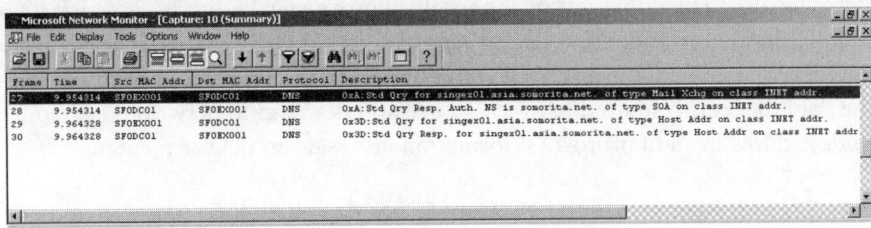

Note that in Figure 14.2, the MX record (type Mail Xchg) is queried first (Frame 27). Since there is not an MX record for that host, a host record is requested next in Frame 29.

Viewing MX Records for a Domain   From an Exchange server command prompt, you can test the records that are returned to the Exchange server from the DNS server. Here is an example using the NSLOOKUP command to query MX records for the domain somorita.com:

```
C:\>nslookup -q=mx somorita.com
Server:  dns1.bobsboogieboardscom
Address:  10.0.0.3


somorita.com  MX preference = 10, mail exchanger = mail1.somorita.com
somorita.com  MX preference = 10, mail exchanger = mail2.somorita.com
somorita.com  MX preference = 20, mail exchanger = mail3.somorita.com
mail1.somorita.com    internet address = 192.168.47.10
mail2.somorita.com    internet address = 192.168.101.37
mail3.somorita.com    internet address = 192.168.210.23
```

In this case, there are three servers that can accept inbound mail for somorita.com. The first two servers in the list (mail1.somorita.com and mail2.somorita.com) have an equal preference value, so the SMTP virtual server will randomly pick one or the other. If neither destination SMTP server is available, then the transmitting SMTP virtual server will use mail3.somorita.com.

SMTP Sessions

An SMTP session is really just what the protocol says it is: simple. The session consists of a conversation between the SMTP client (the sender) and the SMTP server (the recipient server or a relay server). The following steps outline the communication that occurs between two Exchange 2000 servers using SMTP. I have eliminated queries to the Global Catalog server and focused only on the communication necessary to transfer a message. The

Connectivity

PART 4

Global Catalog server lookup was necessary to determine on which home server the recipient was located. This conversation is partially illustrated in Figure 14.3, which summarizes the SMTP communication between the sending host (SFOEX001) and the destination host (SINGEX01). Figure 14.3 shows the frames between the source and destination. A *frame* is the data that is transmitted between source and destination networked computers; it includes addressing and protocol information necessary to deliver the data.

Figure 14.3   SMTP conversation between SFOEX001 and SINGEX01

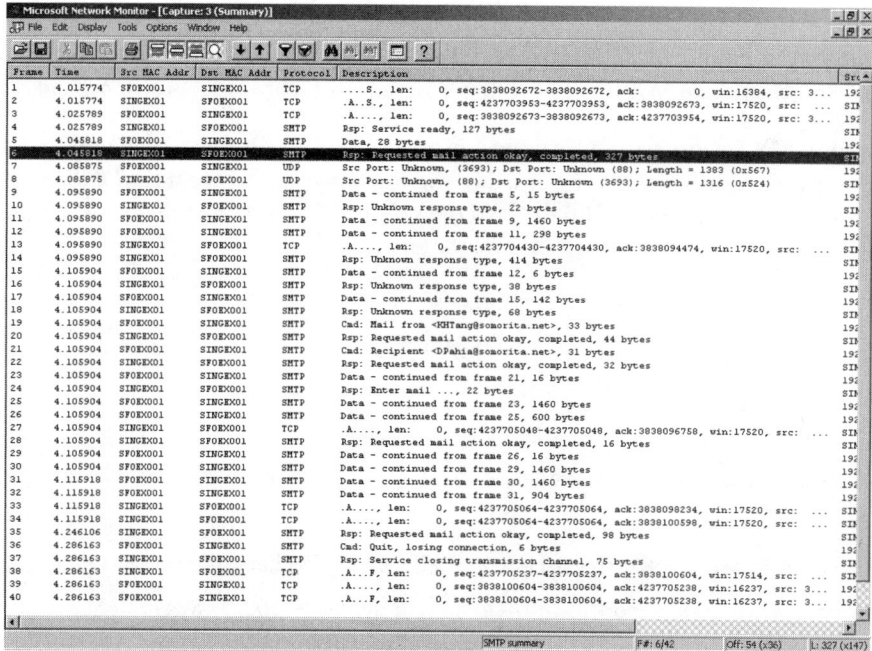

1. The source computer performs a DNS query for MX record first, then a DNS query for the host record of the destination server (shown in Figure 14.2).

2. A TCP three-way handshake is used to establish sequence numbers and acknowledgments (frames 1 through 3).

3. Frame 4 is the initial banner from the destination SMTP server.

4. In frame 5, the SMTP client (SFOEX001) sends the introduction command EHLO SFOEX001.SOMORITA.NET.

5. In frame 6, the SMTP server responds with a list of extensions that it supports. Note that the server is responding to the client with a Hello [192.168.2.2]. This is because the server was unable to perform a reverse DNS lookup on the IP address, or it was configured not to perform reverse DNS lookups.

6. In frames 7 through 16, the SMTP client performs a Kerberos authentication with the SMTP server. Exchange 2000 SMTP virtual servers within the same Active Directory (AD) forest will always perform authentication. Frames 7 and 8 show the client getting a session ticket for the destination SMTP server. SINGEX01 is also the domain controller for this domain.

7. While not obvious from the Network Monitor summary shown in Figure 14.3, frames 17 and 18 are information used by the link-state algorithm. This would be obvious if you opened either frame; you would see the X-LINK2STATE SMTP command verb.

8. Frame 19 is the beginning of the mail transfer; the client has issued the MAIL FROM: <KHTang@Somorita.net> command. The server responds in frame 20 with a 250 2.1.0 KHTang@somorita.net Sender OK response.

9. The client then transmits frame 21; this frame indicates the intended recipient of the message using the RCPT TO: <DPahia@somorita.net> command. The server responds in frame 21 with 250 2.1.5 dpahia@somorita.net.

10. The next phase of the SMTP transmission depends on the extensions supported by the client and the server. Starting in frame 23, the SMTP client issues the XEXCH50 command that indicates it would like to transfer some of the MAPI properties of the message. The server responds in frame 24 that the client can send binary data, and the MAPI properties are transferred in frames 25 through 28.

11. The actual message transfer begins in frame 29, when the client issues the BDAT 3393 LAST command indicating that it is about to transfer 3393 bytes of data. Frame 30 (see Figure 14.4) shows many of the properties of the message such as subject, message ID, and date. The data continues its transfer through frame 35, where the SMTP server indicates that the message is queued for delivery.

12. Frames 36 and 37 in this transmission represent the termination of the SMTP session, and frames 38 through 40 represent the termination of the TCP session.

> **NOTE**   To review this SMTP transfer yourself, you can download the file from www.somorita.com/downloads/smtp1.cap.

If the above SMTP session had been to an SMTP server that was not in the same Exchange organization, you would not have seen the XEXCH50 command verb. Depending on the receiving system, you may have seen the BDAT or the DATA commands. You may also be able to see the entire text of the message. Figure 14.5 shows a frame from Network Monitor in which you can see the entire RFC-822 message including the message subject, message ID, date, time, MIME information, sender, recipient, and the message body.

Connectivity

PART 4

Figure 14.4 First frame of data actually carrying the message data

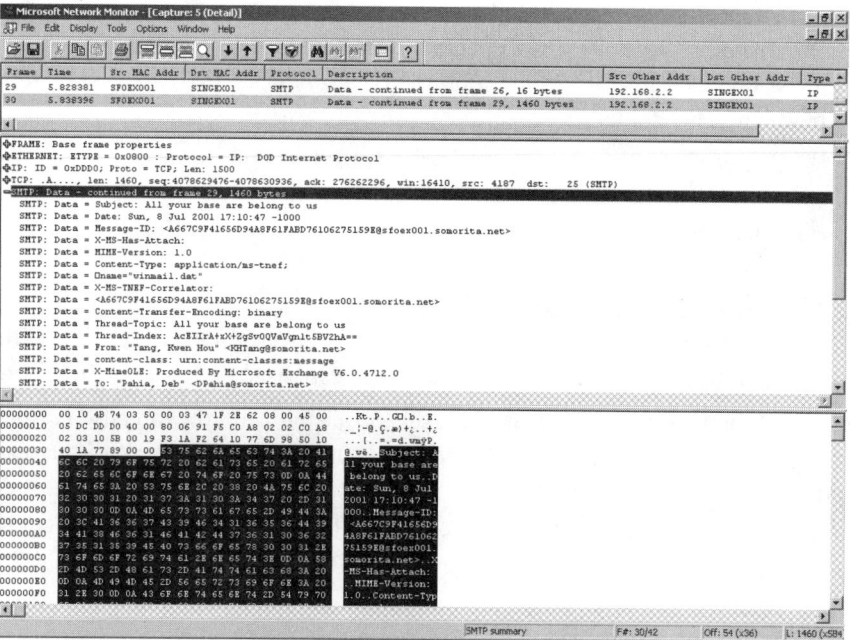

Figure 14.5 Network Monitor trace of an entire message

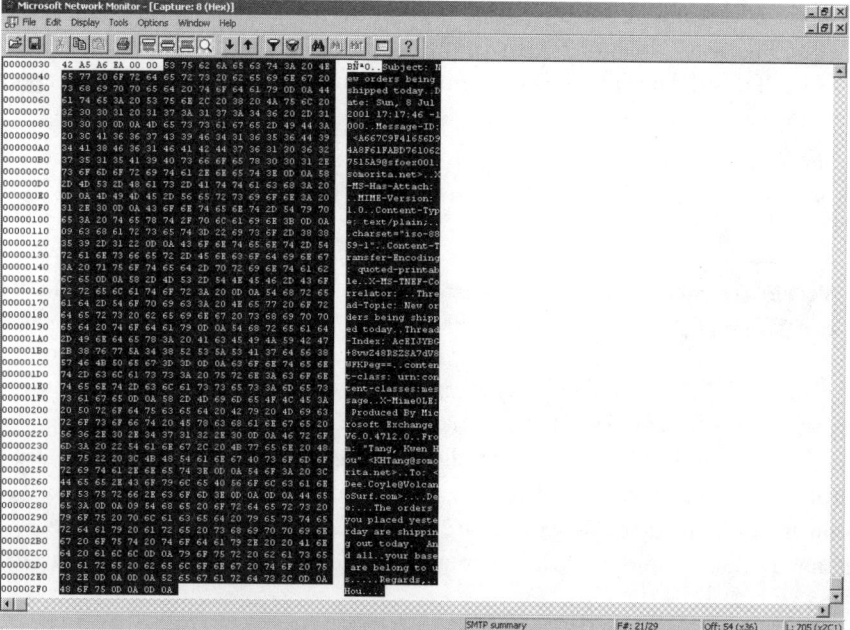

SMTP Virtual Servers

By default, each Exchange 2000 server has a single SMTP virtual server instance; this should be sufficient for most organizations. On each Exchange 2000 server you can configure additional SMTP virtual servers, but there are only a few situations in which you would actually need them. Since IIS and the SMTP components are multi-threaded, additional SMTP virtual servers will *not* improve performance or increase the number of messages the server can handle. You may want to create additional SMTP virtual servers if:

- You need to implement different SMTP virtual servers with different configurations, such as one that requires authentication and encryption and another that does not.
- You have an application that requires the use of an SMTP server and requires a specific configuration.

Though each SMTP virtual server runs as a process under IIS, you must still use Exchange System Manager to create and change their properties. To create a new SMTP virtual server, follow these instructions:

1. Locate the Exchange 2000 server on which you want to create a new SMTP virtual server and open that server's Protocols ➤ SMTP container.

2. Highlight the SMTP container, right-click, and choose New ➤ SMTP Virtual Server.

3. Enter a name for the SMTP virtual server and click Next.

4. Select an IP address for this virtual server (make sure that another SMTP virtual server is not using the IP address and TCP port number you have chosen) and click Finish.

5. If you require a different port number for this SMTP virtual server, right-click the newly created virtual server and choose Properties. Click the Advanced button and edit the TCP port number. Click OK twice when finished.

NOTE The default SMTP virtual server is defined to listen on all IP addresses and TCP port 25.

The SMTP virtual server may not be available to be started immediately. You may have to wait until the DS2MB process replicates the information to the server's IIS Metabase. If the yellow envelope icon has a yellow question mark on it, this means that the information has not yet replicated to the IIS Metabase. If the icon has a red and white X on it, this means it is ready to be started.

Table 14.2 shows the properties and features that can be defined for an SMTP virtual server. Many of the default restrictions that you may be familiar with from the Windows 2000 IIS SMTP server are changed once Exchange 2000 is installed.

Connectivity

PART 4

Table 14.2   Properties and Features of an SMTP Virtual Server

Page	Property	Function
General	IP address	Allows you to select which IP address the virtual server uses.
General	Advanced button	Allows you to specify a custom list of IP addresses, TCP port numbers, and if SMTP domain filtering is enabled for an IP address.
General	Limit number of connections	Specifies the maximum number of simultaneous SMTP connections.
General	Connection time-out	Specifies the maximum number of minutes that a connection can remain idle before the SMTP virtual server will drop the connection.
General	Enable logging	Enables logging of SMTP activity to a log file.
General	Active log format	Allows you to specify the format for the SMTP log file; the W3C Extended Log File Format is the most common.
General	Properties button	Specifies the log creation interval, directory for log files, and the data that should be recorded in the log file. See Chapter 13, "Securing Your Exchange Servers," for more information about logging and security.
Access	Authentication button	Specifies supported authentication mechanisms. By default, Anonymous, Basic, and integrated Windows authentication are all enabled.
Access	Certificate button	Allows you to request a certificate for supporting TLS/SSL.

Table 14.2   Properties and Features of an SMTP Virtual Server *(continued)*

Page	Property	Function
Access	Communication button	Specifies that TLS/SSL is required. (The virtual server must be assigned a certificate before you can enable TLS/SSL.)
Access	Connection button	Restricts access to this SMTP virtual server by IP address.
Access	Relay	Specifies whether SMTP relay is allowed.
Messages	Limit message size	Specifies the maximum size of an SMTP message that this virtual server will process. The default is no maximum size.
Messages	Limit session size to	Specifies the amount of data that can be transferred in a single SMTP session. The default does not limit the amount of data.
Messages	Limit number of messages per connection	Specifies the maximum number of messages per SMTP session; if the SMTP client has more than this number of messages to transfer, it must disconnect and reconnect. The default is 20.
Messages	Limit number of recipients per message	Sets the maximum number of recipients per message. The default is 64,000.
Messages	Send a copy of Non-Delivery Report to	Sends NDRs (non-delivery reports) to a specified SMTP address.
Messages	Badmail directory	Specifies a directory for SMTP messages that could not be delivered, such as malformed messages.
Messages	Forward all mail with unresolved recipients to host	Specifies a host name (outside of your Exchange organization) that will accept mail that could not be delivered by this SMTP virtual server. This feature is useful if you are sharing a single SMTP domain with another host. You might use this feature during a migration.

Connectivity

PART 4

Table 14.2   Properties and Features of an SMTP Virtual Server *(continued)*

Page	Property	Function
Delivery	First second, third, and subsequent retry intervals	The SMTP virtual server will attempt to send the message immediately. If it is not deliverable, then the SMTP virtual server will attempt to deliver it after waiting the first retry interval (by default 10 minutes), then retry again after waiting the second retry interval and then again after the third retry interval. Subsequent attempts will be made after the first, second, and third attempts. The default for each of these is 10 minutes.
Delivery	Delay Notification	Notifies users of messages that are queued to be delivered to remote servers (in the Exchange organization or outside) if the message is queued for a certain period of time. The default is 12 hours.
Delivery	Expiration	Specifies interval after which outbound messages that are not delivered should be returned to the sender with an NDR. The default is 2 days.
Delivery	Local Delay Notification	Notifies users of messages that are queued to be delivered to local mailbox and public folder stores if the message is queued for a certain period of time. The default is 12 hours.
Delivery	Local Expiration	For messages that are queued for delivery to other mailbox or public folder stores on this server, sends an NDR if the message is queued longer than this value. The default is 2 days.

Table 14.2   Properties and Features of an SMTP Virtual Server *(continued)*

Page	Property	Function
Delivery	Outbound Security button	Specifies security for outbound connections. Anonymous authentication should remain the default for any virtual server that will be used for connectivity to the Internet.
Delivery	Outbound Connections button	Specifies maximum number of simultaneous outbound connections (default is 1000), outbound idle session timeout (default is 10 minutes), maximum number of simultaneous connections per domain (default is 100), and outgoing TCP port number (default is 25).
Delivery ➤ Advanced button	Maximum hop count	Specifies the maximum number of hops that an SMTP message can take before reaching this SMTP virtual server. Each hop adds an additional header to an SMTP message. Once the hop count exceeds this value, an NDR is issued to the sender. The default is 15.
Delivery ➤ Advanced button	Masquerade domain	Allows NDR reports to be returned to an alternative domain rather than the domain from which the message originated.
Delivery ➤ Advanced button	Fully-qualified domain name	This field specifies the name that this SMTP virtual server will use when it contacts other SMTP servers and issues the ELHO or HELO commands.
Delivery ➤ Advanced button	Smart host	Specifies that the SMTP virtual server should deliver messages to this host rather than attempting to send them directly.

Connectivity

PART 4

Table 14.2   Properties and Features of an SMTP Virtual Server *(continued)*

Page	Property	Function
Delivery ➢ Advanced button	Attempt direct delivery before sending to smart host	If a smart host is specified, then this check box is active. This allows the SMTP virtual server to attempt to deliver the message first; if it fails, the message will be delivered to the smart host.
Delivery ➢ Advanced button	Perform reverse DNS lookup on incoming messages	Instructs the SMTP virtual server to do a reverse lookup on each inbound IP address so that it can report the host name. This host name will be displayed in the messages' headers.
Delivery ➢ Advanced button	Configure external DNS servers	Specifies external DNS servers for this SMTP virtual server to use. This allows other components of this server to use one DNS server (specified in the IP properties), but allows message delivery components to use a different set of DNS servers.

NOTE   For more detailed information on creating SMTP virtual servers, see Microsoft Knowledge Base articles Q266686 and Q268163.

SMTP and Diagnostics Logging

If you need to configure diagnostics logging for STMP virtual servers, SMTP Connectors, the Routing Group Connectors (RGCs), or the message transport in general, you will need to configure these properties on the Exchange 2000 server's Diagnostics Logging property tab. The categories you want to look at for providing SMTP diagnostics logging are under MSExchangeTransport; these categories are explained in Table 14.3.

Table 14.3 MSExchangeTransport Diagnostics Logging Categories

Category	Function
Routing Engine/Service	Records events related to the Routing Engine.
Categorizer	Records events related to the use of the Message Categorizer.
Connection Manager	Records events related to the use of the Connection Manager, including moving messages into link queues.
Queuing Engine	Events related to the AQE, including moving messages between queues and components.
Exchange Store Driver	Records events related to messages being moved between the Exchange store and the message transport.
SMTP Protocol	Records events related to the use of the SMTP protocol, including protocol errors.
NTFS Store Driver	Records events related to the storage of inbound messages.

SMTP Virtual Server Configuration Recommendations

The default configuration for the SMTP virtual server will suit most organizations. Yet there may be options that you wish to change depending on your configuration and your organization. Below is a list of some of these options and circumstances in which you might (or might not) want to change them.

- Should you enable SMTP logging? Doing so will add more overhead to your system and take up additional disk space. These logs are not automatically deleted, so you must make sure that you delete or archive them on a regular basis. However, in several instances I have needed information about inbound mail (for security reasons), but did not have the protocol logs available. For this reason, I recommend turning on protocol logging for at least any SMTP virtual server that will be delivering mail to the Internet. Try the W3C Extended Log File Format and the following extended properties (set through the Extended Properties property page): Date, Time, Client IP Address, User Name, Service Name, Server Name, Server IP Address, Method, URI Stem, URI Query, Protocol Status, Bytes Sent, Bytes Received, Time Taken, and Protocol Version.

- Many organizations are restricting the maximum message size that their users can send. While this can be set for each individual user, you may also consider setting a maximum limit on the SMTP virtual servers. I am seeing organizations imposing limits between 5MB and 20MB for a maximum message size. Organizations setting limits below 5MB often find this is too small.

- The maximum session size restricts the maximum amount of data that can be transmitted in a single session. This limit may be useful for virtual servers that are connected to the Internet, but I would be reluctant to set it for internal servers that are generating a lot of traffic, since there would be additional overhead incurred setting up new sessions each time the limit is reached.

- For servers that send and receive a lot of mail traffic (such as a bridgehead or connector server), limiting the number of messages per connection may also cause additional overhead. The default is 20 messages, but you may consider raising this or even removing the limit all together.

- Create an alias that can be used for NDR reports. For a smaller organization (under 200 mailboxes), the same alias you use for the postmaster may be fine for NDR reports, but a larger organization may want a special mailbox. This is configured on the SMTP virtual server's Messages property page.

- On the Delivery property page, I recommend raising the Subsequent Retry Interval to 120 minutes (two hours). The default is 15 minutes, but if a remote server is unavailable, attempting to deliver messages every 15 minutes may generate excessive network traffic. The default for the Exchange 5.5 Internet Mail Service (IMS) is actually four hours for subsequent retries.

- Also on the Delivery page, set both of the Expiration Timeout values to 3 days. The only time a message will time out locally is if the mailbox or public folder store it is being delivered to is not mounted. However, outbound delivery of messages will timeout if the remote host is offline, or if you are experiencing network problems.

- If you click the Advanced button on the Delivery property page, you will see the Advanced Delivery options of the SMTP virtual server. The Fully-Qualified Domain Name field allows you to specify the name that the virtual server uses to introduce itself to remote hosts when it establishes an outbound connection. If the Full-Qualified Domain Name field contains singex01.asia.somorita.com, this server will issue an EHLO command that looks like this: EHLO `singex01.asia.somorita.com`. There are some SMTP servers and firewall products that will perform a reverse DNS lookup and confirm that the server's IP address is really registered to that host name. If the PTR (DNS pointer record) and the name that the server introduces itself as do not match, the host will not accept the message.

- One Advanced Delivery options check box that I configure for SMTP virtual servers that will be connected to the Internet is Perform Reverse DNS Lookup On Incoming Messages. This causes a slight performance hit on inbound messages, because each inbound SMTP session will require that the connecting server's IP address be resolved to a host name. While this does cause a performance hit, it allows the SMTP headers of messages received from the Internet to be much more easily read. You should balance your need for performance with your desire to have easily read SMTP headers.

WARNING It is absolutely critical that the name that the server introduces itself as in the EHLO command match exactly the PTR record of the server.

NOTE You may want to create dedicated SMTP virtual servers for connectivity with the Internet. This will allow you to set different limits and relay restrictions on SMTP virtual servers that are exposed to the Internet. Outbound mail can be focused through specific SMTP virtual servers using the SMTP Connector. Inbound mail is directed to SMTP virtual servers using DNS MX records.

Using the SMTP Virtual Server Pickup Directory

Chapter 5, "Status Monitoring and Reporting," discussed a couple of ways that you could send a mail message using a command-line interface or a script. The SMTP virtual server provides an additional way to do this through the \Pickup directory. This directory is found in each SMTP virtual server and is provided for applications to drop in a properly formatted text file; the SMTP virtual server will up pick the file and deliver it. The directory is found (by default) in \Exchsrvr\Mailroot\VSI 1\Pickup.

To use this feature, you must format the file that you will place in the pickup directory as an RFC-822 formatted message. The SMTP service will take care of properly formatting it for transmission. The file must be a text file. The filename and extension are irrelevant; the file will be assimilated by the SMTP service as long as it is formatted correctly. Here is a sample RFC-822 formatted message:

```
Date: 9 Mar 02 0852 HST
To: "Manfred Estrada" <MEstrada@bobsboogieboards.com>
From: "Riley Jean Spottiswood" <RJSpots@barbarylane.com>
Cc: "Suriya Supatanasakul" <SuriyaS@triplecrownofsurfing.com>
Subject: Meet me at China Court for lunch
I know this great place for us to eat. All your base are belong to us. It is
called China Court. It is right down the street from Dorothy's place.
```

Connectivity

PART 4

Customizing SMTP and SMTP Virtual Servers

There are a number of different things that you may want to do to customize the use of SMTP in your organization. These may include specifying custom message formats for specific domains, applying per-domain message filtering, defining recipient policies, and changing the SMTP banner.

Global Settings

Directly under the Exchange organization object in Exchange System Manager, you will find the Global Settings container, which holds configuration items that are global to the entire organization. A couple of the important things that you can configure here are the global messaging defaults and message filtering. In this container is the Message Delivery object; display its properties and choose the Defaults property page (shown in Figure 14.6).

Figure 14.6 Message Delivery properties Defaults tab

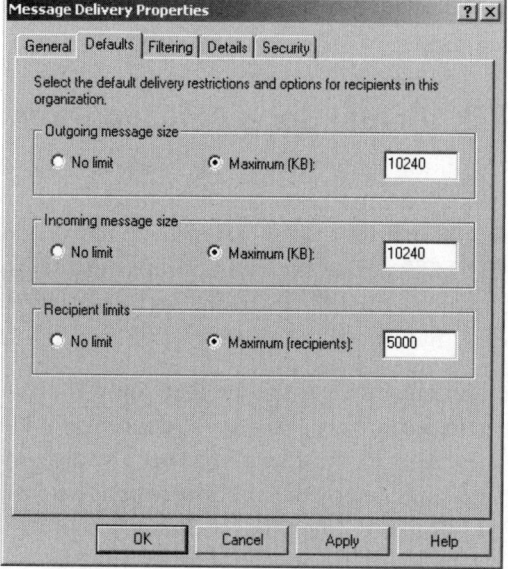

On the Defaults property page, you can specify three global message defaults:

- The maximum size of an outgoing message (the default is no limit).
- The maximum size of an incoming message (the default is no limit).
- The maximum number of recipients per message after mail-enabled group expansion (the default is 5000 recipients).

The maximum number of recipients per message can be overridden per mailbox-enabled user by displaying the properties of that user in Active Directory Users And Computers, choosing the Exchange General property page, and clicking the Delivery Options button. The maximum message-size limits can also be overridden per mail-enabled recipient by locating the Exchange General property page of that user and clicking the Delivery Restrictions button. The values shown in Figure 14.9 are the ones that I recommend for an organization that wants to limit the maximum message size to 10MB and the maximum recipients per message to 5000.

Filtering

The Filtering tab page of the Message Delivery properties allows you to specify SMTP addresses or domains from which you want to reject inbound SMTP messages. This feature was called *turfing* in Exchange 5.5 and was implemented as an anti-spam feature. Figure 14.7 shows the Filtering property page, which is where you can enter a list of SMTP addresses or domain names from which you want to reject mail. Note that the @ sign is required in front of the domain name.

Figure 14.7   Message Delivery properties Filtering tab

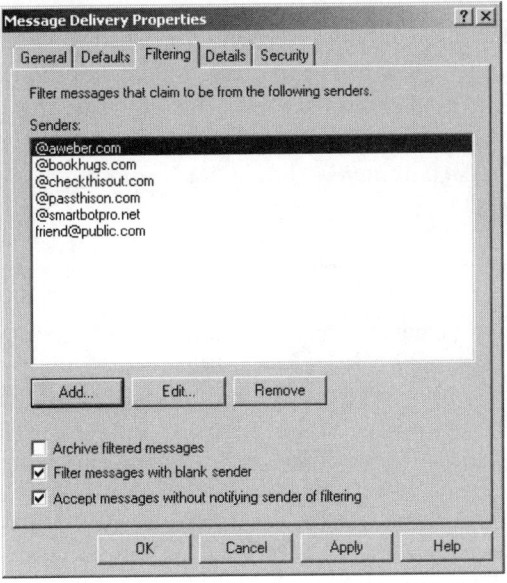

There are three check boxes on the Filtering property page:

- The Archive Filtered Messages check box instructs the SMTP virtual server to put a copy of the "turfed" message in the \Exchsrvr\Mailroot\VSI 1\Filter directory (or the appropriate virtual server directory). Be careful of this option: It means that you will have to periodically clean out all the \Filter directories where these messages are archived. I recommend using this option so that you can periodically inspect the messages that were filtered.

- The Filter Messages With Blank Sender check box instructs the SMTP virtual server to turf any message that doesn't have a Sender field. Spam messages are often sent this way. This is a useful option, but keep in mind that certain types of NDRs are sent to a blank sender (and BCCed to the recipient) to prevent mail loops. I recommend enabling this option.

- The Accept Messages Without Notifying Sender Of Filtering check box instructs the SMTP virtual server to accept the message but not to send an NDR report to the sender. I typically recommend enabling this option unless you specifically want someone to know you are rejecting their mail.

Message Format

Under the Global Settings container is a container called Internet Message Formats. The objects in this container allow you to specify formats of outbound messages to particular domains. All SMTP virtual servers in the organization use these message formats. By default, the only object found in the Internet Message Format container is the default message format. The Default object should not be modified or deleted, since this will cause the Exchange 2000 transport to fail.

NOTE   Most of these settings could be configured in Exchange 5.5, but they had to be configured for each Exchange 5.5 Internet Mail Service individually.

There are two primary property pages on the message format that are relevant to customizing Exchange message formats: Message Format and Advanced. From the Message Formats tab (shown in Figure 14.8), you can specify the default outgoing message format.

The Message Encoding options allow you to specify whether you want the message to be sent as MIME message or a uuencode message. If you select MIME, you need to choose whether you want the message body to be sent as plaintext, HTML, or both. Today, most e-mail systems and clients can accept a message that is formatted as a MIME message with HTML formatting.

Figure 14.8 Message Formats property page

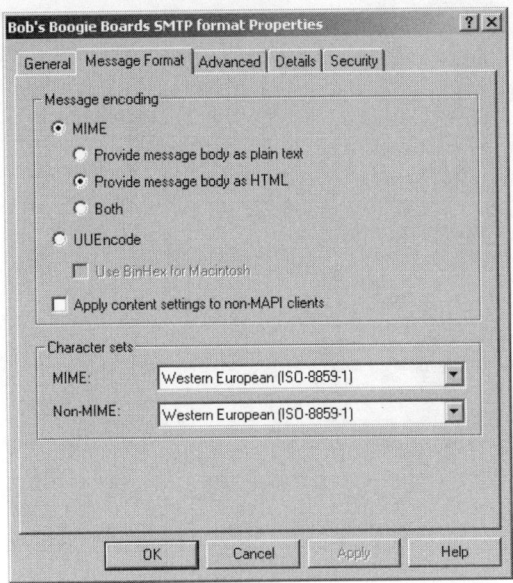

NOTE The default message format is a MIME message with plain-text body. I recommend changing this to provide the message body as both plaintext and HTML. This does increase the size of outbound messages, but it guarantees compatibility with old mail systems that may not support HTML formatted messages.

The Apply Content Settings To Non-MAPI Clients check box tells the SMTP virtual server to use these settings even if a message was sent by a POP3 or IMAP4 client. Unless you feel you have a specific reason to convert all messages to your preferred content selection, leave this setting unchecked.

The MIME and Non-Mime Character Sets tell the SMTP virtual server what character sets to use. Unless you have specific reasons to change these, I recommend that you use Western European (ISO-8859-1).

The Advanced property page (see Figure 14.9) allows you to specify options relating to rich-text formatting, message wrap, automatic reply options, and delivery report options.

Connectivity

PART 4

Figure 14.9 Advanced property page of the default message format

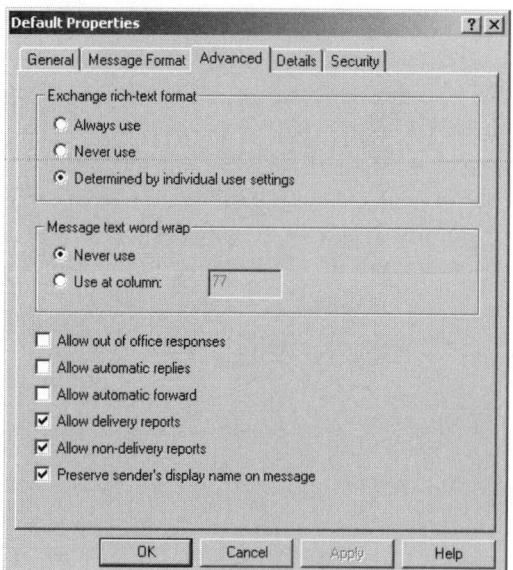

The following Advanced options should be considered carefully before enabling them, as many of them, if configured improperly, will generate some support issues.

- Why are Internet users not getting my out office replies? Probably because the default message format's Allow Out Of Office Responses option is unchecked.

- Why are automatic replies or forward messages not being sent to the Internet? The default is that these are not allowed; you must check the Allow Automatic Replies and/or Allow Automatic Forwards check boxes in order to enable these. Enable this only after careful consideration: Allowing automatic forwarding/replying can result in a mail loop that can cause the server to run out of disk space or the queues to become clogged with messages.

- Why are users not being notified of successful or failed deliveries to remote domains? This can happen if the Allow Delivery Reports and Allow Non-Delivery Reports check boxes are cleared.

- If users do not wish for their display name to be displayed on messages to the Internet, clear the Preserve Sender's Display Name On Message check box.

NOTE Each of the options on both the Message Format and the Advanced property pages can be customized by creating an Internet Message Format object for the specific domain to which you want the custom settings to apply.

Allowing SMTP Relay

One of the biggest headaches that I had to deal with in Exchange 5.5 was that the IMS was automatically configured as an open relay. This means that any SMTP client could send a message destined for any SMTP recipient to the IMS, and the IMS would deliver that message for that client. The problem that I continually experienced was that someone would reconfigure the IMS and leave it open for relay. Then an unscrupulous company on the Internet would find this open relay and use it to send tens of thousands of spam messages. Inevitably, my customer's site would be reported as an open relay to one of the black hole lists, and their site would be blocked by anyone using these lists (see Chapter 13 for more on black hole lists).

Exchange 2000 virtual servers are automatically configured to allow relay *only* for users that successfully authenticate. However, it is still easy to accidentally open up the server for relay by anyone. POP3 and IMAP4 clients such as Outlook Express, Eudora, and Netscape Communicator require relay, and it is very tempting for the Exchange administrator to merely open up relay for anyone rather than go the extra step to allow relay for the authorized users and block it for others. Another way to address clients who need to relay through an SMTP virtual server is to create one that is only accessible from the internal network and then enable that virtual server for relay.

Relay restrictions are set for each SMTP virtual server; simply open the Access property page and click the Relay button. The default relay restriction is that only clients that successfully authenticate can relay; this default must be left in place because Exchange 2000 servers automatically authenticate with one another. You can also allow relay based on a single IP address, an IP subnet, or a domain name.

If you allow relay based on domain name, the SMTP virtual server must perform a reverse DNS lookup on each client, and the client must have a PTR record that points to a permitted domain name.

Defining Inbound SMTP Domains

In Exchange 5.5, to define an inbound SMTP domain you had to define the domain on each IMS's Routing property tab. This allowed that specific IMS to accept inbound SMTP mail for that domain. Once that was defined, you then had to define how those messages to that domain would be handled (either accepted inbound for local recipients or forwarded to other hosts).

Exchange 2000 has a much more universal way to define the inbound SMTP domains: *recipient policies*. Recipient policies are defined for the entire Exchange 2000 organization; they define inbound SMTP domains and Mailbox Manager settings. Recipient policies are defined using Exchange System Manager (in the Recipients ➤ Recipient Policies container) and are global for the entire organization. Each recipient policy can define more than one inbound SMTP domain.

TIP   You should not create more than 999 recipient policies; doing so results in some policies not being applied.

The default policy, found in the Recipients container, can be modified to add more SMTP domains, but you cannot change the filter to which this policy applies.

There are three different types of domains for which you may want to accept inbound SMTP messages: domains for which you have local recipients, domains for which you will forward all mail to another SMTP system (such as relaying or queuing for remote delivery), and domains in which you share SMTP mail with another SMTP system outside of your Exchange 2000 organization.

NOTE   One feature of the Exchange 5.5 IMS that is no longer available in Exchange 2000 is the ability to configure the IMS to re-route incoming mail to an internal domain. This feature would rewrite the recipient's address. You can still re-route mail for an incoming SMTP domain using either recipient policies (if the message is to an internal recipient) or a mail-enabled contact object.

Local Recipients

You must define inbound SMTP domains that your Exchange servers will accept mail for and deliver locally. You do this by editing an existing policy (such as the default policy) or creating a new policy that affects only the users you want the policy to affect. This is useful if you are hosting multiple organizations or if you want your users to have an additional e-mail address. For example, if I wanted all of my users to have two SMTP addresses (one that is *alias*@somorita.com and the other that is *firstname.lastname*@somorita.com), I would simply modify the default policy's E-mail Addresses property page to include an additional SMTP address, as shown in Figure 14.10.

You can define an SMTP address by itself (such as @somorita.com), and the Exchange alias will be used to create the SMTP address, or you can use the following variables:

%g	Given name (first name)
%i	Middle initial
%s	Surname (last name)
%m	Exchange alias
%d	Display name (the spaces and commas are removed)

You can also combine these, such as %g.%s for *firstname.lastname* or %1g%s for first initial followed by last name.

Figure 14.10 E-mail Addresses (Policy) property page

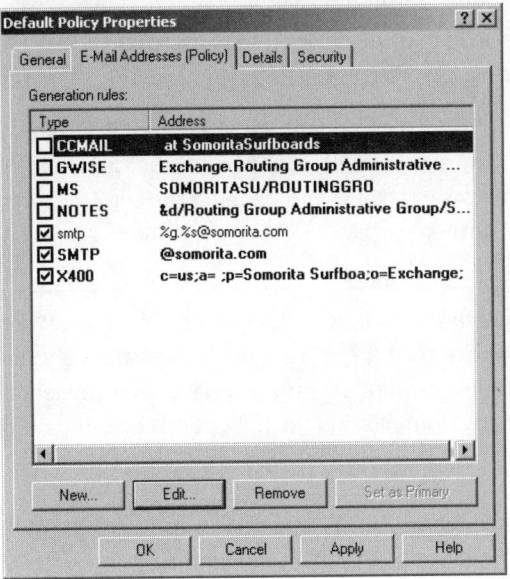

You can create additional policies if you want to only assign addresses to a subset of your users. To best explain this, let's say that I want to host an additional SMTP domain for my server; all users whose Company Name field is Scully Surfboards should have an SMTP address of *firstname.lastname@scullysurfboards.com*. To create an additional recipient policy, follow these steps:

1. Using Exchange System Manager, open the Recipients Policies container.

2. Right-click the Recipients Policies container and choose New ➢ Recipients Policy.

3. Select the E-mail Addresses property page (the Mailbox Manager Settings may not be necessary), then click OK.

4. Assign the policy a descriptive name in the Name field.

5. Click the Modify button to modify the filter rules.

6. Select the Advanced property page on the Find Exchange Recipients dialog box.

7. Select the User field Company, confirm that the Condition is Starts With, enter **Scully Surfboards** in the Value box, and then click the Add button. Click OK to close the Find Exchange Recipients dialog box.

8. Click the E-mail Addresses property page, click New, select SMTP Address, and enter **%g.%s@scullysurfboards.com** in the Address box.

Connectivity

PART 4

9. Make sure that the This Exchange Organization Is Responsible For All Mail Delivery To This Address check box is selected, and click OK.

10. To enable the SMTP address, make sure that you select the check box next to it. Click OK to close the Recipient Policy dialog box.

Notice in the Generation Rules list (shown in Figure 14.13) that only one address of each type is the primary address. You can change another address (one that is not in bold) to the primary address by selecting it and clicking the Set As Primary button. You can only have one primary address.

NOTE   Once you have multiple recipient policies, you will notice that the policies in the list have a priority. If there is a conflict between policies (such as assigning the primary address), the highest priority policy takes precedence. You can change a policy's priority by right-clicking the policy and choosing All Tasks ➢ Move Up (or Move Down).

NOTE   You cannot remove the This Exchange Server Is Responsible For All Mail Delivery To This Address check box if the address is the primary address for the recipient policy. If you need to do this, set another address to be the primary address, and remove the check on the check box.

TIP   You can decrease the amount of time it takes for these policies to be put in place; locate the Recipient Update Service (RUS) for each domain, right-click that service, and choose Update Now.

Relay Domains

You can set up other domains for which you want to store messages for ETRN, or TURN, or to be forwarded. These domains are not domains for which you accept messages locally. In order for your Exchange servers to accept messages inbound for this domain, you must configure a recipient policy; in Exchange 5.5, you would have modified the Exchange 5.5 IMS Routing property tab. To do this in Exchange 2000, follow the same steps as you would to create an additional recipient policy, but don't create any filter rules for this address. On the E-mail Addresses (Policy) property page, create a new SMTP address and make sure that the This Exchange Organization Is Responsible For All Mail Delivery To This Address check box is selected on the SMTP Address dialog box.

The final two steps required are to configure the remote domain's SMTP server to pick up its mail via ETRN and to configure an SMTP Connector to deliver the messages to this domain.

Shared Domains

You can configure Exchange 2000 to accommodate an environment in which you are in the process of migrating or are just sharing an SMTP domain name with a different mail platform. In this type of environment, you want inbound mail to come into an SMTP virtual server and let the Message Categorizer check to see if the recipient is local. If the recipient is not local, you want the message forwarded to the other system's SMTP host.

This scenario requires that you configure a recipient policy for this particular domain and then make sure that the This Exchange Organization Is Responsible For All Mail Delivery To This Address check box is cleared. If this is a Mixed-mode Exchange organization, you will not be able to modify the highest priority recipient policy. Further, you will need to configure the SMTP virtual server that will be accepting mail for this domain (the one that the MX record is pointing to) with a host to which unresolved recipients are forwarded. This is done on the SMTP virtual server's Messages property page by filling in the fully qualified domain name (FQDN) of the host that will accept the messages in the Forward All Mail With Unresolved Recipients To Host box.

Resolving Inbound SMTP Addresses

When a message is received from an STMP recipient, the AQE queries Active Directory to see if that SMTP recipient has an object in AD (such as a mail-enabled contact object). If the SMTP address exists in AD, the From address is replaced with the object's display name. If you wish to disable this feature, it must be done in the Registry on each Exchange server and for each SMTP virtual server that is created.

Each SMTP virtual server instance has its own Registry key; for example, the default virtual server will have the following Registry key:

```
HKLM\System\CurrentControlSet\Services\MSExchangeTransport\Parameters\VSI 1
```

If the value is not already present, create a value type of REG_DWORD called ResolveP2. The default value is 1, which enables the sender to be resolved. Change this value to 0 if you do not want any P2 addresses resolved. You can customize which of the P2 headers you want resolved; consult Microsoft Knowledge Base article Q174755 for more information.

Typically, this setting would be configured on an Exchange server that was dedicated to be the SMTP gateway to the Internet for your organization. This would prevent messages from the Internet from being sent inbound with display names that might mask the true sender. Among servers internally, the ResolveP2 settings are not typically used.

Connectivity

PART 4

Changing the SMTP Banner

When an SMTP client connects to an SMTP server, or when you telnet to an SMTP server's port 25, the SMTP server introduces itself to you with its SMTP banner, which looks something like this (depending on your version of Windows 2000):

```
220 sfoex001.somorita.net Microsoft ESMTP MAIL Service Version:
5.0.2195.2966 ready at Mon, 29 Oct 2001 23:19:14 - 1000
```

You might want to modify this banner, since it gives away some information that you might not want displayed, specifically the SMTP server program (Microsoft ESMTP Mail Service) and the version (5.0.2195.2966). However, an experienced hacker will have many tools at their disposal for learning the software and version you are running on your SMTP server, so don't get lured into feeling that you are more secure just because you changed your SMTP banner. You may also want to change this banner to display a custom message. This is doable, but you cannot remove the FQDN of the server or the date and time.

To change the SMTP banner, you must edit the IIS Metabase for each virtual server on which you want to customize the message. Simply follow these steps:

1. Using the IIS MetaEdit utility from the Windows 2000 Resource Kit, locate the SMTP virtual server you wish to change. This will be in the \Lm\Smtpsvc\1 folder if you are modifying the first SMTP virtual server.

2. Highlight the 1 folder and click Edit ➢ New ➢ Choose String.

3. In the Edit Metabase Data window's ID drop-down list box, make sure that (Other) is selected. In the box to the right of the ID box, enter **36907**.

4. In the Data box, type the banner information that you want displayed, and then click OK. A completed dialog box looks like this:

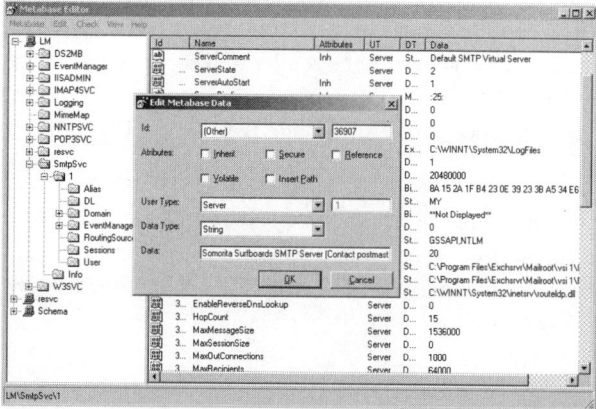

5. Using Exchange System Manager, stop and restart the virtual server that you just updated.

6. Using Telnet, connect to port 25 (or the appropriate port on that server) and confirm that the banner has been changed.

> **WARNING** You may notice a lot of things that you can customize through the IIS MetaEdit program. The master copies of many SMTP virtual server settings are actually stored in AD and are replicated to the IIS Metabase. If you change something in the Metabase that is actually mastered in AD, it will be overwritten.

Disabling Extended SMTP Command Verbs

For either security reasons or compatibility reasons, you may want to disable some of the SMTP command verbs that are advertised by default. Table 14.4 lists the SMTP command verbs and extensions that you can disable along with a value that you must use in order to disable the command.

Table 14.4   SMTP Command Verbs That Can Be Disabled

Verb/Extension	Decimal Value
DSN	64
ETRN	128
TURN/ATRN	1024
ENHANCEDSTATUSCODES	4096
CHUNKING	1048576
BINARYMIME	2097152
8bitmime	4194304

The code that enables or disables these extensions is stored in the Metabase for each SMTP virtual server; the key name it is stored in is `SmtpInboundCommandSupportOptions`. This particular Metabase value is also stored in the Configuration partition of the Active

Connectivity

PART 4

Directory for each SMTP virtual server and is updated using the DS2MB process. This means that changes must be made by modifying the SMTP virtual server in AD. To do this, use a utility such as the ADSIEDIT console and follow these steps:

1. Browse through the Configuration partition until you find the SMTP virtual server instance for which you want to disable a SMTP command verb.

2. Display the properties of that SMTP virtual server and locate the property msExchSmtpInboundCommandSupportOptions.

3. In the Edit Attribute box, enter a value that represents which verbs should be enabled. Click the Set button and click OK.

The challenge here is determining what number you must put into the Value(s) field. The default is 7697601, which enables all of the command verbs. If you want to disable ETRN, for example, subtract 1024 from 7697601 and enter the result (7696577). If you wanted to disable ETRN and TURN, you would have to subtract 1024 + 128 from 7697601 and enter the resulting value in the value field. If you want to disable all SMTP command verbs, you would enter 352257, which is 7697601 - (64 + 128 + 1024 + 4096 + 1048576 + 2097152 + 4194304).

Once this has been changed in AD, you have to wait for the Configuration partition to replicate to the domain controller the Exchange 2000 server is using for its configuration information, and you will have to wait for the DS2MB process to run.

NOTE   For more detailed information on this customization, see Microsoft Knowledge Base article Q257569.

WARNING   Be careful not to customize SMTP virtual servers that are not dedicated to Exchange.

Routing Groups

Routing groups were introduced to give Exchange architects more flexibility when building a large Exchange 2000 organization. With the help of administrative groups (collections of Exchange 2000 servers that are all administered by the same user or group), routing groups separate message routing functions from administrative functions. An Exchange 2000 routing group is a collection of Exchange 2000 servers that are separated by permanent, full-time connectivity.

NOTE Exchange 2000 servers can be moved between routing groups, but the organization should be in Native mode.

Designing an Effective Routing Group

Many organizations will have sufficient bandwidth between all of their Exchange servers so that they will not need multiple routing groups. However, there are some reasons why you might want to break up your organization into multiple routing groups:

- Your organization has multiple sites connected by WAN links whose available bandwidth is often below 64KB of available bandwidth.
- You have remote locations that are not connected via full-time connectivity, or the connectivity is not reliable.
- You need to schedule when messages are sent to another group of servers, or you wish to schedule when messages larger than a specified size are sent to those servers.
- You want to restrict the message size or sender of a message to servers in a specific group.
- You want to control when certain types of messages (such as public-folder replication messages) are transferred.
- You have remote locations that are connected via an X.25 connection.
- You want to focus public-folder connectivity to a certain group of public folder servers.
- You want to control the message path through bridgeheads or over more than one hop.

When you begin to split any Exchange organization into routing groups, you want the structure to be as efficient as possible and to meet the needs of your organization. One of the most common questions I am asked is "What is sufficient bandwidth for servers within a routing group?" I have never seen an official recommendation from Microsoft on this, so I have to fall back on my old reliable answer: It depends on the reasons you are breaking up the organization in the first place (focusing public folder connectivity, the size of your messages, the amount of bandwidth, etc.) I have heard figures as low as 28.8Kb *available* bandwidth, but I would have to recommend about 64Kb.

NOTE Active Directory sites and Exchange 2000 routing groups may share the same architecture, but essentially they bear no relationship to one another.

Here are some things to consider and plan for when designing routing groups:

- Network connectivity should be full-time, reliable, and low-latency.
- There should be at least one Global Catalog server located within each routing group.
- All servers in a routing group communicate with one another point-to-point (in a full mesh).
- Communications between servers in a routing group cannot be scheduled.

Administrating Routing Groups

To ease administration of routing groups and connectors, you may want to consider creating a separate administrative group called Routing Group Administrative Group or Message Routing Administration. Assign Exchange Admin permissions only to the people who will need to manage connectors and routing groups. Then, in that administrative group, create a routing groups container in which you'll create the routing groups you wish to use. Figure 14.11 shows Exchange System Manager and the Message Routing Administration administrative group.

Figure 14.11   Message Routing Administration administrative group

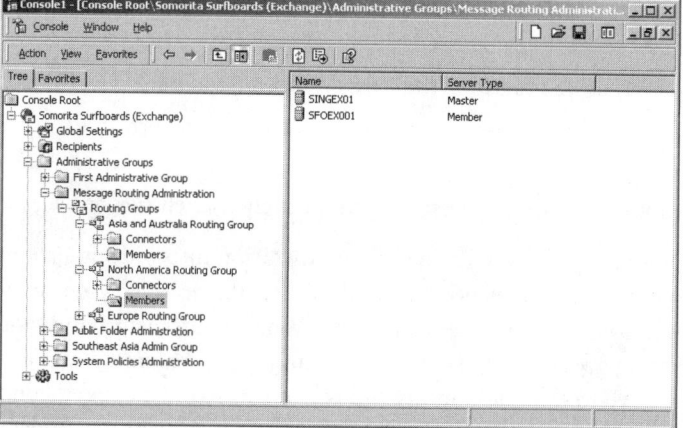

Moving Servers

Once routing groups are created, moving Exchange 2000 servers between them is simple. I find it easiest if I have both routing groups open so that I can see their Members containers (see Figure 14.11); to move a routing group, click and hold it, drag the server to another routing group's Members container, and then release. In order to move a server between routing groups, the administrator performing the move must have at least write permissions on each of the routing groups' objects. Either the Exchange Administrator or Exchange Full Administrator roles will allow you to move servers between routing groups.

You will not be able to move the server between routing groups if that server is acting as bridgehead server for any connectors that join routing groups. Further, if that particular server is responsible for monitoring servers or connectors in its routing group, you should make sure that responsibility is assigned to a server that will remain in the routing group.

The Link State Table

The Exchange 5.5 MTA (and earlier versions of Exchange) used a routing table called the *Gateway Address Routing Table (GWART)* to determine the best route to deliver a message to an Exchange 5.5 server in a remote site. The Exchange 5.5 GWART consists of an address space (such as EX:/O=SomoritaSurfboards/OU=PacificRegion), a connector (or connectors) that could deliver a message to that address space, and a cost associated with using that particular route. Unfortunately, the transmitting MTA had no way to know whether or not any of the remote connectors were operational, so the message began its journey with no guarantee that it would actually arrive at its destination. If there were alternate routes to deliver a message and those routes were also unavailable, then the message could end up ping-ponging between two Exchange servers.

To address this problem, Exchange 2000 introduced a new routing calculation system that helps the Exchange 2000 Routing Engine perform efficient routing of messages based not only on the available routes, but also on the current network conditions (whether a connection is available or not). The Exchange 2000 Routing Engine maintains a table of available routes and their current state called the *Link State Table (LST)*, which is built and updated using the *Link State Algorithm (LSA)*. LSA is based on a well-known, widely accepted method for calculating least-cost routes between nodes in a network called Dijkstra's algorithm. It is very similar to the OSPF (Open Shortest Path First) algorithm used in IP routers. Each routing group in an Exchange 2000 organization is treated as a network node much like a router is considered by OSPF. The algorithm prevents looping and incorporates dynamic re-routing. You can think of the LST as a map of all of the routing groups in an Exchange 2000 organization, the connectors between those routing groups, and the current state (up or down, as described below) of those connectors.

NOTE   For more information on Dijkstra's algorithm along with some interesting demos, visit www-b2.is.tokushima-u.ac.jp/~ikeda/suuri/dijkstra/ Dijkstra.shtml.

Connectivity

PART 4

The LST is built and stored in the Exchange server's memory; no copies of it are written anywhere. The Routing Engine builds the LST from information about routing groups and connectors in AD's Configuration partition. In each routing group, the Routing Group Master server distributes updates (state of connectors) to the Routing Engine. The Routing Engine uses TCP port 691 to send updates within the routing group. Between routing groups, the SMTP X-LINK2STATE command verb or an X.400 message (between X.400 Connectors) is used to send updates.

> **TIP**   You can force a server to rebuild its Link State Table by stopping and restarting the Microsoft Exchange Routing Engine service.

The Routing Group Master server contacts each of the servers in the routing group once every 10 minutes to confirm that they have the latest updates for link state information. Though this might sound like a fairly high-overhead process, the amount of data is actually quite small; this consists of the GUID (globally unique identifier) of the connector and servers, address spaces, and the state of connectors. Only the Routing Group Master server can send updates to other members of the routing group. Each entry in the LST is about 32 bytes, so even an organization totaling 500 routing groups, Exchange servers, and connectors will only have a 16K LST.

> **NOTE**   You can change the server that is the Routing Group Master by right-clicking the server in the Members container and choosing Set As Master.

Updating the Link State Table

By default, the Routing Engine considers all links, servers, and address spaces to be "up," or available. When a server, connector, or address space becomes unavailable, other servers in the organization have to be notified that the server, connector, or address space is "down." Consider the organization shown in Figure 14.12, this organization has three routing groups,s and each routing group is connected to the other routing groups by means of a Routing Group Connector (RGC).

Figure 14.12 Sample routing groups in an Exchange 2000 organization

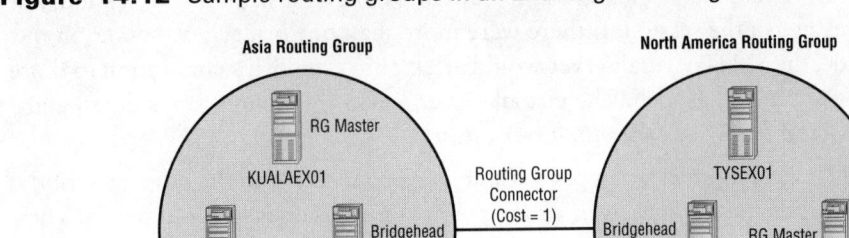

In the Asia Routing Group, a message originating on KUALAEX01 needs to be delivered to a recipient on the TYSEX01 server in the North America Routing Group. The following is the process of attempting to route this message to TYSEX01. In this example, the connectivity to the bridgehead server in the North America Routing Group is down.

1. The Advanced Queuing Engine (AQE) on the KUALEX01 server determines that the message is not to be delivered locally. It consults the Routing Engine to determine the next hop for the message. Within the Asia Routing Group, all of the RGCs are hosted on the SINGEX01 server, so the message is forwarded to that server.

2. The AQE on SINGEX01 consults the Routing Engine and determines that there are two possible routes for this message; one directly to the North America Routing Group and one indirectly through the Europe Routing Group. The AQE checks the connector restrictions to make sure that the message can be sent through both and chooses the cheapest route that it can use. In this example, everything is equal, so the SINGEX01 chooses to send the message to the SEAEX01 server.

3. The SMTP virtual server on SINGEX01 attempts to establish an SMTP session, but fails to establish the session. If there were more than one bridgehead server on the other side, the SMTP virtual server would attempt to establish a connection to those bridgehead servers, as well. The virtual server marks this connector as down and enters what is known as the *glitch retry state*.

4. The SMTP virtual server attempts to establish a connection to the other side of the connector three more times, waiting an interval of 60 seconds between retries. The glitch retry interval defaults to every 60 seconds, but this can be configured for the SMTP service using the GlitchRetrySeconds key (type is REG_DWORD) located in HKLM\System\CurrentControlSet\Services\SMTPSvc\Queuing.

5. If the remote bridgehead servers do not respond after the third glitch retry, the server that determined that the link is down notifies the Routing Group Master server in its own routing group via TCP 691.

6. The routing group's Routing Group Master server notifies all of the other servers in that site that the link is down.

7. The bridgehead servers notify other bridgehead servers in other sites that the link is down by connecting to them, using the SMTP X-LINK2STATE command verb followed by the information about the connector that is down. Once that information is sent to the other routing groups, the remote bridgeheads notify their Routing Group Master servers.

8. In the case of Figure 14.12, there is an alternate route through the Europe Routing Group, so the message is re-routed to the LONEX01 server (the bridgehead for that routing group) unless the connector from Europe to North America is already marked as down. If the Europe Routing Group had previously been marked as down and there were not more alternate routes, the message remains on SINGEX01 until one of the connectors is marked as up again.

9. The Asia Routing Group bridgehead server (in this case, SINGEX01) continues to try to connect using the failed connector even if it has no messages to deliver. It uses the first, second, third, and subsequent retry intervals of the SMTP virtual server.

10. Once the connector is up again, the SMTP virtual server instructs the Routing Engine to mark the state of the connector as up. The Routing Engine then notifies the Routing Group Master server, which in turn notifies the other servers in the routing groups. The remote routing groups are notified via SMTP, and messages start flowing through this connector again.

If the remote server is not back online within the SMTP virtual server's Expiration time-out value found on the Delivery property tab (default is 2 days), the message will be returned to the send with a non-delivery report.

> **NOTE** You can view the Link State Table for each server using the WINROUTE utility, which is found on the Exchange 2000 CD-ROM in the \Support\Utils\ I386 directory.

Connecting Routing Groups

To connect routing groups for messaging, you must decide on the appropriate connector. There are three connectors that are used for messaging connectivity between routing groups:

- Routing Group Connector
- X.400 Connector
- SMTP Connector

Both the SMTP Connector and the RGC use SMTP as their default underlying message transport. The X.400 Connector, naturally, uses the X.400 protocol. If you are upgrading from Exchange 5.5, you will probably already have one of four connector types in place: the site connector, the X.400 Connector, the Internet Mail Service, or the Dynamic RAS Connector.

> **NOTE** The Dynamic RAS Connector is no longer supported in Exchange 2000. Instead, you must choose one of the other three connectors and use a dial-on-demand solution such as Windows 2000's Routing and Remote Access Services (RRAS).

A new content restriction you can place on an Exchange 2000 connector is on its Content Restrictions property page (shown in Figure 14.13). The Allowed Priorities option allows you to specify whether the connector can deliver messages flagged as High, Normal, or Low priority. The other restriction is the Allowed Types option, which allows you to specify whether the connector can deliver system or non-system messages. System messages are public folder replication messages, directory replication messages (Exchange 5.5), delivery reports, and non-delivery reports. Non-system messages are regular e-mail messages to and from mail-enabled users, groups, and contacts.

Connectivity

PART 4

Figure 14.13 Content Restrictions property page

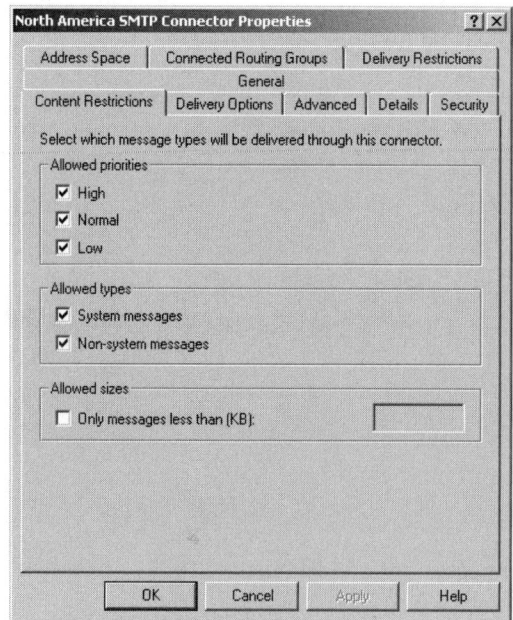

Routing Group Connectors

As you get your organization configured and onto a native Exchange 2000 platform, you will probably find that the Routing Group Connector will become your default connector for connecting routing groups because it is both easy to configure and very versatile. Here is some information about the RGC that may prove relevant when choosing a connector:

- It uses SMTP as the default transport protocol, except in the case of connecting to remote Exchange 5.5 sites that have the site connector installed; then it uses RPCs.
- It's tolerant of low-speed connections (28.8Kb or less).
- It provides scheduling, content, message size, and user restrictions.
- It can have multiple local and remote bridgehead servers.
- It's easy to configure.

Configuring Routing Group Connectors

The Routing Group Connector is fairly easy to configure and offers many configuration options. Before you install the RGC, confirm that you have multiple routing groups created and that each routing group has at least one member. If you have just moved servers into that routing group, you may have to wait until Active Directory replicates before you can configure the RGC.

The RGC requires very little in the way of custom configuration. However, the RGC is unidirectional, so you must create a RGC in both routing groups. To configure the RGC between two routing groups, follow these steps:

1. Using Exchange System Manager, locate the routing group that you want connect to another routing group. Right-click the Connectors container, and choose New ➢ Routing Group Connector. The General property page opens.

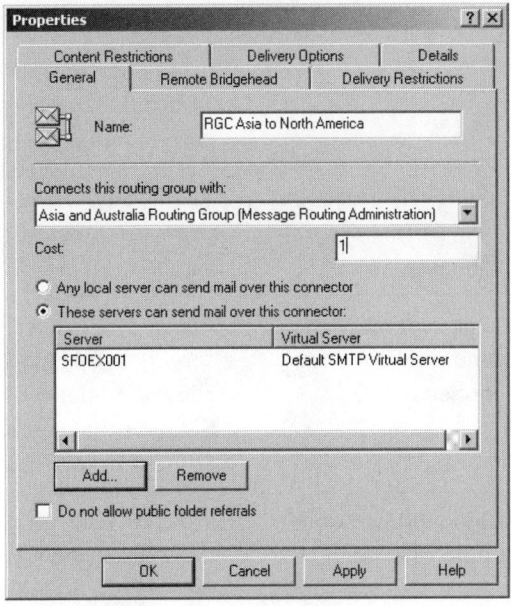

2. Assign this RGC a descriptive name.

3. By default, any server in this routing group can send messages to any remote server. You can specify specific SMTP virtual servers in the local routing group by selecting the These Servers Can Send Mail Over This Connector radio button and then adding a list of SMTP virtual servers that will be used with this RGC.

4. Open the Remote Bridgehead property page and add the appropriate SMTP virtual servers that can be used on the remote routing group. If you do not see all of the SMTP virtual servers, Active Directory may not have fully replicated.

5. Click OK. You will be prompted as to whether or not you want to create the RGC in the remote domain. If you have permission do to this, click Yes. If not, someone with permissions in the remote routing group will have to create the remote RGC.

One the RGC is created, you can go back and configure any customizations that you may need to perform. Table 14.5 shows some of the configuration options for the RGC.

Connectivity

PART 4

Table 14.5   Routing Group Connector Configuration Options

Property Page	Item	Function
General	Connects this routing group with	Drop-down list box that contains a list of all the routing groups to which this connector can connect.
General	Cost	Specifies a cost value associated with using this RGC. This value can be between 1 and 100. Lower cost routes will be used before higher cost routes.
General	Any local server can send mail over this connector	Allows any server in the site to use this connector to send mail to the remote server.
General	These servers can send mail over this connector	Allows you to specify a list of SMTP virtual servers in this routing group that will be allowed to deliver mail to the remote SMTP virtual servers specified on the Remote Bridgehead property page.
General	Do not allow public folder referrals	Prevents users in the local routing group from accessing public folders in the remote routing group.
Remote Bridgehead	Remote bridgeheads	Provides a list of SMTP virtual servers in the remote routing group to which the local bridgehead servers (specified on the General tab) are allowed to connect.
Remote Bridgehead	Override connection credentials for Exchange 5.x	If the Exchange organization is in Mixed mode, this option will be enabled so that you can enter a domain name, username, and password for use when connecting to Exchange 5.5 sites using RPCs.
Delivery Restrictions	By default, all messages from everyone are	Specifies that all messages are either rejected or accepted. You can then specify from which users messages will be accepted.

Table 14.5 Routing Group Connector Configuration Options *(continued)*

Property Page	Item	Function
Delivery Restrictions	Accept messages from	Specifies mail-enabled users and mail-enabled groups of users who are allowed to send messages through this connector.
Delivery Restrictions	Reject messages from	Specifies mail-enabled users and mail-enabled groups of users who are not allowed to send messages through this connector.
Content Restrictions	Allowed priorities	Specifies whether or not High, Normal, and Low priority messages will be delivered through this connector.
Content Restrictions	Allowed types	Specifies whether or not system messages (public folder replication, delivery notifications, non-delivery notifications) and non-system messages (regular e-mail messages) are allowed through this connector.
Content Restrictions	Allowed sizes	Specifies the maximum message size that this connector will transport.
Delivery Options	Connection time	Specifies when the connector will operate.
Delivery Options	User different time for oversize messages	Specifies a size for large messages and when those messages will be delivered.

My favorite feature of the RGC is the Delivery Options property page. This page allows you to specify when this connector will actually deliver messages. If no alternate route is available, then the message will not be delivered until this connector becomes active.

Further, you can configure the connector to use a different delivery time for messages that are over a certain size. In Figure 14.14, messages that are under 5MB in size will be delivered immediately, while messages that are over 5MB in size will be delivered based on a

Connectivity

PART 4

custom schedule. This allows you to keep your WAN bandwidth available for other things during the busiest part of the business day.

Figure 14.14   Configuring the RGC's Delivery Options property tab

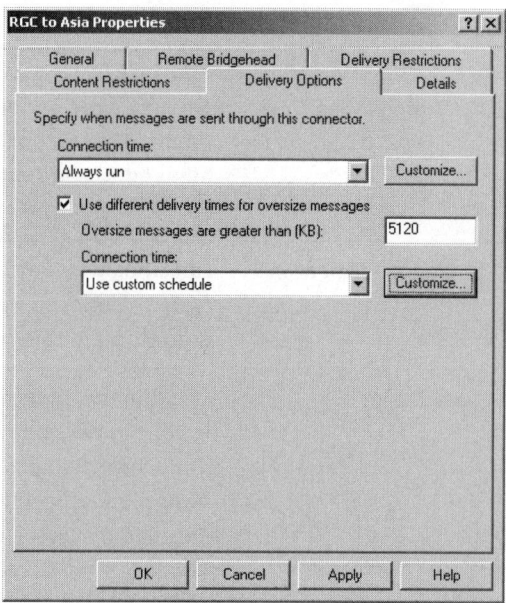

Making Delivery Exceptions   Every organization has exceptions to the rules. While I really like the feature of restricting the maximum message size that can be delivered to a remote site during business hours, there are always one or two users who need to send large messages and want them to get there *immediately* (or maybe sooner—don't you have that time-travel connector installed yet?!!).

For these users, you can create an additional RGC that will deliver messages 24-hours-a-day, 7-days-a-week. The catch is that you have to specify some delivery restrictions. Figure 14.15 shows the Delivery Restrictions tab of an additional RGC. The connector has been configured to reject messages from everyone by default (the Rejected radio button), and then only a list of special people are allowed to send through this RGC (the Allow Messages From list).

Figure 14.15 Applying delivery restrictions to the RGC

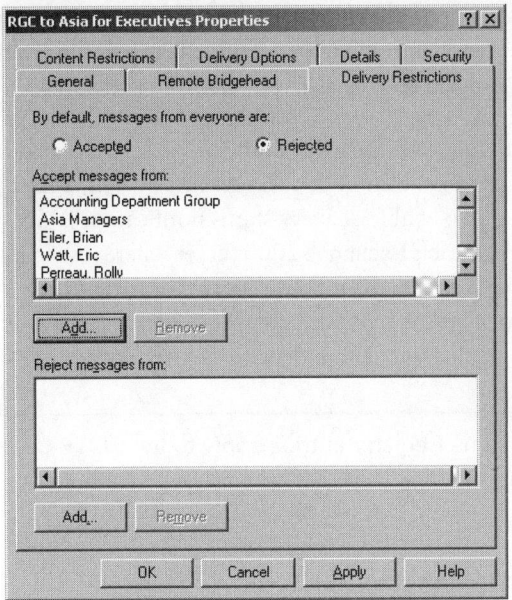

Wait, the Restrictions Aren't Working!   So you have configured the restrictions for the RGC, but they are not working properly. Well, there are a couple of additional things you need to know. The first is that those restrictions will not work until you make a Registry change on all of your Exchange servers. While Exchange System Manager will let you make those restrictions on the Delivery Restrictions property page, the Routing Engine will not pay any attention to them.

To enable the Routing Engine to use these restrictions, you must modify the Registry on each Exchange 2000 server that hosts SMTP virtual servers used by the RGC or the SMTP Connector. Add a value of type REG_DWORD called `CheckConnectorRestrictions` to the `HKLM/System/CurrentControlSet/Services/Resvc/Parameters` key.

To enable checking of restrictions, set this value to 1; to disable it, either delete the Registry value or set it to 0. Once this is enabled, there will be a slight performance drop due to the fact that additional parameter checking has been put in place. For your changes to take effect, stop the Microsoft Exchange Routing Engine service and the Simple Mail Transport Protocol (SMTP) service and restart them.

> **NOTE**   If you do not enable this parameter, you may notice event ID 957 in the application event log from the MSExchangeTransport indicating that connector restrictions are present, but restriction checking is disabled.

Once this parameter is set, only the list of authorized users can send messages through this connector. This may cause a problem if delivery reports or non-delivery reports must pass over a restricted connector. To enable delivery status notification (DSN) messages to pass over a restricted connector, on each Exchange 2000 server where restrictions are being enforced you must create a Registry key called `IgnoreRestrictionforNullDSN` of type REG_DWORD in the `HKLM/System/CurrentControlSet/Services/Resvc/Parameters` key. Set this value to 1 so that the Routing Engine will ignore delivery restrictions for DSN messages.

> **NOTE**   These same Registry entries apply to the SMTP Connector, discussed later in this chapter.

X.400 Connectivity

The X.400 Connector is supported on Exchange 2000 Enterprise servers. The X.400 protocol is based on a series of ITU recommendations for connecting disparate e-mail systems. Though X.400 is difficult to debug and complex to configure, it is used frequently in the messaging industry. X.400 has some distinct advantages over the SMTP protocol, including the fact that it can operate in many types of networks, such as TCP/IP and X.25 (but not the TP4 protocol as was provided with Exchange 5.5). Further, it is very tolerant of low-speed, unreliable network connections. Some of the common uses of the X.400 Connector include:

- Connectivity with X.400 service providers
- Connectivity to Exchange 2000 routing groups and Exchange 5.5 sites

The Exchange 2000 MTA is responsible for managing the X.400 Connectors, but all messages bound for X.400 Connectors still flow through the Advanced Queuing Engine. The Link State Table also contains information about the availability of the X.400 Connectors; link state data is transmitted through "dummy" IPMs (interpersonal messages, or simply X.400 messages).

> **NOTE**   The Exchange 2000 X.400 Connector does not work with current versions of DMS. If you have DMS connectivity requirements, you must use Exchange 5.5 servers.

Configuring X.400 Connectors

Creating X.400 Connectors involves two steps. First, you must create an X.400 transport stack. Once that's configured, you can then create X.400 Connectors that use that transport stack.

NOTE   Unlike the SMTP Connector and the Routing Group Connectors, you cannot have multiple local and remote bridgehead servers.

Creating an X.400 Transport Stack

The X.400 Service Transport Stack tells the MTA which protocol stack the X.400 Connector will use to connect to a remote X.400 host. Exchange 2000 supports two X.400 protocol stacks: TCP/IP X.400 Service Transport Stack and X.25 X.400 Service Transport Stack. If you are going to use X.400 over X.25, you must have special hardware installed (such as the Eicon Technologies X.25 adapter card) and a leased line to an X.25 network provider.

To create the X.400 transport stack, right-click the X.400 Protocols container of an Exchange 2000 Enterprise server and choose New ➢ TCP/IP X.400 Service Transport Stack.

By default, you do not need to configure the name; the default name should work nicely. For connectivity between Exchange 5.5 sites or Exchange 2000 routing groups, simply click OK. For some service providers or for DMS, you must configure the OSI address information. This information is used to further define the connector's addressing information if more than one application is using the same transport stack. Each of these selectors (the T, S, and P selectors) corresponds directly to a layer of the OSI model (Transport, Session, and Presentation, respectively); the X.400 service is, of course, on the Application layer. You can think of these layer identifications as being used much the same way a TCP or UDP port number.

Creating the X.400 Connector

Once the MTA transport stack has been created, you can create the X.400 Connector in the Connectors container of the appropriate routing group. Following these steps will create an X.400 Connector with basic messaging functionality:

1. Using Exchange System Manager, open the routing group in which you wish to create the X.400 Connector.

2. Right-click the Connectors container and choose New ➢ TCP X.400 Connector.

3. On the General property tab, enter a descriptive name in the name property box:

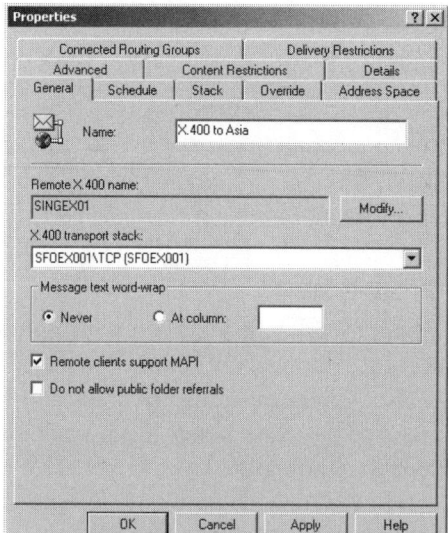

4. Also on the General tab, click the Modify button and enter the remote MTA name. If the remote MTA is an Exchange server, enter the Exchange server's NetBIOS name. If the remote server has a password assigned, enter the password also.

5. On the Stack property tab, enter the remote host name of the X.400 host.

6. On the Address Space property tab, enter the address spaces that this connector supports. If this connector is providing connectivity to an external organization, at a minimum there must be an X.400 address space configured.

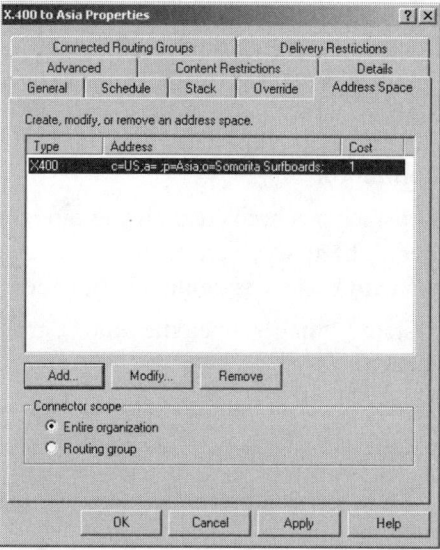

7. If this connector is to be used to connect hosts to a remote Exchange 2000 routing group or an Exchange 5.5 site, on the Connected Routing Groups property tab, provide the name of the routing group or site.

> **NOTE** Both sides of the connection must be configured before messages will flow.

The X.400 Connector has a lot more options than the RGCs. Table 14.6 shows the common X.400 configuration options, though I did leave out some of the more obscure and self-explanatory ones.

Table 14.6 X.400 Connector Configuration Options

Property Page	Option	Function
General	Remote MTA name	Specifies the name (and password) of the remote X.400 MTA.
General	X.400 transport stack	Specifies the name of the X.400 transport stack that you want to use for this X.400 Connector.
General	Remote clients support MAPI	Assumes that the remote clients are Outlook clients and support rich-text formatting.
General	Do not allow public folder referrals	Disables the ability for Outlook clients to connect to public folders in the remote routing group (assuming this X.400 Connector is used to connect routing groups).
General	Schedule	Allows you to schedule when the connector operates. The default is Always; you can select specific times when the connector is active. If you specify Remote Initiated, this connector queues messages and expects the remote connector to retrieve queued messages.
Stack	Remote host name / IP Address	Specifies the remote host name or the IP address of the remote X.400 server.

Connectivity

PART 4

Table 14.6 X.400 Connector Configuration Options *(continued)*

Property Page	Option	Function
Override	Connection retry values	Specifies how often the X.400 Connector will try to deliver messages to the remote X.400 Connector. Maximum Open Retries attempts to deliver a message a 144 times and waits 600 seconds (Open Interval) between retries; this is 24 hours. Once the connection is open, the connector will try to deliver the message twice (Maximum Transfer Retries) waiting 120 seconds between retries (Transfer Interval).
Override	Additional Values button	Specifies values for reliable transfer service (RTS), association and connection lifetime, and transfer timeouts.
Address Space	Create, modify, or remove an address space	Allows you to create a list of address spaces that are supported by this connector.
Address Space	Connector scope	Specifies whether the address spaces supported by this connector will be available for the entire organization or just the routing group.
Advanced	Allow BP-15 (in addition to BP-15)	Specifies that the X.400 host on the other side of this connector can accept attachments formatted as file transfer body part (FTBP or BP-15) as well as simple binary attachments (BP-14).
Advanced	Allow Exchange contents	Allows messages to be transferred in MDBEF format.
Advanced	X.400 conformance	Specifies the MTA's level of X.400 recommendation conformance. Most X.400 systems support 1988 normal mode.

Table 14.6   X.400 Connector Configuration Options *(continued)*

Property Page	Option	Function
Content Restrictions	Allowed priorities	Specifies whether the connector can deliver High, Normal, or Low priority messages.
Content Restrictions	Allowed types	Specifies whether the connector can deliver system messages, non-system messages, or both.
Connected Routing Groups	Create, modify, or remove a connected routing group	Provides a list of Exchange 2000 routing groups or Exchange 5.5 sites to which you can connect through this X.400 Connector.

The maximum number of recipients in a single message that you can send through the Exchange 2000 MTA is 32,000. If you send more to an X.400 host or Exchange 5.5 recipient, the message will be broken into more than one message with no more than 32,000 recipients in each.

> **NOTE**   For information on troubleshooting and monitoring MTA events in the event log, see the document "Exchange 2000 MTA Events" at www.somorita.com.

X.400 Connectivity to Foreign Mail Systems

In the 1980s and early 1990s, X.400 appeared to be the emerging standard in messaging backbones. It was designed to connect many dissimilar messaging systems. Yet the Exchange X.400 Connector can also be used to connect Exchange to foreign X.400 messaging sites. Connectivity between Exchange Server and foreign X.400 e-mail systems is not difficult, but there are a few things you should know prior to attempting this connectivity for the first time. This chapter discusses some topics that may be of interested if you have to configure an X.400 Connector or if you need to diagnose problems related to e-mail messages not converting properly.

Configuring the X.400 Connector for the first time is not for the faint of heart; I recommend having someone around who has done it before (or at the very least, have them available by phone). When connecting to a foreign X.400 system (I am assuming that you

Connectivity

PART 4

will be using X.400 over TCP/IP), you need to be prepared to ask the person on the other side of the connection a few questions, including:

- What is the remote MTA name? The name cannot exceed 32 characters.

- Does the remote MTA have a password? The password cannot exceed 64 characters.

- What is the remote MTA's host name or IP address? If they give you a host name, confirm that you can ping the host name and properly resolve the host's IP address.

- Is custom OSI address information for the Transport, Session, and Presentation selectors (service access points)? The selector fields are quite often left at their defaults (blank). However, if the remote host has these fields set, you must have them set.

- Do the clients know the network you are connecting to support MAPI? Unless they are using a Microsoft messaging system, probably not.

- Can messages be transferred any time of day or night, or do they have to occur on a scheduled basis?

- Is message word wrapping necessary, or do the remote clients insert carriage returns and line feeds automatically? If so, into what column should the carriage returns be inserted? Most modern message systems take care of this automatically.

- Which X.400 recommendation does the remote MTA comply with—1984 or 1988? Most modern X.400 systems comply with the 1988 recommendations.

- Does the remote system support X.400 BP-15 in addition to X.400 BP-14? If not, on the Advanced property page, clear the Allow BP-15 (In Addition To BP-14) check box.

- Is there a maximum message size limit?

- What is the X.400 administrative management domain name (ADMD)? Depending on to whom you're connecting, you may also require their organization name and their private management domain (PRMD).

Chances are good that the person on the other side of the connection will have some questions for you, too. While I cannot give you answers to things such as message size limits or times when you will send and receive, here are some basic X.400 answers relating to Exchange Server:

- The Exchange server's MTA name defaults to the Exchange server NetBIOS name; this can be overridden on the Override property page.

- There is not normally an MTA password, but it can be set for this connection on the Override property page.

- The Exchange server does not require message wrap to be turned on.

- Exchange clients support MAPI (at least Outlook, Exchange client, and Outlook Express do).

- The Exchange server fully conforms to the X.400 1988 recommendations, and it supports BP-15 as well as BP-14 body part encoding standards.

- By default, your private management domain (PRMD) is the same as the first 16 characters of your Exchange organization name.

- The administrative management domain (ADMD) defaults to a single space. This drives administrators of systems that use X.400 crazy, because the single space often simply looks like an empty field.

Message Interoperability

When an X.400 Connector is created, there are a couple of defaults that need to be changed if you are connecting to a foreign X.400 system. These will affect whether the message will actually get delivered and whether the message content will be converted properly. On the Advanced tab of the X.400 Connector property page (see Figure 14.16), there are several important options that must be set properly for the MTA to transfer data to the foreign X.400 system.

Figure 14.16 The Advanced tab of an X.400 Connector's property page

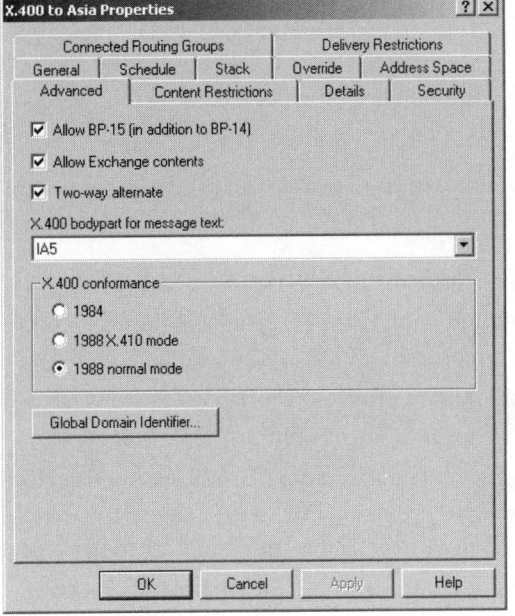

The most critical of these settings is the X.400 Link option called Allow Exchange Contents. When this check box is enabled, the X.400 Connector transfers the message in MDBEF format. This check box should *always* be cleared when connecting to a foreign

X.400 system. This instructs the MTA to convert the message to either an X.400 P2 format (if 1984 conformance is selected) or X.400 P22 format (if 1988 conformance is selected).

Other options that should be confirmed include:

- MTA conformance must be set properly; the majority of the modern MTA software should support the 1988 normal mode. This is configured by selecting the 1988 Normal Mode radio button on the Advanced property tab.
- The X.400 Link option Allow BP-15 (In Addition To BP-14) on the Advanced property tab should be set based on the capabilities of the receiving system. If you don't know if the foreign system can receive BP-15 body parts, clear the check box until you have the connection working. Once the connection is working, send a message to the other side with an embedded file.

Another option that should possibly be cleared is on the X.400 Connector's General property page. This is the Remote Clients Support MAPI check box. If this box is checked, the MTA will transport the message across the connector in Microsoft Transport Neutral Encapsulation Format (TNEF). This means the rich-text formatting is stripped out of the message, and the RTF information is attached to the message as a file called WINMAIL.DAT. If the receiving client supports MAPI and understands the WINMAIL.DAT file, it will automatically re-create the message with rich-text formatting. If the receiving client does not support MAPI, the user will have the WINMAIL.DAT file attached to the messages. While the file is harmless, it will probably generate some help desk calls, so I try to avoid sending this.

If the remote X.400 system is also an Exchange-based system, then you can safely leave this option enabled, allowing RTF messages to be sent to users on the foreign system.

Common X.400 Configuration Problems

Here are some common configuration problems (and potential solutions) that you may encounter when configuring an X.400 Connector:

- The remote host name provided on the Stack tab is not resolvable using DNS or a HOSTS file. Test this when configuring the connector!
- Often, the IP address of the remote X.400 server is entered on the Stack property page, but the Remote Host Name radio button is selected. Make sure that if the IP address is entered that the IP Address radio button is selected.
- Remote clients may report receiving unreadable messages. If you are connecting to non-Exchange systems, you should clear the Remote Clients Support MAPI check box on the General property page and the Allow Exchange Contents check box on the Advanced property page.

- If you find your X.400 Connectors are not delivering messages for remote routing groups, set the X.400 Connector's Connector scope (found on the Address Space tab) to Routing Group.

- Remote users are receiving messages with a `WINMAIL.DAT`. You need to uncheck the Remote Clients Support MAPI check box on the General property page.

Exchange@Work: X.400 and the U.S. Military

In much of the world (at least for small and medium-sized businesses), X.400 is fading from the realm of usability. This is thanks mostly to the wide acceptance of SMTP as a global messaging standard.

As SMTP began to take hold a few years ago, I thought I had seen the last of X.400. However, that was not to be; for the last six years, I have been involved in one capacity or another in the U.S. Department of Defense's DMS (Defense Messaging System) project. DMS is a global, uniform, X.400-based messaging system designed to replace the U.S. DoD's antiquated AUTODIN (Automated Defense Information Network) system. This ambitious project has many components and could itself be the subject of an entire book. The goal is to provide DMS users with a global directory (based on X.500) of all DMS users throughout the world and a standard method (X.400) for securely transmitting messages to those DMS users.

Military commands can pick their own user agents and message servers from a list of approved DMS clients and servers, including Outlook 2000/Exchange Server, GroupWise, and Lotus Notes. Exchange Server has emerged as the preferred choice for the message server; the version that is used is a slightly modified version of Exchange Server 5.5. The Outlook 2000 client has a set of extensions installed so that it can query the DMS X.500 directory and format a military message. The client also requires a PCMCIA reader, since the DMS security is based on a PCMCIA device called a *Fortezza card*, which contains the user's authorization to send DMS messages.

Each Exchange server that connects to the DMS message network (which I have come to call the *DMS cloud*) must have an X.400 Connector installed, which must be configured to connect to a foreign X.400 system.

As of this writing, the primary contractor for DMS (Lockheed Martin, www.1mdms.com) is currently working on a version of DMS (DMS 3.0) that will allow interoperability with Exchange 2000 and DMS, but this version will still require Exchange 5.5 servers to provide X.400 connectivity to the DMS infrastructure.

SMTP Connectivity

All Exchange 2000 servers have at least one SMTP virtual server, so the first question that everyone always asks is "Why do I need an SMTP Connector?" If you do not configure an SMTP Connector, all outbound messages (outbound to the Internet) will be delivered directly from the originating SMTP virtual server. Any server (or all servers) can be configured to receive inbound SMTP mail from the outside merely by pointing an MX record to that server's SMTP virtual server.

The SMTP Connector is quite similar to the Exchange 5.5 Internet Mail Service (IMS). Once the SMTP Connector is installed and configured with an address space, all Exchange 2000 server Routing Engines will direct outbound SMTP messages (messages not meant for an Exchange 2000 recipient) to the SMTP virtual server or servers that host the SMTP Connector.

> **WARNING**   Careful attention should be paid to address spaces for SMTP Connectors that are being configured in organizations with multiple routing groups and multiple SMTP Connectors. Improperly configuring an address space or forgetting to restrict it to a specific routing group may result in your SMTP Connector delivering Internet-bound messages for many remote routing groups.

The Exchange 5.5 IMS allowed you to specify whether a specific IMS would accept messages inbound, deliver messages outbound, or both. The SMTP Connector allows you to specify what types of address spaces are supported (outbound), but the DNS MX records control inbound SMTP connectivity.

The SMTP Connector also sounds sort of like the Routing Group Connector. You can even use the SMTP Connector to deliver messages between routing groups or to an Exchange 5.5 site that is using the IMS as a messaging connector, but the RGC will be much easier to use when connecting routing groups together. In the context of connecting routing groups, the SMTP Connector seldom offers an advantage, and may be at a disadvantage to the RGC. The SMTP Connector is primarily designed to focus outbound SMTP connectivity to the Internet and it can do a few things that the RGC cannot:

- Custom outbound authentication and encryption can be set for each connection.
- The SMTP Connector can be configured to pick up remotely queued mail using TURN or ETRN or to hold mail for a remote server to pick up via ETRN.
- An SMTP smart host can be specified as the delivery point for all outbound messages from an SMTP Connector.
- SMTP Connectors can be used to send SMTP messages to any SMTP server; the RGC only communicates with other Exchange 2000 servers in the same Exchange 2000 organization.

Configuring an SMTP Connector

Configuring an SMTP Connector is pretty simple; there are only a few options necessary to start using the connector. However, there are quite a few options that you may need to configure for the SMTP Connector; these options are listed in Table 14.7. Not all of these configuration options are necessary to create a functional SMTP Connector.

Table 14.7   SMTP Connector Property Pages and Options

Property Page	Option	Function
General	Use DNS to route each address space on this connector	Specifies that this SMTP Connector should deliver messages by using the DNS to query MX records for destination domains. The other option is to use an SMTP smart host to deliver outbound messages on behalf of the SMTP Connector.
General	Forward all mail through this connector to the following smart hosts	Specifies that messages that this connector is processing be forwarded to a smart host rather than relying on local delivery. You can specify the FQDN or the IP of the smart host. Make sure you put the IP address of the smart host in brackets, such as [smarthost .somorita.net]. If the SMTP virtual server is set to use a smart host, this value overrides it.
General	Local bridgeheads	Specifies a list of SMTP virtual servers in the local routing group that can be used by this connector. You should always use at least two local bridgeheads.
General	Do not allow public folder referrals	Specifies whether clients in this routing group can connect to public folder replicas in routing groups listed on the Connected Routing Groups property tab.
Content Restrictions	Allowed priorities	Specifies whether this SMTP Connector can deliver High, Normal, or Low priority messages.

Table 14.7 SMTP Connector Property Pages and Options *(continued)*

Property Page	Option	Function
Content Restrictions	Allowed types	Specifies whether this SMTP Connector can deliver system messages or non-system messages.
Content Restrictions	Allowed size	Specifies the maximum message size this connector will support. This is useful for the SMTP Connector because you may want to restrict message size going out to or in from the Internet (through the SMTP Connector), but not at the SMTP virtual server level.
Delivery Options	Specify when messages are sent through this connector	Specifies a schedule when this connector will deliver all messages.
Delivery Options	Use different delivery times for over-sized messages	Allows you to specify a different schedule for messages that are larger than a specified size. I love this feature!
Delivery Options	Queue mail for remote triggered delivery	Configures this connector to not deliver any messages, but rather to wait for remote domains to connect and issue the TURN command. If this option is configured, you must specify a user account or accounts that these remote domains will use when they connect remotely. You can control which remote domain's mail will queue at this connector using the Address Space property page.
Advanced	Send HELO instead of EHLO	Instructs the SMTP virtual server to introduce itself with a HELO command indicating to the receiving system that this server does not support ESMTP extensions. The HELO command verb is used only when messages are being delivered by the SMTP Connector, not when internal messages are being delivered directly by the SMTP virtual server.

Table 14.7   SMTP Connector Property Pages and Options *(continued)*

Property Page	Option	Function
Advanced	Do no send ETRN/TURN	Disables outgoing TURN or ETRN requests. This is the default and should remain this way for most SMTP Connectors unless you are configuring one that will be used to pick up remotely queued mail.
Advanced	Outbound Security button	Used to specify the type of outbound authentication (Anonymous, Basic, or integrated Windows authentication) and the username and password that are to be used. The default is Anonymous. If you select anything other than the default, the destination SMTP server must be configured to support authentication, and you must be given a username and password on the remote system.
Advanced	Request ETRN/TURN when sending messages	Instructs the SMTP virtual server to issue an ETRN or TURN command to pick up remotely queued mail.
Advanced	Additionally request mail at specified times	Activates the Connection Time drop-down list and Customize button so that you can specify that you want this SMTP Connector to automatically request queued mail even if there is no outgoing mail.
Advanced	Request ETRN/ TURN from a different server	You can use this option when the server that has mail queued for your server is different than the one to which you are connecting. You can enter a host name or an IP address for the remote server. If you enter an IP address, it should be in brackets, such as [192.168.2.200]. This option also actives the Connection Time drop-down list box and the Customize button. This will be necessary when your ISP has separate inbound and outbound hosts; the server you send mail to may not be the same as the server that queues your mail for remote delivery.

Connectivity

PART 4

Table 14.7 SMTP Connector Property Pages and Options *(continued)*

Property Page	Option	Function
Advanced	Specify how to request that remote servers dequeue mail	Specifies that the SMTP virtual server supporting this SMTP Connector use the ETRN or TURN command to dequeue remotely queued mail. If you pick ETRN, you must configure the domains that are to be dequeued using the Domains button.
Advanced	Domains button	Allows you to specify the list of domains that will be used with ETRN to remotely dequeue mail.

If you are configuring an SMTP Connector, you will probably be configuring it for one of four different scenarios. These include standard remote mail delivery, queuing mail for remote pickup, relaying mail, or picking up mail that is queued remotely.

***

NOTE Each SMTP virtual server can be assigned to work with more than one SMTP Connector.

Creating a Standard SMTP Connector

A "standard" STMP Connector is the most common type of SMTP Connector. Once an SMTP Connector is created and an address space is established for that connector (in the case of a standard SMTP Connector, an address space of SMTP:*), the connector will focus all outbound SMTP messages through this connector. By outbound, I mean SMTP messages that are destined for recipients outside of this Exchange organization or routing groups that are connected through this SMTP Connector. Messages within the routing group are still delivered within the routing group using the applicable SMTP virtual server on the originating server.

The following steps create an SMTP Connector that can be used to send messages to the Internet for SMTP addresses:

1. Load Exchange System Manager and navigate to the routing group in which you want the new SMTP Connector to exist.

2. Right-click the Connectors container in the routing group and choose New ➤ SMTP Connector.

3. Enter a name for the connector in the Name field.

4. On the General tab, select the local bridgehead servers that will be used to deliver messages for this SMTP Connector.

5. Click the Address Space tab and choose Add.

6. Choose the SMTP address type and click OK, then click OK again to accept the default address space (*) and cost (1). The SMTP Connector is now ready for use.

If you have more than one Exchange 2000 server in a routing group that contains an SMTP Connector, you should configure the SMTP Connector with at least two SMTP virtual servers in order to provide redundancy.

Connecting Sites and Routing Groups Using the STMP Connector

You can use an SMTP Connector to connect Exchange 2000 routing groups or Exchange 5.5 sites that are using the IMS Connected Sites option. Before you can specify the routing groups to which this SMTP Connector will connect, you must have created the routing groups in Exchange System Manager.

To define a routing group (or Exchange 5.5 site) that an SMTP Connector will connect, display the SMTP Connector's Connected Routing Groups property tab. Add the routing group or Exchange 5.5 site name that will be connected. Then, on the Routing Address property page, specify the name of the e-mail domain. This e-mail domain can either be represented by an MX record or an individual A record, but the SMTP virtual server that will attempt delivery will always perform an MX record lookup first.

Customizing an STMP Connector

There are a couple of ways to customize the SMTP Connector. For example, you may want to restrict the address spaces that the connector supports to be used only within the routing group in which the connector was created. By default, the address spaces will be available to all servers in the Exchange organization. On the Address Space property page (Figure 14.17), there is a radio button selection that lets you define whether or not you want the address spaces on that property page to be visible to the entire organization or just the servers in the routing group. To restrict these address spaces, select the Routing Group radio button.

Figure 14.17   Limiting the scope of the connector's address spaces to only the routing group

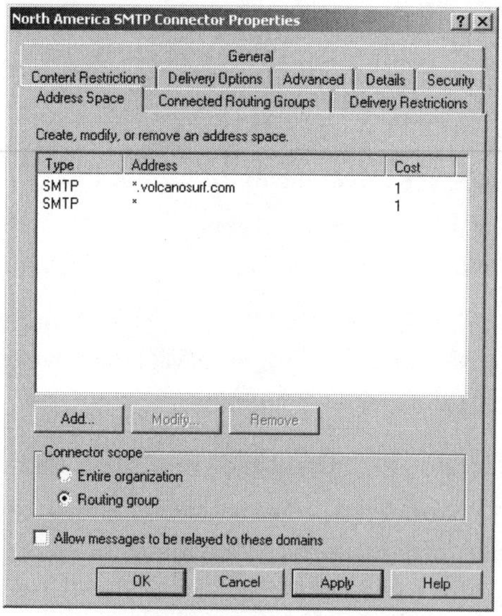

Queuing and Dequeuing Mail

For some organizations, all of the servers may not have full-time network connectivity, or you may not be connected to the Internet and thus may not be able to receive SMTP mail from Internet users. Exchange 2000 supports both the ability to queue messages for remote SMTP servers to retrieve as well as the ability to connect to another server and dequeue messages. The SMTP protocol command verbs that handle this are ETRN and TURN.

If you are planning to use ETRN, you may need a static IP address for the Exchange server that supports the SMTP Connector. (If your server and your provider support dynamic IP services, this may not be necessary.) If you are going to use TURN, the SMTP Connector must authenticate to the server that has the mail queued. This is officially called *authenticated TURN*.

Supporting ETRN or TURN Clients

If you are going to queue SMTP mail for remote clients, you will need to configure an SMTP Connector that will be used to queue the mail. Also, you will need to configure a recipient policy that allows the incoming mail to that remote domain to be accepted and stored. For example, let's say that I am configuring Exchange 2000 to queue mail for an SMTP domain called volcanosurf.com. Since Volcano Surfboards does not have a full-time Internet connection, they cannot receive their SMTP mail, but they will still have to have MX records. Their sister organization (Somorita Surfboards) is going to hold their mail until they can dequeue it using ETRN.

Figure 14.18 shows the configuration of the DNS records and the Exchange 2000 servers. An SMTP server on the Internet needs to send an SMTP message to volcanosurf.com; the SMTP server does an MX record lookup for volcanosurf.com and finds two hosts (hnlex01.volcanosurf.com and sfoex001.somorita.com) can accept mail for that domain. Since hnlex01.volcanosurf.com has a lower MX record, that SMTP server on the Internet attempts to contact hnlex01 first. If that server is not online, then the SMTP server on the Internet contacts sfoex01.somorita.com. Since this sfoex001 is connected to the Internet full-time, it will accept the connection and queue the mail for delivery. At some point in the future (based on the schedule on hnlex01), hnlex01 will dial in and dequeue any mail queued on the sfoex001 server.

Figure 14.18 Mail store and forward configuration for volcanosurf.com

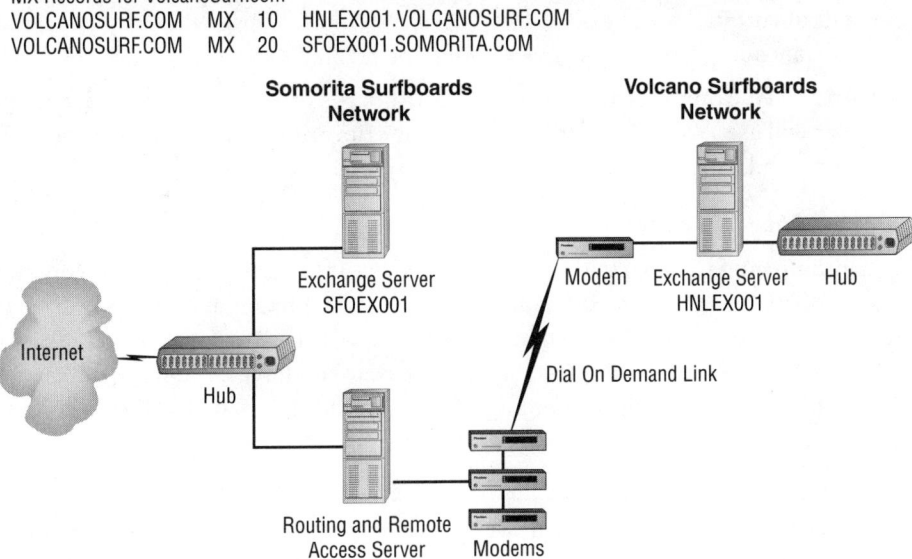

There are a number of things that must be done before the remote Exchange 2000 servers are configured. The following is a basic checklist:

- Windows 2000 RRAS (or some other dial-in solution) must be installed at Somorita Surfboards that will assign a static IP address to the Exchange 2000 server at Volcano Surfboards. Or Volcano Surfboards can alternately dial directly to an ISP and retrieve their mail though the Internet from Somorita Surfboards.

- RRAS should be configured on the Volcano Surfboards Exchange 2000 server and configured for dial-on-demand access to the RRAS server at Somorita Surfboards.

- DNS MX records must be created to identify the servers that will accept mail for volcanosurf.com. Since the SMTP Connector at Somorita Surfboards will accept mail for this domain, it must be listed in the MX records, but the primary record must be the IP address of the Exchange server with the SMTP Connector at Volcano Surfboards. The MX records will look something like this:

   MX10hnlex01.volcanosurf.com

   MX20sfoex01.somorita.com

- A recipient policy must be created in the Somorita Surfboards Exchange organization that allows that organization to accept messages for volcanosurf.com. On this SMTP address's General property page, the This Exchange Organization Is Responsible For All Mail Delivery To This Address check box must be cleared.

- An SMTP Connector must be created in the Somorita Surfboards organization that will queue mail for remote delivery. On the Address Space property page, the volcanosurf.com address space should be created.

- An SMTP Connector in the Volcano Surfboards organization must be configured that will use a smart host (the server at Somorita Surfboards) and will issue an ETRN command for volcanosurf.com.

Queuing Mail

To configure an SMTP virtual server to queue mail for a remote domain, you must create an address space for the domain that you will be queuing mail. This is done on the Address Space property tab. All mail destined for volcanosurf.com will be delivered to this SMTP Connector. In addition, make sure that you have configured a recipient policy for this SMTP domain so that any SMTP virtual servers will know to accept the inbound SMTP domain.

NOTE If you are configuring an SMTP Connector that will store mail for remote dequeuing, I recommend designating only one SMTP virtual server as a bridgehead for this connector. Otherwise the TURN/ETRN remote client may have to connect to two separate servers to dequeue all of their mail.

If the remote clients will be using the TURN command verb, this connector must be dedicated to storing mail only for remote delivery. On the Delivery Options property tab (see Figure 14.19), you will also need to configure the user account that will be used by the remote system to authenticate prior to using the TURN command.

Figure 14.19 Delivery Options configured to support TURN/ATRN clients

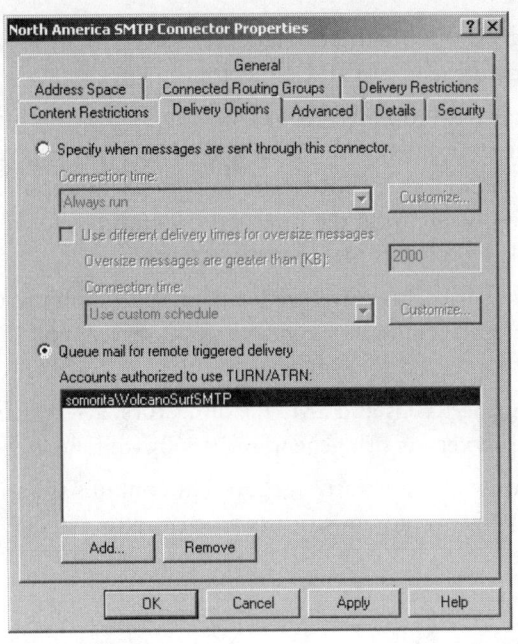

Retrieving Remotely Queued Mail   To configure an Exchange 2000 SMTP virtual server to connect to a remote server and dequeue mail, you must configure an SMTP Connector whose sole purpose is dequeuing mail. Once the connector is created, you will have a couple of additional things you will also have to configure. First, on the SMTP Connector's General property page, you will need to designate the remote host that is queuing mail as the smart host; this must be the FQDN or IP address (in square brackets) of the remote host.

Next, on the Advanced property page, you will need to check the Request ETRN/TURN When Sending Messages radio button. By default, the server will retrieve messages only when it has to connect to the remote host and send messages. However, if you check the Additionally Request Mail At Specified Times option, you can configure the connection time so that messages are requested even if no messages need to be sent. If you are configuring the client for ETRN, you must click the Domains button and specify a list of domain names that will be requested when the client connects to remote server.

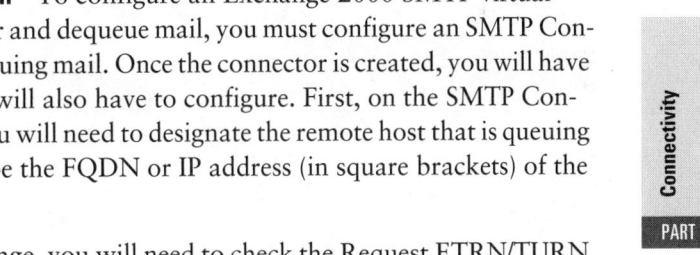

Connectivity Best Practices

Here are some suggestions and best practices to consider when configuring connectivity between routing groups and SMTP Connectors:

- Make sure that you have all of your DNS and name resolution issues resolved. This includes making sure that all Internet-accessible servers have both an address record (an A record) as well as a PTR record (a reverse lookup record), and that these records are resolvable from the Internet. *All* servers should be in the internal DNS and resolvable by any internal Exchange server.

- Confirm that your MX records are functional for inbound mail routing. In an organization with more than one Exchange 2000 server, you should configure at least one backup MX record for redundancy.

- When configuring RGCs and SMTP Connectors, always configure at least two SMTP virtual servers as bridgehead servers for redundancy.

- Create a separate administrative group that contains the routing groups, and delegate authority only to administrators who need to manage the message-routing infrastructure.

15

Internet Client Connectivity

Exchange 5 marked Microsoft's first serious attempt at delivering a messaging system based on Internet client standards. Since that time, Exchange has continued to evolve as a platform for allowing standard Internet clients to send and receive messages. These standard Internet clients include POP3 (Post Office Protocol) and IMAP4 (Internet Message Access Protocol) clients as well as browser-based (HTTP) clients.

Exchange 2000 marks Microsoft's entry into the world of highly scalable Internet servers by providing support not only for POP3, IMAP4, and HTTP but also for new technologies such as HTTP-DAV, front-end servers, and Instant Messaging.

Understanding the particulars of Exchange 2000 Internet client support and when to configure features to support clients is important for Exchange administrators. Over the next few years, I expect that Microsoft will come to rely increasingly on Internet standards–based clients and less on MAPI-based clients. These standard protocols will play an increasing role in the clients that we deploy to our user desktops and thus must support on the Exchange server. This chapter discusses:

- POP3 and IMAP4 virtual servers
- Outlook Web Access
- Front-end and back-end servers
- Instant Messaging

POP3 and IMAP4 Virtual Servers

Exchange 2000 supports both POP3 and IMAP4 for use with Exchange 2000–based mailboxes. Each of these is supported through the use of one or more virtual servers. Virtual servers allow you to create multiple instances of a protocol on an Exchange 2000 server. This is in contrast to Exchange 5.5 in which you could have only a single instance of POP3, IMAP4, NNTP, or the Internet Mail Service (IMS).

Virtual servers should not be used to improve performance or scalability of an Exchange 2000 server. By default, all of the Internet protocols listen on all IP addresses and all IIS processes are multi-threaded so additional virtual servers will not improve performance. Virtual servers may be useful in the following situations:

- You need to configure different virtual servers to support different levels of authentication.
- The virtual servers that users use from the Internet must require Transport Layer Security (TLS), but you do not want the overhead of encryption for users connecting internally.
- You need to configure a virtual server for use with a specific application that may not be constrained by the same rules as the regular users of the Exchange server.
- You want to use a different message format when users connect internally than they receive when they connect from the outside.

Figure 15.1 shows a server configuration that might be implemented for an organization that has POP3 clients who need to access their Exchange mailboxes from both the internal network and the Internet. For security reasons, anyone who connects from the Internet must be required to use TLS/SSL, but to reduce the amount of overhead that encryption places on the server, only external clients should use TLS/SSL.

When configuring the virtual servers for Figure 15.1, the default virtual server would have to be reconfigured to support only a single IP address; the default is (All Unassigned) IP addresses. The virtual server can also be renamed so that its name can better reflect its function.

NOTE   All virtual server configuration is performed through Exchange System Manager and stored in Active Directory's Configuration partition. The DS2MB sub-process of the System Attendant will take this information and create the appropriate entries in the IIS Metabase.

Figure 15.1 Common use of multiple virtual servers

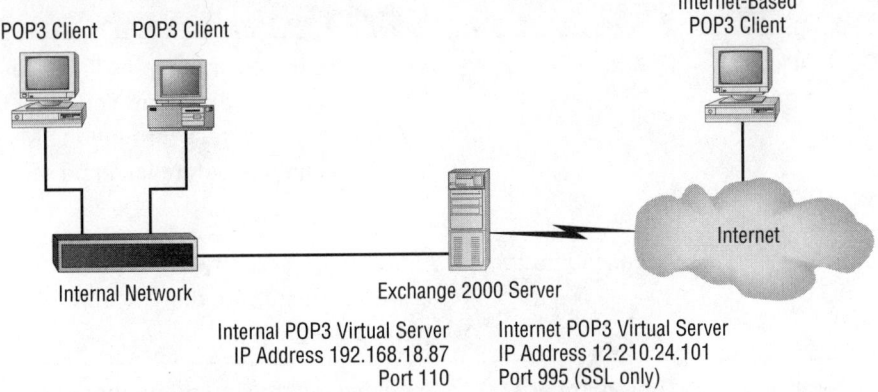

The Microsoft Exchange IMAP4 (IMAP4Svc) and Microsoft Exchange POP3 (POP3Svc) operate as part of the Windows 2000 Internet Information Server (IIS). These services are automatically installed when Exchange 2000 is installed onto Windows 2000.

> **NOTE** For more information on troubleshooting POP3 or IMAP4 client connections, see Chapter 14, "Connectivity" and Chapter 16, "Client Troubleshooting." The POP3 protocol is covered in RFC 1939 with additional discussions in RFCs 1734, 2249, and 2595. The IMAP4 protocol is covered in RFCs 2060 and 2061, and there are other relevant IMAP discussions in RFCs 1731, 2221, 2193, and 2683.

Implementing POP3 and IMAP4 Servers

Before beginning any customization on your POP3 or IMAP4 virtual servers, you should have a good understanding of their configuration options. Further, consider using TLS/SSL when configuring virtual servers that will be accessed by Internet-based users.

Configuring POP3 and IMAP4 Virtual Servers

Configuring POP3 and IMAP4 virtual servers is done through Exchange System Manager; a POP3 or IMAP4 virtual server may need to be configured for each Exchange 2000 server on which you want the specific functionality you are configuring, or you may wish to simply customize the default POP3 or IMAP4 virtual server. Table 15.1 shows the configuration options for POP3 and IMAP4 virtual servers.

Connectivity

PART 4

Table 15.1 POP3 and IMAP4 Virtual Server Configuration Options

Property Page	Option	Description
General	IP Address	Allows you to specify a single IP address or the (All Unassigned) option. You must have assigned an IP address through the My Network Connections before it can be selected in this list.
General	Advanced button	Allows you to specify a group of IP addresses as well as customize the TCP and SSL ports that are used.
General	Limit number of connections	Specifies the maximum number of simultaneous connections to this virtual server. There is no default.
General	Connection timeout	Specifies the time before an inactive client is disconnected. The default is 10 minutes for POP3 virtual servers and 30 minutes for IMAP4 virtual servers. You should not set this value lower than 10 minutes for POP3 or 30 minutes for IMAP4.
General	Include all public folders when a folder list is requested	Sends the entire list of public folders when a client requests the list. This can cause problems for some IMAP4 clients. If this is disabled, only the public folders on the client's home server are listed. This option is only available on IMAP4 virtual servers.
General	Enable fast message retrieval	If checked, the virtual server sends out an estimate of message size (rounded up to the nearest KB) rather than the exact size. Some IMAP4 clients require the exact message size and may not work properly if this is enabled. This option is only available on IMAP4 virtual servers.

Table 15.1 POP3 and IMAP4 Virtual Server Configuration Options *(continued)*

Property Page	Option	Description
Access	Authentication button	Allows you to specify Basic authentication or integrated Windows authentication.
Access	Certificate button	Requests a certificate for use with TLS/SSL. You can request either a certificate immediately from an online authority or send the request to a remote CA.
Access	Communications button	Allows you to specify whether a secure channel is required and whether or not 128-bit encryption is required.
Access	Connection	Allows you to specify which IP addresses, IP networks, or domain names are allowed to access this virtual server. If you specify domain names, the virtual server must perform a reverse name lookup; this can hurt performance. The remote client must also have DNS PTR record.
Message Format	Message encoding - MIME	Converts outbound messages to MIME format. The message body can be provided as plaintext (no formatting codes), HTML (which includes any original formatting codes), or both (which will send a plaintext body as well as an HTML body).
Message Format	Message encoding - UUEncode	Converts the outbound message to a uuencode message and alternatively include BinHex formatting, if the clients retrieving messages through this virtual server are Macintosh clients. This option is only available on POP3 virtual servers.

Connectivity

PART 4

Table 15.1 POP3 and IMAP4 Virtual Server Configuration Options *(continued)*

Property Page	Option	Description
Message Format	Character set	Allows you to select the character set that is used when converting messages sent by Outlook 97 and earlier MAPI clients. If you do not have these clients, you don't need to worry about this option. Exchange 2000 automatically detects the character set used by Outlook 98 and later clients. The default is Western European (ISO-8859-1).
Message Format	Use Exchange rich-text format	Converts outgoing message to Exchange rich-text formatting. Do not use this option if your POP3 or IMAP4 clients all support HTML formatted messages (most modern POP3 and IMAP4 clients do). If you enable this and the clients do not support rich-text formatting, they will get an attachment called `winmail.dat`.
Calendaring	Use recipient's server Use front-end server Front-end server name Use SSL connections	This entire property page allows you to configure how the POP3 or IMAP4 virtual server converts meeting requests. A link to the meeting request is created in the message, and the user can access it through Outlook. You can specify that the URL created points to the recipient's server or a front-end server; you can also specify the name of the front-end server. Further, if you check the Use SSL Connections check box to put an `https` in the URL rather than an `http`.

Here are some other suggestions to keep in mind when implementing POP3 and IMAP4 virtual servers:

- Beware of the Basic authentication option if you're working with public networks. Unless you are also using TLS/SSL, your username and password will be visible to anyone with a network analyzer.
- The integrated Windows authentication option requires a client that supports Windows NT Challenge Response Authentication such as Outlook Express. Without implementing TLS/SSL, event authentication information passed using integrated Windows authentication may be at risk.

Requiring Encryption for POP3 and IMAP4 Clients

I strongly urge you to implement and require encryption on any POP3 or IMAP4 virtual server that is going to have clients connecting to it across a public network, such as the Internet. Unless the clients support Secure Password Authentication (such as Outlook Express), the username and password are transmitted over the network in cleartext.

To require encryption, you must first install a certificate for each virtual server on which you want encryption to be supported. This must be performed on the virtual server's Access property page. Certificates can be installed only at the console of the server on which you are installing the certificate or by connecting remotely using Terminal Services. If the Certificate and Communication buttons are grayed out on the virtual server's Access property tab, then you're not working at the server console.

> **NOTE** The process of installing a certificate is similar for most POP3, IMAP4, NNTP, SMTP, and IIS clients. See Chapter 11, "Security within the Network," for more information on installing certificates. Additional details can be found in the Windows 2000 Server Resource Kit's Microsoft Internet Information Services 5.0 Resource Guide.

To install a new certificate, follow these instructions (keeping in mind that the process has a lot of potential variables):

1. Log on to the console (directly or through Terminal Services) of the Exchange server that has the virtual server on which you want to install a certificate.

2. Using Exchange System Manager, locate the desired virtual server and display its property pages. Display the Access property tab.

3. Click the Certificates button and click Next.

4. Choose the Create New Certificate radio button and click Next.

5. If you have an Enterprise Certificate Authority (a Windows 2000 Certificate server that is visible to Active Directory), you can click the Send The Request Immediately To An Online Certification Authority radio button. Otherwise, click Prepare The Request Now, But Send It Later. This will create a request file that you will have to send to a Certificate Authority (CA). In this case, I am assuming that you have an Enterprise CA, so click Send The Request Immediately To An Online Certification Authority, and then click Next.

Connectivity

PART 4

6. Provide a name for the new certificate. I recommend that you use the same name as the virtual server and that you mention the name of the protocol for which it is being installed. This will make the certificate easier to identify when looking at a list of the installed certificates. Also on this dialog box, you must choose the bit length; 1024 should be sufficient for most cases. Click Next to continue.

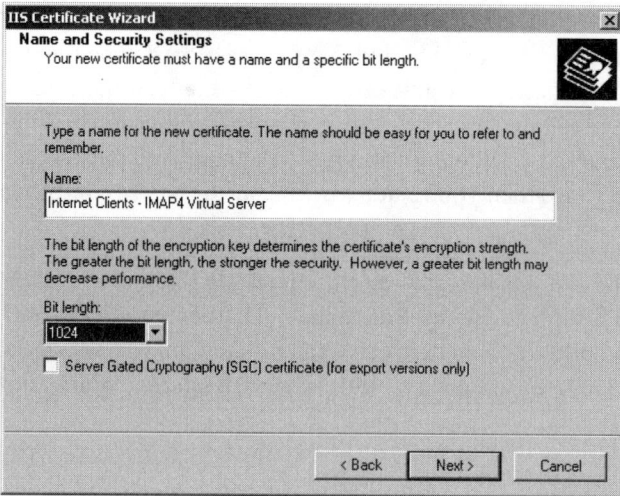

7. Enter the organization (company) name and the organizational unit of your department. If you have previously requested certificates, you can select these from a drop-down list. Click Next to continue.

8. Enter the common name of the server. This name should be the FQDN that the clients use to connect to the server. If this name changes, the certificate should be re-requested with the updated name. If you are using front-end servers, this should be the FQDN name of the front-end server; if you are using load balancing, it should be the name that the clients use. Click Next.

9. Select the country name, state, and city. If you have previously entered city or state names, you can select them through a drop-down list box, or you can enter new ones.

10. Select the name of the CA that will process your request. If you have more than one Enterprise CA in your organization, choose the one that should be issuing certificates for your servers, and then click Next.

11. Review the parameters of your certificate request. Confirm that the common name is correct (Issued To) as well as the CA. Click Next, and then click Finish. If necessary, you can click Back and edit an entry.

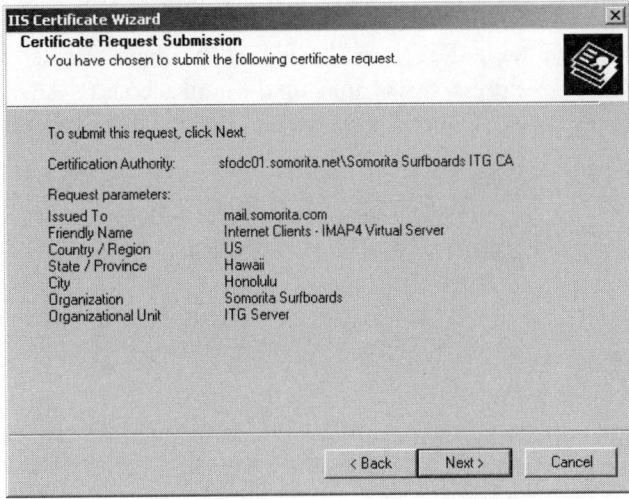

Once this process is completed, clients can request that a secure channel be used to this server. If you want to require the use of SSL/TLS, click the Communication button on the virtual server's Access property tab and click the Require Secure Channel check box (shown in Figure 15.2). If this box is grayed out, then the certificate is not yet installed for this virtual server.

Figure 15.2   Requiring a secure channel

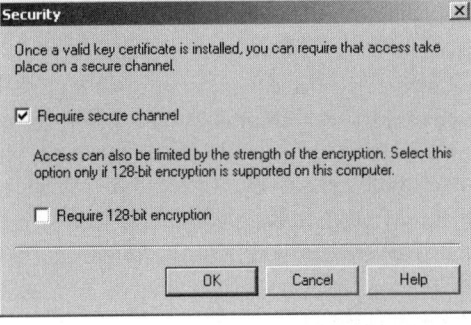

If you check the Require 128-Bit Encryption check box, confirm that the server and all of the clients will support 128-bit encryption. Requiring 128-bit encryption increases the overhead of encryption on the Exchange server, so you may want to consider whether this level of encryption is really necessary in your environment.

Additionally, confirm with all of your clients that they have enabled their clients to support SSL. In Outlook Express, this is done on the mail account's Advanced property tab. You can also specify the SSL port if it is different than the default port (995 for POP3 and 993 for IMAP4).

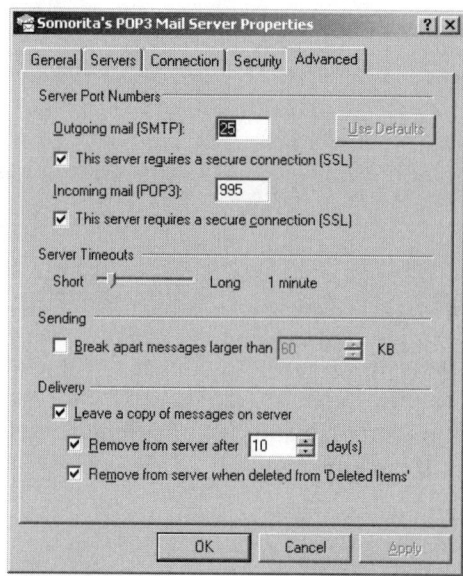

TIP   You can view the currently installed certificates using the Certificates Management console. Certificates used by IIS components are found in the Local Computer certificate store and in the Personal ➢ Certificates folder.

Any certificate you install will have an expiration date associated with it. The default for a certificate issued by the Microsoft Windows 2000 CA is two years from the date of installation. I recommend putting a reminder in your Outlook calendar to notify you a month or two before the expiration to request new certificates before they expire. You can view the certificate expiration dates through the Certificates Management console.

NOTE Alternatives to using TLS/SSL including using IPSec or implementing a vendor-specific VPN solution.

Outlook Web Access

Exchange 2000 Outlook Web Access (OWA) allows users to access their e-mail, calendar, and contacts through a web browser interface. Though this OWA has been supported in all versions of Exchange since Exchange 5, Exchange 2000 has a completely redesigned OWA, and all Exchange 2000 servers automatically support it.

OWA provides a great way for users to access their mailbox and public folders without any special software other than a supported web browser. As a matter of fact, many organizations are moving to supporting much of their user community through OWA. Understanding OWA's limitations and architecture, as well as some ways that you can customize it, will help you to build provide better Web support for your user community.

OWA 2000 Features and Architecture

One of the first things you should understand and convey to your user community is the features that Outlook Web Access supports and, perhaps more important, the ones that it does not support. You have to let people know that OWA is not Outlook, and that they should not expect all or Outlook's really spiffy features.

The following is a list of the major features and capabilities of Outlook Web Access 2000:

- Access to all mailbox folders. Can display e-mail messages, contact items, and appointment items. Public folders that have contact items or calendar items can be viewed.
- Provides a multimedia control for viewing and recording multimedia messages.
- Provides access to mail items using friendly URLs.
- Provides an enhanced interface for Internet Explorer 5 or later, but still supports older web browsers.
- Internet Explorer 5 and later clients support drag and drop between folders in the mailbox, but not between mailbox folders and public folders.
- Provides a Logoff button after Exchange 2000 SP2 or later.
- Supports messages that have embedded items, such as contact items.
- Provides for HTML message formatting.

- Allows users to change their passwords remotely if enabled through IIS. This is not enabled by default.

- Gives new mail notifications and calendar reminders (Exchange 2000 SP2 and later when used with Internet Explorer 5 or later).

- Allows for recovery of deleted items (Exchange 2000 SP1 and later).

- Provides a preview pane and folder views.

- Allows access to the Out of Office Assistant.

- Offers advanced search capabilities (Exchange 2000 SP2 or later).

- Supports Contact Distribution List (Exchange 2000 SP2 or later).

- Supports front-end and back-end configurations.

- Allows restriction of certain features (Exchange 2000 SP2 and later)

NOTE   Exchange 2000 SP2 introduces a number of improvements to the OWA interface including e-mail notifications, calendar reminders, a logoff button, improved calendar printing, and more. To take full advantage of these features, clients should be using Internet Explorer 5.5 SP2 or later.

Understanding what Outlook Web Access *cannot* do is also important, since you need to keep user expectations in check. The following is a list of OWA 2000's limitations:

- Does not display journal items, task items, or sticky notes.

- No offline support.

- Users cannot open up other users' mailbox folders.

- When initially connecting to an OWA server, the browser client will download over 250KB of content, controls, and graphics. This can be very slow for clients connecting to the OWA server through dial-up.

- The envelope icon next to the message list in the Inbox doesn't change when the message is opened, replied to, or forwarded.

- Does not support S/MIME messages, digital signatures, or digital encryption.

- Does not support rules (other than the Out of Office Assistant).

- Cannot browse the address lists.

- Does not support advanced group-scheduling features such as side-by-side displays, appointment list views, track acceptance, tasks lists, or task management.

- Cannot access Exchange 5.5 mailboxes or public folders, only other Exchange 2000 servers.

NOTE A company called Messageware sells an enhancement to Exchange 2000 OWA called Plus Pack. The Plus Pack allows you to perform spell checks, list your contacts when addressing a message, and compress attachments amongst other user-requested features. You can find information about the Plus Pack at www .messageware.com/products/pluspack/pluspack.html.

Rich and Reach Browsers

For a web browser to use OWA, it must support a minimum of HTML 3.2 and JavaScript that is compliant with European Computer Manufacturer Association (ECMA). Browsers later than Internet Explorer 3.02 and Netscape Navigator 4.*x* should work just fine with OWA 2000. Microsoft describes browsers that meet the minimum requirements as *reach browsers* or *down-level clients*; they receive HTML-formatted messages from the OWA server.

Microsoft describes another category of browsers as *rich browsers*. These web browsers support Dynamic HTML (DHTML) and the Extensible Markup Language (XML) to allow the client to support more advanced features. Rich browsers include any browser Internet Explorer 5.*x* or later.

NOTE The user interface for reach browsers looks slightly more basic and has fewer features than rich browsers.

When a browser client connects to a web server, it includes in the HTTP header of the packet a string that identifies the type of web browser the client is using as well as the operating system version. The following is a sample of this string from Internet Explorer 5.5 SP2 running on Windows 2000:

```
User-Agent: Mozilla/4.0 (compatible; MSIE 5.5; Windows NT 5.0)
```

What is Mozilla? Mozilla is Netscape's mascot; Internet Explorer first identifies itself as being compatible with Netscape 4. When the IIS server and OWA components receive this string, they identify the client as a rich browser and know to send it DHTML and XML rather than HTML.

TIP Exchange 2000 SP2 and later allow you to require the clients to use a rich browser. This might be necessary if users encounter a proxy server that does not fully support HTTP 1.1 or HTTP/DAV, and if you want to give users a consistent look and feel and don't want users using down-level browsers.

Connectivity

PART 4

Rich browser clients reduce the processor load on the Exchange 2000 server by allowing it to send DHTML code to the client where the browser client can execute it. An Exchange 2000 OWA server can support more simultaneous rich browser clients than it can reach browser clients. Even though later versions of the Netscape browser supports DHTML, OWA *still* treats the client as a reach browser.

TIP   Your users will have the best results with OWA if you are using Internet Explorer 5.5 SP2 or later.

OWA 2000 Architecture

To fully understand how much more efficient OWA 2000 actually is, you have to appreciate how Exchange 5.5 OWA worked. It used a combination of Active Server Pages (ASP), JavaScript, and Collaborative Data Objects (CDO) to make MAPI function calls to the Exchange information store and directory service. This meant that for each simultaneous OWA 5.5 session, there had to be a MAPI session between the IIS server and the Exchange 5.5 server. This limited the scalability of a single IIS server running OWA to no more than a few hundred OWA clients.

When OWA 2000 was designed, Microsoft's engineers realized that they would have to follow a whole new design paradigm in order to improve the performance and scalability of OWA 2000. Rather than try to improve the existing design, they started over from scratch and used WebDAV rather than standard HTML. WebDAV is a standard set of extensions to HTTP 1.1 that allow additional methods (HTTP commands) for document management, file locking, document property access, folder creation, and more. The new methods included Copy, Mkcol, Propfind, Proppatch, Search, Unlock, Move, and Lock.

NOTE   WebDAV (a.k.a. HTTP-DAV, or just DAV) is described in RFC 2518, and you can find more information at www.webdav.org.

OWA's developers take further advantage of XML and Dynamic HTML to improve performance, offload some rendering tasks to the client, and provide enhanced client features. Where Exchange 5.5 OWA had ASP web pages and JavaScript, Exchange 2000 OWA has a compiled DLL that handles communication between the IIS server and the Exchange server. On a back-end server, this DLL is the DAVEx.DLL; on a front-end server, the EXProx.DLL is responsible for passing requests back to the DAVEx.DLL on the appropriate back-end server. The DAVEx.DLL is responsible for handling all GET and POST requests as well as providing a rendering engine, a template renderer, and a template cache.

Figure 15.3 shows the basics of the Exchange 2000 OWA architecture. Client requests are received by the IIS web server process and are passed to the DAVEx.DLL ISAPI application.

DAVEx then passes the requests through the ExIPC (Exchange Inter-Process Communication) layer to the Exchange information store, where they are handled by the ExOLEDB (Exchange Object Linking and Embedding Database) layer.

Figure 15.3   Exchange 2000 OWA architecture

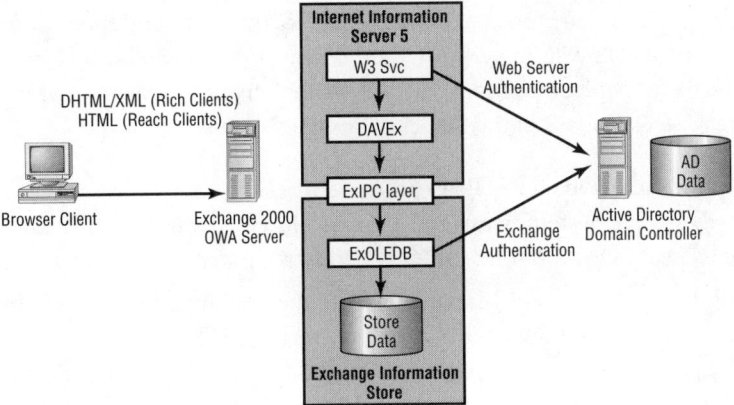

Responses are passed back from the information store to ExOLEDB, then back through the ExIPC layer, and on to DAVEx. DAVEx renders the responses into either DHTML or HTML, depending on the client type, and passes the data back to IIS; then IIS sends the data back to the browser client.

Virtual Directories

By default, when Exchange 2000 is installed, four virtual directories are created on the default website in IIS. Below is an example of the directories that are created on a server whose domain name is somorita.net:

Exchange is mapped to M:\somorita.net\mbx and provides access to mailboxes. This is part of the Exchange Installable File System (ExIFS).

Exchweb is mapped to the \exchsrvr\exchweb directory to provide access to XML style sheets, graphics, language files, and controls.

Public is mapped to the M:\somorita.net\public directory and provides access to the default public folder tree. This access is also provided through ExIFS.

Exadmin is mapped to the \\.\BackOfficeStorage installable file system share and is used by the Exchange System Manager console when managing public folders.

The domain name shown on the M: drive for ExIFS is derived from the default SMTP address in the default policy of the Recipient Policies container. All Exchange 2000 servers in the organization will have the same domain name.

TIP   "Why are their red error signs in IIS on my OWA virtual directories?" When IIS starts, the Exchange information store is not yet started, thus the Exchange, Public, and Exadmin directories are not yet available, and thus IIS marks these virtual directories with little red error signs. While this is not technically a problem, it is annoying. If you stop the default web site, restart it, and then refresh the screen, the errors will go away. If the red error signs really bother you, you can edit the dependencies for the W3Svc in the Registry and make this service depend on the MSExchangeIS in the DependOnService value.

You can create additional HTTP virtual directories for use with Exchange 2000 OWA by using the Exchange System Manager. In the following example, an additional virtual directory is created for a public folder called Surf Spots:

1. Using Exchange System Manager, locate the Exchange server on which the public folder needs to be published. Open that server's HTTP protocol container.

2. Right-click the Exchange virtual server (or other virtual server if others are created) and choose New ➢ Virtual Directory.

3. On the General property page, enter a name for the virtual directory.

4. Click the Public Folder radio button and then click Modify. Browse the public folder hierarchies until you find the folder you want to publish. Highlight that folder and click OK.

5. Click the Access property page and select the Access Control properties and Execute Permissions.

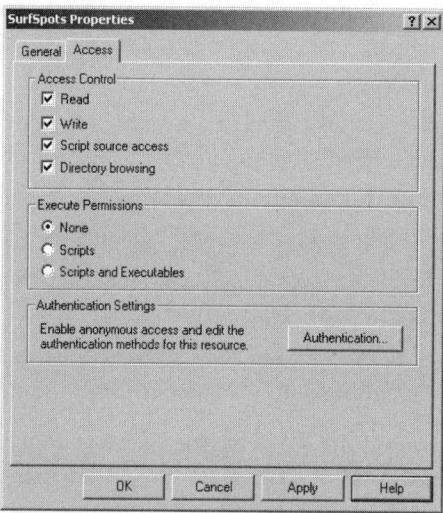

This procedure lets you create a virtual directory that can now be accessed on that server by typing the URL `owa.somorita.net/SurfSpots`. The same method can be used for creating virtual directories to public specific mailboxes, public folders, or additional public folder hierarchies. Here are some additional suggestions and notes relating to creating HTTP virtual servers and virtual directories:

- You can configure a `/public` virtual directory on any new virtual server and point that virtual directory to any point in the public folder hierarchy. This allows users of that virtual server to see only a restricted subset of the public folder tree.

- You can add access to application public folder hierarchies to OWA clients on a particular virtual server by adding a public virtual directory pointing to another public folder tree.

- When creating multiple virtual servers, you may want to set different timeout values for internal and external servers. For example, you may want external virtual servers to timeout clients after 15 minutes, while the internal virtual server times out after 30 minutes.

WARNING Do not attempt to set up multiple virtual servers on a single IP address using host header names. If you configure host header names on the default web site, public folder administration will fail. For Exchange 2000 virtual servers, you should always reserve multiple IP addresses for multiple virtual servers.

Managing OWA Configuration

Just like other IIS services, the virtual server and virtual directory configuration items that are used by OWA are stored in the IIS Metabase. The Exchange System Manager gives you most of the options you need to configure HTTP virtual directory and virtual server information, but certain things will still need to be configured through Internet Services Manager. The problem with this is that if you can also configure those options through Exchange System Manager, the DS2MB process will overwrite any changes you make to the IIS Metabase. The following is a list of configuration changes you must make through Exchange System Manager:

- Creating HTTP virtual servers and virtual directories
- Setting access control settings such as read, write, directory browsing, and script execution controls
- Configuring authentication settings (Anonymous, Basic, and integrated Windows)
- Specifying a path for HTTP virtual directories

The following is a list of common configuration tasks that you will need to configure through Internet Services Manager because the Exchange System Manager does not support configuring these options:

- Enabling Secure Sockets Layer (SSL)
- Enabling HTTP logging
- Changing IP addresses and port numbers
- Setting IP address restrictions, such as blocking access from certain IP addresses
- Specifying connection limits and timeouts

Authentication

The authentication methods that are supported for OWA are configured on each virtual directory. On the Access property page, click the Authentication button to see the Authentication Methods dialog box shown in Figure 15.4.

Figure 15.4   Authentication Methods dialog box

There are three methods of authentication:

- Anonymous access is for use when assigning access to resources to which the anonymous user has been given access, such as to a public folder. You must provide a user account to be used for anonymous access.
- Basic authentication is used for browser clients that do not support NTLM challenge/response authentication and for all Exchange 2000 OWA servers that are running as front-end servers. Passwords are sent over the network as base 64 encoded text, which is easily decoded if captured. See Chapter 11 for more information on password security.

- Integrated Windows authentication is used by Internet Explorer clients that support NTLM challenge/response authentication or by Windows 2000 clients that support Kerberos authentication. Integrated Windows authentication is not supported on front-end servers.

You may notice that under some circumstances you may simply type the URL to your OWA server (such as `owa.somorita.net/exchange`) and be automatically taken to your mailbox. This will happen if integrated Windows authentication is enabled and if you are logged on to your Windows computer in the domain with a username that has a mailbox.

NOTE   Unlike Exchange 5.5 OWA, there is no logon page for Exchange 2000 OWA.

If you wish to log on as someone to access a mailbox other than the one that belongs to the user you are currently logged in as, you can type explicitly the URL to that mailbox, such as `owa.somorita.net/exchange/BrenceJ`.

Any time your users are presented with a login box, they must provide not only their username and password, but also their domain name. You should also caution users about clicking the Save This Password In Your Password List check box, as this presents a potential security problem.

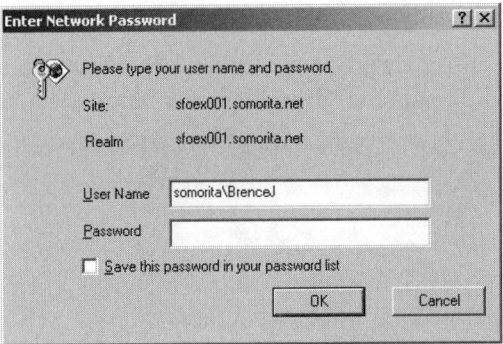

NOTE   For more information about security-related issues and issues with Basic authentication, see Chapter 11. There are also steps in that chapter describing how to enable SSL for a website.

Customizing Outlook Web Access

If you wanted to customize OWA in Exchange 5.5, you had to modify the ASP code that was part of OWA. These scripts no longer exist; their functionality is incorporated into the `DAVEx.DLL` and XML style sheets instead. However, there are still things that you can

Connectivity

PART 4

do to customize OWA for your environment without learning to compile your own DLLs. They include allowing users to change their passwords, changing the default logo, creating and opening messages directly from URLs, and redirecting users to SSL pages.

Changing Passwords

If you click the Options button on the OWA 2000 shortcuts bar and scroll to the bottom of the page, you will see a Change Password button. However, if you click this button, you will get a blank window. That is because this IIS feature is not enabled by default. IIS must be configured to support changing passwords. Follow these steps to enable IIS to support password changes:

1. Configure the default web site to support SSL. This procedure is defined in Chapter 11.

2. Using the Internet Services Manager console, open the default web site.

3. Right-click the default web site and choose New ➤ Virtual Directory, then click Next.

4. In the Alias box, type **IISADMPWD,** then click Next.

5. In the Directory box, enter the path to the password change code. This is located in the `\Winnt\System32\Inetserv\IISADMPWD` directory. Click Next to continue.

6. On the Access Permissions dialog box, take the defaults; the Read and Run Scripts (Such As ASP) check boxes should be checked. Click Next and then click Finish.

7. Right-click the newly created `IISADMPWD` virtual directory and choose Properties.

8. On the Virtual Directory property tab, confirm that the Read button is checked and that the Execute Permissions drop-down list box is set to Scripts Only.

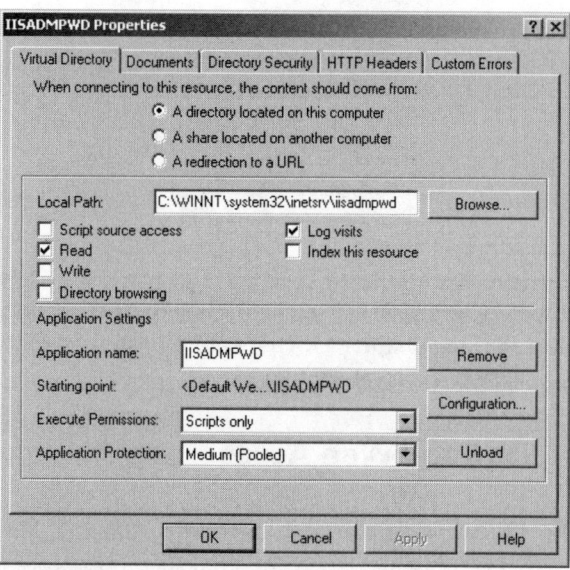

9. Click the Directory Security property tab of the IISADMPWD properties and click the Edit button.

10. Select the Anonymous Access check box. Anonymous access is required or the user will not be able to change their password. Click OK twice to save the changes.

Once this option is enabled, you can change passwords using the Change Password button. The IIS - Authentication Manager dialog box (shown in Figure 15.5) requires the user to enter their domain name, account name, old password, and new password; the currently logged on user information is not passed to this application.

Figure 15.5   Changing a password through IIS

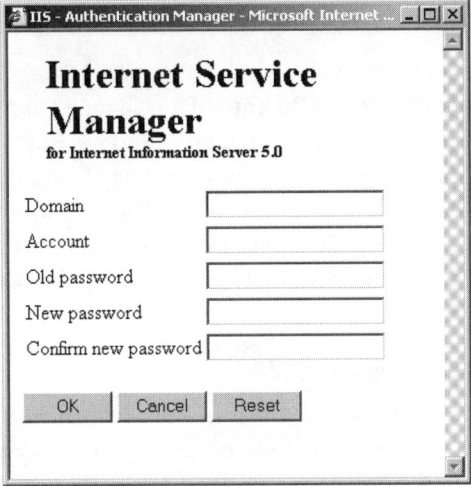

NOTE   See Microsoft Knowledge Base article Q277908 for information about enabling password changes in a clustered environment.

Password Change Latency

If you change your password though IIS, you may notice that you can use either your old password or your new password for up to 15 minutes through Outlook Web Access, but you must use your new password through Outlook. This is a known issue and is designed this way to improve performance. However, you can adjust the interval to decrease the amount of time that IIS keeps the password in cache.

Connectivity

PART 4

Password Change Latency *(continued)*

Using the Registry Editor, add a new value called UserTokenTTL of type REG_DWORD to the key HKLM\SYSTEM\CurrentControlSet\Services\InetInfo\Parameters. This value should be set to the number of seconds that you want IIS to cache the user's credentials. Remember that the value is represented by default in hexadecimal, so don't forget to click the Decimal button. Once applied, this will affect any future users, but the currently logged on users will retain the old value until they log on again. I recommend that you leave this parameter alone unless you have a specific reason to change it. See Microsoft Knowledge Base articles Q152526 and Q267568 for more information.

Removing the Change Password Button   The Change Password button found in the Options box of OWA may just get on your nerves and raise help desk questions from your users. If you are not going to use the password change features, you can remove this button via the Registry, but you must do this on each server. Create a value called DisablePassword in the \HKLM\System\CurrentControlSet\Services\MSExchangeWeb\OWA key. To remove the Change Password button, set this value to 0x1. To display the button, set the value to 0x0, or delete the key.

Restricting Certain Features of OWA

Exchange 2000 SP2 introduces a new feature called *segmentation*, which allows you to disable some of OWA's features, including the Calendar, Contacts, public folders, and Reminders. By default, all of these features are enabled, but you can selectively disable them through the Registry of each OWA server (for all users of that server) or through a user attribute in Active Directory to set the features on a per-user basis.

The features are enabled through a 10-bit mask. For each feature you want to enable, you set the appropriate bit. The following are the 10 bits, their decimal equivalents, and each bit's significance.

Feature	512	256	128	64	32	16	8	4	2	1
Messaging	0	0	0	0	0	0	0	0	0	1
Calendar	0	0	0	0	0	0	0	0	1	1
Contacts	0	0	0	0	0	0	0	1	0	1
Tasks	0	0	0	0	0	0	1	0	0	1

Journal	0	0	0	0	0	1	0	0	0	1
Notes	0	0	0	0	1	0	0	0	0	1
Public folders	0	0	0	1	0	0	0	0	0	1
Calendar reminders	0	0	1	0	0	0	0	0	1	1
E-mail notifications	0	1	0	0	0	0	0	0	0	1
Rich browser UI	1	0	0	0	0	0	0	0	0	1
All	1	1	1	1	1	1	1	1	1	1

In my experience thus far with this feature, the messaging bit (bit 1) must be enabled all the time. Further, I have found that if you don't get the correct number of bits (or the decimal equivalent) into the Registry, you will revert to a reach browser interface, and none of your restrictions will work. Also, you probably noticed that Tasks, Notes, and Journal are included in this list. These features are not supported in OWA as of SP2, but this makes me think that they may be supported in a future release. One of the nice things about restricting the Journal, Tasks, and Notes features is that they don't even show up in the folder list!

To enforce segmenting the OWA features, create a Registry value called DefaultMailbox-FolderSet of type REG_DWORD in the HKLM\System\CurrentControlSet\Services\ MSExchangeWeb\OWA subkey. When you edit the data for this value, set the radio button to Binary and enter the 10-bit binary number that represents your restrictions. Alternatively, if you are good at calculating decimal, you can convert the binary numbers to decimal (or hexadecimal) and enter them that way. Here are a couple of examples of this bit mask:

1000000001 (513 decimal) enables e-mail and allows rich browser clients.

1000000011 (515 decimal) enables e-mail, calendaring, and allows rich browser clients.

1000000101 (517 decimal) enables e-mail, Contacts, and allows rich browser clients.

1001111111 (639 decimal) enables all features except e-mail notifications and calendar reminders.

1110111111 (959 decimal) enables all features except public folders.

NOTE   In order for all of the changes to take effect properly, reboot the Exchange server after making this Registry change.

Segmenting Features Per User Instead of restricting the OWA features for an entire server, you may want to restrict them for only one or two users. This is possible, but doing so may be more trouble than it's worth. You must use ADSIEDIT and manually enter the bit mask for the user attribute ms-Exch-Mailbox-Folder-Set. However, here is the catch: This attribute does not exist with the default Exchange 2000 schema extensions, so you must add the attribute to the Active Directory schema.

There is an LDF file and a script with Exchange 2000 SP2 that will help you do this. These files are found in the \Support\OWASchema directory. To run this script, I recommend that you run them from the domain controller that holds the Schema Master FSMO role; you must be logged in to that machine as a member of both Enterprise Admins as well as Schema Admins.

The script should run very quickly, but it may take 15 minutes or more for this change to replicate to all of your domain controllers. This new attribute *is* flagged as part of the Global Catalog; this will cause your Global Catalog servers to re-replicate from scratch! Of course, your Exchange servers have to be using domain controllers that have had the schema changes replicated to them.

Changing the OWA Logo

The default logo that is shown in the upper left-hand corner of the OWA window directly above the shortcuts is easily changed. This is a nice, easy enhancement to give your users a more familiar feel by adding your company name or logo (as in Figure 15.6).

Figure 15.6 Outlook Web Access with a custom logo

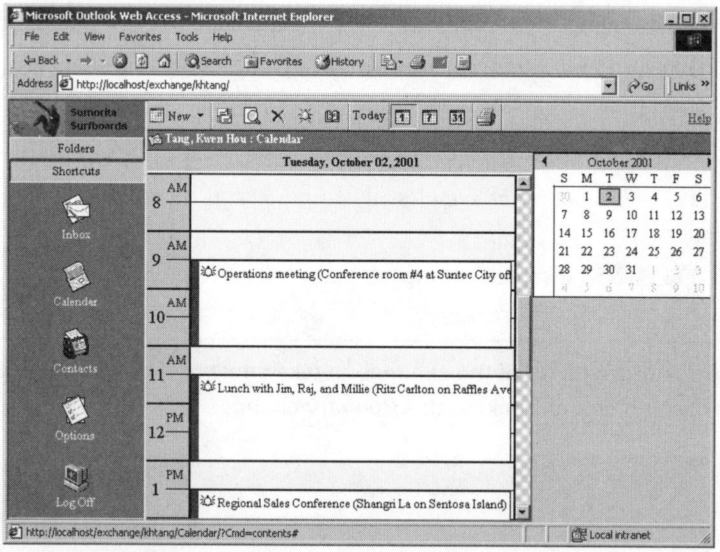

The logo file is located in the \Exchsrvr\Exchweb\Img directory and is called logo-ie5 .gif. You can retrieve this file into Microsoft Paint or some other program that can create GIF files and create your own custom logo; just don't forget to make a backup copy of the file first! The image must not be larger than 148 pixels wide by 38 pixels high.

TIP   Keep a backup copy of this file, because Exchange 2000 service packs will overwrite it.

New Mail and Calendar Reminders

Exchange 2000 SP2 introduced a new feature for rich browser clients that allows the browser to notify the user if new mail arrives or if the user has an appointment reminder. OWA on rich browser clients polls the Exchange server every 15 minutes for new mail. You can change this by creating a Registry key on each OWA server called NewMailNotificationInterval of type REG_DWORD in the subkey HKLM\System\CurrentControlSet\Services\ MSExchangeWeb\OWA. Set this value to the number of minutes that you want the browser to poll the server. Remember that this value defaults to hexadecimal.

When OWA loads on a rich browser client, the browser downloads 24 hours' worth of reminders and then polls the server every 15 minutes for new reminder information. You can change this by creating a value called ReminderPollingInterval of type REG_ DWORD in the subkey HKLM\System\CurrentControlSet\Services\MSExchangeWeb\ OWA. Set this value to the number of minutes you want the browser client to poll for reminders.

Enabling an OWA Logoff Warning

If a user types in a URL and connects to another web page, the session to the OWA server continues to remain open. If that person walks away from the computer without exiting all copies of the web browser, someone else may be able to view that person's mail. The only way to ensure that the session is completely terminated is to close all web browser windows. In Exchange 2000 SP2, there is a Registry key that you can enable that warns the user if OWA detects that you are moving on to another website.

To enable this warning message, in the Registry on the OWA server(s) create a new value called EnableLogoffWarning of type REG_DWORD in the HKLM\System\CurrentControlSet\ Services\MSExchangeWeb\OWA key. Set this value to 0x1 to enable the warning. This feature is not enabled because it may also warn users if they do something as simple as refreshing the screen or closing another browser window.

Connectivity

PART 4

Configuring OWA Inactivity Timeouts

If you have a lot of users who access OWA through a shared kiosk or Internet cafés and the like, you may want to lower the client timeout to reduce the likelihood that someone else can view their mail. Even through we warn our users to close the browser window when they are finished with their mail, they don't always do so. To set a timeout limit, this must be done on each OWA server through the Registry. Create a value called UserContextTimeout of type REG_DWORD in the HKLM\System\CurrentControlSet\ Services\MSExchangeWeb\OWA subkey. Set this value to the number of minutes a user can be inactive before their session times out. If you have a lot of users accessing through kiosks and public-access computers, I recommend setting this value to no more than 10 minutes. If the session does timeout, the user must provide their username and password to continue working.

Forcing Standard HTML Clients

In some circumstances, you may need to force all clients to use the standard HTTP interface, even rich clients. You can force the clients to all be down-level clients through the Registry on each OWA server. Create a value called ForceClientsDownLevel of type REG_DWORD in the HKLM\System\CurrentControlSet\Services\MSExchangeWeb\ OWA subkey. Set this value to 0x1 to enable this functionality or 0x0 to disable forcing clients to be down-level clients. Keep in mind that your user community may not be happy with the loss of functionality that the reach browser interface gives them.

Disabling the OWA Multimedia Control

By default, all clients have the option on the Options screen to download the multimedia control. You may want to disable this control for several reasons, e.g., it may not work on all platforms (such as Unix), or you may not want OWA users sending multimedia messages. To disable the option to download this control, you must edit the Registry of each of the OWA servers. Create a value called DisableMultimedia of type REG_DWORD in the HKLM\System\CurrentControlSet\Services\MSExchangeWeb\OWA subkey. Set this value to 0x1 to disable the ability to download this control.

Manipulating OWA through URLs

Exchange 2000 OWA supports URLs that are easier to remember and use than those that were supported in Exchange 5.5. Exchange 5.5 included a 92-character globally unique identifier (GUID) to uniquely identify the path to a message or folder. OWA 2000 uses the IIS virtual directory and the Exchange folder names.

If you want to open a specific public folder called Exchange 2000, you could type **owa.somorita.net/public/technical/Exchange 2000**. This will automatically open up this folder in the browser window. However, you may note that in the browser's Address box, the URL will appear as `owa.somorita.net/public/technical/Exchange%202000`. The %20 is inserted automatically where the space was because URLs cannot contain a space. You can also open up a message if you know the message subject. For example, if user KHTang knows that there is a message in his Inbox folder called Regional Sales Report, he can enter the following address:

`owa.somorita.net/exchange/khtang/inbox/regional sales report.eml`

The window shown in Figure 15.7 appears.

Figure 15.7   Explicitly entering the path to a message

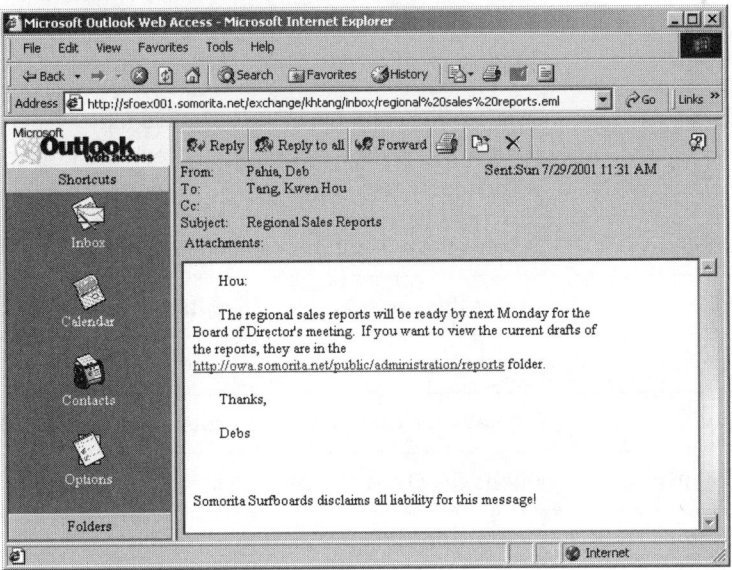

If there were two occurrences of a message whose subject was Regional Sales Report, he would have to enter a -2 on the end of the subject, such as `Regional Sales Report-2 .eml`, if he wanted to open up the second occurrence of the message.

In addition to being able to open messages and folders by entering the correct URL, if you know the syntax, you can create messages, contacts, calendar entries, and public folder postings directly from the browser's Address box. For example, if the user wanted to reply to the above message, she could type **owa.somorita.net/exchange/khtang/inbox/ regional sales report.eml?cmd=reply**. The URL will automatically change from the Inbox folder to the Draft folder; this is normal. If the user wanted to create a new calendar entry, he could type **owa.somorita.net/exchange/khtang/calendar/?cmd=new**.

While most of your user community is not going to switch over to using friendly URLs to open and create message items in OWA, these may be useful for you when creating shortcuts. Table 15.2 shows a list of some of the commands and options you can use for creating custom URLs for OWA. Each of the commands and options in Table 15.2 must be preceded by the appropriate message or folder URL.

Table 15.2 Modifying Outlook Web Access URLs

Suffix	Description
Cmd=New	Creates a new message, contact, appointment, or public folder posting. This option can be used with the Type option to specify the type of item to create (e.g., ?Cmd=New?Type=Message).
Cmd=Contents	Displays the contents of the specified folder. This option can be used with the Page option to display additional pages. (e.g., ?Cmd=contents&Page=2).
Cmd=Delete	Deletes the current or specified item.
Cmd=Edit	Opens the current or specified item in Edit mode.
Cmd=Forward	Forwards the current or specified message.
Cmd=Navbar	Displays the only OWA shortcuts (navigation bar).
Cmd=Options	Opens the OWA options page.
Cmd=Open	Opens a specified item or message.
Cmd=Reply	Replies to sender of the current or selected message.
Cmd=ReplyAll	Replies to all recipients of the current or selected message.
Page=x	Displays the page number of the specified folder.
Sort=x	Species the column name by which you want to sort (e.g., Sort=Subject).
Type=Appointment	Specifies that the type of message you are creating is a calendar item.

Table 15.2 Modifying Outlook Web Access URLs *(continued)*

Suffix	Description
Type=Message	Specifies that the type of message you are creating is an e-mail message item.
Type=Post	Specifies that the type of message you are creating is a public folder posting.

The Type= option will be constrained based on the type of folder in which you are creating an item. For example, you cannot create an appointment in the Inbox folder.

Redirecting to SSL Pages

Throughout this book, I have strongly urged you to use SSL for Internet protocol clients such as OWA. However, it is hard to convince your user community to use HTTPS rather than HTTP when typing in a URL into their OWA server. Yet with a little ingenuity, you can help them along by redirecting them to the secure site. This is especially important if they have already added the non-secure site to the browser's Favorites list.

One of the things that I like to do is to set a DNS alias (a CNAME record) for the OWA server (such as owa.somorita.net) rather than having the user use owa.somorita.net/exchange. This makes it a little easier for users to remember the OWA page. If you are enabling SSL, you must use owa.omorita.net as the common name for the certificate.

There are a couple of approaches to redirecting users. If the virtual server has been set to require security (on the Directory Security property page and behind the Secure Communications Edit button), then when users connect to a non-secure page on that server, they will get the 403.4 - Forbidden: SSL Required web page. This page is nothing more than an HTML file (\Winnt\Help\Iishelp\Common\403-4.htm).

You can either edit this file (or create your own) so that it will direct the user automatically to the correct site. For example, I will create a file in the \Winnt\Help\Iishelp\Common directory called redirect.htm that has the following contents:

```
<html><head>
<meta http-equiv="refresh" content="0";url=https://owa.somorita.com/exchange">
</head></html>
```

Then I have to edit the 403.4 error found on the website's Custom Errors property tab to point it to my custom file. This method works most of the time, but it is slower (since the client has to connect to one page and then to another) and it is not always reliable with older browser clients.

Another method you can use (which may be more reliable and faster) is to create an additional site that redirects the user through the server. First, you need to change the non-secure port of the default website from 80 to something like 8080, and you will probably want to require SSL on that site. Next, you need to create a new virtual server that uses port 80; you can blank out the SSL port because this virtual server does not require SSL security. On the Home Directory property tab of the new virtual server (shown in Figure 15.8), click the A Redirection To A URL button. Enter the path to the original web server including the HTTPS, and click the The Exact URL Entered Above and A Directory Below This One check boxes.

Figure 15.8   Home Directory property page of the Redirect Virtual Web Server

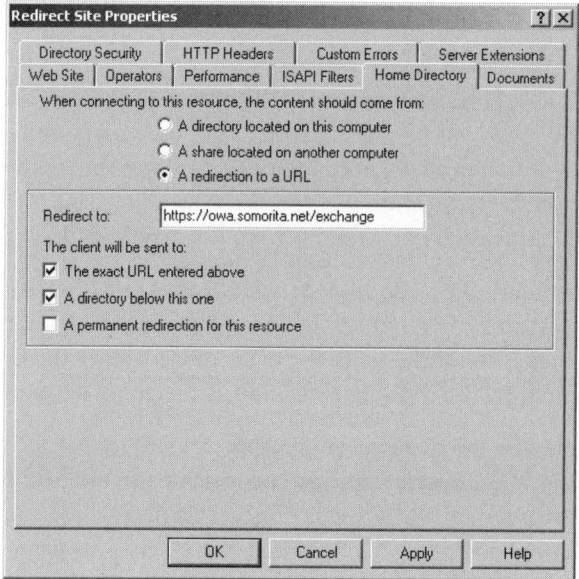

Successfully Deploying OWA 2000

Outlook Web Access 2000 is a powerful part of Exchange 2000, and it can make your users' lives much easier when they need to access their mailboxes from locations other than their own desktop. Many organizations are moving more of their user communities toward stateless clients because maintaining Outlook or Outlook Express configurations for users who roam to many machines is difficult. OWA will be the tool that these organizations use to give their users the functionality they need without increasing the complexity of the client.

Below are some recommendations for successfully deploying Outlook Web Access:

- Set user expectations for the available features.

- Implement and require SSL. Redirect users who connect to the cleartext web page to a secure web page.

- Encourage users to empty their Deleted Items folders often, since OWA does not automatically purge the Deleted Items folder.

- This may sound like my Borg implants are working properly, but I have the best results with later versions of Internet Explorer. IE service packs and updates seem to mysteriously fix weird problems.

- Document and make backup copies of any customizations that you make (such as modifying OWA XML style sheets or customized graphics); these may be overwritten during a service pack installations.

- If you have more than a few hundred simultaneous users, move to a front-end/back-end architecture.

- Advise your dial-in and low-speed connection users that OWA will be slow when initially loading.

- Make changes to web services through Internet Services Manager *only* if the option to configure these changes is not available through Exchange System Manager. Otherwise, the DS2MB process will overwrite them.

Front-End and Back-End Servers

Microsoft introduced the front-end and back-end server architecture to provide additional scalability for your organization. A *front-end server* runs Exchange 2000, but does not host mailboxes or public folders. It accepts requests from Internet clients (POP3, IMAP4, and HTTP clients), performs an Active Directory lookup to find the back-end server that hosts the resource, and passes the request on to the back-end server. The *back-end server* is the Exchange 2000 server that hosts mailboxes and public folders. So in essence, the front-end server is acting like a protocol handler. The clients of a front-end server *never* communicate directly with the back-end servers.

> **NOTE**   MAPI clients always communicate directly with their home mailbox servers. MAPI clients are not "front-endable."

The front-end/back-end architecture is much like the architecture of the web-based mail systems like Yahoo and Hotmail; you connect to one server, but your requests are passed to the back end where the data really resides. This architecture assumes that if you have designated a front-end server, then at least one back-end server exists.

Front-end servers are not for every organization; the following are some reasons why an organization might want to deploy front-end servers:

- You want to offload the overhead of SSL from the back-end servers. SSL causes a server to incur 15% or more additional overhead, depending on the key length. In an environment where SSL is heavily used, consider using SSL co-processing NICs.

- You want to direct all of your Internet clients to a single namespace when they front-end access servers. All clients can be pointed to a single FQDN rather than each user having to know the name of their own home server. If you are using a load balancing service, you can even use a single FQDN to point to more than one front-end server.

- You need to put servers in the perimeter network (DMZ) or outside the firewall (shudder!), but you do not want those servers to have mailboxes on them. Exchange 2000 SP2 servers eliminate the need for RPCs between the front-end servers and the Active Directory domain controllers, so this will make the practice of putting servers in the DMZ more acceptable.

- You have IMAP4 clients that need to access public folders that are not on their own mailbox servers. The front-end server will perform referrals to the appropriate back-end server that contains the public folder content.

Figure 15.9 shows a common use for Exchange 2000 front-end servers. In this configuration, there are three front-end servers in the perimeter network. Each of these servers accepts requests from the Internet for HTTP, POP3, and IMAP4 clients. SSL is required on each of the front-end servers, so the clients must be configured to use SSL. Windows Load Balancing (WLB) is implemented on the front-end servers so that the load is properly balanced and so that a single FQDN can be used to unify the namespace.

Figure 15.9   Front-end/back-end configuration

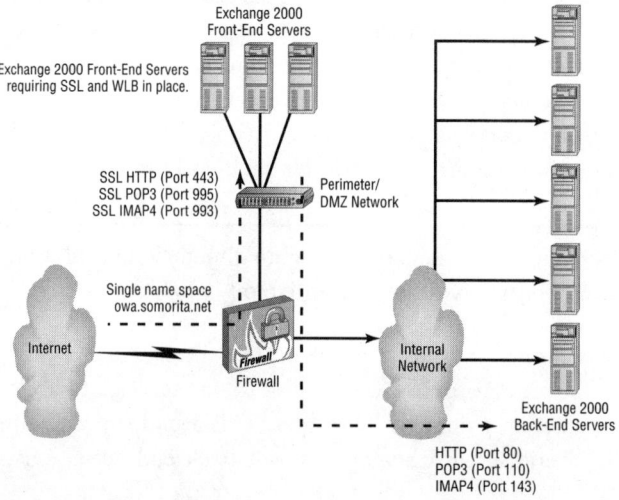

The front-end servers accept the requests from the clients, query Active Directory to determine the appropriate back-end servers, and then pass the request to the appropriate back-end servers. All communication between the front-end and back-end servers takes place over standard ports, not SSL ports. Client authentication between the front-end and the back-end server is handled via cleartext, not integrated Windows authentication.

NOTE   If you configure additional virtual servers on the front-end servers, you must configure identical virtual servers on all back-end servers.

Configuring a Front-End Server

In a default Exchange 2000 configuration, all Exchange 2000 servers are back-end servers. Switching a back-end server to a front-end server is simple; there is only a single check box (This Is A Front-End Server) and a reboot required to switch the server's role. The check box is on the server's General property page (shown in Figure 15.10). Before switching the roles, make sure you have moved all mailboxes off of this server. These mailboxes will not be accessible once the server is in a front-end role, but you can easily switch the server back if you accidentally left a mailbox on a front-end server.

Figure 15.10   Switching to a front-end server role

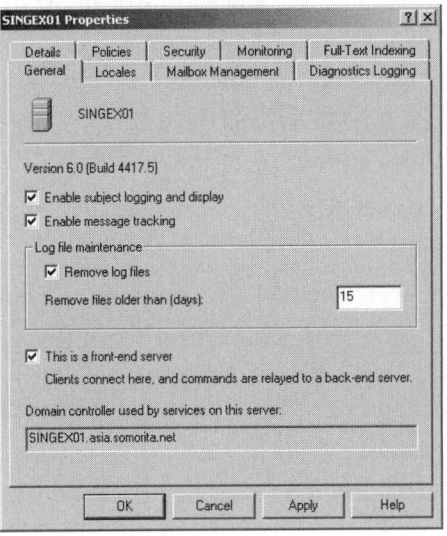

After the server has rebooted, there are a couple of additional things you need to do so that the server operates efficiently:

- Configure any SMTP, POP3, IMAP4, or HTTP virtual servers so that they match the virtual servers on the back-end servers.

- Configure each of the virtual servers with certificates so that they can use SSL. If you have configured additional HTTP virtual directories on any of the back-end servers, make sure you have configured those on the front-end servers as well. Make any SSL configuration changes necessary.

- Unless required, remove Instant Messaging, Chat services, and any mail connectors (Microsoft Mail, Lotus Notes, etc.).

- Remove any application public folder stores from the server.

- Unless you are supporting SMTP or X.400 Connectors, stop and disable the following services:

  - Microsoft Exchange Routing Engine

  - Microsoft Exchange MTA Stacks

  - Simple Mail Transport Protocol (SMTP)

  - Network News Transport Protocol (NNTP)

NOTE If you are planning to use the front-end server as an SMTP relay or inbound SMTP server, both the SMTP and Microsoft Exchange Information Store services must remain running.

- If you are supporting only HTTP clients through the front-end servers, stop and disable the following services:

  - Microsoft Exchange Information Store

  - Microsoft Exchange MTA Stacks

  - Microsoft Exchange IMAP4

  - Microsoft Exchange POP3

  - Microsoft Search

- If you are supporting POP3 or IMAP4 clients, the following services must be running:

  - Microsoft Exchange Information Store (Technically, since there are no local clients, this service does not need to operate, but POP3 and IMAP4 services depend on the information store. This dependency can be changed through the Registry.)

  - Microsoft Exchange IMAP4

  - Microsoft Exchange POP3

NOTE Microsoft has published a white paper on the use of front-end and back-end servers called "Exchange 2000 Front-end and Back-end Topology," which provides good supplemental material for this chapter. Find it on the Web at www.microsoft .com/exchange/techinfo/deployment/2000/E2KFrontBack.asp.

When a back-end server is shut down or rebooted, front-end servers will mark that server as unavailable for up to 10 minutes and will redirect requests to other back-end servers (in the case of public folders). The server may remain unavailable for up to 10 minutes even though it has been brought back online.

Instant Messaging

Instant Messaging (IM) allows you to send and receive messages that do not require an immediate response, but might be more urgent than a telephone call. I like to say that IM is somewhere between an e-mail and online chat or a phone call. While this concept is popular in the business world today, it is not terribly relevant to what most of us do. However, as more people (your customers and clients) are IM enabled, this technology will become more pervasive.

IM also allows users to view information about the users who are on their contact list, indicating if a person is online, out to lunch, out of the office, not receiving calls, etc. The value of this type of "status" information becomes apparent as workflow types of applications are developed that can take advantage of it. For example, an employee could submit a purchase order. Depending on the amount of the purchase order or the items being requested, the workflow process would determine which managers have the authority to approve such a request and route the request to the manager who is currently online.

Microsoft acquired its Instant Messaging technology from a company called Flash; an interesting note is that company's slogan was "Business at the speed of thought." This slogan (also the title of Bill Gates' last book) draws an interesting parallel to the capabilities of IM. AOL reported in 2000 that they were delivering over 750,000,000 instant messages per day, so the potential for business Instant Messaging is substantial.

> **NOTE** Currently, there is an Instant Messaging working group within the IETF working on a protocol called IMPP (Instant Messaging and Presence Protocol), which includes representatives from Microsoft, Lotus, AT&T, and Fujitsu.

How Instant Messaging Works

The Exchange 2000 Instant Messaging server and the Exchange clients for Instant Messaging use HTTP (port 80) to communicate. They rely on a combination of components to relay status information and to pass information between IM clients. The IM communication consists of XML data and WebDAV methods. The protocol that the IM clients speak is called RVP (Rendezvous Vector Protocol).

> **WARNING** All communication between IM clients and the IM servers is in cleartext. Currently, there is no option for providing encryption.

Connectivity

PART 4

The MSN Messenger Service is the client provided by Microsoft that allows you to use Exchange 2000 Instant Messaging Services. You must explicitly use the client provided for Exchange, not the version of the MSN Messenger client that you can download from MSN. However, if you install the MSN Messenger client 3.5 provided with Exchange first, you can then upgrade to the later releases of the client software that are available through MSN and still retain the Exchange features.

On the server side, there are two types of Instant Messaging servers: IM routers and IM home servers. An *IM router* can be thought of as a front-end server for Instant Messaging; it can even run on the same machine as a front-end server. Microsoft estimates that a single, dedicated IM router can handle between 30,000 and 50,000 IM users.

The *IM home server* has a database (the node database) that has information about the user presence information and the user's contacts for each user who uses that server as a home server. A single, dedicated IM home server can support up to 10,000 IM users. The IM home server's database is stored in the \Exchsrvr\Imdata directory in a file called msimnode.edb. Don't forget to back up this database; it is not backed up during an online backup. To back up this file, you must stop the World Wide Web Publishing Service and back up the directory; don't forget to restart the web server when finished.

> **NOTE** The core Exchange 2000 services are not necessary on an IM router or home server.

For most organizations, a single IM home server will probably be sufficient. For organizations with only a few hundred or a few thousand users, the IM server can be one of the more lightly loaded mailbox or public folder servers. I recommend that you consider dedicating a server to IM functions if your total user count rises about 3500 to 4000. Figure 15.11 shows a typical organization that is using both IM home servers and routers

Figure 15.11 Instant Messaging architecture and client operations

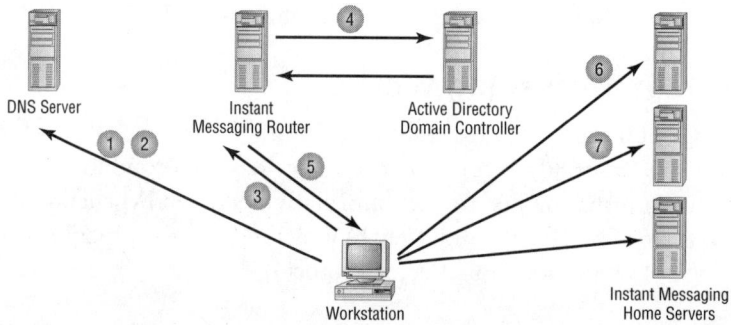

Here are the steps that the IM client goes through to log on and get a list of its contacts' status information (this is illustrated in Figure 15.11):

1. User SuriyaS logs in with his IM address SuriyaS@im.somorita.net. If the IM client is running on a Windows 2000 client, the client does an SRV (Service Location) lookup for _RVP records for the im.somorita.net domain.

2. If the client is not a Windows 2000 client, or if there are no _RVP Service Location records, the client performs an A record lookup for im.somorita.net.

3. The client contacts its IM router server and provides its IM address.

4. The IM router queries Active Directory to determine which IM server is this user's home server. The URL of the user's IM router is returned to the IM router.

5. The IM router returns the user's home server URL to the client.

6. The IM client contacts its home server.

7. The IM home server authenticates the user with an Active Directory domain controller.

8. Once authenticated, the client queries its contacts' IM home servers to determine their current status.

Instant Messaging Name Space

One of the first decisions you will have to make before you deploy Instant Messaging is whether you want the IM address to be the same as the user's e-mail address. This would be simple except for the small fact that in order to match your e-mail domain name with your IM address, you must do one of the following:

- Create RVP SRV records for your domain in DNS, or
- Create an A record for your domain name that points to an IM router.

The problem with creating SRV records is that only Windows 2000 and XP clients use SRV records. The problem with creating A records for the domain name is that often companies are already pointing that to their web server.

So, unless you are a in pure Windows 2000 environment, I recommend creating a child domain called IM, such as im.somorita.net. In that child domain, create an RVP SRV record for each of the IM routers. Then create an A record in the parent domain (somorita.net in my example) that points to one of the IM routers. Figure 15.12 shows an SRV record for the RVP protocol. The service type _RVP is not listed in the Service drop-down list box, but you can enter it manually. The port number is 80.

Figure 15.12 Creating an _RVP SRV record

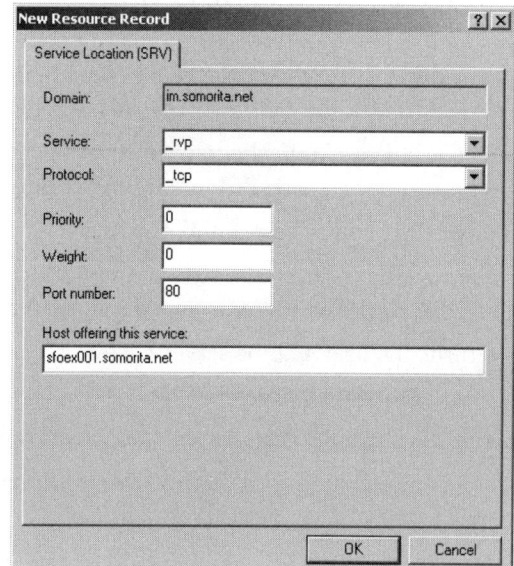

If you are not using an IM router, you may have only one IM home server. If that is the case, then the RVP SRV record would point directly to the IM home server.

> **NOTE** The user interface on the MSN Messenger client is often confusing and will sometimes ask for the e-mail address when it really means the IM address. Users must be trained to know this if their IM address is different from their e-mail address.

Configuring Instant Messaging

To configure Instant Messaging servers, first install the Microsoft Exchange Instant Messaging Service using Exchange 2000 Setup. The Exchange 2000 core components are not required on an IM server (home server or router server). Once the Instant Messaging Service is installed on the machine, you can begin creating Instant Messaging virtual servers on each of the servers on which you installed the IM service. These virtual servers are created in the Instant Messaging (RVP) container under the Protocols container. You can create more than one IM virtual server on each server, but each IM virtual server must use a different HTTP virtual server.

Following is an example of how to create an IM virtual server for the somorita.net organization:

1. Using Exchange System Manager, locate the Instant Messaging (RVP) container. Right-click it and choose New ➢ Instant Messaging virtual server, then click Next.

2. Enter a display name that will be easy to use, then click Next. I include in the name of the virtual server, whether it is an IM home server or an IM router server.

3. Select the IIS website on which this IM virtual server will reside (this is usually the default website), then click Next.

4. Enter the DNS domain name with which the server will be identified through DNS. If this is the only IM home server or the only IM router server, it should identify the IM domain, such as im.somorita.net. Then click Next.

5. If this server is an IM home server, click the Allow This Server To Host User Accounts check box. If it is an IM router server, leave this check box cleared. Click Next, and then click Finish.

Now that the IM virtual server is created, you are ready to enable clients. You must enable each user account that you want to be able to use Instant Messaging. To enable a user, follow these steps:

1. Using Active Directory Users And Computers, locate the user account that you wish to enable.

2. Right-click the user account and choose Exchange Tasks.

3. Choose Enable Instant Messaging and click Next.

4. Click the browse button to select the IM home server. Confirm that the correct instant messaging domain is selected in the Instant Messaging Domain Name field. This will be the address that is used to create the IM addresses. Click Next, and then click Finish.

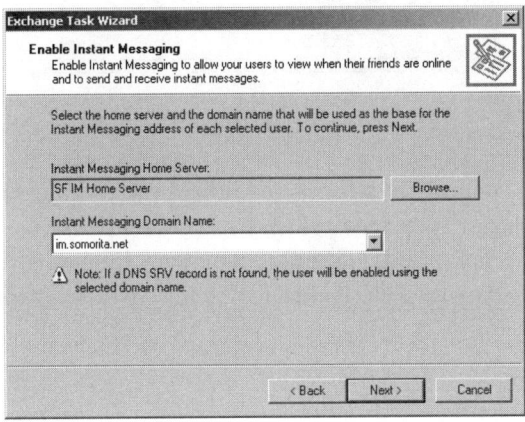

One of the most common problems with IM is that users and administrators don't always know which server is the user's IM home or IM router server. You can display and confirm this information by selecting the user's properties in Active Directory Users And Computers. On the Exchange Features property tab, highlight Instant Messaging and click the Properties button. From the Instant Messaging dialog box (shown in Figure 15.13), you can see the Instant Messaging User Address (`rtyau@im.somorita.net`), the Instant Message URL Address (also known as the IM router; `http://sfoex001.somorita.net/instmsg/aliaes/rtyau`), and the Instant Messaging Home Server URL Address (`http://sfoex001.somorita.net/instmsg/aliaes/rtyau`). In an organization with only one IM server, the IM home server and the IM router will be the same.

From the user's Instant Messaging properties, you can also select the Privacy property page, which allows the administrator to specify a list of IM users and/or IM servers that can communicate with this particular client.

NOTE   More information on troubleshooting IM connectivity can be found in Chapter 16.

Figure 15.13 Instant Messaging user properties

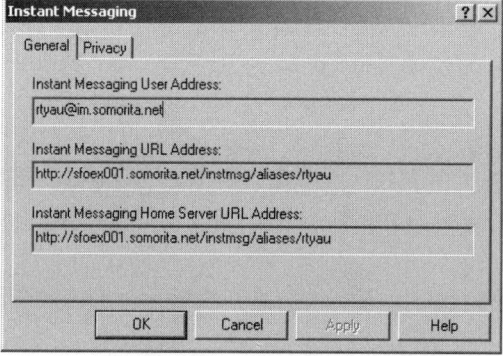

Authentication

Instant Messaging supports two forms of authentication: integrated Windows and Digest. Digest authentication requires that you configure Active Directory to store passwords in reversible encryption; I do not recommend doing this. These forms of authentication are configured on the HTTP virtual directory, which is configurable using Internet Services Manager.

Instant Messaging and Firewalls

When a client makes a connection to an IM router, the IM router returns topology information about the network based on the client's IP address. The IM router has to have a way to know which IP addresses are internal to the network and which are external. This is handled through the Firewall Topology module. Depending on the client's IP address, the following information will be returned to the IM client:

- If the IM client's IP address is inside of the network (behind the firewall), the IM router will return the home server URL of the IM client.

- If the IM client's IP address is outside of the network, the IM router returns the IM domain URL, and thus clients outside the firewall can communicate only with the firewall, and the IM router proxies requests to the IM home server.

To define the IP addresses on the inside of the network, you need to modify the Instant Messaging Settings found under the Global Settings container in Exchange System Manager. From the Instant Messaging settings Firewall Topology property tab (shown in Figure 15.14), you can enter the IP addresses of the internal networks. If outgoing communications should go through an HTTP proxy server, you can also specify the IP address and port number of the HTTP proxy.

Figure 15.14 Configuring the Firewall Topology module

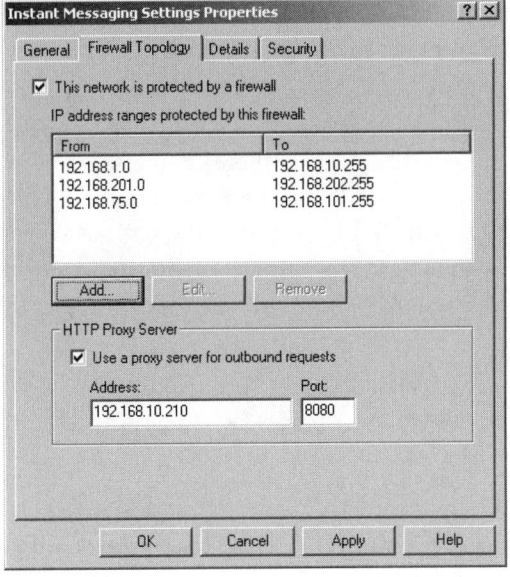

Instant Messaging Client Tuning

Provided you have the MSN Messenger Service client 3.5 or later, there are a number of tuning enhancements you can make to the client to make it slightly more customized to your environment. Appendix A, "Registry Settings," contains a list of Registry settings that affect the IM client but these must be configured at the client, not the IM servers. (Appendix A can be found on the Sybex website, www.sybex.com.) Some of these Registry settings include the ability to configure the client to support polling to receive messages.

Prior to Exchange 2000 SP1, IM clients could not connect to a remote IM server if that client was behind a firewall or proxy server. The IM home server was responsible for initiating a connection to the IM client and sending status change information. This has been updated to provide more flexible methods of communication between the client and the server.

There are three ways that an MSN Messenger Service client and Exchange 2000 SP1 home server can get IM information between the client and the server:

- In the *dynamic* method, the IM client logs on to the home server and gives the server its IP address and the current port number; once this information is registered, the client drops the TCP session. When the server needs to contact the client, it connects to the server via the previously registered IP address and TCP port. This is the default method, but it may not work through firewalls if the firewall is blocking ports above 1024.

- The *fixed port* method is almost the same as the dynamic method, but the server specifies the port number to a value specified in the Registry at the client. The server must also be enabled to support fixed port.

- In the *polling* method, the IM client is configured to poll the IM home server every 10 minutes (configurable) to see if there are messages waiting. The client logs on to the IM home server and sends a POLL request to the IM home server. The client will periodically resend the POLL request to the server to make sure the TCP session remains open. As long as the TCP session is currently open, the IM server can send updates to the client.

Polling support must be enabled through the client and on the server. To enable the polling support on the server, create a new Registry key called PollSupport of type REG_DWORD in HKLM\Software\Microsoft\Exchange\InstantMessaging and configure a value of 1.

To configure polling support on the client, create a new Registry key called Connection Method of type REG_DWORD in HKCU\Software\Microsoft\Exchange\Messenger\Profiles and set this value to 1.

> **NOTE** If you are interested in developing applications that use the IM technologies, there is an IM SDK on the MSDN website at msdn.microsoft.com/exchange.

Estimated Bandwidth Usage   Estimating the amount of bandwidth that IM will consume on your network will depend on a lot of things, including the number of concurrent sessions, the number of contacts each user has, how often they send messages, and if the users are using IM for file transfer.

Microsoft's ITG (Information Technology Group) did some testing during the development of Instant Messaging, and they estimate that IM traffic increased about 12Kbps for each 1000 simultaneous users on a server. This can change dramatically if you implement polling instead of allowing the server to notify the user of new messages.

User Contact Information   The MSN Messenger Service client stores the user's contact information in the local Registry. The contact information is known as a subscription. The Registry key that this information is stored in is HKCU\Software\Microsoft\ Exchange\messenger\profiles\http://im.Somorita.net/instmsg/aliases/Rtyau/ Contacts. Note that the last part of this Registry key is the URL path to the user's IM home server (in this example, user RTyau's home server is im.somorita.net).

> **NOTE** There is a tool on the Exchange 2000 Resource Kit called IM SuperMan that allows users to browse the global address list to add contacts to their contacts list.

Common IM Problems

Problems and Instant Messaging: Those two things certainly tend to go hand in hand. Here is a list of possible problems and things to watch out for with IM:

- The default website that the InstMsg virtual directory creates must be listening on port 80 and must not require SSL.
- Incorrect settings on the Firewall Topology module, or the outgoing HTTP proxy is not configured correctly.
- Make sure that the World Wide Web Publishing Service is started and that the website to which the IM server is running.
- Confirm that the user is using the correct IM address and that the address is correctly resolving to an IM router or the IM home server.

Connectivity

PART 4

- If you are using an _RVP SRV record, confirm that the client can resolve the record by using NSLOOKUP. For example, you can confirm that the record exists by typing **nslookup -q=SRV _rvp._tcp.somorita.net.**

- The MSN Messenger Service client uses the Internet Explorer proxy settings, so make sure that Internet Explorer is configured to bypass local addresses if you have internal IM servers.

NOTE For more information on Instant Messaging and troubleshooting, see Knowledge Base articles Q298421 and Q278974.

Part 5

Troubleshooting

Topics Covered:

- Common Problems and Where to Begin Troubleshooting
- Client Connectivity Problems
- Garbled Messages
- Understanding Non-Delivery Reports
- Troubleshooting MAPI Clients
- Troubleshooting Internet Clients
- Setting Up Internet Client Protocol Logs
- Using Network Monitor
- Remote Procedure Calls and Network Monitor
- Best Practices For Client Troubleshooting
- Solving Problems with Active Directory
- Problems with Exchange Services
- Problems with Message Flow and Stalled Messages

16

Client Troubleshooting

If I had my choice, I would probably hide in the computer room and never show my face near the end users' desks. I have found that network systems operate much more efficiently if there are no end users. Unfortunately I have not found anyone who will let me install Exchange Server to support only myself. So consequently, I'm often stuck solving problems that are generated on the client side of the networking equation.

Troubleshooting client connectivity and odd behavior is something that can drive even the most knowledgeable administrator crazy. Ranking the problems that I've had to trouble-shoot from best to worst, odd client behavior is usually the worst. Thus possessing good client troubleshooting skills is important for all Exchange administrators. The following is a list of things to keep in mind when troubleshooting client-related problems:

- Don't rule out the obvious.
- Keep records of recent changes to the network, servers, and clients in case any of those changes may have caused a new problem to surface.
- Make sure that you have an arsenal of troubleshooting tools—and that you know how to use them.
- Keep records of the most common problems that you experience and how you have solved them in the past.
- Make sure you understand the different types of clients that you have to support (MAPI, POP3, IMAP4, NNTP, or HTTP).

In this chapter, you will learn how to look for these problems and what to do when you find them. Topics in this chapter include:

- Where to start troubleshooting and common problems
- Client connectivity problems
- Garbled messages
- Understanding non-delivery reports
- Troubleshooting MAPI clients
- Troubleshooting Internet clients
- Setting up Internet client protocol logs
- Using Network Monitor
- Remote procedure calls and Network Monitor
- Best practices for client troubleshooting

What To Do First?

When presented with a problem, administrators frequently dive right in and start looking at all the deep, dark network- and server-related configuration issues that might cause that problem to occur. This often costs more time than it is really worth. Here are some issues you should address before troubleshooting the hard stuff:

- Find out if there have been any recent changes and whether the problem you are trying to solve has any similarities to those recent changes. Many problems can be rooted at the same cause. Unfortunately they don't always appear that way.
- Isolate the scope of the problem. Is this problem widespread, or does it affect only a specific network subnet, specific server, or single user?
- Determine the extent of the problem. Does the problem exist only when users attempt to perform a specific action, or does it appear to be random, occurring many times throughout the day?

The answers to these questions often don't tell you what is wrong, but they do provide you with a firm starting point for further troubleshooting.

Fixing Common Problems

When you begin troubleshooting a problem, don't overlook the basics. Some simple but common problems that administrators often overlook in the heat of the moment include:

- Network connectivity problems
- Name resolution problems and service location failures

- Replication delays or problems with Active Directory
- Data in the Exchange 2000 and Windows 2000 resolver caches
- Out-of-sync or out-of-date service packs and/or hot fixes

Network Connectivity

You should confirm that network connectivity exists, that the user has the correct permissions, and that the user was able to do something prior to this problem occurring.

Name Resolution

Without a doubt, name resolution is one of the largest causes of client connection failures. It's really simple: If you can't find the server's IP address, you can't connect to it. This is discussed in greater detail later in this chapter, in the section "Name Resolution Differences," but I want to review connectivity here.

All Exchange clients use DNS to locate a server's IP address. This applies to MAPI, POP3, IMAP4, LDAP, HTTP, and IM (Instant Messaging) clients. The following two areas will hurt you the most:

Client computer TCP/IP settings   The client computers must be configured with accurate DNS servers. Choose DNS servers that are updated regularly or that host Active Directory integrated zones. If you use DHCP in your network, be sure that the correct DNS servers are listed in the scope options.

Errant host records in DNS   Having duplicate host records in DNS for the same server is okay, just so long as both addresses are functional. A large percentage of DNS-related problems stem from someone mistyping the IP address on a host record. Carefully check your host records occasionally to be certain they are accurate and up-to-date.

Testing Name Resolution

Name resolution problems can manifest themselves in many different ways. The problem may be that the client cannot connect to the server at all, or that the client takes a few minutes to connect. One surefire way to test that the problem is related to name resolution is to configure a HOSTS file with the host name of the server and the IP address. If the client connects quickly to the server after the HOSTS file is edited, then the problem is probably related to name resolution, and you need to look at your DNS configuration.

The HOSTS file is located in the \Winnt\System32\Drivers\Etc directory on Windows NT, Windows 2000, and Windows XP clients. The HOSTS file is located in the \Windows directory on Windows 95, 98, and Me clients.

Troubleshooting

PART 5

Active Directory Replication

One of the more frustrating things surrounding client troubleshooting has to be Active Directory replication. Nearly all of us have done it: we make a lot of changes to users and mailboxes and adjust several server-side settings only to find that none of the changes took effect on the other servers. After some fiddling with the other servers, it finally dawns on us that we need to force the replication of Active Directory. Since all of Exchange 2000's configuration data is now stored in Active Directory, Exchange administrators need to understand the replication topology of the network.

Here is a strategy that has worked for me on many occasions: When I'm planning to change multiple users or mailboxes, I group them based on their site topology in Active Directory. I change all the users from one site and then force AD replication to that site. I then repeat this for each site that required changes. This ensures that each site sees their respective data. The downside of this plan is that remote users can run between sites without your knowledge. If you know a group of users to be roaming the countryside, group them together and replicate their changes to all sites when you are completed. As always, if you have the bandwidth to spare, force a total replication for all sites when you have completed making changes to Active Directory.

You can force Active Directory replication in a couple of ways; these methods are discussed in Microsoft Knowledge Base article Q232072. The easiest of these methods is to use the Active Directory Sites And Services console. Locate the server you wish to replicate changes to and open its NTDS Settings container. Right-click any of the connection objects in the left pane and select Replicate Now.

Data in the Exchange 2000 Cache

Exchange 2000 caches data to several places to reduce the load on Active Directory. These include the local mailbox cache (cached items are held for 15 minutes), mailbox limits cache (cached items are held for 60 minutes), and DSAccess cache (cached items are held for five minutes). Keep these cache times in mind when you are waiting for something to happen, such as connecting a user to a server where the mailbox has been recently moved or when you are trying to impose a new mailbox storage limit.

The DSAccess cache can be cleared using the DSCFLUSH utility discussed in Chapter 2, "Active Directory for Exchange 2000 Administrators."

Data in the Windows 2000 Resolver Cache

Windows 2000 will cache recently queried information from DNS servers in order to reduce the number of DNS queries. I have seen this come back and bite me a couple of times. Host records (A records) are cached in the resolver cache for 20 minutes before they are purged. If a mail server's address has recently changed or if it has just been added to DNS, Windows 2000 may keep incorrect information in the resolver cache for up to 20 minutes.

You can view the resolver cache by typing **IPCONFIG/DISPLAYDNS**; clear it by typing **IPCONFIG/FLUSHDNS**.

Service Packs

Before committing a large amount of time trying to figure out a server setting that seems to be malfunctioning, check your service packs. Apply the latest service packs to your server. Be sure that you keep the service pack levels the same across all your servers. Connectivity problems are known to exist when one server has a different service pack version than another. This also applies to hot fixes.

If you apply service packs or hot fixes to one server, apply them to all of your servers. Most of the material in this book assumes you are running at least Exchange 2000 Service Pack 1, especially for servers handling mailbox stores and public folder stores. The Windows 2000 Active Directory servers should have a minimum of Windows 2000 Service Pack 2.

Client Connectivity Problems

Exchange and Windows 2000 come with a number of useful tools for troubleshooting your clients' connections to the Exchange servers. These tools will save you time and help you diagnose connectivity problems with minimal hair loss. But, before I get into the tools of the trade, I must cover a few caveats when implementing Exchange clients with IP Security (IPSec), network address translators (NATs), or firewalls.

Infrastructure Interference

This section may not seem to apply to your network, but please read on; you may save yourself a good deal of time in the future. Firewalls and IPSec are becoming more popular on internal networks. If you implement these technologies in the future, you should be prepared for the fallout.

Connectivity loss can often be attributed to someone activating packet filters or accidentally changing the configuration of your internal routers, as well as firewalls and routers between offices, DMZs (demilitarized zones), and other semi-secure zones. Most external Exchange traffic will pass through a firewall, but the proper TCP/IP ports must be open for the traffic to pass through successfully. The Telnet command (discussed below) will give you the clearest indication of the presence of a firewall. If you cannot connect to the server, either the service is not running on the server, or something is blocking your communication. If you have other clients connecting to that service on the same server, you probably have a firewall in your path. If you do find a firewall, consult with its administrator to open the required TCP/IP ports for your client software.

NOTE Firewalls and networking configurations are discussed in more detail in Chapter 13, "Securing Your Exchange Servers."

A network address translator is a wonderful way to stretch your valuable external IP addresses when communicating with the Internet or other non-private networks. However, NATs are not a good solution for the connectivity for your internal clients. Using a NAT within your private network is frowned upon for a number of reasons, including:

- The server or router performing the network address translation must open the packet and modify the source address. This usually breaks down Netlogon traffic as well as most other RPC communication.

- Network address translation can affect network flexibility and reliability. On a private network, you typically have plenty of internal IP addresses to spare. The added confusion of a NAT when troubleshooting client connections is usually not helpful.

TIP Find more information on NATs and their effect on RPC traffic in Microsoft's Knowledge Base articles Q263293 and Q238390.

Along the same lines, NATs do not work with IPSec. If you must secure your communication with IPSec and you must use NATs, you should use a VPN tunnel. This will allow you the flexibility that you require without letting NATs interfere with your RPC traffic.

The following sections review the troubleshooting tools provided by Exchange and Windows 2000.

Ping

One of the most common tools used to check connectivity to a server is the ping utility, which tests several of the most critical aspects of Exchange connectivity. After you have checked for the common configuration problems, see if the client can even ping the Exchange server. First, ping will check name resolution, and if successful, it will begin sending test packets to the server. Before sending the packets, the client must determine if the server is on the same subnetwork. This tests your subnet mask and default gateway settings. If the connection is successful, you will see replies from the server giving you the latency reading in milliseconds.

Ping tests don't always work, especially when you really need them to. If the ping test fails, you may see one of these error messages:

Request Timed Out   Indicates the client sent a test packet to the server, but it didn't get a response back. This is normally caused by a problem in a router or at the server (in other words, no default gateway or route statement setup on the server).

Destination Host Unreachable   Normally associated with a missing default gateway on the client computer. This means that the client couldn't figure out where to send the packet destined for the server.

Bad IP Address   Indicates that the client was unable to resolve the server's host name to an IP address. This is almost always caused by missing or incorrect DNS settings. Unfortunately, this message can also be raised if the DNS server is unreachable because it is on another subnetwork. The rule of thumb, if the server is on another subnetwork, is to be absolutely certain that your IP address, subnet mask, and default gateway (router) configuration are 100% correct on both the clients and the servers.

Telnet

After verifying that you can ping the server, you know that the infrastructure is in place and that you can at least "see" the server. Now you must determine how much of the server you can really "see." Telnet is an amazing tool for Internet-based clients (POP, IMAP, SMTP, HTTP, NNTP, and LDAP). To use Telnet to your advantage, you must first know the TCP port of each of those services. Table 16.1, below, is a chart of the TCP ports used by these protocols.

To test connectivity, you must specify the port immediately following the server name. For example, if your Exchange server is named sfoex001.somorita.net, and you want to test connectivity to the POP3 service, you would type:

```
telnet sfoex001.somorita.net 110
```

The results of this Telnet session are shown in Figure 16.1. Notice that I was able to log on as a user (user somorita\khtang\khtang) with a password of *password* (pass password). I issued the stat command to see how many messages were waiting, and I retrieved message number 3 (retr 3). If you know the protocol commands, you can read some of your mail through Telnet, though I do not recommend this to end users, since the commands are difficult to use, and some of the mail will be MIME-encoded and unreadable through Telnet.

TIP   You can only use Telnet to connect to POP3, IMAP4, SMTP, and NNTP ports. The other messaging services do not provide any visible response that they are responding.

Troubleshooting

PART 5

Figure 16.1 Sample Telnet session to the POP3 service

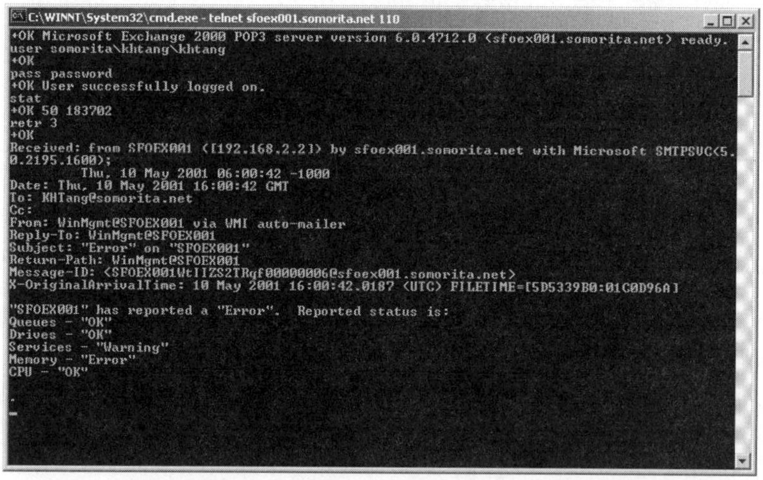

For the most part, checking client connectivity to a service can stop at the server's initial response. When you telnet into a service on an Exchange server, the server will respond with a greeting indicating which service you are using, the server's name, and the version of the software on the server. Because you can only see this information if you successfully connect, this represents the most basic form of testing on the protocol level. If you are experiencing other behavior that requires logging on as a particular user or forcing mail transfers, you can enter the syntax for that service. Each service has been documented in the RFC listings on the Internet. The syntax for the services will be contained within the RFCs. Some of the common port numbers for client applications are shown in Table 16.1; for a complete list of ports used by Exchange, see Chapter 13.

Table 16.1 Protocol TCP Port Numbers

Protocol	Standard Port	Secured Port
POP3	110	995
IMAP4	143	993
SMTP	25	N/A
HTTP	80	443
NNTP	119	563
LDAP	389	636

You will see the following banners if you successfully connect to the POP3, IMAP4, SMTP, or NNTP services. The SMTP banner has been customized; see Chapter 14, "Connectivity within Your Organization," for more information on this feature.

POP3 `+OK Microsoft Exchange 2000 POP3 server version 6.0.4712.0 (sfoex001.somorita.net) ready.`

IMAP4 `* OK Microsoft Exchange 2000 IMAP4rev1 server version 6.0.4712.0 (sfoex001.somorita.net) ready.`

SMTP `220 sfoex001.somorita.net Microsoft ESMTP MAIL Service, Version: 5.0.2195.2966 ready at Wed, 18 Jul 2001 20:46:47 -1000`

NNTP `200 NNTP Service 5.00.0984 Version: 5.0.2195.2966 Posting Allowed`

RPC Ping

Now that we've covered Internet client connectivity, you may be wondering about Outlook and how MAPI clients fit into all this. MAPI uses Remote Procedure Calls (RPCs) for its communication stream. Microsoft developed a tool called RPC Ping that helps us find problems with and verify RPC communication.

TIP Before running the RPC Ping utility, be sure that you can successfully ping the server as noted above. If you cannot ping the server, RPC Ping will almost always fail.

You can find the RPC Ping utility on the Exchange Server CD-ROM in the \Support\ RPCping\Winnt\I386 directory. RPC Ping has two components, the client and the server. You must first run the server-side component at the Exchange server; then you can run the client-side application from the Exchange client. RPC Ping attempts to open a connection to the RPC endpoint mapper (TCP port 135) on the Exchange server. When it does, it receives a set of TCP ports (between 1024 and 65535) that will be used for RPC communication. During the connection, RPC Ping will show the connection status. If it is successful, you know the RPC pathway to the Exchange server is open, and your problems are most likely not RPC-related. Figure 16.2 shows the RPC Ping client after running a successful RPC Ping test to the server SINGEX01.

If the RPC calls fail during any of the tests, something is blocking your requests. This could be a firewall, a NAT, or just simple TCP/IP filtering on the client, server, or router.

Figure 16.2   RPC Ping client

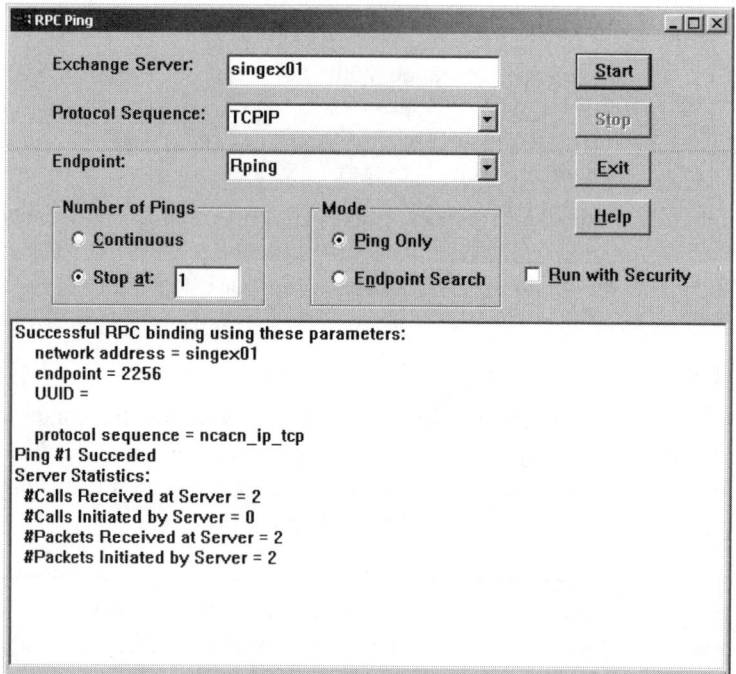

NOTE   You can find more information on the RPC Ping utility in Microsoft Knowledge Base article Q272218 and in the RPCPING.RTF document in the \Support\RPCping directory of the Exchange 2000 CD-ROM.

Garbled Messages

Garbled messages can be a severe annoyance to both users and administrators. They are most often caused by two mail systems failing to interoperate, but they can also be caused by line noise, dropped packets, and so on. You should remember a few things when trying to troubleshoot these problems.

First, not all e-mail systems are created equal. Some use only plaintext while others use extravagant HTML-based messages that seem almost proprietary. When two systems work together properly, they scale backwards to the greatest common denominator (most often plaintext). This usually has the effect of stripping all formatting from the message, but is doesn't normally trash the message.

Inbound messages to Exchange from SMTP and X.400 Connectors should support most standard message formats, such as RTF, uuencode, Binhex, MIME, S/MIME, HTML, and plaintext. The message will be stored in its native format, which will automatically be converted to a format that MAPI clients can understand—if the client is a MAPI client. If the client is an Internet client (such as POP3 or IMAP4), the message will be streamed out to the client in its native format.

When message formats don't work well together, the recipient can receive a message that looks like random characters intermixed with the intended message body. If the original message was formatted in HTML, the result is usually readable, but it shows the HTML formatting (it's possible to read, but certainly annoying). If the original message was formatted in RTF, the users can either receive an apparent random string of characters from the RTF header or a file called WINMAIL.DAT. The message body in both cases will be intact, but that doesn't normally stop people from calling your help desk.

The Mysterious WINMAIL.DAT Attachment

When I hear a user reporting something about a WINMAIL.DAT file accompanying their outbound mail, I immediately know that the problem is incompatibility. The WINMAIL .DAT file comes as an attachment from Outlook client users. This attachment is generated by Outlook, not Exchange, but you can disable this behavior. The attachment is actually a file containing the RTF code, and it is commonly visible on non-Microsoft Macintosh- and Unix-based mail clients. You can open the attachment, but it is nothing more than a binary file containing the formatting for the text-based message.

Some older mail servers are unable to decipher the Windows messaging format. Since most of the e-mail that flows through an Exchange server is also accompanied by its plaintext equivalent, the recipient will normally see the intended message. If you must prevent the attachment from being sent, you can force all messages to a particular recipient to be sent in plaintext mode. This will remove the RTF format from the message and will allow the recipient to view the message properly.

You may also have users reporting MIME attachments called application/tnef. This happens when an Outlook client sends a message using rich text formatting to a MIME client that cannot understand or display the rich text formatting.

Fixing Up Outbound Messages

On a couple of occasions, administrators of other e-mail systems have called my customers to complain that they are receiving unreadable messages. Upon further investigation, we usually found that the other e-mail system was using an older e-mail server or an e-mail client that could support the default outgoing message format (MIME).

Troubleshooting

PART 5

For example, one external mail system was still running a fairly old flavor of Unix. Some of the clients were still using old POP3 mail clients while others were using PINE (a text terminal-based mail client). We could not very well either stop sending them messages or rely on users to make sure that their outgoing messages to this system were always formatted as plaintext.

The solution was to create an Internet Message Format specifically for that domain (the Internet Message Format container is in the Global Settings container of Exchange System Manager). For example, suppose we need to send messages to the domain `VolcanoSurf.com` formatted as uuencode rather than MIME. To create a new message format, right-click the Internet Message Format container, choose New ➤ Domain, and enter the name of the message format and the domain name (`VolcanoSurf.com`).

> **NOTE** The Internet Message Format is configured for the entire Exchange 2000 organization. In Exchange 5.5, this was configured for each Internet Mail Service.

On the Message Format property tab (shown in Figure 16.3), select the UUEncode radio button, and click the Apply Content Settings To Non-MAPI Clients check box. Then select Western European (ISO-8859-1) for the Non-MIME Character Sets drop-down list boxes.

Figure 16.3 Message Format property tab of an Internet Message Format

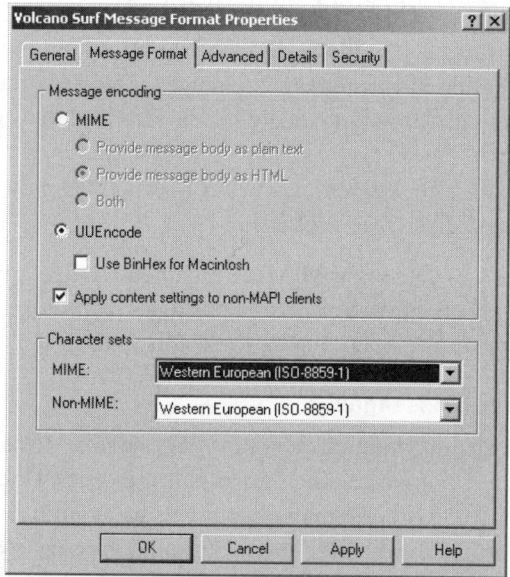

Understanding Non-Delivery Reports

Non-delivery reports (NDRs) are inevitable. These reports indicate that a message did not reach its intended destination. You can only hope that when they do surface you will have a quick answer, especially if the user is your boss. The most common cause of an NDR is a failed mail server on the Internet. I call these *external NDRs*. An external NDR will generally originate from your mail server because the remote mail server was unavailable.

The other type of NDR occurs within your organization. If an internal user receives an NDR while sending a message to another internal user, I call it an *internal NDR*. This is far less common and often only occurs during or shortly after a migration from another mail system. These internal NDRs can be very challenging to resolve. As you will soon see, there are quite a number of things you should do to correctly identify the source of your problems.

> **NOTE**   See Microsoft Knowledge Base article Q281800 for more information on troubleshooting NDRs.

Tracking a Message by Using the NDR

Take a look at the non-delivery report in Figure 16.4. User Kwen Hou Tang sent a message to user Deb Pahia, but received an NDR with the following reason for the undeliverable message:

```
Could not deliver the message in the time limit specified. Please
retry or contact your administrator. <sfoex001.somorita.net #4.4.7>
```

Figure 16.4   Non-delivery report generated within the organization

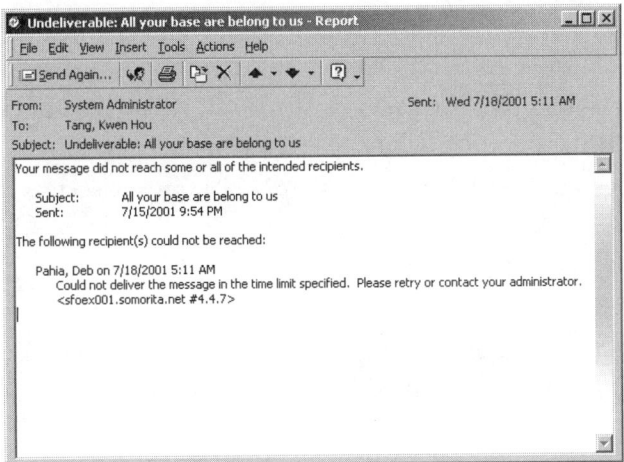

> **NOTE** NDR messages originate from the "System Administrator." Users often want to know if they can respond to these messages. Unfortunately, you cannot create an alias for this user, so you cannot reply to this message.

Though this message may not seem too descriptive, it actually contains some useful information. The bottom line of the message (`<sfoex001.somorita.net #4.4.7>`) indicates the server that generated the message is the sfoex001 server; so I know that this message made it to this server. A little further investigation indicates that this server is a bridge-head server for a Routing Group Connector to the Asia site, which is where Deb Pahia's mailbox is located. This tells me that the message never left the local routing group.

Also in the message is the DSN (delivery status notification) code #4.4.7. The DSN codes are defined in RFC 1893 in order to help SMTP-based mail systems give better diagnostics reporting. The DSN codes are broken up into three positions: $x.y.z$. The x value represents the class of the error code. There are three classes of error codes:

   $2.y.z$ codes represent a success.

   $4.y.z$ codes represent a temporary (transient) failure, such as networking problem.

   $5.y.z$ codes represent a permanent error.

The second part of the code (y) indicates the subject of the failure, and the last part of the code (z) indicates the details of the problem or report.

Seven different types of subjects for these DSNs help identify the major problem:

   $x.1.z$ codes indicate an addressing problem or an incorrect address.

   $x.2.z$ codes indicate a problem with the destination mailbox, such as it is full or cannot accept a message larger than a certain size.

   $x.3.z$ codes indicate a problem with the destination mail system, such as the entire system is down or not accepting messages.

   $x.4.z$ codes indicate a problem with the network, message routing, or delivery time-outs due to a connection failure.

   $x.5.z$ codes indicate problems with the SMTP protocol, such as unsupported SMTP command verbs.

   $x.6.z$ codes indicate problems with conversion or media.

   $x.7.z$ codes indicate a problem with security.

Table 16.2 shows some of the possible codes defined by RFC 1893. Not all of these codes indicate an error, nor are all of them generated by Exchange 2000 servers.

Table 16.2 Second and Third Digits of the DSN Code (Taken from RFC 1893 and KB Q256321)

Code	Explanation
x.1.0	Other address status.
x.1.1	Bad destination mailbox address or mailbox does not exist.
x.1.2	Bad destination system address.
x.1.3	Bad destination mailbox address syntax.
x.1.4	Destination mailbox address valid.
x.1.6	Mailbox has been moved (the mailbox has been moved from the destination system).
x.1.7	Bad sender's mailbox address syntax. Check the format of the message you are sending.
x.1.8	Bad sender's system address.
x.2.0	Other or undefined mailbox status.
x.2.1	Mailbox disabled, not accepting messages.
x.2.2	Mailbox full.
x.2.3	Message length exceeds administrative limit. This is the message Exchange 2000 uses when you send a message to a mailbox that is full or the message is too large.
x.2.4	Mailing list expansion problem.
x.3.0	Other or undefined mail system status.
x.3.1	Mail system full.
x.3.2	System not accepting network messages or administrator deleted the message manually from a queue.
x.3.3	System not capable of selected features.
x.3.4	Message too big for system.

Troubleshooting

PART 5

Table 16.2 Second and Third Digits of the DSN Code (Taken from RFC 1893 and KB Q256321) *(continued)*

Code	Explanation
x.4.0	Other or undefined network, routing status, or host not found.
x.4.1	No answer from host.
x.4.2	Bad connection.
x.4.3	Routing server failure.
x.4.4	Unable to route, no route to message, or next hop not found.
x.4.5	Network congestion.
x.4.6	Routing loop detected. Check DNS.
x.4.7	Delivery time expired.
x.5.0	Other or undefined protocol status.
x.5.1	Invalid command.
x.5.2	Syntax error.
x.5.3	Too many recipients.
x.5.4	Invalid command arguments.
x.5.5	Wrong protocol version.
x.6.0	Other or undefined media error.
x.6.1	Media not supported.
x.6.2	Conversion required and prohibited.
x.6.3	Conversion required but not supported.
x.6.4	Conversion with loss performed. Some data was not converted properly.
x.6.5	Conversion failed.
x.7.0	Other or undefined security status.

Table 16.2   Second and Third Digits of the DSN Code (Taken from RFC 1893 and KB
Q256321) *(continued)*

Code	Explanation
x.7.1	Delivery not authorized, message refused.
x.7.2	Mailing list expansion prohibited. User sent a message to a server or distribution list that cannot be expanded.
x.7.3	Security conversion required but not possible.
x.7.4	Security features not supported.
x.7.5	Cryptographic failure.
x.7.6	Cryptographic algorithm not supported.
x.7.7	Message integrity failure.

Table 16.3 lists some of the more common DSN codes that Exchange 2000 issues. Some
of these codes are displayed only by Exchange 2000 SP1 and SP2 servers.

Table 16.3   Common DSN Codes Used by Exchange 2000

Code	Explanation/Solution
4.3.1	Indicates an out-of-memory or out-of-disk space condition on the Exchange server. On heavily used servers, this might also indicate that the IIS server has run out of file handles.
4.3.2	Message deleted from a queue by the administrator via the Queue Viewer interface in Exchange System Manager.
4.4.1	Host not responding. Check network connectivity. If problem persists, an NDR will be issued.
4.4.2	Connection dropped. Can be caused by temporary network problems.
4.4.6	Maximum hop count for a message has been exceeded. Check the message address, DNS address, and SMTP virtual servers to make sure that nothing is causing the message to loop. The default maximum hop count is 15.

Troubleshooting

PART 5

Table 16.3 Common DSN Codes Used by Exchange 2000 *(continued)*

Code	Explanation/Solution
4.4.7	Message expired, probably because the receiving server is not available. This indicates that the message waited in the queue for the message time-out period. This typically indicates that the remote server is not reachable.
5.0.0	This is a fairly generic message. It may indicate that no route is available to deliver a message or other permanent failure. If it is an outbound SMTP message, make sure that an address space is available. Also check to make sure that routing groups have connectors between them.
5.1.0	Message categorizer failures. Check the destination addresses and try resending the message. If the recipient is local to the Exchange organization, confirm that the recipient has a homeMDB attribute set. The easiest way to correct missing attributes required for mail routing is to force the Recipient Update Service (RUS) to run.
5.1.1	Recipient could not be resolved. Check the destination addresses and try resending the message. This may mean that the e-mail account no longer exists on the destination server.
5.1.3	Bad address. Check the destination addresses and try resending the message.
5.1.4	Duplicate proxy address. Confirm that the address is correct. If this is your system, confirm that there are not two objects in Active Directory that have the same proxy address (you may need to export the directory using LDIFDE.EXE.
5.2.1	Local mail system has refused the message because it is too big. Check the recipient's limits.
5.2.3	Message too large; try sending a smaller message. May also indicate that the recipient's mailbox is disabled because the storage limits have been exceeded.
5.3.3	The remote server has run out of disk space to queue messages, or there may be an SMTP protocol error.
5.3.5	Message loopback detected; the server may be sending messages to itself. Confirm that the connectors are configured properly.

Table 16.3 Common DSN Codes Used by Exchange 2000 *(continued)*

Code	Explanation/Solution
5.4.0	Authoritative host not found; check DNS and check the message. The destination SMTP address may not be correct. This may also mean that an SMTP smarthost could not be found or the IP address of the smarthost is wrong. This may also mean that the remote SMTP domain does not resolve properly to any SMTP address spaces, or it may indicate that lookup of the SMTP virtual server's FQDN failed.
5.4.4	No route found to next hop. Check connectors to make sure connectors are configured correctly. Check that address spaces exist for this type of message.
5.4.6	Categorizer problems with recipient. This problem may be related to a forwarding loop. Make sure the recipient does not have an alternate recipient specified that is looping back to that recipient.
5.4.8	Looping condition detected. This may indicate that the server is trying to forward the message to itself. Check smarthost configuration, FQDN name, DNS host and MX records, and recipient policies. Confirm that the recipient policy does not include the FQDN of the server.
5.5.0	Generic SMTP protocol error.
5.5.2	SMTP protocol error indicating that the SMTP protocol command verbs are being received out of sequence. This may be due to problems on a remote system or to low disk space or low memory.
5.5.3	Too many recipients in the message; the sender is not allowed to send a message to this many recipients.
5.7.1	Access denied, generally because the sender does not have permission to send a message or to send a message to the recipient. May also indicate an SMTP client attempted to send mail without authenticating. See event log error 1709. This may also be seen when someone tries to use an SMTP server to relay messages, but the server does not permit relay.
5.7.3	Access denied because this recipient failed to log in prior to sending SMTP mail to the SMTP virtual server. See application event log error 1710.

Troubleshooting

PART 5

NOTE   For more information on troubleshooting SMTP virtual servers, see Chapter 17, "Server Troubleshooting."

Here are some other possible explanations (and troubleshooting tips) for a message not making its way to its intended recipient:

- Were any other messages successfully delivered to the recipient? Check to see if the e-mail address is incorrect.

- Ask the user if they are using an address copied from the global address list (GAL) into their own personal address book (PAB), the Outlook Contacts folder, or a personal distribution list. Exchange does not update addresses in these personal address books, so it is very possible that the recipient's address has changed and is incorrect in the user's own copy. The user will have to delete the entry in their PAB and re-add it to get the modified address.

- Has the recipient's mail system been down for a few days? This will also cause an NDR. Unfortunately, there is nothing you can do if the recipient's mail system is down or if the recipient no longer receives mail on that system.

- If all else fails, or the NDR is completely useless, continue on to the next section. The next set of instructions will help you solve these problems without the NDRs.

TIP   If addresses are in the GAL, tell users *not* to copy them into a PAB or Outlook Contacts folder. Use the addresses in the GAL to prevent situations where the recipient's address has changed, but that change is not reflected in the user's own copy.

Further Troubleshooting Tips

If you are running a front-end/back-end topology and SMTP mail is delivered at the front-end, the Information Store service must be started. If the service is stopped, NDR messages will *not* be generated if a message cannot be delivered. If you notice that messages are not being delivered and you use the front-end topology for this purpose, start the Information Store service and mount at least one private mailbox store.

The SMTP virtual server's default NDR time-out in Exchange 2000 Server is 48 hours. This means that the sender of an invalid message may not be notified for up to two full days. In that time, Exchange will continue to attempt delivery of the message. Many administrators like to turn off the delay notification for local delivery and outbound delivery. The default for this parameter is 12 hours (shown in Figure 16.5). I think it is better to keep this time-out at 12 hours so that the sender will at least know that their messages are queuing and have not been delivered.

Figure 16.5   SMTP virtual server settings including the delay notification settings.

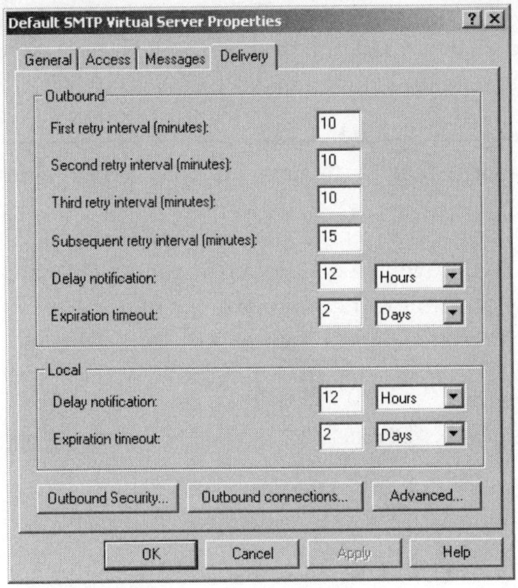

I have also had problems when an external DNS server was overloaded. The DNS server wasn't responding to lookups for MX (mail exchanger) records, so Exchange couldn't locate the remote mail servers. This wasn't immediately apparent since over half the messages made it to their destinations. None of the users were being informed of the failed delivery until the message was two days old. Better late than never? Try telling that to an irate CFO...

TIP   It can't be stated enough: If you are missing messages, check the message queues!

Another location to check is your application logs on the Exchange server. If you are having problems with a service, the service will often log its problems in the event logs. The catch is that you must raise the diagnostic logging level to the maximum to really get much use out of the messages.

Finally, if all else fails, restart the services for your connectors. I have seen this work on occasion. Unfortunately, I have also seen it result in data loss when there was a corrupt message in the SMTP queue.

Troubleshooting

PART 5

Checking Queues

If you find a lot of messages in your SMTP queue, try the following technique. This will indicate if you have a name resolution problem at the server, if you have a protocol blockage at your firewall, or if the remote mail server is down.

> **NOTE** More information on managing queues can be found in Chapter 17.

First, run NSLookup to get the remote domain's mail server location. Be sure to set your TYPE to MX because this will tell NSLookup to query the other name servers specifically for the MX records. The following is an example of using the NSLookup command to check an MX record:

```
C:\>nslookup -q=mx somorita.com
Server:  dns1.Somorita.net
Address:  192.168.24.10


somorita.com    MX preference = 10, mail exchanger =
mail.somorita.com
mail.somorita.com    internet address = 24.183.18.10
```

When you have the MX record, run Telnet and connect to port 25 on the remote mail server. This process is shown in Figure 16.6.

Figure 16.6 Telnet to remote mail server port 25

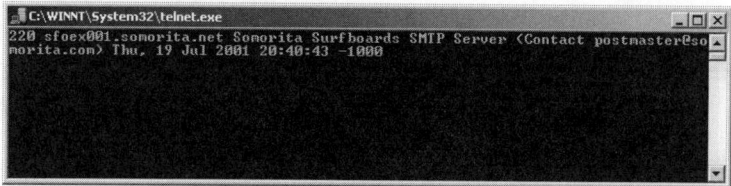

The results shown in the Figure 16.6 indicate that the remote mail server is responding. If Exchange has sent the mail to the remote mail server, the remote mail server should have either delivered the message or sent back an NDR message. Since there is no NDR, the Exchange server must not be able to locate the remote mail server.

The next place to check is the External DNS settings on the SMTP virtual server; select the Delivery tab, click the Advanced button, and then click the External DNS button. The Exchange server will query these DNS servers when sending Internet mail. If the servers are listed incorrectly, Exchange will not deliver the mail, resulting in an automatic NDR 48 hours later. For more information on SMTP and SMTP sessions, see Chapter 14.

If you see an NDR between two internal users, you must determine the location of the Global Catalog (GC) servers that your Exchange server is querying. If the recipient and sender are homed on the same Exchange server, verify that the attributes are correct in Active Directory. Query the local GC to perform this. If the recipient is homed on another Exchange server, determine which GC that server queries. Perform an LDAP query on the recipient at the local GC and the remote GC. Verify that all the attributes match perfectly. If they are different, force AD replication or determine the cause of the replication problem.

If you are running a mixed Exchange 5.5 and Exchange 2000 organization, you should check the Active Directory Connector (ADC) and Site Replication Service (SRS) for failures. Make sure that the SRS is started and that no errors are being logged in the Event Viewer. Verify that the ADC is properly synching between Exchange 5.5 and Active Directory.

If all else fails, set up Regtrace and call Microsoft Product Support. More information can be found in Knowledge Base article Q238614.

MAPI Clients

A MAPI client is any mail client that makes use of the Messaging Application Programming Interface (MAPI) in Windows. The most common MAPI client is Microsoft Outlook. MAPI clients offer the greatest capabilities of all the Exchange clients. A MAPI user can view every type of mail item, all the extended contact and calendaring features, and electronic forms. Microsoft has been trying to incorporate many of these features into their web client, Outlook Web Access (OWA). The characteristic that most greatly separates MAPI and Internet clients (POP3 and IMAP4) would have to be connectivity. A MAPI client must have a constant connection to the Exchange server. This allows many of the advanced features to function properly, including client rules and read notification.

MAPI clients use RPC to communicate to the Exchange server. Even though RPC communication can flow over many transports, you should stick with as few as possible. I recommend using only TCP/IP whenever possible and avoiding NetBEUI like the plague. While RPC is very network intensive, it offers the best functionality for your local area network clients. RPCs are synchronous and tend to time out easily. RPCs typically do not perform well over slow, unreliable links such as dial-up clients that connect at less than 19.2Kbps.

In contrast, Internet clients use a variety of application protocols. In fact, none of the Internet clients use RPC to communicate. This difference allows the Internet clients to make use of the public Internet without regard for performance. The connections are made as needed and broken as soon as the operations are complete. For instance, a POP3

Troubleshooting

PART 5

mail client does not remain connected to the mail server throughout the day. The client software connects on a regular basis (typically every 15 minutes or so), downloads any new mail, and then disconnects. Internet clients are discussed more later in this chapter.

Name Resolution Differences

One of the most common misconceptions about Outlook is that it is a NetBIOS application. Outlook is *not* a NetBIOS application nor does it rely upon NetBIOS name resolution. Outlook uses Windows Sockets (Winsock) function calls and RPC communication. Because it uses Winsock for its connections, it must use DNS for its name resolution. If you are having name resolution problems, check your HOSTS files and/or your DNS server host records. If you notice slow load times on your Outlook client, chances are that your name resolution is configured improperly.

Exchange@Work: Clearing Up Outlook Name Resolution Delays

A very common configuration problem is that the DNS domain name on Windows NT 4.0, 95, 98, and Me clients is either not set or it is set to a domain name that does not include an address record for the Exchange server. When a client queries a DNS server, it must send the query as a fully qualified domain name (FQDN). The client takes the host name of the Exchange server and appends on to the end of it the TCP/IP domain name of the workstation. For example, the name of the Exchange server specified in the Outlook configuration is hnlex01, and the TCP/IP domain name is configured as somorita.net; the DNS query will be for hnlex01.somorita.net. To reduce name resolution errors, make sure there is an address (host) record for hnlex01 in the somorita.net domain.

If the address is set incorrectly, the client may take considerably longer to start if it has to wait for the DNS to time out before it can continue with other name resolution methods.

Because Outlook relies on host name resolution, ping and NSLookup are very effective test utilities. Refer to the beginning of this chapter for the specifics on the usage of each tool.

For those of you unfamiliar with the host resolution process, here's a little recap: Host name resolution is used to resolve TCP/IP names that do not go through the NetBIOS interface. Host name resolution is used by Outlook and Exchange; Internet-type applications such as PING, FTP, and Telnet; and applications using the Winsock (Windows Sockets) API. Most of the time, Exchange clients (such as Outlook) use host name resolution to resolve the Exchange server's address.

To help understand where delays or even initialization failures may occur during name resolution, here are the general steps involved:

1. The client checks to see if the host name in question is its own name. If it is, it stops here.

2. The client searches the HOSTS file. If the name is in the HOSTS file, it stops here. The HOSTS file is found in the `\Windows` directory (for Windows 95/98/Me clients) and in the `\Winnt\System32\Drivers\Etc` directory (for Windows NT/2000/XP clients).

3. If the HOSTS file lookup fails, the client checks the Domain Name Service (DNS). If the DNS server does not have the answer, it will check with other DNS servers, and this can be time-consuming. If the search is successful, DNS returns the address, and the process stops. This is the desired method for name resolution because it is the fastest.

4. Finally, if all this fails, the NetBIOS name resolution process is started as a backup method; the client will consult with the WINS server, do a local broadcast, and scan the LMHOSTS file.

Common Errors and Problems

One of the more popular errors, "Exchange Server not available," still haunts us in Exchange 2000. Though this problem is seen on the client, more often than not it is caused by a server. This error is the most common type of client connectivity error, and it is typically caused by name resolution problems. The error can also be caused by the Exchange services failing or a blockage in connectivity (in other words, a firewall). The key to troubleshooting this error is comparison. Try the same operation on another client computer. If you have similar results, check your Exchange services and then your DNS servers. If all seem fine, run through the steps at the beginning of this chapter. Start by pinging the server and then try the RPC Ping utility.

If you can connect to Exchange, but are prompted with a logon dialog box (shown below) or told that your mailbox cannot be located, you probably have an Active Directory–related problem. This dialog box may also pop up if you are logged in to a Windows-based computer as one user account, but you are attempting to access a mailbox that user account does not have permission to access.

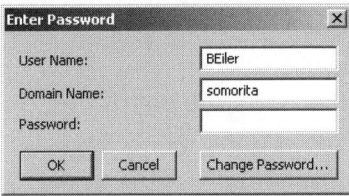

Troubleshooting

PART 5

You may also see a logon dialog box if the client is configured to prompt you for credentials. In Outlook, choose Tools ➢ Services or Control Panel ➢ Mail and configure the Microsoft Exchange Server service properties (on the Advanced tab, shown below). Set the Logon Network Security drop-down list to None if you want to be prompted for your username, domain name, and password each time you launch Outlook.

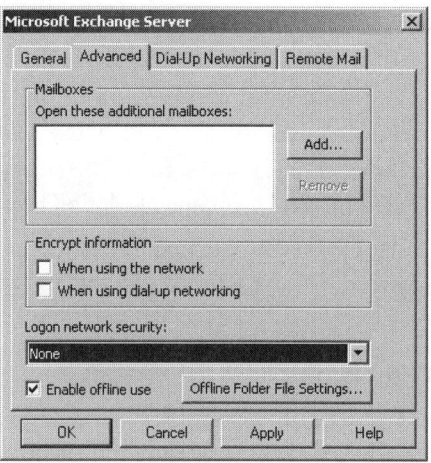

> **TIP** If the login authentication box is not remembering your username and domain name, confirm that there is a Registry key called \HKCU\Software\ Microsoft\Exchange. If there is not a key by this name, create one, and then restart Outlook. After the second restart, Outlook should remember the username and password. See Microsoft Knowledge Base article Q198438 for more information.

This problem was more common in Exchange 5.5 because the Primary Windows NT account field could be easily changed to another user. Now with Active Directory, this error typically indicates an AD replication problem. Here are a few suggestions to try when troubleshooting mailbox logon problems:

- If only one user account is experiencing this problem, check the mailbox properties in Active Directory Users And Computers.

- Try resetting the user's password.

- Verify that the user account is mailbox-enabled. If not, open the Exchange System Manager and "reconnect" the mailbox to the appropriate user account.

- When working with changes to Active Directory, don't forget to force replication to the other servers in your network. If you forget, the users in remote locations may not see your changes for hours depending on the Active Directory replication schedule.

Messages Stuck in the Outbox

Messages hung in your Outbox can indicate either a client-side or a server-side problem. The source of the problem also depends on whether you are working online with server-based message storage, using a PST file, using the Outlook remote mail feature, or working offline with an OST file. If you send a message in Outlook and you are properly connected to the Exchange server, the message will automatically move from your Outbox to the server's SMTP queue for processing. If the message doesn't move, your connection to the server may be severed, or your configuration is preventing Outlook from delivering that message to Exchange. Try restarting the Outlook client. Also verify that the Microsoft Exchange Information Store, the Microsoft Exchange Routing Engine, and the SMTP services on the Exchange server are started.

In Outlook, you can configure your delivery options so that messages will only use specific transports. For example, you might want to send your personal mail via your ISP's mail server, not through your corporate Exchange server. This is valuable for remote users who very rarely connect to the server. Unfortunately, users often adjust settings when they add their personal Internet e-mail accounts. If a user changes the delivery method from using the Exchange server, they may be unable to connect to the other mail server and their mail will stall permanently.

Another reason a message might not leave the Outbox is if the user opens the message in the Outbox folder before it is sent. This will change the status of the message, and it will not be sent. You can check a message's status by looking at its title in the Outbox. If the message title is no longer in *italics*, then the status has been changed. In order to send the message, you must take the following steps to return the message to Send status:

1. Double-click the message to open it in the Outbox.
2. Click the Send button or choose File ➢ Send. This will return the message to Send status, and it should be sent when it connects with the server.

If the user is using an OST file, one final thing to check is to make sure the user is working in online mode. If the user is working in offline mode, they need to reconnect to the server and synchronize or send their mail.

Cleaning Up Problems with Outlook

Outlook is full of features, but where there are features there are also frustrations. Fortunately, the Outlook programmers knew that certain problems were inevitable, so they incorporated several "self-cleaning" functions into the program. For example, to prevent e-mail from building up in users' mailboxes, you can configure Outlook to automatically archive e-mail messages. You can safely and automatically remove a large collection of items from your Exchange mailbox. This frees up precious space on your Exchange server while allowing you to keep your messages in a readily accessible container (the archive personal folder or PST file). However, if you are using this feature, your user community *must* be made aware that items will automatically be archived.

Some problems may occur as a result of a corrupt message, a virus scanner run amok, the reloading of Outlook, or a server crash. These problems may affect some of Outlook's features, such as Reminders or the Outlook Bar. You can fix many of these problems with command-line startup switches for Outlook.

Command-Line Switches

Outlook command-line switches help to diagnose and correct a multitude of problems. To use the switches, you must either run Outlook from the Run menu or from the command prompt. Another option (and possibly simpler way) to use the command-line switches is to first create a shortcut to the OUTLOOK.EXE file on the Desktop. Then modify the executable path to include the desired switch, such as the shortcut shown in Figure 16.7.

Figure 16.7   Creating an Outlook shortcut that includes a command-line switch

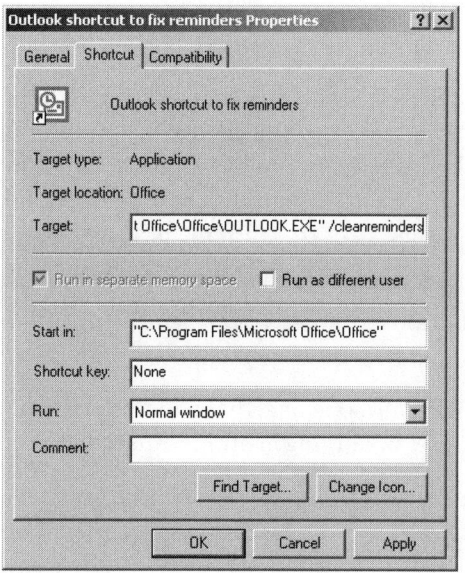

Table 16.4 lists some command-line switches that you can use to clean up erroneous information and to optimize Outlook. But be advised that while creating these shortcuts is great for working around problems, it is not a very permanent solution. In addition, the Microsoft website states that they will not support the Outlook client while you run it

with these switches. To receive support, you must run Outlook without the command-line switches.

Table 16.4   Outlook Command-Line Startup Options

Command-Line Switch	Purpose
/a <*filename*>	Opens a new mail message using the specified filename (Outlook 2002 only).
/c <*messageclass*>	Starts Outlook and creates a message of the specified class (Outlook 2002 only).
/CheckClient	Prompts for default manager of e-mail, news, and contacts.
/Cleanfinders	Removes saved searches from the Exchange Server store.
/CleanFreeBusy	Cleans and regenerates free/busy information.
/CleanReminders	Cleans and regenerates reminders.
/CleanSchedPlus	Deletes all Schedule+ data (free/busy, permissions, and .CAL file) from the server and allows the free/busy information from the Outlook Calendar to be used and viewed by all Schedule+ users.
/CleanViews	Restores default views.
/f <*filename*>	Opens the specified message file (.MSG) (Outlook 2002 only).
/Nopreview	Turns off the Preview pane and removes the option from the View menu. This is useful for organizations that are worried about viruses being launched through the Preview Pane.
/p <*filename*>	Prints the specified message file (.MSG) (Outlook 2002 only).
/Profile <*profilename*>	Starts Outlook using the specified profile name (Outlook 2002 only).

Troubleshooting

PART 5

Table 16.4   Outlook Command-Line Startup Options *(continued)*

Command-Line Switch	Purpose
/Profiles	Automatically shows the MAPI profiles dialog box when Outlook starts (Outlook 2002 only).
/Recycle	Starts Outlook using an existing Outlook window, if one exists.
/ResetFolders	Restores missing folders for the default delivery location.
/ResetOutlookBar	Rebuilds the Outlook Bar. Useful if you have reconfigured Outlook to point to a different message store location.
/s *<filename>*	Specifies a specific Outlook shortcut (.FAV) file (Outlook 2002 only).
/Safe	Launches Outlook safe mode, without extensions, Preview pane, or toolbar customization.

Confusing Form Behavior in Outlook 2000

Outlook forms are wonderful tools that can drastically reduce paper consumption and help the move toward a paperless office. Well, when they work, that is. Unlike their paper counterparts, electronic forms are constantly under construction. Most of the forms I work with are on their tenth to twentieth formal revision. This can pose a real problem for offline Exchange users, not to mention the form designers.

> **NOTE**   In the early 1990s, the paper industry was concerned that the broadening PC market would reduce the need for paper. In the early 2000s, paper demand is at an all-time high.

When you are offline, you can only access the forms that have been copied to your machine. When you reconnect to the Exchange server, your mailbox is synched, but you do not automatically copy down all the new forms. If you receive messages that require custom forms and the forms are not part of the message, you must read those forms online. Unfortunately, that doesn't always happen. If you go offline without opening the latest version of the form, you will not have it downloaded, and therefore you may not be able to see the entire message.

While the following fix is not really specific to Outlook 2000, it will solve this common problem with offline forms. The fix is simple, but it requires a little more storage space for each message that uses a specific form. You can configure your forms to send the form definition with each message. This enables your offline users to view the form without being connected. The best part about this technique is that you can choose to do this on a per form basis. The forms that are only accessed online should remain stored only on the Exchange server. When designing a form with the Outlook Forms Designer, you can choose to include the form definition with the item, as shown in Figure 16.8.

Figure 16.8   Form definition storage in Outlook 2000

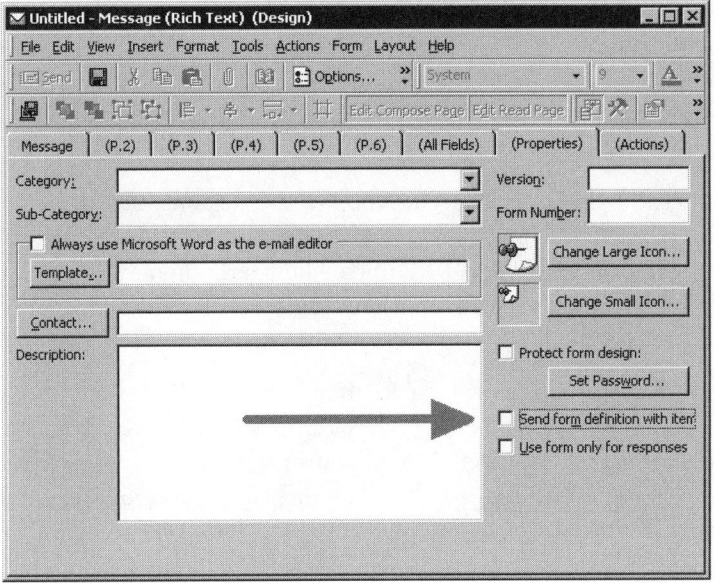

On the other hand, form designers often work with multiple copies of the same form all day long. It can become confusing to even the most experienced Exchange administrator unless you properly document the version number in the form. Even with version numbers, your machine keeps a form cache. If you send a message with a form, that form is inserted into the cache. A common problem when testing the new form is finding that your changes are missing.

WARNING   Form designers should also update the form version any time they publish a new version of an Outlook form.

This is easily fixed in Outlook 2000; in Outlook 2000 Service Release 1 (and Outlook 2002), you have the ability to manage the form cache on your local machine. If you are unable to see your changes on updated forms, you should clear your form cache. With Outlook 2000 SR1, you can solve your form cache problems with the click of a button. Clearing the forms cache can save you a lot of headaches. You can do this from Outlook by choosing Tools ➤ Options ➤ Other, clicking the Advanced Options button, clicking the Custom Forms button, and clicking the Manage Forms button.

For other earlier versions of Outlook, you can simply delete the locally cached copy of the forms from the \Windows\Forms or \Winnt\Forms directories.

Delivery Locations and the Missing E-mail Dilemma

A user calls you and says, "I am missing most of my messages! What did you do to them? I want them back right *now*!" Sound familiar? I have never seen a situation where an Exchange message mysteriously and inexplicably disappeared (possibly alien abduction!?); there is always a rational explanation.

In some cases, the user may be right; you may be responsible for the untimely demise of their messages. If you have implemented Outlook Auto-Archiving, run ExMerge, or are using the Exchange 2000 SP1 Mailbox Manager, you may be responsible for cleaning up some of the user's messages. These tools are discussed in Chapter 4, "Maintenance and Management."

However, in most cases the problem is often related to DEU (defective end user) problems. One common affliction strikes those users who are using personal folders (PST files) as their preferred location for mail delivery. If a user often moves from computer to computer, it is entirely possible that their messages may exist in several different personal folders. You can set a user's mail delivery location by adjusting their Mail Delivery options in the messaging profile. To do so, go to Tools ➤ Services and choose the Delivery tab, or go to Control Panel ➤ Mail (or Mail And Fax) and view the Delivery tab (see Figure 16.9).

In Figure 16.11, since an Exchange Server service and a PST file are configured, the Deliver New Mail To The Following Location drop-down list box has two possible locations for mail delivery: the Exchange server mailbox (Mailbox –Tang, Kwen Hou) and a PST file (Hou's Archive Folder).

NOTE In the delivery location drop-down list, the Exchange server location is always preceded by "Mailbox –".

Figure 16.9   Mail delivery location options

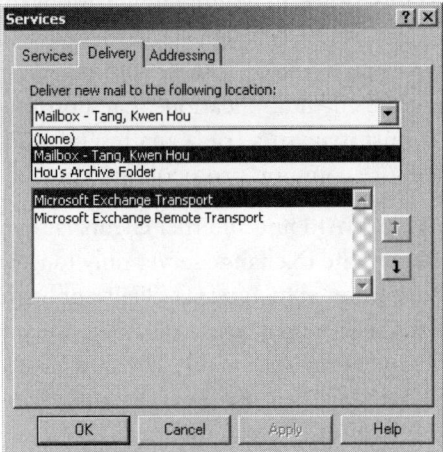

If the PST file is configured locally, and a user has a messaging profile on more than one computer, the PST file should be stored in their home directory on a shared server. If not, the new messages, calendar items, contact items, and so on will only be stored on the copy of the PST file that the user was working on when the message arrived or the item was created.

This problem also occurs if the user has a PST file configured on their desktop at the office, then goes home to use OWA. Since the Exchange server does not have a copy of the messages, the user sees an empty Inbox.

Another common problem occurs when a user uses a POP3 client to retrieve their messages. All of the messages in the Inbox will be downloaded to the POP3 client.

Internet Clients

Unlike MAPI clients, Internet clients were designed for use over slow and often unreliable connections. Internet clients are ideal for Internet users who only need access to their mailbox, calendar, and contacts, but not other features such as the Journal, Notes and Tasks. As I stated before, the Internet protocols supported by Exchange 2000 are POP3, IMAP4, SMTP, NNTP, and HTTP (including IM); the LDAP protocol is supported by Windows 2000 Active Directory. The key to troubleshooting Internet clients is knowing the proper syntax and when to use each protocol.

Troubleshooting

PART 5

Internet Explorer, Netscape Navigator, Outlook Express, Eudora Pro, Netscape Communicator, Opera, and Gravity are all popular applications that allow users to connect to Exchange 2000 messaging services through standardized protocols. The server (not the client) determines the protocol syntax for these Internet clients. This greatly simplifies support if you have multiple client applications. Each protocol has a set of commands that the client software must issue to retrieve mail, send mail, look up names, and so forth. The basics of the more common protocols are covered later in this chapter.

One big difference between MAPI and Internet clients is that Internet clients such as POP3 and IMAP4 connect to the Exchange server only long enough to transfer mail, contacts, or scheduling information. The Internet client applications do not form constant connections with the Exchange server. This cuts down the bandwidth requirements and improves connection reliability for the clients. The downside of this technique is that the client must check for updates to their mailbox. Because there is no constant connection to the Exchange server, new messages and updates are not automatically delivered to the client computer. This means the end user must either force a connection manually or schedule their client software to get the updates and new messages from the server.

Table 16.5 shows the different uses of each protocol. In the table, the HTTP protocol is split into IM and OWA to differentiate its capabilities.

Table 16.5   Internet Client Protocols

Protocol/Port	Description/Purpose
POP3/Port 110	Post Office Protocol. Downloads all messages in the root of the user's Inbox folder only. Does *not* provide access to other folders. Data is typically downloaded to the client machine and then deleted from the Exchange server.
IMAP4/Port 143	Internet Message Access Protocol. Downloads the headers of all messages in the Inbox and allows the user to access other folders in their mailbox and public folders. Unless the user specifies to delete a message item, messages are kept on the Exchange server.
SMTP/Port 25	Simple Mail Transfer Protocol. Used to send mail from an SMTP client to an SMTP server. This is a universal protocol that POP3 and IMAP4 clients require to send messages.

Table 16.5   Internet Client Protocols *(continued)*

Protocol/Port	Description/Purpose
NNTP/Port 119	Network News Transport Protocol. Used to read and submit Usenet news articles from pubic or private news servers. Data is kept on the Exchange server in either a public folder store or the file system.
LDAP/Port 389 or 3268	Lightweight Directory Access Protocol. Used to query directories such as Active Directory or public e-mail directories. All data is kept on the queried server.
HTTP (OWA)/Port 80	Hypertext Transfer Protocol (Outlook Web Access). Permits access to any folder in a user's mailbox, including public folders on the Exchange server. OWA graphically displays the user's calendar and contacts. All data is kept on the server; the web pages can be cached on the client computer.
HTTP (IM)/Port 80	Hypertext Transfer Protocol (Instant Messaging). Permits directed "instant" messages over HTTP. Subscriptions provide status updates and present information to other users (or applications). Unlike other instant messaging applications, message content is not stored on the Exchange server or the client computer.

More complete information on all ports that Exchange 2000 and its clients use can be found in Chapter 13.

Front-End/Back-End Server Issues

The front-end/back-end (FE/BE) topology was designed around Internet client connectivity. To recap, only Internet clients connect to the front-end servers. MAPI clients directly connect to a back-end server. This allows a distributed architecture because the primary users of the Internet protocols exist at the Internet gateway, not the private network. Because all Internet clients connect through the front-end to retrieve their e-mail, you must be sure that the front-end is able to handle user authentication properly. The protocols served by the front-end include POP3, IMAP4, NNTP, SMTP, and HTTP.

Troubleshooting

PART 5

One major consideration for your FE/BE topology is that you should not store users' mailboxes on front-end servers. If you do, the users assigned to those mailboxes will not be able to access them via any Internet mail protocols. However, they will still be able to access them via a MAPI client such as Outlook. This presents a security risk as well. Front-end servers are generally kept in DMZs (perimeter network or screened subnet), where security is much more lax, and backups are run far less frequently.

> **NOTE**   For more detailed information about configuring up front-end servers, see Chapter 15, "Internet Client Connectivity." If your front-end servers are often separated from the back-end servers by a firewall, refer to Chapter 13.

Authentication Problems at the Front-End

For security and performance reasons, most front-end Exchange 2000 servers will not be domain controllers. The front-end server must be able to freely communicate with Active Directory domain controllers and Global Catalog servers. If your front-end server is not a domain controller, you cannot use Windows Integrated authentication (NTLM). NTLM authentication requires that the authenticating server already "knows" the user's password. Because the front-end server is not a domain controller and it cannot authenticate to the back-end server(s), it will not know the user's password. Thus the only option available for authentication when using front-end servers is Basic authentication.

I highly recommend using SSL (Secure Sockets Layer) when the authentication method is Basic authentication. This allows the authentication to occur at the front-end, while providing a secure transport for the user's username and password. Authentication between the front-end and the back-end servers is still in cleartext, but the client-to-front-end-server portion of the conversation is encrypted. (For more information, see Chapter 11.) Basic authentication without the use of SSL allows passwords to be transmitted over the Internet in cleartext format; this is the work of the devil and should be avoided whenever possible.

If you have multiple back-end servers, you can test each server by directly connecting to it. The implementation of the front-end will not disable your ability to directly access your Inbox on the back-end web services.

Authentication and Domain Names

A user may not authenticate properly to a POP3, IMAP4, or NNTP server under a couple of circumstances. These include:

- The Exchange 2000 server is in a different domain than the user's account.
- The user's Exchange alias is different than their Active Directory account name.

In these cases, the user should provide their username in the following format: *DomainName\UserName\ExchangeAlias*. For example, user Andrew's Exchange alias is ARiehemann, and his user account is Andrew, so his POP3 or IMAP4 login name should be Somorita\Andrew\ARiehemann.

Troubleshooting POP3 Clients

POP3 clients are the easiest clients to troubleshoot because the syntax of the protocol is so simple. If a user is unable to download their mail, follow this troubleshooting checklist:

1. Verify that the POP3 server is set to the correct address. Most troubleshooting will stop here. It is very common for remote users to confuse their SMTP and POP3 server addresses, especially if they are supposed to use their ISP's SMTP server to send mail. Figure 16.10 shows the Outlook Express POP3 client's Servers property page; take care to make sure that the Incoming Mail (POP3) box is populated with the client's home mail server or a front-end server.

Figure 16.10 POP3 server configuration for Outlook Express

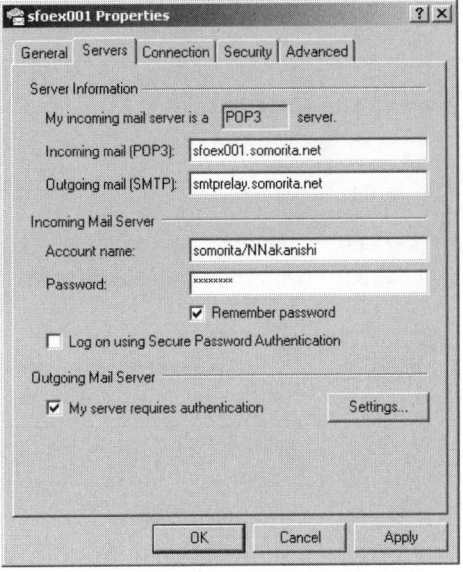

2. Ping the mail server's address. If you can't ping the server, don't panic. There may be a firewall in place that prevents access to the server. This is still a good test because pings are not blocked on every network.

3. Telnet into the mail server using port 110. The remote mail server will send a greeting as shown earlier in this chapter. Issue the commands shown below to determine if the user has any messages in their mailbox:

USER *username*   The user's username must be entered in the form of *domain_name\username*.

PASS *password*   The user's password must be provided.

STAT   Lists the number of messages waiting and the size.

LIST   Lists the size of each message.

RETR *message_number*   Retrieves a message.

DELE *message_number*   Deletes a message.

QUIT   Disconnects the client.

If you receive an error after entering the user's password, verify that the account is enabled and that the password is correct. Here is an example session with local echo turned on to show the command dialog. The bold text indicates commands that I entered.

```
+OK Microsoft Exchange 2000 POP3 server version 6.0.4712.0
(sfoex001.somorita.net) ready.
```
user somorita\kkawabata\kkawabata
```
+OK
```
pass $ecret!!
```
+OK User successfully logged on.
```
stat
```
+OK 2 2679
```
list
```
+OK 2 2679
1 1485
2 1194
.
```
retr 1
```
+OK
Received: by sfoex001.somorita.net
        id <01C1124D.F81F1B68@sfoex001.somorita.net>; Sat, 21 Jul
2001 15:31:02 -1000
```

```
content-class: urn:content-classes:message
Subject: Annual status report
Date: Sat, 21 Jul 2001 15:31:02 -1000
Message-ID:
<A667C9F41656D94A8F61FABD7610627515BE@sfoex001.somorita.net>
MIME-Version: 1.0
Content-Type: text/html;
        charset="iso-8859-1"
Content-Transfer-Encoding: quoted-printable
X-MS-Has-Attach:
X-MS-TNEF-Correlator:
Thread-Topic: Annual status report
Thread-Index: AcESTfgdYqjOG9V+S1iz4+ZRCBEuqQ==
X-MimeOLE: Produced By Microsoft Exchange V6.0.4712.0
From: "Tang, Kwen Hou" <KHTang@somorita.net>
To: "Riehemann, Andrew" <ARiehemann@somorita.net>,
        "Kawabata, Keith" <KKawabata@somorita.net>

<!DOCTYPE HTML PUBLIC "-//W3C//DTD HTML 3.2//EN">
<HTML>
<HEAD>
<META HTTP-EQUIV=3D"Content-Type" CONTENT=3D"text/html; =
charset=3Diso-8859-1">
<META NAME=3D"Generator" CONTENT=3D"MS Exchange Server version =
6.0.4712.0">
<TITLE>Annual status report</TITLE>
</HEAD>
<BODY>
<!-- Converted from text/rtf format -->
<P><FONT SIZE=3D2 FACE=3D"Arial">Keith and Andrew:</FONT>
<BR>        <FONT SIZE=3D2 =
```

```
FACE=3D"Arial">I will have those sales figures before the first of
next

month.  I'm arriving on the 2nd on Delta flight 2131 from =
Atlanta.</FONT></P>

<P><FONT SIZE=3D2 FACE=3D"Arial">Thanks,</FONT>

<BR><FONT SIZE=3D2 FACE=3D"Arial">Hou</FONT>

</P>

</BODY>

</HTML>

.
```

retr 2

```
+OK

Received: by sfoex001.somorita.net
        id <01C1124E.6AC4BD8A@sfoex001.somorita.net>; Sat, 21 Jul
2001 15:34:15 -1000

content-class: urn:content-classes:message

Subject: Boards are shipping

Date: Sat, 21 Jul 2001 15:34:15 -1000

Message-ID:
<A667C9F41656D94A8F61FABD7610627503CC48@sfoex001.somorita.net>

MIME-Version: 1.0

Content-Type: text/html;
        charset="utf-8"

Content-Transfer-Encoding: base64

X-MS-Has-Attach:

X-MS-TNEF-Correlator:

Thread-Topic: Boards are shipping

Thread-Index: AcESTmrDzrLGH6dOSouByZjF8Wd8Mg==

X-MimeOLE: Produced By Microsoft Exchange V6.0.4712.0

From: "Riehemann, Andrew" <ARiehemann@somorita.net>

To: "Kawabata, Keith" <KKawabata@somorita.net>
```

PCFETONUWVBFIEhUTUwgUFVCTElDICItLy9XMOMvLORURCBIVE1MIDQuMCBUcmFuc2l0a
W9uYWwv

LOVOIj48SFRNTD48SEVBRD48TUVUQSBIVFRQLUVRVU1WPSJDb250ZW50LVR5cGUiIENPT
1RFT1Q9

InRleHQvaHRtbDsgY2hhcnNldD11dGYtOCI+PC9IRUFEPjxCT0RZPjxESVY+VGh1IG51d
yAxMCBm

b290IGNvbXBvc210ZSBib2FyZHMgYXJlIHNoaXBwaW5nIGZyb20gClBvcnQgQgS2xhbmcgd
G9kYXku

Jm5ic3A7IFRoZXkgc2hvdWxkIGJJIGluIHN0b3J1cyBieSBTBTZXB0ZW1iZXIuPC9ESVY+C
jxESVY+

Jm5ic3A7PC9ESVY+CjxESVY+UmVnYXJkcywgPC9ESVY+CjxESVY+QW5rcmV3PC9ESVY+C
jxESVY+

Jm5ic3A7PC9ESVY+PC9CT0RZPjwvSFRNTD4=

.

quit

+OK Microsoft Exchange 2000 POP3 server version 6.0.4712.0 signing off.

Connection to host lost.

In this example, I have connected to a mail server and successfully logged on (as user KKawabata). I queried the server for a list of messages and found two new messages in the Inbox. I used the retr 1 command to retrieve the first message, which copied it to the screen only, and then I used the retr 2 command to copy the second message.

One interesting note about this session is that the first message was originally sent by an Outlook 2000 user and formatted as a rich text message. The second message was sent via an OWA client, and thus the message body is completely formatted as an HTML message and is encoded in Base64.

Disappearing E-mail

One common problem that POP3 users experience is disappearing mail. When a POP3 user connects to the Exchange server, the default configuration forces the client application to download all messages and then remove them from the server. If the user moves to a different machine, their Inbox will not follow them because it is stored on the original machine. To give users access to their mail from other machines, clear the option to delete the messages after download. This will also have a negative impact, however, since messages will be continually downloaded without being deleted. If a user must move between computers and still have access to their mail, configure that user for IMAP4 access to the Exchange server.

Troubleshooting

PART 5

Troubleshooting IMAP4 Clients

IMAP4 is not without its own flaws. In fact, IMAP can be just as frustrating if configured improperly. IMAP users typically move between machines and often collect a large amount of mail that is never deleted. If you begin experiencing delays when connecting to your Exchange server via IMAP, you may have too many messages in your Inbox. During the connection to the Exchange server, IMAP pulls the header information from each message. This information is then used to download the full message when the user selects it for reading. To reduce the load time, move some of the messages to subfolders.

If you are unable to connect to your Exchange server via IMAP, check the following: Are your logon name and password correct? Did you enter the correct server name in the IMAP field? Is your Exchange server protected by a firewall, and does it have port 143 open? If none of these cases exist, try a Telnet session to the IMAP service.

One important note about IMAP4 sessions: you must include a "tag" before each command you run. I typically start my commands at a001 and increment from there; it is not necessary to increment tag numbers, but I did so below for clarity. Below is a simple example of an IMAP4 session. The portion of the session in which I entered code is in boldface. If you were wondering if it was tedious to type all of this, you are right.

```
* OK Microsoft Exchange 2000 IMAP4rev1 server version 6.0.4712.0
(sfoex001.somorita.net) ready.
```
a001 LOGIN rtyau password
```
a001 OK LOGIN completed.
```
a002 SELECT inbox
```
* 8 EXISTS
```
```
* 0 RECENT
```
```
* FLAGS (\Seen \Answered \Flagged \Deleted \Draft $MDNSent)
```
```
* OK [PERMANENTFLAGS (\Seen \Answered \Flagged \Deleted \Draft
$MDNSent)] Permanent flags
```
```
* OK [UNSEEN 1] Is the first unseen message
```
```
* OK [UIDVALIDITY 1556] UIDVALIDITY value
```
```
A002 OK [READ-WRITE] SELECT completed.
```
A003 FETCH 8 (body[header.fields (subject)])
```
* 8 FETCH (BODY[HEADER.FIELDS (subject)] {47}
```
```
Subject: New models are shipping next month
```
```
  FLAGS (\Seen))
```
```
A003 OK FETCH completed.
```
a004 FETCH 8 (body[])

```
* 8 FETCH (BODY[] {1309}

Received: by sfoex001.somorita.net

        id <01C11253.AD5282EA@sfoex001.somorita.net>; Sat, 21 Jul
2001 16:11:54 -1000

content-class: urn:content-classes:message

Subject: New models are shipping next month

Date: Sat, 21 Jul 2001 16:11:54 -1000

Message-ID:
<A667C9F41656D94A8F61FABD7610627515BF@sfoex001.somorita.net>

MIME-Version: 1.0

Content-Type: text/html;

        charset="iso-8859-1"

Content-Transfer-Encoding: quoted-printable

X-MS-Has-Attach:

X-MS-TNEF-Correlator:

Thread-Topic: New models are shipping next month

Thread-Index: AcESU601eOOI0T+uR4KjNX4nKEo65Q==

X-MimeOLE: Produced By Microsoft Exchange V6.0.4712.0

From: "Tang, Kwen Hou" <KHTang@somorita.net>

To: "Tyau, Rance" <RTyau@somorita.net>,

        "Wolman, Emily" <EWolman@somorita.net>


<!DOCTYPE HTML PUBLIC "-//W3C//DTD HTML 3.2//EN">

<HTML>

<HEAD>

<META HTTP-EQUIV=3D"Content-Type" CONTENT=3D"text/html; =
charset=3Diso-8859-1">

<META NAME=3D"Generator" CONTENT=3D"MS Exchange Server version =
6.0.4712.0">

<TITLE>New models are shipping next month</TITLE>

</HEAD>

<BODY>

<!-- Converted from text/rtf format -->
```

```
<P><FONT SIZE=3D2 FACE=3D"Arial">The new models of long boards are =
shipping in less than 30 days.  Do we have the invoices for the =
major retailers ready to print?</FONT></P>
<BR>
</BODY>
</HTML>)
a004 OK FETCH completed.
```

a005 STORE 1 +FLAGS (\Deleted)

```
* 1 FETCH (FLAGS (\Seen \Deleted))
a005 OK STORE completed.
```

A006 EXPUNGE

```
* 1 EXPUNGE
* 7 EXISTS
A006 OK EXPUNGE completed.
```

A007 LOGOUT

```
* BYE Microsoft Exchange 2000 IMAP4rev1 server version 6.0.4712.0
signing off.
```

A007 OK LOGOUT completed.

```
Connection to host lost.
```

In step a002, I selected the Inbox folder, and then I retrieved the subject of message number 8 (step a003) and the entire message body (step a004). In step a005 I marked the message for deletion, and then in step a006 I instructed the store to delete (expunge) the message.

IMAP4 is somewhat more complicated than POP3 and has additional commands. The key IMAP4 commands include:

LOGIN *username password*	The user's username and password must be supplied. The user name must be in the form of *domain_name\username*.
SELECT *mailbox*	Selects the location of the mailbox.
FETCH *message arguments*	Retrieves headers/bodies of messages.
STORE *message arguments*	Stores changes/deletion flags on server.
EXPUNGE	Removes messages on the server that the user has marked for deletion.
LOGOUT	Disconnects the client.

TIP More information, including a tutorial on SMTP, IMAP4, and POP3, can be found on the Internet at www.cee.hw.ac.uk/courses/5nn2/7/index.htm. For more information on troubleshooting NNTP clients, see the Troubleshooting NNTP clients document at www.somorita.com.

Troubleshooting HTTP Clients

OWA is one of the most flexible features that Microsoft built into Exchange server. With the latest version, Internet clients have more capabilities than ever before. Unfortunately, these capabilities can cause problems and confusion for your users. One of the most important things that you can do to make your life easier is to clearly define the OWA features to the user community; make sure they know that it does not have the same features as Outlook 2000.

Users may also have to get used to authentication issues. The authentication component in OWA for Exchange 2000 determines the mailbox that users will receive when they connect. By default, the OWA virtual directory is secured with Integrated Windows authentication (for back-end servers). This means that users logged in to the domain will not have to re-enter their credentials when they visit the OWA website. The downside of this feature is that users must log out of the domain before a different user can log on to their mailbox using OWA. Since the NTLM username and password are automatically passed to the web server, there is no logon dialog box. Without a logon box, the connection assumes the credentials of the user actively logged in to the workstation.

Authentication through a Proxy

One problem you may experience occurs when you have to *reach* browser clients connecting to the OWA server through a proxy server. (Reach browser clients including Internet Explorer 4 and earlier as well as the Netscape and Opera browsers.) The client will appear to connect and authenticate, but the browser window will be empty.

There are a couple of possible solutions to this problem. First, you can require everyone to upgrade to at least Internet Explorer 5 (preferably IE 5.5 SP2 or later). Another solution is to have these clients bypass the proxy server when they are accessing the OWA server, but this may not be possible. If you decide to require your users to upgrade to IE 5 or later, you can force Exchange 2000 SP2 and later to accept connections only from *rich* browser clients. For more information on rich and reach browsers, see Chapter 15.

Kiosks

In some situations users do not have their own workstations, such as at a factory or on shop floors where multiple users or supervisors use the same computer to check e-mail. If a user logs on to the machine using their Active Directory user account, they may not log off for days. All the while other users can access that mailbox using OWA.

One simple solution is to make the kiosk workstation a stand-alone computer (not a member of the domain). When any user attempts to log in to OWA, they must provide the full path to their mailbox (for example, `owa.somorita.net/exchange/SMulder`). Then they will be prompted for their username and password, as shown below. It is a good practice to remind users to avoid checking the Save This Password In Your Password List check box.

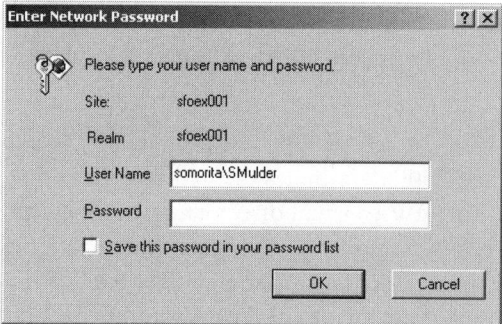

Another solution is also simple but requires a little extra work on your part. If you want to prompt your users to log on each time they access the OWA website, change the authentication method to Basic authentication and then enable SSL to encrypt the communications. To enable SSL, you will need to acquire a certificate based on the fully qualified domain name of the OWA server. Once you have set up Basic authentication, users will be prompted to log on each time they connect to the site.

> **NOTE** The OWA login box may or may not have a field for the domain name. If the domain name field is visible, make sure the users fill it in. If not, they should log in using *domain_name\username*.

Internal HTTP clients rely heavily on proxy settings. If you are using a proxy server, you should configure the clients to bypass proxy for local sites. This will allow you to use NTLM or Basic authentication since most proxy servers do not support passthrough NTLM authentication. Figure 16.11 shows the local area network settings and proxy settings in Internet Explorer. Note that the Bypass Proxy Server For Local Addresses check box is checked.

Figure 16.11 Bypassing the proxy server for local address

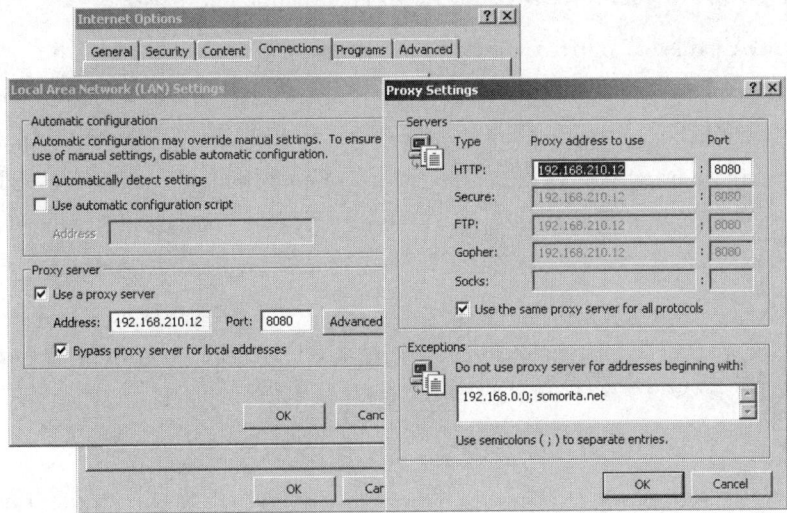

If you cannot connect to the OWA site from any computer, verify that the web services are started on the Exchange OWA server. Then check the sites in Internet Service Manager. The website with the /Exchange virtual directory should be started and authentication should be set to at least NTLM. If all connections fail, create a new website on another TCP/IP port (such as 81) and connect to the default page of this site. If you still cannot connect, refer back to the "Client Connectivity Problems" section of this chapter. Remember, Internet clients use TCP/IP communication and DNS for name resolution.

Troubleshooting SSL Connections

Secure Sockets Layer (SSL) connections are encrypted channels that are used to pass data between clients and servers. SSL connections require a secure key to be issued from a certificate authority. You have the following options when dealing with SSL:

- You can contact a third party like Verisign to issue a certificate (most secure).
- You can create an Enterprise-level certificate authority and generate a private domain certificate.
- You can install Certificate Services as a workgroup and issue a certificate for your web server (least secure).

If you have already acquired your certificate, you may want to verify that it has not expired or been revoked. If you have installed it correctly on your web server, the padlock will appear on the client computer's web browser when they connect to a secured part of

Troubleshooting

PART 5

your web site. The SSL client computer does not need to have a certificate because the certificate is used to guarantee that the server is authentic and trusted.

If you are unable to connect over SSL, you might want to check the following:

- Is port 443 open on the firewall?
- Have you correctly installed the certificate in the Internet Services Manager?
- If you are using host headers, do the host names match the DNS records?
- Are you permitting any encryption level or are you requiring 128-bit?
- Is the client connecting with the most recent web browser version?

These settings are all controlled in the Internet Services Manager. Most are controlled on the site properties, while some can also be controlled at the folder level. Be sure that you do not have conflicting settings in subfolders.

Querying Active Directory Using LDAP

In Windows 2000, the LDAP protocol is used to query Active Directory for user account information, service information, and other activities during logon. End users with an LDAP client can even query Active Directory for information about users in Active Directory, such as when looking for an e-mail address. Exchange 2000 uses LDAP to find the various attributes of mailboxes and groups before sending messages. This section focuses on how the client computer connects to Active Directory for logon and resource location.

NOTE More information on LDAP and its roots in the X.500 community can be found in the Microsoft Knowledge Base article Q196455.

Most LDAP queries can be performed as an anonymous user, but more in-depth access requires a logon and password. This is especially true when working with Active Directory. LDAP is used to modify data as well as read it. As an administrator, you have a couple of tools available to search Active Directory. One of these tools is LDIFDE, a command-line utility mainly used during large change operations. LDIFDE can be used to extract or import large amounts of data to and from Active Directory. The Windows 2000 Support Tools ships with another tool called LDP that provides a graphical interface to LDAP. Table 16.6 shows some LDAP programs and their typical uses.

Table 16.6   LDAP Tools and Clients

Application	Purpose
Outlook Express Address Book	Provides clients using Internet Explorer and Outlook Express the ability to search Active Directory for e-mail addresses, mailing address information, telephone numbers, and more.
LDP	Provides graphical access for LDAP-based queries; it will allow you to connect on any port you choose. This allows you to check Global Catalog queries as well as standard complete data queries. By default, input is taken from the keyboard, and output is sent to the screen.
LDIFDE	Commonly used to work with large amounts of data. Provides import and export capabilities for LDIF files from a command-line.
CSVDE	Imports data into Active Directory. It only works with CSV (comma-separated value) files. By default, input is taken from files, and output is sent to files.

On the client side, the most common LDAP utility that will be use is a utility such as the Outlook Express Address Book. If the clients are on the outside of the firewall, then you must provide access to a domain controller (preferably a Global Catalog server) through the firewall. For most organizations, this will probably not be an acceptable solution. A good alternative to this may be to require users who need to query Active Directory either to use OWA or to connect through a VPN.

If you are going to allow clients to query Active Directory through an LDAP utility such as the Outlook Express Address Book, then you need to understand a few things about configuring the client. You must create a directory service account in Outlook Express. Figure 16.12 shows the General tab of the Active Directory account.

Troubleshooting

PART 5

Figure 16.12 Configuring the General property tab of a directory service in the Address Book

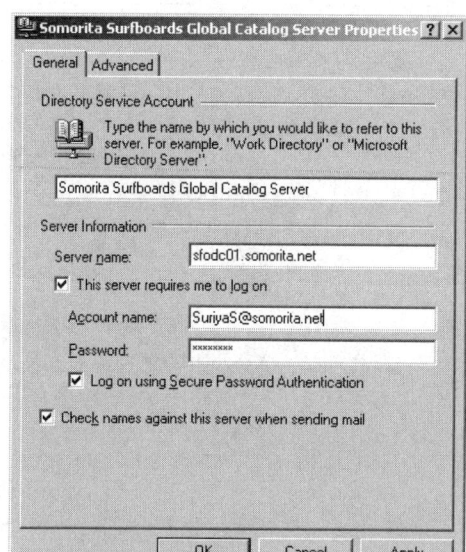

Be sure that the following items are configured correctly on the General property tab, or the user will not be able to perform queries:

- Ensure that the Server Name box is correct and resolvable using DNS or a HOSTS file.

- Enable the This Server Requires Me To Log On check box. By default, domain controllers do not allow anonymous access to Active Directory.

- Confirm that the username is correct in the Account Name box. Note in Figure 16.14 that Active Directory User Principal Name (UPN) is being used.

- Enable the Log On Using Secure Password Authentication check box.

On the Advanced property tab (shown in Figure 16.13), make sure the following are set correctly:

- Confirm that the Directory Service (LDAP) box is set to 3268; this indicates that the client will be querying a Global Catalog server. In a multidomain forest, this ensures that you have access to all of the user information from all domains.

- You can also specify a base organizational unit (OU) from which to begin your search by specifying the Search base.

Figure 16.13 The Advanced property tab of the Address Book account properties

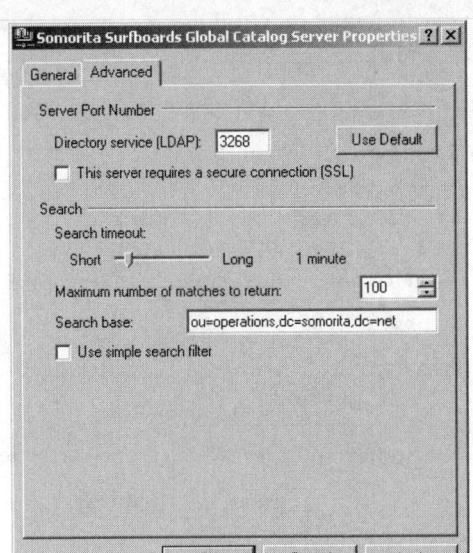

Testing Client-to-Server Connectivity with LDP

To say that Exchange 2000 depends on Active Directory is a bit of an understatement. Every time a client connects to the Exchange server, a directory query is sent from the client to the Exchange server. This query is intercepted by the Directory Store proxy (DSProxy) on the Exchange server. Before Outlook 2000, the query was then sent from the Exchange server to the nearest Global Catalog (GC) server in the forest. If the communication between the Exchange server and the client was okay, there could still be a failure if the Exchange server could not connect to a GC. Microsoft changed this behavior with Outlook 2000. The Outlook 2000 client will query the Exchange server for its preferred GC, and then Outlook will directly communicate with the GC for authentication and directory queries.

Unfortunately, you cannot use Telnet to verify LDAP connectivity. So if you are having problems, you will have to rely on some other methods. If you have verified connectivity from your client computers to the Exchange server, but no one can open their mailboxes, run the following tests, which check if the Exchange server can locate and connect to a GC. Then run a sample query to check for a username-to-mailbox mapping.

1. Run NSLookup on the Exchange server. Set your query type to ALL, and then query for _gc._tcp (you can include the full domain name after this string if the query fails). Below shows the results of such a query:

```
C:\>nslookup -q=all _gc._tcp.somorita.net
Server:   sfodc01.somorita.net
Address:  192.168.2.1


_gc._tcp.somorita.net    SRV service location:
          priority      = 0
          weight        = 100
          port          = 3268
          svr hostname  = sfodc01.somorita.net
sfodc01.somorita.net     internet address = 192.168.2.1
```

TIP   If you didn't get a response from the DNS server, you may have a DNS resolution issue. Verify that you connected to a DNS server that will contain your internal domain resource records. (You may have placed an Internet DNS server above your own internal DNS servers.)

2. Now connect to the Global Catalog server on the port shown in your NSLookup results. Use the LDP utility to do this. Make sure when you connect to a Global Catalog server that you specify port 3268 rather than port 389.

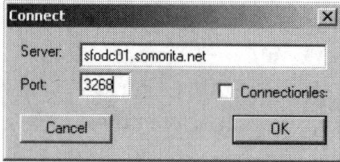

3. You should receive results similar to those shown in Figure 16.14. Notice that the results window indicates the Global Catalog is ready to receive a query. The very last line of the results window shows that the Global Catalog server is ready.

Figure 16.14 LDP utility initially connected to a Global Catalog server

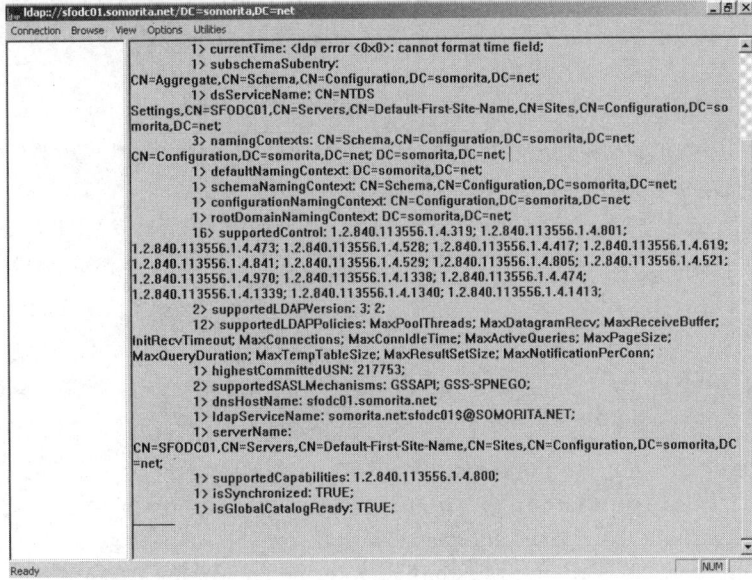

4. You must then bind to the Global Catalog to gain access to Active Directory. This authenticates you to Active Directory.

5. To query the Global Catalog for information, you must first specify the starting point of your searches. To do this, choose View ➢ Tree. When prompted for the Base DN, enter it in X.500 format: ou=sales,dc=somorita,dc=net. (This returns the Sales OU in the somorita.net domain.)

6. When you double-click the node in the left window pane, you will see the child nodes. This may be other OUs or user containers (CNs). If you select a user CN, you will see its properties displayed in the right window pane.

Instant Messaging Clients

Instant Messaging seems simple enough, yet I see so many problems getting clients connected. With problems ranging from logon failure to invalid contact names, it is often difficult to decide where to start troubleshooting. For those of you that don't already know, Instant Messaging (IM) is really a child of the HTTP protocol. In fact, IM uses a virtual directory on the default website for much of its communication. IM operates on port 80, and it uses the same HTTP commands that a web browser would issue. Below I have outlined a typical logon process for an IM client using their SMTP address as their IM logon:

1. The user logs on to the Instant Messaging client using their Instant Messaging addresses, such as kdehlert@sfoex001.somorita.net.

2. The client machine performs a DNS SRV lookup for the associated _rvp._ tcp.sfoex001.somorita.net record, which returns the host name of the Instant Messaging router if that record exists. Otherwise the client looks up the address record of sfoex001.somorita.net.

3. The Instant Messaging client connects to the Instant Messaging router.

4. The Instant Messaging router queries Active Directory for the user's Instant Messaging home server.

5. The Instant Messaging router returns the user's home server URL to the client machine.

6. The client machine uses the home server URL to connect to the Instant Messaging home server.

7. The Instant Messaging home server queries and validates the user's Active Directory username and password.

Before going off and creating a brand new RVP record, you must understand the router and home server relationship. The router is typically found on front-end servers in large environments where firewalls and perimeter networks (DMZs) are in place. The Instant Messaging router is nothing more than an intermediate point for all IM clients. The IM clients must first check the IM router to determine where their home server is located. The home server is also the entry point for all Internet IM users. If you have made your Instant Messaging available to the Internet, you should have directed all IM traffic to a router first.

The home servers contain the node database that determines which users have subscribed to other users' status messages. This database is unique per IM server. If a user on one IM home server attempts to send a message to a user on another server, the connection must first go through the IM router. After the connection is established, it becomes client-to-client and the servers are removed from the process. From that point forward, each client has a TCP port open to each other that will be used by all future messages in that session. That is how you can see if the remote user is typing a message when you have an IM window open. As soon as you close the window, you must reestablish this connection via the IM router.

Troubleshooting Connectivity

As with all the previous sections, connectivity tops the list when it comes to IM traffic. There are a number of reasons for connectivity loss and problems with Instant Messaging:

- The client is unable to connect to a valid DNS server, or the RVP record was not found in DNS.

- The administrator expects to use RVP records with operating systems other than Windows 2000 or Windows XP. If you have Windows NT/95/98/Me, then you must have address records for the domain names.

- Active Directory has not replicated, so the IM router cannot locate the user's home server.
- The user entered the domain name or Instant Messaging incorrectly. The IM address is not always the same as the e-mail address.
- The Web proxy client has not been configured to exclude internal web resources.

Unable to Access DNS

If you do not have proper access to DNS, you will not be able to locate the RVP record. This record tells the IM client where to find the IM router. The RVP records are used when you make the IM username the same as the user's SMTP address. This is often done to simplify the life of the users. If you find an RVP record, verify that it is directed to the exact host name of the IM router. If the user is coming in from the Internet, it is not likely that they will be able to resolve an internal host name. You must be certain to direct the records to resolvable host names.

AD Replication

If you just enabled a series of users for IM, the changes may not be available yet on your remote domain controllers. Force AD replication and see if you are able to connect. When the IM router queries AD, it must be able to locate the home server URL, or the IM client will not be told where to connect.

Incorrect Username

It probably goes without saying, but for completeness, be absolutely sure that the user is entering their username and password correctly. This is a big problem since users will be entering much longer usernames than normal (kdehlert@sfoex001.somorita.net instead of just kdehlert). If you decide not to make the users' SMTP addresses the same as their IM logon, be sure they are entering the proper domain name (kdehlert@sfoex001 .somorita.net). You can confirm the user's IM address by displaying the user's properties in Active Directory Users And Computers. On the Exchange Features property tab, highlight Instant Messaging and click the Properties button. The Instant Messaging General property tab is shown in Figure 16.15. The IM address is in the Instant Messaging User Address field, the IM router is shown in the Instant Messaging URL Address field, and the IM home server is shown in the Instant Messaging Home Server URL Address field. You cannot use these URLs through a Web browser.

On the Privacy property tab, you can specify a list of users or servers that are allowed to communicate with a specific user. So if the problems with IM communications are only affecting some users, check to make sure this has not been configured for one of the users whom people are not able to contact.

Troubleshooting

PART 5

Figure 16.15 Instant Messaging General property tab

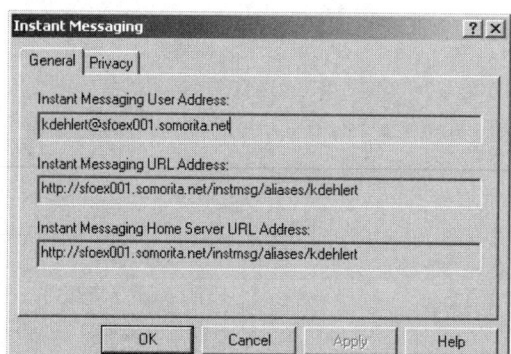

Web Proxy Client Not Configured

One final area that often holds back administrators is the Web proxy settings in Internet Explorer. You must enter an exclusion for your e-mail domain in the proxy settings or disable your web proxy. Proxy servers will forward the IM client requests to the Internet if you do not do this. Common practice is to exclude only the sites that are required (im.mycompany.com or mycompany.com). This way you can still use proxy for all your other web traffic. If you are using only the Winsock Proxy client, you do not have to make adjustments. These changes are only applicable if you have configured Internet Explorer with a web proxy server.

> **NOTE** Make sure you are using a more recent version of the Instant Messaging client. Microsoft ships an updated client with Exchange 2000 Service Pack 1 and later.

Interaction with MSN Messenger

Now that MSN Messenger is so popular, it is becoming almost a requirement to tie your Instant Messaging domains to the Internet. This presents a security risk if not done correctly. I highly recommend placing a firewall between any web-enabled server and the Internet. The Instant Messaging traffic will flow over TCP port 80 without problems, so there are minimal firewall issues.

Since MSN was available before Exchange's Instant Messaging, many of your users may have Hotmail or passport accounts set up at home. Some of these users will *require* that they have access to their "buddies" while at the office. (MSN Messenger, personal buddy lists, and good work ethics; I'm not even going to go there....)

If you want to "fix" your Exchange Instant Messaging client so that it will not accept communication with the MSN service, you're in luck. Here is a Registry hack that you must place on each client computer to be "fixed." (More Registry settings are available in Chapter 15.) Create a value of type REG_DWORD in the key HKLM\Software\ Microsoft\MessengerService\Policies called ExchangeConn and set it to 2.

One of the nicer parts of MSN Messenger is the "follow me anywhere" buddy list. Wherever you go, you still have the same list of contacts. That is because your list of contacts is stored on a Hotmail server when you connect to the MSN Messenger service. Unfortunately, Exchange's Instant Messaging client does not support this same behavior. There is no central place where your contacts are stored. However, you can work around this. Microsoft stores all the clients in a Registry key on your client computer. If you want to take them with you, export that key and then reimport it on the other computer. While this isn't the most effective way to have your users move their contacts, it is the fastest. The key that you need to copy is this:

```
HKCU\Software\Microsoft\Exchange\Messenger\Profiles\http://
im.company.com/instmsg/aliases/alias/contacts
```

where *im.company.com* is the IM domain, and *alias* is with the Exchange alias of the user in question.

NOTE If you have Instant Messaging clients separated from their IM Home servers by a firewall, reference Microsoft Knowledge Base article Q283022. This article contains information on client status polling and assigning static TCP/IP ports to the IM client.

Internet Client Protocol Logs

Each virtual server in Exchange 2000 has the ability to log client connections. The information in the logs can also be controlled. If you're stumped and can't seem to figure out what's going on, try enabling these logs. The information can seem a bit cryptic at times, but it can be a lifesaver when nothing else makes sense.

How to Set Up Logging

Let's just run through the services again. We have SMTP, NNTP, POP3, IMAP4, and HTTP (including IM).

SMTP and NNTP Logging

Logging for the SMTP and NNTP protocols is controlled through Exchange System Manager. To enable logging, open Exchange System Manger and navigate to the virtual server that is giving you headaches. On the General tab (shown in Figure 16.16), virtual server you check the Enable Logging check box and select the log file format; I recommend the W3C Extended Log File Format.

Figure 16.16 The SMTP virtual server General property tab is where you enable logging.

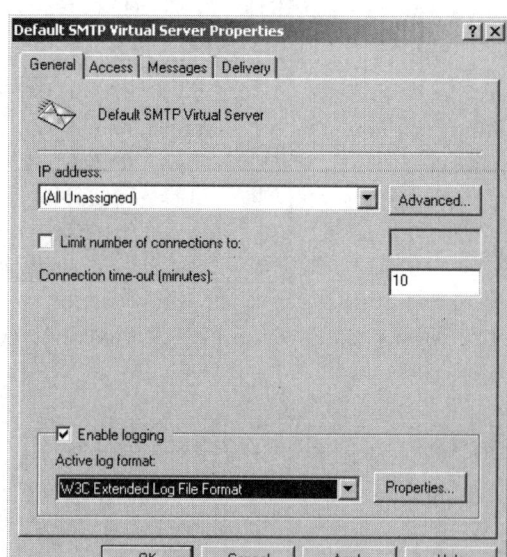

The logs are stored in the \Winnt\System32\Logfiles folder on the Exchange server and are cycled each day. You can change this log file location and see the specific subdirectory that the log files will be stored in by clicking the Properties button on the virtual server's General tab. On the General Properties tab (shown below), you can also control how often a new log file is created and whether or not the local time is used to name the log file and to start a new file.

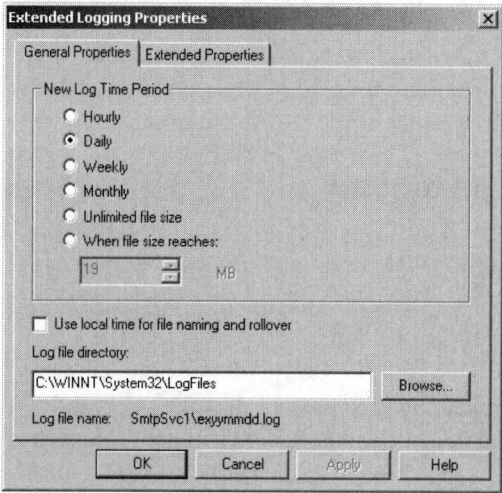

Be sure to disable these controls when you are done investigating your problem, or you will quickly eat up a lot of disk space. The more information that you choose to track in the log file, the larger the log files will be. On the SMTP virtual server's logging options Extended Properties tab (shown in Figure 16.17), you can select the Extended Logging Options to specify what you want recorded in the log file. For troubleshooting SMTP- and NNTP-related problems, I recommend at a minimum the options shown in Table 16.7.

Figure 16.17 Extended Properties tab for creating logs in an SMTP virtual server

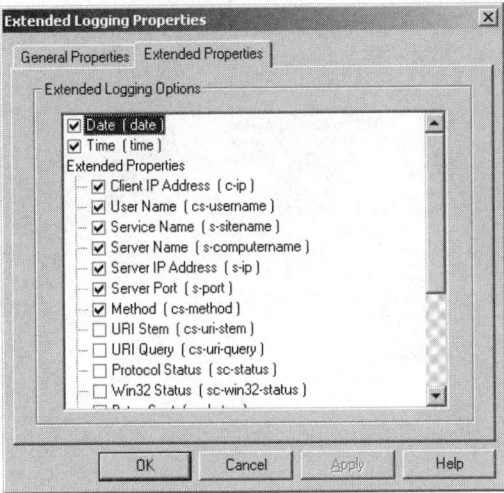

Table 16.7 Recommended Logging Options for Tracking Basic SMTP and NNTP Problems

Option	Column Header	Description
Date	Date	Date of the connection
Time	Time	Time of the connection
Client IP	c-ip	IP address of the client
User Name	cs-username	The name that the client introduces itself as
Method	cs-method	The commands used by the client (such as EHLO, DATA, MAIL FROM)
URI Query	cs-uri-query	Options used with the cs-method, such as MAIL FROM: <khtang@Somorita.net>

Troubleshooting

PART 5

POP3 and IMAP4 Logging

The POP3 and IMAP4 protocols are enabled in the Exchange System Manager, but you must navigate to the server object above the protocol and storage group containers. When you open the properties of the server, select the Diagnostic Logging tab, which displays a listing of the Exchange services (see Figure 16.18). To display the logging categories, you must select one of the services (POP3Svc or IMAP4Svc).

Figure 16.18 Diagnostics logging for the IMAP4Svc

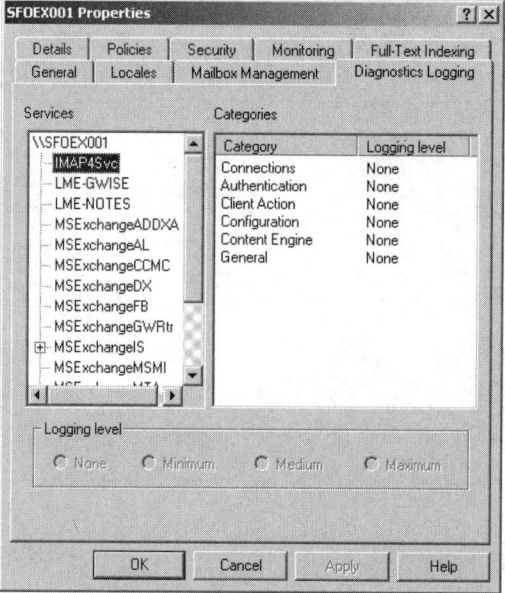

Adjusting the logging level at the bottom of the window allows independent control of each logging category. Be careful when setting all the categories to Maximum, as this will quickly fill up your Exchange server's application log. The best practice here is to enable only the categories that deal with your specific problem. If you are experiencing connectivity issues, enable logging on the Connections or Authentication categories. Also, setting the logging level to Maximum will yield the most results, but you may not need that much information. Start out with lower logging levels and increase them if you don't see the information that you need.

You can also enable protocol logging for POP3 and IMAP4, but you cannot do this through Exchange System Manager. Instead, you must create Registry keys. To enable protocol logging for POP3, open the Registry editor on the Exchange 2000 server on which you wish to enable logging and create two new keys: POP3 Protocol Logging Level of type REG_DWORD and POP3 Protocol Log Path of type REG_SZ. These should be in the following key:

    HKLM\System\CurrentControlSet\Services\Pop3svc\Parameters

Set the path to the directory in which you want the log files created by creating the POP3 Protocol Log Path value. To enable logging, set the value of POP3 Protocol Logging Level value between 0 (no logging) and 5 (maximum logging).

To enable protocol logging for the IMAP4 protocol, the procedure is very similar. On the Exchange 2000 server, create two new values: IMAP Protocol Logging Level of type REG_DWORD and IMAP Protocol Log Path of type REG_SZ. These should be in the following key:

    HKLM\System\CurrentControlSet\Services\IMAPsvc\Parameters

Set the path to the directory to which you want the log files created by creating the IMAP Protocol Log Path value; To enable logging, set the value of IMAP Protocol Logging Level value between 0 (no logging) and 5 (maximum logging).

Logging level 3 will report basic connection information while logging level 4 will include the POP3 or IMAP4 commands that were issued. Logging level 5 includes not only the POP3 or IMAP4 commands, but also the message data that is transferred.

You should stop and restart the "Microsoft Exchange IMAP4" or "Microsoft Exchange POP3" service when you enable or disable logging; however, once enabled, it appears that you can change logging levels without stopping and restarting.

HTTP Logging

Logging for HTTP (to track OWA usage or Instant Messaging) must be enabled in the Internet Services Manager, not the Exchange System Manager. All IM activity is logged with the website that you specified when you created the IM Virtual Server (typically the Default Web Site). To enable logging on a website, open the Internet Service Manager. Select the appropriate website and open its property tab. On the General tab, you will be given the option to Enable Logging and select the log file format. Check this box and then select the type of log you wish to receive; I recommend using the W3C Extended Log File Format. As I mentioned before, the defaults are good unless you have a specific problem. These logs are also stored in the \Winnt\System32\LogFiles folder on the Exchange server and are cycled each day by default. Be sure to disable them when you are done investigating your problem to avoid using a lot of disk space.

TIP Protocol logs for the SMTP, NNTP, IMAP4, POP3, and HTTP Virtual Servers are tab-delimited, so you can open them in a spreadsheet application such as Microsoft Excel.

How to Interpret the Logs

The SMTP, NNTP, and HTTP logs are written sequentially so that each connection takes exactly one line in the log file. The data is tab-delimited for readability, and the columns or fields can be adjusted on the Virtual Server as noted above. Remember that Internet client protocol sessions will consist of several connections to and from the server. There will be one connection for each command issued from the client to the server, and another one for the response. For example, a typical SMTP session will consist of at least the EHLO, MAIL, RCPT, DATA, and QUIT command verbs plus all the server responses to each command. Figure 16.19 shows a simple SMTP protocol log that represents an Outlook Express client connecting to the SMTP virtual server and transferring a single mail message. This makes troubleshooting more difficult, but it will also give you the most information possible.

Figure 16.19 SMTP protocol log for a single mail message from Outlook Express

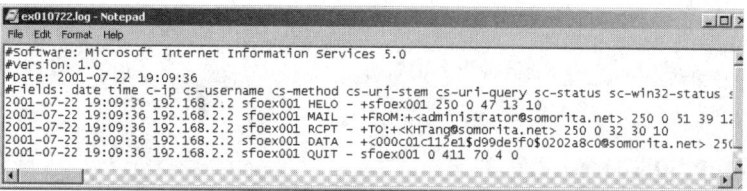

NOTE Times in the log files are GMT (Greenwich Mean Time, a.k.a. Zulu time or UTC).

The logs for POP3 and IMAP4 are a little easier to control because you can determine the amount of information that you receive. The logs are also contained in a more graphical mode, the Exchange server's Application Log; however, you cannot export the logs to a database server as easily. Some administrators require that all server logs be kept for review. This is easily done if the logs are comma-delimited, which works well with most database applications. When you store the data in the event log, however, it becomes pretty difficult to work with. Fortunately these services are rarely hacked, so historic logging is not nearly as important.

When viewing these event logs and protocol logs, be sure to note which dialog you are watching. The logs are not always written together. They are recorded as the server processes the information, so it is possible to have an extraneous log message inserted into logs at any point. Figure 16.20 shows a sample POP3 protocol log; the logging level was set to 3.

Figure 16.20 Sample POP3 protocol log

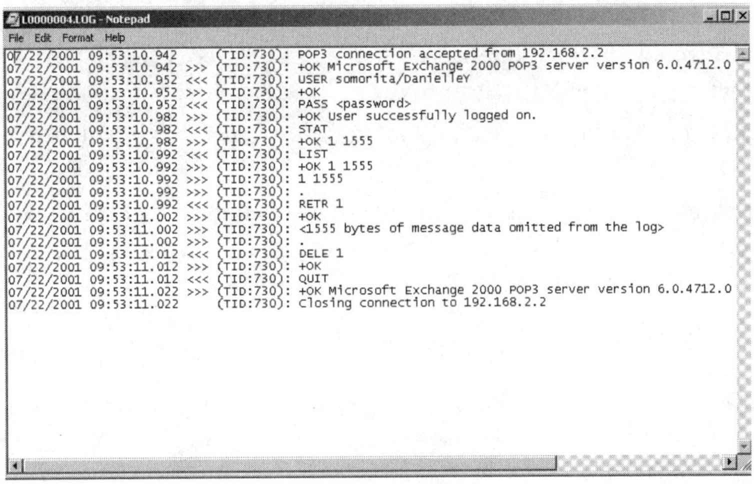

When you examine a POP3 or IMAP4 protocol log, the text "`>>>`" indicates something that the server has transmitted while the text "`<<<`" indicates something that the server has received from the client. In both cases, the logs will show you what is happening at the server-side of the communication. If you believe that the client machine is connecting to the server, but the connection is being lost, protocol logging is for you. If, however, you feel your data is being lost between the server and the client, read on.

> **NOTE** If you are not familiar with the Microsoft Network Monitor tool, then you should become familiar with it. Network Monitor is an incredibly powerful utility. For more information on using Network Monitor, see the document "Using Network Monitor to Troubleshoot" at www.somorita.com.

Best Practices

Troubleshooting client problems can be a royal pain in the neck—especially problems that are intermittent. Here is a list of best practices and approaches to solving problems.

- Isolate the problem to determine how many users, servers, or network segments are actually affected.

- Always verify connectivity using PING. Use PING to verify that the IP address will respond and that you can look up the host name. Connectivity problems rank in the top of the types of problems that affect clients.

- Always verify IP address resolution to all systems involved including the Exchange server, Global Catalog server, and domain controllers.

- When troubleshooting Internet clients such as SMTP, POP3, IMAP4, and NNTP, Telnet is your friend. Use it to confirm that the service is responding.

- Confirm authentication-related configuration items including username, domain name and password.

- Check to see if a server is requiring SSL. If so, confirm that the client is configured to use SSL.

17

Server Troubleshooting

Though there are fewer primary components in an Exchange 2000 server than there were in an Exchange 5.5 server, Exchange 2000 has a lot of dependencies. If Active Directory (AD), DNS, IIS, SMTP, or a whole slew of Windows 2000 services do not respond properly, Exchange 2000 may be rendered non-functional.

When things go wrong, you have to be able to narrow down the source of a problem quickly. The problem may be the result of Exchange-related issues, or it may be the result of a dependency service not working properly.

Unfortunately, without making the troubleshooting chapter of this book 500 pages, I had to figure out a way to adequately cover each of the dependencies. So throughout this entire book, I have discussed things you need to do in order to ensure that Exchange 2000 operates properly. Chapter 2, "Active Directory for Exchange 2000 Administrators," focuses on Exchange 2000's dependencies on AD. Chapter 5, "Status Monitoring and Reporting," covers tools and techniques to help you know quickly when a problem is afoot, while Chapter 6, "Performance Monitoring and Optimization," makes some recommendations for counters to monitor to ensure that Windows 2000 and Exchange 2000 run efficiently. When dealing with message transport issues, both Chapter 14, "Connectivity within Your Organization," and Chapter 16, "Client Troubleshooting," help with troubleshooting message transport and connectivity problems.

This chapter presents some basic troubleshooting steps from the perspective of solving problems related to the Exchange server. Topics include:

- Things to check first
- Active Directory and DNS troubleshooting
- Exchange services
- Troubleshooting message flow problems

First Things First

When you have problems with Exchange 2000, there are a couple of basic things you need to do and check. Before you start troubleshooting more complicated scenarios, here is a list of suggestions that may help you isolate the source of a problem:

- Look in the Windows 2000 system and application event logs for errors (red events) and warnings (yellow events) that affect directory, networking, and Exchange 2000 components.
- Confirm Exchange 2000 connectivity to the network and with AD.
- Confirm that DNS queries are working; if they're not, try clearing the DNS resolver cache, or flushing the DNS server cache. Troubleshoot DNS problems from the Exchange server console.
- Confirm that all of the disk drives have sufficient free disk space; I get worried if the hard disk is below 500MB of free disk space.
- Check the Services console to see that all Exchange 2000 services are started.
- Enable diagnostics logging for the service that is not functioning properly. Start with minimum diagnostics logging.
- Enable protocol logging for protocols such as SMTP, POP3, IMAP4, HTTP, and NNTP.
- Remember that different Exchange 2000 components (e.g., DSAccess, the information store, message categorizer) cache information for different durations.
- If the message is related to message transport, stop and restart the Microsoft Exchange Routing Engine and the Simple Mail Transport Service (SMTP) services.
- If the problem is related to communication with Exchange 5.5 servers in the same site or X.400 connections, stop and restart the Microsoft Exchange MTA Stacks service.
- If all else fails, reboot the server.

> ***TIP*** Perhaps one of the most important things you can do when you begin to troubleshoot a problem is to check in the Exchange server's application and system event logs for events that may be relevant to your current problem.

Know the Code

If the problem you are experiencing has generated a specific error number, you're in luck! Well, sometimes you are. Try performing a Microsoft Knowledge Base search on that error code. If this search fails to yield any significant results, there is still hope. On the Exchange 2000 CD-ROM (or the appropriate Service Pack), there is a utility called ERROR.EXE, which decodes cryptic error codes into not-quite-as-cryptic message strings.

This utility decodes many (but not all) of the error codes that Exchange and Exchange-related programs will toss at you. For example, if you see a message in the event log that indicates an error code 0x80004005, the following is an example of using the ERROR.EXE program and its output:

```
C:\>error 0x80004005

Error -2147467259 (0x80004005) = ecError-MAPI_E_CALL_FAILED
```

The resulting text indicates that error 0x80004005 is a MAPI_E_CALL_FAILED problem; in English, a MAPI function call failed. This may be due to client security, or the information store may not be available. When you enter an error code, make sure to include the 0x if it is part of the error number, otherwise the error converted will assume that the number is a decimal number.

If the Microsoft Knowledge Base fails to yield any clues, all is not lost. The next place to search is www.google.com. Google's index of the Usenet newsgroups and the Knowledge Base is quite useful, but it includes the websites as well as newsgroup content, so be sure to narrow your search appropriately. A Google search may yield results even in the Microsoft Knowledge Base that a regular Knowledge Base search does not.

DNS and AD Troubleshooting

Exchange 2000 is far more dependent on DNS than its predecessors were. And Exchange 2000 is so tightly coupled with Active Directory that if an Exchange 2000 server cannot communicate with the domain controllers and Global Catalog servers, services will stop responding, and mail will not be delivered.

Troubleshooting

PART 5

Understanding how to recognize and troubleshoot common problems relating to AD and DNS will help you resolve problems quickly. Troubleshooting these problems includes learning which domain controllers an Exchange server is using and how Exchange resolves IP addresses using DNS.

Active Directory Troubleshooting

Exchange Server must be able to query Active Directory; not only does the Exchange server rely on AD for logon authentication, but it relies on AD for information about configuration and mail-enabled objects. This means that your Exchange server must be able to query domain controllers and Global Catalog servers. Active Directory must be accessible and the servers must be up-to-date in order for queries to be answered successfully.

Active Directory Connectivity

There are a couple of utilities that you can use to verify that AD is accessible by an Exchange 2000 server. The first of these utilities can be found on the www.exinternals .com website; it is called *DSADiag* and is used to list up to 10 domain controllers and Global Catalog servers. It also shows the current configuration domain controller. This information is contained in the DSAccess cache. Download the DSADiag tool and copy it into the \Exchsrvr\Bin directory. The program has two command-line options:

- DSADiag 1 lists the current domain controllers, Global Catalog servers, and the configuration domain controller.
- DSADiag 2 forces DSAccess to rediscover the topology.

Here is a sample output from DSADiag:

```
C:\Program Files\Exchsrvr\BIN>dsadiag 1
.......
Working DC's:
UP FAST DOWN InSync    Name
X  X         X         sfodc01.somorita.net


Working GC's:
UP FAST DOWN InSync    Name
X  X         X         sfodc01.somorita.net
Config DC:

                       sfodc01.somorita.net

Done
```

The UP column means that the server is currently available; the FAST column means that the server is responding to LDAP queries within two seconds.

> **NOTE** Starting with Exchange 2000 SP2, DSADiag functionality is now included on the Directory Access property page of the server's properties.

Another useful utility is NLTEST, which is found with the Windows 2000 Support Tools on the Windows 2000 CD-ROM in the \Support\Tools directory. This utility does a lot of things that are not relevant to this text, yet it performs a couple of useful diagnostic functions that can help you to ensure that your Net Logon service is indeed finding domain controllers and Global Catalog servers. Following are some examples of using NLTEST in a domain called somorita.net:

nltest/dclist:somorita.net	Lists the domain controllers in the somorita.net domain.
nltest/dsgetsite	Displays the current site name.
nltest/dsgetdc:somorita.net	Lists detailed information about each domain controller.

> **NOTE** For more examples of using NLTEST, see Chapter 2.

Names Not Appearing in Address Lists

Mail-enabled objects may not appear in the global address list (GAL) or other address lists for a couple of reasons, including:

- The Recipient Update Service (RUS) has not yet updated the mail-enabled object.
- Replication has not yet occurred to the Global Catalog server that the Exchange server is using or to which the Outlook client is being referred.
- Users do not have the appropriate permissions to the Active Directory object.
- The LDAP query that forms the address list may be incorrect.

Forcing the Recipient Update Service to Run   In a small environment with only one or two domain controllers, if a mail-enabled object does not appear in the address lists after a few minutes, the problem may be related to the RUS. Each domain should have at least one RUS configured to run, and there should be an Enterprise Configuration RUS configured.

Troubleshooting

PART 5

To force the RUS to run, right-click the appropriate RUS and choose either Update Now or Rebuild. Update Now will check for changes, but I have seen instances where an entire Rebuild was necessary. However, in a domain with more than a few thousand mail-enabled objects, a complete Rebuild can take 15 minutes or more.

Replication Issues   Active Directory replication is far too complex a topic to delve into too much depth in an Exchange 2000 book. That is somewhat unfortunate considering how intertwined the fates of the two products actually are. Nonetheless, understanding some of the delays within an AD domain can help you to troubleshoot problems. Or, better yet, just tell your users to be patient and wait it out.

In an organization with a single AD site, generally, you can count on replication completing within about 20 minutes. This means that if you added a new mailbox, it should appear in the GAL in about 20 minutes (worst case).

In an organization with more than one AD site, replication depends mostly on the site link replication schedules. That said, you can force replication in a couple of ways, but the simplest approach is to use the ReplMon utility from the Windows 2000 Support Tools. ReplMon also tells you the last time that this server performed a replication. To do this, open ReplMon, right-click the Monitored Server container and choose Add Monitored Server. Either search for the server you are looking for in the Active Directory or enter the server's name explicitly. The ReplMon main screen is shown in Figure 17.1.

Figure 17.1   The Windows 2000 Support Tools Replication Monitor

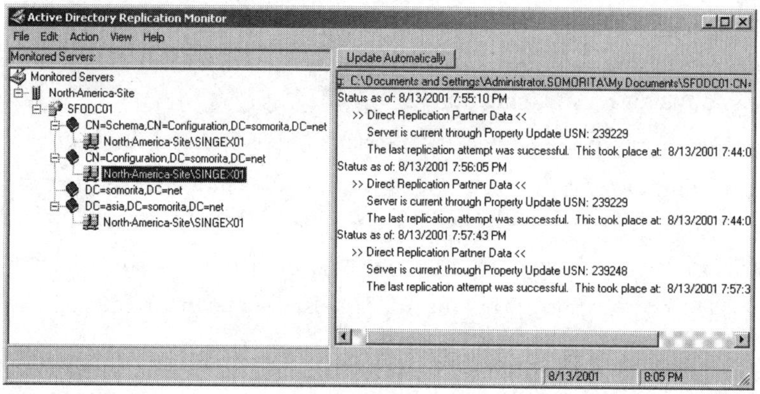

Once you have the server information on the screen, open the container you are interested in seeing if it has replicated. This will be either the Configuration partition or the domain partition. Under each partition, there will be a list of replication partners. In Figure 17.1, the server SFODC01 has a replication partner for the Configuration partition called SINGEX01. In the right pane, you can see that the most recent replication occurred at 8/13/2001 at 7:57 P.M.

Figure 17.1 shows an extremely simple replication topology. In an Active Directory site with more than three domain controllers, replication will not always be directly from the source to each destination server. To better understand AD replication, invest in a copy of *Mastering Active Directory* by Robert King (Sybex, 2000). This book has detailed information about Active Directory domain and site design as well as building a solid replication architecture.

> **TIP** You can force replication using either ReplMon or Active Directory Sites And Services.

DNS Name Resolution

Name-to-IP address resolution is of critical importance on a Windows 2000 network. If an Exchange server cannot resolve IP addresses, it will not be able to deliver mail properly and may even cease to function at all. This section includes some information that you can use to confirm that DNS name resolution is working properly.

> **TIP** You should always troubleshoot DNS problems at the Exchange server console (or through a Terminals Services connection to the console). Differences in network topology, operating systems, caching values, and other factors may not yield successful troubleshooting results from your workstation.

Looking Up Domain Controllers

From the console of the Exchange server, you should be able to perform an NSLOOKUP query for SRV records relating to the Exchange server's domain and relating to Global Catalog servers. The following DNS query (LDAP SRV records) helps to confirm that you can query domain controller information for a given domain (somorita.net):

```
C:\>nslookup -q=ALL _ldap._tcp.somorita.net
Server:  sfodc01.somorita.net
Address:  192.168.2.1


_ldap._tcp.somorita.net SRV service location:
        priority      = 0
        weight        = 100
        port          = 389
        svr hostname  = sfodc01.somorita.net
```

Troubleshooting

PART 5

```
    _ldap._tcp.somorita.net        SRV service location:
            priority       = 0
            weight         = 100
            port           = 389
            svr hostname   = sfodc02.cta.net
    sfodc01.somorita.net    internet address = 192.168.2.1
    sfodc02.somorita.net    internet address = 192.168.10.13
```

This listing shows two domain controllers available for the domain somorita.net. You can also perform the same type of query for Global Catalog servers. The results are very similar, except that the port numbers are different:

```
C:\>nslookup -q=SRV _gc._tcp.somorita.net
Server:   sfodc01.somorita.net
Address:  192.168.2.1


    _gc._tcp.somorita.net          SRV service location:
            priority       = 0
            weight         = 100
            port           = 3268
            svr hostname   = sfodc01.somorita.net
    _gc._tcp.cta.net          SRV service location:
            priority       = 0
            weight         = 100
            port           = 3268
            svr hostname   = sfodc01.somorita.net
    sfodc01.somorita.net    internet address = 192.168.2.1
    sfodc02.somorita.net    internet address = 192.168.10.13
```

If both of these queries are successful, this means you have no problems with basic DNS name resolution. If the Exchange server cannot successfully resolve domain related records, here are a couple of things to try:

- Confirm that the IP address of the DNS server is correct and that it is pointing to an internal DNS that is capable of resolving domain-related records.

- At the Exchange server command prompt, flush the resolver cache by typing **IPCONFIG /FLUSHDNS**.

- Stop and restart the Net Logon service on the Exchange server.

- Confirm that the DNS server is responding and that the DNS server service is operational.

- Confirm on the DNS server that the appropriate A and SRV records exist in the DNS zone.

- Flush the DNS cache on the DNS server.

Sending Mail to External Organizations

If the Exchange 2000 server is sending mail to an outside organization, the SMTP virtual server must perform a DNS query called an MX record. For example, let's say that the message a user is sending is destined for Novell (`novell.com`). To test to see if this domain can be resolved, you could type the following query. It is best to run this at the console of the Exchange server that has the SMTP virtual server that is sending the message.

```
C:\>nslookup -q=mx novell.com
Server:  dns4.somorita.net
Address:  192.168.10.4


Non-authoritative answer:
novell.com  MX preference = 5, mail exchanger = prv-mx.provo.novell.com
novell.com  MX preference = 5, mail exchanger = prv1-mx.provo.novell.com
novell.com  MX preference = 10, mail exchanger = prv2-mx.provo.novell.com
novell.com  MX preference = 20, mail exchanger = cp1-mx.novell.nl
prv-mx.provo.novell.com        internet address = 192.233.80.8
prv1-mx.provo.novell.com       internet address = 192.233.80.9
prv2-mx.provo.novell.com       internet address = 192.233.80.18
cp1-mx.novell.nl               internet address = 195.109.215.67
```

This query tells me that there are four hosts accepting mail for `novell.com`. The first two have a preference of 5; this means that the Exchange 2000 SMTP virtual server will randomly pick between prv-mx or prv1-mx. If neither of these hosts is available, the SMTP virtual server will pick the next highest MX record (prv2-mx); it will pick cp1-mx if all else fails.

Troubleshooting

PART 5

Exchange Services

If you are having trouble starting an Exchange 2000 service, you may be having a problem with some dependencies. Chapter 1, "Getting Started with Exchange 2000," discusses Windows 2000 services and on which of these the Exchange 2000 services depend. Here is a list of suggestions for troubleshooting Exchange services:

- Check the application and system event logs for messages.
- Configure diagnostics logging for the component that is failing.
- Confirm Active Directory and DNS connectivity.
- Confirm that the service packs and hot fixes have been applied properly and are up-to-date.

Some Common Problems

While no single issue sticks out in my mind as causing most Exchange 2000 problems (except for maybe Active Directory communications), I see a couple of things generated over and over again. This section discusses some of these problems and possible solutions.

Low Disk Space

A potential Exchange server killer is available disk space on the server quickly sneaking down to a point below which Exchange 2000 can no longer operate. Some things that can cause this to happen include:

- Tape backup problems cause the transaction logs to not be purged.
- Virus outbreaks may cause the virus quarantine to become full of infected messages.
- A mail storm occurs where a user accidentally sends a large message to the Internet and gets dozens or hundreds of rejected messages. These can quickly fill up the disk with the SMTP inbound queue directory, the log files disk, or even the disk with the mailbox store. Be especially careful of this if you are running Exchange 2000 Server due to the 16GB maximum size limit on the mailbox store.
- An administrator can move a large number of mailboxes to a server, which can cause a large number of transaction logs to be generated in a short period of time.

The long-term solution to running out of disk space is to make sure that you watch your disks carefully and implement some sort of monitoring system so that when disk space begins to get low you will be notified. See Chapter 5 for more information.

Database Problems

A database problem can manifest itself in one of a couple of ways. First, you may notice error events in the application event logs. Database errors in the event logs are often reporting during an online backup. Second, the database may not remount after it has been dismounted or the server has been restarted. In either case, the first thing you need to do is to gather as much information about the problem as possible. Things to note include:

- Confirm that there is free disk space on all drives that Exchange is using.

- What are the error messages that are in the Event Viewer? Are there any messages showing up when you try to mount the database?

- Can you perform an online backup? If so, do that immediately. If you cannot, then perform an offline backup immediately. Even though the database may be generating errors, you may still need these files later.

- Restart the information store service.

If the application event log is displaying error codes relating to the ESE98 database engine, refer to Microsoft Knowledge Base articles Q266361 and Q266367 for additional information. Table 17.1 lists some common errors that may be reported by the MSExchangeIS Mailbox or MSExchangeIS Public event sources along with a suggested action. These actions require the ISINTEG utility and that the database be dismounted.

Table 17.1   Event IDs Reported by Either MSExchangeIS Mailbox or MSExchangeIS Public and Suggested ISINTEG Options

Event ID	Recommended Command
1025	Isinteg -fix -test search
1186	Isinteg -fix -test acllistref or Isinteg -fix -test aclitemref
1198	Isinteg -fix -test folder
7200	Isinteg -fix -test mailbox or Isinteg -fix -test folder
7201	Isinteg -fix -test folder,artidx or Isinteg -fix -test rowcounts,dumpsterref
8500, 8501, 8502, or 8503	Isinteg -fix -test message
8504 or 8505	Isinteg -fix -test folder
8506 or 8507	Isinteg -fix -test folder,message
8508 or 8509	Isinteg -fix -test attach

Troubleshooting

PART 5

WARNING   The golden rule of data recovery is "Do no further harm." Do not perform any database maintenance without first performing a backup. If any error persists after you think you have taken appropriate action, contact Microsoft Product Support Services (PSS).

NOTE   Refer to Chapter 7, "Backup and Recovery," for more information on recovering from database problems and the ISINTEG utility.

Moving Mailboxes

Problems are popping up with a lot of Exchange administrators trying to move mailboxes between Exchange 5.5 and Exchange 2000 servers, or even just between Exchange 2000 servers. Here are a couple of things that you should keep in mind when moving mailboxes and diagnosing related problems:

- While RPC connectivity is not required between Exchange servers in a Native-mode organization, it is required when moving mailboxes. Confirm that RPC communication can occur between servers.

- The information store service caches the names of the local mailboxes, so that user may not be able to access their mailbox for up to 15 minutes.

- Different permissions are required to move a mailbox to another mailbox store than are required to initially create a mailbox. In addition to needing permission to modify the Active Directory user object, you must have administrative permissions on the machine on which you are running Exchange System Manager. Further, you must have the Exchange Administrator role on the administrative groups that contain both the source and destination mailbox stores.

Missing Files

If any of the event logs indicate that a file is missing (such as a DLL or an EXE file), then you may have to replace the files. Unless you know exactly which file is missing, you should run the Exchange 2000 Setup program again and choose the Reinstall option. Once the reinstall is complete, immediately reapply any service packs and hot fixes.

File System Permissions

A common problem I have seen with Exchange is that an administrator, in an effort to tighten security, restricts NTFS permissions to the local hard disk to only the Administrators local group. Exchange 2000 services all operate under the SYSTEM account's security context, so if this account does not have permissions to the file system, Exchange 2000 will not function.

Diagnostics Logging

When Exchange starts behaving strangely, Exchange 2000 diagnostics logging will become your best friend. There are several different services to which you can apply diagnostics logging, each of which has up to eight different categories of logging that can be enabled. Diagnostics logging for these services can be configured through Exchange System Manager by displaying the properties of the Exchange server and choosing the Diagnostics Logging tab (shown in Figure 17.2).

Figure 17.2   Diagnostics logging for a typical Exchange 2000 server

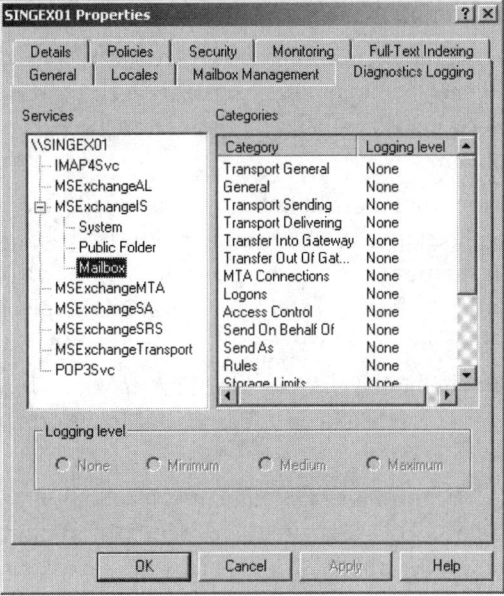

On some Exchange servers, you may see additional services; this depends on the additional Exchange services that are installed. These services are as follows:

IMAP4Svc and **POP3Svc** include categories for monitoring IMAP4 and POP3 activity.

MSExchangeAL includes categories for monitoring the RUS.

MSExchangeIS includes categories for the system (information store service as a whole), public folder (public folder store monitoring), and mailbox (mailbox store monitoring).

MSExchangeMTA includes categories for monitoring the MTA. Monitoring this service will be useful only if you have X.400 Connectors or Exchange 5.5 servers in the same site/administrative group.

Troubleshooting

PART 5

MSExchangeSA includes categories for monitoring the DSProxy and referral interface as well as the offline address book generator.

MSExchangeSRS includes categories for monitoring the Site Replication Service (SRS). Monitoring this service will be useful only if you have Exchange 5.5 servers in the site/administrative group.

MSExchangeTransport includes categories for monitoring the SMTP protocol, Routing Engine, categorizer, and Advanced Queuing Engine.

There are five main logging levels that can be set through the Exchange System Manager console; many of the categories support a higher level of logging called *field engineering* that can only be set through the Registry:

None specifies that only errors and critical events are logged to the application event log. This level is specified in the Registry as level zero. By default, logging for all categories is set to None. Logging levels should remain at None unless you are trying to debug a problem.

Minimum specifies that more detail will be reported; any event with a logging level of 1 or lower will be logged when Minimum is set. These types of events are usually summaries, informational, or warning events. When configuring diagnostics logging, try the minimum level of logging first to see if this gives you the information for which you are looking.

Medium specifies higher levels of logging (events with a logging level of 3 or less). If a Minimum level of logging does not give you the information you are seeking, switch to Medium logging.

Maximum specifies the highest documented level of logging (events with a logging level of 5 or lower). This generates a tremendous amount of information in the application log, causes application logs to fill quickly, and may adversely affect performance.

Field Engineering specifies the maximum amount of logging. This value cannot be set through Exchange System Manager. Each category must be set manually in the Registry by setting the level to 7, and not all categories will provide any more information than the Maximum setting. For categories that do support field engineering, this level generates huge amounts of event log entries on even a moderately busy Exchange server. Most of these events will be useful only when analyzed by Microsoft PSS.

WARNING   When you have completed diagnostics logging, don't forget to set the logging level back to None. This will ensure that you don't adversely affect performance during normal operations.

Microsoft Exchange Recipient Update Service

The Recipient Update Service (known during the early beta period as the Address List Service) is responsible for updating mail-enabled objects to reflect the address lists they are part of as well as updating other attributes of mail-enabled objects. By default, it checks once per minute for changes in the domain that may require that the RUS process. The diagnostics logging category for the RUS is MSExchangeAL. Table 17.2 lists the diagnostics logging categories and what they report.

Table 17.2   Diagnostics Logging for the Recipient Update Service (MSExchangeAL)

Category	Explanation
Ldap Operations	Reports on connections to domain controllers, initiating LDAP queries, and LDAP queries made to domain controllers as well as information relating to servers and port numbers used by the RUS.
Service Control	Reports on which calling policy provider initiated an LDAP query (recipients policies, system policies, etc.).
Attribute Mapping	Reports on the attribute mapping performed by the RUS. I have never seen this category generate any events during normal operation.
Account Management	Reports on the account management activities that the RUS performs. I have never seen this category generate any events during normal operation.
Address List Synchronization	Reports information on the initiation or shutdown of the RUS service.

Microsoft Exchange Information Store

The Information Store Service contains a lot of diagnostic logging categories on which you can choose to respond. These categories are broken down into three basic categories: system-related, public folder–related, and mailbox-related. Table 17.3 shows the diagnostic logging categories for the Information Store Service.

Table 17.3 Diagnostics Logging for the Information Store Service

Category	Explanation
System/Recovery	Reports transaction log recovery operations that occur if a database is mounted when the database is not consistent.
System/General	Reports general information about information store operation.
System/Connections	Tracks information about users connecting to the Information Store Service.
System/Table Cache	Displays information about sessions and tables in each public and mailbox database.
System/Content Engine	Reports on errors that occur when the information store IMAIL process converts messages to Internet format.
System/Performance Monitor	Reports problems related to Windows 2000 Performance Monitor counters.
System/Move Mailbox	Reports when a mailbox has been moved from one mailbox store to another.
System/Virus Scanning	Reports events related to the Antivirus API 2 installed with Exchange 2000 SP1.
Public Folder/Transport General	Reports general message transport–related events in the public folder stores.
Public Folder/General	Reports general public folder store–related tasks, such as online maintenance information.
Public Folder/Replication Incoming Messages	Tracks inbound replication messages and the destination public folder.
Public Folder/Replication Outgoing Messages	Tracks outbound replication messages and the folder from which the replication message originated.

Table 17.3 Diagnostics Logging for the Information Store Service *(continued)*

Category	Explanation
Public Folder/Non-Delivery Reports	Reports public folder replication messages that were returned with an NDR.
Public Folder/Transport Sending	Reports problems sending messages outbound that originated from public folders.
Public Folder/Transport Delivering	Reports problems delivering inbound messages to public folders.
Public Folder/MTA Connections	Reports connections from the MTA where messages are transferred from gateways to the public folder store or from the public store to a gateway.
Public Folders/Logons	Reports logons to the public folder store.
Public Folders/Access Control	Displays reports of users accessing public folders and the access rights they required for the particular task they tried to perform.
Public Folders/Send On Behalf Of	Reports any time a user uses the Send On Behalf Of privilege for a public folder.
Public Folders/Send As	Reports any time a user sends a message where the From address is the address of a public folder.
Public Folders/Rules	Reports which rules fired when a message enters a public folder; if rules were skipped, this information is logged.
Public Folders/Storage Limits	Reports when public folders are over their storage limits.
Public Folders/Replication Site Folders	Reports errors and status when system public folders are replicated.
Public Folders/Replication Expiry	Reports the processing of messages in public folders that have exceeded the permitted age limit for a folder and are being expired.

Troubleshooting

PART 5

Table 17.3 Diagnostics Logging for the Information Store Service *(continued)*

Category	Explanation
Public Folders/Replication Conflicts	Reports the public folder conflicts for messages and design conflicts.
Public Folders/Replication Backfill	Reports events when the public information store attempts to fill a newly created replica or to synchronize a replica if it has missed replication updates.
Public Folders/Background Cleanup	Reports cleanup of public folders and folder content that are eligible to be purged from the deleted item cache.
Public Folders/Replication Errors	Reports general replication errors with public folders.
Public Folders/Views	Reports when a user creates, modifies, or deletes views on a public folder.
Public Folders/ General Replication	Reports general replication problems.
Mailbox/General	Reports general information about activities affecting mailbox stores, such as creating and deleting mailboxes and mailbox store online maintenance tasks.
Mailbox/Transport Sending	Reports problems delivering outbound messages originating from mailboxes on this server.
Mailbox/Transport Delivering	Reports problems delivering inbound messages to mailboxes.
Mailbox/Transfer Into Gateway	Displays information about messages being transferred from the mailbox store into a gateway or third-party connector.
Mailbox/Transfer Out Of Gateway	Displays information about messages being transferred *in* from a gateway or third-party connector. Also reports on information about threads, wait times, and items queued to be delivered to the information store.

Table 17.3 Diagnostics Logging for the Information Store Service *(continued)*

Category	Explanation
Mailbox/MTA Connections	Reports connections from the MTA where messages are transferred from gateways to the information store or from the information store to a gateway.
Mailbox/Logons	Reports mailbox store logons and mailbox access by users other than the primary user.
Mailbox/Access Control	Displays reports of users accessing mailboxes and the access rights they required for the particular task they tried to perform.
Mailbox/Send On Behalf Of	Reports any time a user sends a message on behalf of someone else's mailbox.
Mailbox/Send As	Reports any time a user sends a message either from someone else's mailbox or from their own mailbox.
Mailbox/Rules	Reports which rules fired when a message enters a mailbox; if rules were skipped, this information is logged. Setting this category to at least medium is very useful in diagnosing why some rules are not being processed.
Mailbox/Storage Limits	Reports any time storage warning limits that are generated.
Mailbox/Background Cleanup	Reports on cleanup of mailboxes and folders that are eligible to be purged from the deleted item cache.
Mailbox/Views	Reports when a user creates, modifies, or deletes views on a public folder.

Microsoft Exchange System Attendant

The System Attendant performs a lot of odd jobs on an Exchange 2000 server including running DSAccess, DSProxy, the DSProxy referral interface, offline address book generation, and mailbox management tasks. Table 17.4 shows a list of the diagnostics logging categories that can be enabled for the System Attendant. DSAccess is enabled separately using the MSExchangeAL category.

Troubleshooting

PART 5

Table 17.4 System Attendant Diagnostics Logging Categories

Category	Explanation
NSPI Proxy	Reports operation of the DSProxy interface, including establishing/terminating sessions and reporting which Global Catalog servers are being used.
RFR Interface	Reports the use of the DSProxy RFR (referral) interface for Outlook 2000 and later clients. Details of the event include the Global Catalog server to which the client was referred.
OAL Generator	Reports when the System Attendant runs the offline address book generator.
Mailbox Management	Reports when mailbox management operations are performed, including reports of how many mailboxes and messages were processed.

Microsoft Exchange Transport

When you have to diagnose problems relating to message delivery, the categorizer or the SMTP protocol, you will need to enable diagnostics logging for categories found in the MSExchange Transport. Table 17.5 shows a list of the diagnostics logging categories that can be enabled.

Table 17.5 Message Transport Diagnostics Logging Categories

Category	Explanation
Routing Engine/Service	Displays information such as calculation of next hop for SMTP addresses.
Categorizer	Reports usage of the message categorizer, distribution list expansion, and message routing.
Connection Manager	Reports on connectivity problems (such as dropped connections) between SMTP clients and servers.
Queuing Engine	Reports problems with the queuing engine.

Table 17.5   Message Transport Diagnostics Logging Categories *(continued)*

Category	Explanation
Exchange Store Driver	Reports problems with the Exchange store driver (this is the IIS interface to the information store through ExIPC).
SMTP Protocol	Reports errors with the SMTP protocol. Microsoft PSS has a DLL called PROTOLOG.DLL that can be loaded as an event sink that provides detailed SMTP troubleshooting. PROTOLOG.DLL is not currently available without assistance from PSS.
NTFS Store Driver	Reports problems with the NTFS store driver that is used when messages arrive on the server via SMTP.

NOTE   For diagnostics information relating to the Exchange 2000 MTA, see the document "Exchange 2000 MTA Diagnostics" at www.somorita.com.

Active Directory Connector Logging

If you are in the middle of a migration from Exchange 5.5 to Exchange 2000, you are probably using the Active Directory Connector (ADC). In my experience, once it is set up and stable, the ADC is fairly trouble-free. However, in case you need to diagnose ADC-related problems, you can enable diagnostics logging just like you can for Exchange 2000 components. Enabling diagnostics logging is done from the ADC Management console. Simply right-click the Active Directory object in the left pane, select Properties, and then choose the Diagnostics Logging property tab. Table 17.6 shows the categories that you can choose for diagnostics logging on the ADC.

Table 17.6   Active Directory Connector Diagnostics Logging Categories

Category	Explanation
Replication	Reports events occurring when the ADC was initiating replication between Exchange 5.5 and Windows 2000 Active Directory, or vice versa.
Account Management	Reports events occurring while performing activities relating to AD or Exchange 5.5 account management, such as creating or deleting accounts or mailboxes.

Troubleshooting

PART 5

Table 17.6 Active Directory Connector Diagnostics Logging Categories *(continued)*

Category	Explanation
Attribute Mapping	Reports events occurring when mapping attributes from the Exchange 5.5 directory to AD attributes, or vice versa.
Service Controller	Reports events occurring when the ADC service starts or stops.
LDAP Operations	Reports events occurring when LDAP queries are generated from the ADC to Exchange 5.5 or the Active Directory, including queries and connection to servers.

Message Flow Problems

Exchange server is not very useful if user messages are not being delivered to their intended locations. Since all messages on Exchange 2000 have to be routed through the Advanced Queuing Engine, even local delivery may be affected if some components are not working properly. There are a couple of different types of problems that you may encounter when debugging message flow problems. Here are some common problems along with some things to do in order to begin troubleshooting:

Problem	Things to Check
Messages disappearing	Use Message Tracking. Restart the Simple Mail Transport Protocol (SMTP) service. Restart the Microsoft Exchange Routing Engine. Check the queues. Check the antivirus software message quarantine.
Messages stuck in Outlook Outbox	Open the message and click Send. Restart the SMTP service. Confirm that the server has sufficient disk space. Confirm that the client is in online mode rather than offline mode if using a PST or OST file.
Non-delivery reports (NDRs)	Look at the error codes and the server name that generated the NDR report (see the common NDRs in Chapter 16). Use Message Tracking.

TIP If you want to reset the Link State Table, stop and restart the Microsoft Exchange Routing Engine on the Routing Group Master server in the routing group.

Check the Object in Active Directory

If the object that is being addressed was selected from the global address list, you may want to check that the object has all of the necessary attributes for categorizing the message and sending a message to the recipient. This means that you need to dump the attributes of the message. The simplest way to get a list of the object's attributes is to use the LDIFDE utility and dump the object's attributes to an LDF file. You must know the object's distinguished name (DN) in order to do this. In the following example, we dump a recipient whose RDN (relative distinguished name) is Phillip Zaw and the organizational unit is Operations. To do this, at the command prompt, type:

```
ldifde -f output.ldf -d cn=Phillip
Zaw,ou=operations,dc=somorita,dc=net
```

This will dump the output to a file called output.ldf; this file can have quite a few lines depending on the number of attributes that have been populated with data. Now you need to look through this file to make sure that the object has all of the necessary attributes populated in Active Directory. The following attributes are necessary for mailbox-enabled objects:

LegacyExchangeDn	HomeMdb
HomeMta	mailNickName
ProxyAddress	msExchHomeServerName
MsExchMailboxSecurityDescriptor	msExchMailboxGuid

If these attributes are not present, the message categorizer will not be able to correctly categorize and route the message to another Active Directory mail-enabled recipient. What to do? Here are a couple of suggestions:

1. Confirm that Active Directory has replicated the data to the local Global Catalog server.
2. Run the correct domain's RUS in Update Now mode.
3. Run the correct domain's RUS in Rebuild mode.

Monitoring Queues Using the Queue Viewer

One of the daily tasks that an administrator should perform is making sure that the queues are not backing up. As you recall from Chapter 5, you can configure notifications to tell you if a queue is growing, and there are tools for monitoring queue totals through a web page. However, the simplest way to monitor queues is to use the Queue Viewer tool, which is integrated into Exchange System Manager.

The Queue Viewer is a nice addition to Exchange System Manager, and it lets you do some nice things with the queues, but it is awkward to use since you must select each SMTP or X.400 virtual server separately in order to view their queues. Perhaps some third-party (hint, hint) will write a Queue Management console someday.

The Queue Viewer interface (see Figure 17.3) shows an SMTP virtual server. From here you can see the messages that are queued up for server-to-server delivery, delivery to other routing groups, or delivery to the SMTP Connector. This interface shows you the following types of queues:

- The *local delivery* queue holds messages that are awaiting delivery to a local public folder, mailbox store, the MTA's mailbox, or the mailbox of a connector.

- The *messages awaiting directory lookup* queue holds message that have not yet been categorized. This queue may also be referred to as the pre-cat queue.

- The *messages waiting to be routed* queue holds messages that have been categorized and are now waiting to be placed into the destination message queues and eventually the link queues. This queue is also called the post-cat queue, post-categorizer queue, or the pre-routing queue.

- The *final destination unreachable* queue contains messages for which the Routing Engine could not figure out the correct next hop. These messages may be in this queue as a result of a server recently being moved to another routing group or an incorrect DNS entry.

- The *pre-submission* queue holds messages that have been streamed in from outside SMTP sources, but have not yet been moved to the pre-cat queue. The OnSubmission event sinks have not yet picked up the messages sitting in this queue. This queue does not always appear in the Queue Viewer; if you are not running Exchange 2000 SP2, you will not see it.

- The *PendingRerouteQ* (X.400/MAPI queues only) contains messages that are waiting to be rerouted. You will see messages in this queue if one link has failed and the MTA is rerouting messages to another queue.

- The *link queues* are for remote delivery; these are named based on the name of the destination server or the name of the connector. Figure 17.3 shows a few of these queues.

    - The singex01.asia.somorita.net is for messages going to another server in the organization. If the SMTP Connector is not installed, you will also see queues for remote SMTP domains here as well.

    - The *North America SMTP Connector* queue is for messages that are currently held in the queue for an SMTP Connector. You will see one of these queues for each destination host. This queue list is refreshed, and unused link queues are removed about once a minute.

Figure 17.3   Queue Viewer interface

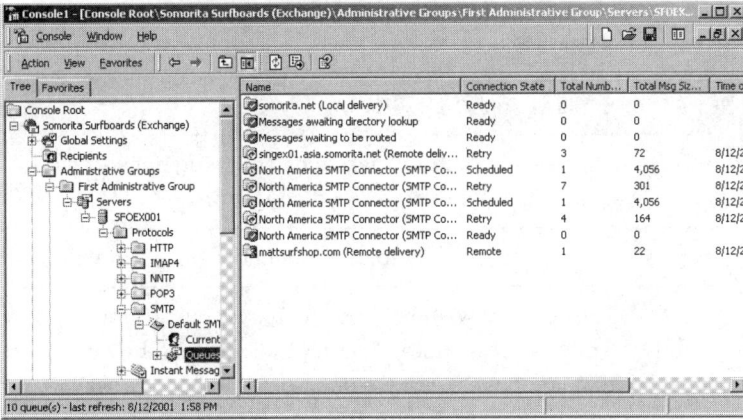

If you are viewing the queues for other connectors, such as the connectors for Lotus Notes, cc:Mail, or GroupWise, you will see the following queues:

- The *MTS-IN* queue contains messages that have been sent to the Exchange server from a remote e-mail system. These messages are inbound to the Exchange server for either Exchange-based recipients or to be routed by other Exchange connectors.

- The *MTS-OUT* queue contains messages that have been routed through the Exchange server and are destined for recipients of the foreign e-mail system.

- The *READY-IN* queue contains messages that have been sent from a remote e-mail system. The messages have been converted to Exchange messages, and their attributes have been mapped to Exchange message attributes, but the recipients have not yet been resolved.

Troubleshooting

PART 5

- The *READY-OUT* queue holds messages that are queued for delivery to external e-mail systems. These messages have been resolved to the correct remote address, but they have not been converted to the remote e-mail system's native message format.

- The *BADMAIL* queue contains messages that generated an error when the connector software attempted to convert the message or to resolve a recipient. This queue should be checked periodically and cleaned. If this queue has more than a few messages in it over a period of a few days or weeks, you should take steps to find out why the messages are not being delivered properly. This may be the result of upgraded client software on the foreign e-mail system that Exchange 2000 does not support, or it may be the result of a bug in the Exchange 2000 connector software.

In the Connection State column of the Queue Viewer, you can see the current state of each individual link queue. Table 17.7 shows a list of the possible states of a queue.

Table 17.7 Possible Queue States

Queue State	Explanation
Active	The queue is active, messages are being delivered normally, and the queue has not encountered any errors.
Ready	The queue is ready for a connection to be initiated.
Retry	The queue is waiting to try and reconnect to a remote server. If you see a queue in this state, this may indicate that the remote server is down, that you have a name resolution problem, or that this server is experiencing network connectivity problems.
Scheduled	The queue is waiting until the next scheduled time window so that it can go active.
Remote	The queue is holding messages that will be retrieved by a remote system using ETRN or TURN/ATRN. This server will not attempt to deliver these messages.
Frozen	The administrator has frozen the queue so that no messages will be delivered through it; however, messages will continue to flow into the queue.
Disabled	The queue has been disabled, and no messages will leave it.

> **TIP**   If the remote SMTP domain name does not exist, if it does not have an MX record, or if the MX record points to a nonexistent A record, Exchange 2000 will immediately NDR the message, giving a #5.4.0 DSN code and stating that "The e-mail system was unable to deliver the message, but did not report a specific reason. Check the address and try again." This is usually due to the fact that the sender has typed in the wrong SMTP address, but it can be DNS related, also.

Managing the Queues

From the Queue Viewer interface, the administrator can perform certain actions on each queue. First, if you right-click the Queues container, you will have two choices that may prove useful. You can either Disable All Connections or Enable All Connections. These choices allow you to stop all messages from being delivered through this virtual server or connector. If you right-click any queue, you will see the context menu for the queues.

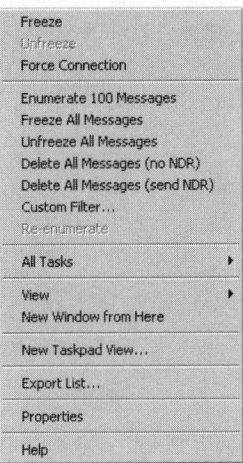

The number of choices available on the context menu vary based on the type of queue and the queue's current state. Table 17.8 shows a list of the options on the context menu.

Table 17.8   Queue Context Menu Choices

Menu Option	Explanation
Freeze	Stops this queue from processing outbound messages. If the queue is currently active and transferring messages, it will abort the transfer of any messages currently being processed.

Troubleshooting

PART 5

Table 17.8 Queue Context Menu Choices *(continued)*

Menu Option	Explanation
Unfreeze	Allows the queue to start processing outbound messages if it has been frozen.
Force Connection	Forces the virtual server to immediately retry to make a connection rather than waiting until the next connection retry time (if the queue state is Retry), the next scheduled time the connector is supposed to operate (if the state is Scheduled), or until the remote server connects to dequeue the messages (if the state is Remote).
Enumerate 100 Messages	Lists the first 100 messages in the queue (the messages appear in the right pane).
Freeze All Messages	Freezes the messages currently in the queue.
Unfreeze All Messages	Unfreezes all the messages in the queue that have been frozen.
Delete All Messages (no NDR)	Deletes all queued messages, but does not send a non-delivery report.
Delete All Messages (send NDR)	Deletes all queued messages and sends the original sender a message indicating that the message was not delivered. (The message does not indicate that the administrator deleted the message.)
Custom Filter	Allows you to apply a custom filter if you only want to display, delete, freeze, or unfreeze messages that meet specific criteria. If you are trying to delete a message, you should freeze the entire queue first before trying to find the message; otherwise the message may be delivered while you are looking for it.
Re-enumerate	Refreshes the list of queued messages.
Properties	Displays the properties of the queue including the status of the queue, and the next connection retry time.

You can also highlight an individual message, right-click it, and get the context menu on which you can select Freeze, Unfreeze, Delete (send NDR), and Delete (no NDR). You can also display the message properties. Figure 17.4 shows the General property tab of a message. From here you can see the Message ID, sender, subject (if enabled), priority, message size, number of recipients, and the message recipients. On the Details property page, you can also display the submission and expiration time.

Figure 17.4   Queued message properties

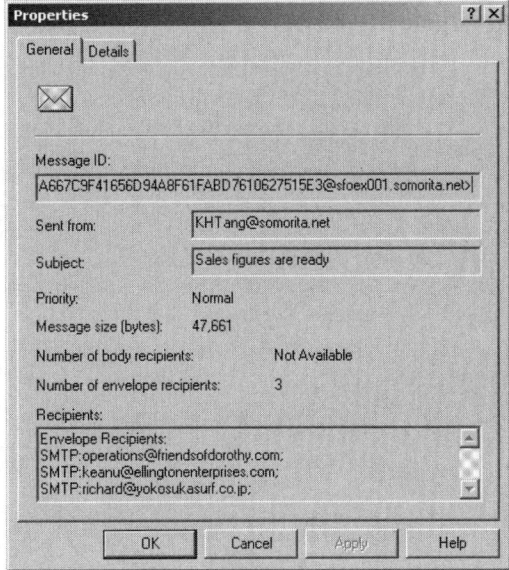

Diagnosing NDRs

One of the most maddening things that you can troubleshoot is the non-delivery report (NDR), an indication that a message did not make it to its final destination. Seeing the actual NDR message is critical to troubleshooting NDR problems, as it usually gives an error code indicating why the message was not delivered. These error codes can be quite cryptic; a list of the common error codes is shown in Chapter 16.

If the message is not leaving a local server, another option is to use diagnostics logging on your server to determine why the message is not being delivered. To do this, on the MSExchange Transport category, set the Categorizer category to Maximum. This may yield the information necessary to diagnose this problem. However, you may have to set the diagnostic level to Field Engineering to get any real results.

To set diagnostics logging for the Categorizer to the Field Engineering level, locate the HKLM\System\CurrentControlSet\MSExchangeTransport\Diagnostics Registry key and change the Categorizer value to 0x7. This generates a lot of information in the application event log, so make sure that you have set this back to 0x0 when you are finished.

> **NOTE** Microsoft published a Troubleshooter Home Page (support.microsoft .com/support/tshoot/) containing some steps that may be useful for Exchange 2000 as well as other technologies. Though this page is currently a little spartan, hopefully Microsoft will continue to enhance the information.

Index

Note to the Reader: Throughout this index **boldfaced** page numbers indicate primary discussions of a topic. *Italicized* page numbers indicate illustrations.

The Mark Minasi
Windows® Administrator Series

First Three Titles of an Expanding Series

By Jeremy Moskowitz
0-7821-2881-5 • $49.99

By Christa Anderson
0-7821-2885-8 • $49.99

*By J. Peter Bruzzese
and Chris Wolfe*
0-7821-2883-1 • $49.99

- **Mark Minasi** serves as the series editor, chooses topics and authors, and reviews each book

- Concise, focused material based upon real-world implementation of Windows 2000 Server

- Designed to provide Windows 2000 Systems Administrators with specific in-depth technical solutions

Mark Minasi, MCSE, is recognized as one of the world's best teachers of NT/2000. He teaches NT/2000 classes in 15 countries. His best-selling *Mastering Windows 2000 Server* books have more than 500,000 copies in print.

SYBEX®
WWW.SYBEX.COM

TELL US WHAT YOU THINK!

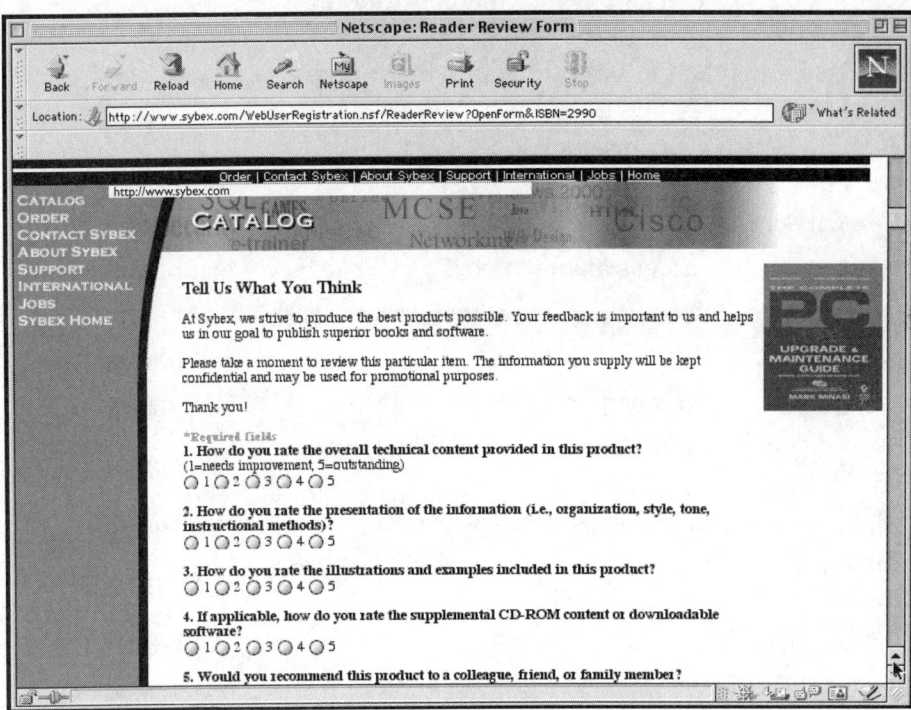

Your feedback is critical to our efforts to provide you with the best books and software on the market. Tell us what you think about the products you've purchased. It's simple:

1. Visit the Sybex website
2. Go to the product page
3. Click on **Submit a Review**
4. Fill out the questionnaire and comments
5. Click **Submit**

With your feedback, we can continue to publish the highest quality computer books and software products that today's busy IT professionals deserve.

www.sybex.com

SYBEX Inc. • 1151 Marina Village Parkway, Alameda, CA 94501 • 510-523-8233

How to...